Miscarriages of Justice

A Review of Justice in Error

Edited by

Clive Walker

Professor and Director of the Centre for Criminal Justice Studies,
University of Leeds

and

Keir Starmer

Barrister, Doughty Street Chambers,
and Research Fellow, Essex University

BLACKSTONE
PRESS LIMITED

First published in Great Britain 1999 by Blackstone Press Limited,
Aldine Place, London W12 8AA. Telephone 081–740 2277
www.blackstonepress.com

© Blackstone Press Limited, 1999
The contributors hold the copyright for their respective chapters.

ISBN: 1 85431 687 7

British Library Cataloguing in Publication Data
A CIP catalogue record for this book is available from the British Library

Typeset by Style Photosetting Limited, Mayfield, East Sussex
Printed by Ashford Colour Press, Gosport, Hants

Contents

List of Contributors

John Bell is Professor at the Faculty of Law, University of Leeds. He previously lectured at Oxford University. His areas of expertise are the legal system and comparative law, especially French law, as described in his books, *French Administrative Law* (with Neville Brown, 4th ed., Clarendon, Oxford, 1993) and *French Constitutional Law* (2nd ed., Clarendon Press, Oxford, 1995)

Lee Bridges is a Professor and Director of the Legal Research Institute, University of Warwick. He previously lectured at Birmingham University and has acted as consultant to many bodies, including the Legal Aid Board. He is a member of the Management Committee of the Legal Action Group. His writings on the criminal justice system include *Standing Accused: The Organisation and Practices of Criminal Defence Lawyers in Britain* (Clarendon Press, Oxford, 1994) and *Criminal Justice in Crisis* (edited with Mike McConville, Edward Elgar, Aldershot, 1994), and he has conducted several empirical studies on the provision of police station legal advice.

Brice Dickson is Professor of Law at the University of Ulster and in 1999 was appointed Chief Commissioner of the Northern Ireland Human Rights Commission. He formerly lectured at the University of Leicester and Queen's University, Belfast. His main interests are in the fields of the legal system, civil liberties, criminal justice and comparative law. He is the author of the leading work, *The Legal System of Northern Ireland* (3rd ed., SLS, Belfast, 1993) and is editor of *Civil Liberties in Northern Ireland: The CAJ Handbook* (3rd ed., CAJ, Belfast, 1997).

David Dixon is Associate Professor, Faculty of Law, University of New South Wales. Until 1989, he was a lecturer in law at the University of Hull. He has researched and written extensively on policing, including *From Prohibition to Regulation* (Clarendon Press, Oxford, 1991), *Law in Policing: Legal Regulation and Police Practices* (Clarendon Press, Oxford, 1997) and *Ann Hai: Young Indo-Chinese People's Perceptions and Experiences of Policing* (with L. Maher, UNSW, Sydney, 1997).

Ben Fitzpatrick is a Lecturer in Criminal Justice Studies at the University of Leeds. His interests lie in the fields of criminal justice, crime and evidence.

Peter Hill is a journalist who has investigated and reported on many miscarriages of justice. He originated the programme, *Rough Justice*, in 1980 and has written about some of the cases in *Rough Justice* (with Martin Young, Ariel Books, London, 1983) and *More Rough Justice* (with Martin Young and Tom Sargant, Penguin, Harmondsworth, 1985).

John Jackson is Professor in Law at Queen's University, Belfast. His main research interests lie in the fields of criminal process and evidence. He has written on the impact of 'Diplock' courts in these respects (with Sean Doran) in *Judge without Jury* (Clarendon Press, Oxford, 1995).

Helena Kennedy is a barrister practising predominantly in the criminal law and also holds the posts of chair of the British Council and Chancellor of Oxford Brookes University. She became a life peer (as Baroness Kennedy of The Shaws) in November 1997. She has acted in many prominent cases during the last decade including the *Guildford Four* appeal. A frequent broadcaster and journalist on law and women's rights, her book, *Eve Was Framed* (Vintage, London, 1993) was about women and British justice.

Michael Mansfield is a barrister practising at 14 Tooks Court. He has acted in many of the recent miscarriage of justice cases. From his experiences, he has compiled his own remedies for the criminal justice system in *Presumed Guilty* (Heinemann, London, 1993).

Geoffrey Robertson is the head of chambers at Doughty Street Chambers. He is well-known for his work in human rights and media-related cases, a collection of which was published as *The Justice Game* (Chatto & Windus, London, 1998).

Andrew Sanders is Professor of Criminal Law and Criminology at the University of Bristol and a Fellow of Pembroke College, Oxford. He formerly lectured at Birmingham and Oxford Universities. He is a member of the Parole Board. He has co-authored (with Mike McConville and Roger Leng) *The Case for the Prosecution* (Routledge, London, 1991) and (with Richard Young) the definitive *Criminal Justice* (Butterworths, London, 1994).

Keir Starmer is a barrister specialising in European human rights law at Doughty Street Chambers. In 1996 he published *The Three Pillars of Liberty: Political Rights and Freedoms in the UK* (with Francesca Klug and Stuart Weir, Routledge, London, 1996) and in 1999 he published *European Human Rights Law* (Legal Action Group, London, 1999). He is also a research fellow at the Human Rights Centre at Essex University.

Mark Stephens is the senior partner at solicitors, Stephens Innocent, which specialises in complex litigation particularly in the arts and also human rights. He is renowned for his work for Michelle and Lisa Taylor, the Brent Spar case (involving Greenpeace), Friendly Fire and the Sinn Féin broadcasting ban.

Russell Stockdale is a partner of Forensic Access, a group of independent scientific consultants to the legal profession.

Nicholas Taylor is a lecturer in law at the Centre for Criminal Justice Studies, University of Leeds. He has written and researched on miscarriages of justice and policing, human rights and the legal system.

Clive Walker is Professor of the Faculty of Law and Director of the Centre for Criminal Justice Studies, University of Leeds. He previously lectured at Manchester University and practised as a solicitor. Apart from an interest in miscarriages of justice (which led to the book with Keir Starmer, *Justice in Error* (Blackstone Press, London, 1993)) he has written extensively about terrorism, including *The Prevention of Terrorism in British Law* (2nd ed., Manchester University Press, 1992).

Dermot Walsh is a barrister and a Professor in Law at the University of Limerick where he is also the Director of the Centre for Criminal Justice. He was formerly a Senior Lecturer in Legal Studies at the University of Ulster, a lecturer in law at University College, Cork and the holder of the Cobden Trust Studentship at Queen's University, Belfast. He is the author of *The Irish Police* (Round Hall Sweet & Maxwell, Dublin, 1998).

James Wood is a barrister practising in the Doughty Street Chambers and an executive member of Liberty. He has acted in several of the prominent miscarriage of justice cases.

Mitchell Woolf is a solicitor specialising in human rights law. He is a researcher at Doughty Street Chambers and teaches part-time at the School of Oriental and African Studies in London.

Table of Cases

Table of Statutes

Table of Secondary Legislation and other Rules

Part One

THE NATURE OF MISCARRIAGES OF JUSTICE

1

The Agenda of Miscarriages of Justice

Clive Walker

. . . it's true all the stories that you tell come back to haunt you.[1]

Justice in Error was published in early 1993, a very significant year for miscarriages of justice. As described on the very first page of that book, we were working in the shadow of the Royal Commission on Criminal Justice, which had been established in 1991 under the chairmanship of Lord Runciman with the following terms of reference:

> To examine the effectiveness of the criminal justice system in England and Wales in securing the conviction of those guilty of criminal offences and the acquittal of those who are innocent, having regard to the efficient use of resources, and in particular to consider whether changes are needed in
> i   the conduct of police investigations . . .
> ii   the role of the prosecutor . . .
> iii the role of experts . . .
> iv   the arrangements for the defence . . .
> v   the opportunities available for an accused person to state his position . . .
> vi   the powers of the courts in directing proceedings . . .
> vii the role of the Court of Appeal . . .
> viii the arrangements for considering and investigating miscarriages of justice
>   . . .

Our aim was to make a contribution to the ongoing debate by documenting and analysing miscarriages of justice in two ways. The first was by accounting for those features in the system which are capable of giving rise to miscarriages. Secondly, we offered suggestions as to the avoidance of errors in the future.

Those two aims remain true of the current work, and our cast list is also intended to be reflective of the same mixture of backgrounds, academics, campaigners and practitioners, as before. However, many other circumstances have changed. The

---

[1] Blunt, M., Bookes, J., Burgess, T., Collins, M. and Collins, R., *Tellin' Stories* (Beggars Banquet, London, 1997).

eagerly-awaited Royal Commission reported in July 1993,[2] and there followed not
only conferences and commentaries akin to our own but also, and more significantly, the outlines of the response of the Conservative Government, signalled
politically by the Home Secretary, Michael Howard, in his speech to the Conservative Party conference in October 1993.[3] It has since been implemented by
legislation, principally in the shape of the Criminal Justice and Public Order Act
1994, the Criminal Appeal Act 1995, and the Criminal Procedure and Investigations Act 1996. In the light of all of these changes, it was necessary for us to make
a fresh start, signalled by a new title. So, this book is not simply a second edition
of *Justice in Error* but differs in at least three respects. First, the agenda is wider,
with more issues being covered to give a better picture of the polycentric issue of
miscarriages of justice. Secondly, in so far as the same issues are rehearsed as
before, most of the relevant chapters have been revised substantially to take
account of the *Runciman Report* and later developments. Thirdly, there is no
attendant Royal Commission to which to express our concerns. So, the aim must
now be to address the Labour Government which took office in May 1997, though
the task will be difficult as the Government's initial stance has been to retain many
of the same policies as its predecessor.[4]

We have endeavoured to cover circumstances comprehensively up to 31
December 1997, though most significant events up to 1 January 1999 have been
mentioned (including the impact of the European Convention through the Human
Rights Act 1998). As before, the views of individual chapter authors or of the
editors are not necessarily shared by other contributors. Readers who find our
views unpalatable at least have the consolation of knowing that royalties from the
sale of this book are being donated to the Prison Reform Trust. In the compilation
of this book, I must thank on behalf of myself and my co-editor all who have
contributed to this work. I personally would also like to thank my close colleagues
at the Centre for Criminal Justice Studies here in Leeds, especially, Professor John
Bell, Dr Adam Crawford, Ben Fitzpatrick, Nick Taylor and Dr David Wall.

The remainder of this chapter will give an outline of the issues tackled in this
book. The rest of Part I on 'The nature of miscarriages of justice' is completed by
the chapter, 'Miscarriages of Justice in Principle and Practice', which attempts a
rights-based definition and typology of the phenomenon of miscarriages of justice.
After outlining the *causes célèbres* and diagnosing the common causes, attention is
turned to the process of reform which was centred on the Runciman Commission.
Its shortcomings and the political aftermath are analysed. Further details as to its
recommendations and the official responses are contained in the survey in Part II.

**Part II – The Criminal Justice Process in England and Wales and
Miscarriages of Justice**

Part II begins with a critique by David Dixon of police investigative procedures
(Chapter 3), which focuses upon police powers and processes of investigation by

---

[2] Cm 2263, HMSO, London, 1993.
[3] *The Daily Telegraph*, 7 October 1993, p. 12.
[4] This faith in the value of reform is itself contentious; compare: McConville, M., Sanders, A., and
Leng, R., *The Case for the Prosecution* (Routledge, London, 1991) ch. 10; Craig, P.P., *Public Law
and Democracy in the UK and the USA* (Clarendon, Oxford, 1990) p. 130.

way of arrest, detention and interrogation. There is also an assessment of the regulation of the processes either by the primarily internal mechanism of the Codes of Practice under the Police and Criminal Evidence Act 1984 (PACE) or by external judicial oversight.

The police are generally the gatekeepers to the criminal justice system, so there is a danger that mistakes at this point will become pervasive and amplified. Nevertheless, in line with the reassuring messages from official agencies such as the Crown Prosecution Service and the police that the PACE regime was already tough enough,[5] the Runciman Commission proposed only modest changes,[6] even though there was an emergent catalogue of PACE-era miscarriages of justice and even though the police sometimes condoned abuses committed through the 'noblest cause'.[7]

Thus, radical changes are either treated cursorily or are ignored altogether. These include additional control strategies such as the role of outside scrutiny by the police complaints system[8] or by lay visitors.[9] Redesignation as independent civilian officers of the pivotal custody officers who are charged with overseeing and safeguarding the treatment and welfare of prisoners would be a further possibility.[10] The use of non-police custodians is happening to some extent anyway because of civilianisation (though civilians do, of course remain subject to police orders).[11] But the *Runciman Report*[12] did not recommend any such system: 'To make another body responsible for the custody officer role would mean a serious risk that the police would no longer regard the responsibility for ensuring fair treatment of suspects as being theirs.'. Ironically, this concern for police responsibility was based more on ensuring the integrity (and admissibility) of evidence than on the fair treatment of suspects.

Substantial developments in police interrogation or investigative strategies which were occurring in the early 1990s also largely bypassed the Runciman Commission. As for interrogation, the growing emphasis upon ethical and investigative interviewing[13] is to be welcomed but is problematic as it attempts to assign a quasi-inquisitorial, neutral role to police officers which is unrealistic.[14] Nor is

---

[5] *Submission to Runciman Commission* (1990) para. 3.1.1. The Police Service also viewed the regulation of PACE as strict: *Submission* (1991) para. 1.1.5.

[6] These have been largely implemented but reform is still awaited on s. 77 (protection for persons who are mentally ill or disordered as well as those who are mentally handicapped): *Runciman Report*, ch. 4 para. 40.

[7] Alderson, J., 'The police' in Stockdale, E. and Casale, S., *Criminal Justice under Stress* (Blackstone Press, London, 1992) at p. 13. Similar problems are experienced in the USA: Huff, C.R., Rattner, A. and Sagarin, E., *Convicted But Innocent: Wrongful Conviction and Public Policy* (Sage, Thousand Oaks, 1996) at p. 64; Johnson, G., 'False confessions and fundamental fairness' (1997) 6 *Boston University Public Interest Law Journal* 719; White, W.S., 'False confessions and the constitution' (1997) 32 *Harvard Civil Rights – Civil Liberties Law Review* 185.

[8] See: Goldsmith, A.J (ed.), *Complaints Against the Police* (Oxford Univ Press, 1991); Maguire, M. and Corbett, C., *A Study of the Police Complaints System* (HMSO, London, 1991); Hayes, M., *A Police Ombudsman for Northern Ireland?* (Northern Ireland Office, Belfast, 1997); Home Affairs Committee, *Police Disciplinary and Complaints Procedures* (1997–98 HC 409).

[9] Kemp, C. and Morgan, R, *Lay Visitors to Police Stations* (Bristol University, 1990): Walker, C., 'Police and community in Northern Ireland' (1990) 41 *Northern Ireland Legal Quarterly* 105.

[10] See further Walker, C., and Starmer, K., *Justice in Error* (Blackstone Press, London, 1993) p. 34.

[11] Graham, V., 'Civvy streak' (1995) 103 *Police Review*, 25 August 16.

[12] *Runciman Report*, ch. 3 para. 25.

[13] See Home Office Central Planning and Training Unit, *The Interviewer's Rule Book* (1992); Home Office Central Planning and Training Unit, *A Guide to Interviewing* (1992); Home Office Circular 7/1992, 'Investigative interviewing'.

there sufficient training or disciplinary force behind the ethics at the heart of the project.[15] If confessions offer such fallible evidence, why rely on them at all as evidence proffered on behalf of the State in court? One response might be that other forms of evidence turn out also to be fallible and subject to manipulation. This is true of forensic evidence, as discussed in Chapter 6. 'Independent' third party witnesses equally involve drawbacks. In so far as the witnesses are confederates of the defendants, professional informers or cell-mates, the perils of unreliable evidence have been exemplified in terrorist cases by the widespread use of 'supergrasses' in Northern Ireland between 1981 and 1986.[16] Not only did they fail to secure convictions on the basis of their highly dubious testimony, but they tarnished the reputation of the criminal justice system in the minds of many sections of society. As for genuinely independent third parties (assuming they exist, are not ignored by the police in favour of confessions[17] and are willing to testify), the different problems arise of how the police select which persons to interview and then compile statements from them. Without a rival team of defence investigators to keep a check, there is always the possibility that the police will try to construct a case from witnesses sympathetic to their analysis and will pressure or ignore 'hostile' persons.[18] There are also remarkably scant controls governing the taking of witness statements, and so all the pre-PACE dangers of inaccurate records, pressure and verballing remain.[19]

A further strategy for avoiding dependence upon confessions would be to catch criminals *in flagrante*. Yet, this most direct form of evidence can also lead to acute dilemmas in two directions. First, the 'criminals' may only be effectively caught in this way if their criminality can be channelled by the police in ways which are manageable in relation to their evidence-gathering capabilities. The danger thus arises that the police will induce crime of a kind and in a location which would otherwise never have occurred. Examples include the setting up of bogus second-hand dealers, encouraging the trade in stolen goods[20] or the temptation of unguarded goods on the back of a van.[21] A second, equally serious problem is that where the criminals or terrorists have not been set up by the police, then any police intervention at the point of fruition of the crime may well put at deadly peril the police themselves, members of the public and, of course, the criminals or terrorists.[22]

One might next rely upon the uncovering of physical evidence by way of searches. However, though the evidence found, if any, might be less controversial, the search powers utilised are often open to abuse. For example, there remains a

---

[14] Compare Williamson, T., 'Investigative interviewing' (1992) 8 *Policing* 286; 'Police investigation' in Leishman, F., Loveday, B. and Savage, S., *Core Issues in Policing* (Longman, London, 1996) p. 37; Shepherd, E., 'The trouble with PEACE' (1996) 104 *Police Review* 26 July 14.

[15] Newton, T., 'The place of ethics in investigative interviewing by police officers' (1998) 37 *Howard Journal* 52.

[16] See: Hogan, G. and Walker, C., *Political Violence and the Law in Ireland* (Manchester, 1989) pp. 123 to 126; Carrington, K., *et al.*, *Travesty!* (Pluto Press, Leichhardt, 1991) ch. 11; Greer, S.C., *Supergrasses: a study in anti-terrorist law enforcement in Northern Ireland* (Clarendon Press, Oxford, 1994).

[17] Sargant, T. and Hill, P., *Criminal Trials* (Fabian Research Series No. 348, London, 1986) p. 4.

[18] See: *ibid.*, p. 10; McConville, M., Sanders, A. and Leng, R., *The Case for the Prosecution* (Routledge, London, 1991).

[19] Moston, S. and Stephenson, G.M., *The Questioning and Interviewing of Suspects outside the Police Station* (Royal Commission on Criminal Justice Research Study No. 22, HMSO, London, 1993).

[20] See *R v Christou* [1992] 2 WLR 228.

[21] *R v Williams* [1993] 3 All ER 365.

[22] See: Amnesty International, *Killings by Security Forces and Supergrass Trials* (London, 1988).

strong case for reducing or abolishing the available powers to stop and search, and the regulatory regime is equally deficient in regard to searches of physical property.[23] The treatment of individuals in custody in terms of searches of them for incriminating evidence is even more scandalous and seems to stem from English law's blindness to the value of privacy.[24] Accordingly, those powers in sections 32, 54, and 61 to 63 of PACE which self-authorise police searches of prisoners should be reformulated, except perhaps in a serious emergency or for items designed to injure or effect an escape. The idea that procedures such as fingerprinting and other bodily samples should require judicial authorisation, as was the case before 1984[25] was strongly opposed by the Police Service and Home Office submissions to the Runciman Commission,[26] and the Criminal Justice and Public Order Act 1994 has stepped decisively in the opposite direction.

Rather than seeking to avoid interrogation processes altogether, it might be more sensible to ask, why rely on confessions in the absence of some form of independent confirmation of guilt or other limit upon reliance on the veracity of a statement alone, such as a rule requiring corroboration,[27] a warning to the jury, the requirement of the presence of a lawyer[28] or a formal reaffirmation before a magistrate? Many of these restrictions were advocated in submissions to the Runciman Commission,[29] though none is without its own drawbacks. A majority of the Royal Commission concluded that confession evidence *per se* should continue to found convictions without corroboration but with a warning as to unreliability to the jury.[30] In response, the Government rejected the recommendation, stating that '. . . if a confession has passed all the tests in PACE . . . it is difficult to see why a jury should be warned of the dangers of convicting on it.'[31] The answer is that this view ignores the difference between the admissibility of evidence and the weight to be accorded to evidence. It also turn a blind eye to practices which have brought into disrepute the integrity of criminal justice within the past decade.

If confessions and statements are to continue in use, then good records are essential. However, the Runciman Commission viewed the extension of tape recording requirements to suspects or witnesses beyond the police station as impractical and costly,[32] even though the lack of a good record is alleged to be a

---

[23] See further, Walker, C., and Starmer, K., (eds.) *Justice in Error* (Blackstone Press, London, 1993) pp. 32–3.

[24] *Malone* v *MPC (No. 2)* [1979] ch. 344.

[25] See: Magistrates' Courts Act 1980, s. 49.

[26] Police Service, *Evidence* (1991) pp. 68–71; Home Office, *Memoranda* (1991) para. 1.14. See also the assertion that more protection should be afforded to property than to body as a site of privacy in Redmayne, M., 'The DNA Database' [1998] *Criminal Law Review* 437 at p. 444.

[27] Pattenden, R, 'Should confessions be corroborated?' (1991) 107 *Law Quarterly Review* 317. Few cases lack corroboration: JUSTICE, *Unreliable Evidence? Confessions and the Safety of Convictions* (London, 1994) p. 26.

[28] But this might not be effective as most produce guilty pleas: Huff, C.R, Rattner, A. and Sagarin, E., *Convicted But Innocent: Wrongful Conviction and Public Policy* (Sage, Thousand Oaks, 1996) at p. 138.

[29] See Mansfield, M., *Presumed Guilty* (Heinemann, London, 1993) pp. 95–6; Dennis, I., 'Miscarriages of justice and the law of confessions' [1993] *Public Law* 291.

[30] *Runciman Report*, ch. 4 paras. 77, 85, 87. See Jackson, J., 'Royal Commission on Criminal Justice: the evidence recommendations' [1993] *Criminal Law Review* 817.

[31] Lord Chancellor's Department, Home Office and Law Officers' Department, *The Royal Commission on Criminal Justice: Final Government Response* (Home Office, London, 1996) para. 48.

[32] *Runciman Report*, ch. 2 para. 15, ch. 3 para. 12. Compare Fenwick, H., 'Confessions, recording rules and miscarriages of justice' [1993] *Criminal Law Review* 174; Wolchover, D. and Heaton-Armstrong, A., 'Tape-recording witness statements' (1997) 147 *New Law Journal* 855, 894.

major cause of wrongful acquittals, since evidence of prosecution witnesses can be undermined by lack of recollection or fidelity to police statements.

We must also think in terms other than traditional questioning of suspects in police stations,[33] and this 'multi-faceted and multi-functional' range of policing tactics has been very much fostered by the Audit Commission's police studies.[34] These other approaches principally include more proactive techniques such as surveillance,[35] targeting, crime pattern analysis, informants, police cell stooges[36] and undercover agents.[37] All await the public debate, if not the control and rationalisation which PACE achieved in regard to police station detention. Such tactics often involve specialist police squads, the insularity of which breeds abuses, as illustrated in the West Midlands cases. Endorsed by the Runciman Commission, HM Inspectorate of Constabulary has called for published terms of reference, clearer rules as to staff selection and turnover, and clearer lines of supervision and internal inspection.[38]

Though methods of police investigation may be increasingly divorced from the police station, the adversarial system is unlikely to swing into operation until the conflict reaches that point. The story is taken up in Chapter 4, 'The Right to Legal Advice'. In an adversarial system, fairness surely requires that professionalisation within the police and prosecution services be matched by the defence, especially through the provision of adequate legal assistance.[39] In this way, the premise is that the intervention by solicitors provides a major safeguard against miscarriages of justice and provides a core protection for the detainee.[40] Certainly, the courts have depicted defence lawyers in that light, most notably in *R v Samuel*.[41] There is also empirical evidence to support this link. In a survey by JUSTICE of 89 cases in which there was an allegation of a miscarriage of justice,[42] in 33 out of 71 post-PACE cases surveyed, legal advice was allegedly refused or not reasonably arranged; it equally found, agreeing with Chapter 4, passivity on the part of lawyers whose services were obtained and lack of knowledge of the facts of the client's case.

Changes within the PACE regime are therefore still necessary to achieve a more effective equality of arms. Aside from those considered in Chapter 4, others might include police notification of rights at the moment of arrest rather than on arrival

---

[33] *Ibid.* at p. 894.
[34] Audit Commission, *Helping with Enquiries* (London, 1993), *Streetwise* (London, 1996).
[35] Police Act 1997, pt. III.
[36] *R v Morley* [1994] *Criminal Law Review* 919; *R v Parker* [1995] *Criminal Law Review* 233; *R v Roberts* [1997] *Criminal Law Review* 222.
[37] See Dunnington, C. and Norris, C., 'The nark's game' (1996) 146 *New Law Journal* 402, 456; Sharpe, S., 'Covert police operations and the discretionary exclusion of evidence' [1994] *Criminal Law Review* 793; Robertson, G., 'Entrapment evidence' [1994] *Criminal Law Review* 805.
[38] Letter to chief officers 18 February 1992, as reported in *Runciman Report*, ch. 2, paras. 63–5.
[39] The role of the appropriate adult could also be strengthened. See Gudjonsson, G., Clare, C., Rutter, S., and Pearse, J., *Persons at Risk During Interviews in Police Custody* (Royal Commission on Criminal Justice Research Study No. 12, HMSO, London, 1992); *Runicman Report* ch. 3 para. 86 (suggesting local panels of lay persons or of duty solicitors); Nemitz, T. and Bean, P., 'The use of the "appropriate adult" scheme (a preliminary report)' (1994) 34 *Medicine Science & Law* 161; Littlechild, B., 'Reassessing the role of the appropriate adult' [1995] *Criminal Law Review* 540; Thomas, T., 'The continuing story of the "appropriate adult"?' (1995) 34 *Howard Journal* 151; Palmer, C., 'Still vulnerable after all these years' [1996] *Criminal Law Review* 633; Hodgson, J., 'Vulnerable suspects and the appropriate adult' [1997] *Criminal Law Review* 785.
[40] See Berger, M., 'Legislating confession law in Great Britain' (1990) 24 *University of Michigan Journal of Law Reform* 1 at p. 59.
[41] [1988] 2 WLR 920. See also *Director of Public Prosecutions v Billington* [1988] 1 All ER 435; *R v Parris* (1989) 89 Cr App R 68; *R v Raghip, Silcott and Braithwaite, The Times*, 9 December 1991.
[42] JUSTICE, *Unreliable Evidence? Confessions and the Safety of Convictions* (London, 1994) ch. 2.

at the police station,[43] effective early disclosure of the police case,[44] no waiver of the right without advice from a solicitor[45] and denial of access (admittedly now rare) to be confirmed by a judge.[46] Commentators have also suggested that no interrogation should take place or perhaps no statement be admissible unless a lawyer is present.[47] There may be a host of other reforms necessary to make legal assistance effective, such as legal aid funding at adequate levels[48] and the extension of rights of audience for solicitor-advocates.[49] At the later stages of the process, the propensity of barristers to inflict late changes in personnel on hapless defendants has come under scrutiny.[50] The problem may be alleviated by better trial listing practices and greater use of pre-trial reviews (discussed further in Chapter 9) but must also be a matter of personal professional responsibility.

Even when experienced lawyers do make an appearance at the police station, and accreditation schemes and conditions of attendance attached to legal aid have improved their performance in this respect,[51] Chapter 4 grieves their lack of an adversarial approach.[52] This phenomenon has been recognised in other contexts and is said to result from the 'local legal culture' that inevitably arises.[53] The effect is that the practices of actors within the criminal justice system are to be understood in terms of their common expectations, workgroup practices and social relations, which mean that they strive for co-operation and negotiation rather than conflict and confrontation. The lawyer is on police territory and in need of their beneficence in order to make professional life liveable.[54] By comparison, the client is a transient and socially remote character who is unlikely to influence prevailing outlooks.

---

[43] See submissions to the Runciman Commission from Amnesty International (para. 4.1.1), Law Society (para. 1.118), CPS (para. 3.6.11); Police Service (p. 83). The Law Society (para. 1.14) also called for a video record to be made of the processing of the suspect on arrival at the station.

[44] There is a right to see the custody record and record of interview: PACE Code C para. 2.4 (1995 ed.). But see also *Runciman Report*, ch. 3 paras. 52, 53; Hodgson, J., 'No defence for the Royal Commission' in McConville, M. and Bridges, L., (eds.) *Criminal Justice in Crisis* (Edward Elgar, Aldershot, 1994); Ede, R., 'New improved PACE' (1995) 139 *Solicitors' Journal* 298; Wolchover, D. and Heaton-Armstrong, A., 'Questioning and identification: changes under PACE 95' [1995] *Criminal Law Review* 356.

[45] Law Society, *Evidence* (1991) para. 1.24; Liberty, *Submission* p. 21.

[46] Amnesty International, *Submission* (1991) para. 4.2.3.

[47] See Sanders, A. and Young, R, *Criminal Justice* (Butterworths, London, 1994) p. 203.

[48] The *Runciman Report* (ch. 8 para. 94) recognises that the level of fees is a disincentive to criminal practice, but no concession has been made to this point: Lord Chancellor's Department, Home Office and Law Officers' Department, *The Royal Commission on Criminal Justice: Final Government Response* (Home Office, London, 1996) para. 138.

[49] Courts and Legal Services Act 1990, s. 67.

[50] Zander ('The Royal Commission's Crown Court survey' (1992) 142 *New Law Journal* 1730) found that 50 per cent of barristers were first briefed within 24 hours of the trial, though 95 per cent of defendants felt they had been properly represented.

[51] Lord Chancellor's Department, Home Office and Law Officers' Department, *The Royal Commission on Criminal Justice: Final Government Response* (Home Office, London, 1996) para. 33.

[52] This includes undue trust in the accuracy of transcripts from taped interviews: Baldwin J., *Preparing the Record of Taped Interviews* (Royal Commission on Criminal Justice Research Study No. 2, HMSO, London, 1992). The *Runciman Report*, ch. 3 para. 86, suggests further consideration.

[53] See: Blumberg, A., 'The practice of law as a confidence game' (1967) 1 *Law and Society Review* 15; Skolnik, J., 'Social control in the adversary system' (1967) 11 *Journal of Conflict Resolution* 52; Baldwin, J. and McConville, M., *Negotiated Justice* (Martin Robertson, London, 1977); McConville M., *et al.*, *The Case for the Prosecution* (Routledge, London, 1991), p. 167.

[54] See Cape, E., 'Defence services' in McConville, M. and Bridges, L., (eds.) *Criminal Justice in Crisis* (Edward Elgar, Aldershot, 1994). Other reasons may include the professional distance from clients and (in the case of barristers) the willingness to act for prosecution or defence: Pizzi, W., 'Discovering who we are: an English perspective on the Simpson trial' (1996) 63 *University of Colorado Law Review* 1027.

One lesson would seem to be the importance of constant retraining in the ethos of the defender, so as to achieve some distance between lawyer and police and greater commitment to the client.[55] A public defender system, as in the USA,[56] presents a more radical solution. However, such a system is vulnerable to State manipulation in terms of funding and so may not be able to attract the calibre of recruit necessary or may not equip them with adequate resources.[57] Nevertheless, a pilot public defender scheme has now been established under the Crime and Punishment (Scotland) Act 1997. The Legal Aid Board's proposals for franchising or block contracting specialist legal services[58] may reduce the dangers of financial manipulation in a specific case but at some cost to choice for defendants (especially in difficult and non-routine cases) and the professional autonomy to act extensively and obstructively in the interests of the client. If the defendant fails to receive competent legal assistance through no fault of his or her own (such as failure to give full instructions), then an equality of arms has not been secured.[59] Accordingly, significant mistakes or failures by lawyers who are said to be 'gravely at fault', as in the *Cardiff Three* case,[60] should provide a ground for appeal.[61]

Most of the safeguards for the accused, including those just proposed, only bite in the context of a regulated detention in the police station. Where interrogation takes place outside that context, especially at the scene of a crime or in a police car following 'the scenic route' back to the police station, then few checks and balances are possible.[62] Another vulnerable group are prisoners held by the Prison Service.[63] These form an available population replete with intelligence about crimes, and, as the prison population increases, the temptation will be to see them as easy prey for evidence. It is arguable that a confession alone should not be sufficient evidence for a conviction in these circumstances and that some form of corroboration should be demanded. This matter will be considered further in Chapter 9. In the meantime, attention will be turned to the exercise of 'the right to silence', which is often linked to the grudging improvement in the availability of legal advice.[64] That link has now been touched upon, but the fundamental worth of a right to silence is yet to be determined. The issue is taken up in Chapter 5, 'The Right to Silence'.

---

[55] There are now plans to measure client satisfaction: Lord Chancellor's Department, *Striking the Balance: The Future of Legal Aid in England and Wales* (Cm 3305, HMSO, London, 1996) para. 3.18.

[56] See: McIntyre, L., *The Public Defender* (University of Chicago Press, 1987); Spangenberg, R., 'Indigent defence systems in the US' (1995) 58 *Law and Contemporary Problems* 32; Watson, A., 'Public defender schemes in the United States: lesson for Britain?' (1997) 161 *Justice of the Peace* 1031.

[57] See Wall, D., 'Legal aid, social policy and the architecture of criminal justice' (1996) 23 *Journal of Law & Society* 549 at p. 561.

[58] See: Lord Chancellor's Department, *Striking the Balance: The Future of Legal Aid in England and Wales* (Cm 3305, HMSO, London, 1996) ch. 3; Wall, D., 'Legal aid, social policy and the architecture of criminal justice' (1996) 23 *Journal of Law & Society* 549 at p. 560.

[59] See *Neimeister v Austria*, Appl. no. 1936/63, Ser. A vol. 8 (1968).

[60] *R v Paris, Miller, Abdullahi*, The Times, [1993] 97 Cr App R 99.

[61] LAG, Submission to the Runciman Commission (1991).

[62] The most recent version of PACE Code C para. 11.1 is subject to a restrictive definition of 'interview', is subject to exceptions and is not automatically enforceable by exclusion. The submissions of the CPS (para. 3.6.3) and Law Society (para. 1.120) suggested that the suspect should be invited to repeat any admission on tape in the station; compare Police Service, p. 217.

[63] See e.g. *R v Rowe* [1994] *Criminal Law Review* 837; Lidstone, K. and Palmer, C., *The Investigation of Crime* (2nd ed., Butterworths, London, 1996) p. 499.

[64] Friendly, H., 'The Fifth Amendment Tomorrow: The Case for Constitutional Change' (1968) 37 *University of Cincinnati Law Review* 671.

As has been pointed out elsewhere,[65] the role of the right to silence in a criminal justice system ultimately depends on whether it is recognised as a fundamental right or is viewed in instrumental, often utilitarian, terms. English law has been traditionally reluctant to confer a meta-legal status upon any claim against the State. However, the vital nature of the privilege against self incrimination in a common law adversarial system[66] is confirmed by its expression in the Fifth Amendment to the US Constitution, 'no person . . . shall be compelled in any criminal cases to be a witness against himself . . . '. If the case for the right to silence in rights terms is accepted, then it should not be restricted or abolished for utilitarian gain, such as to make the police more efficient. However, even if a utilitarian approach were adopted, one may still doubt on the evidence whether the benefits are certain or substantial enough to outweigh the costs of aggressive police forces and miscarriages of justice.

The proposals before the Runciman Commission neatly illustrated that divergence of viewpoints,[67] and the role of the right to silence in the criminal justice process turned out to be one of the most closely debated issues. Reflecting the division of views, the *Runciman Report* set out arguments in favour of change (the need to tap a potential source of information and to test known information against that testimony in a way which reduces the pressure for a confession and is subject to all the safeguards of PACE) and also the arguments against (the recognition that there can be legitimate reasons for silence and the need to encourage the police to look for evidence beyond the suspect).[68] Bolstered by research findings that silence is not disproportionately a resort of professional criminals nor indeed does it increase the chances of acquittal,[69] the majority of Commissioners opposed any change, believing that the risks of adverse comment on silence would be too great, especially for 'the less experienced and more vulnerable suspects'.[70] However, even the majority thought that silence at trial should be treated differently, with the possibility of adverse inferences being drawn from it.[71] This proposed amendment was said to ensure earlier and better preparation of cases (or the disposal of weak

---

[65] See: Easton, S.M., *The Right to Silence* (Avebury, Aldershot, 1991) ch. 6. For appraisals of these arguments, see Friendly, H.J., 'The Fifth Amendment Tomorrow: The Case for Constitutional Change' (1968) 37 *University of Cincinnati Law Review* 671; Greenawalt, R.K., 'Silence As a Moral and Constitutional Right' (1981) 23 *William & Mary Law Review* 15; Arenella, P., 'Schmerber and the Privilege Against Self-Incrimination: A Reappraisal' (1982) 20 *American Criminal Law Review* 31; Dolinko, D., 'Is There a Rationale for the Privilege Against Self-Incrimination?' (1986) 33 *UCLA Law Review* 1063 (1986); Dripps, D.A., 'Against Police Interrogation – And the Privilege Against Self-Incrimination' (1988) 78 *Journal of Criminal Law & Criminology* 699; Allen, R.J., 'Reform: the system: the Simpson affair, reform of the criminal justice process, and magic bullets' (1996) 67 *Colorado Law Review* 989.

[66] It is implicit in the European Convention on Human Rights (1950) Art. 6.

[67] See Walker, C., and Starmer, K., (eds.) *Justice in Error* (Blackstone Press, London, 1993) pp. 72–4.

[68] *Runciman Report*, ch. 4 paras. 6–14.

[69] *Runciman Report*, ch. 4 para. 19. See Leng, R, *The Right to Silence in Police Interrogation* (Royal Commission on Criminal Justice Research Study No. 10, HMSO, London, 1993) p. 73. The difference made by the presence of legal advisers was viewed as more equivocal, but two research studies strongly suggested that silence was not commonly advised and arose from lack of legal experience or an information deficit about the case rather than as an obstructive tactic; see: Baldwin, J., *The Role of Legal Representatives at the Police Station* (Royal Commission on Criminal Justice Research Study No. 3, HMSO, London, 1993) pp. 37–41; McConville, M. and Hodgson, J, *Custodial Legal Advice and the Right to Silence* (Royal Commission on Criminal Justice Research Study No. 16, HMSO, London, 1993) chs. 5, 6.

[70] Runciman Report, ch. 4 para. 23.

[71] *Ibid.* paras. 26–27, ch. 6 paras. 2, 70.

ones), more accurate trial estimates and more focused trials. By way of dissent, it was suggested that the burden of proof was unconscionably affected, that there was no evidence that ambush defences were a significant problem or that the minimal requirements of disclosure would help when an ambush did occur.[72] In the event, and as delineated in Chapter 5, the Criminal Justice and Public Order Act 1994 brings about the evisceration of the right to silence, overriding the Runciman Commission's caution against inferences from pre-trial silence and implementing the suggested changes to trial rules. The changes have implications for the very nature of the criminal justice system which throws into question the recognition of fundamental precepts and rights,[73] though, as outlined in Chapters 2 and 5, these concerns must be understood in the light of both politics and recent legal history.[74]

It is right to question the panic over the loss of the 'right to silence' and to ask how silence relates to miscarriages of justice. The answer must lie in three respects. First, there is a danger that suspects will be pressured to speak, leading to false confessions. A post-1994 Act survey by the London Criminal Courts Solicitors' Association found that fewer clients made or were advised to engage in 'No Comment' strategies (down from 71 per cent to 35 per cent), as a result of which 84 per cent of solicitors surveyed thought more innocent persons would be convicted.[75] Confessions should not be excluded as sources of evidence, but the more involuntary the circumstances in which they are obtained, the more dubious their evidential value. Thus, the system should provide for an effective right to silence, which takes us back to issues of conditions of detention and especially the presence of legal advice.[76] The second danger is that the system will be viewed as lacking in integrity having regard to its adversarial credentials. The prosecution is no longer proving its case and should not be allowed to call in aid silences. There may also be damage from the encouragement of perjured evidence by the guilty (though inference from silence may conversely discourage perjury at the later trial).[77] Thirdly there is the danger that mistakes will be made in the inferences drawn from silence, the evidential value of which is far from self-evident:[78]

There are many valid reasons why even an innocent person may choose not to testify. Timid or nervous witnesses often do not fare well on the witness stand.

---

[72] See Note of Dissent to the *Runciman Report* given by Professor Michael Zander at p. 222. See further Zander, M., 'You have no right to remain silent' (1996) 40 *Saint Louis University Law Review* 659.

[73] See O'Reilly, G.W., 'England limits the right to silence and moves towards an inquisitorial system of justice' (1994) 85 *Journal of Criminal Law & Criminology* 402. Compare Ingraham, B.L., 'The right of silence, the presumption of innocence, the burden of proof, and a modest proposal: a reply to O'Reilly' (1996) 86 *Journal of Criminal Law & Criminology* 559; O'Reilly, G.W., 'Criminal law: comment on Ingraham's "moral duty" to talk and the right to silence' (1997) 87 *Journal of Criminal Law & Criminology* 521.

[74] The change has also been raised in the USA: United States Department of Justice, Office of Legal Policy, 'Adverse Inferences from Silence' (1989) 22 *University of Michigan Journal of Law Reform* 1005, 1120–1.

[75] Williams, J., 'Inferences from silence' (1997) 141 *Solicitors' Journal* 566. Bucke, T. and Brown, D., *In police custody: police powers and suspects' rights under the revised PACE codes of practice* (Home Office Research Study 174, Home Office, 1998) confirm that the refusal to answer all questions has become less common.

[76] See Chase, C.A., 'Hearing the "sounds of silence" in criminal trials: a look at recent British law reforms with an eye toward reforming the American criminal justice system' (1996) 44 *Kansas Law Review* 929 at p. 947.

[77] *Ibid.* at pp. 945, 946.

[78] *Ibid.* at p. 944. Consider also the failure to give a sample in *R* v *McGranaghan (note)* [1995] 1 Cr App Rep 559.

Their timidity or nervousness may often be mistaken for evasiveness or deception. Even a confident, self-assured witness can be confused or embarrassed by a skilful cross-examiner.

Certainly the potential link with miscarriages of justice was seen by the future Lord Chancellor in 1994: 'The confused, the inarticulate, the weak and the inadequate are prone to suggestion and bullying; and they need the right to silence.'.[79] As Chapter 5 concludes, the European Convention and the Human Rights Act 1998 demand reform before further harm is done.

Forensic evidence is the focus of Chapter 6. The emphasis on this mode of crime investigation has increased considerably in recent years, not least because of the development of DNA analysis and storage. There are those who have viewed the progress of forensic science as the saviour of the criminal justice system, especially by circumventing the problems of confessions and police malpractices. Yet, Chapter 6 demonstrates that this view is facile, as it ignores the uncertainties inherent within forensic evidence and also the failures on the part of scientists which have themselves created miscarriages of justice such as in the cases of the *Maguire Seven* and *Judith Ward*.[80] The response of the Runciman Commission was radical and ambitious. It called for a statutory Forensic Science Advisory Council which could set and audit high standards both for personnel and for laboratories. Yet, the Government of the day stood firmly against the model of statutory regulation and accepted only in lukewarm terms the value of a non-statutory body performing some of the same roles. However, the disquiet about this neglectful attitude, strongly expressed in Professor Caddy's report,[81] has shaken this complacency though not to the extent of any firm promises to legislate. Accordingly, even five years after the *Runciman Report*, there is still no official movement in these areas, though the forensic professions themselves are now moving towards more systematic self-regulation. It is suggested that the principal explanation for the failure to act is cost. One might concede with some wry regret that the episode provides some vindication of the Commission's steadfastness in having regard to the consideration of due economy, for in one of the two areas where significant and wholly new public spending is adventurously required (the other being the Criminal Cases Review Commission, as discussed in Chapter 10), it has not been forthcoming.

The issues in Chapter 7, 'Disclosure: Principles, Processes and Politics', in several ways take us back to the debates in chapter 5, though many of the problems concerning non-disclosure have centred on forensic evidence. One may start again with the proposition that full prosecution disclosure of the evidence gathered by the agencies of the State is an integral part of a right to a fair trial. This proposition has been accepted under the European Convention on Human Rights,[82] but even without its intercession, disclosure rights have already been recognised as part of English common law by Lord Justice Steyn in *R v Brown (Winston)*:[83]

---

[79] HL Debs. vol. 554 col. 502, 25 April 1994, Lord Irvine.
[80] See also Chapter 2 for details of these cases and also *R v McGranaghan (note)* [1995] 1 Cr App R 559.
[81] See Caddy, B., *Assessment and Implications of Centrifuge Contamination in the Trace Explosive Section of the Forensic Explosives Laboratory at Fort Halstead* (Cm 3491, HMSO, London 1996) Appendix 4.
[82] See *Edwards v United Kingdom*, Appl. no. 13071/87, Ser. A no. 247-B, (1993) 15 EHRR 417.
[83] [1994] 1 WLR 1599 at p. 1606.

In our adversarial system, in which the police and the prosecution control the investigatory process, an accused's right to fair disclosure is an inseparable part of his right to a fair trial.

The reverse proposition is also true – that non disclosure results in miscarriages of justice is illustrated by several of the prominent cases detailed in Chapter 2, especially the *Judith Ward* and *Guildford* and *Maguire* cases.[84]

One would suppose that any opposition to fulsome prosecution disclosure would be unthinkable in the light of these events, but when the courts edged towards demanding it in cases such as *Ward*,[85] there ensued a backlash. The police especially began to balk at this prospect of stronger and more enforceable rules and sought to have trimmed the expanding duties which they said had caused up to 60 major cases to be dropped so as to protect witnesses and informants,[86] and which had also produced severe administrative burdens.[87] As Chapter 7 describes, faced with a mixture of 'law and order' and efficiency concerns, it should be no surprise that a Conservative administration was readily persuaded of the need for change. The resultant Criminal Procedure and Investigations Act 1996 delivers a number of reforms, but two are most prominent. One is the narrowing of the duty to disclose. Even more controversially, the Act imposes a requirement on the defence to carry out its own disclosure so as to secure fuller prosecution disclosure and in any event to avoid adverse comment or inferences in court. The implications of the latter are severe; the requirement alters the balance of forces between prosecution and defence, despite giving the latter no extra resources to carry out independent investigations.[88] The Act fatally fails to understand that the defendant is essentially reactive and has few resources to investigate *de novo*; consequently, it should be up to the prosecution to make out the case in every respect in the absence of an impartial third force for investigation.[89]

Aside from objections in principle, there are also grave doubts about whether even the more miserly levels of disclosure will be delivered. Police disclosure officers may be subject to a code of conduct, but it does not mention the fundamental right to disclosure of the defence or more general ethical concerns to act fairly. In turn, prosecutors are not investigators, and so must rely upon the

---

[84] For more comprehensive lists, see Gershman, B.L., 'The New Prosecutors' (1992) 53 *University of Pittsburg Law Review* 393, at pp. 451–4; JUSTICE, *Disclosure: A Consultation Paper, the JUSTICE Response* (London, 1995); Niblett, J., *Disclosure in Criminal Proceedings* (Blackstone Press, London, 1997) ch. 3. See also May, Sir John, *Report of the inquiry into the circumstances surrounding the convictions arising out of the bomb attacks in Guildford and Woolwich in 1974, Interim Report* (HC 556 of 1989–90) chs.11–13.

[85] (1992) 96 Cr. App. R 1. See also *R* v *Keane* [1994] 1 WLR 746; *R* v *Brown (Winston)* [1994] 1 WLR 1599. Similar changes occurred in Northern Ireland; see *R* v *Harper and another* [1994] NI 199.

[86] See Police Service, *Submission*, para. 2.3.2, p. 133; Rozenberg, J., *The Search for Justice* (Hodder & Stoughton, London, 1994) p. 341; Pollard, C., 'A case for disclosure' [1994] *Criminal Law Review* 42.

[87] Lord Chancellor's Department, Home Office and Law Officers' Department, *The Royal Commission on Criminal Justice: Final Government Response* (Home Office, London, 1996) para. 75.

[88] See Leng, R., 'Losing sight of the defendant' [1995] *Criminal Law Review* 704; Redmayne, M., 'Process gains and process values' (1997) 60 *Modern Law Review* 79.

[89] See further Young, R, and Sanders, A., 'Boxing in the defence: the Royal Commission, disclosure and the lessons of research' (1994) 50 *Criminal Lawyer* 3 (a survey of criminal legal aid applications suggested defendants would fare badly if defence solicitors were required to disclose their case by completing a standard form as the Runciman Commission proposed).

evidence passed on by the disclosure officers. Acute problems of disclosure may arise when the investigators include non-police experts, such as forensic scientists. How does a scientist know what is material unless aware of the whole of case from both sides? In reality, they will not be fully aware of the police case, but their duty is to reveal to the prosecution which may then filter the evidence thence to the prosecutor and the court.[90] Even the courts seem to be losing the stomach for a fight against unethical behaviour. In *R v Mills; R v Poole*,[91] the Court of Appeal found a risk of injustice from the non-disclosure of the statement of a witness thought to be untruthful but went on to uphold the conviction as safe.

Other adversarial jurisdictions have recognised the importance of disclosure. The US Supreme Court has recognised constitutional duties to disclose. Such a duty in Federal cases was imposed in *Jencks v US* in respect of prior statements of witnesses.[92] This duty, with some modifications, is now contained in the 'Jencks' Act.[93] Next the Court decided that it would be a violation of due process for the prosecution to fail to disclose evidence in its possession that testimony given on its behalf was perjured.[94] Eventually, however, the Court developed a wider duty to disclose any evidence sufficient to create 'a reasonable doubt that did not otherwise exist' as to the guilt of the defendant.[95] This level of disclosure is no longer on offer in England and Wales, but pressure from the European Convention may eventually swing back the law in this direction.

The closely related Chapter 8, on 'Public Interest Immunity and Criminal Justice', considers the significant and growing impact of this doctrine in recent years. Rather like the arguments in relation to disclosure generally, it must be recognised that defendants in criminal prosecutions are not the paradigm voluntary and equal suitors of civil litigation. Accordingly, the laws of public interest immunity (PII), which have been largely developed in the civil courts and have crept into criminal process without clear understanding or purpose, must be modified if miscarriages of justice are not to occur. A major miscarriage of justice did occur from a failure to have regard to this distinction. It concerned the directors of the Matrix Churchill company who were prosecuted over selling equipment to Iraq. They were eventually acquitted, though only after suffering great personal anxiety and effort but also inflicting great political discomfort and damage on the Conservative Government. Chapter 8 relates that some of the governmental practices have changed for the better. But neither laws nor practices are either

---

[90] See Jones, C.A.G., *Expert Witnesses* (Clarendon Press, Oxford, 1994) pp. 191–2; Lawson, E., 'Third party disclosure' (1997) 37 *Medicine Science and Law* 120.

[91] [1997] 3 All ER 780.

[92] 353 US 657 (1957). See notes at (1959) 11 *Stanford Law Review* 257; (1979) 54 *New York University Law Review* 801.

[93] 18 USCA s. 3500. See note at (1958) 67 *Yale Law Journal* 674; (1960) 38 *Texas Law Review* 595; Traynor, R.J., 'Ground lost and found in criminal discovery' (1964) 39 *New York University Law Review* 228.

[94] *Alcorta v Texas* 355 US 28 (1957); *Nagua v Illinois* 360 US 264 (1959); *Miller v Pate* 386 US 1 (1967).

[95] *US v Agurs* 427 US 97 (1976). The more limited rules imposed in State trials require proof that the favourable evidence could reasonably be taken to put the whole case in such a different light as to undermine confidence in the verdict: *Brady v Maryland* 373 US 82 (1963); *Giles v Maryland* 386 US 66 (1967); *US v Bagley* 473 US 39 (1985); *Pennsylvania v Ritchie* 480 US 39 (1987); *Kyles v Whitley* 514 US 419 (1995). See Givelber, D., 'Meaningless acquittals, meaningful convictions: do we reliably acquit the innocent?' (1997) 49 *Rutgers Law Review* 1317 at p. 1386. For allegations of defence abuse, see Mullenix, L.S., 'Discovery in disarray: the pervasive myth of pervasive discovery abuse and the consequences for unfounded rulemaking' (1994) 46 *Stanford Law Review* 1393.

clearer or satisfactory, and it may again take a more distant and impartial hard look from the European Court of Human Rights to bring about more systematic reform.

A duty to disclose by the prosecution is of limited utility if the investigators have closed their eyes to all avenues of exploration promising to the defendant. This dilemma raises the fundamental issue of whether an adversarial system is the best that can be designed to discover the truth or whether an inquisitorial system might be preferable. The conduct of trials in England and Wales under the adversarial model is taken up in the next chapter; the attractions of inquisitorial systems are considered in Part III of the book.

The case for adversarial justice, especially within the context of trial procedures, is the subject of Chapter 9. The chapter considers a variety of features which may dim the supposed beneficial effects of adversarial justice, including modes of trial, the phenomenon of plea bargaining, the rules of evidence and the role of the judge.

As for modes of trial, the assumption is generally that Crown Courts, despite all their imperfections,[96] offer clear advantages to defendants over trial by magistrates because of their more accentuated adversarial features such as a jury and umpireal judge. Indeed, Professor Jackson is keen to reinvigorate the role of jury and judge in fact-finding, the judge being more adept at 'technical' issues such as identification or forensic evidence, while the jury's strength lies in issues of credibility.[97] Likewise the Government recognises the jury (albeit in a paper on *Juries in Serious Fraud Trials* which envisages their curtailment) as 'a cornerstone of our criminal justice system' and as assisting with fairness, independence, democracy, openness, intelligibility and public confidence.[98] However, such mechanisms turn out often to be expensive, so Chapter 9 considers the pressure to diminish jury trials and also questions some of their credentials as superior tribunals of fact to magistrates.[99]

The controversial practices of plea bargaining are next considered in Chapter 9. The pressures towards some form of plea bargaining seem to be growing. There is now the standing statutory offer of a discount for a guilty plea set out in the Criminal Justice and Public Order Act 1994, s. 48. In addition, the experimentation with pre-trial reviews (PTR) is spreading from the magistrates' courts[100] into the Crown Court,[101] given impetus by managerial pressures[102] in favour of PTRs,

---

[96] There is still no commitment to research into the jury, while idea of express inclusion of ethnic minority jurors has been rejected: Lord Chancellor's Department, Home Office and Law Officer's Department, *The Royal Commission on Criminal Justice: Final Government Response* (Home Office, London, 1996) paras. 6, 130.

[97] Jackson, J. and Doran, S., 'Judge and jury' (1997) 60 *Modern Law Review* 759. See also Strier, F., *Reconstructing Justice* (University of Chicago Press, 1996).

[98] Home Office, *Juries in Serious Fraud Trials* (London, 1998) para. 2.2.

[99] See Narey, M., *Review of Delay in the Criminal Justice Process* (Home Office, London, 1997) ch. 6. Other concerns arising from Crown Court trials include the prejudicial impression given by placing the defendant in the dock: Sargant, T. and Hill, P., *Criminal Trials* (Fabian Research Series, 1986) p. 12; Law Society, *Submission* (1991) para. 3.79; Liberty, *Submission* (1991) p. 46. It is now accepted that the defendant should be sited in court close to counsel: Lord Chancellor's Department, Home Office and Law Officers' Department, *The Royal Commission on Criminal Justice: Final Government Response* (Home Office, London, 1996) para. 151.

[100] See: Baldwin, J, *Pre-trial Justice* (Blackwell, Oxford, 1985); Mulcahy A., Brownlee I.D. and Walker C.P., 'PTRs, court efficiency and justice' (1994) 33 *Howard Journal of Criminal Justice* 109.

[101] For earlier rules see *R v Thorn* (1977) 66 Cr App R 6; *R v Atkinson* (1977) 67 Cr App R 200; Practice Rules dated 21 November 1977.

[102] See Le Vay, *Magistrates' Courts: Report of a Scrutiny* (Home Office, London, 1989); Home Affairs Committee, *Home Office Expenditure* (1988–89 HC 314); Home Office Working Group on Pre-Trial Issues (Home Office, 1991); Raine, J., and Wilson, M., *Managing Criminal Justice* (Harvester, Hemel Hampstead, 1993), 'Beyond managerialism in criminal justice' (1997) 36 *Howard Journal*

which are seen to offer a focus for case-settlement or, in default, the identification of issues in contention and fewer 'cracked' trials.[103] The PTR provides the opportunity for bargaining as to charge, fact or plea, and, as argued elsewhere,[104] the system may tend towards a crime control ethos and certainly tends towards professional corporatism.[105] Therefore, the model of case management as used in serious frauds litigation pursuant to s. 7 of the Criminal Justice Act 1987[106] has now been extended to all potentially long and complex cases by the Criminal Procedure and Investigations Act 1996,[107] as described in Chapter 9.

Whilst delay and the minimisation of costs are related to the value of justice,[108] the relevant issue which arises is whether PTRs are likely to inflict injustice or unfairness especially towards the defendant. Possible benefits from PTRs may include keeping defendants better informed and thereby enhancing their confidence in the courts. A fuller exchange of information may also enhance the quality of decision-making by improving the understanding of the professionals handling the case. Conversely, the non-confrontational atmosphere of the PTR may encourage defence solicitors to weaken their guard and to feel a greater antipathy towards their defendant-client than towards the prosecution representatives, who are their social peers. The Law Society has issued stern warnings about this danger,[109] but there is a fear that the local legal culture of co-operation (already referred to) may prevail over the demands of an adversarial system. The most serious dangers of miscarriage of justice – convicting the innocent when the guilty plea is given under duress of circumstances[110] – arise mainly if the defence professionals involved do not serve their clients appropriately; in other words, that they act out of motives of convenience or financial gain. There is as yet little evidence that this is so, or at least no more so than in a trial process. At least it should be recognised by the courts that plea-bargaining exists and is not necessarily unjust,[111] so long as the defendant is professionally advised[112] and has time for reflection[113] and so long as

---

80. For the application of these concerns to the committal stage, see Brownlee, I. and Furniss, C., 'Committed to committals?' [1997] *Criminal Law Review* 3.

[103] See the *Submissions* of the Bar Council (para. 169), CPS (paras. 8.3.3., 8.3.6), Justices' Clerks' Society (para. 2.1), Law Society (para. 3.41) and Police Service (p. 1). See further Bredar, J., 'Moving up the day of reckoning' [1992] *Criminal Law Review* 153; Bock, B.P., *Ordered and directed acquittals in the Crown Court* (Royal Commission on Criminal Justice Research Study No. 15, HMSO, London, 1993).

[104] Walker, C., and Starmer, K., (eds.) *Justice in Error* (Blackstone Press, London, 1993) at p. 158.

[105] Mulcahy, A., 'The justifications of justice' (1994) 34 *British Journal of Criminology* 411.

[106] Jones, A., 'The decline and fall of the preparatory hearing' [1996] *Criminal Law Review* 460.

[107] See Lord Chancellor's Department, Home Office and Law Officers' Department, *The Royal Commission on Criminal Justice: Final Government Response* (Home Office, London, 1996) paras. 84, 85.

[108] See Narey, M., *Review of Delay in the Criminal Justice Process* (Home Office, London, 1997).

[109] 'Pre-trial reviews in the Magistrates' Courts: guidance for defence solicitors' (1983) 80 *Law Society's Gazette* 2330.

[110] See McConville, M. and Mirsky, C., 'Redefining and structuring guilt in systematic terms' in McConville, M. and Bridges, L. (eds.), *Criminal Justice in Crisis* (Edward Elgar, London, 1994) at p. 272. See also Sanders, A. and Young, R., *Criminal Justice* (Butterworths, London, 1994) p. 391.

[111] *Ibid.*, p. 281. The proportion of 'innocent' defendants who plead guilty is most marked with unrepresented defendants and those who change their plea at a late stage: Zander, M. and Henderson, P., *Crown Court Study* (Royal Commission on Criminal Justice Research Study No. 19, HMSO, London, 1993).

[112] See Mulcahy, A., 'The justifications of justice' (1994) 34 *British Journal of Criminology* 411; Huff, C.R., Rattner, A. and Sagarin, E., *Convicted But Innocent: Wrongful Conviction and Public Policy* (Sage, Thousand Oaks, 1996) at p. 155.

[113] See Bar Council Working Group, *Efficient Disposal of Business in the Crown Court* (1992); Law

any discount should relate to the interests of victims rather than economic savings.[114]

As reflected further in Chapter 9, many of the controversies to reach the courts and indeed many of the recent miscarriages of justice cases have concerned the admissibility of evidence, especially confessions. Suggestions to bolster their weighting as evidence include corroboration, a warning to the jury or a formal reaffirmation of their veracity to a magistrate. The *Fisher Inquiry* into the *Confait* case also recommended 'supporting evidence' where confessions had been secured in the following circumstances: in breach of police rules; from young or mentally handicapped persons without the presence of an adult; or where the confession was not taped.[115] For reasons cited in Chapter 9,[116] the *Runciman Report* rejected a corroboration requirement in favour of a special warning to juries, though this was in turn rejected as unnecessary by the Government. Any changes must also face up to the police view that confessions remain 'a vital tool of justice'.[117] The result is to leave suspects especially vulnerable in at least four situations.[118] One is where the detainee is interviewed in the absence of a solicitor, as commonly occurs. The second arises where verbal exchanges take place outside the police station or within the station but outside the interview room; either way, recording and supervisory arrangements envisaged by PACE do not effectively operate.[119] The third concerns detainees under the Prevention of Terrorism Act (Temporary Provisions) 1989, who are by design not accorded the same protective regime as ordinary suspects.[120] Finally, where the detainee has been detained for more than 24 hours, there exists the inherent likelihood of excessive pressures and oppression.

The fallibility of confessions do not exhaust the evidential mistakes behind miscarriages of justice. Eyewitness identification remains a prime cause, according to some studies, far exceeding coerced confessions, which also far outweigh forensic science error.[121]

Some of the points in Chapter 9 are taken up again in Chapter 10, 'The Judiciary'. The highly contrasting nature and roles of the judiciary in magistrates' courts and the Crown Court, which may well have an impact on mode of trial decisions, is considered here. However, there is some contrast to Chapter 9 which deals with the conduct and practices of the judiciary, whereas the emphasis in Chapter 10 is on personnel, standards and training of these professionals at the core of the criminal justice system. There are, of course, other important professional

---

Reform Commission of Canada, Working Paper 60: *Plea Discussions and Agreements* (Ottawa, 1989).

[114] See *Runciman Report*, ch. 6 para. 41.

[115] 1977–78 HC 90, para. 2.26. See also Evans, R., *The Conduct of Police Interviews with Juveniles* (Royal Commission on Criminal Justice Research Study No. 8, HMSO, London, 1992).

[116] See also Walker, C., and Starmer, K., (eds.) *Justice in Error* (Blackstone Press, London, 1993) p. 149.

[117] Sir J. Woodcock, 'Why we need a revolution' (1992) 100 *Police Review* 1932.

[118] See: *Submissions* by JUSTICE, para. 2; Liberty, p. 54; Law Society, paras. 1.20, 1.120; General Council of the Bar, paras. 104, 105; Justices' Clerks' Society, para. 1.4; NACRO, para. 8.

[119] See Moston, S. and Stephenson, G.M., *The Questioning and Interviewing of Suspects outside the Police Station* (Royal Commission on Criminal Justice Research Study No. 22, HMSO, London, 1993).

[120] See Chapter 9.

[121] See Huff, C.R., Rattner, A. and Sagarin, E., *Convicted But Innocent: Wrongful Conviction and Public Policy* (Sage, Thousand Oaks, 1996) p. 64 (the sources of the respective errors are given as 54 per cent, 8 per cent and 2 per cent).

groups within the criminal justice system who contribute to the avoidance or causation of miscarriages of justice, including principally[122] the Crown Prosecution Service[123] and the legal professions,[124] but a full assessment of them will have to be left to others.

Whatever the causation, it should be abundantly clear by now that systems of criminal justice, whether adversarial or inquisitorial, are fallible. The existence and effectiveness of appeals and post-appeal reviews are therefore considered next.

Chapter 11 considers the processes of appeal and thereafter arising from finding of guilt after trial on indictment in the Crown Court where most is at stake in terms of the consequences of mistake. However, note should also be taken of the larger group of appeals from the Crown Court to the Court of Appeal on sentence (in 1996, there were 7252 appeals (10 per cent of those sentenced) of which 1350 (19 per cent) had their conviction quashed or sentence varied).[125] There were also many more appeals from magistrates – largely to the Crown Court (in 1996, there were 10,441 appeals against conviction (under 1 per cent), with 3494 resulting in a quashed conviction (33 per cent), and 14193 appeals against sentence (1 per cent) of which 6071 (43 per cent) had their conviction quashed or sentence varied). It takes a society which is confident in its own values and is open in its style of Government to admit that mistakes may have been made during its criminal justice process. Given the nature of political society in this country, it is not surprising that the structures for addressing allegations of injustice have operated in a half-hearted and secretive fashion. Facing the Runciman Commission were problems in at least four areas.

One was the physical treatment of the convicted and the obstacles caused by the processes of incarceration or defaults on the part of professionals. Some of these

---

[122] For forensic scientists, see Chapter 6. Other professional groups not otherwise mentioned include interpreters; see Butler, I. and Noaks, L., *Silence in court? A study of interpreting in the courts of England and Wales* (Nuffield Interpreter Project, Cardiff, 1992); Morris, R, 'Interpreters and the legal process' (1996) 146 *New Law Journal* 1310. Independent accreditation of interpreters is being taken forward through the Nuffield Interpreter Project which has given way to a scheme, the National Register of Public Service Interpreters, which is run by the Institute of Linguists. As with forensic scientists, the Government has seemingly disclaimed responsibility for the maintenance of standards and is happy to leave the matter to the efforts (and budgets) of private bodies (see Lord Chancellor's Department, Home Office and Law Officers' Department, *The Royal Commission on Criminal Justice: Final Government Response* (Home Office, London, 1996) para. 30). For community psychiatric nurses and police surgeons, see Robertson, G., *The Role of Police Surgeons* (Royal Commission on Criminal Justice Research Study No. 6, HMSO, London, 1993); Kelly, K., Moon, G., Savage, S. and Bradshaw, Y., 'The role of the police surgeon' (1993) 9 *Policing* 148; Laing, J.M., 'The mentally disordered suspect at the police station' [1995] *Criminal Law Review* 371 and 'The police surgeon and mentally disordered suspects: an adequate safeguard?' (1996) 1 *Web Journal of Current Legal Issues*; Norfolk, G.A., '"Fitness to be interviewed" – a proposed definition and scheme of examination' (1997) 37 *Medicine Science & Law* 228.

[123] See Mullin, C., 'Miscarriages of justice in the UK' (1996) 2(2) *Journal of Legislative Studies* 8 at p. 16; Blake, M. and Ashworth, A., 'Some ethical issues in prosecuting and defending criminal cases' [1998] *Criminal Law Review* 16. Review of the Crown Prosecutions Service (Cm 3972, Stationery Office, London, 1998).

[124] In regard to barristers, the *Runciman Report* (ch. 8) calls for a restriction on work undertaken by newly qualified barristers, more monitoring of pupils and more continuing education (paras. 86–8), but these are all to be achieved without official intervention (Lord Chancellor's Department, Home Office and Law Officers' Department, *The Royal Commission on Criminal Justice: Final Government Response* (Home Office, London, 1996) para. 138). In regard to solicitors, a code of conduct for advocates has been introduced (*Runciman Report*, ch. 8 para. 90). But there has been no discernible change in regard to legal training in forensic science: *Runciman Report*, ch. 8 para. 89; Lord Chancellor's Department, Home Office and Law Officers' Department, *The Royal Commission on Criminal Justice: Final Government Response* (Home Office, London, 1996) para. 139.

[125] Source: Home Office, *Criminal Appeals, England and Wales 1995 and 1996* (Research and Statistics Directorate, London, 1998).

obstacles are inevitable, but the Commission alarmingly found that 9 per cent of prisoners received no cell visit after conviction, a further 23 per cent received no advice about appeal during such a visit, and almost 90 per cent received no written information.[126] The Commission felt that there should be a clearer duty on both solicitor and counsel to give advice and that it should be both orally and in writing. The Commission was also alarmed at the confusion over the possible penalty that time spent in custody pending an appeal which is considered frivolous would not count as part of the sentence. The Commission suggested that the penalty be limited to 90 days, in the light of the facts that any penalty of this kind is rarely applied and commonly for only 28 days.[127] Another important problem is the difficulty experienced by lawyers in locating their client within the prison system.[128] The response to most of these recommendations has taken the form of guidelines, whether by the Bar Council and Law Society or by the Prison Service. However, the maximum limit on time loss was rejected as unnecessary.[129]

The second issue tackled by the Runciman Commission concerned what counts as relevant reasons for reinquiry, referral or retrial. Here, the problem was the narrowness of the grounds. For example, there may be limits on the admission of evidence not previously heard if it was available but unused at the original trial. The refusal to take account of any but the most flagrant of failings in defence lawyers is also problematic.[130] As is related in Chapter 11, the grounds of appeal have been duly changed but without any clear signal that they are to be treated as much wider than the previous wording. It is suggested that more crucial is the attitude of the appellate judges; if so, one must not expect much change in the light of the failure to reform the appointments and training systems as outlined in Chapter 10.

The next stage is the receptivity of the system to evidence that there has been a miscarriage of justice. Certainly, the fitful scrutiny by the Home Secretary's backroom staff and the politically-charged reluctance to use the referral power under (the now abolished) s. 17 of the Criminal Appeal Act 1968 was far from convincing in the view of many.[131] A government reply in 1983 dismissed reform and made the empty promise that the Home Secretary and Court of Appeal would be more receptive to petitions and referrals.[132] However, the model of an independent tribunal eventually came back into official favour,[133] and was given

---

[126] *Runciman Report*, ch. 10 para. 13. See Plotnikoff, J. and Woolfson, R., *Information and advice for prisoners about grounds for appeal and the appeals process* (Royal Commission on Criminal Justice Research Study No. 18, HMSO, London, 1993).

[127] *Runciman Report*, ch. 10 para. 19.

[128] *Runciman Report*, ch. 10 para. 22.

[129] Lord Chancellor's Department, Home Office and Law Officers' Department, *The Royal Commission on Criminal Justice: Final Government Response* (Home Office, London, 1996) para. 176.

[130] See: *R v Ensor* [1989] 2 All ER 586; *R v Clinton* [1993] 2 All ER 998; *McLeish v Amoo-Gottfried & Co. The Times*, 13 October, 1993; *US v Cronic* 466 US 648 (1984); *Strickland v Washington* 466 US 668 (1984); Law Society, *Submission* (1991) para. 5.21. The *Runciman Report* suggested a greater readiness to interpret 'unsafeness' as applying to mistakes by lawyers: para. 10.59. It is perhaps odd that the integrity of lawyers in court is treated as more important than the integrity of the police whose actions effectively determine the vast majority of cases.

[131] See Home Affairs Committee, *Miscarriages of Justice* (1981–82 HC 421) and *Government Reply* (Cmnd 8856, 1983); JUSTICE, *Miscarriages of Justice* (London, 1989); Woffinden, B., 'Independent review tribunal' (1989) 139 *New Law Journal* 1108; Police Complaints Authority, *Annual Report 1991* (1992–93 HC 15) para. 6.8.

[132] Cmnd 8856.

[133] See Home Office, *Memoranda* (1991) paras. 4.47, 4.48, 4.62, 4.67, 4.80; Law Society, *Submission* (1991) paras. 5.20, 5.24, 5.31; General Council of the Bar, *Submission* (1992) para. 208.

personal support given by the Home Secretary in reaction to the Second Report of the May Inquiry,[134] which also endorsed the principle of independent investigative machinery in place of the Home Office.[135] The *Runciman Report* acceded to these pressures and recommended a replacement for the reviews and referrals through the Home Office.[136] The idea has been implemented in the shape of the Criminal Cases Review Commission by part II of the Criminal Appeal Act 1995.[137]

The Criminal Cases Review Commission is perhaps the most important positive outcome of the *Runciman Report*, and it was important to concentrate some effort here.[138] In its work to date, the Commission has undoubtedly been more active, effective and open than the Home Office. However, Chapter 11 points out at least two central shortcomings. One is a lack of resources, which renders it reliant upon the police for investigation[139] and also leaves it struggling to cope with the caseload.[140] The second is that its power ends with a referral, so that it is ultimately dependent on the performance of the Court of Appeal, which is confined under s. 23 of the 1968 Act to evidence which is capable of belief[141] and in any event admissible and, if previously adduced at trial, where there is a reasonable explanation for failure to adduce it earlier.

So, the fourth problem area concerned the procedures and performance of the Court of Appeal.[142] But as noted earlier, despite calls for changes in its ground rules[143] and even some suggestions that its role in miscarriage cases should be taken over by other forms of dispute resolution,[144] the Court of Appeal has emerged relatively unscathed. Thus, the *Runciman Report* politely suggested that the Court of Appeal should be readier to overturn verdicts but then, in order to achieve this, suggested changes to the wording of s. 2 of the Criminal Appeal Act 1968 (in part implemented by s. 2 of the Criminal Appeal Act 1995[145]) which arguably

---

[134] *The Times*, 4 December 1992, p. 2.

[135] May, Sir John, *Report of the inquiry into the circumstances surrounding the convictions arising out of the bomb attacks in Guildford and Woolwich in 1974, Second Report* (1992–93 HC 296) paras. 10.6, 12.24.

[136] *Runciman Report*, ch. 11.

[137] See Home Office, *Criminal Appeals and the Establishment of a Criminal Cases Review Authority* (1994); Thornton, P., 'Righting the wrongs' in Birks, P.B.H. (ed.), *Pressing Problems in the Law Volume 1: Criminal Justice and Human Rights* (Oxford University Press, 1995); Owers, A., 'Not completely appealing' (1995) 145 *New Law Journal* 353; Smith, J.C., 'Criminal appeals and the CCRC' (1995) 145 *New Law Journal* 533, 572; 'Appeals against conviction' [1995] *Criminal Law Review* 920; Malleson, K., 'A broad framework' (1997) 147 *Justice of the Peace* 1023; Bindman, D., 'Righting wrongs' (1997) *Law Soc Gazette* 94/2 12; Malet, D., 'The new regime for the correction of miscarriages of justice' (1995) 159 *Justice of the Peace* 716, 735.

[138] Wisotsky, S., 'Criminal law symposium: miscarriages of justice: their causes and cures' (1997) 9 *St. Thomas Law Review* 547 at pp. 555, 556.

[139] Investigators were once available to the Court of Appeal (see Criminal Appeal Act 1907, s. 9, repealed in 1968). The Court of Appeal can now direct the CCRC to carry out investigations: Criminal Appeal Act 1968 (as amended), s. 23A.

[140] By 31 March 1998, it had received 1348 applications (as well as 252 passed from the Home Office), completed around 300, and referred 12.

[141] *Runciman Report*, para. 10.60.

[142] See Pattenden, R., *English Criminal Appeals 1844–1994* (Clarendon Press, Oxford, 1996).

[143] See: Home Office, *Memoranda* (1991) para. 4.84.

[144] The CPS suggestion (*Submission* (1991) paras. 14.4.11, 14.4.8) was for fresh evidence cases to be tried by a new, intermediate court; a new review body is to look at allegations, so the powers of the Home Office could be abolished. See also: JUSTICE, *Submission* (1991) para. 5.

[145] The *Runciman Report*, ch. 10 para. 32 wanted a test of 'is or may be unsafe' but s. 2 states only 'is unsafe'. The proviso is abolished: ch. 10 para. 31.

would have the opposite effect[146] and indeed have since been interpreted in a conservative way.[147] Wider grounds for appeal to the House of Lords were also rejected.[148]

Some say that none of these reforms is likely to change the practices of the Court of Appeal and that effective reform is impossible,[149] and it must be expected that a Court of Appeal is hardly likely to accept that the system is endemically, as opposed to accidentally, rotten. Of course, it cannot be sufficient for a convicted person simply to claim innocence – the appeal courts demand finality and respect for the jury[150] and no longer operate a presumption of innocence.[151] But there is no reason why balances cannot shift or why rhetoric should be unaffected by events such as the chastening experience of miscarriages of justice in the last decade. For example, it would be possible to alter the system of sifting by leave to appeal whereby papers which must be lodged within 28 days are referred to a single judge and can be dealt with without a hearing; though the application may then be renewed before a bench of judges, less than one half of appellants take this option. If more time for preparation was afforded to defendants who are probably distressed and being moved around the prison system and if the process were more open, then a fairer system would result. Likewise, significant changes could be secured through the provision of more legal advice[152] and clearer rules about the possible penalties arising from appeal.[153] There could have been greater encouragement for retrials,[154] and even a rule that, if impractical, the person must be

---

[146] The new formulation rules out appeals being granted on a disciplinary basis and also seems to ignore the value of the integrity of the system, which requires more than that the conviction is factually grounded and could be supported by the erstwhile concept of an 'unsatisfactory' conviction. See *Runciman Report*, ch. 10 paras. 38, 46. In the view of the Government, the new wording 'reflects the current practice of the Court of Appeal': Lord Chancellor's Department, Home Office and Law Officers' Department, *The Royal Commission on Criminal Justice: Final Government Response* (Home Office, London, 1996) paras. 178, 180.

[147] See Chapter 10.

[148] *Runciman Report*, ch. 10 para. 79; Lord Chancellor's Department, Home Office and Law Officers' Department, *The Royal Commission on Criminal Justice: Final Government Response* (Home Office, London, 1996) para. 186.

[149] See Nobles, R., 'The inevitability of crisis in criminal appeals' (1993) 21(1) *International Journal of the Sociology of Law* 1; Schiff, D., and Nobles, R., 'Criminal Appeal Act 1995' (1996) 59 *Modern Law Review* 573; Nobles, R. and Schiff, D., 'The never ending story' (1997) 60 *Modern Law Review* 293 at p. 295.

[150] Friendly, H.J., 'Is innocence irrelevant? Collateral attack on criminal judgments' (1970) 38 *University of Chicago Law Review* 142.

[151] *Herrera v Collins* 506 US 390 (1993).

[152] Appellants are much less likely to succeed if they are not represented – 19 per cent as against 55 per cent. *Practice Direction* [1974] 2 All ER 805 states that the trial barrister should see the client at end of trial in the cells and advise in writing on chances of appeal, but up to 32 per cent received no such advice. See Malleson, K., *Appeals against Conviction and the Principle of Finality* (Royal Commission on Criminal Justice Research Study No. 17, HMSO, London, 1993); *Runciman Report*, paras. 10.15–16. There is no legal aid if the defendant wishes to appeal against advice; the *Runciman Report*, para. 10.24, recommended that it should be available for drafting only if the solicitor disagrees with the barrister.

[153] Lawyers warn appellants that they might lose time spent in custody during appeal time as a penalty awarded under the Criminal Appeal Act 1968, s. 29; see *Practice Note* [1980] 1 All ER 555. But this rarely happens (see Plotnikoff, J. and Woolfson, R, *Information and advice for prisoners about grounds for appeal and the appeals process* (Royal Commission on Criminal Justice Research Study No. 18, HMSO, London, 1993), and so the *Runciman Report*, paras. 10.19, 10.26 suggests that a further Practice Direction should make this clearer and limit any loss to 90 days.

[154] But retrials are increasing, partly through the Court's own discretion and partly through the encouragement of the Criminal Justice Act 1988, s. 43.

acquitted rather than allowing the Court of Appeal to pretend that it can act as a trial by peers.[155]

An emergent agenda which naturally flows from the belated recognition of the perpetration of miscarriages of justice in the United Kingdom is the compensation of the wrongfully imprisoned and abused. In Chapter 12, 'Victims of Miscarriages of Justice', the authors describe how two systems exist for compensation but how neither addresses the wrongs which have been suffered.[156] The schemes are niggardly in their scope, grossly inefficient in their operation, with few of the major miscarriage of justice cases being settled to date,[157] and fail to recognise the wider and more radical interests of restorative justice. These deficiencies are all the more serious since, in *Silcott* v *Commissioner of Police for the Metropolis*,[158] the courts have refused to allow the development of compensation at common law. Some of the wider issues of redress have been revealed by countries which have sought to respond fully to patterns of gross violations of human rights. A prominent example is the Truth and Reconciliation Committee in South Africa,[159] whose Reparation and Rehabilitation Committee took account of five distinct categories of reparation:[160]

Redress which is the right to fair and adequate compensation.

Restitution which is the right to the re-establishment, as far as possible, of the situation that existed for the beneficiary prior to the violation.

Rehabilitation which is the right to the provision of medical and psychological care and fulfilment of significant personal and community needs.

Restoration of dignity which could include symbolic forms of reparation; and

Reassurance of non-repetition which includes the creation of legislative and administrative measures, which contribute to the maintenance of a stable society and the prevention of the re-occurrence of human rights violations.

Redress and restitution involving financial restitution for the wrongfully imprisoned are at the core of the mechanisms that exist in the United Kingdom. However, as pointed out in Chapter 12, there is no attempt at personal or social rehabilitation, while the process of dealing with claims almost seems counterproductive in achieving the restoration of dignity and has not included any grand gestures of apology or generosity. Perhaps the greatest failure, however, is to secure a reassurance of non-repetition. This is not only of importance as an aspect

---

[155] This was accepted in the *Runciman Report* in regard to appeals only where there was no fresh evidence paras. 10.63, 10.66 (the Commission was split 6–5 on this issue). Compare Lord Chancellor's Department, Home Office and Law Officers' Department, *The Royal Commission on Criminal Justice: Final Government Response* (Home Office, London, 1996) para. 182.

[156] Compare the schemes in California, Illinois, New York, Tennessee and Wisconsin: Huff, C.R., Rattner, A. and Sagarin, E., *Convicted But Innocent: Wrongful Conviction and Public Policy* (Sage, Thousand Oaks, 1996) p. 156.

[157] Under the Criminal Justice Act 1988 scheme as at 21 May 1997, there were 156 outstanding cases (59 applications where a decision had still to be taken on whether the applicants qualified for compensation; 27 finalised claims yet to be submitted by successful applicants; 18 claims either with, or in the process of being prepared for, the independent assessor; 52 arising from a number of cases in Greater Manchester where drink-driving convictions were quashed following possible contamination of blood samples): HC Debs vol. 294 col. 77wa, 21 May 1996, Mr Alan Michael.

[158] *The Times*, 9 July 1996.

[159] See Promotion of National Unity and Reconciliation Act 1995 (no. 34); http://www.truth.org.za/. For other examples, see: Hayner, P.B., 'Fifteen truth commissions – 1974–1994' (1994) 16 *Human Rights Quarterly* 597.

[160] Truth and Reconciliation Commission, *Proposed Policy for UIR and Final Reparation* (Pretoria, 1997) para. 4.1.

of reparation to the victim of a miscarriage of justice but also, of course, to the strengthening of societal institutions as a whole.[161] Yet, the truth has never been established or even fully investigated in many of the major miscarriage of justice cases, so it is difficult to see how one can be sure that the reforms which have taken place address the real problems. One cannot realistically now expect the Criminal Cases Review Commission to take on this separate agenda,[162] but one would hope that for the future the Commission will be prepared to make thematic inquiries and recommendations where it recognises patterns of abuses or error.

The final contribution to Part II, 'The Role and Impact of Journalism' deals both with potentially adverse effects on the trial process, as well as more positive investigative aspects of media intervention, especially post-trial. Both sections provide insights into how the criminal justice system is viewed from within and without and how it should be shaped in the light of experience of the impacts of the media.

The media have undoubtedly become more interested in criminal justice issues and have tended to report on them more extensively.[163] It is more difficult to adjudge whether the media have become more 'critical', though the O.J. Simpson trial[164] and the decision by the *Daily Mail* to label as the racist murderers of the black teenager, Stephen Lawrence, five identified individuals – 'if we are wrong, let them sue us' – does suggest a bolder approach.[165] Is it wrong for the media to express opinions in this way about the results of litigation? Why should issues which are of enormous public concern be placed off limits, any more than we must close public discussion because Parliament has or has not decided to pass an Act of Parliament?[166] It must be recognised that law is a partial representation of life which requires its distillation into a court trial and always a conventionally certain outcome. Of course, the media will tend to focus on the strength of either the prosecution or defence case and will underplay the role of the jury. Given that jury deliberations are secret, this is understandable but is no reason for closure to public, as opposed to legal, debate.[167] Journalists will also focus on convictions as the most dramatic (newsworthy) moment of the process and ignore much of what has gone on before. The media (especially television programmes about possible miscarriages of justice) were accused by Lord Chief Justice Lane as being 'a mere entertainment'; this is half true, but only half true.[168] None of this attention is any 'misreading' of a system by an outsider, though the outsider may have different interests and priorities. In fact, the outsiders have had real insights – for example, two cases taken up by the Channel 4 programme, *Trial and Error* in the early 1990s have resulted in several acquittals.[169]

---

[161] See Zalaquett, J., 'Balancing ethical imperatives and political constraints' (1992) 43 *Hastings Law Journal* 1430; Mendez, J., 'Accountability for past abuses' (1997) 19 *Human Rights Quarterly* 255.

[162] See Mullin, C., 'Miscarriages of justice in the UK' (1996) 2(2) *Journal of Legislative Studies* 8 at p. 12.

[163] See Reiner, R., 'Media made criminality' in Maguire, M., Morgan, R. and Reiner, R., *The Oxford Handbook of Criminology* (2nd ed., Oxford UP, 1997).

[164] Compare Evans, K., 'The publicity is the problem' (1995) 145 *New Law Journal* 992; Mason, K., 'Free speech, fair trial and O.J Simpson' (1995) 69 *Australian Law Journal* 157.

[165] *The Times*, 15 February 1997 pp. 1, 2. Common law contempt proceedings are said to be pending: *The Times*, 13 March 1997 p. 9.

[166] See further Jessel, D., 'The Lund Lecture: television, science and the law' (1997) 37 *Medicine, Science and the Law* 4.

[167] Compare Nobles, R. and Schiff, D., 'Miscarriages of justice: a systems approach' (1996) 59 *Modern Law Review* 299 at p. 312.

[168] Jessel, D., *Trial and Error* (Headline, London, 1994) p. 49.

[169] See the cases of Mark Cleary and Sheila Bowler in *ibid* (also described in Chapter 2).

Whatever might be the legal community's distaste for media clamour, which includes hankering after tighter contempt rules on witnesses and the resurrection of pre-censorship through common law sub judice rules,[170] the reality is that media fragmentation and globalisation will never again permit effective intervention in these ways.[171] These factors point towards alternative legal strategies such as postponement and change of venue, media self-regulation, and better lawyer training to handle media pressures.[172] The alternatives may prove more costly in financial terms,[173] but the accentuation of accessibility would be valuable as a form of civic education. If the courts refuse to provide proper access not just to its press and public benches but to its documentation, then they should not complain if the press mishear, misunderstand or misinterpret. One regrets that the *Runciman Report* remained largely silent on media relations with criminal justice, which have had a lasting and profound impact on the system,[174] aside from a call for possible research into the workings of the jury system.[175]

Part III, 'Miscarriages of Justice in Other Jurisdictions'

The major shortcomings in English criminal justice which can (and do) lead to miscarriages of justice have now been explained. The remainder of this book examines whether other jurisdictions have fared any better, hopefully without taking these other systems out of context and discovering faultless panaceas.[176] The chosen jurisdictions are Northern Ireland and the Republic of Ireland, which share similar legal traditions, though are subject to distinct policing arrangements and problems, and France and Scotland, which in part offer a contrasting model for criminal investigation and adjudication.

A major reason for considering 'Miscarriages of Justice in Northern Ireland' (Chapter 14), is that its criminal justice system has been modified in directions often followed later in England and Wales. This is especially true of the changes to the 'right to silence' and perhaps will become true of reliance at summary level upon resident/stipendiary magistrates. There may be other important and instructive differences, such as over the interpretation and practical application of PACE powers, but the absence of research is a fact of much legal life in Northern Ireland, which was also formally beyond the remit of the Runciman Commission, though the promise was made by the Northern Ireland Secretary to take careful account of its findings.[177]

A further feature of Northern Ireland which is worth scrutiny is that, in response to paramilitary activity, the jurisdiction has relied heavily upon extraordinary

---

[170] See Lord Chancellor's Department, *Payments to Witnesses* (London, 1996); National Heritage Committee, *Press activity affecting court cases* (1996–97 HC 86).

[171] Walker, C.P., 'Fundamental rights, fair trials, and the new audio-visual sector' (1996) 59 *Modern Law Review* 517, 'Cybercontempt: fair trials and the internet' (1997–8) 3 *Oxford Yearbook of Media and Entertainment Law* p. 1.

[172] Compare *Hunt* v *NBC* 872 F 2d 289 (1989) where a court refused to restrain the making of a 'docudrama' before trial.

[173] The sequestering of the jury in the O.J Simpson trial had to persist for nine months: Whittell, G., 'Prisoners of OJ trial' *The Times*, 29 September 1995 p. 16.

[174] Compare Nobles, R. and Schiff, D., 'Miscarriages of justice: a systems approach' (1996) 59 *Modern Law Review* 299 at p. 313.

[175] At ch. 1 para. 8.

[176] This is not to say that the English model is so fault-ridden that nothing can be learnt from it. See Strier, F., *Reconstructing Justice* (University of Chicago Press, 1996) p. 231.

[177] *The Times*, 30 July, 1992 p. 1.

powers, now set out in the Prevention of Terrorism (Temporary Provisions) Act (PTA) 1989 and the Northern Ireland (Emergency Provisions) Act (EPA) 1996–8.[178] One might consider these measures as potentially relevant to miscarriages of justice in two senses.[179] The first is that their contents are inherently and intentionally inimical to the rights of suspects. 'Draconian' was how one former Home Secretary put it,[180] and the characteristic is also reflected in the derogation from the European Convention on Human Rights now enshrined in the Human Rights Act 1998, schedule 2. Secondly, the operation of the legislation in practice may incorporate features or even an 'ethos' which tend towards miscarriages in the sense of an unjustifiable conviction in a court. The special powers of arrest under the PTA 1989, s. 14,[181] coupled with extraordinary detention powers, inadequate record-keeping and limited rights of access to lawyers, come under close scrutiny as possible progenitors of miscarriages of justice through false statements.

In the light of the history of the cases which prompted the Runciman Commission's establishment, its lack of attention accorded to the operation of the PTA 1989 or the forerunners to the EPA 1998 almost beggars belief. The terms of reference devised by the Home Secretary were silent on the issue, and none of the 88 interrogatories issued by the Commission itself made reference to the Acts. At least the May Inquiry rightly expressed grave concern.[182] Several remedies could be suggested. With the advent of a comprehensive code of arrest powers in PACE (apart from Scotland), it is doubtful whether arrests on the basis of 'terrorism' are either necessary in most cases or desirable in any. Similarly, now that four day detentions have become part of the regular law, it may also be doubted whether more extensive detentions are justifiable. At the very least, it might be argued that any confession should be corroborated and any which is made after four days should not be admissible at all in the light of the oppressive circumstances. Other changes could include extensions being authorised by judges, the abolition of the special rules about access to lawyers, the full recording of interviews, regular medical checks, access by lay visitors in Northern Ireland and a greater readiness on the part of the courts to act and penalise the police when ill-treatment is alleged.[183] With the establishment of a paramilitary ceasefire and a British-Irish Agreement on future constitutional and security arrangements,[184] it is to be hoped that the special legislation will both lapse and be replaced.[185]

---

[178] See Hogan, G. and Walker, C., *Political Violence and the Law in Ireland* (1989, Manchester University Press); Walker, C., *The Prevention of Terrorism in British Law* (2nd ed., 1992, Manchester University Press).

[179] But there were few campaigns against miscarriages until the late 1980s: Jackson J. and Doran, S., *Judge without Jury* (Clarendon Press, Oxford, 1995) at p. 51. For a possible explanantion for this apparent quiescence (which masked a far higher rate and greater depth of dissatisfaction with the criminal justice system than in Britain), see Walker, C., and Starmer, K., (eds.) *Justice in Error* (Blackstone Press, London, 1993) pp. 224, 225.

[180] HC Debs. col. 35, 25 November 1974, Roy Jenkins.

[181] For further details, see Walker, C., and Starmer, K., (eds.) *Justice in Error* (Blackstone Press, London, 1993) pp. 195–202.

[182] See May, Sir John, *Report of the inquiry into the circumstances surrounding the convictions arising out of the bomb attacks in Guildford and Woolwich in 1974, Final Report* (HC 449 of 1993–94) paras. 4.19, 21.9.

[183] Compare: *In re Gillen's Application* [1988] 1 NIJB 47; *Wheldon v Home Office* [1990] 3 WLR 465.

[184] See *British-Irish Agreement reached in the multi-party negotiations* (Cm 3883, HMSO, London, 1998).

[185] This fate should even apply to the Criminal Justice (Terrorism and Conspiracy) Act 1998, which was passed after the Omagh bombing of August 1998. For a review, see Walker, C., 'Criminal

The implications of the *Runciman Report* for Northern Ireland's 'ordinary' criminal justice system has at least been considered more fully by the Standing Advisory Commission on Human Rights (SACHR). But its programme of study has lacked principle and cohesion in a way reminiscent of the *Runciman Report* itself, and one finds both a crime control and due process agenda being pursued at the same time.[186] Perhaps the most useful discussion concerned the application of the Criminal Cases Review Commission to Northern Ireland;[187] the model adopted does not entail any structure exclusive to Northern Ireland contrary to the view of the SACHR, though there is an appointee specifically from the Province.[188]

Having seen in Chapter 14 how miscarriages of justice arise and are handled in one Irish jurisdiction, the position in the other Irish jurisdiction is next raised. The Irish Republic (see Chapter 15) again provides an interesting mix of similarities (often retaining ancient common law principles and rules as well as pre-1922 UK statutes) and differences (increasingly based on the same sorts of rights granted by the 1937 Constitution which are now making an entrance into UK law by the Human Rights Act 1998).[189] Of course, there are also parallels with Northern Ireland in that special legislation, the Offences against the State Acts,[190] is used far more widely than originally envisaged. As related in Chapter 15, much of the focus has been on the case of the *Tallaght Two*,[191] who have tested both old and new laws dealing with identification evidence, reviews of miscarriages of justice and compensation for those unjustly convicted. In addition, the *Runciman Report* and later English reforms have had some influence,[192] and so interesting comparisons can be made with the (Irish) Criminal Procedure Act 1993 and the Criminal Appeals Act 1995.

Moving from Ireland to Scotland (chapter 16), there may be again at least two points of general interest in relation to miscarriages of justice. One is to see whether the underlying system gives rise to them to a greater or lesser extent. The other is to consider any responses which differ from recent English patterns.

From an English lawyer's perspective, some of the interesting features of the Scottish system include the potential use of judicial examination and the rules on the corroboration of confession, both of which might protect against miscarriage of justice arising from the predominantly police-based interrogation. Judicial examination was revived in 1980 and is now set out in sections 35 to 39 of the Criminal Procedure (Scotland) Act 1995. But its impact is limited, and it has certainly not replaced or curtailed police questioning, which continues to grow despite the traditional strictures against any form of 'cross-examination' in Scottish

---

Justice (Terrorism and Conspiracy) Act 1998 in *Current Law Statutes Annotated* (Sweet & Maxwell, London, 1998) ch. 40.

[186] Compare the treatment of plea bargaining and disclosure: *ibid.*, paras. 12, 13.

[187] Northern Ireland Office, *Criminal Appeals and Arrangements for Dealing with Alleged Miscarriages of Justice in Northern Ireland* (Belfast, 1994) For official proposals, see *Legislation against Terrorism* (Cm 4178, Stationery Office, London, 1998).

[188] Standing Advisory Commission on Human Rights, *19th Report* (1993–94 HC 495) ch. 3 para. 18. This was also recommended later by the Standing Advisory Commission on Human Rights, *20th Report* (1994–95 HC 506) ch. 3; *21st Report* (1995–96 HC 467) ch. 4.

[189] Kelly, J M., *The Irish Constitution* (3rd ed. by Hogan and Whyte, Butterworths, Dublin, 1994).

[190] See Hogan, G. and Walker, C., *Political Violence and the Law in Ireland* (Manchester, 1989).

[191] See Henry, M., *The Tallaght Two* (Gill & MacMillan, Dublin, 1995).

[192] See O'Malley, T., 'The Royal Commission on Criminal Justice' (1994) 3(2) *Irish Criminal Law Journal* 97.

law.[193] Therefore, the main attention of English lawyers has tended to focus on the rules about corroboration of confessions, a concept which, it will be recalled, was rejected by the Runciman Commission. Corroboration in the law in Scotland demands that there must be 'some independent fact incriminating the accused, altogether apart from the statements or confessions which he may have made'.[194] However, the message from chapter 16 is that the corroboration rule has been progressively weakened, especially by the widening of the so-called self-corroborating confession exception whereby the accused reveals through the confession facts which only the perpetrator of the crime could know.

As for recent responses to miscarriages of justice, the reform programme in Scotland has lagged very much behind that of England and Wales, and it is notable that there has been no Scottish Runciman despite published cases of miscarriage. Several Scottish Office reviews have been held,[195] and some reforms reminiscent of England and Wales have been pursued. These include an emphasis on crime control measures, such as disposal by way of fixed fines and the use of DNA sampling, though there is also a pragmatic mix of other measures.[196] Conversely, matters not seriously taken up in England have equally been left to lie in Scotland, and some matters, such as disclosure and the impact of imcompetent lawyers, have been left to the happenstance of judicial development. The only independent review, the Sutherland Committee,[197] was confined to the issues of appeals and referrals back. Its recommendations were largely implemented by the Crime and Punishment (Scotland) Act 1997, but the impact of these reforms is far from certain.

In the light of the successive scandals arising out of miscarriages of justice in recent years, some maintain that the English system of criminal justice has totally failed and can be salvaged only by fundamental change rather than revision.[198] Amongst the faults inevitably associated with adversarial systems[199] are slanted and self-serving investigative processes, unequal resources as between prosecution and defence and a commitment to orality in evidence-giving which generates strict and apparently artificial rules as to relevance as well as a limited use of experts.[200] The Philips Commission endorsed without argument the view that an adversarial

---

[193] *Chalmers v HM Advocate* 1954 JC 66; *Hartley v HM Advocate* 1979 SLT 26.

[194] *Manuel v HM Advocate* 1958 JC 41.

[195] Scottish Office, *Appeals in the Scottish Criminal Courts* (HMSO, Edinburgh, 1993), *Juries and Verdicts* (HMSO, Edinburgh, 1993), *Review of Criminal Evidence and Criminal Procedure* (HMSO, Edinburgh, 1993), *Firm and Fair* (HMSO, Edinburgh, 1994).

[196] Scottish Office, *Firm and Fair* (Edinburgh, HMSO, 1994) ch. 8, para. 9.21; Criminal Procedure (Scotland) Act 1995 Pt. II.

[197] Committee on Criminal Appeals and Alleged Miscarriages of Justice, *Report* (Cm. 3245, HMSO, Edinburgh, 1996) ('*Sutherland Report*'). This followed an earlier inconclusive review, Scottish Office, *Sentencing and Appeals* (Edinburgh, HMSO, 1994): Scottish Office, *Firm and Fair* (Edinburgh, HMSO, 1994) paras 6.2, 6.6, 6.17.

[198] For example: Mansfield, M., 'Presumed Innocent', on Inside Story (BBC television) 9 October 1991; Lawton, Sir F., 'What follows the Judith Ward case?' (1992) 136 *Solicitor's Journal* 616 Mansfield, M., *Presumed Guilty* (Heinemann, London, 1993) chs 4, 6.

[199] It follows that the problems are not unique to England. Infamous miscarriages elsewhere include the cases of Sacco and Vanzetti in the USA (see: Ehrmann, H.B., *The Case That Will Not Die* (W.H. Allen, London, 1970) and Lindy Chamberlain in Australia (see: Carrington, K. *et al.*, *Travesty!* (Pluto Press, NSW, 1991).

[200] See: Frankel, M.E., 'The search for the truth' (1975) 123 *University of Penn. Law Review* 1031; Golding, M.P., 'On the adversary system and justice' in Bronaugh, R., (ed.), *Philosophical Law* (1978); Sargant, T., and Hill, P., *Criminal Trials* (Fabian Society, London, 1986) ch. 4; McEwan, J, *Evidence and the Adversarial Process* (Blackwell, Oxford, 1992).

form of justice should be maintained.[201] However, curiosity in inquisitorial systems[202] was again revived at the invitation of the Runciman Commission. The issue is taken up in connection with French criminal process in Chapter 17.

The resultant submissions[203] and research studies[204] soon dampened interest in the light of further reflection upon shortcomings in the Continental alternatives. In the end, the *Runciman Report,* pragmatic and incremental in its approach,[205] stuck with adversarialism as it feared 'an unsuccessful cultural transplant', believed in the efficacy of the separation of powers, and recognised that inquisitorial systems had been recently borrowing from English models.[206] Nevertheless, several features (the restriction of the right to silence and defence disclosure, to name but two) have emerged which are reminiscent of Continental procedures, even if the prime motivation for them tended to be crime control or managerialism rather than the importation of new models of justice. Certainly, there has been little enthusiasm for police reinvestigation[207] or for any outside agency to take over, direct or supervise police investigations *à la juge d'instruction,*[208] though the Crown Prosecution Service has been administratively empowered to clear up inconsistencies in the papers forwarded to them by asking the police for further investigations to be carried out.[209] In any event, Professor Bell concludes that the system of the single pre-trial case-file, cumbersome though this can be, has merits which are worth exploring more than the system of the investigating magistrate. It remains to be seen if the governance of record-keeping under the Criminal Procedure and Investigations Act 1996 will go any way to achieving such benefits, though the chances look slim as the files are compiled and held by the police for police purposes in the first instance.

In principle, both inquisitorial pursuit of the 'truth' and accusatorial suspicion

---

[201] Cmnd 8091, 1981 paras. 1.6–1.8.

[202] There is of course a tendency towards over-simplification in these labels. See Damaska, M.J., *The Faces of Justice and State Authority* (Yale Univ Press, 1986). The possibility of convergence is considered by Fennell, P., Harding, C., Jorg, N. and Swart, B., (eds.), *Criminal Justice in Europe: A Comparative Study* (Clarendon Press, Oxford, 1994); van den Wyngaert, C, *Criminal Procedure Systems in the European Community* (Butterworths, London, 1993) p. 1.

[203] CPS, *Submission* (1991) para. 7.2.11; General Council of the Bar, *Submission* (1992) para. 33; Law Society, *Submission* (1991) para. 2.4; Liberty, *Submission* (1991) p. 4. Academic support likewise became muted: Zander, M., 'From inquisitorial to adversarial – the Italian system' (1991) 141 *New Law Journal* 678; Monahan, J, 'Sanctioning injustice' (1991) *New Law Journal* 678; Gow, N., 'The revival of examinations' (1991) 141 *New Law Journal* 680; Zuckerman, A.S., 'Miscarriages of justice – a root treatment' [1992] *Criminal Law Review* 323.

[204] Leigh, L.H. and Zedner, L., Report on the Administration of Criminal Justice in the Pre-Trial Phase in France and Germany (Royal Commission on Criminal Justice Research Study No. 1, HMSO, London, 1992); Osner, N., Quinn, A., and Crown, G. (eds), *Criminal Justice Systems in Other Jurisdictions* (HMSO, London, 1993).

[205] Rose, D., *In the Name of the Law* (Jonathan Cape, London, 1996) p. 317.

[206] *Runciman Report,* ch. 1, para. 14. See further Jones, R.L., 'Criminal appeals in England and France' (1995) 159 *Justice of the Peace* 683; Kramer, P., and Rushe, R., 'French inquisition' (1997) 94/10 *Law Society's Gazette* 22.

[207] See Zuckerman, A.S., 'Miscarriages of justice – a root treatment' [1992] *Criminal Law Review* 323; Walker, C., and Starmer, K., (eds.) *Justice in Error* (Blackstone Press, London, 1993) p. 247.

[208] But see Sanders, A., 'Access to justice in the police station – an elusive dream?' in Young, R. and Wall, D., *Access to Justice* (Blackstone Press, London, 1996) p. 274.

[209] Procedures were agreed in 1994: Lord Chancellor's Department, Home Office and Law Officers' Department, *The Royal Commission on Criminal Justice: Final Government Response* (Home Office, London, 1996) para. 53. Compare Police (Scotland) Act 1967, s.17.

of the state's motivations each have their good and bad points,[210] so issues of professional and ethical standards may be ultimately more important in both systems – the effectiveness, honesty and openness of individuals. An American survey of miscarriages of justice concludes:[211]

> If we were to isolate a single 'system dynamic' that pervades large numbers of these cases, we would probably describe it as police and prosecution over-zealousness: the anxiety to solve a case; the ease with which one having such an anxiety is willing to believe, on the slightest evidence of the most negligible value, that the culprit is in hand; the willingness to use improper, unethical and illegal means to obtain a conviction when one believes that the person at the bar is guilty.

These failings could and do arise in any criminal justice system, adversarial or inquisitorial. Other causes of error, such as the unreliability of eyewitnesses, are also not evidently solved by the choice of system.

Part IV, 'Miscarriages of Justice in Summary'

An overview is provided in Chapter 18. Without pre-empting the contents of that chapter, I would adopt the summary that 'it would be wrong to pretend that nothing has changed for the better since the great scandals of the early 1990s . . . It must be said, however, that progress has been painfully slow.'[212] One might add that change has not been unidirectional, and so progress must also be balanced with retrograde measures, such as modifications to the right to silence and to prosecution disclosure. The consolation is that the criminal justice system has at least become more open in recent times. Therefore, the hope for the future is not that miscarriages will never occur but that their occurrence will become more evident more quickly than in the very dim but not so distant past.

---

[210] Stephenson, G.M., *The Psychology of Criminal Justice* (Blackwell, Oxford, 1992) p. 114; Sprack, J., 'The trial process' in Stockdale, E. and Casale, S., *Criminal Justice under Stress* (Blackstone Press, London, 1992) p. 70.

[211] Huff, C.R, Rattner, A. and Sagarin, E., *Convicted But Innocent: Wrongful Conviction and Public Policy* (Sage, Thousand Oaks, 1996) p. 64.

[212] Mullin, C., 'Miscarriages of justice in the UK' (1996) 2(2) *Journal of Legislative Studies* 8.

2

Miscarriages of Justice in Principle and Practice

Clive Walker

The issue of miscarriages of justice has been at the heart of much recent discussion – legal, political and social – concerning the criminal justice process in England and Wales. Such has been the depth of the crisis of confidence that it has prompted attempts to re-establish legitimacy, including by such tried and tested methods as changes of personnel,[1] and the appointment of a wide-ranging Royal Commission on Criminal Justice (the Runciman Commission)[2] which followed the more focused May Inquiry.[3] This book concentrates on how the criminal justice system creates and responds to miscarriages of justice. But before embarking on a detailed survey, this chapter will outline what is meant by 'miscarriages of justice' and will catalogue the recurrent causative factors as well as some prominent cases in which they have impacted.

The Nature of Miscarriages of Justice

Definitions and Categorisation

A 'miscarriage' means literally a failure to reach an intended destination or goal. A miscarriage of justice is therefore, *mutatis mutandis*, a failure to attain the desired end result of 'justice'. The meanings of justice and the ways in which it may be denied need to be dissected further, since the desired ends will inherently affect what counts as a miscarriage.

Justice is about distributions – according persons their fair shares and treatment. As far as the impact of the criminal justice system is concerned, one could argue that fair treatment in the dispensation of criminal justice in a liberal, democratic society means that the State should treat individuals with equal respect for their

---

[1] Lord Lane, LCJ, who was associated with the rejection of the *Birmingham Six* appeals (see: *R v Callaghan and others* (1988) 88 Cr App R 40) was succeeded by Lord Taylor in 1992.

[2] The Commission was established in 1991 and reported in 1993 (Cm 2263).

[3] Sir John May, *Report of the inquiry into the circumstances surrounding the convictions arising out of the bomb attacks in Guildford and Woolwich in 1974*, *Interim Report* (1989–90 HC 556), *Second Report* (1992–93 HC 296), *Final Report* (1993-94 HC 449).

rights and for the rights of others.[4] Conversely, theories of justice which elevate in priority general, collective interest (such as utility)[5] or which define rights in terms of class, rather than individual, interests (Marxism-Leninism) must be discarded,[6] though this does not entail the rejection of rights to basic welfare provision for individuals.[7] It does not follow that individual, liberal rights must always be treated as absolute,[8] for it is rationally coherent to accept limitations for the sake of preserving the rights of others or competing rights. More controversially, it has been argued that an exercise of a right might be disallowed if its social costs (such as the downfall of a liberal society by inciting disaffection in wartime) are greater than the cost paid to grant the original right.[9] Hopefully, a sceptical attitude will be taken to claims of catastrophic damage through the observance of rights in a stable, well-established polity such as the United Kingdom. However, one can readily find evidence that episodes of national xenophobia and hysteria affect the courts as much as other branches of the State,[10] and one often looks in vain for an echo of the sentiments expressed two centuries earlier by Lord Mansfield in *R* v *Wilkes* that:[11]

We must not regard political consequences; however formidable soever they may be; if rebellion was the certain consequence, we are bound to say *'fiat justitia, ruat caelum'*.

As for rights potentially affected by the operation of the criminal justice system, several are at risk,[12] including humane treatment, liberty, privacy and family life and even the very right to existence in those jurisdictions which operate capital punishment.[13] The potential costs to the individual will be substantial if subjected to the criminal justice system. Nevertheless, criminal and anti-social activities also have a real adverse effect on the enjoyment of rights by others. Hence, it is justifiable and necessary for the criminal justice process to take steps against the

---

[4] See: Dworkin, R, *Taking Rights Seriously* (Duckworth, London, 1977) chs. 7, 12.

[5] See: Smart, J.J.C. and Williams, B., *Utilitarianism: For and Against* (Cambridge University Press, 1973); Lyons, D., 'Human rights and the general welfare' (1976–77) 6 *Philosophy & Public Affairs* 113.

[6] See: Markovits, I., 'Socialist vs. bourgeois rights' (1978) 45 *University of Chicago Law Review* 612; Osakwe, C., 'The Soviet view of human rights law' (1981) 56 *Tulane Law Review* 299.

[7] Scheffler, S., 'Natural rights, equality and the minimal state' (1976) 6 *Canadian Journal of Philosophy* 59.

[8] But see European Convention on Human Rights and Fundamental Freedoms (Cmd 8969, ETS 5, 1950) Art. 3.

[9] Dworkin, R, *Taking Rights Seriously* (Duckworth, London, 1977) p. 200. This idea is also reflected in the European Convention on Human Rights (1950) Art. 17.

[10] *R* v *Secretary of State for the Home Department, ex parte Cheblak* [1991] 2 All ER 319.

[11] (1770) 98 ER 327 at p. 347 ('Though the heavens fall, let justice be done'). This is an 'irresponsible' maxim to those with priorities of finality and stability: Nobles, R. and Schiff, D., 'The never ending story' (1997) 60 *Modern Law Review* 293 at p. 300.

[12] These rights are delineated *infra* by reference to the European Convention on Human Rights.

[13] See Radelet, M.L. and Bedau, H.G., *In spite of Innocence: Erroneous Convictions in Capital Cases* (Northeastern University Press, Boston, 1992); Gross, S.R., 'The risks of death: why erroneous convictions are common in capital cases' (1996) 44 *Buffalo Law Review* 469; Bandes, S., 'Simple murder: a comment on the legality of executing the innocent' (1996) 44 *Buffalo Law Review* 501; Palacios, V.J., 'Faith in fantasy: The Supreme Court's reliance on commutation to ensure justice in death penalty cases' (1996) 49 *Vanderbilt Law Review* 311. In the view of Rose LJ in *R* v *Mattan The Times*, 5 March 1998, 'capital punishment was not perhaps a prudent culmination for a criminal justice system which is human and therefore fallible'.

rights of suspects and convicts – by way of loss of liberty, property or other proportionate means – in order to protect the rights of others.

At the same time, it is wise to recognise that the responsibility on the State to treat its citizens justly is awesome. So if 'the justifications offered for a finding of guilt or non-guilt are seriously defective'[14] and their treatment is unwarranted by, or disproportionate to, the need to protect the rights of others, then serious damage will be inflicted not only on the individual but on society (all citizens) as a whole. The ever-present jeopardy of mistakes in the criminal justice system is reflected in the aphorism that 'It is better that ten guilty persons escape than that one innocent suffer.'[15] It may also be reflected in features such as the burden of proof and the privilege against self-incrimination, though the rational connection between these features and the ethos of the system has become controversial.[16]

Leaving aside issues of evidence and proof, one possible definition of 'miscarriage' in the context of criminal justice will now be suggested, and it is one which reflects an individualistic rights-based approach to miscarriages of justice.[17] A miscarriage occurs as follows: whenever suspects or defendants or convicts are treated by the State in breach of their rights, whether because of, first, deficient processes or, second, the laws which are applied to them or, third, because there is no factual justification for the applied treatment or punishment; fourth, whenever suspects or defendants or convicts are treated adversely by the State to a disproportionate extent in comparison with the need to protect the rights of others; fifth, whenever the rights of others are not effectively or proportionately protected or vindicated by State action against wrongdoers or, sixth, by State law itself. Each of these six categories will now be illustrated.

The treatment of individuals in breach of their rights because of unfair processes will occur when individuals are subjected to arrest or detention without due cause. For example, there is evidence that young black males are subjected to an unsupportable degree of police attention because of the colour of their skin.[18] Police actions after detention may also be injurious to rights, especially through unfair treatment to procure confessions or in the production of unsound forensic evidence or through the non-disclosure of evidence. A breach of due process may occur at the stage of a trial. Failures have arisen through biased or ineffective judges, perverse juries and the mishandling of forensic evidence. A defendant may also be failed by lawyers who fail to advocate effectively through inadequate preparation or performance. The resultant conviction of a defendant following such failures can realistically be viewed as a miscarriage of justice, even in respect of

---

[14] Greer, S., 'Miscarriages of justice reconsidered' (1994) 57 *Modern Law Review* 58 at p. 61.

[15] Blackstone, *Commentaries on the Law of England* (1765–9) Vol. iv p. 27. See also: Stephen, Sir J, *History of the Criminal Law of England* (Macmillan, London, 1883) Vol.I p. 438; Fletcher, G.P., 'Two kinds of legal rules' (1968) 77 *Yale Law Journal* 880; Shavario, D., 'Statistical probability evidence and the appearance of justice' (1989–90) 103 *Harvard Law Review* 530; Ingraham, B.L., 'The right of silence, the presumption of innocence, the burden of proof, and a modest proposal: a reply to O'Reilly' (1996) 86 *Journal of Criminal Law & Criminology* 559 at pp. 562, 576.

[16] See Chapter 4.

[17] See also the definition in Chapter 14 and the statements of ethics in Ashworth, A., *The Criminal Process: An Evaluative Study* (2nd ed., Clarendon Press, Oxford, 1998) ch. 3. This definition is meant to expand upon, but not in any way contradict, that in *Justice in Error*, p. 4. For a valuable critique, see Schiff, D. and Nobles, R., '*Review: Justice in Error*' (1994) 34 *British Journal of Criminology* 383.

[18] See Jefferson, T, and Walker, M.A., 'Ethnic minorities in the criminal justice system' [1992] *Criminal Law Review* 83.

a person who has committed the elements of a crime. Some observers attempt to distinguish between those who are really 'innocent' and the wrongfully convicted – those who are acquitted 'on a technicality' – say, because of a misleading direction in law by a judge to a jury.[19] However, the emphasis here is on the breach of rights, and rights to due process have central importance in assuring righteous treatment. Accordingly, even a person who has in fact and with intent committed a crime could be said to have suffered a miscarriage of justice if convicted by processes which did not respect basic rights,[20] though the misdirection of a jury may have more or less impact on rights in the fullness of any case. A much narrower variant of this view is put forward by the *May Report*, which, though not requiring 'innocence', does demand that 'something goes seriously wrong in the criminal justice process which may have affected the result of the trial, even though one cannot be sure that it has done so.'.[21] Nevertheless, breaches of rights not falling under the *May Report* formula may still fall within an indirect meaning of miscarriages of justice discussed later.

Another conceivable category of persons suffering a miscarriage of justice because of a denial of their rights concerns those who fall foul of laws which are inherently unjust rather than unjustly applied. In a responsive, liberal democracy, such failures of the system should be few and far between. However, claims along these lines have been made in recent years by: persons convicted of failure to pay the poll tax or taxes to finance nuclear weapons;[22] women provoked (in fact but not so defined in law until the Court of Appeal changed its mind in 1995 on the referral back of Sarah Thornton's case) into retaliation by the violence of male relatives;[23] those involved in prosecutions for homosexual activities by persons aged 16–21;[24] or soldiers in Northern Ireland (or indeed 'joyriders') whose fate is determined by the application of the law of murder in situations of excessive force.[25] This book will mainly reflect upon dysfunctions in the application of laws, but some space is afforded to laws which some people view as inherently unfair, for example the Prevention of Terrorism (Temporary Provisions) Acts 1974–89.[26] A more blatant example may be South African apartheid, which involved many

---

[19] There may be arguments for a retrial where the acquittal is through error of law or the misconduct of the defendant or defence counsel: DiBiagio, T.M., 'Judicial equity: an argument for post-acquittal retrial when the judicial process is fundamentally defective' (1996) 46 *Catholic University Law Review* 77. By contrast, retrials following acquittals tainted by criminal interferences by the defendant under the Criminal Procedure and Investigations Act 1996 ss. 54–7 do not require proof of a connection between the interference and the acquittal (and see also *Runciman Report*, ch. 10 para. 72).

[20] In this way, mistakes of law do not have meaning just for lawyers, since any citizen could surely understand that persons should be convicted on the basis of the law as it is and not as some foolish judge says it is. Compare Sir John May, *Report of the inquiry into the circumstances surrounding the convictions arising out of the bomb attacks in Guildford and Woolwich in 1974, Final Report* (1993–94 HC 449) ch. 13 (concerning admissions by Gerard Conlon of IRA involvement); Nobles, R. and Schiff, D., 'Miscarriages of justice: a systems approach' (1996) 59 *Modern Law Review* 299 at p. 302.

[21] Sir John May, *'Report'* (see footnote 20, above), para. 21.3–4.

[22] See: *Cheney v Conn* [1968] 1 All ER 779; Dignan, J., 'A right not to render unto Caesar' (1983) 34 *Northern Ireland Legal Quarterly* 20; Finnis, J. *et al.*, *Nuclear Deterrence, Morality and Realism* (Oxford University Press, 1987).

[23] *R v Thornton* [1992] 1 All ER 306, (No. 2), [1996] 1 WLR 1174. See also *R v Ahluwalia* [1992] 4 All ER 889; *R v Humphreys* [1995] 4 All ER 108.

[24] See *Sutherland v UK*, Appl. no. 25186/94.

[25] *R v Clegg* [1995] 2 WLR 80.

[26] See Chapter 14.

denials of rights and thereby miscarriages. That system was often rational and predictable according to its own lights, but to label it 'just' because it observed regular and solemn procedures would be blinkered.[27] Laws such as these often deepen the injustice by the conferment of wide and low-visibility discretion, which undermines public accountability or redress.[28]

The third category of miscarriage of justice occurs where there is no factual justification for the treatment or punishment. A conviction – perhaps because of mistaken identity – of a person who is in fact innocent would obviously fall into this category of breach of rights (ultimately of humanity and liberty) and indeed might be defined as a core case.[29] Persons enjoy a 'profound right not to be convicted of crimes of which they are innocent.'.[30] Perhaps the only qualification which may be entered at this point is that one must allow the system some time to correct itself, whether through acquittal or the payment of damages, and so the notion of 'miscarriage' involves a completion of a process (in failure) and not simply a mistake. Furthermore, there must be some kind of State responsibility for the conviction, but this should be defined in wide terms. For instance, the jury might be viewed as a State agency even though it normally produces verdicts which are largely independent. Nonetheless, the jury is part of the State's criminal process, and the State retains a responsibility to ensure various safeguards against inaccurate decision-making, including the avoidance of bias,[31] the provision of adequate facilities for lay decision-making and a willingness to reconsider perverse convictions. Similarly, a conviction brought about by a defendant who falsely confesses or by a mendacious informer or unreliable eyewitness can also be counted as a potential miscarriage of justice, since the State has chosen to rely upon facts which have not been subjected to adequate processes of scrutiny or review.

Illustrations of miscarriages of justice resulting from disproportionate treatment in terms of rights might include the granting of arrest or extensive search powers in respect of trivial anti-social conduct[32] or excessively harsh charges or sentences.[33] Similarly, the imposition of conditions during punishment which serve little purpose other than degradation and therefore do not ultimately bolster respect for rights should be treated as a miscarriage of justice. It should be noted that sentencing and penal regimes are not covered in the remainder of this book, which concentrates mainly upon the first, process-related type of miscarriage. This focus is adopted since it is at the heart of the controversial cases, reviews and reforms over the past decade, even though it is arguable that these other forms of miscarriage are more endemic.

---

[27] See: Mathews, A.S., *Freedom, State Security and the Rule of Law* (Sweet & Maxwell, London, 1988); Dyzenhaus, D., *Hard Cases and Wicked Legal Systems* (Clarendon, Oxford, 1991).

[28] Stenning, PC (ed.), *Accountability for Criminal Justice* (University of Toronto Press, 1995) p. 6.

[29] Compare: Brandon, R. and Davies, C., *Wrongful Imprisonment* (Allen, London, 1973) p. 19.

[30] Dworkin, R., *A Matter of Principle* (Clarendon Press, Oxford, 1986) p. 72; *Herrera v Collins* (1993) 506 US 390 at p. 398.

[31] Failures in this regard may arise from ethnic composition (see: *R v Ford* [1989] 3 WLR 762, and Commission for Racial Equality, *Submission to the Royal Commission* (1991)), the abolition of the defence's rights to peremptory challenge (Criminal Justice Act 1988, s.118) and the rules about jury vetting (*Practice Direction* [1988] 3 All ER 1086).

[32] Consider some of the powers in the Police and Criminal Evidence Act 1984, s. 25.

[33] In regard to excessive charges, consider the consensual sado-masochists in *R v Brown* [1994] 1 AC 212; *R v Wilson* [1996] 3 WLR 125; but see also *Laskey, Jaggard and Brown v UK*, Appl. no. 21627/93, 21826/93, 21974/93, 1997–I, *The Times* 20 February 1997; as regards sentences, consider the penalties for breach of Anti-Social Behaviour Orders in the Crime and Disorder Act 1998.

The fifth type of miscarriage of justice, a failure to protect and vindicate the rights of potential or actual victims, can arise in various ways. For example, a lack of police officers to guard against violent attackers could be a breach of rights,[34] though recent neo-Liberalism has sought to resurrect a heavier burden of self-responsibility for security.[35] A refusal to prosecute particular types of suspects, whether through intimidation, bias or political manipulation or corruption,[36] may also be viewed as a miscarriage. Such a situation arose in 1988, when the Attorney-General blocked proceedings against RUC officers accused by the Stalker/Sampson inquiry of perverting the course of justice and obstruction of the police investigation.[37] There was also a failure to prosecute persons involved in the racist murder of Stephen Lawrence in 1993.[38] These decisions may have been fair to the accused, but they did result in a failure to protect the rights of others because of State mismanagement of the process.[39] A failure to vindicate rights may equally occur when a jury perversely refuses to convict an individual, through intimidation or bias.[40] Disregard for the rights of Rodney King, a black suspect beaten severely by four white policemen, sparked riots in Los Angeles in May 1992 when they were acquitted,[41] and criticisms in some quarters were also expressed in response to the acquittals of Ponting in 1985[42] and Randle and Pottle in 1991,[43] though it could be argued that in these cases one 'miscarriage' prevented another – that of disproportionate treatment. Another controversial acquittal of the 'obviously guilty'[44] was that of O.J Simpson in Los Angeles in 1995, probably heavily motivated by a wish on the part of the jury to discipline the police or at least to demonstrate that the police lacked credibility and thereby to uphold the integrity of the process.[45] As well as substantive outcomes, victims may also be treated unjustly by the process, a point which is often raised in relation to rape survivors especially those who have to face the cross-examination of their alleged assailants[46] or are required to produce corroboration.[47]

[34] See: *X v UK and Ireland*, Appl. no. 9825/82, (1986) 8 EHRR 49.
[35] O'Malley, P., 'Risk, power and crime prevention' (1992) 21 *Economy and Society* 252.
[36] For some extreme pressures and responses, see Savona, E.U. (ed.), *Mafia Issues* (ISPAC, Milan, 1992).
[37] See: HC Debs. vol. 126 col. 21, 25 January 1988. See also, in Australia: Carrington, K. *et al.*, *Travesty!* (Pluto Press, NSW, 1991) chs. 11, 12.
[38] See *Report by the Police Complaints Authority on the investigation of a complaint against the Metropolitan Police Service by Mr N and Mrs D Lawrence* (Cm 3822, HMSO, London, 1997).
[39] CPS, *Annual Report for 1990-91* (London, 1991) p. 28.
[40] Such is alleged to be an ever-present danger in Northern Ireland: *Report of the Commission to consider legal procedures to deal with terrorist activities in Northern Ireland* (Cmnd 5185) (1972).
[41] *The Times*, 1 May 1992 p. 1; *United States v Koon* 34 F.3d 1416 (9th Cir. 1994); Davis, P.L., 'Rodney King and the decriminalization of police brutality in America' (1994) 53 *Maryland Law Review* 271.
[42] [1985] *Criminal Law Review* 318, [1986] *Criminal Law Review* 491.
[43] *The Times*, 27 June 1991 p. 24.
[44] Allen, J., 'Reform: the system: the Simpson affair, reform of the criminal justice process, and magic bullets' (1996) 67 *University of Colorado Law Review* 989. Also see Chapter 13.
[45] See *California v Simpson*, No. BA097211, 1995 WL 672670 (Cal. Super. Ct., 1995); Dershowitz, A.M., *Reasonable Doubt: The OJ Simpson Case and the Criminal Justice System* (Simon & Schuster, New York, 1996); Uelmen, G.F., *Lessons from the Trial* (Andrews and McMeel, Kansas, 1996). See also: Devlin, P., 'The conscience of the jury' (1991) 107 *Law Quarterly Review* 398.
[46] See for example the case of Milton Brown, whose cross-examination of his victims was described by the Home Secretary as a 'traumatising experience': *The Times*, 17 January 1998 p. 7. Reforms are suggested by the Report of the Interdeparmtental Working Group on the Treatment of Vulnerable or Intimidated Witnesses in the Criminal Justice System, *Speaking Up for Justice* (Home Office, London, 1998).
[47] The Home Secretary, Michael Howard, was critical of the corroboration rule in 1993: 'The other day

A sixth type of miscarriage of justice is the existence and application of laws which are inherently unfair to victims. To continue the theme raised in the last category, the treatment of the sexual history of rape survivors has been problematised,[48] though the difficulty of balancing fairness to the accused is acute at this point. A less controversial example may be the (now repealed) legal rule within the law of murder that the victim must have died within a year and a day.[49]

These six categories, which revolve around themes of breach of rights of suspects/defendants, the disproportionate treatment of suspects/defendants or the non-vindication of the rights of victims, might be termed direct miscarriages. In addition, it may be possible to derive from their infliction a seventh, indirect miscarriage which affects the community as a whole. A conviction arising from deceit or illegalities is corrosive of the State's claims to legitimacy on the basis of its criminal justice system's values such as respect for individual rights. In this way, as well as the undesirable fate of the individual, the 'moral integrity of the criminal process' suffers harm.[50] Moreover, there may be practical detriment in terms of diminished confidence in the forces of law and order leading to fewer active citizens aiding the police and fewer jurors willing to convict even the blatantly 'guilty'. It is arguable that this indirect form of miscarriage can exist independently as well as contingently in two respects. One is that a breach of 'the principle of judicial legitimacy'[51] should be of concern even if there is an accurate and fair determination of guilt or innocence. Secondly, it still produces a great moral harm even if, so far as the individual is concerned, there is a mistake but no real harm is inflicted (say, when a person imprisoned for life is wrongfully convicted soon afterwards of a minor motoring offence). It is therefore argued that the State itself should avoid actions or processes which might damage the integrity of the system. Consistent with this concern, lawyers, whether acting for prosecution or defence, are reminded that they are not the ciphers of their clients but owe duties of integrity to the system.[52]

In summary, there are four points to infer from the definitions of 'miscarriages' adopted in this chapter. First, the meaning is not confined to miscarriages in court or in the penal system. Miscarriages can arise on the street when the police unjustly exercise their coercive powers, as may be increasingly the case if the rationale of criminal justice is switched from conviction to surveillance.[53] Secondly, miscarriages can be institutionalised within laws as well as ensue from failures in the application of laws. Thirdly, a miscarriage of justice must involve a shortcoming for which there is a degree of State responsibility. In these days of private security

---

a woman judge said she almost choked every time she gave the warning. It is offensive. It cannot be justified. It must go.' (*The Daily Telegraph*, 7 October 1993 p. 12.) See Lees, S., *Ruling Passions* (Open University Press, Buckingham, 1997).

[48] Temkin, J., 'Sexual history evidence' [1993] *Criminal Law Review* 3; McColgan, A., 'Common law and the relevance of sexual history evidence' (1996) 16 *Oxford Journal of Legal Studies* 275.

[49] Law Reform (Year and a Day Rule) Act 1996.

[50] Choo, A.L-T., *Abuse of Process and Judicial Stays of Criminal Proceedings* (Clarendon Press, Oxford, 1993) p. 10. See also Packer, H.L., *The Limits of the Criminal Sanction* (Stanford University Press, 1969) p. 166; Sprack, J, 'The trial process' in Stockdale, E. and Casale, S., *Criminal Justice under Stress* (Blackstone Press, London, 1992) p. 65.

[51] Choo, A.L.T., *Abuse of Process* (see footnote 50 above), p. 13.

[52] See for example Crown Prosecution Service, *Statement of Purpose and Values* (1997): 'We are committed to providing a high quality prosecution service, working in the interests of justice . . . We will act with integrity and objectivity . . .'.

[53] Ericson, R.V. and Haggerty, K.D., *Policing the Risk Society* (Clarendon, Oxford, 1997).

services and prisons and other forms of 'hollowing out' of government, it is not essential that an official agency was involved in the proximate cause of the miscarriage so long as the function leading to the miscarriage was of a public nature and sanctioned by the State.[54] But deceit, neglect or violence by private persons or bodies may inflict gross hardship and unfairness yet are not necessarily attributable to any deficiency in the criminal justice system. We do not normally assign the phrase 'miscarriage of justice' to a breach of contract or a trespass – unless a public agency was to blame or the State failed to offer any system for resolution or redress. The fourth point is to reiterate what was asserted at the outset: justice and failures of justice should primarily be defined with respect to rights. This last claim will now be explored further, but, if substantiated, will imply a strong duty on the part of the State to be vigilant about miscarriages and to be willing to rectify them, even if at some cost to aggregate happiness and traditions of utilitarian calculus.

Critique of an Individualistic Rights-based Approach to Miscarriages of Justice

Reliance upon theories of individual rights in an analysis of the criminal justice system is in some senses unremarkable. The discourse of rights is increasingly pervasive, as it has been applied under the influence of the European Convention on Human Rights[55] whose impact will be augmented by the Human Rights Act 1998. The rights of most relevance are as follows: Articles 2 (life), 3 (humane treatment), 5 (liberty and security of the person), 6 (fair trials, and importing a concern for fairness and equality of arms throughout the pre-trial process),[56] 7 (non-retrospective penalties), and 8 (privacy and freedom from intrusion). Aside from common usage, one can argue for a rights-based approach on the grounds that the sanctions of the criminal justice system are often designed in terms of loss of rights – whether liberty (imprisonment) or property (fines): 'Judges, whatever else they do, deal in fear and pain and death.'.[57] So, a focus on rights seems appropriate, since it coheres with the overall function of the State which is the protection of citizens not just collectively but also as atomistic individuals. The criminal justice process provides a fundamental aspect of that protection by deterring or punishing persons who violate the rights of others, but it would be counter-productive and abusive to sanction the innocent, as well as undermining the integrity and legitimacy of the system.[58] More consequentialist strategies can be adopted after conviction whereupon individual rights may be legitimately restrained,[59] but only

---

[54] Compare Human Rights Act 1998, s.6.

[55] See Harris, D.J, O'Boyle, M. and Warbrick, C., *Law of the European Convention on Human Rights* (Butterworth, London, 1995).

[56] See *Edwards* v *UK*, Appl. no. 13071/87, Ser.A vol. 247B, (1993) 16 EHRR 47, *John Murray* v *UK*, Appl. no. 18731/91, 1996-I, (1996) 22 EHRR 29, *Saunders* v *UK*, Appl. no. 19187/91, 1997-VI, (1997) 23 EHRR 313.

[57] Douzinas, C. and Warrington, R., 'A well-founded fear of justice: law and ethics in postmodernity' in Leonard, J (ed.), *Legal Studies as Cultural Studies* (State University of New York, Albany, 1995) at p. 198.

[58] See Ashworth, A., *The Criminal Process: An Evaluative Study* (2nd ed., Clarendon Press, Oxford, 1998) at p. 32. These are arguably independent values, but a system lacking integrity and legitimacy will not serve the interests of individuals either as defendants or as victims.

[59] See Braithwaite, J. and Pettit, P., *Not Just Deserts: A Republican Theory of Criminal Justice* (Oxford University Press, 1990).

assuming it is a safe and legitimate conviction and subject to normative constraints as to treatment.

The ethical priority given to the interests of the individual also correlates with the taxonomy for criminal justice derived from Packer's 'normative antinomy' between the due process model and the crime control model.[60] The primacy of individual autonomy and rights is central to the due process model, which recognises that the possibility of human fallibility and error can thereby yield grave injustice, as when the system convicts the innocent or even convicts without respecting procedural rights. So, the emphasis must be on the quality of justice and on the deterrence of abuses of official power rather than the grant of wide, deterrent powers to catch criminals. Consistent with this due process model are a number of features, including, in England and Wales (as well as many other common law jurisdictions, including Northern Ireland, the Republic of Ireland and the USA),[61] an adversarial approach to the determination of issues within the criminal justice system.[62] In other words, the process is organised around the concept of two opposing sides, each freely and openly presenting in words their own contested case (hi)stories[63] in order to convince the impartial decision-maker at a trial. The rivalry of arguments in the curial marketplace is designed to expose the true facts and laws relevant to the case[64] and is thought to avoid any form of complacency or bias by official inquisitors, including even judicial figures such as investigating magistrates. The central role of the defendant within the process necessarily entails a recognition of that person's individual autonomy and interests. At the same time, the two sides are hardly equal in terms of powers and resources, so the imbalance is corrected by procedural and evidential rules, including the burden of proof, disclosure by the prosecution and legal assistance from public funds.[65]

The due process model fits well with the first and third of the definitions of miscarriage of justice outlined earlier. Treatment in breach of, or disproportionately to, rights, whether because of factual errors or because of a failure to secure rightful treatment (such as legal representation) is a core concern of the due process model which seeks to stamp out oppression on the part of the State and to provide an 'obstacle course' for any conviction.[66] By contrast, inaccurate decision-making by the tribunal of fact is less readily treated as a miscarriage under the definitions and under the due process model, though the State may have responsibility through its prior actions for prompting the verdict and certainly has a responsibility after

---

[60] Packer, H.L., *The Limits of the Criminal Sanction* (Stanford University Press, 1969) p. 153. See also Damaska, M.J., *The Faces of Justice and State Authority* (Yale University Press, 1986) chs. 4, 5.

[61] But contrast the positions in Scotland and France: Chapters 16, 17.

[62] See Packer, H.L., *The Limits of the Criminal Sanction* (Stanford University Press, 1969) p. 157; Jorg, N., Field, S. and Harding, C., 'Are inquisitorial and adversarial systems converging?' in Fennell, P., Harding, C., Jorg, N. and Swart, B., (eds.), *Criminal Justice in Europe: A Comparative Study* (Clarendon Press, Oxford, 1994) p. 42; Uglow, S., *Criminal Justice* (Sweet & Maxwell, London, 1995) p. 130.

[63] See Bennett, W.L. and Feldman, M., *Reconstructing Reality in the Courtroom* (Rutgers University Press, New Brunswick, 1981); Stephenson, G., *The Psychology of Criminal Justice* (Blackwell, Oxford, 1992).

[64] See McEwan, J, *Evidence and the Adversarial Process* (Blackwell, London, 1992).

[65] These supportive features have been categorised as 'result-efficacious' (those that contribute to accurate convictions or acquittals) and 'dignitary' (those that ensure ethical treatment even if impairing the determination of facts): Arenella, P., 'Rethinking the functions of criminal procedure' (1983) 72 *Georgetown Law Journal* 185.

[66] Packer, H.L., *The Limits of the Criminal Sanction* (Stanford University Press, 1969) p. 163.

it is reached for reviewing it in the light of respect for rights, whether of a defendant or a victim. The other definitions relate less to process and more to substantive ends or relate more to victims than to suspects; these concerns are outside the core of the due process model and can more readily be explained by the human rights focus which is ultimately adopted in this chapter. In addition, an emphasis upon the protection of rights rather than due process *per se* may avoid a degeneration into legal formalism whereby established processes rather than ultimate values become venerated.[67]

The competing crime control model stresses the effective and efficient control and punishment of crime so as to minimise violations of the rights of victims and to maximise the deterrent impact of the criminal justice system. It follows that a great deal of trust has to be placed in the accurate screening of guilty from innocent by the police and other pre-trial gatekeepers of the system;[68] this point is highlighted by Ericson who argues that surveillance and record-keeping are now the primary functions of criminal justice and may even be independent of crime control which still envisages a court lawsuit.[69] Once a person has entered the system, the emphasis is upon summary and speedy disposal (often without a rigid demarcation between agencies or parties). Mistakes which abnegate the procedural rights of individuals can be tolerated so long as the individual is factually 'guilty' and so long as the failings in the process do not undermine public confidence. The rightful treatment of the accused is not necessarily paramount unlike under the due process model, though complete miscarriages are to be avoided as wasteful of resources.[70]

Of course, neither due process nor crime control model exhausts the possible stances of a criminal justice system[71] nor indeed fully explains its workings or purposes.[72] Other archetypes (or 'polarities'[73]) include the rehabilitative model[74] (often of importance for young offenders)[75] and the bureaucratic model (reminiscent perhaps of the New Public Management of the 1980s as applied especially to magistrates' courts).[76] The interests of victims do not fit easily with either model. Centrality for the interests of victims under a restorative justice model[77] might well

---

[67] Greer, S., 'Miscarriages of justice reconsidered' (1994) 57 *Modern Law Review* 58 at p. 60.

[68] King, M., *The Framework of Criminal Justice* (Croom Helm, London, 1981) p. 127.

[69] Ericson, R.V., 'The Royal Commission on Criminal Justice: system surveillance' in McConville, M. and Bridges, L., (eds.) *Criminal Justice in Crisis* (Edward Elgar, Aldershot, 1994) at p. 113.

[70] But defendants may be viewed under this view as inevitably guilty of some crime: Givelber, D., 'Meaningless acquittals, meaningful convictions: do we reliably acquit the innocent?' (1997) 49 *Rutgers Law Review* 1317 at p. 1330.

[71] For a wider categorisation, see King, M., *The Framework of Criminal Justice* (Croom Helm, London, 1981); Davies, M., Croall, H. and Tyrer, J, *Criminal Justice* (2nd ed., Longman, London, 1998) ch. 1.

[72] See Damaska, M., 'Evidentiary barriers to conviction and two models of criminal procedure' (1973) 121 *University of Pennsylvania Law Review* 516. For an explanation of purposes, see Home Office, *Report for 1992* (Cm 1909, HMSO, London); Davies, M., Croall, H. and Tyrer, J., *Criminal Justice* (2nd ed., Longman, London, 1998) p. 21.

[73] Packer, H.L., *The Limits of the Criminal Sanction* (Stanford University Press, 1969) p. 153.

[74] See Griffiths, J., 'A third model of criminal justice' (1970) 79 *Yale Law Journal* 359; Foote, D.H., 'The benevolent paternalism of Japanese criminal justice' (1989) 80 *California Law Review* 317.

[75] See Home Office, *No More Excuses* (Cm 3809, HMSO, 1997).

[76] See: Raine, J.W., and Wilson, M.J., *Managing Criminal Justice* (Harvester Wheatsheaf, London, 1993), 'Beyond managerialism in criminal justice' (1997) 36 *Howard Journal* 80.

[77] See Wright, M., *Justice for Victims and Offenders* (2nd ed., Open University Press, 1996); Miers, D.M., *State Compensation for Criminal Injuries* (Butterworths, 1996) Davis, R.C., Lurigio, S. and Skogan, R.C., *Victims of Crime* (2nd ed., Sage, London, 1997); Fenwick, H., 'Procedural "rights" of victims of crime' (1997) 60 *Modern Law Review* 317; JUSTICE, *Victims in Criminal Justice* (London, 1998).

conflict with basic due process features such as the presumption of innocence and open confrontation. Equally crime control focuses on the more collective (though not necessarily communitarian)[78] interests of deterrence and security; individual determinations may not accurately reflect the injury suffered. Nor can it be claimed convincingly that one model is, or should be, wholly dominant within a given system,[79] and one can immediately see from the examples given that the models depend on value judgments about rights as against other considerations which may come into play according to the level of the court, consequences of the decision and type of offender. There is next the concern that models, especially the due process version, are little more than propaganda designed to engender legitimacy for inherently oppressive societies and their coercive agencies.[80] In a system which in fact processes most suspects without troubling the courts, and, even less often, jurors,[81] the crime control model in fact predominates and may even be the underlying purpose of the system as a whole.[82] Further, it would be a delusion, especially in a book about miscarriages of justice, to pretend that, even where relevant, the due process model is perfectly observed. At the same time, it is maintained that the due process ideology is in fact taken seriously throughout much of the system and is arguably the dominant ethic of the more serious end of the criminal justice process – the Crown Court and appeals and post-appeals systems which have produced the caseload to be described next.[83] In addition, these stages of criminal justice involve the most dramatic impacts in terms of rights, and so that agenda is again to the fore. Due process as a relevant value was not extinguished by the miscarriages of justice of the last two decades, but it is true that more mixed stances both in terms of the values of the criminal justice system and therefore of the meanings of miscarriages were re-established by the close of the Runciman Commission in 1993 and were certainly reflected in the legislative programme which followed it, as will be described later.

To conclude, the due process model does not underpin much of the daily operation of the criminal justice system, especially those parts of the system which involve routinised and unsupervised encounters between police and citizen. Yet, it should certainly be to the fore when those encounters become more formalised and more is at stake in terms of rights, such as by detention in a police station or when the suspect becomes formally charged, especially if liberty is at stake.[84]

Though one can tally the due process/crime control debate with the rights-based conception of miscarriages of justice put forward in this chapter, there may be

---

[78] See Braithwaite, J., and Pettit, P., *Not Just Deserts: A Republican Theory of Criminal Justice* (Oxford University Press, 1990) p. 112; Lacey, N. and Zedner, L., 'Discourses of community in criminal justice' (1995) 22 *Journal of Law and Society* 301; Raine, J.W. and Wilson, M.J., 'Beyond managerialism in criminal justice' (1997) 36 *Howard Journal* 80.

[79] Damaska, M.J., *The Faces of Justice and State Authority* (Yale University Press, 1986) p. 241.

[80] McBarnett, D.J, *Conviction: Law, the State and the Construction of Justice* (Macmillan, London, 1981).

[81] Of offences committed in 1994, only around 47 per cent are reported to the police, only 27 per cent are recorded, only 2.7 per cent result in conviction or cautioning: Home Office, *Information on the Criminal Justice System in England and Wales* (London, 1995) p. 25. In addition, out of 1.95m defendants who were prosecuted in 1994, just 88,000 were tried in the Crown Court, of whom 55 per cent pleaded guilty: pp. 33, 34.

[82] Ashworth, A., *The Criminal Process: An Evaluative Study* (2nd ed., Clarendon Press, Oxford, 1998) p. 27.

[83] See Sanders, A. and Young, R., *Criminal Justice* (Butterworths, London, 1994) chs. 7, 9.

[84] Sanders, A. and Young, R., *Criminal Justice* (Butterworths, London, 1994) ch. 1, p. 463.

other conceptions of miscarriages of justice which are more difficult to subsume. One such alternative approach is taken by Nobles and Schiff.[85] They argue that the controversies in cases like the *Birmingham Six* were essentially 'evidential': 'that there was either insufficient evidence to accept their guilt or (in the minds of some) that there was good reason to believe them innocent.'. So, miscarriages of justice are about 'evidence and proof' rather than the recognition or denial of rights, as suggested in this chapter. If this alternative conception can be called a definition at all, then it must be one of the shallowest definitions imaginable. It is shallow in that it wholly ignores two important aspects of miscarriages of justice firmly within the definitions set out earlier – namely, miscarriages which arise through the operation of laws which are inherently unjust, and miscarriages through the failure to vindicate the rights of victims. Their definition is equally inadequate even in regard to the first and fourth categories of miscarriages, namely those where individuals are treated without any or proportionate regard to their rights. Putting the boot on the other foot, we should now ask, 'what evidence' and 'what proof'? For example, would one want to embrace as 'evidence' confessions obtained as a result of torture? What about forensic 'evidence' from an incompetent scientist or by means of unreliable techniques? Should we define silence as 'evidence', and if so how much does it count for? There seems to be a fundamental flaw here; it is implied that matters of 'evidence and proof' are self-evident and self-contained and are more fundamental than matters of 'rights'. However, it is central to the definition in this chapter that evidence and proof should reflect rights rather than the reverse. As recognised by others,[86] only on the basis of deeper values within the criminal justice system can cogent answers be given to the questions 'what evidence' and 'what proof'. Otherwise, the door is opened to Home Secretaries who wish to dress up repressive legislation as merely technical adjustments.

A later, more sophisticated attempt by Nobles and Schiff to explain miscarriages of justice draws heavily upon theories of autopoiesis and so elucidates the inward-looking disposition of the earlier attempt.[87] This theoretical basis is most unpromising as a way of explaining causes of injustice or how to remedy them.[88] Looking at law, or indeed any social system,[89] as 'a system of self-referential communications'[90] is hardly likely to explain the complex inter-play of law, politics and culture which has impacted upon the criminal justice system during the last decade. The theory of autopoiesis also requires the arid and misleading drawing of 'system' boundaries, which confuses and underplays the impact of, for example, academic and journalistic legal writing, legal political pressure groups and politician-lawyers (such as the former Home Secretary, Michael Howard, and the present incumbent, Jack Straw) and suggests that mere journalists or politicians cannot inspire reforms appropriate to an alien system (the law), except perhaps through exceptional 'linkage institutions' such as Royal Commissions.[91] It also

---

[85] Schiff, D. and Nobles, R., Review: *Justice in Error* (1994) 34 *British Journal of Criminology* 383.
[86] Greer, S., 'Miscarriages of justice reconsidered' (1994) 57 *Modern Law Review* 58.
[87] Nobles, R. and Schiff, D., 'Miscarriages of justice: a systems approach' (1996) 59 *Modern Law Review* 299.
[88] King, M., 'The truth about autopoiesis' (1993) 20 *Journal of Law and Society* 218 at pp. 229–230.
[89] James, A., 'An open and shut case? Law as an autopoietic system' (1992) 19 *Journal of Law and Society* 271 at p. 275.
[90] Nobles, R. and Schiff, D., 'Miscarriages of justice: a systems approach' (1996) 59 *Modern Law Review* 299 at p. 300.
[91] *Ibid.* at p. 314.

suggests a rigid binary divide between lawful/unlawful which does not tally with how unfair convictions are in fact viewed, whether by lawyers or others. More fundamentally, the ultimate values shaping the criminal justice process, individual rights, cannot easily be contained within a second-order autopoietic system such as law, since rights draw their normative meaning from other 'systems' which interact and coalesce.[92] Therefore, the authors seek refuge in much narrower values, such as finality (of verdicts) and workability (of rules of evidence and process), as the basis for the maintenance of the authority of criminal justice. But these will not suffice; as the *Birmingham Six* case well illustrates, no matter how final the Lord Chief Justice's pronouncements were in dismissing the appeals, the case kept coming back whenever there was new evidence that they had not been accorded their rights. Such uncertainty and scepticism is only 'threatening' to the system if one's ultimate values emphasise finality but not respect for rights.[93] More interestingly, it is suggested that the problem for the legal system is that the conception of justice is based increasingly on scientific truth rather than fairness or rights.[94] However, the problem with this assertion is not just some abstruse systems incompatibility but the failure to appreciate the limits in the value of scientific 'truth' as a form of factual and especially legal proof,[95] a point taken up in Chapter 6. In this way, the assumed 'unresolved conflict between due process and truth'[96] should be resolved in favour of individual rights, having regard both to the commitment of the system to their value (which is certainly more than a 'technicality') and also having regard to the constructed nature of both 'truth' as well as 'guilt'[97] which can only be settled within a hierarchy of values (though that is not to say that those values are unique to one system).[98]

In contrast to autopoiesis, more radical critiques of Liberalism,[99] based in critical legal studies or postmodernism, accept that legal actions are far from closed either in influence or impact.[100] But the 'ethics of alterity'[101] in the context of miscar-

---

[92] Compare King, M., 'The truth about autopoiesis' (1993) 20 *Journal of Law and Society* 218 at pp. 224, 227.

[93] Nobles, R., and Schiff, D., 'Miscarriages of justice: a systems approach' (see footnote 90, above) at pp. 301, 306.

[94] *Ibid.* at p. 304. But compare the impact of PACE, s. 78 in Chapter 10.

[95] Ashworth, A., 'Crime, community and creeping consequentialism' [1996] *Criminal Law Review* 220 at p. 227; Jones, C.A.G., *Expert Witnesses* (Clarendon Press, Oxford, 1994) p. 5.

[96] Nobles, R., and Schiff, D., 'Miscarriages of justice: a systems approach' (see footnote 90, above) at p. 317. Others depict law, more consistently with this chapter, as 'a search for justice': Rozenberg, J., *The Search for Justice* (Hodder & Stoughton, London, 1994) p. 1.

[97] McConville, M., Sanders, A. & Leng, R., *The Case for the Prosecution* (Routledge, London, 1991) p. 11; Givelber, D., 'Meaningless acquittals, meaningful convictions: do we reliably acquit the innocent?' (1997) 49 *Rutgers Law Review* 1317 at p. 1323. The same has been argued in relation to the physical sciences: Kuhn, T., 'Scientific paradigms' in Barnes, B., (ed.), *Sociology of Science* (Penguin, London, 1972); *The Essential Tension: selected studies in scientific tradition and change* (University of Chicago Press, 1977), *The Structure of Scientific Revolutions* (3rd ed., University of Chicago Press, 1996). See further Chapter 6.

[98] According to Sir John May, *Report of the Inquiry into the circumstances surrounding the convictions arising out of the bomb attacks in Guildford and Woolwich in 1974, Final Report* (1993–94 HC 449) para. 21.28, the truth ultimately remains 'a matter for the consciences of all those involved'.

[99] For the sustainability of this claim to radicalism, see Goodrich, P., 'Sleeping with the enemy' (1993) 68 *New York University Law Review* 389.

[100] See Douzinas, C., and Warrington, R., 'A well-founded fear of justice: law and ethics in postmodernity' in Leonard, J. (ed.), *Legal Studies as Cultural Studies* (State University of New York, Albany, 1995); *Justice Miscarried* (Harvester Wheatsheaf, London, 1994).

[101] Douzinas, C. and Warrington, R., 'A well-founded fear of justice: law and ethics in postmodernity' in Leonard, J. (ed.), *Legal Studies as Cultural Studies* (State University of New York Press, Albany, 1995) at p. 200.

riages seem to impose constraints against silencing and disrespect which are not so far distant from notions of due process. Of course, Liberalism ultimately demands attention for a universal standard, which, translated into law, can become a form of political repression of opposed viewpoints.[102] Douzinas and Warrington cite the case of X v Morgan-Grampian[103] as an illustration of the denunciatory power of law in the face of competing values. However, whilst the judgment inadequately weighed the competing values,[104] it is wholly acceptable that the judges should have preferred the legislation of Parliament to the code of the National Union of Journalists which in fact influenced the defendant journalist to withhold the source of his confidential information in defiance of a court order. On the same basis, one would hope there would be something to choose between the ethics of parliamentary democracy and, say, the Cosa Nostra or the Ku Klux Klan. The critique does, however, usefully remind us that the prior morality of law cannot be assumed, a point fully recognised in the fourth and sixth meanings of 'miscarriages of justice'.

Even if one accepts the predominance of an individual rights discourse, there are still rivalries between competing right-holders to be determined. Within criminal justice, these may increasingly relate to the rights of, on the one hand, suspects/convicts and, on the other hand, victims. In this discussion, the rights of the former have tended to be treated as more important. One might offer two reasons for this ordering: that the loss of rights tends to be more acute in the case of the suspect or convicted person in the sense that, for example, liberty is immediately threatened; secondly, the loss of rights is entirely a matter of State responsibility whereas the victim has suffered primarily through the actions of third parties.

A competing conception of rights raised earlier is the communitarian perspective, which involves 'freedom holistically conceived: not the liberal conception of freedom as the condition of the atomistic individual, but a republican conception of freedom as freedom of the city, freedom in a social world.'.[105] This conception does share several deontological features with due process such as the constraint (of 'parsimony') that the onus of proof is against intervention and also the need to check State power. But amongst the less palatable features propounded by at least some of its proponents[106] are the exclusionary emphasis upon 'citizenship' (or, on a more localised basis, 'community'[107]) and the willingness to promote state intervention (often in the form of surveillance) to protect the ill-defined 'province of others', which may encourage intervention on the basis of vague notions of 'anti-social conduct' such as appear in the Crime and Disorder Act 1998.

---

[102] Macedo, S., Liberal Virtues (Clarendon Press, Oxford, 1990).
[103] [1990] 2 WLR 1000.
[104] See Goodwin v UK, Appl. no. 17488/90, 1996–II, (1996) 22 EHRR 123, The Times, 28 March 1996.
[105] Braithwaite, J. and Pettit, P., Not Just Deserts: A Republican Theory of Criminal Justice (Oxford University Press, 1990) p. 9. See also Braithwaite, J., 'Inequality and Republican criminology' in Hagan, J., and Peterson, R.D. (eds.), Crime and Inequality (Stanford University Press, 1995); Lacey, N., and Zedner, L., 'Discourses of community in criminal justice' (1995) 22 Journal of Law and Society 301; Raine, J.W., and Wilson, M.J., 'Beyond managerialism in criminal justice' (1997) 36 Howard Journal 80.
[106] But other versions more reassuringly depict communitarianism as not only consistent with the enjoyment of individual rights but as a necessary condition: Etzioni, A., The Spirit of Community (Fontana, London, 1995) pp. x, 15.
[107] Crawford, A., The Local Governance of Crime (Clarendon Press, Oxford, 1997) chs. 5, 8.

The Crisis in Criminal Justice – a Chronology of *Causes Célèbres*

It is not intended in this commentary to go further back than those cases which fed the instability leading to the Runciman Commission. The deadline may be taken to be around 1981, when the last major inquiry, the Royal Commission on Criminal Procedure (the *'Philips Report'*) was published.[108] That Commission had in turn been mainly prompted by a miscarriage of justice in the *Confait* case (see below), and the *Philips Report* did promote sweeping changes in terms of police powers (the Police and Criminal Evidence Act 1984 – PACE) and a new Crown Prosecution Service (the Prosecution of Offences Act 1985).[109] Accordingly, this book will tend to focus upon later re-appeal or referral back cases[110] which were the most compelling in shaping proposals to the Runciman Commission, as well as subsequent cases which have actually been returned to the appeal courts.[111] Another reason for this selection is that many earlier miscarriages are already the subject of voluminous documentation. Famous cases in this category include those of *Rowland* (1947),[112] *Evans* (1950),[113] *Bentley* (1952),[114] *Hanratty* (1962),[115]

---

[108] Cmnd 8092.

[109] But note that the Philips Commission accepted without argument that an adversarial form of justice should be maintained and that its focus should be on pre-court issues: paras. 1.6–1.8.

[110] So as to keep the list manageable and to focus on the cases involving the greatest damage to rights and illustrating best the failure of process inherent in the term 'miscarriage', the catalogue does not include those detained without proper cause, those held in custody pending eventual acquittal or those acquitted on first appeal. But this is not to say that miscarriages only arise through convictions: compare Schiff, D. and Nobles, R., *Review: Justice in Error* (1994) 34 *British Journal of Criminology* 383 at p. 383.

[111] There are of course hundreds of other notable cases not covered here. The following have been perhaps the most publicised: Terry Allen (Jessel, D., *Trial and Error* (Headline, London, 1994) ch. 5); Paul Blackburn (Jessel, D., *ibid* ch. 10); Mary Druhan (Jessel, D., *Trial and Error* (Headline, London, 1994) ch. 2); Peter Fell (Jessel, D., *ibid.,* ch. 4); Alf Fox (see Rose, D., *In the Name of the Law* (Jonathan Cape, London, 1996) p. 35); Eddie Guilfoyle (see *R* v *Guilfoyle* [1996] 3 All ER 883); Colin James (see *The Express*, 8 February 1997 pp. 22, 23); Paul Malone (McConville, M. and Bridges, L., 'Another miscarriage of justice' *The Times*, 26 July 1994 p. 37; Hill, P., 'Taking the politics out of justice' (1994) 144 *New Law Journal* 1270); Gary Mills and Tony Poole (see Jessel, D., *Trial and Error* (Headline, London, 1994) ch. 7, *R* v *Mills*; *R* v *Poole* [1997] 3 All ER 780); Matthew Richardson (Jessel, D., *Trial and Error* (Headline, London, 1994) ch. 9); Anthony Steel (see Hill, P., 'Finding finality' (1996) 146 *New Law Journal* 1552); Colin Wallace (see Fod, P., *Who Framed Colin Wallace?* MacMillan, London, 1989). Other campaigns are listed by *Scandals in Justice* (http://www.scandals.demon.co.uk/); *The Guardian*, 19 April 1994 p. 4; Pattendon, R., *English Criminal Appeals 1844–1994* (Clarendon Press, Oxford, 1996) pp. 353–359.

[112] See: *Report of an Inquiry by J.C. Jolly* (Cmd 7049, 1947); Cecil, H. (ed.), *The Trial of Walter Graham Rowland* (David and Charles, Newton Abbot, 1975); Cotton, P., 'The Deansgate mistake' (1990) 98 *Police Review* 1104.

[113] See: *Report of an Inquiry by Scott Henderson* (Cmd 8896 and 8946, 1953); Paget, R.T. and Silverman, S., *Hanged and Innocent?* (Gollancz, London, 1953); Eddowes, M., *The Man on Your Conscience* (Cassell, London, 1955); Grigg, J., and Gilmour, I., *The Case of Timothy Evans* (Spectator, London, 1956); Tennyson, F.J, *The Trials of Timothy John Evans and John Reginald Christie* (Hodge, London, 1957); Hale, L., *Hanged in Error* (Penguin, London, 1961); Kennedy, L., *Ten Rillington Place* (Gollancz, London, 1961); *Report of an Inquiry by Mr Justice Brabin* (Cmnd 3101, 1966); Eddowes, J., *The Two Killers of Rillington Place* (Little Brown, 1994).

[114] See: Yallop, D., *To Encourage the Others* (W.H. Allen, London, 1972); Trow, M.J., 'Let Him Have It, Chris' (Constable, London, 1990); Parris, J., *Scapegoat* (Duckworth, London, 1991); Bentley, I., *Let Him Have Justice* (Sidgwick & Jackson, London, 1995). The Home Secretary's initial failure to consider all relevant forms of pardon was quashed on review: *R* v *Secretary of State for the Home Department ex parte Bentley* [1993] 4 All ER 442. The Court of Appeal overturned the conviction because of errors in the summing up by the trial judge, Lord Goddard: *R* v *Bentley, The Times*, 31 July 1998.

[115] See: Blom Cooper, L., *The A6 Murder* (Penguin, London, 1963); Russell, E.F.L., *Deadman's Hill* (Secker & Warburg, London, 1965); Foot, P., *Who Killed Hanratty?* (Cape, London, 1971); *Report*

Stafford and Luvaglio (1967),[116] *Murphy, McMahon and Cooper* (the Luton Post Office murder in 1970),[117] *Lattimore, Salih and Leighton* (the *Confait* case in 1972),[118] *Dougherty* (1973),[119] and *Maynard and Dudley* (the *Legal and General Gang* in 1977).[120] Although no description will be given of the foregoing, one should not assume that all (or even any) of the problems illustrated by them have been solved by previous inquiries or legislation. Indeed, most of the present concerns were equally current during the previous two decades. Accordingly, some of the aforementioned cases will appear in the following chapters.

As for the more recent cases which will figure more prominently in this book, the list may begin with the *Guildford Four* and *Maguire Seven*. The *Guildford Four* (Paul Hill, Carole Richardson, Gerard Conlon and Patrick Armstrong)[121] were convicted of pub bombings on behalf of the IRA in Guildford and Woolwich. An appeal against conviction failed in 1977 despite the fact that other IRA defendants awaiting trial had by then claimed responsibility.[122] However, other new evidence was eventually amassed (including of alibis and medical conditions)[123] which convinced the Home Secretary to order further investigations and a referral back to the Court of Appeal. Once it was discovered that detectives in the Surrey Police involved in the case had fabricated statements (especially of Armstrong) and suppressed possible exculpatory evidence, the Director of Public Prosecutions decided not to contest the convictions, which were quashed in 1989. This outcome immediately prompted reconsideration of the *Maguire Seven* case.[124] Suspicion first fell on the Maguire household when Gerard Conlon (one of the *Guildford Four*)

---

     of Mr C. Hawser Q.C. (Cmnd 5021, 1975); Woffinden, B., *Hanratty: The Final Verdict* (Macmillan, London, 1997).

[116] See: [1968] 3 All ER 752, [1972] 1 WLR 1649, [1974] AC 878; Lewis, D. and Hughman, P., *Most Unnatural* (Penguin, London, 1971).

[117] (1975) 65 Cr App R 215, (1978) 68 Cr App R 18.

[118] See: (1975) 62 Cr App R 53; *Report of an Inquiry by the Hon. Sir Henry Fisher* (1977–78 HC 90).

[119] See: *Report of the Departmental Committee on evidence of identification in criminal cases* (the *Devlin Report*) (1975–76 HC 338).

[120] See: (1979) 69 Cr App R 309; Hilliard, B., 'Criminal complicity' (1992) 100 *Police Review* 1226; Wickstead, A., 'Truth and the torsos' (1992) 100 *Police Review* 1370: Goldberg, J, 'Brief's nightmare' (1992) 100 *Police Review* 1506.

[121] See: *R v Hill and others, The Times*, 23 October 1975 p. 1, *The Times*, 28 February 1977 p. 2, *The Times*, 20 October 1989; Kee, R., *Trial and Error* (2nd ed., Penguin, London, 1989); McKee, G. and Franey, R., *Time Bombs* (Bloomsbury, London, 1988); Lords Devlin and Scarman, 'Justice and the Guildford Four' (1988) *The Times*, 30 November 1988 p. 16; Scrivener, A.,'The Guildford Four' (1989) *Counsel* November p. 15; Hilliard, B., 'The time bomb goes off' (1989) 97 *Police Review* 2174; Hill, P. and Burnett, R, *Stolen Years* (Doubleday, London, 1990); Conlon, G., *Proved Innocent* (Hamish Hamilton, London, 1990); Rozenberg, J., 'Miscarriages of justice' in Stockdale, E., and Casale, S., *Criminal Justice under Stress* (Blackstone Press, London, 1992) p. 92; Bennett, R, *Double Jeopardy* (Penguin, London, 1993); Logan, A., 'In the Name of the Father' (1994) 144 *New Law Journal* 294. The prosecution of three police detectives involved in the case was abandoned: *R v Read, Morris and Woodwiss* (1993) *The Times*, 8 October pp. 1, 3; Sir John May, *Report of the Inquiry into the circumstances surrounding the convictions arising out of the bomb attacks in Guildford and Woolwich in 1974, Final Report* (1993–94 HC 449) para. 1.12.

[122] Sir John May, *Report of the Inquiry into the circumstances surrounding the convictions arising out of the bomb attacks in Guildford and Woolwich in 1974, Final Report* (1993–94 HC 449) ch. 17.

[123] *Ibid.*, chs. 7–11,19. The existence of the alibi witness, Charles Burke, was expressly disclosed in 1989 following the referral: 19.82.

[124] *R v Maguire, The Times*, 5 March 1976 p. 1, *The Times*, 28 June 1977; [1992] 2 All ER 433. See: Kee, R., *op. cit.* footnote 121 above; Rozenberg, J., 'Miscarriages of justice' in Stockdale, E., and Casale, S., *Criminal Justice under Stress* (Blackstone Press, London, 1992) p. 98; Maguire, A., *Miscarriage of Justice: An Irish Family's Story of Wrongful Conviction As IRA Terrorists* (Roberts Rinehart, Colorado, 1994).

made statements to the police that his aunt, Anne Maguire, had taught him to manufacture bombs.[125] The police raided her house, and convictions were obtained mainly on the basis of forensic tests which were said to show traces of nitroglycerine. The Court of Appeal, on a reference back in 1990,[126] grudgingly overturned the convictions because of the possibility that third parties had left the traces in the house and so caused innocent contamination (the non-disclosure of evidence was also a material irregularity in the case). However, the May Inquiry's *Interim* and *Second Reports* on the Maguire case more realistically cast doubt on whether the tests used could in any event be taken to be conclusive proof of the knowing handling of explosives.[127]

The next blow to confidence in the criminal justice system was the *Birmingham Six* case in 1991.[128] The six (Patrick Hill, Gerry Hunter, Richard McIlkenny, Billy Power, Johnny Walker and Hughie Callaghan) had been convicted along with three others of bombings in two Birmingham pubs in 1974. The attacks had caused the most deaths of any IRA incident in Britain and were the signal for the passing of the Prevention of Terrorism Acts.[129] The prosecution evidence rested upon three legs: confessions which the defendants claimed had been beaten out of them; forensic tests which the defendants claimed were inherently unreliable and had been performed negligently by Dr Skuse; and highly circumstantial evidence, such as links to known Republicans, their movements and demeanour. After being refused leave to appeal in 1976, they ploughed a furrow in the civil courts by way of a claim for damages for assault against the police and prison warders. However, their path was eventually blocked by the House of Lords as an abuse of process, since any civil victory would undermine the finality of their criminal conviction. Their focus then switched back to the criminal courts, and there was a referral back to the Court of Appeal in 1988. The Court was then not persuaded, but further revelations about the police fabrication of statements (especially of McIlkenny) and new uncertainties about the quality of the forensic tests eventually secured

---

[125] See Sir John May, *op. cit.* footnote 122 above, para. 4.5.

[126] *The Times* 28 June, [1992] 2 All ER 433. The defendants had all by then served their sentences, but one, Giuseppe Conlon (father of Gerard) had died in prison in 1980. Three police officers were acquitted of conspiracy to pervert the course of justice: *R v Attwell, Donaldson and Style, The Times,* 20 May 1993 p. 1.

[127] 1989–90 HC 556; 1992–93 HC 296. This argument was expressly rejected by the Court of Appeal: [1992] 2 All ER at p. 444, which judgment the *Second Report* in turn criticises: [1992–93] paras. 1.6–8, 3.16.

[128] See: *R v Hill and others, The Times,* 16 August 1975 p. 1, *The Times,* 31 March 1976 p. 9; *McIlkenny and others v Chief Constable, West Midlands* [1980] 2 All ER 227; *Hunter and others v Chief Constable, West Midlands* [1981] 3 WLR 906; *R v Callaghan and others* [1988] 1 WLR 1, *The Times,* 29 January 1988 p. 5, *The Times,* 22 March 1988 p. 1; *R v Callaghan and others* (1988) 88 Cr App R 40, *The Times,* 1 April 1991; *R v McIlkenny and others* [1992] 2 All ER 417. Commentaries include: Gibson, B., *The Birmingham Bombs* (Rose Chichester, 1976); Yahuda, J., 'The Birmingham bombers' (1988) 152 *Justice of the Peace* 230; Hilliard, B., 'Soldiers of nothing' (1990) 140 *New Law Journal* 160; Dunne, D., *The Birmingham Six* (Birmingham Six Committee, Dublin, 2nd ed., 1989); Mullin, C., *Error of Judgment* (3rd ed., Poolbeg, Dublin, 1990); Rozenberg, J., 'Miscarriages of justice' in Stockdale, E. and Casale, S., *Criminal Justice under Stress* (Blackstone Press, London, 1992) p. 103; Blom-Cooper, Sir L., *The Birmingham Six and other Cases: Victims of Circumstances* (Duckworth, London, 1997). The prosecution of three of the detectives involved in the case was abandoned: *R v Read, Morris and Woodwiss, The Times,* 8 October 1993 pp. 1, 3, Rozenberg, J., *The Search for Justice* (Hodder & Stoughton, London, 1994) p. 314.

[129] See: chapter 9; Walker, C., *The Prevention of Terrorism in British Law* (2nd ed., Manchester University Press, 1992) ch. 4.

their release in 1991. That outcome was swiftly followed by the establishment of the Runciman Commission.

A further Irish-related case of relevance is that of Judith Ward, who was convicted in 1974 for delivering the bombs which resulted in 12 deaths on an Army coach travelling along the M62 in Yorkshire.[130] The conviction was once again undermined by the unreliability of the forensic evidence (Skuse's name appears once more) and of the confessions Ward made (though this time more because of her mental instability than because of police mistreatment of her). In the background were allegations of non-disclosure. Ward's case was referred to the Court of Appeal unilaterally by the Home Office, and she was released in 1992 after the prosecution declined to contest the matter. The Court's judgment was particularly censorious of the non-disclosure of evidence by named forensic scientists and prosecution counsel.

The final case arising from Irish paramilitary activities concerns the *UDR Four*– Neil Latimer, Alfred Allen, Noel Bell and James Hegan.[131] The four defendants were members of the UDR who were convicted of the murder in Armagh city of Adrian Carroll, whom they believed to be active in the IRA.[132] Their allegations of injustice arose from three main concerns. First, Latimer pointed to conflicting identification evidence and oppressive treatment during his police interrogation. Further, it was shown that the police had tampered with the confessions by rewriting some notes, deleting references to requests to see solicitors and attaching false authentications. After referral back to the Court of Appeal in 1992, Allen, Bell and Hegan were all freed on the basis that the police had indeed tampered with the evidence, but Latimer's conviction was not overturned in the light of the identification evidence against him, his confirmation of his admission at the original trial in 1985 and the finding that he had lied to the court.[133]

It will be evident that the largest catalogue of contemporary miscarriages of justice has concerned Irish 'terrorist' cases. Amongst the reasons behind this tendency to lapse from acceptable standards are, first, that terrorist action creates, and is designed to create, extraordinary tension, fear and panic. These reactions are to be induced in the forces of authority, such as the police, just as much as in sectors of the public. Accordingly, a police overreaction generated by irrationality and characterised as lawless and oppressive is an intended objective and sometimes the prize secured by terrorist action. Secondly, official reaction to terrorism often involves a conscious departure from the normal due process ideology of the criminal justice system and a tendency towards the holding of grand 'State trials'.[134] Considerations such as the primacy of the individual and the desire to stack the odds in favour of the innocent in part thereby give way to conflicting goal-based rather than rights-based factors.[135] The relevant goals include the strategy of the criminalisation of terrorists – the policy of the condemnation of the

---

[130] *R v Ward, The Times*, 5 November 1974 p. 4, *The Times*, 12 May p. 1, (1992) 96 Cr App R 1; Rozenberg, J., 'Miscarriages of justice' in Stockdale, E., and Casale, S., *Criminal Justice under Stress* (Blackstone Press, London, 1992) p. 107.

[131] [1986] 9 NIJB 1 (trial); [1988] 11 NIJB 1 (appeal). For other cases, see Chapter 14.

[132] His brother, Roddy, was shot by the RUC in 1982: Stalker, J., *Stalker* (Penguin, London, 1988).

[133] *The Times*, 30 July 1992 pp. 1, 2. See Chapter 14.

[134] See: Kirchheimer, V., *Political Justice* (Princeton University Press, 1961); Allen, F.A., *The Crimes of Politics* (Harvard University Press, 1974).

[135] See: Packer, H.L., *The Limits of the Criminal Sanction* (Stanford University Press, 1969); King, M., *The Framework of Criminal Justice* (Croom Helm, London, 1981).

motives and values held by the defendants and their kind together with the reinforcement of State legitimacy. There is also the 'presentational' aspect[136] – the desire to be seen to be taking effective action against terrorists. Even if the official action is in reality worthless, it can still relieve public frustrations and fears. Hence, Lord Denning's comment in response to the *Guildford Four* case was that even if the wrong people were convicted, 'the whole community would be satisfied'.[137] These wider societal considerations may also explain why miscarriages seem so hard to remedy. The problem is not simply stubbornness, but that an acquittal becomes particularly costly to the State in terms of damage to its legitimacy and prestige. These same factors may apply to marginalised groups other than Irish Republicans, such as ethnic minority defendants. The fact that such groups form a large part of the non-motoring business within the criminal justice system refutes those who attempt to draw clear distinctions between 'ordinary run-of-the-mill criminal cases [and] atypical . . . *causes célèbres'*.[138] What is special in terrorist cases is not so much the forensic science techniques in play but the police and court perceptions and processes.

Next, there have occurred various miscarriages which do not relate to Irish terrorism. Though less prominently discussed, this catalogue of cases may in a sense be even more significant since they have occurred in more commonplace circumstances and sometimes under the 'normal' regime of PACE.

Perhaps the longest-running case, and one which incidentally predates PACE, is that involving the murder of Carl Bridgewater, a newspaper delivery boy who was killed when he interrupted a burglary at Yew Tree Farm, near Stourbridge.[139] Michael Hickey, Vincent Hickey, James Robinson and Patrick Molloy were imprisoned in 1979. The convictions rested largely on the confessions of Molloy, who died in prison in 1981. Molloy, who was denied access to a solicitor, later retracted his confession and claimed he had been tricked by police (members of the West Midlands Serious Crime Squad) who showed him a confession by Vincent Hickey, and his refutation was given credence by later electrostatic tests on the police papers, which revealed the imprint of a fake confession. The case was referred back to the Court of Appeal in 1996 (leave to appeal had been refused in 1981, and an appeal had been refused in 1989 following a referral back in 1987) after the Home Secretary had been mauled by the Divisional Court for his secretive and grudging treatment of the available evidence.[140] The men were released in 1997, though with some qualms on the part of Lord Justice Rock in respect of the guilt of Vincent Hickey.[141]

The business of the West Midlands Police Serious Crime Squad has also provided most of the cases during the more contemporary era of PACE, since its activities have given rise to 91 complaints about beatings, the fabrication of

---

[136] See: Review of the Operation of the Prevention of Terrorism (Temporary Provisions) Act 1976 (Cmnd 8803, 1983) paras. 207, 208.

[137] *The Times*, 17 August 1990 p. 14.

[138] Roberts, P. and Willmore, C., *The role of forensic science evidence in criminal proceedings* (RCCJ Research Study no. 11, 1993) at p. 1.

[139] See Foot, P., *Murder at the Farm* (Penguin, London, 1988); Morrell, J., *The Wrong Men* (Bridgewater Four Support Group, Birmingham, 1993).

[140] *R v Secretary of State for the Home Department, ex parte Hickey (no. 2)* [1995] 1 WLR 735.

[141] *The Times*, 21 February 1997 pp. 1,4, 22 February 1997 pp. 1, 6, 7, 31 July 1997 p. 4; Hilliard, B., 'Trial and error' (1997) 105 *Police Review* 28 February p. 16.

evidence and denial of access to lawyers.[142] Some of those affected have had their convictions quashed.[143] An investigation into the conduct of the police resulted in the disbandment of the Squad in 1989 but no convictions of officers.[144] However, the award of civil damages for assault to Derek Treadaway in 1994 proved very significant. First, his conviction was quashed in 1996, following a reference back to the Court of Appeal, and then the refusal to prosecute five officers, who were alleged to have handcuffed the applicant and to have placed a plastic bag over his head so as to subject him to suffocation, was overturned on review in 1997 as not adequately taking account of the civil court's findings against the police.[145]

Another well-publicised case dealt with under a PACE-type regime, and one with racial overtones akin to the Irish cases, is that of the *Tottenham Three* (Engin Raghip, Winston Silcott and Mark Braithwaite), who were convicted of the murder of PC Blakelock during the Broadwater Farm riot in 1985.[146] On a referral back to the Court of Appeal in 1991,[147] it was shown that notes of the interview were altered by the police in the case of Silcott; that Raghip's confession was negated by his mental state; and that Braithwaite had been unfairly denied a lawyer. Two police officers were charged with perversion of the course of justice; the officers were acquitted after a trial,[148] and Silcott was not allowed to bring a civil action for conspiracy and misfeasance.[149] There were also allegations that the Home Office officials gravely doubted the strength of the prosecution case long before the referral back.[150]

Release after an even longer period of imprisonment, 13 years after his original appeal, was ordered in the case of Stefan Kiszko.[151] His conviction for murder was accepted as unsustainable in the light of the medical evidence that he was unable to produce the sperm found on the murdered victim. The processing of this evidence by the prosecution counsel also gave rise to concern. Both a detective and a forensic scientist were charged with perverting the course of justice, but the case was halted as an abuse of process (because of delay) by the committing magistrate.[152]

The remaining cases to be mentioned are difficult to catalogue as often multiple causes of miscarriages of justice have occurred. However, a substantial strand of them relates to the circumstances of confessions. One such case concerns the

---

[142] See: *R v Khan*, *The Independent*, 2 March 1990; *R v Edwards* [1991] 1 WLR 207; *R v Binham* (1991) NLJ 189; *R v Wellington*, *The Times*, 26 March 1991 p. 7; *R v Lynch*, *The Times*, 22 October 1991 p. 3; *Ex parte Coventry Newspapers Ltd.* [1992] 3 WLR 916; Kirby, T., 'The force of corruption', *The Independent Magazine*, 14 October 1989 p. 14; Kaye, T., *Unsafe and Unsatisfactory* (Civil Liberties Trust, 1991); Maloney, J., 'The squad that lost its way' (1991) 99 *Police Review* 2234.

[143] See *R v Fryer, Francis and Jeffers*, *The Times*, 28 April 1993 p. 2.

[144] See: *R v Mills*, *The Times*, 21 June 1991 p. 3; *The Times*, 20 May 1992 pp. 1, 3; (1992) *Law Society's Gazette* 27 May p. 10.

[145] *R v Director of Public Prosecutions, ex parte Treadaway* (1997, LEXIS, QBD, *The Times* 1 August 1997 p. 1).

[146] See Lord Gifford, *The Broadwater Farm Inquiry* (Karia Press, London, 1986); Rose, D., *A Climate of Fear* (Bloomsbury Press, London, 1992); Rozenberg, J., 'Miscarriages of justice' in Stockdale, E. and Casale, S., *Criminal Justice under Stress* (Blackstone Press, London, 1992) p. 108.

[147] *The Times*, 9 December 1991.

[148] *R v Melvin and Dingle*, *The Times*, 27 July 1994 pp. 1, 3.

[149] *The Times*, 9 July 1996 CA.

[150] See *The Guardian*, 9 August 1994 pp. 1, 2, 19.

[151] See: (1979) 68 Cr App R 62; *The Times*, 18 February 1992 p. 5, 19 February 1992 p. 3; Rose, J., *Innocents* (Fourth Estate, London, 1997).

[152] *R v Holland and Outteridge*, *The Times*, 12 May 1994 p. 5, 2 May 1995 p. 2.

Darvell brothers, Wayne and Paul,[153] who had been convicted in Swansea Crown Court in June 1986 of murdering the manageress of a sex shop. Their convictions were overturned after an uncontested appeal in 1992. Evidence was then presented that police notes about the investigation and a confession had been redrafted at a later date, that police witnesses who had identified the brothers as being in the area of the murder at the crucial time were in fact nine miles away and that fingerprint evidence at the scene of the crime which pointed elsewhere was not disclosed to the defence, was not fully investigated and was even destroyed before the trial. A pre-PACE confession was also at the centre of the case of Mark Cleary, who was convicted of murder in 1985 (along with a co-accused, Philip Atherton who had implicated him). It was alleged in the television programme, *Trial and Error*, in 1993 that the timings and other details suggested by the defendant did not stand serious scrutiny and the conviction was quashed.[154] Cleary, described as a person of limited intelligence, had been pressured by the police into making a statement which he then retracted. Next, the convictions in 1990 of the *Cardiff Three* for the murder of a prostitute were overturned in December 1992 on referral to the Court of Appeal.[155] The Court expressed itself as horrified by evidence of oppression from the police interview tapes. Unreliable confessions by a suspect, George Long, with a history of mental instability who had been refused access to a solicitor resulted in the quashing of the conviction for murder in 1995.

Non-disclosure of evidence affecting the reliability of a prosecution witness was at the heart of the appeal of Michelle and Lisa Taylor, convicted of the murder of Alison Shaughnessy but acquitted in 1994 in the light of the suppression of evidence (an inconsistent statement) and the unremitting, extensive, sensational, inaccurate and misleading media coverage and its impact on the trial.[156]

Evidence from eyewitnesses remains a cause of difficulty, as it has done since cases like Luke Dougherty and Laslo Virag.[157] John McGranaghan was released in 1991 after a conviction for rape on the basis of victim identification was shown to be false by forensic evidence which had not previously been disclosed by the prosecution.[158] The acquittal of Eddie Browning in 1994, after his conviction of the murder of a stranded female motorist in 1988, turned on the unreliability of an off-duty police witness, who had also been hypnotised in order to recall vital details, especially of a car registration number.[159] Sam Hill was released in 1995 after his conviction in 1988 for 'Borden baseball bat murder' during a gang fight; the Court of Appeal, after rejecting an earlier appeal, was not satisfied that the direction in regard to identification was sufficiently fair and clear.[160]

The fallibility of expert evidence was illustrated again in an extraordinary way in the case of Kevin Callan, who was freed in 1995 after being sentenced to life imprisonment for the murder of his girlfriend's daughter in 1992.[161] Evidence from

---

[153] See: *The Times*, 15 July 1993 pp. 1, 3. An earlier appeal had been rejected in 1987, but a further investigation had been ordered after a *Rough Justice* television programme on the case.

[154] Jessel, D., *Trial and Error* (Headline, London, 1994) chs. 1, 12; *The Guardian*, 4 May 1994 p. 8.

[155] *R v Paris, Yusef, Abdullahi and Miller* [1993] 97 Cr App R 99.

[156] See *R v Taylor and Taylor* (1993) 98 Cr App Rep 361. See also Chapter 13 and *R v Solicitor General, ex parte Taylor and Another*, *The Times*, 14 August 1995.

[157] *Devlin Report*, ch. 5.

[158] [1995] 1 Cr App R 559. See Davies, G.M., 'Mistaken identification' (1996) *Howard Journal* 232.

[159] Editorial, 'Dangerous evidence' (1994) 144 *New Law Journal* 661; *The Times*, 14 May 1994 p. 3.

[160] *The Times*, 21 November 1995 p. 3.

[161] *The Times*, 7 April 1995 p. 6; Sage, H., 'How infallible is the expert's voice?' (1996) *The Lawyer* 12 March.

the Home Office pathologist (unaccredited in this particular field) suggested that the child had been shaken to death but Callan's own studies of medicine whilst in prison demonstrated other possible causes of death such as injury from cerebral palsy. Lack of convincing forensic evidence – that Sheila Bowler murdered her senile and disabled aunt-in-law by pushing her into a river after trekking some distance over difficult terrain – prompted the quashing of a conviction and eventual acquittal at retrial.[162]

Aside from these notorious cases, some indication should be given of the number of miscarriages produced overall. In a Report in 1989, the organisation, JUSTICE, estimated that up to 15 defendants a year sentenced to four years or more on indictment have been wrongly convicted.[163] Just over 1 per cent of those convicted on indictment fall into this sentencing band, so the total number of miscarriages in the Crown Court may be well over 1000 a year. No attempt has been made to estimate the rate in magistrates' courts where over 90 per cent of cases are heard.[164] More recently, the Society of Prison Officers has estimated that there might be up to 700 innocent persons in prisons after conviction.[165] Likewise, the Home Office has revealed that it receives about 700 to 800 petitions a year.[166] In 1992, Liberty compiled a dossier of 163 cases which it intended to pursue.[167] Evidence presented to the Runciman Commission from a survey of Crown Court cases found that 'problematic' convictions occurred at a rate of 2 per cent (250 cases a year) in the view of judges and 17 per cent (about 2000) in the view of defence lawyers.[168] By March 1998 (after just under one year of operation), the Criminal Cases Review Commission had received 1304 applications, though around 240 cases had been transmitted from the Home Office.

Part III of this book will examine the corresponding cases and rates of incidence in selected jurisdictions outside England and Wales. There are some variations, but the principal causes (summarised below) are largely constant.

Recurrent Forms of Miscarriage in Practice – a Summary

Miscarriages result from a multiplicity of causes, and individual prisoners have often been subjected to more than one form of abuse of authority. The problems arise from the very outset of contact with police, with allegations of harassment and assault, to the very end of entanglement with the State, when machinery to reopen problematical judgments has been shown to be unfair and inappropriate.

---

[162] Jessel, D., *Trial and Error* (Headline, London, 1994) ch. 11; *The Times*, 6 February 1998 pp. 1, 5; Devin, A. and Devlin, T., *Anybody's Nightmare* (Taverner, London, 1998).

[163] *Miscarriages of Justice*, p. 1 and see also App. 1.

[164] But note that disputed confessions are far rarer: CPS, *Submission to the Royal Commission* (1991) Vol. I ch. 10. In the USA, it is reckoned that 0.5 per cent of felony convictions are wrongful: Huff, C.R., Rattner, A., Sagarin, E., *Convicted But Innocent: Wrongful Conviction and Public Policy* (Sage, Thousand Oaks, 1996) p. 61.

[165] *The Independent*, 19 March 1992 p. 31.

[166] Memoranda (1991) para. 4.47.

[167] (1992) *The Lawyer* 17 November p. 7.

[168] Zander, M. and Henderson, P., *Crown Court Study* (Royal Commission on Criminal Justice Research Study No. 19, HMSO, London, 1993) p. 171 (for problematic acquittals, see p. 169). See also Baldwin, J. & McConville, M., *Jury Trials* (Clarendon Press, Oxford, 1979: 5.9 per cent following trial in Birmingham), 'Doubtful Convictions by Jury' [1979] *Criminal Law Review*: 230 (5.3 per cent following trial in London).

The JUSTICE *Report on Miscarriages of Justice*[169] highlighted five 'common threads' which ran through most of the allegations made over the years: wrongful identification, false confessions, perjury by witnesses, police misconduct and bad trial tactics. The Runciman Commission was based upon terms of reference which focused upon the following: the conduct of police investigations; the role of the prosecutor; the role of experts; the arrangements for defence; statements by the accused and the right to silence; the powers of the courts and directing proceedings; the role of the Court of Appeal; and arrangements post-appeal. These pointers in turn were translated into no fewer than 88 specific questions on which views were sought. Without delineating in detail all these possible issues, it is clear from the cases already given that there are some common themes which are outlined below.

1 *The most obvious danger is the fabrication of evidence.* It has been recognised for some time that informers who are co-accused may well have self-serving reasons for exaggerating the role of the defendant, though this lesson did have to be relearnt in response to the 'supergrasses' who emerged in Northern Ireland between 1981 and 1986.[170] Supergrasses were also relied upon in the West Midlands cases but later came to be viewed as gravely tainted. The police are also in a powerful position to manipulate evidence, for example by 'verballing' the accused – inventing damning statements or passages within them. The *Birmingham Six, Tottenham Three, Armagh Four,* Darvell brothers and several West Midlands cases all involve allegations along these lines. As well as these gross and intentional violations, fabrication can come about through a more subtle process of 'police and prosecutorial overzealousness . . . the willingness to use improper, unethical and illegal means to obtain a conviction when one believes that the person at the bar is guilty.'.[171]

2 *Both the police and lay witnesses may prove to be unreliable when attempting to identify an offender.* This has been recognised by the Criminal Law Revision Committee[172] and the Devlin Committee of Inquiry set up following the cases of Dougherty and Virag, though the implementation of the Committee's recommendations in *Turnbull* leaves much to be desired.[173] In the USA, it is suggested that about a half of wrongful convictions fall into this category.[174]

3 *The evidential value of expert testimony has also been overestimated* in a number of instances only for it later to emerge that the tests being used were

---

[169] 1989, pp. 3, 4. Compare: Borchard, E.M., *Convicting the Innocent* (1932, reprinted by Da Capo Press, New York, 1970); Donnelly, R.C., 'Unconvicting the Innocent' (1952) 6 *Vanderbilt Law Review* 20; Frank, J. & Frank, B., *Not Guilty* (1957, reprinted by Da Capo Press, New York, 1971); Radin, E.D., *The Innocents* (Morrow, New York, 1964); Sargant, T. and Hill, P. *Criminal Trials* (Fabian Research Series, 1986) ch. 2.

[170] See: Hogan, G. and Walker, C., *Political Violence and the Law in Ireland* (Manchester Univ Press, 1989) pp. 123–6.

[171] Huff, C.R., Rattner, A. and Sagarin, E., *Convicted But Innocent: Wrongful Conviction and Public Policy* (Sage, Thousand Oaks, 1996) p. 64, ch. 4.

[172] 11th Report: *Evidence (General)* (Cmnd 4991, 1972) para. 196.

[173] [1977] QB 224. See: *Justice* Report, *op. cit.* (footnote 164 above) pp. 24–7.

[174] Huff, C.R, Rattner, A. and Sagarin, E. (footnote 173, above) pp. 64, 66; Givelber, D., 'Meaningless acquittals, meaningful convictions: do we reliably acquit the innocent?' (1997) 49 *Rutgers Law Review* 1317 at p. 1352 (86 per cent). See also O'Hagan, C.J., 'When Seeing is Not Believing: The Case for Eyewitness Expert Testimony' (1993) 81 *Georgia Law Journal* 741.

inherently unreliable, that the scientists conducting them were inefficient or both. The *Maguire Seven, Birmingham Six,* Ward, Callan and Kiszko cases all fit into this category.[175]

4 *Unreliable confessions as a result of police pressure, physiological or mental instability or a combination of all* are the next common factor. Examples include the *Guildford Four, Birmingham Six,* Ward, Treadaway, *Tottenham Three* and *Cardiff Three* cases.[176]

5 *The non-disclosure of relevant evidence by the police or prosecution to the defence* may be a further issue. The investigation of a case is by and large reliant on the police – they speak to all possible witnesses and arrange for all manner of forensic testing. The defence have neither the financial resources to undertake such work nor the opportunities in terms of access – indeed, approaches to prosecution witnesses might well be construed as attempts to pervert the course of justice. Yet, several cases – the *Guildford Four, Maguire Seven,* Darvell brothers and Ward in particular[177] – demonstrate that the police, forensic scientists and prosecution cannot be relied upon fairly to pass on evidence which might be helpful to the accused, despite there being no other agency which might uncover it in the interests of justice.

6 *The conduct of the trial may produce miscarriages.* For example, judges are sometimes prone to favour the prosecution evidence rather than acting as impartial umpires, as is alleged in connection with the *Birmingham Six.* A failure to appreciate the defence's submissions either in law or fact can result in unfairness in judges' rulings or directions to the jury, as in the *Maguire Seven* case. Equally, defence lawyers are not always beyond reproach. Lack of legal aid funding has made defence work the Cinderella service of the criminal justice system, so it is not surprising that the quality of defence lawyers is not always as good as it should be. Yet, defendants select (or more likely are assigned) lawyers at their own risk. In *R v Ensor,*[178] the Court of Appeal said that defence counsel must be 'flagrantly incompetent', not just unwise or mistaken, before the Court will overturn conviction.[179]

7 *The presentation of defendants in a prejudicial manner* is the next problem. An insidious way of achieving this effect is the pejorative labelling of them as 'terrorists'. Similarly, the obvious and heavy-handed security arrangements accompanying trips to court and the defendants' quarantined appearance in the dock inevitably convey an impression of guilt and menace. These problems could be alleviated by advice to the media and by different physical arrangements in court, but little has yet been done. Prejudice can also arise through comments on the case.

---

[175] See also Connors, E., Lundregan, T., Miller, N. and McEwan, T., *Convicted by Juries, Exonerated by Science* (NIJ, Washington, 1996).

[176] Huff, C.R., Rattner, A. and Sagarin, E., (footnote 164 above), ch. 5.

[177] Note also the case of George Lindo: Hansen, O., 'Justice delayed – justice denied' (1980) *Legal Action Group Bulletin* 83.

[178] [1989] 2 All ER 586. See also Chapter 7.

[179] [1989] 2 All ER at p. 590. Defiance of instructions would be a further reason for intervention: *R v Clinton* [1993] 2 All ER 998.

The law of contempt may temper excessive behaviour, but the courts should be more concerned about securing a fair trial rather than punishing contemnors. At least in the cases of the *Winchester Three* and Taylor sisters, comment did result in the overturning of convictions.[180] Intervention in this way has become more common,[181] but though fairness to the individual accused should predominate, the deleterious impact on victims and community confidence suggest that other protective strategies (aimed at the jury) should be developed.

8 *There are the problems associated with appeals and the procedures thereafter.* Common difficulties include the lack of access to lawyers and limited legal aid funding, so there has to be reliance on extra-legal campaigns which may or may not be taken up by the media dependent upon factors which have little to do with the strength of the case. The Court of Appeal has made life even more difficult because of its interpretations of the grounds for appeal. Once the courts are exhausted, complainants have, until recently, had to rely upon a ramshackle and secretive review by Home Office officials rather than an independent inquiry.

9 *Finally, a miscarriage can occur through the failure of State agencies to vindicate or protect rights* or through laws which are inherently contradictory to the concept of individual rights. Examples have already been adduced.

This list might be described as the direct causes of concern. However, there are several underlying issues not all of which can be taken up within the confines of this book and, more disappointingly, virtually none of which figure as part of the agenda of the inquiries envisaged by the Runciman Commission. Such matters include the particular difficulties arising in Northern Ireland and Scotland; police institutional issues, such as accountability and the investigation of complaints; the funding of legal aid; and the penal system.

The Runciman Commission

The details of the *Report* are for later chapters. Here it will be considered how far the *Report* assisted with the conceptualisation of miscarriages of justice or focused on an appropriate agenda of issues.

Conceptualisation

The *Runciman Report* does little more than restate the guiding principles set out in its terms of reference which, it will be recalled, emphasised 'the effectiveness of the criminal justice system in England and Wales in securing the conviction of those guilty of criminal offences and the acquittal of those who are innocent', as well as 'the efficient use of resources'.[182] The only gloss on these statements is the

---

[180] *R v McCann* (1991) 92 Cr App R 239. See: Woffinden, B., 'The case of the Winchester Three' (1990) 140 NLJ 164. Compare the appeal of those convicted of the Brighton bombing: *R v Anderson* [1988] 2 WLR 1017.

[181] *R v Wood, The Times,* 11 July 1995; *R v Knights, The Times,* 5 October 1995 p. 1; *R v West, The Times,* 3 April 1996; Corker, D. and Levi, M., 'Pre-trial publicity and its treatment in the English courts' [1996] *Criminal Law Review* 622.

[182] *Report,* ch. 1 paras. 5, 16.

addition that it is necessary to secure a process which treats people fairly, reasonably and without discrimination.[183] To become meaningful in a given context, these three precepts obviously needed further elaboration and also further explanation in terms of their respective roles and weights. Unlike the *Report* of the Philips Commission (which talked in terms of openness, workability and fairness),[184] there was in the event no discussion in either respect, the explanation for which was that the criteria were incapable of being balanced in any consistent manner; Packer's models and bench-marking documents such as the European Convention on Human Rights were likewise felt to be unavailing.[185] The approach was essentially pragmatic and piecemeal rather than principled: 'It must always be a matter of determining in the light of the particular topic which consideration is to be given priority.'.[186] Best judgment as to competing considerations was exercised,[187] no doubt informed technocratically by the research studies which had been commissioned.[188] But it was not informed by any overall conception of what values should underlie the system, what priority they should be given nor what results overall should be achieved in the interests of justice.

The approach of the Commissioners was criticised sharply.[189] Values such as crime control or due process are at the foundation of any criminal justice system. One might debate which should prevail overall or at any one point, but to ignore that debate risks damage to the legitimacy and coherence of the system. More specifically, McConville and Mirsky argued that the Commission had misread its terms of reference which they interpreted as prioritising the aim of ensuring that innocent persons are not wrongfully convicted, an aim which was not simply to be put into the balance but had already been balanced as receiving priority over cost considerations. Cost considerations cannot be ignored but should be applied proportionately and ultimately without detriment to fundamental rights rather than in trade-offs with them.[190] Thus, if the courts or prison systems cannot cope fairly with the number of cases being presented to them, then the answer must be to reduce the number of prosecutions rather than the observance of rights or the expenditure per case.[191]

Some commentators have taken issue with critics who have demanded costly reforms, especially in the areas of forensic science and prosecution disclosure.[192]

---

[183] *Report*, ch. 1 para. 25.

[184] Royal Commission on Criminal Procedure, *Report* (Cmnd 8092, HMSO, 1981).

[185] Zander, M., 'Where the critics got it wrong' (1993) 143 *New Law Journal* 1338, 1364.

[186] *Ibid*. Compare Young, R. and Sanders, A., 'The Royal Commission on Criminal Justice' (1994) 14 *Oxford Journal of Legal Studies* 435.

[187] Zander, M., 'The Royal Commission strikes back' (1993) 143 *New Law Journal* 1507.

[188] Lacey, N., 'Missing the wood' in McConville, M., and Bridges, L., (eds.) *Criminal Justice in Crisis* (Edward Elgar, Aldershot, 1994).

[189] McConville, M. and Mirsky, C., 'The disordering of criminal justice' (1993) 143 *New Law Journal* 1446, 'Balancing acts and constitutionalism' (1993) 143 *New Law Journal* 1579; Young, R. and Sanders, A., The Royal Commission on Criminal Justice' (1994) 14 *Oxford Journal of Legal Studies* 435; Rozenberg, J, *The Search for Justice* (Hodder & Stoughton, London, 1994) p. 323.

[190] Council of Europe, *The Management of Criminal Justice* (R (95)12, Strasbourg, 1995) p. 71; Ashworth, A., *The Criminal Process: An Evaluative Study* (2nd ed., Clarendon Press, Oxford, 1998) at p. 306.

[191] Gordon, G.H., 'The Report of the Royal Commission: a view from Scotland' in Birks, P.B.H. (ed.), *Pressing Problems in the Law Volume 1: Criminal Justice and Human Rights* (Oxford University Press, 1995) at p. 3; Allen, R.J., 'Reform: the system: the Simpson affair, reform of the criminal justice process, and magic bullets' (1996) 67 *Colorado Law Review* 989 at p. 992.

[192] Schiff, D. and Nobles, R, Review: *Justice in Error* (1994) 34 *British Journal of Criminology* 383.

This difference in approach again reflects distinct theoretical foundations. This chapter's analysis takes a rights-based stance, which gives a moral priority to rights claims over utility, whereas the reviewers seem to rest upon some variant of utility – spend enough money (but no more) to find enough 'evidence and proof' to put before the courts. If a convincing story can be told, then it would only cause unhappiness to spend more money so that the defence can attempt to undermine the prosecution story. In this way, some reviewers adopt a position more openly hostile to rights than the rather undeveloped position of the Royal Commission.

Agenda

Compared with the terms of reference (set out at the start of Chapter 1 of this book), the Commission's agenda seems haphazard[193] and to have 'ducked the challenge' of dealing with the real issues of miscarriages in favour of a more bureaucratic tinkering with the system.[194]

On some issues very worthy of exploration, there is silence. So, there is no inquiry into the leading cases, including even the *Birmingham Six* who triggered the setting up of the Commission. Consequently, the Commission's findings often seem strangely detached from the concerns of miscarriages – it became a fragmented audit rather than a sustained review which reacts to identified shortcomings. One might contrast the *May Inquiry*, which published three reports just to unravel the *Guildford* and *Maguire* cases.

As a result of the demotion of the agenda of miscarriages, the Commission left itself open to lobbying on a very wide range of issues. It follows that several recommendations emerged which had no aetiology in past cases, were not clearly signalled by the terms of reference of the Commission and which had not been researched save by the lobbyists themselves. As expected, the police and the Home Office proved to be two of the strongest and most effective communicators, and issues which were eventually to form a part of the *Report* included the taking of bodily samples and changes to pre-trial process. Other important issues which had been threaded through several miscarriage cases, notably, the quality of defence solicitors and the powers of detention under the Prevention of Terrorism Acts, were not tackled but were remitted to others; there was also a blind belief in the ability of magistrates' courts to try virtually any case.[195]

Impact of the Report and Subsequent Legislation

The absence of principled argument was a wasted opportunity for civic education, but more dangerous in the short-term, it left the field of reform fairly free for political choice. If the *Report's* findings were based on little more than either a sincerely held belief or a 'contingent fact'[196] arising from a research study, it was

---

[193] See McConville, M. and Bridges, L., 'Keeping faith with their own convictions' in McConville, M. and Bridges, L., (eds.) *Criminal Justice in Crisis* (Edward Elgar, Aldershot, 1994).

[194] Ashworth, A., 'Principles, practice and criminal justice' in Birks, P.B.H. (ed.), *Pressing Problems in the Law Volume 1: Criminal Justice and Human Rights* (Oxford University Press, 1995) p. 45; Rose, D., *In the Name of the Law* (Jonathan Cape, London, 1996) p. 16.

[195] *Runciman Report*, ch. 3 paras. 63, 95, ch. 6 para. 18.

[196] Ashworth, A., *The Criminal Process: An Evaluative Study* (2nd ed., Clarendon Press, Oxford, 1998) at p. 100.

always open to a politician to challenge them on an equally sincerely held belief or perhaps to trump them on the basis of further and better empirical research. Thus, the Commission left itself very open to being overruled or 'cannibalised'[197] because of its mode of decision-making. This weakness was not, however, an inherent design fault in either the personnel or terms of reference of the Commission which meant that the entire process was a charade or that recommendations unpalatable to the Home Office were out of bounds or could never conceivably be implemented.[198] Nevertheless, the publication of the *Report* coincided with the advent of a period of attempted populist repression by the Home Office, which found the *Report* to be suitably malleable for its purposes to achieve its own agenda without having to snub the Commission.[199]

In terms of impact in relation to some of the models outlined earlier, there are plenty of indications (such as the new powers to take bodily samples, the abolition of committals and case-management by judges, and discounts for guilty pleas)[200] that the trend of the subsequent legislation was towards crime control and away from due process, though it is less certain that this outcome (or indeed any consistent outcome) was intended by the Commission itself.[201] Assuming this analysis to be correct, two questions arise.

The first is, 'is the trend desirable?'. Given the philosophy behind crime control, the short answer is that the trend is not desirable in a system which already perceives itself to be undermined by miscarriages of justice arising from the abuses of rights of suspects, detainees and prisoners. The danger is that even more people will be abused and wrongly convicted of crimes they did not commit. It is possible that this danger can be averted through the introduction of new mechanisms to protect rights or to make their exercise more viable. These could have included: the restriction of admissible confessions to those in the presence of a solicitor;[202] the custody of detainees to be made the responsibility of an independent agency; the independent scrutiny of forensic services and further legal aid to assist with testing; effective and independent powers of investigation and disposal of cases post-appeal. A few of these ideas were indeed suggested by the Runciman Committee, but none has been implemented.[203] Of course, it is difficult to find any panacea for the balancing of due process and crime control. Both are legitimate considerations within a Liberal democracy; crime control touches on individual lives and interests (especially of victims and the law-abiding) just as does the concern for due process. There are indeed no 'magic bullets', and 'difficult and tragic choices' must be made.[204] So, the arguments for change tend ultimately to be a

---

[197] Field, S. and Thomas, P.A., (eds.), *Justice and Efficiency* (1994) 21(1) *Journal of Law & Society* 21(1) (special issue, Blackwell, London) at p. 7.

[198] See Runciman, W.G., 'An outsider's view of the criminal justice system' (1994) 57 *Modern Law Review* 1 at p. 5.

[199] By 1996, 204 out of 352 recommendations had been accepted with more to be legislated that year: Lord Chancellor's Department, Home Office and Law Officer's Department, *The Royal Commission on Criminal Justice: Final Government Response* (Home Office, London, 1996) para. 5.

[200] See further Chapter 9. See also Home Office, *Improving the Effectiveness of Pre Trial Hearings in the Crown Court* (Cm 2924, HMSO, London, 1995); Home Office, *Mode of Trial* (Cm 2908, HMSO, London, 1995).

[201] Compare Sanders, A., 'Thinking about criminal justice' and Wadham, J., 'Miscarriages of justice: pre-trial and trial stages' in McConville, M. and Bridges, L., (eds.) *Criminal Justice in Crisis* (Edward Elgar, Aldershot, 1994) at pp. 146, 245.

[202] See Mansfield, M., *Presumed Guilty* (Heinemann, London, 1993) pp. 95, 96.

[203] See further Chapter 14.

[204] Allen, R.J., 'Reform: the system: the Simpson affair, reform of the criminal justice process, and magic bullets' (1996) 67 *Colorado Law Review* 989 at p. 1024.

mixture of philosophical, political and factual judgments. But in the process of reform after 1991, too much emphasis was placed on the political and not enough on the philosophical and factual. The political assertion that too many advantages had shifted the way of the defence and this imbalance had to be corrected with a move towards crime control values was stated most forcefully by the Home Secretary, Michael Howard, in outlining his 27-point reform package to the Conservative Party Conference in 1993:[205]

> In the last 30 years the balance in the criminal justice system has been tilted too far in favour of the criminal and against the protection of the public. The time has come to put that right.

It will be noted that there was no such overall finding either in philosophy or fact after two years of contemplation and research by the Runciman Commission, though there were strong echoes from police chiefs.[206] Consequently, the proposals appeared in a philosophical vacuum without an appreciation of the value of individual rights and their relationship to consequentialist arguments. There is also much force in the constitutional perspective inherent in due process arguments that above all it is important to check abuses of power by the State, even at the cost of truth-finding within the criminal justice system.[207] Besides, account should be taken of how the system is factually working and how any changes are likely to impact upon it. In this way, one might accept that a rapidly rising crime rate is a cause for concern, though one must always be wary of the political interpretations of the statistics. Equally, one must test whether erosions of specified features – such as the right to silence[208] – in the pre-reformed system really are justified by the seriousness of the offences where they commonly arise, the difficulty of obtaining evidence or the sophistication of suspects.[209] Factual justification must also be available in terms of what supposed reforms are likely to achieve and the objectives set for them. In any event, one should be sceptical that crime control perspectives bring a more accurate determination of guilt or innocence. Truth is not an absolute in the socially constructed world of criminal justice. Nor is it necessarily always the predominant value within the criminal justice system, for it may be properly be overridden by concerns for individual rights or the integrity of the system.

The second question is, what has become of the criminal justice system in terms of the antinomies of crime control/due process and adversarial/inquisitorial? The reform programme does list at least four features apparently contradictory of due process tenets. These included the abolition of the right to silence:[210]

---

[205] *The Daily Telegraph*, 7 October 1993 p. 12. See Newburn, T., *Crime and Criminal Justice Policy* (Longman, London, 1995) p. 178.

[206] See Reiner, R., 'The politics of the Act' [1985] *Public Law* 394 at p. 396; Pollard, C., 'Public safety, accountability and the courts' [1996] *Criminal Law Review* 152.

[207] See Frank, J., *Courts on Trial* (Princeton UP, 1949); King, M., *The Framework of Criminal Justice* (Croom Helm, London, 1981) p. 126.

[208] See Criminal Law Revision Committee, *Eleventh Report: Evidence (General)* (Cmnd 4991, HMSO, London, 1972) para. 21; Zander, M., 'The Criminal Law Revision Committee Report – a survey of reactions' (1974) 71 *Law Society's Gazette* 954.

[209] See Ashworth, A., 'Crime, community and creeping consequentialism' [1996] *Criminal Law Review* 220.

[210] *The Daily Telegraph*, 7 October 1993 p. 12.

What fools [criminals] must think we are. It is time to call a halt to this charade. The innocent have nothing to hide and that is exactly the point the prosecution will be able to make in future.

They also included the taking of DNA samples without consent in connection with all recordable criminal offences so as to bring 'the full force of modern science to bear on the modern criminal'. Third, the judges were asked to take a more active role in case management, an apparent departure from their aloof and umpireal due process stance. Fourth, victims were to be given a more prominent role in the system.[211] Yet, for all these changes, the due process, adversarial model of opposing parties presenting contending views of case history and even the concern for 'greater fairness in procedures and practices to prevent miscarriages of justice'[212] survives for the most part in the higher criminal courts' process. There are still such cornerstones as the presumption of innocence and the burden and standard of proof. Whilst on the one hand, they are now narrower through changes to the right to silence (though the defendant still cannot be called as a witness and in that sense remains in control[213]), on the other hand, they are becoming more enforceable under the Human Rights Act. Likewise, the availability of legal aid and representation has actually increased enormously since the advent of the Police and Criminal Evidence Act 1984,[214] alongside, of course, its incursion into rights by the granting of more police powers. The judges have also sent mixed messages, becoming more activist in protecting the interests of defendants but refusing to penalise *per se* all breaches of due process,[215] becoming more prominent in the administrative management of serious cases[216] but not metamorphosing into inquisitors. Much depends on whether, overall, the balance between the parties remains an equal one, and the shifting focus towards police interrogation, which has developed throughout most of this century, demands a commensurate emphasis on equality of arms which once primarily related to the courthouse. It may be that, especially in the light of the changes to the right to silence, the days of the English criminal justice system being categorised as 'accusatorial' are on the wane.[217] This is self-evidently the case if such a system is defined as one which 'imposes on the Government the burden of proving a case through witnesses and extrinsic evidence',[218] since the English system has increasingly recognised and encouraged police interrogation. But whether this undoubted trend negates the adversarial

---

[211] For tangible results, see Wright, M., 'The rights of witnesses' (1996) 22 *Criminal Justice Matters* 4; Lord Chancellor's Department, Home Office and Law Officers' Department, *The Royal Commission on Criminal Justice: Final Government Response* (Home Office, London, 1996) paras. 57–61, 116–122.

[212] Home Office, *Protecting the Public* (Cm 3190, HMSO, London, 1996) para. 1.9.

[213] Damaska, M.J., *The Faces of Justice and State Authority* (Yale University Press, 1986) p. 127. See further Chapter 5.

[214] See Chapters 3, 4.

[215] See Chapter 10.

[216] See Criminal Justice Act 1987; Criminal Procedure and Investigation Act 1996, s.29.

[217] Compare: O'Reilly, G.W., 'England limits the rights to silence and moves towards an inquisitorial system of justice' (1994) 85 *Journal of Criminal Law & Criminology* 402 at p. 405; Ingraham, B.L., 'The right of silence, the presumption of innocence, the burden of proof, and a modest proposal: a reply to O'Reilly' (1996) 86 *Journal of Criminal Law & Criminology* 559; O'Reilly, G.W., 'Criminal law: comment on Ingraham's "moral duty" to talk and the right to silence' (1997) 87 *Journal of Criminal Law & Criminology* 521.

[218] O' Reilly, G.W., 'England limits the right to silence and moves towards an inquisitorial system of justice' (1994) 85 *Journal of Criminal Law & Criminology* 402 at p. 419.

nature of the process is debatable, since adversarial and accusatorial influences are distinct.[219] After all, it is still the police, rather than a judicial officer, performing the questioning, and, as the case of *John Murray* v *United Kingdom*[220] recognises, even the possibility of adverse inferences from silence can be fair in an adversarial system provided there are new balancing safeguards such as the presence of a solicitor.

The real agenda for the Runciman Commission was to restore the balance of an adversarial system in a way which gave meaning to the basic rights of citizens. Instead, it treated issues piecemeal and in isolation, just as the research it commissioned.[221] Then came the Home Office with a more selective approach, very much guided by notions of crime control. So what went wrong? At the outset, one must reject the assertion that miscarriages of justice cannot be utilised heuristically as bases for analysis and progress.[222] These failures provide good opportunities both to examine our catalogues of principles and policies towards crime and also to accord a higher priority to that examination. It is notable that it is miscarriages of justice which have prompted the last two Royal Commissions on the crime-related processes and that major reforms have followed the two reports. Nor is it always the case that a rights agenda (or due process values) has been consistently ignored because lawyers, speaking from their 'system', have failed to appeal to the values of other 'systems', such as the media and politics. In fact, the agenda and values are not specific to law, but it is true that journalists and politicians often act for short-term and unprincipled reasons. In conclusion, there was no necessary or catastrophic failure on the part of the Runciman Commission, but it did fail to seize the opportunity which its authority conferred and acted without any sense of its own importance or authority to draw out of a conflictual situation a set of common standards and a programme of action based on them. If the game was simply to second-guess what the Government of the day would accept, then why have a Royal Commission? By contrast, the Home Office seized the opportunity thus presented and manipulated the outcome for political advantage which it undoubtedly gained but at some cost to individual rights and to the integrity of the system.

Conclusions

Assertions that the British system of justice is the best in the world or that miscarriages of justice are few and far between can no longer be sustained without argument. Criminal justice systems should be judged, *inter alia*, on the number of injustices produced by them in the first place, and, secondly, on their willingness to recognise and correct those mistakes. The British system scores badly on both counts, as will be explained in the following chapters. How it performs in comparison with other systems will also be considered. More generally, it is hoped that this book will assist the reader to understand the reasons behind the recurrent crises and to choose amongst the possible solutions to them.[223] There is no

---

[219] Goldstein, A.S., 'Reflections on the two models' (1974) 26 *Stanford Law Review* 1009.

[220] *John Murray* v *UK*, Appl. no. 18731/91, 1996–I, (1996) 22 EHRR 29.

[221] Hodgson, J., 'Justice undermined' (1997) 29 *Criminal Justice Matters* 4.

[222] Compare Nobles, R., and Schiff, D., 'Miscarriages of justice: a systems approach' (1996) 59 *Modern Law Review* 299 at p. 320.

[223] This faith in the value of reform is itself contentious (see: McConville, M., Sanders, A. and Leng, R., *The Case for the Prosecution* (Routledge, London, 1991, ch. 10), but even sceptics may prefer not to leave the field open to administrative fiat or the powerful clients of Government (see: Craig, P.P., *Public Law and Democracy in the UK and the USA* (Clarendon Press, Oxford, 1990) p. 130).

expectation that miscarriages can be abolished in any sense,[224] but there should be a constant demand to respect and reflect the hallowed values of the criminal justice system, especially the right of the innocent not to be convicted. It is not the case that the English criminal justice system is in a constant state of crisis without precedent,[225] but it is the case that recurrent crises are likely and that the changes to the system during the course of this decade have made the possibility of crisis more, rather than less, likely.

For the future, a sudden change of heart on the part of the Home Office is most unlikely – the Crime and Disorder Act 1998 at least suggests otherwise. It has also been suggested that a standing Royal Commission on Crime and Punishment should be resurrected in order to wrest policy back from 'the cockpit of competitive party politics' and the desire to be seen as the toughest on crime, no matter what the cost to rights.[226] Perhaps more faith can be placed in the reinvigoration of fundamental values via the Human Rights Act 1998. One might predict that the criminal process will become the most fecund area of rights litigation and, no matter what the success rate, it will serve as a constant reminder to the legal system of the values to be respected and furthered. Albeit piecemeal, it is possible that Act will eventually achieve what the Runciman Commission left undone.

---

[224] Greer, S., 'Miscarriages of justice reconsidered' (1994) 57 *Modern Law Review* 58 at p. 73.

[225] Compare Rose, D., *In the Name of the Law* (Jonathan Cape, London, 1996) p. ix.

[226] Blom Cooper, Sir L. and McConville, S., *A Case for a Royal Commission on Crime and Punishment* (Prison Reform Trust, London, 1997) p. 3. There is as yet no evidence that the Criminal Justice Consultative Councils will rise above administrative matters; see Farquharson, D., 'The Criminal Justice Consultative Councils' (1993) 49(2) *The Magistrate* 26.

Part Two

THE CRIMINAL JUSTICE PROCESS IN ENGLAND AND WALES AND MISCARRIAGES OF JUSTICE

3

Police Investigative Procedures: Changing Legal and Political Contexts of Policing Practices

David Dixon

There have been two turning points in the recent history of police investigative procedures: the implementation of the Police and Criminal Evidence Act (PACE) in 1986 with its codification of many police powers and suspects' rights, and a series of developments beginning in 1993 which brought about a decisive shift in the dominant discourse about and within policing. The relationship between police investigative procedures and miscarriages of justice was significant at both stages. Concern about the consequences of not providing substantial protections for suspects[1] (along with police pressure for more powers and a more general interest in the renovation of criminal justice processes) structured the debates which led to PACE. In the early 1990s, it seemed possible that the belated acknowledgement that incompetent police investigations had produced numerous serious miscarriages was going to provoke some fundamental reform. This was not to be: in a formidable display of the British State's capacity for deflecting or absorbing threats, the Government turned instead to renewed law and order campaigning and a programme of reforming criminal justice according to the dictates of an economically constructed 'efficiency'.[2] In both respects, the focus on a narrow conception of crime control threatens some of the gains made in the earlier period. This chapter seeks to review briefly some of these developments, placing police investigative procedures in the changing legal and political contexts of policing practices.

---

[1] Exemplified by the case of *R v Lattimore, Salih and Leighton* (1975) 62 Cr App R 53(the Confait case): see *Report of an Inquiry by the Hon. Sir Henry Fisher* (1977–78 HC 90); Baxter, J. and Koffman, L., (1983) 'The Confait inheritance' 14 *Cambrian Law Review* 11.

[2] At the time of writing, it appears that the new Labour Government will make little substantial difference in this respect.

Assessing PACE's Impact on Investigations

A considerable body of research on PACE[3] has now accumulated.[4] Studies of the impact of PACE on stop and search and search of premises found that the legislators had assumed an inaccurate conception of policing practices; consequently, formal police powers were extended, but the accompanying safeguards have been of limited effect.[5] The more extensive research on detention and questioning has been inconveniently, but not surprisingly,[6] inconclusive. Summarising crudely, there are three broad interpretations.

The first presents PACE as a 'sea-change' in policing: it argues that PACE fundamentally changed criminal investigation, shifting towards a putatively American model of due process.[7] While there has been some academic support for this approach (notably in Irving and McKenzie's early research[8]), its main exponents have been police officers who have used (and abused[9]) research to bolster their campaigns for legislation to redress what they viewed as the consequent 'imbalance' in criminal justice. According to Tom Williamson, a key figure in police responses to PACE, a 'new climate has been created in which there is strict adherence to the new rules'.[10]

In very considerable contrast, McConville, Sanders and Leng argue that PACE has been 'easily absorbed by the police' and that the dominance of police priorities, culture and crime-control commitments has not been challenged: 'Apart from changes to bureaucratic recording practices . . . the basic message from our research is of the *non-impact* of PACE on police practices'.[11] Rather than regulating policing, PACE has served to facilitate and legitimate powers and practices adopted by the police in their culturally-driven commitment to crime control. Key features identified by this school of analysis include: a fundamental similarity between (highly discretionary and experienced-based rather than rule-based) policing on the street and in the station; change by PACE of procedures, but not of substance; police domination of the process by which cases are constructed and processed; police resistance to and evasion of attempts to control their activities; the inefficacy of supervisory and managerial controls, particularly in an adversary system; the degeneration of provisions which notionally protect

---

[3] For a description of its legal provisions, see Lidstone, K. and Palmer, C., *The Investigation of Crime* (2nd ed., Butterworths, London, 1996); Zander, M., *The Police and Criminal Evidence Act 1984* (3rd ed., Sweet & Maxwell, London 1995).

[4] See Brown, D., *PACE Ten Years On: A Review of the Research* (Home Office Research Study No. 155, HMSO, London, 1997).

[5] See Dixon, D. *et al.*, 'Reality and rules in the construction and regulation of police suspicion' (1989) 17 *International Journal of the Sociology of Law* 185; Bottomley, K., *et al.* The *Impact of PACE* (Centre for Criminology, Hull, 1991) chs. 2 & 3; Brown, D., *op. cit.* (footnote 4 above); Lidstone, K., and Bevan, V., *Search and Seizure under the PACE Act 1984* (University of Sheffield, 1990); Dixon, D., *Law in Policing: Legal Regulation and Police Practices* (Clarendon Press, Oxford, 1997) ch. 3.

[6] See Maguire, M. and Norris, C., 'Police investigations: practice and malpractice' (1994) 21 *Journal of Law & Society* 72 at p. 75; Dixon, D., *op. cit.* (footnote 5 above) at pp. 152–69.

[7] For example McKenzie, I. and Gallagher, G. P., *Behind the Uniform* (Harvester, Hemel Hempstead, 1989) pp. 11, 136–7; compare Dixon, D., *op. cit.* (footnote 5 above) pp. 152–4.

[8] Irving, B. and McKenzie, I., *Police Interrogation* (Police Foundation, London, 1989).

[9] See Dixon, D., *op. cit.* (footnote 5 above) pp. 231–3.

[10] Williamson, T., *Strategic changes in police interrogation* (Ph.D. thesis University of Kent, 1990) p. 1.

[11] McConville, M., Sanders, A. and Leng, R, *The Case for the Prosecution* (Routledge, London, 1991) p. 189. See also Sanders, A. and Young, R., *Criminal Justice* (Butterworths, London, 1994).

suspects' rights (such as legal advice and electronic recording of questioning) into mechanisms of crime control; and the operational bias of criminal justice against the socially and economically marginal. The implications for those interested in using law to control policing are made clear:[12]

> The assumption underlying the reforms of the 1980s is that police and prosecutors are susceptible to control by law and administrative guidelines, and that the practices of these agencies may be changed by tightening the law . . . Our major finding is that these assumptions are wrong.

This account, and particularly its presentation in their major work, *The Case for the Prosecution*, has been both influential and controversial.[13]

The third interpretation presents a critical, but guardedly positive, assessment of PACE.[14] The accumulated research certainly illustrates the limited effectiveness of PACE's control mechanisms, including the routinisation of supervisory controls and the minimal use of disciplinary sanctions. However, this must not be overstated: the PACE reforms are flawed, but potential exists for them to be given more (or less) substance. The substantial right of access to legal advice, electronic recording of custodial interrogation, and the custody officer's role in regulating investigative detention are – despite the serious deficiencies which have been identified – significant developments. In particular, criticism of legal advisers should not lose sight of how remarkable it was that a right to legal advice backed by a publicly-funded scheme should have been conferred[15] during Thatcher's administration with its commitment to rolling back the frontiers of the State. A comparative perspective is instructive on this point; in the contemporary reforms of Australian criminal procedure, public funding for legal advice at police stations is routinely recommended by law reform commissions but is not even seriously considered by legislators.[16]

This third interpretation is a more optimistic view of the potential for police reform attainable by regulation and internal supervision. External controls and accountability mechanisms (desirable as considerably strengthened forms of them are) cannot be expected to be effective unless police organisations are themselves involved in the process: this is the clear lesson to be learnt from studies of regulation in other areas. Change in institutions is a complex phenomenon: people may change their behaviour without being culturally or ideologically committed to such change, but values and beliefs may then shift too. At the same time, attempting to change by using highly prescriptive and punitive rules may well provoke cultural resistance rather than change. Compliance has to be sought by skilfully blending negotiation and imposition.[17]

---

[12] Leng, R., McConville, M. and Sanders, A., 'Researching the discretion to charge and to prosecute', in Downes, D., (ed.), *Unravelling Criminal Justice* (Macmillan, London, 1992) p. 119 at pp. 134–5.

[13] The debate surrounding it is fully rehearsed in Dixon, D., *op. cit.* (footnote 5 above), pp. 155–69; Noaks, L., *et al.*, (eds.) *Contemporary Issues in Criminology* (Wales University Press, Cardiff, 1995) chs. 9–13.

[14] Brown, D., *op. cit.* (footnote 4 above); Dixon., D., *op. cit.* (footnote 5 above) ch. 4; Dixon, D., *et al.*, 'Safeguarding the rights of suspects in police custody' (1990) 1 *Policing & Society* 115; Reiner, R. and Leigh, L., 'Police power', in McCrudden, C. and Chambers, G., (eds.), *Individual Rights and the Law in Britain* (Clarendon Press, Oxford, 1994) pp. 69–108.

[15] PACE, s. 59. Now see the Legal Aid Act 1988, sch. 6.

[16] Dixon, D., *op. cit.* (footnote 5 above), ch. 5.

Procedural changes have to be placed in a broader cultural context. PACE contributed to some significant changes in policing practices and cultures. When officers speak of a new 'professionalism' in police work, their terminology may be questionable, but they do refer to a perceptible shift. This must not be overstated: I would not (as has been suggested) argue that 'PACE has ushered in a new era of police professionalism' which is 'sweeping though the ranks'.[18] It is altogether a more modest claim, one which accords with Maguire and Norris's perceptive discussion of detective work. They found 'signs of genuine commitment among junior officers, in principle at least, to the new styles of working, centred around the concept of "crime management"'.[19] Crucially, there has been a shift in evaluations of investigative methods: the tradition of arresting on hunches, interrogating, and giving weak cases 'a run' has been challenged by according status to officers who investigate and collect evidence more carefully before arrest, rely less on interrogation, find ways of working within the rules, and produce evidence which survives judical scrutiny and convictions which cannot be successfully challenged on appeal. One has by no means replaced the other; but there is a significant tension which indicates shifts and variations within police cultures. Obviously, this is not a declaration of a simple faith in 'progress'. It is not necessary to say that things have changed for the better to accept that there has been change: this requires recognition (not necessarily applause) so that analysis can address the new situation. The 'new professional' is not necessarily a 'nice cop'.[20] He or she may be one who resents the restrictions of PACE and who ruthlessly exploits the resources which it provides, in very much the way that McConville, Sanders and Leng describe. Nor need it be claimed that changes are pervasive. Maguire and Norris found that some detectives maintain 'the "traditional detective culture" of secretiveness, individualism and beliefs in the "Ways and Means Act"'.[21] This is not a homogeneous group: as well as the 'dinosaurs', it includes some more influential officers.[22] A larger group (a majority of Maguire and Norris's interviewees) treated PACE as what the Policy Studies Institute called 'inhibitory' rules: they 'followed the rules because they had to, rather than because they believed in them'.[23] However, alongside the grumbling acquiescence, there has been some attitudinal and behavioural change. As time passes, PACE becomes normality, rather than an imposition, particularly for younger officers inducted into its regime from the outset.[24]

---

[17] Ayres, I. and Braithwaite, J., *Responsive Regulation* (Oxford University Press, New York, 1992); Dixon, D., *op. cit.* (footnote 5 above), ch. 7.

[18] Leng, R., 'Pessimism or professionalism?', in Noaks, L., *et al.*, (eds.) *Contemporary Issues in Criminology* (Wales University Press, Cardiff, 1995) at pp. 206, 208.

[19] Maguire, M. and Norris, C., *The Conduct and Supervision of Criminal Investigations* (Royal Commission on Criminal Justice Research Study No. 5, HMSO, London, 1992) p. 42.

[20] Compare Williamson, T., 'Are nice cops winning?' paper presented to the British Psychological Society (1990).

[21] Maguire, M. and Norris, C., *The Conduct and Supervision of Criminal Investigations* (Royal Commission on Criminal Justice Research Study No. 5, HMSO, London, 1992) p. 41.

[22] A notable example of this group was a detective sergeant whom I encountered during our PACE project: realising that I had seen him leaving a cell after a 'welfare' visit to a suspect, he engaged in a lengthy inquiry into what my 'brief' was which provided a good insight into this group.

[23] Maguire, M. and Norris, C., *The Conduct and Supervision of Criminal Investigations* (Royal Commission on Criminal Justice Research Study No. 5, HMSO, London, 1992) at p. 42; compare Smith, D.J, and Gray, J., *Police and People in London* (Policy Studies Institute, London, 1985).

[24] Maguire, M. and Norris, C., 'Police investigations: practice and malpractice' (1994) 21 *Journal of Law & Society* 72 at p. 82.

Given the parochialism of most debates about policing in Britain, a comparative perspective might be useful in choosing between the three interpretations so far on offer. A similar process of normalisation as in the third interpretation has been noted in studies (by authors who are far from being police apologists) of the long-term effects of procedural reform which followed the landmark decision in *Miranda* v *Arizona*[25] in the United States Supreme Court:[26]

> . . . virtually all of today's police interrogators have known no law other than *Miranda*. The discourse of *Miranda* has . . . by now suffused police conscious-ness so much that it has become second nature to them . . . *Miranda* has helped generate a professional ethic of physical restraint in policing that has changed the social organization and moral ordering of detective work.

While officers grumble about restraints upon them, 'underneath the veneer of "prime time" cop talk, one discovers that police at all levels demonstrate a routine awareness of procedural tasks that have become as much part of the job as using the radio or completing paper work'.[27] As Walker argues, to assess the impact of the Warren Court's reforms of criminal procedure, it is necessary to look at their continuing, indirect effects.[28] The cases led police organisations to improve their training, supervisory practices, and general professionalism. They encouraged a cultural shift towards the acceptance of accountability and legality: Skolnick writes of a 'legal archipelago . . . sets of islands of legal values . . . distributed throughout the broad experience of policing'.[29] Equally importantly, public expectations of police performance developed.

Richard Leo's important research charts a shift in US interrogation practices from coercion to 'manipulation, deception and persuasion'.[30] As the terminology suggests, this cannot be neatly categorised as 'progress': it is part of a more general reconstitution of techniques of power and processes of control. Simple moral judgments are unhelpful: while 'contemporary interrogation tactics are undeniably more humane and civilised than the coercive practices they have replaced', they are ethically questionable, notably in their reliance upon deception. These tactics

---

[25] *Miranda* v *Arizona* 384 US 436 (1966).

[26] Leo, R., 'Police interrogation and social control' (1994) 3 *Social & Legal Studies* 93 at p. 114.

[27] Skolnick, J., 'Justice without trial revisited', in Weisburd, D. and Uchida, C., (eds.), *Police Innovation and Control of the Police* (Springer-Verlag, New York, 1993) p. 196.

[28] Walker, S., *Popular Justice* (Oxford University Press, New York, 1980) pp. 229–32; Walker, S., *Taming the System* (Oxford University Press, New York, 1993). *Miranda*'s thirtieth birthday was marked by some significant studies into its impact: see Cassell, P.G., '*Miranda*'s social costs' (1996) 90 *Northwestern University Law Review* 387; Cassell, P.G. and Hayman, B.S., 'Police interrogation in the 1990s' (1996) 43 *University of California Law Review* 839; Leo, R., 'The impact of *Miranda* revisited' (1996) 86 *Journal of Criminal Law & Criminology* 621; Schulhofer, S.J., '*Miranda*'s practical effect' (1996) 90 *Northwestern University Law Review* 500; Huff, C.R., Rattner, A. and Sagarin, E., *Convicted But Innocent: Wrongful Conviction and Public Policy* (Sage, Thousand Oaks, 1996) ch. 5; Leo, R.A. and Thomas, G.C. (eds.), *The Miranda Debate* (Northwestern University Press, Boston, 1998).

[29] Skolnick, J., 'Justice without trial revisited', in Weisburd, D. and Uchida, C., (eds.), *Police Innovation and Control of the Police* (Springer-Verlag, New York, 1993) at p. 196.

[30] Leo, R., '*Miranda*'s revenge' (1996) 30 *Law & Society Review* 259 at p. 284; Leo, R., 'From coercion to deception' (1992) 18 *Crime, Law & Social Change* 35; Leo, R., 'Police interrogation and social control' (1994) 3 *Social & Legal Studies* 93; Leo, R., 'Inside the interrogation room' (1996) 86 *Journal of Criminal Law & Criminology* 266; Leo, R., 'The impact of *Miranda* revisited' (1996) 86 *Journal of Criminal Law & Criminology* 621.

legitimate the use of interrogation and represent more effective modes of police power. Yet they also provide the possibility of their further transformation by being opened to the influence of 'legal institutions, professional standards and social norms'.[31] But, of course, there are other possibilities: developments are rarely linear, and such change as there has been can be reversed or undermined. The detrimental effect which the 'war on drugs' has had on the 'legal professionalism' of US police provides clear evidence of this.[32] Similarly, Maguire stressed that the toehold of reforms in English policing was precarious: they were 'by no means so well established, nor is the commitment to them by the police service so secure, that one can be confident that the momentum will be maintained. Priorities in the police service change quickly, and are strongly influenced by the political "mood"'.[33]

Crime Control, Managerialism, and Efficiency

The political mood on criminal justice in England and Wales shifted decisively in 1993, triggered by two related factors which ended a period during which the police had been on the back foot from public and judicial criticism resulting from the miscarriage of justice cases. The first factor was the Report of the Royal Commission on Criminal Justice ('the Runciman Commission');[34] the second was a significant shift in the political discourse about, and within, policing.

The Runciman Commission

The pressure on the police arising from the series of miscarriage cases around the start of the decade was dissipated by the Royal Commission on Criminal Justice's Report. Established after the release of the *Birmingham Six*,[35] and chaired by a distinguished sociologist, much had been expected of this Royal Commission. In its treatment of police investigative procedures, the Royal Commission generally adopted a rather superficial interpretation of the third view outlined above. The 'implicit assumption seems to have been that problems revealed by the miscarriage of justice cases had been largely addressed by PACE and that only minor adjustment was required'.[36] Therefore, the Commission looked to enhanced implementation of the PACE strategy by means of further inquiry by other bodies, detailed regulatory change, and improved training and supervision. Its recommendations led to (or strengthened existing tendencies towards) measures designed to improve the quality of legal advice at stations, new techniques for questioning suspects and witnesses, the video-recording of charge rooms,[37] numerous detailed

---

[31] Leo, R., 'Police interrogation and social control' (1994) 3 *Social & Legal Studies* 93 at p. 117.

[32] Skolnick, J., 'Justice without trial revisited', in Weisburd, D. and Uchida, C., (eds.), *Police Innovation and Control of the Police* (Springer-Verlag, New York, 1993) at p. 205.

[33] Maguire, M., 'The wrong message at the wrong time?', in Morgan, D. and Stephenson, G., (eds), *Suspicion and Silence* (Blackstone, London, 1994) 39 at p. 47.

[34] Cm 2263, HMSO, London, 1993.

[35] See Chapter 2.

[36] Field, S. and Thomas, P.A., 'Justice and efficiency?' (1994) 21 *Journal of Law & Society* 1 at p. 3; compare *Runciman Report*, ch. 4 para. 33. See also Reiner, R., 'Royal Commission on Criminal Justice: investigative powers and safeguards for suspects' [1993] *Criminal Law Review* 808.

[37] But not of interrogations, in recognition of technological and (more significant) interpretive problems in using video: see Baldwin, J., *Video-taping Police Interviews with Suspects* (Police Research Series

amendments to PACE Code C,[38] and changes in training, supervision, and equipment.

Widespread disappointment and criticism greeted the Report of the Runciman Commission, which is likely to be used by political scientists as a classic example of the political and symbolic functions of such inquiries 'in reassuring the world that the State is examining the entrails and that all will shortly be well'[39] and of their vulnerability to capture by Government (in this case, the Home Office).[40] The Commission's approach had three major weaknesses of direct relevance to consideration of investigative procedures and practices. First, it allowed miscarriage of justice to slip from its central focus, as it became obsessed with a narrowly-defined 'efficiency' in crime control and wholly failed to carry out any analysis of the *Birmingham Six* case or similar miscarriages.[41] These criticisms have been made in detail elsewhere;[42] for present purposes, the primary significance of the Royal Commission was that it relieved the pressure for fundamental change in investigative practice.

Secondly, the Royal Commission's widely-criticised lack of articulated theory or principle meant that its account of policing and criminal procedure was threadbare: there was no sense of the significance of the structural and cultural contexts in which investigative procedures were deployed, and from which miscarriages of justice emerged. Notably:[43]

. . . despite the centrality of malpractice to the problem of miscarriages, the Commission's report spends remarkably little time in analysing how and why it may occur. It does not look in detail at the mechanics of investigations, at the various social and organisational contexts in which they take place, nor at the aims and attitudes of – or pressures upon – those managing or conducting them.

As Lacey suggests, the focus on specific measures to counter malpractice excluded broader questions which 'have to do with why abuses occur in the first place, and they can only be addressed through reflection on issues such as the way in which policing is socially constructed within a society preoccupied by "law and order" as a major social problem; how adequate and humane policing is defined and

No. 1, HMSO, London, 1992); *Runciman Report*, ch. 3 paras. 65–72; Dixon, D. and Travis, G., *The Impact of the Electronic Recording of Police Questioning of Suspects on Criminal Justice in New South Wales* (University of New South Wales, Sydney, forthcoming). There is continuing Home Office interest in video; see Home Office Circular 6/1993, *Video-Recording of Interviews with Suspects*. By contrast, video-recording of interrogations concerning indictable offences is already standard in several Australian jurisdictions.

[38] See Home Office Circular 13/1995, *PACE 1984: Revised Codes of Practice;* Home Office Circular 26/1995, *Tape Recording of Interviews*.

[39] Sedley, S., 'Whose Justice?' (1993) *London Review of Books* 23 Sept. 1993 at p. 5. See also Burton, F. and Carlen, P., *Official Discourse* (Routledge and Kegan Paul, London, 1979).

[40] As detailed in the bibliography of *Justice in Error* (Blackstone Press, London, 1993) (at p. 249), there was also a substantial submission to the Runciman Commission in the name of the 'Police Service', some of which was confidential.

[41] The failure was wilful as it viewed itself as not appointed to consider individual cases, passing that responsibility to Sir John May, even though he was confined to the *Maguire* and *Guildford* cases: see *Runciman Report*, ch. 1 para. 3.

[42] See Field, S. and Thomas, P.A., (eds.), *Justice and Efficiency* (1994) 21(1) *Journal of Law & Society* 21(1) (special issue); McConville, M. and Bridges, L., (eds.) *Criminal Justice in Crisis* (Edward Elgar, Aldershot, 1994); Ashworth, A., *The Criminal Process* (2nd ed., Clarendon Press, Oxford, 1998); Sanders, A. and Young, R., *Criminal Justice* (Butterworths, London, 1994).

[43] Maguire, M. and Norris, C., 'Police investigations: practice and malpractice' (1994) 21 *Journal of Law & Society* 72 at p. 73. Like other authors of Runciman Commission Research Reports, Maguire and Norris were justifiably disappointed at the Commission's treatment of their work.

rewarded; (and) the institutional culture of the police and police work.'.[44] These, surely, were appropriate for a Royal Commission to consider.

Thirdly, there were serious empirical as well as theoretical gaps in the Commission's account. If, as was assumed, the general PACE strategy was correct, one might have expected significant discussion of specific major problems identified in the research literature. For example, a major opportunity to take serious account of the need for special attention to be paid to vulnerable suspects was missed: this issue will be addressed below. In addition, it had been pointed out that police can sidestep legal regulation by relying on 'consent'.[45] The extent to which 'voluntary attendance' still occurs is unclear, and the Commission simply ignored this issue. Other investigative practices which rely heavily on 'consent' – stop and search on the street and search of private premises – were treated as being beyond its terms of reference. There should have been some interest in the use of powers which research showed to be extremely problematic.[46] The oversight of stop and search was particularly surprising, given that its recorded use had more than trebled since 1986.[47] In retrospect, the omission was particularly unfortunate given the likely impact of the currently fashionable 'zero-tolerance' policing on the use of stop and search. The purported success of 'broken windows' strategies in reducing serious crime in New York City makes the need to understand the links between street policing and crime investigation particularly pressing.[48] The links between street policing and investigative detention have to be understood, because pre-arrest and arrest decisions may structure individual cases and because both regulation of custodial interrogation and the restriction of the right to silence increase the incentive for 'preparatory' interviewing outside the police station.[49]

While overlooking routine powers, the Commission also barely touched on 'exceptional' powers which will often be available in cases of the kind which, in the past, produced miscarriages. Having offered its opinion that PACE safeguards should apply to terrorism inquiries, the Commission went no further in either investigation or recommendation on the grounds that these issues were considered by Parliament in its annual review of the Prevention of Terrorism Acts.[50] One might have expected a Royal Commission on Criminal Justice to have paid attention to

---

[44] Lacey, N., 'Missing the wood', in McConville, M. and Bridges, L., (eds.), *Criminal Justice in Crisis* (Edward Elgar, Aldershot, 1994) at p. 35.

[45] Dixon. D. *et al.*, 'Consent and the legal regulation of policing' (1990) 17 *Journal of Law & Society* 345; McKenzie, I. *et al.*, 'Helping police with their inquiries' [1990] *Criminal Law Review* 22.

[46] See Dixon, D. *et al.*, 'Reality and rules in the construction and regulation of police suspicion' (1989) *International Journal of the Sociology of Law* 185–206; Bottomley, K., *et al. The Impact of PACE* (Centre for Criminology, Hull, 1991); Lidstone, K. and Bevan, V., *Search and Seizure under the PACE Act 1984* (University of Sheffield, 1990); Dixon, *op. cit.* (footnote 5 above) ch. 3.

[47] See Home Office Statistical Bulletin 21/93; the rate of increase has continued: see Statistical Bulletin 27/97.

[48] Kelling, G. L. and Coles, C. M., *Fixing Broken Windows* (Free Press, New York, 1996) Dixon, D., 'Broken Windows, zero tolerance, and the New York miracle' (1997) 10 *Current Issues in Criminal Justice* 96.

[49] See Brogden, M., 'Gatekeeping and the seamless web of criminal justice' and Singh, S., 'Understanding the long-term relationship between police and policed', both in McConville, M. and Bridges, L., (eds.), *Criminal Justice in Crisis* (Edward Elgar, Aldershot, 1994) at pp. 152–61, 162–70.

[50] *Runciman Report*, ch. 3 paras. 93–5. This was perhaps the most disingenuous of the Commission's numerous recommendations that other bodies should take responsibility for various matters, especially given their poor record to date; see: Walker, C.P., 'Constitutional governance and special powers against terrorism' (1997) 35 *Columbia Journal of Transnational Law* 1.

some of the following issues: the well-documented limitation of key safeguards in a type of case in which pressures to miscarry have previously been overwhelming and frequent;[51] the acceptability of powers, the use of which had been held to be contrary to the European Convention on Human Rights;[52] and the connections between exceptional and 'normal' powers.[53]

The Commission's faulty understanding of criminal justice was further indicated by the strange recommendation that questioning after charge should be routinely permissible. This was 'put forward in an almost casual, common-sense manner'[54] which suggests that the Commission did not understand either the significance invested in in-station charging by the mid-nineteenth century transfer of duties from magistrates to police, or the impact of such a recommendation if adopted on PACE's scheme of time-limits on investigative detention or on custodial legal advice schemes.[55]

Changes in the Political Discourse about Policing

The Royal Commission produced its report in a political context quite different from that surrounding its establishment. The political and professional consensus about the need for criminal justice reform had broken down 'in an outbreak of populist anti-reformism'[56] triggered by moral panics over sentencing, juvenile crime, and bail. A new Home Secretary, Michael Howard, encouraged renewed populist obsession with law and order as the Government struggled to rekindle electoral popularity and to improve relations with a police service which was not enjoying its subjection to the new managerialism (see below). The police received a 'veritable avalanche of "gifts"'[57] including new powers to stop and search and to take samples from suspects, new equipment, additional offences with their consequential extension of police authority (like most gifts, not all of these were welcome), and, most notably, the restriction of the right to silence.[58]

In the mid-1990s, the message to the police from Government was approval of a simple-minded 'toughness' on crime:[59]

---

[51] See Walker, C.P., *The Prevention of Terrorism in British Law* (2nd ed., Manchester University Press, 1992).

[52] *Brogan, Coyle, McFadden & Tracey* v *UK* Appl. nos. 11209/84, 11234/84, 11266/84, 11386/85, Judgment of Court Ser. A vol. 145-B, *The Times*, 30 November 1988, (1988) 11 EHRR 117. But see also *Brannigan and McBride* v *UK* Appl. nos 14553–4/89, Judgment of Court Ser. A vol 258-B, (1994) 17 EHRR 539, *The Times*, 28 May 1993.

[53] Walker, C.P., *The Prevention of Terrorism in British Law* (2nd ed., Manchester University Press, 1992); Hillyard, P., *Suspect Community* (Pluto Press, London 1993); Hillyard, P., 'The politics of criminal injustice' in McConville, M., and Bridges, L,, (eds.), *Criminal Justice in Crisis* (Edward Elgar, Aldershot, 1994).

[54] Bridges, L., 'The Royal Commission's approach to criminal defence services', in McConville, M., and Bridges, L,, (eds.), *Criminal Justice in Crisis* (Edward Elgar, Aldershot, 1994), p. 282; compare *Runciman Report*, ch. 2 para. 42.

[55] See Bridges, L., 'The Royal Commission's approach to criminal defence services', in McConville, M., and Bridges, L,, (eds.), *Criminal Justice in Crisis* (Edward Elgar, Aldershot, 1994); Dixon *op. cit.* (footnote 5 above), ch. 4. Australian experience provides a warning about how police may be encouraged to arrest at times when no magistrate will be available at the end of any detention period, so allowing continued questioning by default: see *ibid.*, ch. 5.

[56] Bridges, L., and McConville, M., 'Keeping faith with their own convictions' (1994) 57 *Modern Law Review* 75 at p. 76.

[57] Leishman, F., Loveday, B. and Savage, S.P., (eds.), *Core Issues in Policing* (Longman, London, 1996) at p. 3.

[58] See Chapter 5.

[59] Maguire, M., 'The wrong message at the wrong time?', in Morgan, D. and Stephenson, G., (eds), *Suspicion and Silence* (Blackstone, London, 1994) at p. 48.

If such messages were accompanied by firm statements of commitment to fair and open investigations and the protection of suspects' rights, there would be less reason to fear backtracking by the police from commitment to investigative reform. However, not only are statements of this kind virtually absent, but specific proposals appear to send out quite opposite messages.

Among these, the restriction of the right to silence in 1994 was emblematic. Given how few suspects remain silent and the diversity of their reasons for doing so,[60] the more significant effects of restricting the right to silence are likely to be those which are indirect. At the level of police practice, it 'encourages a reversal of the move away from reliance upon confessions as the central plank of investigative strategy . . . (I)t returns the focus to the interview room, with all the attendant dangers of oppressive questioning, false confessions, and so on.'.[61] The right to silence had become such a King Charles's head to the police that they may have underestimated the implications of its restriction. For inferences to be properly drawn from silence, the quality of police questioning needs significant improvement. If 'questioning is rambling and vague' or if officers get angry with uncooperative suspects, or 'make their disdain apparent, it may be difficult to hold any subsequent silences against the suspect.'.[62]

At the political level, police success in the long campaign against the right to silence encouraged senior officers in the mid-1990s to launch renewed and increasingly sophisticated campaigns against the 'imbalance' of the criminal justice process.[63] They sought to draw a line demarcating the problems of the past from the needs of the present and future: according to such accounts, the miscarriage cases were the result of practices and procedures replaced by PACE and, as such, an unfortunate but increasingly irrelevant diversion from current concerns.[64]

In 1993, the police lost their long exemption from the new managerialism which had swept through other public services. The familiar concerns for efficiency and effectiveness[65] coupled now with the designation of 'core functions' were deployed in a particularly unfortunate way: crime fighting was identified as the 'core business' of the police and success measured by calculating arrest, clear-up, and crime rates. Ignoring the key message of police research since the 1960s (that crime-fighting is no more than one part of a broad police mandate) and its strategic product (as reflected in attempts to implement new and more enlightened models

---

[60] See Dixon *op. cit.* (footnote 5 above), ch. 6; Leng, R, *The Right to Silence in Police Interrogation* (Royal Commission on Criminal Justice Research Study No. 10, HMSO, London, 1993).

[61] Maguire, M., 'The wrong message at the wrong time?', in Morgan, D. and Stephenson, G., (eds), *Suspicion and Silence* (Blackstone, London, 1994), p. 48.

[62] Addison, N., 'Beat the defence' (1995) 103 *Police Review* 14 April 1995 20–1, at p. 21. For a critique of police questioning, see Baldwin, J., 'Police interview techniques' (1993) 33 *British Journal of Criminology* 325.

[63] See for example Pollard, C., 'Public safety, accountability and the courts' [1996] *Criminal Law Review* 152.

[64] Maguire, M. and Norris, C., *The Conduct and Supervision of Criminal Investigations* (Royal Commission on Criminal Justice Research Study No. 5, HMSO, London, 1992) pp. 27, 38, 108–9. Post-1986 cases are ignored or explained as products of changing judicial standards: see Williamson, T., 'Police investigation: the changing criminal justice context', in Leishman, F., Loveday, B. and Savage, S.P., (eds.), *Core Issues in Policing* (Longman, London, 1996) 26–38 at p. 36.

[65] See especially, Home Office Circular 114/1983, *Manpower Effectiveness and Efficiency in the Police Service* (Home Office, London, 1983); Audit Commission, *Police Papers No. 8: Effective Policing* (HMSO, London, 1990).

of community and problem-oriented policing),[66] the 1993 White Paper on Police Reform stated bluntly that the 'main job of the police is to catch criminals'.[67] As Leishman *et al.* wryly comment:[68]

> the discovery that the search for core duties could lead to major reductions in resources appeared to concentrate police minds wonderfully. Reclaiming the 'rubbish' of social service (and other) functions frequently dismissed by the police as not 'real police work' has been one interesting consequence of the Government's review.

While the police (in a notable demonstration of their political power) managed to resist a radical managerialist redefinition of policing (as reflected in new terms of contract and disciplinary codes),[69] the episode had a significant effect in shifting discourse about policing: managerialism dovetailed with law and order politics in undermining the advances made during 1986-93.[70]

Once again, it is the indirect effects of developments which are most significant. Maguire and Norris noted potential benefits of a shift in investigative practices away from reacting to crime reports, going through the motions of investigating even hopeless cases (such as most burglaries), and relying on interrogation, towards ' "crime management' methods, based on the improvement and rationalisation of intelligence gathering and on careful analysis of intelligence and crime patterns . . . (and) more use of methods such as targeted surveillance and a greater focus on physical and documentary evidence'.[71] The danger is that, in the context of a shifting discourse about policing, crime management can merely provide new tactics to supplement traditional methods, rather than a new strategy which displaces them. For example, proactive surveillance and suspect targeting may simply feed into and strengthen interrogation as a primary investigative method. The dangers of expanding the use of informers without fundamentally reviewing investigative practice are considerable.[72] Inappropriate activities by covert investigators have attracted criticism.[73] Forensic science remains an under-funded and under-utilised resource.[74] Moreover, so long as 'the clear-up rate remains the key statistic' in assessing CID performance, pressure for quantity rather than quality in

---

[66] See Morgan, R. and Newburn, T., *The Future of Policing* (Clarendon Press, Oxford, 1997).

[67] (Cm 2281, HMSO, London) para. 2.3. Compare Audit Commission, *Helping With Enquiries: Tackling Crime Effectively* (HMSO, London, 1993).

[68] Leishman, F., Loveday, B., and Savage, S.P., (eds.), *Core Issues in Policing* (Longman, London, 1996), p. 2.

[69] See (Sheehy) Inquiry into Policing Responsibilities and Rewards, *Report* (Cm 2280, HMSO, London, 1993); Leishman, F., *et al.*, *op. cit.* (footnote 57 above), pp. 9–25; Walker, N., 'Defining core police tasks' (1996) 6 *Policing & Society* 53; Home Office, *Review of Police Core and Ancillary Tasks: Final Report* (HMSO, London, 1995).

[70] See Lacey, N., 'Missing the wood', in McConville, M., and Bridges, L., (eds.), *Criminal Justice in Crisis* (Edward Elgar, Aldershot, 1994).

[71] Maguire, M. and Norris, C., *The Conduct and Supervision of Criminal Investigations* (Royal Commission on Criminal Justice Research Study No. 5, HMSO, London, 1992) at p. 118, see also *ibid.* at pp. 28, 32, 42; Matthews, R., *Armed Robbery* (Home Office, London, 1996).

[72] See Dunnighan, C. and Norris, C., 'The detective, the snout and the Audit Commission', paper presented to the British Criminology Conference (1995); Brown, D. B. and Duffy, B., 'Privatising police verbal: the growth industry in prison informants', in Carrington, K. *et al.*, (eds.), *Travesty!* (Pluto Press, Leichhardt, 1991).

[73] Armstrong, G. and Hobbs, D.,. 'Tackled from behind', in Giulianotti, R, *et al.* (eds.), *Football, Violence and Social Identity* (Routledge, London, 1994); see also the Stagg and Hall investigations, *The Times*, 10 October 1994.

[74] See ACPO/FSS, *Using Forensic Science Effectively* (FSS, Birmingham, 1996). See further Chapter 6.

clear-ups will continue to undermine the benefits of crime management.[75] Other contemporary developments serve to focus attention on crime-fighting even more closely: organisation of a National Crime Squad and the National Criminal Intelligence Service,[76] links with Europol,[77] and new legal powers of electronic surveillance[78] will have little direct effect on the work of a sub-divisional officer. But their indirect effect on police culture may well be significant.

Judicial Control of Interrogation

An unexpectedly significant element of the story of police investigative procedures since 1986 has been the role of the courts. Judges have been much more willing than was predicted to exclude evidence and to interpret sections of PACE and the Codes in ways which constrain police activity.[79] Such judicial activism is neither consistent nor uniform, but it is significant.

For present purposes, it is appropriate to comment on just two cases. Their importance for investigative practice is that the officers involved thought that they were working within PACE,[80] but the courts disagreed, resulting in much-publicised acquittals. In *R v Paris* (the *'Cardiff Three'* case),[81] it was held that Stephen Miller's 'confession' concerning the murder of a prostitute should have been excluded as having been obtained by oppression in a 'travesty of an interview'. The Lord Chief Justice commented that he was 'horrified' by the interrogation: '[s]hort of physical violence, it is hard to conceive of a more hostile and intimidating approach by officers to a suspect'.[82] Yet the investigating officers presumably thought their tactics were unexceptionable, in that the interviews were recorded on audio-tape, Miller's solicitor sat passively through the objectionable interrogations, and, at trial, Miller's counsel did not submit crucial sections of the tapes as evidence. All seemed to have viewed it as merely business as usual, the way that the criminal justice system was accustomed to dealing with this kind of defendant (three black men from Cardiff's 'notorious' Butetown).

The *Paris* decision achieved real impact on many police officers through its application in another murder case, *Heron*.[83] (This was perhaps not unrelated to

[75] Maguire, M. and Norris, C., *The Conduct and Supervision of Criminal Investigations* (Royal Commission on Criminal Justice Research Study No. 5, HMSO, London, 1992) at p. 34. On the manipulation of clear-ups, see *ibid.*; Coleman, C. and Moynihan, J., *Understanding Crime Data* (Open University Press, Buckingham, 1996) ch. 2; Maguire, M., *et al.., Assessing Investigative Performance* (University of Wales, Cardiff, 1991); Brown, D., *Investigating Burglary* (Home Office Research Study no. 123, HMSO, London, 1991).

[76] See Police Act 1997 pts.I and II.

[77] Convention based on Article K.3 of the Treaty on European Union, on the Establishment of a European Police Office (Europol Convention) with Declarations (Cm 3050, 1995). See House of Lords Select Committee on the EC, Europol (1994–95 HL 51); Anderson, M., *et al., Policing the European Union* (Clarendon Press, Oxford, 1995).

[78] Police Act 1997, pt. III.

[79] See Feldman, D., 'Regulating treatment of suspects in police stations' [1990] *Criminal Law Review* 452–71; Dixon, *op. cit.* (footnote 5 above), pp. 169–77. See further Chapter 10.

[80] Compare *R v Canale* [1990] 2 All ER 187 (Court of Appeal excluded evidence of unrecorded interviews where police had acted in blatant disregard of PACE which they viewed as not setting appropriate procedures) and *R v Keenan* [1989] 3 WLR 1193 (Court of Appeal excluded a confession under s. 78 where no contemporaneous notes taken because police said they had never heard of the PACE code).

[81] [1993] 97 Cr App R 99 at p. 103.

[82] *Ibid.*, at p. 104 per Taylor LCJ.

[83] Unreported, Leeds Crown Court, 1993 (but see *The Guardian*, 22 November 1993 p. 2). The decision

the fact that while the victim in the former was a drug-using prostitute, in the latter the victim was a seven-year-old girl). In *Heron*, the trial judge excluded the defendant's 'confessions' as oppressive because the investigating officers misrepresented the strength of the evidence against him, repeatedly asserted his guilt, asked offensive questions about his sex life, and suggested that it was in his own interest to confess. Heron had been questioned in detention for a total of almost eight hours in five interviews over three days, during which he denied the murder some 120 times. As the Northumbria Police's report on the case commented drily, the decision 'undoubtedly came as a surprise to many of those involved in the case'.[84] Here, the principal interviewers were a detective chief inspector and a detective inspector (rather than the detective constables in the *Cardiff Three* case); again, a legal adviser (though the judge strongly criticised the fact that this was not a solicitor) had been present during audio-taped interviews and made no complaint; the tapes were 'vetted' by the Crown Prosecution Service and a psychologist acting as an 'independent assessor'; and the head of Northumbria CID insisted that '[t]hese interviews were conducted properly by police in accordance with the Police and Criminal Evidence Act'.[85]

What *Heron* starkly illustrates is the way in which electronic recording has made problematic the traditional distinction between what has been accepted as appropriate interaction between investigating officer and suspect in the privacy of the interview room and that between prosecutor and defendant in the courtroom. Electronic recording means that interrogations are available for the court to hear (and perhaps see). Procedure in the police station and at the subsequent trial can no longer be distinct.[86] Restrictions on cross-examination by prosecutors have little value if the court is presented with an audio-visual record of cross-examination and vigorous interrogation by police officers. The seemingly inevitable outcome is the (doctrinal if not practical) dominance of curial standards, at least in interrogations which are recorded. In turn, this will provide a dilemma for trial judges in choosing between the rhetoric of legality and perceived requirements of crime control, and further incentives for officers to rehearse formal 'interviews' by interrogating in the cells[87] or before reaching the station.[88]

---

in *Paris* came between George Heron's interrogation and his trial. Comments on this case also draw on the records of interview, the report of Northumbria Police's inquiry into the case, and interviews with the principal investigating officer, Detective Superintendent John Renwick, and Heron's counsel, Roger Thorn QC and Robin Patton. I am grateful to them for their assistance, but the interpretation is mine. See also Dixon *op. cit.* (footnote 5 above), pp. 172–7.

[84] Northumbria Police, *Report of an Enquiry* (Northumbria Police, Ponteland,1994) at p. 25.

[85] Detective Superintendent Barry Stewart, quoted in *The Times*, 2 November 1993, p. 3.

[86] This is so despite the Home Office's assertion that officers questioning suspects 'are not constrained by the rules applied to lawyers in court': see HO Circular 2/1992, *Principles of Investigative Interviewing.*

[87] *R v Williams, The Times*, 6 February 1992; *R v Conway* [1994] *Criminal Law Review* 838; *R v Campbell* [1995] *Criminal Law Review* 157.

[88] See Moston S.L. and Stephenson S., *The Questioning and Interviewing of Suspects outside the Police Station* (Royal Commission on Criminal Justice Research Study No. 22, HMSO, London, 1993); *Runciman Report*, ch. 3 para. 7; Fenwick, H., 'Confessions, recording rules and miscarriages of justice' [1993] Crim. L. R 174; Field, S., 'Defining interviews under PACE' (1993) 13 *Legal Studies* 254; JUSTICE, *Unreliable Evidence? Confessions and the Safety of Convictions* (London, 1994) ch. 3. For judicial views, see *R v Parchment* [1989] Crim LR 290; *R v Brezeaunu & Francis* [1989] *Criminal Law Review* 650; *R v Kingsley Brown* [1989] *Criminal Law Review* 500; *R v Maguire* [1989] *Criminal Law Review* 815; *R v Absolam* (1989) 88 Cr App R 332; *R v Manji* [1990] *Criminal Law Review* 512; *R v Cohen* [1993] *Criminal Law Review* 768; *R v Oransaye* [1993] *Criminal Law Review* 772; *R v Goddard* [1994] *Criminal Law Review* 46.

The formal Home Office and police response has been to encourage the further development of 'investigative' and 'ethical' rather than 'persuasive' interviewing.[89] There is considerable enthusiasm for these techniques, which is hardly surprising given the poor quality of 'traditional' interviewing reported by researchers.[90] However, no substantial research is yet available on the effectiveness of the 'new interviewing'.[91] While recognising the problems of 'persuasive interviewing', it must be doubted whether investigative interviewing can tackle the (admittedly rare, but significant) resistant suspect. As Simon suggests in his comment on a detective using a show of loud anger to produce a confession from a suspect who was impervious to interrogation according to the training manuals: 'science, deliberation and precision are not enough. Whether he (sic) likes it or not, a good detective eventually has to pull the trigger'.[92] This raises two problems. First, neither the courts nor the Runciman Commission gave clear and detailed guidance to the police as to what constitutes 'oppression'.[93] Investigating officers were (as the officer who carried out the subsequent inquiry into *Heron* commented) left in 'a sea of uncertainty'.[94] This lack of regulatory or judicial guidance encourages police cynicism about the justice process. Secondly, there may be a fundamental problem in using confessional evidence: the point at which interrogation could become effective in difficult cases is also the point at which its results become potentially unreliable.[95] Introducing a corroboration rule is an obvious response, but experience elsewhere must qualify expectations about its potential impact.[96]

Conclusions

These concluding comments raise some more general issues relevant to future discussions of the link between investigative procedures and miscarriages of justice.

Efficiency and Justice

For those concerned about miscarriages of justice, current trends in policing give cause for considerable disquiet. One significant response is to argue that 'efficiency' in criminal justice cannot be defined merely in managerialist, economic terms. The provision of justice should be fundamental to such a definition. But justice must refer to more than individualistic, civil libertarian concerns for those

---

[89] See Home Office Central Planning and Training Unit, *The Interviewer's Rule Book* (1992), Home Office Central Planning and Training Unit, *A Guide to Interviewing* (1992); Home Office Circular 7/1993, 'Investigative interviewing'; Williamson, T., 'Investigative interviewing' (1992) 8 *Policing* 280; Williamson, T., 'From interrogation to investigative interviewing' (1993) 3 *Journal of Community & Applied Social Psychology* 89; Mortimer, A., 'Asking the right questions' (1994) 10 *Policing* 111.

[90] See *Runciman Report*, ch. 2 para. 23; Baldwin, *op. cit.* footnote 62 above.

[91] Compare McGurk, B. *et al.*, *Investigative Interviewing Courses for Police Officers* (Police Research Series Paper 4, Home Office, London, 1993).

[92] Simon, D., *Homicide* (Houghton Mifflin, Boston, 1991) at p. 558.

[93] But see *R v Fulling* [1987] 2 WLR 923; *R v Davison* [1988] *Criminal Law Review* 442; *R v Glaves* [1993] *Criminal Law Review* 685; *R v Paris* (1993) 97 Cr App R 99.

[94] Northumbria Police, *op. cit* (footnote 84 above), p. 9. The phrase is Professor John Baldwin's.

[95] See Gudjonsson, G., *The Psychology of Interrogations, Confessions and Testimony* (John Wiley, Chichester, 1992); JUSTICE, *Unreliable Evidence? Confessions and the Safety of Convictions* (London, 1994).

[96] McConville, M., *Corroboration and Confessions* (Royal Commission on Criminal Justice Research Study No. 13, HMSO, London, 1993). See further Chapter 16.

wrongly convicted. A developed conception of justice also includes concern that the guilty should be punished.[97] If failure to provide suspects with substantial rights leads to a wrongful conviction, then those really guilty escape justice (usually for ever, because the investigation has been misdirected for so long). This failure to appreciate 'the double-sided nature of miscarriages of justice . . . serves to perpetuate a . . . misleading dichotomy between ''soft'' and ''tough'' measures, between effective crime control and civil liberties'.[98] This needs elaboration which is not possible here, because it can degenerate into simplistic crime control rhetoric.[99] This is not inevitable, and it is particularly important to strengthen the toehold which PACE helped to create in police cultures for the view that police work can be done more efficiently within rules which, *inter alia*, provide suspects with substantial safeguards.

New Policing

Like much research and comment, this chapter has focused on detention and questioning. This is justifiable given interrogation's instrumental and ideological significance in police investigations. However, other methods of investigation (such as forensic science, electronic surveillance, and identification procedures) need more empirical study.

More is involved than a broadening of the empirical focus to cover a variety of investigative tactics. Some developments in investigative activity are part of changes noted above towards proactive, intelligence-led policing. However, such changes must in turn be put into broader contexts. Commentators increasingly identify fundamental shifts in the criminal process which include the growth of informalism and diversion, the decline of adversary justice, blurring of boundaries between criminal justice and other agencies and techniques of control, the growth of private security, and the demotion of individualistic concepts of guilt, responsibility and desert in favour of 'techniques for identifying, classifying and managing groups assorted by levels of dangerousness'.[100] From this perspective, intensive use of informants and of human and electronic surveillance expresses fundamental shifts in social relations which have blurred the boundaries between private and public. Such accounts run the risk of exaggerating the pace and uniformity of change. Nonetheless, it is increasingly clear that the relatively simple concept of criminal process which has informed previous analyses of miscarriage of justice needs to be replaced by one which recognizes its changing, multi-faceted and multi-functional character.

---

[97] This assumes that a crime has been committed, which will not always be so, as in the cases of the Ananda Marga (see Carrington, K. *et al.*, *Travesty!* (Pluto Press, Leichhardt, 1991)) and Errol Madden (details of the latter are in *R v Police Complaints Board, ex parte Madden* [1983] 2 All ER 353 at 365).

[98] Hogg, R., 'Law and order and the fallibility of the justice system', in Brown, D.B. *et al.*, *Criminal Laws* (Federation, Annandale, NSW, 1996) 309 at p. 314.

[99] See criticism of the Runciman Commission by Lacey, N., 'Missing the wood', in McConville, M., and Bridges, L., (eds.), *Criminal Justice in Crisis* (Edward Elgar, Aldershot, 1994), p. 33. Such elaboration would connect with critiques of 'balance' metaphors: see Ashworth, A., *The Criminal Process* (2nd ed., Clarendon Press, Oxford 1998); Jackson, J.D., 'Getting criminal justice out of balance' in Livingstone, S. and Morison, J., (eds.), *Law, Society and Change* (Dartmouth, Aldershot, 1990); Dixon, *op. cit.* (footnote 5 above), pp. 283–5.

[100] Feeley, M. and Simon, J., 'Actuarial justice', in Nelken, D., (ed.), *The Futures of Criminology* (Sage, London, 1994) 173–201, at p. 173. See also Dixon, D., 'Criminal law and policing in sociological perspective' in Tomasic, R., (ed.), *The Sociology of Law* (Sage, London, forthcoming).

Case Theories and Changing Investigative Practice

If any one factor in investigative practice had to be nominated as most responsible for leading to miscarriages, it would have to be the tendency for investigators to commit themselves to belief in a suspect's guilt in a way which blinds them to other possibilities.[101] 'Case theories'[102] are inevitable in any system, adversarial or inquisitorial: police officers will always have to make significant decisions before a prosecutor or other external body has an opportunity to assess the investigation. As Greer suggests:[103]

> . . . no criminal justice system could function without them. The dangers stem instead from the highly charged atmosphere surrounding the investigation, the haste with which the theory has been formed and the tenacity with which the police have clung to their original view in spite of strong countervailing evidence.

A key issue is how investigative practice can be changed in order to prevent case theories leading investigations astray. Irving and Dunningham suggest that this would require improving the quality of officers' reasoning and decision-making by challenging the occupational 'common sense' about criminals and crimes and the detective craft's 'working rules about causation, about suspicion and guilt, about patterns of behaviour and behavioural signatures . . . [which] are passed from experienced to inexperienced officers'.[104] Better supervision and training are the obvious tools. Lessons for everyday investigative practice may be learnt from major inquiry systems by adapting procedures ensuring transparency, systematic cross-checking, and peer review. Active, skilful supervision which sets the 'ethos' of the unit could put 'as much emphasis . . . upon ensuring procedural and legal compliance as upon securing results'.[105] This would promote conditions from which miscarriages are less likely to emerge. However, the effectiveness of specific reforms in supervision and training depends upon a broader change in policing.[106] Chan's work is particularly valuable here in replacing the usual clichés about police culture with a theoretically sophisticated account of police culture as constituted by the interaction between the legal and political contexts of policing and police organisational knowledge. This informs her account of the possibilities and limits of police reform.[107]

---

[101] Sedley, S., 'Whose Justice?' (1993) *London Review of Books* 23 Sept. 1993 5 at p. 6.

[102] See McConville, M., Sanders, A. and Leng, R., *The Case for the Prosecution* (Routledge, London, 1991); McConville, M., 'Weaknesses in the British judicial system' *Times Higher Education Supplement*, 3 November 1989; Irving, B. and Dunnighan, C., *Human factors in the quality control of CID investigations and a brief review of relevant police training* (Royal Commission on Criminal Justice Research Study No. 21, HMSO, London, 1993) at p. 10.

[103] Greer, S., 'Miscarriages of criminal justice reconsidered' (1994) 57 *Modern Law Review* 58 at p. 71.

[104] Irving, B. and Dunnighan, C., *Human factors in the quality control of CID investigations and a brief review of relevant police training* (Royal Commission on Criminal Justice Research Study No. 21, HMSO, London, 1993) at p. 17.

[105] Maguire, M. and Norris, C., *The Conduct and Supervision of Criminal Investigations* (Royal Commission on Criminal Justice Research Study No. 5, HMSO, London, 1992) at p. 115; Stockdale, J.E., *Management and Supervision of Police Interviews* (Police Research Series No. 5, Home Office, London, 1993); Baldwin, J. and Moloney, T., *Supervision of Police Investigation in Serious Criminal Cases* (Royal Commission Research Study No. 4, HMSO, London, 1992).

[106] Maguire, M. and Norris, C., 'Police investigations: practice and malpractice' (1994) 21 *Journal of Law & Society* 72 at p. 81.

[107] Chan, J., *Changing Police Culture* (Cambridge University Press, Melbourne, 1997).

Everyday (In)justice

Even a superficial reading of literature in criminal justice over the last two decades would make clear the inadequacy of focusing only on 'serious' cases which go to trial in the Crown Court. The starting point for analysis is recognition that the mass of criminal justice is administered by police and magistrates, that the process is structured around guilty pleas, and that pressures for the expansion of summary justice and the encouragement of guilty pleas are characteristic of the trends towards 'technocratic' or 'actuarial' justice noted above (and which the Runciman Commission's recommendations hasten). The scale of the injustice done to individuals in the publicised miscarriage cases has drawn attention away from the potential for injustice in 'everyday', 'minor' matters: the Runciman Commission largely took for granted the probity of summary justice and ignored the possibility of miscarriage in its realm.[108] Lack of appeal or public complaint hardly justifies the sociologically and politically naïve assertion that the 'great majority of criminal trials are conducted in a manner which all participants regard as fair'.[109] In everyday criminal justice, there may be more room for mistakes and malpractice: the 'sheer volume of cases' and police attitudes towards suspects 'tends to place their rights and welfare low on the list of police priorities',[110] and there is 'little time for thorough checking of evidence, and where solicitors are less often present at interviews than in major cases'.[111]

A related issue is the need to focus more closely upon the diversity of suspects, rather than on the one-dimensional figure of the 'normal' (male, adult, mentally competent) suspect which inquiries typically take for granted.[112] PACE safeguards for young people, the mentally ill, and the intellectually disabled continue to be problematic.[113] The Runciman Commission paid insufficient attention to the damning findings of its own research studies on the problems experienced by intellectually disabled suspects and on how young people are treated during police investigations.[114] As regards the latter, as Evans points out, there is not even the notional possibility of most such cases being inspected by a court because they are dealt with by caution: diversion, another central feature of the new criminal justice, was overlooked by a Commission fixated on trials for serious offences.[115]

The conclusion of this account is ambivalent. On one hand, there is evidence that police investigative practices and procedures developed after PACE's implementation in ways which should have somewhat reduced the potential for

---

[108] *Runciman Report*, ch. 1 para. 7.

[109] *Runciman Report*, ch. 1 para. 23.

[110] Maguire, M. and Norris, C., 'Police investigations: practice and malpractice' (1994) 21 *Journal of Law & Society* 72 at p. 10, compare at p. 62.

[111] *Ibid.* at p. 99.

[112] For example, the Runciman Commission delegated responsibility for considering vulnerable suspects to a Home Office working party: ch. 3 para. 86.

[113] See Irving, B. and McKenzie, I., *Police Interrogation* (Police Foundation, London, 1989) pp. 219–34; Dixon, D., 'Juvenile suspects and the Police and Criminal Evidence Act' in Freestone, D.A.C., (ed.), *Children and the Law* (Hull University Press, Hull, 1990) 107–29.

[114] Evans, R., *The Conduct of Police Interviews with Juveniles* (Royal Commission on Criminal Justice Research Study No. 8, HMSO, London, 1992); Gudjonsson, G. *et al.*, *Persons at Risk During Interviews in Police Custody* (Royal Commission on Criminal Justice Research Study No. 12, HMSO, London, 1992).

[115] Evans, R., 'Police interrogations and the Royal Commission on Criminal Justice' (1994) 4 *Policing and Society* 73.

miscarriages. On the other hand, more recent trends in the political environment of policing and in the character of criminal justice provide considerable grounds for concern. Those concerned about miscarriages of justice now face an increasingly powerful and confident police leadership, and a series of new challenges as investigative practice develops new techniques and tactics. For all the talk of a 'crisis in criminal justice', the Home Office, police and courts have continued to display remarkable equanimity and complacency.[116] This is not conducive to fundamental reform of police investigative practices: without such reform, miscarriages of justice will recur.

---

[116] Sections of the media, ignored by the Runciman Commission, have contributed significantly. The *Daily Telegraph* greeted the release of the *Bridgewater Three* as demonstrating a distinctively British ability to 'own up' to 'mistakes' ('human nature being fallible, no system can guarantee absolute justice') and to take remedial measures: 'In many countries there would be an insuperable reluctance to admit that the state had been in error; not in Britain . . . That should be cause for reassurance and quiet pride.' (*Weekly Telegraph*, 26 February 1997). 'Whispering campaigns' about the 'real guilt' of the *Guildford Four* and others have also played their part: see Bennett, R., 'Criminal justice' *London Review of Books* 24 June 1993, 3–15. See further Chapter 13.

4

The Right to Legal Advice

Andrew Sanders and Lee Bridges

Introduction

Prior to the Police and Criminal Evidence Act 1984 ('PACE'), access to legal advice was allowed by the quasi-legal Judges' Rules only provided that 'no unreasonable delay or hindrance' be thereby suffered by the police.[1] This gave the police considerable latitude for which they were rarely called to account. There are no reliable figures for the numbers of suspects requesting or receiving advice before 1984, but Softley found that only seven per cent of suspects requested advice in the late 1970s in his study of four police stations.[2] Nearly one in five requests was refused by the police. The Judges' Rules also provided that all suspects should 'be informed orally of the rights and facilities available to them'. However, in Softley's study all suspects were informed of their rights in only one station. In that station the request rate was three times higher than in the other three. So, when the police informed suspects of their rights, the request rate rose, but the police could not be relied upon to do this. More commonly, the police often broke and 'bent' the law (both on informing suspects of their rights and on allowing access when it was requested). In this chapter we will be concerned with the changes under PACE which superseded the Judges' Rules and how effective those changes have been.

Exercising the Right

The Effect of PACE on Request Rates

PACE, section 58(1) provides that 'A person arrested and held in custody . . . shall be entitled, if he so requests, to consult a solicitor privately at any time.'[3] Section 58(6) and (8) allow the police to delay access, rather than to deny it, and to do so

---

[1] Home Office, *Judges' Rules and Administrative Directions to the Police* (HO Circular 89/1978, HMSO, London, 1978).

[2] Softley, P., *Police Interrogation: An Observational Study in Four Police Stations: Royal Commission on Criminal Procedure Research Study No 4* (HMSO, London, 1981).

[3] These statutory rights do not entirely supplant common law rights: *R v Chief Constable of South Wales, ex parte* Merrick [1994] 1 WLR 663.

only in very restricted circumstances. Further, PACE Code C, the Code of Practice for the Detention, Treatment and Questioning of Persons by the Police ('COP') obliges the police to inform suspects of their rights.[4] This is done orally by a custody officer and by a written notice. Apart from the fact that there is no specific remedy or enforcement mechanism for ensuring compliance with these provisions,[5] there is now, for the first time, an absolute right to legal advice and to be informed of that right. Moreover, section 59 (as amended by the Legal Aid Act 1988, schedule 6) provides for free legal aid for suspects, enabling duty solicitor schemes to be established. Many more suspects are now able to see solicitors than were able to do so prior to PACE.

In addition to the right to advice in section 58, there are important new rights to consult the COP itself,[6] to have someone informed of one's arrest[7] and to speak to a relative or friend on the telephone.[8] All these rules apply to every arrested person, regardless of age or suspected offence (and extra protections are provided for juveniles and other vulnerable individuals), with two exceptions. The first is a suspect who is 'incapable . . . of understanding what is said to him or is violent or likely to become violent'.[9] The second is that rights are severely curtailed in respect of suspects detained under the Prevention of Terrorism (Temporary Provisions) Act 1989.[10] Until recently, access has been delayed in many cases, as have requests to have friends or family members informed of arrests. Frequently, no reason is given for this[11] Since this is covered in Chapter 14 we will not discuss it further here. It is worth observing, however, that these categories of suspect remain as vulnerable as all suspects were in the 1970s and early 1980s.

Since there are no national data on arrests and requests for advice, we have to rely on research studies of particular police stations for a picture of the working of these rights. In research carried out soon after PACE was introduced, Brown found that, on average, around 25 per cent of all suspects requested advice, and that around 21 per cent secured it (although only 17.5 per cent did so prior to charge).[12] In subsequent research, in which we observed the processing of suspects and interviewed officers, solicitors, and suspects, in 10 police stations for 45 days each throughout 1988, we secured similar results.[13] However, as a result of this research, the Code of Practice was revised in 1991.[14] Many of the rights of suspects

---

[4] Home Office, *Codes of Practice, Code C* (HO Circular 13/1995, HMSO, London, 1995) para. 3.1. This is the third revision of the Codes which first came into operation in 1986. See further, Brown, D., Ellis, T. and Larcombe, K., *Changing the Code – Police Detention under the Revised PACE Codes of Practice* (Home Office Research Study 129, HMSO, London, 1993).

[5] Sanders, A., 'Rights, Remedies and the PACE Act' [1988] *Criminal Law Review* 802.

[6] Home Office, *Codes of Practice, Code C* (HO Circular 13/1995, HMSO, London, 1995) para. 1.2.

[7] Home Office, *Codes of Practice, Code C* (HO Circular 13/1995, HMSO, London, 1995) para. 3.1.

[8] PACE, s.56. See Bottomley, K. *et al.*, 'The detention of suspects in police custody' (1991) 31 *British Journal of Criminology* 347.

[9] Home Office, *Codes of Practice, Code C* (HO Circular 13/1995, HMSO, London, 1995) para. 1.8.

[10] See especially Brown, D., *Detention under the PTA 1989* (Home Office Research and Planning Unit 75, HMSO, London, 1993).

[11] Brown, D., *PACE Ten Years On: A Review of the Research* (Home Office Research Study 155, HMSO, London, 1997) pp 84–5.

[12] Brown, D., *Detention at the Police Station under the PACE Act 1984* (Home Office Research Study No. 104, HMSO, London, 1989).

[13] Sanders, A., Bridges L., Mulvaney, A. and Crozier, G., *Advice and Assistance at Police Stations and the 24 Hour Solicitor Scheme,* (Lord Chancellor's Department, London, 1989).

[14] See Home Office, *Police and Criminal Evidence Act 1984: Revised Codes of Practice A-D* (HO Circular 15/1991, HMSO, London).

were clarified, and the obligations on the police to inform them of their rights were increased. The result of this, and perhaps of a general increase in knowledge of one's rights,[15] has led to significant increases in request rates. Brown et al.'s study in 1991 found a request rate in twelve stations of 32 per cent on average,[16] while a further study by Phillips and Brown in 1993–4 of ten stations found an average request rate of 38 per cent.[17]

It is interesting to see that all of these research studies have found great variations between police stations. Phillips and Brown, for instance, found that in the 'worst' police station the request rate was 22 per cent, while in the 'best' it was over twice as high, at 50 per cent. Some of these differences can be explained by reference to the type of offence (request rates are higher for more serious offences) and alleged offender (ethnic minority suspects and adults request advice more often than do white suspects and juveniles). Some can be explained by the behaviour of the police officers in those stations and the lawyers servicing them. But much remains inexplicable. Although a 38 per cent request rate represents a dramatic increase over the pre-PACE situation, nearly two out of three suspects still appear to be refusing a free gift, and a further 6–8 per cent who accept the offer fail to receive it in time or do not receive it at all.

Out of the 103 suspects interviewed by Sanders et al., 60 said that they knew that they had a right to legal advice, and only two said that they did not. However, 14 of the 60 (23.3 per cent) only knew this because the police had told them, and 12 out of 38 (31.6 per cent) still remained ignorant that the service was free.[18] It is clearly still important that suspects be given all relevant information by the police if they are to make informed decisions. Although, as we saw above, the general level of awareness of rights has increased since 1988, Brown et al. found in 1991 that the police gave suspects more information than they were routinely given in 1988. However, over one quarter were not told that the advice was free and that it was a continuing right, and nearly half were not told that advice could be given in private.

Factors Influencing Request Rates

Little is known about how suspects decide whether or not to request advice. Sanders et al. found that many suspects declined advice because of the triviality of their offences. They may not have done so had they realised that it would be free. In their words:

> Something like drunk and disorderly is not really worth it because you don't get legal aid for things like that.
> It's not a serious offence anyway . . . not worth seeking advice and spending money for in my opinion.

---

[15] Brown, D., PACE Ten Years On: A Review of the Research (Home Office Research Study 155, HMSO, London, 1997) pp. 94–5.

[16] Brown, D. et al., Changing the Code – Police Detention under the revised PACE Codes of Practice (Home Office Research Study 129, HMSO, London, 1992).

[17] Phillips, C. and Brown, D., Entry into the Criminal Justice System (Home Office, Research Study 185, HMSO, London, 1998).

[18] The numbers do not 'add up' because in a large number of interviews no comprehensive responses could be secured.

. . . I work and I'd have to pay for a solicitor.

Notwithstanding the above concern, many suspects would not have wanted a solicitor under any circumstances. Some are too fatalistic, while others are remarkably confident. Here are some typical responses:

There was nothing to hide.'
I think they [the police] have been very good to me and I'm quite happy.
I don't see the point . . . I was going to admit to it.
I knew what I was going to tell them . . . I was involved but I didn't put it into his face. They [the police] were trying to tell me that I had stuck it into his face. *Q.* Do you think a solicitor could have helped? *A.* No. *Q.* Did you actually admit the offence? *A.* They sort of put words into my mouth.

As some of these examples indicate, confidence (or, indeed, fatalism) may sometimes be misplaced. Many suspects are unaware of how helpful a solicitor could be in ensuring that their stories are told properly.

For some suspects it is not that legal help is unwelcome in principle, rather, that solicitors as such are disliked and distrusted: 'They [solicitors] are a waste of time . . . most are there just to earn their money.'. Some suspects differentiate duty solicitors from their own solicitors. As we shall see, there is some basis in fact for this view, and the following suspects capture the feelings of many:

Q. Would you ask for a duty solicitor again? *A.* No, I'd ask for my own. *Q.* Why? *A.* Because he weren't no bloody good!
. . . I told my mother to get me one . . . When I was arrested before, the police put their own man in . . . and he acted like a policeman.

Perhaps the most important influence on suspects is the time factor. Suspects who believed that a solicitor would shorten their time in custody (for example, by securing bail) usually asked for one, while those who believed the opposite (perhaps because they would have to wait for one to arrive) usually did not:

Detainee 1: Is it going to take time to get one [a solicitor]?
Officer: . . . I haven't got one in the cupboard . . . I'll call one . . .
Detainee 2: I'll have one when I'm charged . . .
Officer: I asked you if you wanted a solicitor.
Detainee 2: It depends how long I'm in here . . .
Detainee 3: One thing that put me off seeing a solicitor is that I would have been longer here.

One suspect wrote on the custody record, 'I agree to be interviewed without the presence of a solicitor only on provision that I am released a.s.a.p.'. Needless to say, she was not. It follows from this evidence that suspects who do ask for solicitors usually do so if they are scared of the police, afraid of being detained overnight, or if they recognise specific problems with which they need immediate help. Only occasionally do suspects (usually the more experienced ones) ask for advice simply because it is free or in an attempt to obstruct the police. Some suspects are so indecisive that they seek advice from the police on whether they should seek advice!

The conundrum, then, is this: why are fewer than four out of ten suspects afraid of being unaided? Why are over half of suspects so trusting of the police, distrustful of solicitors or confident of their own abilities, when objectively so many could benefit from advice? The answer lies, in part, with the police: as we shall see, they often play on fears about delay and cost. It also lies with solicitors: many do take time to arrive or do not arrive at all, and others simply 'advise' suspects to confess. But most important of all is a joint message from both: that what happens in the station is really not that important, and court is where guilt and innocence is decided. This is far from the truth, as the centrality of 'confession evidence' in the recent miscarriage cases shows. But it suits the police, the legal profession, and the State to maintain this false ideology.[19]

The Responses of the Police

Under PACE, access to a solicitor is not automatic. It has to be positively requested by the suspect. This requires the negotiation of several obstacles. First, suspects need to know their rights. Secondly, they need to make and then maintain their requests unambiguously in the face of possible police obstruction. Thirdly, they need the police to act on those requests by actually contacting a solicitor. We saw earlier that the COP requires the police to tell suspects about all of their several rights – not only that they can see a solicitor, but that the advice will be free, given in private, that it is a continuing right, and so forth. This has to be done orally and in the form of a written notice. As a safeguard, suspects are asked to sign the custody record to confirm that the police have complied. The overwhelming majority do so. As we have seen, though, this does not guarantee that a suspect has been informed of *all* of his or her rights. The custody record does not require a signature to verify each right separately, and it does not specify what these rights are. Only suspects with prior knowledge, or who read and take in the written information given to them by the police, will realise if they have been informed of only some of their rights. Moreover, Sanders *et al.* found that some suspects were told to 'sign here, here and here' without being told their rights orally at all and without being given the written information. Brown *et al.*, in research carried out to evaluate the impact of the revisions to the Code of Practice which were aimed at eliminating these malpractices, found the same in relation to the written, but not oral information.[20] The numbers are small, but as Brown points out '. . . the presence of the detainee's signature is not itself a guarantee that a written notice of rights was in fact given.'.[21] We suggest that it is also no guarantee that

---

[19] McConville, M., Sanders, A. and Leng, E., *The Case for the Prosecution* (Routledge, London, 1991); McConville, M., Hodgson, J., Bridges, L. and Pavlovic, A. *Studying Accused: The Organization and Practices of Criminal Defence Courses in Britain* (Clarendon Press, Oxford, 1994).

[20] Brown, D. *et al.*, *Changing the Code – Police Detention under the revised PACE Codes of Practice* (Home Office Research Study 129, HMSO, London, 1992). This study, and that by Sanders *et al.*, (Sanders, A., Bridges L., Mulvaney, A., Crozier, G., *Advice and Assistance at Police Stations and the 24 Hour Solicitor Scheme*, (Lord Chancellor's Department, London, 1989)), observed the processing of suspects following arrest and compared what the police actually did with what their records claimed they did. There is, of course, the danger that the police modified their practices when they were observed.

[21] Brown, D., *PACE Ten Years On: A Review of the Research* (Home Office Research Study 155,

suspects were orally informed of their rights, though Brown appears to believe that this is very rare indeed. There are two important issues here. First, as we have seen, failure to notify suspects of their rights (or to do so completely) makes it less likely that those rights will be asserted. Secondly, the level of unlawful failure to notify suspects of their rights is higher in reality than custody records reveal. In other words, the police sometimes either falsify or wrongly complete custody records, making it appear that they are more law-abiding than they really are. Sanders *et al.* found that, rather than breaching COP in 2.9 per cent of cases (according to custody records), the police actually breached it in 10.5 per cent of cases.

Police Ploys: the Initial Impact of PACE

It would be misleading simply to concentrate on formal compliance. Being *informed* of one's rights is not the same as *understanding* those rights. For example, the written information given to suspects is too complicated for most suspects with a lower than average IQ to understand.[22] Furthermore, Sanders *et al.* found that the oral provision of information by custody officers was often too garbled and/or hurried to be understood. Among various 'ploys' used by the police to dissuade suspects from seeking advice, the incomplete or incomprehensible reading of rights were the most common, but there are many others, such as statements like:

It's not a very serious charge
You'll have to wait in the cells until the solicitor gets here
We won't be able to get a solicitor at this time/none of them will come out/he won't be in his office.

Altogether, Sanders *et al.* observed one or more ploys being used in 41.4 per cent of cases, and two or more in 9.3 per cent.

Not only do ploys obstruct suspects' understanding of their rights (misleading suspects as to the cost of advice being another example), but they are also designed to dissuade suspects from making requests and to persuade them to cancel such requests as have been made. Being told to 'sign here, here and here', for instance, is difficult to resist even when one knows one may be signing away one's rights. Moreover, some ploys, such as being told they will have to wait, reinforce the negative aspects of seeking advice. Others, by reassurance, bolster the naïve feeling of confidence possessed by many suspects (telling suspects that they can have a solicitor later even though the police rarely repeat the offer later).

These ploys have not been perceived as being so Machiavellian by all researchers.[23] Others see 'ploys' as simply the provision of information (the likely delay in securing a solicitor, for instance). At one level we would not disagree. And as we observed earlier, the police cannot be faulted for engaging in discussion when so many suspects ask for their advice! The problem is the information which

HMSO, London, 1997) p. 77.

[22] Clare, I. and Gudjonsson, G., *Devising and piloting an experimental version of the notice to detained persons* (Royal Commission on Criminal Justice Research Study No. 7, HMSO, London, 1993).

[23] Morgan, R., Reiner, R. and McKenzie, I., *Report to ESRC: A Study of the Work of Custody Officers* (unpublished); Dixon, D., Bottomley, K., Coleman, C., Gill, M. and Wall, D., 'Safeguarding the rights of suspects in police custody' (1990) 1 *Policing and Society* 2.

is *not* provided by the police. Suspects are *not* told that they will spend hours in the cells awaiting interview regardless of whether or not they request advice. Suspects are *not* told that telephone advice can be secured with virtually no delay at all. Suspects are *not* told that a solicitor is far more useful in the station than in the court. Inarticulate, confused and indecisive suspects are not assumed to want,

Table 4.1: Types of police ploys

Ploy	Frequency of use (principal ploy only) %
1. Rights told too quickly/incomprehensibly/incompletely	142 (42.9%)
2. Suspect query answered unhelpfully/incorrectly	5 (1.5%)
3. Inability of suspect to name own solicitor	2 (0.6%)
4. 'It's not a very serious charge'	1 (0.3%)
5. 'You'll have to wait in the cells until the solicitor gets here'	13 (3.9%)
6. 'You don't have to make up your mind now. You can have one later if you want to'	27 (8.2%)
7. 'You're only going to be here a short time'	25 (7.6%)
8. 'You're only here to be charged/interviewed'	14 (4.2%)
9. (To juvenile) 'You'll have to [or 'do you want to'] wait until an adult gets here'	18 (5.4%)
10. (To adult) ['Juvenile] has said he doesn't want one'	8 (2.4%)
11. Combination of 9 and 10	4 (1.2%)
12. 'We won't be able to get a solicitor at this time/none of them will come out/he won't be in his office'	6 (1.8%)
13. 'You don't need one for this type of offence'	2 (0.6%)
14. 'Sign here, here and here' (no information given)	7 (2.1%)
15. 'You don't have to have one'	4 (1.2%)
16. 'You're being transferred to another station – wait until you get there'	6 (1.8%)
17. Custody officer interprets indecision/silence as refusal	9 (2.7%)
18. 'You're not going to be interviewed/charged'	1 (0.3%)
19. 'You can go and see a solicitor when you get out/at court'	9 (2.7%)
20. 'You're (probably) going to get bail'	6 (1.8%)
21. Gives suspects Solicitors' Directory or list of solicitors without explanation/assistance	3 (0.9%)
22. Other	19 (5.7%)
Total	331 (100.0%)

or told that they should seek, advice. This is not necessarily a criticism of the police, for the COP does not require them to tell suspects these things.

On closer inspection, Dixon *et al.* found police practices similar to those we observed, although they did not attempt to quantify them. Morgan *et al.* found 'active discouragement, leading questions or incomplete statement of rights . . . in about 14 per cent of observed cases'.[24] In the 'overwhelming majority of cases', they say, rights are stated in a way that anyone in a reasonable state of mind would comprehend. But they concede that 'few suspects are in a "reasonable" frame of mind at the time. There is usually no attempt to make sure the statement has been understood'.[25] Behind the different emphasis of other researchers there is, then, no fundamental disagreement: in many cases – perhaps the majority – the police allow suspects who are unsure of their rights to remain unsure.

Sanders *et al.* found little correlation between the use of just one ploy and requests for advice. However, when police officers have a particular interest in preventing or delaying access, they tend to use several ploys together to discourage a request or, if a request has already been made, to secure cancellation or a waiver of the suspect's right to delay interrogation until the solicitor's arrival. There was a strong correlation between the use of multiple ploys and failures to request/ cancellations/waivers. The point was made earlier that police behaviour may have been modified when under observation. Some suspects who initially insisted on seeing a solicitor were hustled out of sight of researchers, only to be returned a few minutes later with a new willingness to waive their rights!

Lastly, in a small but significant number of cases the police fail to record requests (for instance by crossing out the wrong line on the custody record) and fail to secure legal advice when requested and recorded. Now that outright refusal of access is unlawful, and delay under section 58(6) and (8) is restricted to exceptional circumstances (3 per cent of requests or fewer), it seems that the police resort to less overt, but equally effective, denials of access.[26]

Attempts to Curb the Influence of the Police

Since the research discussed above was completed, the COP has been revised twice.[27] Several ploys are now outlawed. For instance, rights must be read 'clearly' and must include the fact that advice is free;[28] the written information provided also now includes this fact;[29] the custody officer is responsible for ensuring that suspects sign 'in the correct place'[30] and he 'must act without delay to secure the provision' of advice when requested;[31] and the right of juveniles and other vulnerable suspects to advice prior to the arrival of an 'appropriate adult' has been clarified.[32]

---

[24] Morgan, R. *et al.*, *Report to ESRC: A Study of the Work of Custody Officers* (unpublished), p. 22.

[25] *Ibid.*, p. 23.

[26] See, for details, Sanders, A., Bridges L., Mulvaney, A. and Crozier, G., *Advice and Assistance at Police Stations and the 24 Hour Solicitor Scheme,* (Lord Chancellor's Department, London, 1989). Also see Maguire, M., 'Effects of the PACE provisions on detention and questioning' (1988) 28 *British Journal of Criminology* 19.

[27] Home Office, *Police and Criminal Evidence Act 1984: Revised Codes of Practice A–D* (HO Circular 15/1991, HMSO, London); Home Office, *Codes of Practice* (HO Circular 13/1995, HMSO, London, 1995). See further Ede, R., 'New improved PACE' (1995) 139 *Solicitors' Journal* 298; Wolchover, D. and Heaton-Armstrong, A., 'Questioning and identification: changes under PACE 95' [1995] *Criminal Law Review* 356.

[28] Home Office, *Codes of Practice*, Code C (HO Circular 13/1995, HMSO, London, 1995) para. 3.1.

[29] *Ibid.*, para. 3.2.

[30] *Ibid.*, para. 3.5.

[31] *Ibid.*, para. 6.5.

[32] *Ibid.*, note 3G.

It is one thing to say what the police should, and should not, do. Ensuring that they comply with the rules is, as we have seen, another matter. It cannot be denied that the proportion of suspects requesting and securing advice has risen considerably. On the other hand, more recent research has found that the way in which the police present information is still unclear or discouraging. Brown *et al.* found 'inadequacies' in 16 per cent of cases just before the COP was revised in 1991, but in around 25 per cent afterwards. In around 28 per cent of cases prior to the 1991 revisions, and 35 per cent afterwards, suspects may have been influenced against seeking advice by the police.[33] Although it appears that standards of police behaviour declined, this trend really reflects an inadequate response on the part of custody officers to the increased obligations placed on them by the revised COP. Understandable though this is, it shows that both the letter and spirit of the law will always be breached by the police in a significant minority of cases.

Even if the police had complied both in letter and spirit with the COP, two basic problems would remain. One is that there are non-monetary costs attached to seeking advice (in person, at any rate – see later). The other is that the presumption in PACE, the COP and in actual police behaviour is against having advice. If PACE required a positive decision to refuse advice, the take-up rate would probably rise still further.

It is not our belief that the police discourage access in all (or even most) cases. Thus it is not surprising that the changes to COP influenced police behaviour at the margins. However, when the police strongly wish to confront suspects on their own, they have many opportunities to do so – before a request is made, before the solicitor arrives, and between interrogations. In addition, 'informal' interviewing – uncontrolled interrogation outside the surveillance of tape recorders – still goes on.[34] The revised COP attempts to restrict it but affords several loopholes for the police. Also, when the police do behave improperly, if the suspect's solicitor finds out about the wrongdoing, s/he rarely tackles the police. There are rarely adverse repercussions for officers who evade the COP.[35] The small number of cases where this happens may make little statistical impact on rates of access, but if miscarriages arise from the police's determination from the moment of initial detention to secure incriminating statements from selected suspects in major crimes, clearly the current arrangements for access will not stop this. It is worth remembering that none of the suspects in the *Birmingham, Guildford or Tottenham* cases, and very few in the *West Midlands Serious Crime Squad* cases,[36] were allowed initially to see a solicitor.

---

[33] Brown, D. *et al.*, *Changing the Code–Police Detention under the revised PACE Codes of Practice* (Home Office Research Study 129, HMSO, London, 1992).

[34] See Kaye, T., *Unsafe and Unsatisfactory? Report of the Independent Inquiry into the Working Practices of the West Midlands Police Serious Crime Squad* (Civil Liberties Trust, London, 1991). Also see Evans, R. and Ferguson, T., *Comparing Different Juvenile Cautioning Systems in One Police Force Area* (Research and Planning Unit, Home Office, 1991); McConville, M., Sanders, A. and Leng, E., *The Case for the Prosecution* (Routledge, London, 1991); McConville, M., Hodgson, J., Bridges, L. and Pavlovic, A., *Standing Accused: The Organization and Practices of Criminal Defence Lawyers in Britain* (Clarendon Press, Oxford, 1994); Sanders, A., Bridges L., Mulvaney, A. and Crozier, G., *Advice and Assistance at Police Stations and the 24 Hour Solicitor Scheme,* (Lord Chancellor's Department, London, 1989); Moston, S., and Stephenson, G.M., *The Questioning and Interviewing of Suspects outside the Police Station* (Royal Commission on Criminal Justice Research Study No. 22, HMSO, London, 1993); McConville, M., 'Videotaping Interrogations' [1992] *Criminal Law Review* 532.

[35] McConville, M., Hodgson, J., Bridges, L. and Pavlovic, A. *Standing Accused: The Organization and Practices of Criminal Defence Lawyers in Britain* (Clarendon Press, Oxford, 1994).

The Responses of Solicitors

It is no use having a right to a solicitor if none can be found when needed or if the service is too expensive. This point was recognised by the Government, which provided for free advice and assistance from either one's own solicitor or a duty solicitor.[37] Existing duty solicitor schemes covering magistrates' courts were extended to cover nearly every police station in the country shortly after the coming into force of PACE in 1986. On a rota scheme there is always someone on duty who is obliged to provide advice and who receives a 'stand by' payment as well as a specific payment for each suspect assisted. With panel schemes no single solicitor is on duty, and there is no 'stand by' payment. When suspects request duty solicitors, custody officers contact a national telephone service which attempts to find a duty solicitor. That solicitor will then phone the station and speak to the custody officer and/or the suspect.

Of the 25 per cent approximately of suspects who requested advice prior to 1 April 1991 (when the revised Code took effect), around 19 per cent actually secured advice prior to charge. As we have seen, police malpractices (sometimes blatant law-breaking) explain the gap in part. However, the contribution to miscarriages of justice made by the absence of meaningful legal assistance cannot be blamed on the police alone. The legal profession is equally responsible.

Perhaps the clearest example of this shortcoming is to be found in the case of the *Cardiff Three*.[38] In that case one of the defendants was, according to the Lord Chief Justice, Lord Taylor, 'bullied and hectored' by the police in a series of long interviews, including asking him no fewer than 300 times whether he had committed a murder.[39] As Lord Taylor said, 'Short of physical violence, it is hard to conceive of a more hostile and intimidating approach by officers to a suspect.'.[40] Yet, unlike many of his counterparts, this suspect had asked for legal advice and was attended at the police station and during the interviews by a fully qualified solicitor (rather than an unqualified clerk), but one who according to the Court of Appeal sat 'passively through this travesty of an interview'.[41] For many other suspects, the problems they face with their legal advisers start many steps back in the process.

Delay

Some requests fail because suspects will not wait for the arrival of the solicitor. In our pre-1991 study we found that of those solicitors who attend the station, fewer than 60 per cent managed it within one hour of being contacted (and contact itself took over one hour in 7 per cent of requests). This cannot be entirely the fault of the profession but, significantly, suspects' own solicitors tended to be quicker at getting to the station than duty solicitors. If delay were a product solely of factors beyond lawyers' control, it should be randomly spread rather than patterned in this

---

[36] Kaye, T., *Unsafe and Unsatisfactory? Report of the Independent Inquiry into the Working Practices of the West Midlands Police Serious Crime Squad* (Civil Liberties Trust, London, 1991).
[37] Originally provided in PACE, s. 59. Now see the Legal Aid Act 1988, sch. 6.
[38] *R v Paris, Abdullahi, and Miller* (1993) 97 Cr App R 99.
[39] *Ibid.*, at p. 103.
[40] *Ibid.*, at p. 103.
[41] *Ibid.*, at p. 104.

way. The inference is that if the suspect is not the private client of the solicitor in question the suspect is given a lower priority.[42]

Delay is a problem not just because it leads to overall dissatisfaction with the legal profession and an unwillingness to wait for, or even to request, a solicitor. It also leaves suspects vulnerable to police malpractice. In particular, the police are more easily able to 'get at' a suspect and secure incriminating statements if the suspect is anxiously waiting for his solicitor, not knowing when (or if) he or she is going to turn up.

No Solicitor Available

The second problem is that there is sometimes no solicitor available (or willing) to advise. Suspects' own solicitors are unavailable more often than duty solicitors, though the difference is not as great as one would expect, for duty solicitor unavailability ought to approach zero. Anyone unavailable when on duty on a rota could be excluded from the scheme, which ought to be an important deterrent. In practice, though, local administrators tended, at least at the beginning of the schemes, to be afraid of alienating their duty solicitors in case so few remained that schemes became unviable, as shown by these comments from our research about unavailability made by two different administrators:

> *Administrator 1*: I will certainly mention the matter at an appropriate local committee meeting. I am not convinced that there is a great deal I can do about the matter or indeed that it would be politic for me to write to the individual participants. I fear that a letter from me might be wrongly construed as criticism.
> *Administrator 2*: I am quite relieved that there were only four occasions, given the number of solicitors now participating in the scheme. Looking at my list, F, S, G, V, M and S all prosecute one or two days a week and I am thus not at all surprised that [the telephone service] had difficulty in getting anybody.

One of these schemes, covering a large town, had dropped from 30 participating solicitors to 13. Another scheme was down to three solicitors.

Telephone Advice

The third problem is the manner in which advice is delivered. Solicitors may advise on the phone or attend the station (or both). When at the station they are entitled to advise the suspect privately, to attend the interrogation and provide support for as long as the suspect is in police custody. None of this is possible via the phone, yet around 30 per cent of advice in our pre-1991 study was by telephone alone. Even in serious cases phone advice alone was used in 20 per cent of cases. National data shows that the overall rate of telephone advice only cases recorded on legal aid claims has remained consistent at about 23 per cent every year from

---

[42] Following this research, new performance indicators were introduced by the Legal Aid Board to monitor the work of duty solicitors, including targets for the time taken by the national telephone service to contact a duty solicitor able to provide advice. However, there is no mechanism available to monitor the time it takes a solicitor, once s/he has accepted a referral, to contact the police or suspect or to attend the police station.

1989 through to 1996.[43] This is despite the fact that new guidelines issued to duty solicitors in 1992 required them to attend the police station whenever requested to do so by a suspect; where the offence is arrestable and the suspect is due to be interrogated by the police; where an identification parade is due to be held; or where the suspect complains of serious maltreatment.[44] Moreover, throughout the history of the scheme, duty solicitors have consistently tended to provide phone advice far more frequently than do suspects' own solicitors, despite the fact that there is no evidence to indicate that they tend to receive requests from suspects involved in less serious offences than do own solicitors.

According to both the Law Society and the Legal Aid Board,[45] solicitors should consider what type of advice and assistance is required in each case and then decide whether to attend in person or not (or to send a representative or not, as discussed below) on that basis. In fact, financial factors are at least as influential. Solicitors broadly do what is in their economic interest, as one would expect of a small business. Advice on the telephone is paid at a fixed fee, with a lower rate for 'routine' calls and a higher rate for 'advice and assistance' calls. On the other hand, attendance on the suspect is paid on the basis of time actually expended on the case. Thus, solicitors have a capacity to earn more by attending the police station, although the fixed telephone fee, especially for 'advice and assistance' calls, may amount to a higher rate for time spent on the case than would be received when actually attending the police station.[46] Perhaps a more significant variable for solicitors is that of retaining client loyalty. Duty solicitors may have less incentive to attend on suspects in police stations (who often return to their own solicitors for later stages of the case) than do own solicitors, who will not wish to risk dissatisfying established clients. This became apparent in conversation with solicitors, one of whom referred to attending his own clients as a 'public relations exercise'. Another told us that:

> I would always go down for my own clients purely because they are my seed corn, if you like. With the DS scheme I don't feel the same level of loyalty although I wouldn't like to think that people didn't get proper service.

Another solicitor was critical of his colleagues: 'I fear that there are certain people . . . who would just speak to everyone on the telephone.'

Many suspects, not surprisingly, founder when confronted with the police. A phone conversation, often with an anonymous voice to which neither name nor face can be put, is not much help. As one in our mid-1980s research put it, had his solicitor attended, 'you could have talked to him, you know, tell him more things you wouldn't say on the phone . . . If you met him face to face you could talk.' Another said,

---

[43] This figure is consistent with the finding of most recent research as reported by Brown, D., *PACE Ten Years On: A Review of the Research* (Home Office Research Study 155, HMSO, London, 1997) p. 105.

[44] Duty Solicitor Arrangements 1992 (Legal Aid Board, London, 1992).

[45] Law Society, *Advising a Suspect in the Police Station* (3rd ed., Law Society, London, 1991); Shepherd, E., Ede, R. and Edwards, A., *Police Station Skills for Legal Advisers* (2nd ed., Law Society, London, 1996) and Duty Solicitor Arrangements, (Legal Aid Board, London, 1992).

[46] Recent work carried out by one of the authors shows that the actual rate paid to two London firms for 'advice and assistance' telephone calls ranged between £220 and £305 an hour, whereas the highest rate available for actually attending the police station was just over £60 per hour. Legal aid rates in criminal work were a concern of the Royal Commission on Criminal Justice, *Report* (Cm 2263, HMSO, London, 1993) ('*Runciman Report*'), ch. 7 para. 73.

. . . he gave me a certain amount of advice. But obviously I wasn't going to say a lot over the phone to anybody . . . Well you never know do you? I could have been speaking to another policeman, you never know.

Moreover, the phone advice which was provided was often valueless:

Detainee 1: He said basically stick to your story and hopefully you'll get bailed and that was most of what he said . . . If I got charged with it I was to take the charge-sheet down to him.
Detainee 2: I thought they automatically came down but we only spoke on the phone. He said 'You're making a mountain out of a molehill. Probably what you'll be fined is £10 . . . It's only a minor offence.'. I suppose it is minor but these people are making a big issue out of it saying 'It's a criminal offence' . . . I think if it happened again I would arrange to have a solicitor with me at all times because the ordinary man in the street doesn't stand a chance once they get their teeth into him.

A point emphasised in all the official guidance and by solicitors in conversation is the importance of a solicitor in the interrogation. Yet not only did solicitors fail to attend one-third of suspects who asked for advice and who were interrogated, they also attended only 80 per cent of the interrogations in cases where they did in fact go out to the station. This meant that, overall, only 14 per cent of interrogated suspects in our study had a lawyer or other legal adviser present with them in the interrogation. Brown recorded in his 1989 study an even lower figure of 12 per cent of interrogations having a legal adviser present.[47] He also found that, prior to the introduction of the revised COP in 1991, legal advisers stayed on for interviews in only 60 per cent of the cases in which they actually attended the police station, with this rate actually falling to 42 per cent after the change in the COP.[48] Brown suggested that this was the result of a higher demand for legal advice and greater pressures on legal advisers not to prolong their stays at police stations.

The distress caused by solicitor responses is sometimes harrowing. We saw far more suspects upset by the failures of lawyers than by police action, although we cannot discount the fact that the police knew we were watching and the lawyers did not. Many suspects were advised on the phone to stay silent, but of course they rarely did once under police pressure. Some of these suspects tried refusing interrogation on the ground that their solicitors were not there, but of course the police refused to accept this. Other suspects were hardly advised at all. We asked the mother of one suspect what advice the solicitor provided, and she replied,

Not a lot really. Mainly her choices: she could either say nothing in the interview or she could make it easy on herself.

Quality of Advice and Advisers

The fourth problem is the competence and approach of the legal adviser. This is an area in which, partly as a result of our and other research and the recommen-

---
[47] As reported in Brown, D., *PACE Ten Years On: A Review of the Research* (Home Office Research Study 155, HMSO, London, 1997) p. 106.
[48] *Ibid.*

dations of the Royal Commission on Criminal Justice,[49] major efforts have been
made to improve the situation over recent years. Legal executives, trainee
solicitors, and other 'representatives' were used in over one-third of all cases in
our study.[50] From the beginning of the scheme, duty solicitors have been restricted
in the extent to which they can use such representatives: in many parts of the
country, substitution is not allowed at all, and where it is permitted the representative must be someone who has been vetted and approved by a local duty solicitor
committee. Own solicitors, on the other hand, were completely unrestricted up to
1995 in both the extent of their use of representatives and whom they could use
to perform this role. Not surprisingly, as many as 55 per cent of the own solicitor
cases in our study that entailed a visit to the police station, and where the status
of the adviser was known, were dealt with by representatives. Other research has
shown widely varying rates of use of non-solicitor staff in providing police station
legal advice, a fact that may be due as much to differences in the methodology
employed in the various studies as to real underlying variations in the practices of
solicitors' firms. The highest rate of use of representatives was found by McConville and Hodgson, where three-quarters of cases were handled by non-solicitors in
a sample based on mainly very large criminal defence practices and which
over-represented own solicitor work.[51] The more recent research by Brown and
Phillips found that 26 per cent of those attending police stations to give legal
advice were non-solicitors.[52]

Not all representatives are necessarily worse at giving advice than qualified
solicitors. Indeed, since 1995 a rolling programme for training and accrediting
non-solicitor staff used in the provision of custodial legal advice has been
implemented by the Law Society and the Legal Aid Board.[53] It is perhaps an
indicator of the poor quality of much of the advice given by such staff previously
that 44 per cent of those who initially entered on the scheme failed to become
accredited and are now excluded from this work.[54] More importantly, there is no
similar national scheme for training or accrediting solicitors for police station
advice work. Many solicitors will have been approved by local committees made
up of their peers to act as duty solicitors, but it remains the case that any solicitor,
whether regularly practising in criminal law or not, can provide and be paid legal
aid for custodial legal advice when acting as an own solicitor.

One of the key features of the new training scheme for non-solicitor police
station advisers is to instil in them a professional, adversarial approach to their
work which much of the research on custodial legal advice has shown to be
missing. Both solicitors and other advisers, even when they have attended police
interviews, have tended to be passive and to let the police set the agenda. As shown
dramatically in the *Cardiff Three* case, they rarely intervened in interrogations, to
remind clients of their rights or to prevent them being brow-beaten. Their advice

---

[49] *Runciman Report*, Recommendations 61–8, especially at ch. 3 paras. 60, 61.

[50] See also *R v Chief Constable of Avon & Somerset ex parte Robinson* [1989] 1 WLR 793.

[51] McConville, M. and Hodgson, J., *Custodial Legal Advice and the Right to Silence* (Royal
Commission on Criminal Justice Research Study No. 16, HMSO, London, 1993).

[52] As reported in Brown, D., *PACE Ten Years On: A Review of the Research* (Home Office Research
Study 155, HMSO, London, 1997) p. 108.

[53] For details of this programme, see Sheppherd, E., *Becoming Skilled* (Law Society, London, 1994);
Bridges, L. and Hodgson, J., 'Improving custodial legal advice' [1995] *Criminal Law Review* 101.

[54] (1995) *The Lawyer* 5 September p. 1.

to their clients has often been to confess, and rarely to remain silent (even before the rules on silence were changed).[55] In one typical case in our study, when asked what advice the solicitor provided, the suspect replied, 'He just asked me to plead guilty.'. In another the suspect actually argued with her solicitor who put the police case to her. As she put it in interview with us, 'But I hadn't admitted it . . . it was all hearsay.'. The custody officer told us that 'nine times out of 10 . . . he says "well do as the policeman says and be a good boy and you'll be out soon".'

Unlike the new accreditation scheme for non-solicitor advisers, the process of selecting duty solicitors through local committees may have placed less emphasis, at least during the initial stages, on quality and adversariness than on numerically smaller issues (unavailability) or on matters of purely professional concern (ensuring that duty solicitors did not 'poach' other solicitors' clients). This may have reflected a lack of interest in the quality of advice because of the absence of financial incentive, or, as with unavailability, the fear that imposition of high standards could have led to even smaller numbers of solicitors being willing to participate in local schemes.[56] On the other hand, it may also reflect a fundamental and long-standing problem – that many defence lawyers do not, in reality, subscribe to the due process adversarial values that supposedly underpin the system. They rarely operate with a presumption of innocence and are loath to make the police prove their case, unless the client convinces them that he or she is innocent.[57] As has been commented elsewhere, this may have important implications for the ultimate success of the new training and accreditation scheme for non-solicitor advisers in raising the standards of custodial legal advice:[58]

Evidence in other fields . . . shows that, unless the positive effects of training are continuously reinforced by the routines of daily practice, they rapidly dissipate and are overtaken by negative features of organisational and occupational culture. This points to the need to locate the improvement of custodial legal advice in wider reforms of criminal defence practice as a whole.

Conclusion

We have seen that the practices of both police officers and the legal profession have led to what is still only a minority of suspects securing legal advice prior to interrogations. Attempts to tighten the rules have led to more suspects seeking and securing advice, but the proportion of those advised who actually see a solicitor or clerk does not seem to have risen dramatically. When we did our original research in the mid-1980s, 14 per cent of suspects were accompanied by a legal adviser in interrogation, and it is doubtful whether that figure has subsequently risen by a

---

[55] See especially Baldwin, J., *The role of legal representatives at the police station* (Royal Commission on Criminal Justice Research Study No. 3, HMSO, London, 1993); Roberts, D., 'Questioning the suspect: the solicitor's role' [1993] *Criminal Law Review* 368; Baldwin, J., 'Legal advice at the police station' [1993] *Criminal Law Review* 371. For a review of the research evidence on this point, see Brown, D., *PACE Ten Years On: A Review of the Research* (Home Office Research Study 155, HMSO, London, 1997) pp. 113–115.

[56] Cape, E., 'New duties for duty solicitors' (1991) 91/13 *Law Society's Gazette* 19.

[57] McConville, M., Hodgson, J., Bridges, L. and Pavlovic, A., *Standing Accused: The Organization and Practices of Criminal Defence Lawyers in Britain* (Clarendon Press, Oxford, 1994).

[58] Bridges, L. and Hodgson, J., 'Improving custodial legal advice' [1995] *Criminal Law Review* 101 at p. 113.

significant extent. It is true that many suspects choose not to seek advice or to wait for it. However, the practices we have described are bound to increase the numbers who do not consider it worth asking and waiting for. Even when a solicitor is secured speedily, does come to the station, and does attend the interrogation – and at each stage the numbers get smaller – if the solicitor adopts a non-adversarial approach, it really will not have been worth the effort.

It is not clear why some solicitors are so non-adversarial. It is possible that it is not in the financial interest of lawyers to be adversarial in the station. It is indeed ironic that a solicitor who does a good job at this early stage may succeed in ensuring that the suspect is never charged, while the one who does a poor job, with the result that his or her client is charged, may subsequently obtain further financial benefit under a legal aid order for defending the case in court. But the problems of delay, unavailability, phone advice and use of representatives may also arise from the generally low priority given to what is regarded as relatively low paid work. Only a minority of practices specialise in criminal work and, with few worthy exceptions, these tend to adopt bureaucratic, rather than adversarial, procedures to keep themselves afloat financially. It may also be that some solicitors, including even some in the notorious miscarriage of justice cases, are out of sympathy with suspects and/or convinced of their guilt because of the power of the police/media machine.[59]

In so many miscarriage cases, 'confessions' are virtually the only evidence.[60] If the falsification of evidence by the police and/or the dubious circumstances in which it is obtained is to be prevented or uncovered, then at a minimum a competent and adversarial legal adviser must be present prior to and during interrogations. Providing advice only over the telephone will hardly ever be sufficient, and waiting until after charge will certainly be too late. Yet, as many of the extracts in this chapter indicate, police officers and lawyers often suggest that suspects can see lawyers 'later', or 'in court', of 'if you are charged'. One suspect, when asked how he felt about the non-appearance of his lawyer, replied that he did not mind as 'nothing happened'. In fact he had been interrogated and charged as a result of what he told the police.

The police still have opportunities to 'get at' suspects in the absence of a legal adviser. Police freedom here is not unfettered but is made considerably wider by the practices of some solicitors. It may have been a mistake to think that the system of private practice-based criminal defence and court duty solicitors could be automatically extended to incorporate custodial legal advice on the scale that was required under PACE. More recent reforms, in particular the introduction of the training and accreditation scheme for non-solicitor police station representatives, may have begun to remedy some the structural failings of this system.[61] At a minimum these need to be extended to cover other areas of criminal work and

---

[59] For further discussion see Sanders, A., 'Access to Justice in the Police Station – An Elusive Dream?' in Young, R. and Wall, D., *Access to Justice* (Blackstone Press, London, 1996).

[60] Kaye, T., *Unsafe and Unsatisfactory? Report of the Independent Inquiry into the Working Practices of the West Midlands Police Serious Crime Squad* (Civil Liberties Trust, London, 1991) p. 4.

[61] See Bridges, L. and Choongh, S., *Improving Police Station Legal Advice: The Impact of the Accreditation Scheme for Police Station Advisers* (Law Society and Legal Aid Board, London, 1998). This study shows significant improvements in many aspects of custodial legal advice provision but also continuing high rates of non-compliance among all types of legal advisers with some key elements of Law Society performance standards for police station advisers.

especially solicitors as well as their unqualified staff, whether through a rigorous criminal defence specialisation scheme (self-)imposed on the profession by the Law Society or through the Legal Aid Board imposing new quality standards through mechanisms such as franchising and contracting with major providers of these services.[62]

None of this will change the fact that, under PACE and the Codes of Practice, the police are able to determine most of the conditions under which legal advice is sought and provided. This puts lawyers and suspects at a disadvantage. So, for instance, waiting for a solicitor is particularly distressing for suspects because it takes place in a cell, rather than at home. And defence solicitors have to respond to what the police say and do, rather than being able to take the initiative themselves. PACE and the Codes of Practice attempt on one hand to establish an equality between police and suspects through the provision of police station advice. But this is, and will always remain, an illusory equality whilst PACE allows the police to dictate terms of their encounters with suspects, and thereby to influence the relationship between suspects and their solicitors.[63] Under these circumstances, the scope for miscarriages of justice is plain to see.

---

[62] See *Modernising Justice: The Government's plans for reforming legal Services and the courts* (Cm 4155, Stationery Office, London, 1998). This White Paper confirms the Government's intention that criminal defence services, including custodial legal advice, should in future be delivered exclusively under contracts by private solicitors who will meet improved quality standards imposed by the Legal Aid Board or by salaried public defenders.

[63] See Sanders, A., Bridges L., Mulvaney, A. and Crozier, G., *Advice and Assistance at Police Stations and the 24 Hour Solicitor Scheme* (Lord Chancellor's Department, London, 1989); Sanders, A. and Young R., 'The Rule of Law, Due Process and Pre-Trial Criminal Justice' (1994) 47 *Current Legal Problems* 125.

5

The Right to Silence

Keir Starmer and Mitchell Woolf

Introduction

In the sense of a right that can be freely exercised without sanction, it is questionable whether a 'right' to silence has ever really existed. Even before the radical changes brought about by the Criminal Evidence (Northern Ireland) Order 1988,[1] the Criminal Justice and Public Order Act 1994 and the Criminal Procedure and Investigations Act 1996, all discussed below, failure to give information to the police or other investigators in the course of criminal inquiries – including failure to answer questions – has always come at a price.

Analysis of the price of silence – that is, the application, or threat, of sanctions – lies at the heart of the debate about the privilege against self-incrimination. In this chapter we examine the effect of the profound changes of the last 15 years, which came about despite opposition from the Runciman Commission,[2] and question whether the present provisions can survive incorporation of the European Convention on Human Rights into United Kingdom law.

The Old Regime[3]

Under the Police and Criminal Evidence Act 1984 ('PACE'), the police have power to detain a suspect to obtain evidence by questioning.[4] This power has been interpreted as permitting the police to continue to question a suspect after he has indicated that he does not wish to answer, and also as permitting further detention (within the time limits laid down by PACE) for the purpose of re-interview after a lapse of time. In other words, PACE implicitly permits the police to hold a silent

---

[1] SI No. 1987.

[2] Royal Commission on Criminal Justice, *Report* (Cm 2263, HMSO, London, 1993) ch. 4 (*Runciman Report*). See further Chapter 1.

[3] See Easton, S.M., *The Right to Silence* (Avebury, Aldershot, 1991); Walker, C., and Starmer, K., (eds.) *Justice in Error* (Blackstone Press, London, 1993) ch. 4; Morgan, D., and Stephenson, G., (eds.), *Suspicion and Silence: the right to silence in criminal investigations* (Blackstone Press, London, 1994); Langbein, J.H., 'The historical origins of the privilege against self-incrimination at common law' (1994) 92 *Michigan Law Review* 1047.

[4] Section 37(2) (subject to the qualification that detention must be considered necessary).

suspect in the hope of overcoming the individual's silence.[5] Detention for the purpose of placing psychological pressure on suspects to provide answers is regarded as lawful.[6]

Silence in the face of accusations maintained by a person speaking on 'even terms' has always come at an even higher price. In *Norton*[7] it was accepted that the silence of the accused 'on an occasion which demanded an answer' might be conduct from which an inference of acknowledgement might be drawn. This principle was derived from *Mitchell*,[8] where Cave J said:

> Undoubtedly, when persons are speaking on even terms, and a.charge is made, and the person charged says nothing, and expresses no indignation, and does nothing to repel the charge, that is some evidence to show that he admits the charge to be true.[9]

Mitchell was approved by the Privy Council in *Parkes v The Queen*[10] where the defendant's failure to comment when accused of injuring the deceased by her mother was held to be one of the matters to be taken into account by the jury in deciding whether he had committed murder. In the same year, the Court of Appeal observed in *Chandler*,[11] that, although the right not to incriminate oneself was well established, it 'does not follow that a failure to answer an accusation or question when an answer could reasonably be expected may not provide some evidence in support of the accusation'.[12]

Even failure to testify at court has never been completely without sanction. The Criminal Evidence Act 1898 abolished the common law prohibition on defendants giving evidence on oath but provided that failure to testify was not to be made the subject of any comment by the prosecution. Comment by the judge was permissible – but its scope was limited. It had to be accompanied with a reminder that the accused was not bound to give evidence and that, while the jury had been deprived of the opportunity of hearing his story tested in cross-examination, they were not to assume that he was guilty because he had not gone into the witness box.[13] Stronger comment was permitted only where the accused bears the burden of proof on any issue. In *Bathurst*,[14] the Court of Appeal approved the comment that '[the accused] is not bound to go into the witness box, nobody can force him [to do so], but the burden is on him, and if he does not, he runs the risk of not being able to prove his case'.

The existence of such venerable sanctions for silence was expressly recognised by the then Lord Chief Justice, Lord Taylor, in one of the early test cases after the enactment of the Criminal Justice and Public Order Act 1994. In *Cowan*,[15]

---

[5] See Leng, R., *The Right to Silence in Police Interrogation: A study of some of the issues underlying the debate* (Royal Commission on Criminal Justice Research Study No. 10, HMSO, London, 1993); Hodgson, J. and McConville, M., 'Silence and the Suspect' (1993) 143 *New Law Journal* 659.
[6] *Holgate-Mohammed v Duke* [1984] 1 All ER 1054.
[7] [1910] 2 KB 496.
[8] (1892) 17 Cox CC 503.
[9] *Ibid.* at p. 508.
[10] [1976] 1 WLR 1251.
[11] [1976] 1 WLR 585. See also *R v Gilbert* (1977) 66 Cr App R 237.
[12] *Ibid.* at p. 589.
[13] *R v Bathurst* [1968] 2 QB 99.
[14] *Ibid.*
[15] [1995] 4 All ER 939.

rejecting the proposition that the new provisions should only be applied in 'exceptional' cases because they breached long-established principles, Lord Taylor remarked:

> As to inhibitions affecting a defendant's decision to testify or not, some existed before the 1994 Act. On the one hand, a defendant whose case involved an attack on the character of a prosecution witness could well be inhibited from giving evidence by fear of cross-examination as to his record. On the other hand, in certain cases, judges were entitled to comment on the defendant's failure to testify . . . Arguably, this put pressure on a defendant to give evidence. Even in a case calling only for the classic *Bathurst* direction . . . , a defendant might be inhibited from remaining silent for fear the jury would hold it against him that he chose to leave the prosecution evidence uncontradicted.[16]

On the broader issue of failing to give information to the police in the course of criminal investigations, a range of coercive measures also exists.[17] Subject to various procedural safeguards, force can be used to take a suspect's fingerprints after arrest,[18] after charge[19] and after conviction[20] for a recordable offence. Similar powers now exist for the taking of 'non-intimate' samples such as hair (excluding pubic hair), nails (including samples from under nails), swabs from any part of the body (including the mouth but no other orifice) and saliva.[21]

Even before these provisions permitting the use of force were introduced, adverse inferences could be drawn at common law from unco-operative conduct other than silence. In *Smith*,[22] the defendant was asked in the presence of his solicitor if he was willing to provide a sample of hair for comparison with hairs found at the scene of the robbery of which he was suspected. He refused. The Court of Appeal, emphasising that since the defendant had his solicitor present he was on 'even terms' (within the *Mitchell* meaning) with the police, considered that it would be 'contrary to good sense' to prohibit the drawing of inferences. This approach was given statutory force in relation to 'intimate' samples by section 62 of PACE which provides that where a suspect in custody refuses consent to provide intimate samples such as blood, semen or other tissue fluid, urine, pubic hair or a swab taken from body orifices, 'without good cause' a court or jury determining guilt, 'may draw such inferences as appear proper'.[23]

The New Regime

In the mid-1980s, growing concern about the extent of, and difficulties of investigation into, corporate fraud led to the first of a series of further statutory

---

[16] *Ibid.* at p. 942.
[17] See *Runciman Report*, ch. 2 paras. 25–38; Lidstone, K. and Palmer, C., *The Investigation of Crime* (2nd ed., Butterworths, London, 1996) pp. 461–74.
[18] PACE, ss. 61(3)(a), (4) and 117.
[19] PACE, ss. 61(3) and 117.
[20] PACE, ss. 61(6) and 117.
[21] PACE, s. 63 originally restricted the use of force to cases where the accused was suspected of involvement in a 'serious arrestable offence'. See Walker, C. and Cram, I., 'DNA profiling and police powers' [1990] *Criminal Law Review* 479. As amended by the Criminal Justice and Public Order Act 1994, it now applies where the accused is suspected of involvement in a 'recordable' offence.
[22] (1985) 81 Cr App R 286.
[23] PACE, s. 62(10).

restrictions on the privilege against self-incrimination. Following the report of the Roskill Committee,[24] the Serious Fraud Office ('SFO') was established under the Criminal Justice Act 1987 to facilitate the investigation and prosecution of complex fraud.[25] Section 2(2) gives the Director of the SFO inquisitorial powers to obtain evidence in relation to serious fraud.[26] The extent to which these powers may affect the privilege against self-incrimination, albeit that they are not exercisable by police constables,[27] was explored by the House of Lords in *R v Director of the Serious Fraud Office, ex parte Smith*[28] where their Lordships unanimously held that section 2(2) gives the Director the power to compel a person under investigation to answer questions and, further, that this power does not cease when the defendant has been charged or even has been put on trial. Failure to comply with an investigation is a criminal offence in itself.[29] In *Hamilton v Naviede*[30] (on appeal from *Re Arrows Ltd (No. 4)*), this principle was extended when the House of Lords held that self-incriminating answers obtained under the Insolvency Act 1986 are admissible against the defendant in criminal proceedings.

For similar reasons to do with the possible complexity and seriousness of fraud and the assumption that such white-collar fraudsters can take care of themselves,[31] there is no right to silence in inquisitorial proceedings by the Commissioner of Customs and Excise established by the Purchase Tax Act 1963,[32] during examination by the Department of Trade and Industry under the Companies Act 1985,[33] during an examination of the Bank of England under the Banking Act 1987[34] or under the Financial Services Act 1986 and the Friendly Societies Act 1992.

Set against this background, the changes brought about by the Criminal Evidence (Northern Ireland) Order 1988, the Criminal Justice and Public Order Act 1994 and the Criminal Procedure and Investigations Act 1996 can be seen in their proper context. They do not represent the introduction of sanctions into an area of the law where before there were none. Rather they represent a shift – albeit a significant shift – along the continuum of coercive measures available for dealing with failure to give information to those vested with investigative powers, including failure to answer questions and failure to testify.

---

[24] Roskill Committee, *Fraud Trials Report* (HMSO, London, 1986).

[25] See Wood, J., 'The Serious Fraud Office' [1989] *Criminal Law Review* 175; Graham, C. and Walker, C., 'The continued assault on the vaults' [1989] *Criminal Law Review* 185; Staples, G., 'Serious and complex fraud' (1993) 56 *Modern Law Review* 127; Kirk, D.N. and Woodcock, A.J.J., *Serious Fraud: investigation and trial* (2nd ed., Butterworths, London, 1997).

[26] There is no form of hearing or representation before a case is embarked upon or copies of notices issued to third parties: *R v Director of S.F.O. ex parte Nadir, The Independent* 16 October 1990.

[27] See s.2(11). The *Runciman Report* (ch. 2 para. 69) called for an end to this disability, but no change has occurred. See further Levi, M., *The investigation, prosecution and trial of serious fraud* (Royal Commission on Criminal Justice Research Study No. 14, HMSO, London, 1993) pp. 168, 169.

[28] [1993] AC 1. See also *R v S.F.O., ex parte Saunders, The Times*, 1 August 1988.

[29] Section 2(13). But the evidence cannot be used as the basis for prosecution: s.2(8). See *Runciman Report*, ch. 4 para. 29.

[30] [1995] 2 AC 75.

[31] See Smith, A.T.H., 'The right to silence in cases of serious fraud' in Birks, P.B.H. (ed.), *Pressing Problems in the Law Volume 1: Criminal Justice and Human Rights* (Oxford University Press, 1995).

[32] *R v Harz; R v Power* [1967] 1 AC 760.

[33] *R v Seelig* [1991] 4 All ER 429; *In Re London United Investments plc* [1992] Ch 578; *R v Saunders and others* [1996] 1 Cr App Rep 463; *R v Secretary of State for Trade and Industry, ex parte McCormick, The Times*, 10 February 1998.

[34] *Bank of England v Riley* [1992] Ch 475.

The Criminal Justice and Public Order Act 1994

Sections 34 to 39 of the Criminal Justice and Public Order Act 1994 entail the most far-reaching changes to the consequences of silence.[35] In relation to pre-trial investigations, section 34 provides that a court or jury may draw such inferences as appear proper from evidence that the accused failed, on being questioned under caution or on being charged with the offence, to mention any fact relied on in his or her defence, being a fact which in the circumstances existing at the time he or she could reasonably have been expected to mention. The inferences may be drawn both in determining whether there is a case to answer and in determining whether the accused is guilty of the offence charged. The provision applies in relation to questioning by constables and by other persons with the duty of investigating offences or charging offenders.

Section 35 deals with silence at trial. If the accused chooses not to give evidence, or, having been sworn, refuses to answer any question without good cause, the court or jury may draw such inferences as appear proper from the failure to do so. A decision not to testify will not, however, be something that can be taken into account in determining whether there is a case to answer. Under section 35, the court is obliged to satisfy itself that a defendant who has not indicated that he or she intends to give evidence understands the consequences of declining to do so.[36] The burden of explaining the law to the defendant rests, in the case of a legally represented defendant, with the legal representative.[37]

The provisions of sections 36 and 37 of the 1994 Act relate to the accused's failure to account for objects, substances or marks, or physical presence at a particular place, in circumstances where such matters are reasonably believed by an investigating constable to be incriminating. Such failures, like failure to mention facts relied upon subsequently, may lead to adverse inferences both in determining whether there is a case to answer and in determining the guilt of the accused.

A common feature of sections 34 to 37 of the 1994 Act is that no-one can be convicted solely on the basis of an adverse inference.[38] Beyond that rule, the circumstances in which adverse inferences can properly be drawn, and the strength of the inference that should be drawn where permitted, will vary on a case-by-case basis. However, some guide as to how the Act will be interpreted and applied can be gained from Northern Ireland, since sections 34 to 39 of the Criminal Justice and Public Order Act 1994 are modelled on the provisions of the Criminal Evidence (Northern Ireland) Order 1988 (with minor modifications).[39] The operation of the Criminal Evidence (Northern Ireland) Order 1988 over the last ten years gives a fairly clear indication of the scope for drawing adverse inferences both under the Order itself and under the 1994 Criminal Justice and Public Order Act. As will be seen, whilst the initial inclination of the judiciary in Northern

---

[35] See Wasik, M. and Taylor, R.D., *Blackstone's Guide to the Criminal Justice & Public Order Act 1994* (Blackstone Press, London, 1995) ch. 3; Dennis, I., 'The CJ & POA' [1995] *Criminal Law Review* 4; Pattenden, R., 'Inferences from silence' [1995] *Criminal Law Review* 602.

[36] Section 35(2) and (3) and *Practice Direction (Crown Court: Defendant's Evidence)* [1995] 1 WLR 657.

[37] *Ibid.*, paras 2–4.

[38] CJPOA 1994, s. 38.

[39] The most significant is the requirement that the accused must have been cautioned before inferences can be drawn from his failure to mention facts when questioned about the offence.

Ireland was to draw an inference from silence only in finely balanced cases, this soon gave way to a more robust approach.

The Northern Ireland Experience[40]

Although the 1988 Order came into effect in December 1988, it was not until October 1989 that it was first invoked to support a conviction.[41] Before then Nicholson LJ had held, in *MacDonald*,[42] that an inference should not be drawn under the Order unless the other evidence in a case pointed to 'probable' guilt. Kelly LJ had appeared to go even further. In his judgment in *Smith*,[43] he stated that an inference under the Order should only be taken into account where the standard of evidence adduced by the prosecution, without the inference, rested on the brink of being 'beyond reasonable doubt'. In other words, the inference was only to be used as the final 'weight' in an otherwise finely balanced case.

Within a relatively short period of time, however, the judiciary in Northern Ireland began to change tack. In *Gamble*,[44] the first case in which an inference was actually drawn, Carswell J. drew an inference not from the accused's refusal to answer police questions (he had done so) but from his decision not to testify in court. And in *McLernon*[45] Kelly LJ began to distance himself from his own judgment in *Smith* – stating that he had never intended that case to limit the application of the 1988 Order. His revised view in *McLernon* was that a refusal to answer questions may be taken into account where it *merely* adds weight to the prosecution case.

Kelly LJ's *volte face* was completed in *Kevin Sean Murray*,[46] where thumb-prints of the accused and fibres from his clothing had allegedly been found on the car of a murder victim. The defendant advanced various explanations during interrogation, but gave no evidence at trial. Kelly LJ drew strong adverse inferences from this and went on to assert, in broader terms, that the 1988 Order was not limited to situations of 'confess and avoid' (in other words, where an explanation was clearly called for on the evidence) but that it might be used, and Parliament had intended it to be used, much more generally.

The *Murray* case was appealed to the House of Lords,[47] where their Lordships considered the inference drawn in the court below to have been justified. The 1988 Order was intended to change the law and practice and, under the new regime, the consequences of silence are not simply that specific inferences may be drawn from

---

[40] See Jackson, J.D., 'Curtailing the right to silence' [1991] *Criminal Law Review* 404; 'Inferences from silence' (1993) 44 *Northern Ireland Legal Quarterly* 103; 'Interpreting the silence provisions' [1995] *Criminal Law Review* 587.

[41] *R v Gamble and others*, [1989] NI 268, reported in Haldane Society of Socialist Lawyers, *Upholding the Rule of Law?, Northern Ireland: Criminal Justice under the 'Emergency Powers' in the 1990s* (London, 1992) at p. 44.

[42] *Ibid.*

[43] *Ibid.*, 20 October 1989.

[44] *loc. cit.*

[45] [1990] 10 NIJB 91, upheld by the Northern Ireland Court of Appeal at [1992] NI 168.

[46] (1991) 2 BNIL n51, The Northen Ireland Court of Appeal upheld the assertion that there was no requirement that the Crown case should have created a situation which at common law would be regarded as 'confession and avoidance': [1993] NI 105. See further *R v McLaughlin* [1991] 8 NIJB 20; *R v Gamble* (1991) 2 BNIL 20; *R v Martin and others* (1992) 7 BNIL 42; *R v Murphy and McKinley* (1994) 10 BNIL n56; *R v McAnoy* (1996) 6 BNIL n50.

[47] *Kevin Sean Murray v Director of Public Prosecutions* [1994] 1 WLR 1.

specific facts, but include, in a proper case, the inference that the accused is guilty. As to what is proper, Lord Slynn said:

> If there is no *prima facie* case shown by the prosecution there is no case to answer. Equally, if parts of the prosecution case had so little evidential value that they called for no answer, a failure to deal with those specific matters cannot justify an inference of guilt.
>
> On the other hand, if aspects of the evidence taken alone or in combination with other facts clearly call for an explanation which the accused ought to be in a position to give, if an explanation exists, then a failure to give any explanation may, as a matter of common sense, allow the drawing of an inference that there is no explanation and that the accused is guilty.[48]

Lord Mustill, for his part, suggested that it was impossible to generalise about the question of what inferences might be 'proper'. In his view:

> [Everything] depends on the nature of the issue, the weight of the evidence adduced by the prosecution upon it . . . and the extent to which the defendant should in the nature of things be able to give his own account of the particular matter in question. It is impossible to generalise, for dependent upon the circumstances the failure of the defendant to give evidence may found no inference at all, or one which is for all practical purposes fatal.[49]

On the facts of the case, the House of Lords took the view that the evidence adduced by the prosecution established a clear *prima facie* case which called for an explanation from the accused. Since the accused ought to have been in a position to give an explanation if one existed his failure to do so justified a 'common-sense' inference that there was no explanation and that he was guilty.

The case law under the Criminal Justice and Public Order Act is still emerging. However, it is clear that the House of Lords intended the case of *Murray* to be of general application, and there is little scope for distinguishing between the 1988 Order and the 1994 Act in principle. The fact that under the 1994 Act adverse inferences may be drawn by juries (rather than judges under an obligation to give reasoned decisions) has meant that the early cases under the Act have emphasised the need for careful jury directions.

As to silence when questioned or charged, in *Argent*,[50] the Court of Appeal indicated that there are six formal conditions that must be met before adverse inferences can be drawn:

(a)   there must be criminal proceedings against the accused;

(b)   the accused must fail to mention a fact when questioned before a charge is made;

(c)   the accused must have been questioned under caution by a constable or any other person within section 34(4) of the 1994 Act;

(d)   the questioning must have been directed to trying to discover whether or by whom the alleged offence was committed;[51]

---

[48] *Ibid.* at p. 11.
[49] *Ibid.* at p. 5.
[50] [1997] 2 Cr. App. R 27. See Broome, K., 'An inference of guilt' (1997) 141 *Solicitor's Journal* 202.
[51] See *R v Pointer* [1997] *Criminal Law Review* 676.

(e)   at trial the accused must rely on the fact which he did not mention to the police when so questioned;[52]

(f)   in the circumstances existing at the time of the questioning it must have been reasonable to expect the accused to have mentioned that fact.

As to the last requirement, the Court of Appeal indicated that courts should not construe the expression 'in the circumstances existing at the time' restrictively, and that amongst the personal factors which might be relevant to an assessment of what an individual could reasonably have been expected to mention were age, experience, mental capacity, state of health, sobriety, tiredness and personality. However, these factors are not to be used so as to marginalise section 34; in *R v Friend*[53] inferences were drawn under section 35 against a defendant aged 14 and with a mental age of 9.

The Court of Appeal's approach to the difficult issue of what use, if any, can be made of a 'no comment' interview in which the accused remains silent on legal advice has been less protective of the accused. In *Condron*,[54] the defendants were advised to remain silent by their solicitor who considered that their drug withdrawal symptoms rendered them unfit to be interviewed despite being passed fit by the Forensic Medical Examiner. The Court of Appeal held that the fact that the defendants' silence followed legal advice did not of itself preclude the drawing of inferences. It depended on the reasons for the advice. This raises a thorny issue – whether in adducing reasons for advice to remain silent a defendant waives his or her legal professional privilege. A bare assertion by a defendant that he or she had been advised to remain silent cannot, following the Court of Appeal decisions in *Condron* and *Argent*, amount to waiver. Equally, however, such a bare assertion would be unlikely to carry much weight. In *Condron*, Stuart-Smith LJ stated that, in order to invite the court not to draw an adverse inference, an accused would probably have to call the solicitor to give reasons for the advice. In his view, this would involve waiving the shield of legal privilege, which might well, in turn, provide the prosecution with fertile ground for cross-examination. This creates a tricky dilemma for defendant and solicitor. A defendant is left with an unenviable choice between exposure to the risk of adverse inferences being drawn from silence and waiving his legal professional privilege, only recently described as a fundamental condition of the administration of justice.[55] Solicitors are put in potential breach of their professional code of conduct which requires that solicitors should not act for a person if they may be a material witness in the court case.[56]

Moving on to a defendant's failure to testify at trial, the Court of Appeal in *Cowan*[57] identified five essential points which a trial judge must relay to the jury before an adverse inference can be drawn under section 35 of the 1994 Act, namely:

---

[52] See *R v N, The Times*, 13 February 1998; *R v Daniel, The Times*, 10 April 1998.

[53] [1997] 1 WLR 1433. See also *R v A* [1997] *Criminal Law Review* 883.

[54] [1997] 1 WLR 827. See Spencer, J.N., 'The right to silence, legal privilege and the decision in *Condron*' (1996) 160 *Justice of the Peace* 1167.

[55] *R v Derby Magistrates' Court, ex parte B* [1996] 1 AC 487 at p. 507 per Lord Taylor.

[56] Law Society, *The Guide to the Professional Conduct of Solicitors* (7th ed., Law Society, London, 1996) para. 21.12. See Tregilgas-Davey, M.I., 'Adverse inferences and the ''No Comment'' interview' [1997] 141 *Solicitors' Journal* 500; 'Inferences from the silence of suspects' (1997) 161 *Justice of the Peace* 525.

[57] [1995] 3 WLR 818. See also *R v Birchall, The Times*, 10 February 1998.

(a)   the burden of proof must remain on the prosecution at all times;

(b)   the defendant is entitled to remain silent;

(c)   an inference from failure to give evidence cannot on its own prove guilt;

(d)   the jury must be satisfied that the prosecution has established a case to answer before drawing any inferences from silence; and

(e)   the jury may draw an adverse inference, if despite any evidence relied upon by the accused to explain his silence or in the absence of such evidence, the jury conclude the silence can only sensibly be attributed to the accused having no answer or none that would stand up to cross-examination.

Having said this, the Court of Appeal emphasised that it is impossible to anticipate all possible circumstances in which a judge might think it right to direct or advise a jury against drawing an adverse inference.

The Criminal Procedure and Investigations Act 1996

Whatever view one takes of the 1988 Order and the 1994 Act, there can be little doubt but that the Criminal Procedure and Investigations Act 1996 effectively marks the end of the so-called right to silence in England, Wales and Northern Ireland. This Act creates a new framework for disclosure in criminal cases, significantly restricting the prosecution duty of disclosure, and imposing a duty of defence disclosure in most Crown Court cases.[58]

Under the Act, a distinction is made between disclosure of material which might undermine the prosecution case (primary disclosure) and disclosure of material which might assist the defence case (secondary disclosure). Primary disclosure is automatic. But secondary disclosure is conditional on the defendant making a 'defence statement'. A defence statement is a written statement setting out in general terms the nature of the accused's defence; indicating the matters on which he takes issue with the prosecution; and setting out, in the case of each such matter, the reason why he takes issue.[59] No defence statement means no secondary disclosure (there is no relief for exceptional circumstances). This, in itself, is probably a breach of the European Convention on Human Rights, as discussed below.

A secondary enforcement mechanism under the 1996 Act is the threat of adverse comments and inferences for non-compliance with its provisions. Consequently, if a defence statement is not made, or is made late, or if at trial the defendant advances a defence inconsistent with it, the court (or with leave of the court any other party) may make such comment as appears appropriate[60] and the court or jury may draw such inferences as appear proper in deciding whether the accused is guilty of the offence concerned.[61] Clearly, these provisions are modelled on the Criminal Justice and Public Order Act 1994, though, as with that Act, no-one may be convicted solely on the basis of an adverse inference.[62]

The 1996 Act also changed the law relating to alibi evidence. Although for many years it has been a statutory requirement under the Criminal Justice Act 1967,

---

[58] See further Chapter 7.

[59] Criminal Procedure and Investigations Act 1996 (CPIA 1996), s. 5(6).

[60] CPIA 1996, s. 11(3)(a).

[61] CPIA 1996, s. 11(3)(b).

[62] CPIA 1996, s. 11(5).

section 11, that the defence give particulars of alibi evidence to the prosecution before trial, the sanction for failure to comply with notice requirements was that leave had to be sought from the trial judge to adduce alibi evidence – with the risk that such leave would not be given. Under the 1996 Act comment may be made or permitted or adverse inferences drawn to the same extent and in the same way as comment and inferences can be made and drawn in relation to failure to make a defence statement.

The European Convention on Human Rights

The extent to which the Criminal Justice and Public Order Act 1994 and the Criminal Procedure and Investigation Act 1996 comply with the fair trial provisions of the European Convention on Human Rights has yet to be tested. However, judging by the clear principles emerging from Strasbourg – including those enunciated by the European Court of Human Rights in the only case under the Criminal Evidence (Northern Ireland) Order 1988 yet to reach it – it seems unlikely that they will easily survive challenge.

Article 6 of the Convention, which guarantees the general right to a fair trial, was based on the 1949 version of the United Nations Human Rights Committee's draft of the International Covenant on Civil and Political Rights which, at that stage, did not expressly set out the prohibition on self-incrimination. Later, that safeguard was added to the draft International Covenant and subsequently adopted as Article 14(3)(g) which requires that in the determination of any criminal charge against him, everyone shall be entitled 'not to be compelled to testify against himself or to confess guilt'.[63] It is now clearly accepted that Article 6 of the European Convention implicitly includes this prohibition as a necessary precursor of a fair trial.

In *Funke* v *France*,[64] the European Court of Human Rights found a breach of Article 6 of the Convention where the applicant was prosecuted and fined for failing to co-operate with French customs officers seeking information about his interests in a number of foreign bank accounts. The European Court (disagreeing with the Commission) held that the right to a fair trial under Article 6 includes 'the right of anyone charged with a criminal offence . . . to remain silent and not to contribute to incriminating himself'.

In *Saunders* v *United Kingdom*,[65] the European Court expanded on this notion in a case concerning the powers of compulsory questioning under the Companies Act 1985. In December 1986 inspectors appointed by the DTI began an inquiry into allegations that, during a corporate take-over battle, Guinness had artificially maintained or inflated its share price by means of an unlawful share support operation. In the first six months of 1987, the applicant was interviewed by the

---

[63] The Criminal Evidence (Northern Ireland) Order 1988 has been condemned as in breach: Cumaraswamy, P., *Report on the mission of the Special Rapporteur to the United Kingdom of Great Britain and Northern Ireland* (E/CN.4/1998/39/Add.4, UN Economic and Social Council, Geneva, 1998) para. 79.

[64] Appl. no. 10828/84, Ser. A vol. 256-A, (1993) 16 EHRR 297. See Warbrick, C., 'Self incrimination and the European Convention on Human Rights' in Birks, P.B.H. (ed.), *Pressing Problems in the Law Volume 1: Criminal Justice and Human Rights* (Oxford University Press, 1995).

[65] Appl. no. 19187/91, 1997-VI (1997) 23 EHRR 313. Nash, S. and Furse, M., 'Self incrimination, corporate misconduct and the ECHR' [1995] *Criminal Law Review* 854; Munday, R., 'Inferences from silence and the European Human Rights law' [1996] *Criminal Law Review* 370.

inspectors nine times. He was required by law to answer the questions put to him – under threat of punishment akin to contempt of court or a fine.[66]

In January 1987 the DTI inspectors notified the Secretary of State that they had found evidence of possible criminal offences and passed transcripts of the applicant's interviews to the CPS. The applicant was subsequently charged with several counts of false accounting and conspiracy. At trial, the applicant denied any wrongdoing, and the prosecution sought to prove the case against him using the transcripts of his interviews with DTI inspectors. Despite the applicant's objections, the court admitted these documents into evidence on the basis of section 431(5) of the Companies Act 1985 which provides that 'an answer given by a person to a question put to him in the exercise of powers conferred by this section . . . may be used in evidence against him'. The applicant was subsequently convicted. His appeal that this conflation of powers was an abuse of process or inflicted 'such an adverse effect on the fairness of the proceedings that the court ought not to admit it' under section 78 of PACE was later rejected.[67]

The European Court of Human Rights, finding for the applicant, stressed that the right not to incriminate oneself was a generally recognised international standard which lay at the heart of the notion of a fair procedure under Article 6 of the Convention. In the Court's opinion, whether or not the applicant's right not to incriminate himself had been unjustifiably infringed in the circumstances of the case depended on the use made by the prosecution at the trial of the statements which he had been obliged to give to the inspectors. It was irrelevant that they may not have been self-incriminating in themselves. In the Court's view, the right not to incriminate oneself extends to 'neutral' evidence which might be deployed in a way which supported the prosecution case. On the facts it was clear that the prosecution had employed the transcripts of the applicant's interviews with DTI inspectors in an incriminating manner in order to cast doubt on his honesty and to establish his involvement in the unlawful share support operation. Accordingly, the Court considered that there had been an infringement of the applicant's right not to incriminate himself, and the public interest in combating fraud could not be invoked to justify the use of answers obtained under powers of compulsory questioning in a non-judicial investigation to incriminate him at his trial.

The case law of the Court and Commission on the question of drawing adverse inferences from silence is less extensive. In *John Murray* v *United Kingdom*,[68] (not to be confused with *Kevin Sean Murray* v *Director of Public Prosecutions* – the House of Lords case) the European Court examined the provisions of the Criminal Evidence (Northern Ireland) Order 1988. The applicant had been arrested in a house in which a Provisional IRA informer had been held captive. He was taken to Castlereagh police office, where his access to a solicitor was delayed for 48 hours pursuant to the Northern Ireland (Emergency Provisions) Act 1987. He was cautioned under the 1988 Order and then interviewed 12 times. He remained silent throughout. At his trial he elected not to give evidence. The Lord Chief Justice of Northern Ireland (trying the case without a jury) exercised his discretion under the 1988 Order to draw adverse inferences from the applicant's silence and convicted him of aiding and abetting the false imprisonment of the informer.

---

[66] See Companies Act 1985, ss.432(2) and 436(3).
[67] *R* v *Saunders and others* [1996] 1 Cr App Rep 463.
[68] Appl. no. 18731/91, 1996–I, (1996) 22 EHRR 29.

The European Court carefully confined its attention to the facts of the case, emphasising that it was not its role to examine whether, in general, the drawing of inferences under the 1988 Order was compatible with the notion of a fair hearing under Article 6. In so far as it laid down any principles of general application, the Court held[69] that it was self-evident, on the one hand, that it was incompatible with immunity from self-incrimination to base a conviction solely or mainly on the accused's silence or on a refusal to answer questions or to give evidence at trial. On the other hand, the Court deemed it equally obvious that such immunity could not and should not prevent the accused's silence, in situations which clearly called for an explanation from him, being taken into account in assessing the persuasiveness of the evidence adduced by the prosecution. Wherever the line between these two extremes is to be drawn, it followed from this understanding of the right to silence, that, in the Court's view, the question whether the right was absolute had to be answered in the negative.

As to the degree of compulsion involved in the applicant's case, the Court noted that he was in fact able to remain silent and that he remained a non-compellable witness. The Court also observed that:[70]

In Northern Ireland, where trial judges sit without a jury, the judge must explain the reasons for the decision to draw inferences and the weight attached to them. The exercise of discretion in this regard is subject to review by the appellate court.

In the present case, the evidence presented against the applicant by the prosecution was considered by the Court of Appeal to constitute a 'formidable' case against him . . .

In the circumstances, the Court found that, 'having regard to the weight of the evidence against the applicant', the drawing of inferences from his refusal, at arrest, during police questioning and at trial, to provide an explanation for his presence in the house in which the informer was held was 'a matter of common sense' and could not be regarded as unfair or unreasonable in the circumstances.[71] The substantive challenge to the 1988 Order therefore failed.

However, the Court went on to find that the adverse inferences drawn in the applicant's case significantly contributed to a violation of Article 6(1) and 6(3)(c) which arose from the delayed access to a solicitor at the police station. In the Court's view:[72]

[T]he scheme contained in the [1988] Order is such that it is of paramount importance for the rights of the defence that an accused has access to a lawyer at the initial stages of police interrogation. It observes in this context that, under the Order, an accused is confronted with a fundamental dilemma relating to his defence. If he chooses to remain silent adverse inferences may be drawn against him in accordance with the provisions of the Order. On the other hand, if the accused opts to break his silence during the course of interrogation, he runs the

---

[69] *Ibid.* para. 47.
[70] *Ibid.* paras. 51, 52.
[71] *Ibid.* para. 54.
[72] *Ibid.* para. 66.

risk of prejudicing his defence without necessarily removing the possibility of inferences being drawn against him.

Under such conditions the concept of fairness enshrined in Article 6 requires that an accused person has the benefit of the assistance of a lawyer at the initial stage of police interrogation. To deny access to a lawyer for the first 48 hours of police questioning, in a situation where the rights of the defence may well be irretrievably prejudiced, is – whatever the justification for such denial – incompatible with the rights of the accused under Article 6.

The Question of Compulsion

At the heart of the distinction drawn by the European Court and the European Commission on Human Rights between powers of compulsory questioning and the power to draw inferences from silence is the question, or definition, of 'compulsion'. In the *Saunders* case, the Commission emphasised that:[73]

> [T]he privilege against self-incrimination is an important element in safeguarding an accused from oppression and coercion during criminal proceedings. The very basis of a fair trial presupposes that the accused is afforded the opportunity of defending himself against the charges brought against him. The position of the defence is undermined if the accused is under compulsion, or has been compelled to incriminate himself . . . Whether a particular applicant has been subject to compulsion to incriminate himself and whether the use made of the incriminating material has rendered criminal proceedings unfair will depend on an assessment of each case as a whole.

Similarly, in *Murray*, the Court drew a distinction between 'proper' compulsion (permitted under Article 6) and 'improper' compulsion (not permitted). Where the line lies between the two is difficult to discern. However, the following conclusions can be tentatively drawn.

Compulsory Questioning on Pain of Criminal Proceedings

Most (if not all) of the powers of compulsory questioning violate the European Convention in so far as they permit the use in criminal proceedings of statements or documents obtained by the use of such powers. Whether those statements or documents are incriminating on their face is irrelevant if they are used to support the prosecution case. The Court of Appeal (in *R v Staines, R v Morrissey*[74]) accepts that there is a breach of the Convention but disclaims any power to disapply the relevant legislation. The Government likewise accepts this interpretation. In a statement to Parliament on 4 February 1998, the Attorney-General disclosed that he had issued new guidance to prosecuting authorities in light of the judgment of the European Court in *Saunders*. The Attorney-General told the House of Commons that:[75]

---

[73] *Ibid.* para. 72.

[74] *The Times*, 1 May 1997.

[75] HC Debs. vol. 305 col. 640w.a., 4 February 1998, John Morris. The Lord Advocate is to issue similar guidance in Scotland.

The Government proposes to bring forward legislation when a suitable opportunity arises to ensure that the domestic law, which was in issue in *Saunders* v *UK*, is fully compatible with our obligations under the European Convention on Human Rights. As an interim measure, I have today promulgated to prosecuting authorities guidance about the handling of cases where the evidence available to the prosecution includes answers obtained by the exercise of compulsory powers . . .

. . . Its effect is that answers obtained pursuant to a procedure which includes the power to compel answers, whatever the investigative or regulatory regime, cannot be used in subsequent criminal proceedings as part of the prosecution case except for the very limited purposes of proceedings for offences arising out of the giving of the evidence (e.g. perjury). The Guidance therefore covers not only evidence obtained by the exercise of powers under section 434 of the Companies Act 1985, which was in issue in *Saunders* v *UK*, but also evidence obtained under analogous powers. In addition, the guidance restricts the use by prosecutors of compulsorily acquired answers for the purpose of cross-examination . . .

The guidance contains numerous examples of 'answers obtained under compulsory powers' but extends to any such answers obtained through any other procedure in legislation concerned with the regulation of commercial or financial activities carried on by companies or individuals, or with the investigation of the financial affairs of companies or individuals which includes the powers to compel answers.

Bodily Evidence

By contrast from the Strasbourg standpoint, the use in evidence of fingerprints, intimate and non-intimate samples would not appear to infringe the privilege against self-incrimination. On the basis that the privilege against self-incrimination is primarily concerned with respecting the will of an accused person to remain silent, in the *Saunders* case, the European Court took the view that:[76]

[I]t does not extend to the use in criminal proceedings of material which may be obtained from the accused through the use of compulsory powers but which has an existence independent of the will of the suspect such as, *inter alia*, documents acquired pursuant to a warrant, breath, blood and urine samples and bodily tissues for the purpose of DNA testing.

The Court did not comment on the legitimacy of the *means* for obtaining such evidence. It may be that PACE powers enabling police officers to use force to take non-intimate samples such as hair or body swabs infringe other rights under the Convention such as privacy rights under Article 8.

Adverse Inferences from Silence

The legitimacy, in Convention terms, of drawing adverse inferences from silence during police questioning or failing to testify at trial under the Criminal Evidence

---

[76] Appl. no. 19187/91, 1996–VI, (1997) 23 EHRR 313 at para. 69.

(Northern Ireland) Order 1988 and the Criminal Justice and Public Order Act 1994 is less clear-cut. In *Murray*, the European Court based its decision primarily on the strength of the evidence against the applicant. Since this constituted a 'formidable case against him' it called 'as a matter of common sense' for an explanation. Yet under the 1988 Order and the 1994 Act, so long as there is a *prima facie* case, there is no *requirement* for the prosecution evidence to reach such a high threshold before adverse inferences are drawn. On the contrary, as noted above, the judiciary in Northern Ireland have rejected the 'confess and avoid' approach initially advocated by Kelly LJ in *Smith*.[77] And, in the case of *Byrne*[78] in which inferences were drawn under the 1994 Act, the Court of Appeal held that the strength or weakness of the prosecution case is not, of itself, a general ground for requiring a judge to advise or direct the jury that they ought not to draw any adverse inference from the failure of the defendant to give evidence. According to Lord Chief Justice Taylor, 'We do not consider that the strength or weakness of the prosecution would, of itself, be any general ground for requiring a judge to take a particular course in regard to his directions on drawing inferences.'

Furthermore, the European Court emphasised in *Murray* the need for safeguards such as the right to legal advice before adverse inferences could be drawn from failure to answer police questions. This raises a number of interrelated issues yet to be resolved. As Roger Ede has pointed out,[79] as a result of the Criminal Justice and Public Order Act 1994, a suspect is expected to know and disclose the details of what the defence will be without any corresponding obligation on the prosecution to disclose details of the case which the suspect is expected to answer. Investigating officers are advised to disclose the minimum necessary to avoid a 'no comment' interview and ensure that the possibility of an adverse inference being drawn at trial is not ruled out.

In addition, it is well-recognised that suspects about to face questioning, with or without legal assistance, are often emotional, confused, suggestible, intimidated or intellectually disadvantaged. Research for the Runciman Commission found the average IQ of suspects to be within the bottom 5 per cent of the general population; indeed, the researchers classified one in three suspects as being 'intellectually disadvantaged'.[80] Further research found that many suspects did not understand the old caution which was relatively simple.[81] And a recent study has revealed that when the caution was recited in full, 86 per cent of the general population did not understand the meaning of the second sentence – 'But it may harm your defence if you do not mention when questioned something which you later rely on in court'.[82]

---

[77] See above (footnote 43) reported in Haldane Society of Socialist Lawyers, *Upholding the Rule of Law?, Northern Ireland: Criminal Justice under the 'Emergency Powers' in the 1990's* (London, 1992) at p. 44.

[78] 21 November 1995 (95/4159/W4, LEXIS).

[79] Ede R., 'Silent Danger' (1997) 94/6 *Law Society's Gazette* 22.

[80] See Gudjonsson, G. *et al.*, *Persons at Risk During Interviews in Police Custody* (Royal Commission on Criminal Justice Research Study No. 12, HMSO, London, 1992) p. 24.

[81] *Ibid.* pp. 17, 18. 20 per cent did not fully appreciate the meaning of the right to silence and 55 per cent could not distinguish between moral and legal obligation. See also on the difficulties of comprehending notices as to rights in custody, Clare, I. and Gudjonsson, G., *Devising and Piloting an Experimental version of the notice to detained persons* (Royal Commission on Criminal Justice Research Study No. 7, HMSO, London, 1993).

[82] Ede, R., 'Silent Danger', LSG 94/6, 12 February 1997.

Moreover, available research suggests that the conceptual approach of the European Court in *Murray* may be flawed. The Criminal Law Review Committee in 1972 recognised that there are numerous innocent reasons why people in custody may refuse to answer questions.[83] More recent research suggested that up to 12 per cent of suspects remain silent to protect others.[84] Other motives such as distrust of the police cannot be discounted. And in Northern Ireland, plausible, exculpatory pretexts for silence can be suggested – for example, the low proportion of charges arising from Prevention of Terrorism Act detentions[85] tends to suggest that the police often select for interrogation those who have no direct knowledge of terrorism but who may be too intimidated by terrorists to co-operate in any way with the police. Drawing inferences of guilt from silence in such circumstances carries an obvious risk of injustice.

In summary, the conclusion that where the prosecution evidence is sufficiently strong, inferences can safely be drawn as a matter of common sense may be too simplistic in some cases. It may be partly in recognition of this possibility that the European Court in *Murray* noted and emphasised that, in Northern Ireland, the 'Diplock' judge (who determines factual as well as legal issues)[86] must state the reasons for his decision to draw adverse inferences and explain what weight he attaches to them. Absent this safeguard under the 1994 Act (and neither juries nor lay magistrates offer reasons), the European Court and Commission may be more inclined to find a violation of the fair trial guarantees in Article 6 of the Convention. In this regard it should be noted that in July 1995 the United Nation's Human Rights Committee considered the United Kingdom's fourth periodic report under the International Covenant on Civil and Political Rights and noted 'with concern' that:[87]

> [T]he provisions of the Criminal Justice and Public Order Act 1994 . . . whereby inferences may be drawn from the silence of persons accused of crimes, violates various provisions in article 14 of the Covenant, despite the range of safeguards built into the legislation and the rules enacted thereunder.

Defence Statements

The issues arising from the requirement for, and use of, 'defence statements' under the Criminal Procedure and Investigations Act 1996 are more complicated still. As with the 1988 Order and 1994 Act, there is no *requirement* for the prosecution evidence to reach a certain threshold before adverse inferences are drawn from a failure to provide a defence statement. Consequently, the 1996 Act may also fail to meet the *Murray* criteria for compliance with Article 6. In addition, under the 1996 Act, adverse inferences can be drawn where the defendant at trial advances a defence inconsistent with the defence statement. Arguably, such use of the defence statement comes very close to the use of statements obtained by powers of compulsory questioning in criminal proceedings disapproved of by the European

---

[83] Criminal Law Revision Committee, *Eleventh Report: Evidence: General* (Cmnd 4991, HMSO, London, 1972).

[84] Leng, R., *The Right to Silence in Police Interrogation* (Royal Commission on Criminal Justice Research Study No. 10, HMSO, London, 1993).

[85] See Chapter 14.

[86] See Northern Ireland (Emergency Provisions) Act 1998, s.10.

[87] Human Rights Committee, *19th Annual Report* (A/50/40, New York, 3 October 1995) para. 424. The UK report is at CCPR/C/95/Add.3.

Court in *Murray*. Whilst the sanction of withholding material which might assist the defence case where no defence statement is made is less extreme than the threat of imprisonment or a fine which underpinned the powers of compulsory questioning in *Saunders*, it may be no less effective. If a fair trial is to be guaranteed, all relevant evidence should be disclosed. Failure to do so frustrates preparation for trial and increases the risk of a miscarriage of justice.[88]

This broad principle was recognised by the European Court in *Edwards v UK*[89] where two significant pieces of information had been withheld from the applicant: the fact that (contrary to evidence given at the applicant's trial) fingerprints had been found at the scene of a burglary; and the fact that (again contrary to evidence given at trial) one of the victims of a robbery had not identified the applicant when shown a photograph of him. The European Court held that it was a requirement of fairness under Article 6(1) of the Convention that the prosecution disclose to the defence 'all material evidence for or against the accused' and that failure to do so in the applicant's case gave rise to a defect in the trial proceedings.[90]

Since the information withheld in the *Edwards* case undermined the prosecution case, it may well come within the definition of 'primary' rather than 'secondary' disclosure under the 1996 Act. However, if the broad principle in *Edwards* holds, the threat under the Act is of an unfair trial. Drawing on the European Court's reasoning in *Saunders* – that the right not to incriminate oneself cannot be confined to statements or admissions of wrongdoing or to remarks which were directly incriminating but extends to evidence which might be deployed in a way which supported the prosecution case – the use of defence statements made under the 1996 Act to support the prosecution case or undermine the defence case probably violates Article 6 of the Convention.

The Political Dimension

How has it come about that in the 1990s the UK Government is instructing public prosecutors to disapply some provisions of the powers of compulsory questioning legislation passed in the 1980s? Examination of the political dimension suggests an answer – namely that, driven by an unsubstantiated belief that numerous criminals were escaping justice by remaining silent, successive Governments ignored much of the available research and all advice against restricting the privilege against self-incrimination.

The drive for reform began with the Criminal Law Revision Committee in 1972.[91] This body, which comprised people with very similar ages and backgrounds, recommended that both the prosecution and the judge be permitted to draw adverse inferences from silence. They quoted with approval the comment of Jeremy Bentham that 'innocence claims the right of speaking, as guilt invokes the privilege of silence.'. At the time, the Committee's report was denounced by almost all commentators[92] and its recommendations never implemented.

---

[88] See Chapter 7.

[89] Appl. no. 13071/87, Ser.A vol.247-B, (1993) 15 EHRR 417.

[90] *Ibid.* at para. 36.

[91] Criminal Law Revision Committee, *Eleventh Report: Evidence (General)* (Cmnd 4991, HMSO, London, 1972).

[92] For a more detailed history see Zander, M., 'Abolition of the right to silence, 1972–1994' in Morgan, D. and Stephenson, G., (eds.), *Suspicion & Silence:The Right to Silence in Criminal Investigations* (Blackstone Press, London, 1994).

The Philips Royal Commission, which led to the enactment of PACE, returned to the issue in its Report in 1981.[93] It recommended that the privilege against self-incrimination remain unaltered. In its view, the risk inherent in any change was that the innocent and vulnerable would suffer, not the guilty. The Conservative Government adopted the advice, but the privilege against self-incrimination was not enshrined in PACE. Nonetheless, the police caution reflected the old rule.

In spite of the long public debate which had resulted in the findings of the Philips Commission, the Government embarked on a concerted effort to render the right to silence impotent. In 1987 the then Home Secretary, Douglas Hurd, announced in a speech to the Police Federation that there should be a public debate about the right to silence.[94] Significantly, the terms of reference for the Home Office Working Group set up in May 1988 were not to consider the merits of the right to silence but to formulate the changes in the law necessary to abolish it. Additionally, the Government introduced the Criminal Evidence (Northern Ireland) Order 1988. Although, apparently, in response to concern over the high level of terrorism and other serious crime, and in particular racketeering, the Order was made applicable against all criminal suspects in the region.

The eagerness of the Government to introduce the 1988 Order was highlighted by the manner of its implementation. Without having conducted any empirical research, it dispensed with the parliamentary procedure of circulating the draft Order in advance which was designed to allow comment and amendment. Indeed, the Order was introduced to the surprise of the Standing Advisory Commission on Human Rights (SACHR). The SACHR was specifically established to advise the Government on such issues, but was not given any effective opportunity to raise its concerns about the draft Order. The Government's intention to apply the same reform to England was frustrated by the much publicised miscarriages of justice involving the *Maguire Seven*, the *Guildford Four* and the *Birmingham Six*. Instead, the Prime Minister announced the setting up of the Royal Commission on Criminal Justice.

The research sponsored by the Runciman Commission suggested that 'the right to silence is rarely exercised . . . that about half of those who exercise it are convicted' and that 'there is little evidence that the prospects for conviction would be enhanced by inducing the suspect to speak or by treating his silence as evidence against him'.[95] The Commission concluded by a majority of 9–2 that:[96]

. . . the possibility of an increase in the convictions of the guilty is outweighed by the risk that the extra pressure on the suspects to talk in the police station and the adverse inferences invited if they do not may result in more convictions of the innocent.

In response, the then Home Secretary, Michael Howard, declared in his speech to the Conservative Party conference in Autumn 1993 that he intended to adopt the view of the minority of the Commission. The speed with which the Criminal

---

[93] Royal Commission on Criminal Procedure, *Report* (Cmnd 8092, HMSO, London, 1981) para. 4.53.

[94] 'Right to silence' (1987) 84 *Law Society's Gazette* 3298.

[95] Leng, R., *The Right to Silence in Police Interrogation: A study of some of the issues underlying the debate* (Royal Commission on Criminal Justice Research Study No. 10, HMSO, London, 1993) p. 79.

[96] *Runciman Report*, ch. 4 para. 22.

Justice and Public Order Act 1994 was enacted ignored the concerns raised by MPs that the proposals violated the European Convention on Human Rights and, in particular, the warnings of Gerald Bermingham and Stephen Byers that it would be prudent to wait for the cases of *Saunders* and *Murray* which had been declared admissible by the European Commission on Human Rights to be decided by the Strasbourg authorities.

Conclusion

Whether or not a 'right' to silence existed prior to the radical developments of the last 15 years is open to question. However, what is clear, is that the cumulative effect of the powers of compulsory questioning, the Criminal Evidence (Northern Ireland) Order 1988, the Criminal Justice and Public Order Act 1994 and the Criminal Procedure and Investigations Act 1996 has been to remove the privilege against self-incrimination as understood by the Strasbourg institutions.[97]

The recent guidelines issued by the Attorney-General to the CPS in relation to powers of compulsory questioning – effectively directing them to disapply clear legislative provisions – indicate the scale of the problem faced by a Government now committed to incorporation of the European Convention on Human Rights by means of the Human Rights Act 1998. Similar measures may soon be required to deal with emerging problems under the 1988 Order, the 1994 Act and the 1996 Act. Ultimately, a wholesale revision of the law on the right to silence is necessary and desirable.

---

[97] The pressure for change is likely to continue as two further cases are pending: *Sean Kevin Murray v UK*, Appl. no. 22384/93, *Dermot Quinn v UK*, Appl. no. 23496/94.

6

Forensic Evidence

Clive Walker and Russell Stockdale[*]

The Problems of Police Interrogation and the Place of Forensic Science

As discussed in the previous chapters, some of the deepest and most persistent causes of miscarriages of justice relate to the interrogation practices of the police and the evidential value of the self-incriminatory oral testimony or in later years the silences thereby produced. A number of alternative investigative strategies were outlined in Chapter 1, including a greater reliance upon forensic science to provide the necessary evidence against criminality. The role of forensic science in crime investigation is indeed growing in importance because of two factors. One is the development of wholly novel forensic sciences. The second factor involves more efficient and effective ways of performing and applying old forensic sciences. Standing in the former category is, above all, the invention of DNA profiling. Successive phases of development have rendered this technique widely accessible and applicable. Its utilisation is now pervasive, with a National DNA database which will hold up to five million records.[1] In the category of improvements of old, established techniques might be the development of automatic fingerprint recognition, which promises to revitalise the interest in taking prints in the first place and seeking matches in the second.[2] In these ways, the picture seems to have changed from a decade or so ago, when a study for the Philips Royal Commission in 1980 suggested the utilisation of forensic science was rare,[3] and when there was not only limited value but police ignorance of feasible applications.[4] However,

---

[*] An earlier version of this chapter appeared as 'Forensic science and miscarriages of justice' (1995) 54 *Cambridge Law Journal* 69.

[1] See Home Office Circular No. 16/95, *National DNA Database* (1995). See Police and Criminal Evidence Act 1984, s.63(3A), (3B); Redmayne, M., 'The DNA Database' [1998] *Criminal Law Review* 437. There is a US Federal equivalent: Shapiro, E.D. and Reifler, S., 'Forensic DNA analysis and the US Government' (1996) 36 *Medicine, Science and the Law* 43.

[2] The technology has proven very problematic with competing systems being sponsored by a police force consortia (the AFR Consortium) and the Home Office (the National Automatic Fingerprint Identification System), though the latter will prevail by the end of the decade: Hook, P., 'Fingertip precision' (1997) 105 *Police Review* 17 January p. 25. The value of fingerprint checks has been widened by the Criminal Procedure and Investigations Act 1996, s. 64.

[3] Steer, D., *Uncovering Crime* (Royal Commission on Criminal Procedure Research Study No. 7, HMSO, 1980).

[4] Ramsay, M., *The Effectiveness of the Forensic Science Service* (Home Office Research Study No.

because of the factors indicated, it is now understood that forensic science is potentially available in a much broader range of cases, though the emphasis is often on its efficient application rather than its use in greater volume.[5] Perhaps an exception is Northern Ireland, where the expanding facilities of the Northern Ireland Forensic Science Agency (FSANI) received some unwelcome recognition of their growing relevance by the fact that the IRA arranged for the laboratories to be laid waste by a large bomb in 1992.[6]

On the face of it, this evidential avenue seems to offer great promise for the avoidance of miscarriages of justice. On the one hand, it avoids several human fallibilities, such as memories or responses affected by fright or lapse of time or self-condemnatory statements induced by disorientation or undue pressure. On the other hand, it calls in aid the wonders of modern science with its allure of cold detachment and technical probity and precision. Yet even this most apparently objective category of prosecution evidence has been shown to be very fallible, especially in terrorist cases. The purpose of this chapter is to elucidate the nature of forensic science, to describe some of the fallibilities with which it must grapple and to draw lessons for the future avoidance of miscarriages of justice.

Nature of Forensic Science[7]

Forensic scientists are regarded as expert witnesses, consequently they occupy a special position in court in that they may give evidence of opinion as well as fact. Dangers arise if the court, and perhaps the scientists themselves, are unclear as to which is which, their evidence being regarded as somehow infallible and the pristine truth. The main danger is that when considering any piece of scientific work, it is tempting to dwell on the analytical tests employed and the manner in which these were carried out, matters which are often unimpeachable,[8] without giving sufficient weight to the provenance of the material under test, how this was collected and presented and what inferences may be safely drawn from the results obtained.[9] The effect is rather like focusing on the making of a cake without being unduly concerned about the quality of its ingredients, what it tasted like and whether it was suitable for the specific purpose for which it had been made. These dangers are belatedly being recognised by the courts. As Lord Justice Glidewell commented in the *Ward* case:[10]

For lawyers, jurors and judges a forensic scientist conjures up the image of a man in a white coat working in a laboratory, approaching his task with cold

92, 1987) ch. 2

[5] See ACPO/FSS, *Using Forensic Science Effectively* (FSS, Birmingham, 1996).

[6] See http://www.nics.gov uk/forensic/forensic.htm. The FSANI is larger in proportion to the police force served by it than any other laboratory in the UK: House of Lords Select Committee on Science and Technology (hereafter cited as 'H.L. Select Committee'), *Forensic Science* (1992–93 H.L. 24) para. 2.15. It became a Next Steps agency in 1995.

[7] See: Phillips, J.H. and Bowen, J.K., *Forensic Science and the Expert Witness* (Sweet & Maxwell, London, 1985); Kind, S.S., *The Scientific Investigation of Crime* (Forensic Science Services, Harrogate, 1987); Hodkinson, T., *Expert Evidence* (Sweet & Maxwell, London, 1990) ch. 14; Aitken, C.C.G. and Stoney, D.A., (eds.), *The Use of Statistics in Forensic Science* (E. Horwood, New York, 1991); Kaye, B.H., *Science and the Detective* (VCH, New York, 1995).

[8] See: Whitehead, P.H., 'Ten years of forensic science 1974–83' [1984] *Criminal Law Review* 663.

[9] See: Robertson, B. and Vignaux, G.A., 'Expert evidence' (1992) 12 *Oxford Journal of Legal Science* 392.

[10] (1992) 96 Cr App R 1 at p. 51. But the aura of science may be exaggerated: 'Note: Standards for admitting scientific evidence' (1983) 28 *Villanova Law Review* 554.

neutrality, and dedicated only to the pursuit of the truth. It is a sombre thought that the reality is somewhat different. Forensic scientists may become partisan.

In most fields of scientific endeavour the scientist has a large measure of control over the nature and condition of the raw materials in his or her tests. By contrast, the raw materials of forensic science are the stuff of everyday life, and the forensic scientist has to take them in the state they are in and to recognise them for what they are. There can be considerable difficulties in deciding what should be looked at in the first place, and what inferences – matters of opinion – might safely be drawn from test results in the second. In reality, and as in every other field of professional endeavour, different forensic scientists presented with the same sets of data can and do come to different views and express different opinions based on them. Moreover, the interpretation of their results and the significance they attach to these will depend upon the quality and extent of the information they have received about the case at issue. In this way, science is 'not . . . an independent, self-regulating producer of truths about the natural world, but . . . a dynamic social institution fully engaged with other mechanisms for creating social and epistemological order . . . '.[11]

All this means that forensic science evidence, like any other, must be thoroughly probed and tested in order to expose weaknesses or room for reasonable doubt. These can lie hidden from the lay observer, behind an apparently unassailable façade of scientific precision and accuracy. At this point it is necessary to look more closely at the nature of forensic science and the different demands placed upon its practitioners by the police/prosecution on the one hand and by the defence on the other.

By way of definition, forensic science can be said to be the systematic and painstaking identification, analysis and comparison of the physical residues of crime in order to establish what happened, when, where and how it happened, and who might have been involved. In criminal cases its purpose is to assist the court in deciding upon the guilt or otherwise of those brought before it. Nonetheless, forensic science has other important functions to fulfil well before any such proceedings are in view and usually starting with the police investigation. This view is reflected in evidence to the Home Affairs Committee[12] in which the Home Office said that the main functions of the Forensic Science Service were '. . . to provide resources to assist the police in the investigation and detection of crime and to assist the courts in the administration of justice.'.[13] In summary,[14] one might accept the response of the House of Lords Select Committee on Science and Technology that:[15]

The task of forensic science is to serve the interests of justice by providing scientifically based evidence relating to criminal activity.

---

[11] Jasanoff, S., *Science at the Bar* (Harvard University Press, 1995) p. xv. See also Wynne, B., 'Establishing the rules of law constructing expert authority' in Smith, R. and Wynne, B. (eds.), *Expert Evidence* (Routledge, London, 1989).

[12] *The Forensic Science Service* (1988–89 HC 26).

[13] *Ibid.* Vol. II at p. 1.

[14] See also: Phillips, J.H. and Bowen, J.K., *Forensic Science and the Expert Witness* (Sweet & Maxwell, London, 1985); Kind, S.S., *The Scientific Investigation of Crime* (Forensic Science Services, Harrogate, 1987); Hodgkinson, T., *Expert Evidence* (Sweet & Maxwell, London, 1990) ch. 14; Aitken, C.C.G. and Stoney, D.A., (eds.), *The Use of Statistics in Forensic Science* (E. Horwood, New York, 1991).

[15] H.L. Select Committee, para. 1.5.

Recognition that forensic scientists' terms of reference are not confined to the trial process alone is at the root of understanding the differences between the roles of scientists advising the police/prosecution and those engaged, usually at a much later stage, by the defence.

Forensic Science for the Police/Prosecution

Traditionally, the Crown has provided forensic science resources to assist the police and the prosecution.[16] This public sector work is now carried out in two main organisations.[17] One is the Forensic Science Service (FSS), an agency created in April 1991 under the Next Steps Programme in succession to the Home Office laboratories.[18] Secondly, there are police-owned laboratories. By far the largest used to be the Metropolitan Police Forensic Science Laboratory (MPFSL), but in 1996 this was merged with the FSS[19] leaving police-based laboratories exclusively in Scotland. The defence on the other hand has relied on what has been available in the private sector.[20]

The job of the scientist advising the police/prosecution begins far from the laboratory bench. In the first instance it will involve helping to train specialist scenes of crime officers (SOCOs – sometimes now called Scenes of Crime Examiners or SCEs) and detective officers to select and recover those items which are likely to be of most use in clarifying issues for the investigating officer and, ultimately, the court. The better this training, the higher the quality of starting materials the scientist will have to work with.[21]

In the early stages of a police enquiry, the forensic scientist is part of the investigating officer's team of specialist advisers to the extent of helping to determine whether or not a crime has been committed at all and, if so, which one and how. In a suspected murder case for example, the scientist is probably most effective working at the investigating officer's side – at the scene looking for clues, pointing out features and material likely to be of evidential value and generally trying to piece together precisely what has happened and, wherever possible on the information available, suggesting directions in which police enquiries might usefully proceed. This means that from the outset the forensic scientist is, and arguably should remain, actively engaged in the identification and investigation of crime. The nature of this aspect of the job requires close involvement with, and deep commitment to, the investigative process.[22] In order to make an effective

---

[16] Forensic laboratories began in 1931 as a common service (now see Police Act 1996, s. 57).

[17] Other relevant organisations are the Central Research and Support Establishment (described below), the Defence Research Agency (which supersedes the Royal Armament Research and Development Establishment and tests explosives) and the Northern Ireland Office Forensic Science Laboratory Agency. Account should also be taken of the Laboratory of the Government Chemist which became a Next Steps agency in 1989 but in 1996 was sold to LGC (Holdings) Ltd, a consortium consisting of Laboratory managers, 3I Group plc and the Royal Society of Chemistry.

[18] See: Home Affairs Committee, *The Forensic Science Service* (1988–89 HC 26); *The Forensic Science Service* (Cm 699, 1989). The FSS operates at six different sites and employs about 400 scientists (see http://www.fss.org.uk/).

[19] See FSS, *Annual Report* (1995–96 HC 551). The former MPFSL was possibly the largest single forensic establishment in Europe, with over 300 scientists.

[20] This remains very small by comparison: McCulloch, H., *Police Use of Forensic Science* (Police Research Group, Paper no. 19, London, 1996).

[21] Training is raised as an issue but without any detail in ACPO/FSS, *Using Forensic Science Effectively* (FSS, Birmingham, 1996) para. 3.3.

[22] See ACPO/FSS, *Using Forensic Science Effectively* (FSS, Birmingham, 1996) p. 42.

contribution, the scientist cannot stand on the side-lines with the lofty detachment of a disinterested observer.

When the items – several hundred in a large, serious case – arrive at the laboratory, the scientist must decide which it would be most profitable to examine, and for what. If all items were to be examined and in all respects, a single case could turn into a lifetime's work. Selections made at this stage depend, again, on experience and on the amount and quality of the information the scientist has received about the case; decisions at this step can dramatically affect the quality and usefulness of the evidence subsequently produced.

It is only at this stage that analytical procedures begin to be applied. Tests must be chosen carefully, and great care and attention paid to the manner in which they are carried out, the equipment used and so on. The results they provide must then be interpreted, but this may be far from straightforward. No two cases are ever precisely the same; they each have their own peculiarities, and it is only by investigating many cases of the same general type that the effects of these can be appreciated and a balanced conclusion reached.

Next the scientist will prepare a written report on the findings, selecting only the ones which are considered to be most pertinent. It would not be practicable to try to report on everything seen and found. Again, decisions as to what to include and what to omit will depend very much on the information received and perceptions of the matters at issue. This may be the last ever heard of the case. Alternatively, the scientist may be called to give oral evidence. If so, then the amount and type of information he or she is able to impart will be conditioned by the questions put and by the latitude allowed in making replies.

The overall quality of the scientific evidence which emerges from the prosecution's scientist will depend upon many variables. One is knowledge of the circumstances of the case and, against this background, the scientist's (and/or that of others, such as SOCOs/SCEs) initial selection of which items to submit to the laboratory. Others involve the selection of which tests to apply to which items, the conduct of the tests themselves, the interpretation of the test results, the drawing of inferences from these interpretations in the context of the case, the selection of information to impart in the written report, and the nature of questions put to the scientist at court and the latitude allowed in framing responses.

Much of the recent criticism of FSS and other public sector forensic scientists has arisen, albeit rather late in the day, as a result of whether and to what extent the evidence they gave was balanced. Clearly, there have been occasions when it was not. But, arguably, in the generality of cases it is perhaps too much to expect of anyone actively involved as a matter of course in the identification and investigation of crime, and the hunt for the perpetrator, to present all the evidence to the entire satisfaction of both prosecuting and defending counsel alike. That would be like expecting the hound who has just caught what he believes to be the hare to set to with a will to give it the kiss of life.[23] However intellectually

[23] See further: Stockdale, R., 'Running with the hounds' (1991) 141 *New Law Journal* 772. Prosecution bias was likewise uncovered in the Office of the Inspector General of the Department of Justice; see *The FBI Laboratory: An Investigation into laboratory practices and alleged misconduct in explosives-related and other cases* (Washington, 1997); Kelly, J.F. and Wearne, P.K., *Tainting Evidence* (Free Press, New York, 1998).

independent and scientifically objective FSS and police scientists may strive to be, their 'hunting' role is inescapable. As such, they are neither in a position, nor necessarily have sufficient information of the right kind, to determine whether their evidence and stance are balanced or whether they list slightly to one side.

An emergent problem being faced on the public/prosecution side is that funding for forensic work allocated by the police is under great pressure. This pressure has resulted, for example, in fewer scenes of crimes visits,[24] the non-submission of potential forensic evidence, the limiting of tests to be performed on the instructions of the customer[25] or its submission to inappropriate scientists.[26] Though the problems of the defence may be even more acute, undue economies on the part of the prosecution will have an enduring and pervasive impact on the quality of forensic evidence on both sides.

Forensic Science for the Defence

There are three main strands comprising the role of forensic scientists engaged by the defence. These are:

(a) to check the analytical results emerging from the police/prosecution scientist's work, and to undertake any such further tests as may be warranted;

(b) to clarify the nature of the police/prosecution scientist's findings and the interpretation of them;

(c) to assess and to advise on the significance of the scientific evidence overall in the light of all the circumstances.

(a) *Checking analytical results.* The standard of analytical work coming from the FSS laboratories generally is very high. It is rare for there to be much margin for quibble about, for example, the reported identity and purity of a particular drug, the DNA profile of a blood stain, or the conclusion that one particular fibre is indistinguishable from another. Nonetheless, the analytical procedures employed must always be scrutinised as to their appropriateness, and the results obtained checked to see how far they support what has been reported.

Unfortunately, there is a strong tendency for scientists consequently employed by the defence and who have little or no forensic science training and experience to want to repeat, willy-nilly, the primary work of the police scientists. In most cases, this is impracticable and/or uninformative for various reasons. For instance, the relevant material might all have been used up; or it might have deteriorated to a point beyond which any results obtained would be meaningful; or, owing to repeated handling and testing, the integrity of the material can no longer be assured. So, it is often more important to focus on the detailed records of analyses already carried out than slavishly to repeat them. This is not to say that there will not be other separate and specific tests which the defence scientist will need to carry out to assess the strength of the links the prosecution has proposed, such as

[24] See Weddell, R.J., 'The way forward – raising educational standards for scientific support personnel in the UK' (1997) 37(1) *Science and Justice* 9 at p. 10.

[25] See Lucas, D.M., 'The ethical responsibilities of the forensic scientist' (1989) 34(3) *Journal of Forensic Sciences* 719 at p. 720.

[26] See Gallop, A.M.C., 'Market forensics' (1994) 34(2) *Journal of the Forensic Science Society* 121; Blakey, D.C., 'Does forensic science give value for money?' (1995) 35(1) *Science and Justice* 1.

investigating possible alternative and innocent sources of seemingly incriminating trace evidence.

Some cases involve protracted scientific examinations but, as matters stand and unless formal interim reports are issued, the defence will have no knowledge of, or access to, the analyses in progress. In these circumstances, it would seem to be reasonable for the defence scientist to be admitted to the examination as it proceeds. As to cases in which the police/prosecution scientist's examinations are complete, the defence scientist should have full and ready access to all the working notes and be able to request copies of these as required. Until recently, access to such papers in the FSS depended very much on how the police/prosecution scientist was disposed to opening his or her file.

The position in which the defence inevitably finds itself thus underscores the need to appoint properly trained and thoroughly experienced forensic scientists who will be completely familiar with all the procedures adopted by the FSS. It also emphasises the special nature and weight of the responsibility placed upon the police/prosecution's scientists by virtue of their having the first and possibly only opportunity to examine materials in their original state.

(b) *Clarifying the nature of scientific evidence.*   A number of lawyers admit that they regard forensic science evidence very much as a closed book, dealing with it as quickly as possible and avoiding tackling it head-on. One of the reasons for this might be that scientists' reports have tended to be short on explanations and long on jargon. Another is the almost total absence of training of lawyers in forensic science, either at university or in professional courses. This 'scientific illiteracy'[27] renders lawyers (and judges) handicapped in terms of comprehending the significance and meaning of forensic evidence. The point is well-illustrated by the inept handling of the *Maguire Seven* final appeal. Even with the benefit of the *Interim Report* of the May Committee on the Maguire case,[28] full argumentation from counsel and the considerable blessing of hindsight, the Court of Appeal failed to grasp how the undermining of the specificity of the forensic tests for nitroglycerine tainted the whole evidence for the prosecution. Instead, the Court took refuge in the possibility of contamination, despite (or perhaps because of) its unwarranted overtones that, if not guilty, the defendants had undesirable associates. The Court's interpretation was in turn criticised by the May Inquiry's *Second Report*, which more realistically cast doubt on whether the tests used could provide conclusive proof of guilt.[29] Accordingly, an important part of the defence scientist's work is to ensure that all concerned on behalf of the defendant fully understand what the prosecution's scientific evidence means and feel thoroughly at home with the principles behind it. In this way, counsel will be best supported and equipped to cross-examine on the evidence confidently and effectively and thus expose any weaknesses inherent in it.

(c) *Interpretation and significance.* Another essential part of the defence scientist's job is to bring a fresh eye to the interpretation of the scientific evidence and the significance laid upon it. In particular, he or she should assess its significance

[27] Memorandum of the Forensic Science Society to the H.L. Committee (1992), p. 67.
[28] *Interim Report on the Maguire Case* (1989–90 HC 556) (*Interim Report*).
[29] (1992–93 HC 296) paras. 1.6–1.8 (*Second Report*).

in the context of all the circumstances, including the results of any further tests carried out for the defence and in the light of, for example, the defendant's last word on the matter which the police/prosecution scientist may not have had the opportunity to consider. Depending upon those findings, the defence scientist too may be required to give oral evidence or, at least, to advise counsel while he tackles what the prosecution's scientist has to say.

The overall quality of the advice and/or evidence which emerges from the defence scientist will depend upon qualifications and experience in the field, knowledge of the case at issue and, against this background, checking of the prosecution's analytical procedures; clarifying the extent and nature of the police scientist's findings and the interpretations which have been placed on these; and assessment and advice as to the significance of the scientific evidence in the light of all the circumstances.

The Fallibility of Forensic Evidence

In the wake of a number of well-publicised cases in which, on closer scrutiny, the prosecution's scientific evidence was found wanting,[30] forensic science has been variously labelled as potentially unreliable, partial and misleading. It is difficult to say whether the rate of challenge is increasing or has remained stable, but it is becoming more noticeable because of the proportion of serious crime cases in which forensic science is utilised.[31] Either way, the possibility of unreliability is disturbing. The problem is also deep-seated in that it is often alleged to be inherent in the nature of the evidence and its analysis. So, the removal of a few 'bad apple' scientists[32] will help but will not solve all the potential weaknesses. Further, the problem seems to be pervasive. It does not simply apply to the forms of forensic evidence common in terrorist cases, in other words the analysis of traces of explosives or firearms discharges. Other forms of material can equally give rise to dispute, such as the DNA samples which are now the common fare of contemporary rape and child abuse trials. As a result, one should take issue with the blinkered premise of the House of Lords Select Committee on Science and Technology that forensic science primarily suffers from an 'image problem'.[33] In fact the problems are substantive and serious. While forensic science is an increasingly powerful tool for clarifying issues before the courts, there is a popular misconception that it provides an especially pure and objective form of evidence and has the capacity to give universally accepted, clear-cut answers leaving no doubt.[34]

---

[30] See especially: *R v Maguire* [1992] 2 All ER 433; *R v McIlkenney* [1992] 2 All ER 417.

[31] See: H.L. Select Committee, p. 17. Zander ('The Royal Commission Crown Court survey' (1992) 142 *New Law Journal* 1730) suggests its use in a third of cases surveyed and challenges in a quarter of those, but these data are dubiously drawn from the impressions of participants rather than court records.

[32] Candidates for this title have been alleged to include Dr Frank Skuse, whose evidence was described as in 'grave doubt' in the *Birmingham Six* case (*R v McIlkenney* [1992] 2 All ER 417 at p. 432) and as 'valueless' in the *Ward* case ((1992) 96 Cr App R 1 at p. 53). A *World in Action* programme along similar lines prompted an action for libel which was later dropped: *Skuse v Granada TV, The Independent*, 2 April 1993, *The Times*, 18 October 1994 p. 5, [1994] 1 WLR 1156. The prosecution of Ronald Outteridge arising out of the *Kiszko* case was stayed by a magistrate: (1995) *The Independent* 2 May p. 2.

[33] H.L. Select Committee, para. 1.33.

[34] The HL Select Committee, para. 1.26, found that the FSS provided conclusive evidence in 61 per cent of the cases in which it is involved and strong evidence in a further 14 per cent.

Several recent miscarriages of justice have occurred because scientific evidence adduced at trial was not properly tested or understood. There have been at least four features which have led to both mistakes by the police/prosecution and a failure on the part of the defence to expose them. One is that it is the police/prosecution who take the initiative in the collection of evidence, which can lead to unsuspected contamination and significant omissions. In addition, the quality and competency of forensic scientists causes concern. There are also recurrent misunderstandings, both by scientists and lawyers, as to how forensic evidence translates into proof. Finally, funding for the needs of the defence is inadequate.

Contamination and Omissions

The collection of the materials which will eventually be tested in forensic laboratories is primarily a matter for the discretion of the police.[35] Thus, the obvious dangers arise that non-scientists will accidentally contaminate evidence or that they will fail to appreciate the value of such evidence as is available and will fail to forward it to the laboratory. To some extent, the dangers have been decreased in recent years because of the changing profile of the SOCOs/SCEs who perform the task. In the first place, the post has been civilianised in many forces, allowing the appointment of individuals with specialised knowledge.[36] Secondly, their training was significantly improved in 1990 when a new and more substantial course was inaugurated at the National Training Centre for Scientific Support to Crime Investigation at Durham.[37] Nevertheless, the raising of the quality of SOCOs/SCEs by no means solves all the problems, since they attend only a minority of crimes and arrive at selected sites only after other police officers have visited.[38] Thus, training should be increased throughout the police service to ensure that patrol officers are fully aware of forensic science principles and practices and act in accordance with them.[39]

Contamination is less likely to occur through the operations of the FSS, the Laboratory of the Government Chemist[40] or the Defence Research Agency (including the Forensic Explosives Laboratory and the Royal Armament Research and Development Establishment). Moreover, there seems to be a willingness to investigate without waiting for acquittals or judicial criticisms. Thus, the possibility of contamination of a centrifuge at Fort Halstead used to test for explosives residue in eight cases involving alleged IRA activity was considered in an independent inquiry by Professor Caddy.[41] The inquiry found high standards at the laboratories and that control samples did not reveal contamination.

---

[35] Serious Crime Units in the FSS London Laboratory and FSANI allow their scientists to work alongside police collectors of evidence. Scientists from FSS laboratories have attended major crime scenes as a matter of course for many years.

[36] See: Ramsay, M., *The Effectiveness of the Forensic Science Service* (Home Office Research Study No. 92, 1987) p. 32.

[37] ACPO/FSS, *Using Forensic Science Effectively* (FSS, Birmingham, 1996) p. 95. NVQs have been developed for fingerprinting and other scientific work: Lord Chancellor's Department, Home Office and Law Officers' Department, *The Royal Commission on Criminal Justice: Final Government Response* (Home Office, London, 1996) para. 158.

[38] See: Sargant, T. and Hill, P., *Criminal Trials* (Fabian Research Series No. 348, London, 1986) p. 18. See ACPO/FSS, *Using Forensic Science Effectively* (FSS, Birmingham, 1996) p. 29.

[39] See *ibid.*, 23.

[40] This agency (of the DTI) has actively sought new customers in the forensic sector: (1992–93 HC 809) p. 12. Its work mainly concerns substance and document testing: (1994–95 HC 660) p. 5.

[41] Caddy, B., *Assessment and Implications of Centrifuge Contamination in the Trace Explosive Section of the Forensic Explosives Laboratory at Fort Halstead* (Cm 3491, HMSO, London, 1996).

Quality and Competence

Concerns about the quality and competence of forensic science personnel apply to personnel in the profession in general. Additional problems arise from the operations of public or private sector scientists respectively. It is undoubtedly true that in international terms, UK standards are very high,[42] but that achievement must be set in the context of an adversarial system which in respect of forensic investigations places many of the trump cards in the hands of the police/ prosecution.

Amongst the general concerns are whether people of the necessarily high calibre can be recruited and retained by the forensic science community and the levels of education and training of entrants into the profession. On the latter point, first or even postgraduate degrees are not enough. Though postgraduate courses in forensic science are useful in so far as they give potential forensic scientists a flavour of the job, they are no substitute for the necessary long professional apprenticeship which all newcomers to the profession need to undergo before they can properly offer themselves to the courts as forensic scientists. The primary and initial sources of relevant job training are total immersion in the casework of the FSS and police laboratories: forensic scientists cannot be bought off university shelves. In any event, existing vocational qualifications and recognitions are far from satisfactory,[43] so additional National Vocational Qualifications (NVQs) are being developed.[44] While these might be appropriate for technicians and assistants,[45] it is difficult to see that they would be relevant at the professional, court-going level where more sustained and sophisticated professional education is required.

Even if the requisite personnel is available, professional standards should demand rigorous staff development and training. In the past, in-service education and training in the FSS have appeared to be adequate, but whether or not the present 'small team structure' of the Service will adequately expose trainees to sufficient depth in any particular subject area remains to be seen. Moreover, there are worrying signs that individual laboratories within the FSS may be extending the range of services they offer without ensuring that the necessary skills and experience are in place. Furthermore, in the light of criticisms concerning, *inter alia*, less than full disclosure by forensic scientists,[46] some attention needs to be given to clear direction and instruction in their legal responsibilities to the courts.

Essential features of a healthy profession include the encouragement of research and technical development as well as the maintenance of standards. In the past British research in forensic science, centred mainly at the Central Research and Support Establishment (CRSE) of the FSS, enjoyed an unassailable prime position.

---

[42] House of Lords Select Committee, para. 2.1.

[43] The Forensic Science Society offers Diplomas on Document Examination and Scenes of Crime Examination. It also compiles (as does the Law Society) a register of experts, though makes no inquiry into their competence. The University of Durham offers a Diploma in Scientific Support Skills.

[44] Hadley, K., 'Vocational qualifications in forensic science' (1994) 34 *Journal of the Forensic Science Society* 5.

[45] See Weddell, R.J., 'The way forward – raising educational standards for scientific support personnel in the UK' (1997) 37(1) *Science and Justice* 9; Horswell, J, and Edwards, M., 'Development of quality systems accreditation for crime scene investigators in Australia' (1997) 37(1) *Science & Justice* 3.

[46] See chapter 7.

With the introduction of agency status, the title CRSE was lost, and its work, which was transferred to the Birmingham branch of the FSS, has been run down to the extent that, save for a rump of DNA-oriented projects, little research work is being undertaken there or anywhere else in the Service. Moreover, a once thriving Information Division within the CRSE, catering for the needs of research and operational scientists alike, has now apparently been substantially reduced. Other former CRSE functions are as a source of unimpeachable materials standards for reference purposes against which quality in routine casework procedures can be assessed and assured,[47] and for trouble-shooting when potential anomalies arise in the course of casework. The House of Lords Select Committee's response to these concerns arising from the commercial pressures on the FSS was to recommend that a new centre for forensic research be established.[48] However, a less costly and perhaps more sensible solution is to locate research where there is most expertise and need for research – in other words within the FSS; this solution could be achieved by the specification of minimum research fund allocation within the framework agreement between Home Office and FSS. Research and development within the FSS exists but still does not figure expressly in its Aims and Objectives, nor is a specified budget allocated according to FFS annual reports, nor does it sit easily with the language of performance indicators which are pitched in terms of customer satisfaction and response times.

Turning towards particular concerns about scientists working in the public sector, the FSS laboratories are very well equipped, and procedures for handling and testing materials well-defined and carefully controlled and monitored. However, a number of unpalatable developments traceable to the agency status of the FSS may be occurring.[49] As already mentioned, problems include the loss or dislocation of experienced staff, as well as the effective demise of research on new scientific developments and technologies. The FSS laboratories are also no longer capable individually of undertaking a broad range of work, and specialist services are now located in national centres (such as DNA profiling only at London and Wetherby). This has led to the routine fragmentation of cases and the evidence in them. Another danger is that cost implications are restricting the extent to which police employ FSS scientists,[50] seek assistance from them at scenes of crime or are prepared to submit items for examination, thereby compromising the scope of scientific investigations and the safety of the inferences drawn from these.[51] It

---

[47] Assurance requires more in the way of publication of results and oversight: HL Select Committee, para. 3.13.

[48] HL Select Committee, paras. 2.48, 2.51.

[49] Agency status was approved by the Home Affairs Committee, *The Forensic Science Service* (1988–89 HC 26) para. 101.

[50] The appointment of Scientific Support Managers within police forces has the potential for benefits in terms of efficiency and the raising of standards, but the fear is that the trend is mainly motivated by rationing and cost-reduction: House of Lords Select Committee, paras. 2.11, 2.17. There is a warning against undue screening on cost grounds in ACPO/FSS, *Using Forensic Science Effectively* (FSS, Birmingham, 1996) p. 55.

[51] Between April and September 1991, the FSS suffered a 13 per cent drop in case referrals by the police, and about one half of police forces have expressed criticisms of the FSS on cost grounds: H.L. Committee, pp. 58, 181, 182. Before 1989, the Home Affairs Committee, *The Forensic Science Service* (1988–89 HC 26) had reported increasing caseloads because of the growth in reported crime, new police powers, new forensic techniques and the demands of the CPS But since 1991, the total case submissions have barely risen, while the number of items submitted per case has fallen: Weddell, R.J., 'The way forward – raising educational standards for scientific support personnel in the UK' (1997) 37(1) *Science and Justice* 9 at p. 12.

cannot be viewed as satisfactory that an ability to pay may sometimes replace the criterion of seriousness of the case[52] as the determining factor in the reference from the police to the FSS. A further consequence is a trend towards in-house police scientists,[53] and even independent forensic scientists – sometimes little better than 'enthusiastic amateurs'.[54] Disquiet about quality is immediately aroused, and there are also more pragmatic reasons to be wary of the proliferation of police laboratories in terms of the efficiency and capabilities of small scientific units.[55] The House of Lords Select Committee was unable to reach any firm conclusion as to whether the MPFSL with its well-established reputation should be merged with the FSS, judging the arguments to be 'finely balanced'.[56] Nevertheless, it was more clearly hostile to the proliferation of small, ill-founded, police-dominated labora-tories.[57] The Runciman Commission decided against the merger of police labora-tories into the FSS. Not only would it be difficult to produce a single comprehensive agency, since the smaller police outlets and the specialised Laboratory of the Government Chemist and the Defence Research Agency would remain outside, but also consolidation of the MPFSL into the FSS would not in any way remove the perceived link with the police/prosecution.[58] In the event, these recommendations were wholly ignored, and, following a secretive review, the subsumption of the MPFSL within the FSS was brought about on 1 April 1996.[59] The merger followed an internal review by the Home Office in which only the MPFSL, police and FSS were represented and which was predicated on the need to put the MPFSL 'on a business-like footing', though the distancing of scientists from the police was also seen as advantageous.[60] In this way, it would seem that a major change to the configuration of forensic services was implemented without any public discussion and no reference even in private to the concerns of the Runciman Commission. It may be that the option chosen was the best, and it would certainly have been more difficult to combine the MPFSL with other governmental laboratories or to float it off as an independent institute. However, these alterna-tives might have been more seriously considered if a wider range of voices could have been heard.

As with all public expenditure, there is a balance to be struck here. On the one hand, forensic testing has the potential to expand and thereby to increase its demand on scarce resources. In response the agency status of the FSS is endorsed by the Runciman Commission as appropriate in terms of encouraging transparency in accounting and competition and efficiency in the provision of services.[61] On the other hand, this support overlooks somewhat the concerns already expressed about the viability of abstract research in a market environment and about the danger that

[52] See: Ramsay, M., *The Effectiveness of the Forensic Science Service* (Home Office Research Study No. 92, 1987) ch. 2.

[53] See: Pereira, M., 'Forensic science: our changing world' (1993) 33 *Journal of the Forensic Science Society* 117; Stockdale, R., 'Exploding myths' (1997) 37 *Science and Justice* 139.

[54] Stockdale, R., 'Exploding myths' (1997) 37 *Science and Justice* 139 at p. 142.

[55] See: Home Office, *Memoranda to the Royal Commission* (1991) Annex E para. 5.

[56] HL Select Committee, para. 4.26.

[57] *Ibid.* para. 4.13.

[58] Royal Commission on Criminal Justice, *Report* (Cm 2260, 1993) ('*Runciman Report*'), ch. 9 paras. 14–17; LGC, *Annual Report* (1992–93 HC 809) p. 12.

[59] See HC Debs. vol. 254 col. 426 w.a. 10 February 1995, Michael Howard.

[60] Home Office, *Review of the Merger of the Forensic Science Service with the Metropolitan Police Forensic Science Laboratory* (1994) paras. 2, 3.

[61] *Runciman Report*, ch. 9 paras. 22, 23.

charging might induce greater selectivity in the referral of materials.[62] As for other laboratories to whom some police forces are turning on cost grounds, these are in the main poorly equipped, and their scientists lack the necessary skills and experience to do the job properly. Subject to adequate resourcing, it might be argued that in an adversarial system it is proper for the police to have the full range of investigative techniques at their disposal, at least if balanced by equal facilities for the defence, if subject to adequate and enforceable professional standards and if checked by an independent prosecution service which can undertake an independent and thorough review of what evidence has, and has not, been sought or secured. However, it is far from clear that these conditions are met. The Runciman Commission likewise voiced its support for police laboratories in this conditional mode. Whether the conditions are adequately met seems doubtful.

By contrast to the FSS, the very few independent firms properly qualified to act for the defence on the majority of forensic science evidence are often short of equipment and resources. This is a reflection of the uncertain and poor remuneration for the large majority of their work which is funded by legal aid but barely pays for scientists' time, let alone necessary overheads, and leaves nothing for essential investment in equipment, research, and library and reference materials. So-called defence experts are a mixed bag. While the best might be genuinely familiar with the materials they contract to examine, few of them can properly claim anywhere near sufficient or appropriate training and experience to be able to assess the significance of these in the circumstances of the case at issue.[63] Moreover, a worrying number are ready to advance opinions in fields of expertise well outside their own.

With the advent of agency status, the FSS now offers to undertake some work for the defence. However, both the Home Affairs Committee[64] and the Royal Commission's Research Study[65] found that most defence lawyers viewed the FSS as too close to the police, especially because of its practice, until recently, of disclosing defence examination reports to the prosecution. Not surprisingly, defence-related customers form a small majority of FSS turnover – despite early optimism, the total is still well below 5 per cent of customers.[66] At best, agency status does mean that independent practitioners can now make use of the FSS's specialised equipment to carry out checks on their work. Whether the FSS's response to pressing police needs should be diluted by outside commissions is open to debate.

In summary, the attempt to foster quality and efficiency in forensic science by market competition has an uncertain prospect of success given that the FSS has no real rival and given that consumers have little interest in research and development.[67] In common with the treatment of other imperfect public service markets,

---

[62] There was a sharp fall in items submitted to the FSS in 1991–92, which was mainly reversed in 1992–93 (*Annual Report* (1992-93 HC 761) p. 12), but demand is still depressed given the background increase in crime rates.

[63] See: JUSTICE, *A Public Defender* (London, 1987) p. 10.

[64] *The Forensic Science Service* (1988–89 HC 26) para. 80.

[65] Roberts, P. and Willmore, C., *The role of forensic science evidence in criminal proceedings* (Royal Commission on Criminal Justice Research Study No. 11 HMSO, London, 1993) p. 139. See further Roberts, P., 'Science in the criminal process' (1994) 14 *Oxford Journal of Legal Science* 469; Jones, C.A.G., *Expert Witnesses* (Clarendon Press, Oxford, 1994) pp. 212, 222.

[66] *Annual Report* (HC 761 of 1992–93) p. 10.

[67] Jones, C.A.G., *Expert Witnesses* (Clarendon Press, Oxford, 1994) p. 95; Roberts, P., 'What price a

such as power utilities or health services, some form of regulation seems preferable, as will be considered later.

Translation into Proof

One of the ways in which quality of personnel and of management oversight has impacted on trials is in respect of the interface between forensic science and criminal evidence. In other words, mistakes have been made in the process of translating scientific (often chemical) experimentation into legal proof. Misinterpretations can arise at various stages. There may be misguided views about how a substance came to be present in the first place, or the nature of that substance or the extent to which it meets the requisite standard of proof. On matters such as these:[68]

> . . . there can be genuine disagreement between forensic scientists just as there can be disagreement between nuclear physicists or art historians.

Accordingly, it is important for the courts to have the benefit of opinions which are expert but which admit to the margin of appreciation within which opinions may be fairly asserted.

Relevant illustrations may be taken from the *Maguire* and *Birmingham* cases.[69] In *Maguire*, the essence of the prosecution case was that the defendants had knowingly handled nitroglycerine (NG) for an unlawful purpose contrary to section 4 of the Explosive Substances Act 1883. This charge not only required scientific evidence of a positive tracing consistent with the presence of NG on each defendant's body or clothing but also that the trace could not be excused as innocent contamination or as attributable to the presence of some other substance which mimics the chemical make-up of NG. It was on the issue of innocent contamination that the convictions were eventually set aside, but there is now considerable doubt as to the verdict on some of the other grounds. Indeed, the May Inquiry criticised the Court of Appeal for not fully recognising the total improbability of the prosecution's case, given the backgrounds of the defendants, their movements, later tests (undisclosed at the original trial) which proved negative[70] and the lack of other forensic evidence from the Maguire household, without resort to a contamination theory which, of course, continues to impugn the character of someone connected with the household.[71]

Turning first to the issue of contamination, the prosecution's contention at the trial in 1975 was that traces of NG had been discovered underneath the fingernails of most of the defendants.[72] This presence in such a shielded part of the body could only arise, it was said, from substantial, direct and intentional contact with NG, such as by shaping or kneading it or by inserting a detonator.[73] Although that

---

free market in forensic science' (1996) 36 *British Journal of Criminology* 37.

[68] Roberts P. and Willmore, C., *the role of forensic science evidence in criminal proceedings* (Royal Commission on Criminal Justice Research Study No. 11 HMSO, London, 1993) p. 135.

[69] *Ibid.*

[70] *Interim Report*, chaps.11, 12.

[71] *Second Report*, para. 1.6.

[72] In the case of Anne Maguire, the traces were on the plastic gloves used by her: May Inquiry, *Interim Report*, ch. 7.

contention was sustained at trial and was a major factor in securing a conviction, later tests commissioned by the May Inquiry demonstrated repeatedly the brittle nature of legal extrapolation from scientific fact. Thus, the *Interim Report* of Sir John May, published in 1990, related the details of an investigation by a forensic scientist, Professor Thorburn Burns, commissioned by the Inquiry to re-examine the scientific evidence.[74] The tests were reported by the Professor and by the May Inquiry in unequivocal terms; they 'demonstrated' that significant traces of NG could be picked up from a towel (such as used communally in a bathroom) and that, having picked up traces in this way, NG readily migrates under the fingernails.[75] This assertion was echoed by the Court of Appeal when, in 1991, it set the convictions aside solely on this ground. However, the ground had shifted startlingly by the time of the *Second Report* of the May Inquiry in 1992. With the benefit of further tests conducted by a team including Professor Thorburn Burns and chaired by Professor West, it was concluded that contamination with NG under the fingernails was more likely to be a product of the swabbing techniques used to take the samples to be tested rather than from a contaminated towel (or soap).[76] Indeed, it was latterly felt to be improbable that traces under fingernails could have originated from a towel.[77] Nonetheless, the May Inquiry remained convinced that, whatever its origins, contamination had been a real danger and that, in any event, the prosecution's case was improbable as a whole.

In summary, this almost dialectical process of experimentation and interpretation illustrates well the perilous interface between scientific discovery and legal proof. One important salutary lesson to be drawn is that even an inquisitorial tribunal, with no vested interest in sustaining a conviction and with lavish resources to engage with forensic science, still found it difficult to draw appropriate conclusions. Thus, one should not assume that the answer lies purely in resources and independence, though they undoubtedly will assist.

Further salutary lessons along these lines can be derived from the *Birmingham Six* case. Aside from falsification of the interview record, which ultimately precipitated the quashing of the convictions, there was again anxiety that scientific assertions of the presence of NG had been overstated and that the tests used were less specific (or precise) than the impression given to the trial judge and jury. The specificity of the so-called Greiss Test (which is designed to detect for NG via the presence of nitrate observed through a chemical colour change)[78] had been disputed at trial in 1975 without success.[79] Dr Skuse, the main prosecution scientific witness at the original trial, had convinced the judge with the following words: 'I am 99 per cent certain that shows the presence of nitro-glycerine.'.[80] However, a

---

[73] *Second Report*, ch. 7.

[74] *Interim Report*, ch. 9.

[75] *Ibid.* para. 9.5. The latter point was already well known to the prosection scientists, some of whom had carried out further tests and even proclaimed them to the world (Twibell, J.D., Home, J.M., Smalldon, K.W. and Higgs, D.G., 'Transfer of nitroglycerine to hands during contact with commercial explosives' (1982) 27 *Journal of Forensic Sciences* 783). The matter had first been considered by them in 1977: *Second Report*, para. 11.17.

[76] *Second Report*, paras. 3.3, 3.6.

[77] *Second Report*, para. 3.7.

[78] See: *R v McIlkenny* [1992] 2 All ER 417 at p. 422.

[79] See: Mullin, C., *Error of Judgment* (3rd ed., Poolbeg, Dublin, 1990) ch. 27.

[80] *Skuse v Granada TV, The Independent*, 2 April 1993, *The Times*, 18 October 1994 p. 5, [1994] 1 WLR 1156.

prosecution review of the evidence in 1990[81] suggested that the nitrate in soap or detergent could give positive results, and so contamination could have arisen from the process of cleaning the bowls employed in the testing process. In the eyes of the Court of Appeal, this finding put the evidence of Dr Skuse 'in grave doubt',[82] and the Greiss test, so convincing in the 1975 bag of forensic science tricks, is now apparently considered to be never more than a preliminary screening test.

In fairness to the prosecution, the Greiss test did not stand alone in the *Birmingham Six* case. A more sophisticated analysis is offered by the use of thin layer chromatology (TLC). This process separates substances left after the evaporation of an ether solution by applying them to one side of a flat plate coated with silica or alumina. The plate is placed in a solvent (an eluant), and different chemical substances travel by capillary action different detectable and measurable distances (and perhaps rates of travel) up the plate for each substance.[83] Even more sensitive and complex is Gas Chromatography/Mass Spectometry (GCMS), which attempts to indicate the precise atomic mass of each substance under examination. Yet, paradoxically, the greater sophistication of these tests creates further room for human errors of contamination, interpretation or downright incomprehension.

Some of the complexities are further illustrated by the *Maguire* cases. For example, room for doubt can arise over the definition of a positive finding of the presence of NG. The May Inquiry's *Interim Report* noted disturbingly wide parameters for designating a TLC test as 'positive', which meant that the swabs from one defendant were treated as positive whereas random samples with like values were treated as negative.[84] Similar problems arose in the *Birmingham Six* case concerning the interpretation of GCMS readings.[85]

Even deeper disputes arose in connection with the specificity of the TLC test for NG. Evidence was produced fairly late during the original *Maguire* trial in 1975 that another high explosive, PETN (pentaerythritol tetranitrate), could produce positive results on tests for NG.[86] This revelation initially caused consternation, and at least two forms of disputes arose. One concerned whether the two explosives were in fact distinguishable on the TLC test. At least one prosecution scientist voiced the opinion in the May Inquiry's *Interim Report* that the rate of colour development could be used in this way, though more scientists doubted this possibility or at least averred that it would be an extremely subjective test and therefore of low probative value.[87] The sands had shifted by the time of the *Second Report*, in which the appointed committee of scientific experts concluded that differentiation was possible but that the scientist had not properly calibrated for this differentiation in the original test.[88]

A second, and fundamental dispute as to interpretation and legal inferences arose. In theory, one could no longer claim that the TLC test was specific for NG. But the only other substance thought to produce similar readings was PETN.

[81] Similar tests had been undertaken by World in Action in 1985: Mullin, C., *Error of Judgment* (3rd ed., Poolbeg, Dublin, 1990) ch. 37.
[82] *R v McIlkenny* [1992] 2 All ER 417 at p. 432.
[83] See: May Inquiry, *Interim Report*, para. 6.1.
[84] *Ibid.* paras. 11.22, 11.28.
[85] See: Mullin, C., *Error of Judgment* (3rd ed., Poolbeg, Dublin, 1990) pp. 239, 297.
[86] May Inquiry, *Interim Report*, ch. 10.
[87] May Inquiry, *Interim Report*, paras. 6.8, 11.23.
[88] May Inquiry, *Second Report*, para. 3.10.

Neither the prosecution nor the defence wished to suggest that PETN was actually present. The prosecution had no interest since it could only confuse by reference to irrelevant conjecture (there was no record of that explosive being used by the IRA until about 1979)[89] the clarity of its forensic evidence. For the defence, it might appear to the jury to be a rather damning admission to claim that another high explosive had possibly been handled. So, the issue was largely discounted at the trial 'as a red herring'.[90] This topic was taken up in the *Interim Report* of the May Inquiry, which was critical of the fact that at the time both the scientists and the lawyers seemed not fully to appreciate at the time that the discovery undermined the prosecution's assertion that the forensic tests showed that NG uniquely had been handled.[91] As the Report puts it:[92]

It is now clear on the evidence the Crown was unable to prove a material allegation in the indictment namely the presence of NG. It was far too late at this stage in the trial to amend the indictment.

Thus, neither the scientists nor lawyers fully appreciated the interpretative implications for the case of the scientific debate. One should not be too critical of the individuals concerned in the trial in 1975. After all, the Court of Appeal in 1991 still failed to grasp the point properly even when it had been spelled out by counsel and the May Inquiry. Thus, it stuck to the line that the TLC test had provided reliable evidence that the traces found were of NG and could be of nothing else.[93] The May Inquiry's *Second Report* was scathing about how the Court of Appeal had failed to appreciate the legal implications for the case as it had been pleaded, but even the May Inquiry largely dismissed the possibility of factual confusion on the grounds that there was no evidence of the presence of PETN or indeed any other substance which might be confused with NG.[94] This revision stands in contrast to the finding of the Court of Appeal in the *Ward* case just a few months earlier. In the *Ward* appeal, it emerged that certain black shoe polishes and other household items could produce TLC results very similar to NG; though the conviction was quashed on grounds of non-disclosure of evidence by the prosecution, the possibilities of confusion helped to discredit the forensic evidence.

To reiterate a point made earlier, these problems are not unique to terrorist cases, though clearly the precise tests in respect of high explosives are more common in that context than in any other. However, difficulties of the same nature do arise in connection with other forms of forensic science testing, interpretation and presentation of evidence. A comparison might be made with DNA profiling. Though the technique certainly has potential for good in the sense of providing strong evidence of crimes and even assisting in the reexamination of cases where there is an alleged miscarriage of justice,[95] it has equally engendered disputes about its evidential

---

[89] *Ibid*, para. 11.20.
[90] May Inquiry, *Interim Report*, para. 10.8.
[91] *Ibid.*, ch. 10.
[92] *Ibid.*, para. 10.17.
[93] [1992] 2 All ER 433 at p. 444.
[94] *Second Report*, para. 3.9.
[95] It is estimated that 28 convicted persons have been since exonerated in this way in the USA: Connors, E., Lundregan, T., Miller, N. and McEwan, T., *Convicted by Juries, Exonerated by Science* (NIJ, Washington, 1996).

value. These disputes relate principally to the definition of a visually 'matching' profile,[96] the statistical probabilities of matching within endogamous groups,[97] and the translation of the probabilities of a chemical match into legal proof of guilt. The latter point was especially seized upon by the Court of Appeal in *R v Deen*,[98] wherein it warned scientists not to fall into the trap of 'the prosecutor's fallacy' – in other words, confusing 'the match probability' that an innocent person would match the DNA sample from the scene of the crime, a matter on which they can act as experts, with 'the likelihood ratio' which is the probability that the matching individual before the court is innocent, a matter of weighing all the evidence and of applying common sense by the jury rather than scientists. As always, there is also a need for full disclosure of the circumstances of the provenance of samples, as well as the ways in which they have been processed.[99] In summary, the expansion of DNA profiling, especially as fostered by sections 54 to 59 of the Criminal Justice and Public Order Act 1994, will no more necessarily ensure that the innocent never reach trial or are acquitted than will any other type of evidence gathered and explained by fallible human beings.[100]

Funding for Defence Forensic Work

Access by the defence to properly qualified, experienced forensic scientists is hampered by inadequate funding.[101] In most criminal cases, the cost of the defence is met from public funds administered by local legal aid authorities and the Crown Courts. In the worst cases, legal aid authorities may withhold funds altogether on the grounds that, for example, the scientific evidence is, in their (lay) view, unassailable. Even when funds are forthcoming, the defence may be required to instruct a 'local expert', whose advice could be inadequate, incompetent, or both.[102]

Further obstacles result from the scandalously slow and arbitrary system of payment from legal aid funds. In simple contractual terms, instructing solicitors are responsible for meeting experts' fees and costs, but they are often not in a position to settle unless and until, some months later, they themselves are placed in funds, subject to taxation, by the relevant Crown Court. Furthermore, in 1995, a system

---

[96] See: *Jakobetz v US* (1992) 955 F.2d 786, cert. den. 113 S. Ct. 104; *R v Deen, The Times*, 10 January 1994; *R v Gordon, The Times*, 27 May 1994; Cooke, G., 'The length of the genetic string we can't yet measure', *The Times*, 19 May 1992 p. 27; Ames, J, 'DNA evidence under scrutiny' (1992) 89/46 *Law Society's Gazette* 16 Dec. p. 7; Dawson, T.C., 'DNA profiling – evidence for the prosecution' (1993) 33 *Journal of the Forensic Science Society* 238; Redmayne, M., 'Doubts and burdens: DNA evidence, probability and the courts' [1995] *Criminal Law Review* 464 at p. 466.

[97] See: *Jakobetz v US* (1992) 955 F.2d 786, cert. den. 113 S. Ct. 104; Hoeffel, JC, 'The dark side of DNA profiling' (1990) 42 *Stanford Law Review* 465; Robertson, B. and Vignaux, T., 'Why the NRCC Report on DNA is wrong' (1992) 142 *New Law Journal* 1619; Redmayne, M., 'Doubts and burdens: DNA evidence, probability and the courts' [1995] *Criminal Law Review* 464.

[98] *The Times*, 10 January 1994. See Balding, D.J and Donnelly, P., 'The prosecutor's fallacy and DNA evidence' [1994] *Criminal Law Review* 711.

[99] See: *R v Borham and Hammond* (1992), reported in (1992) 89/46 *Law Society's Gazette* 16 Dec. p. 7, Farrington, D., 'Unacceptable evidence' (1993) 143 *New Law Journal* 806, 857.

[100] Compare: Mills, B., 'Justice for all' (1994) 144 *New Law Journal* 1670; Rozenberg, J., *The Search for Justice* (Hodder & Stoughton, London, 1994) p. 350.

[101] See also: Steventon, B., *The Ability to Challenge DNA Evidence* (Royal Commission on Criminal Justice Research Study No. 9, 1993) pp. 40, 42; Roberts, P. and Willmore, C., *The role of forensic science evidence in criminal proceedings* (Royal Commission on Criminal Justice Research Study No. 11 HMSO, London, 1993) p. 139.

[102] Mansfield, M., *Presumed Guilty* (Heinemann, London, 1993) p. 174.

of prior authority was introduced in which solicitors had to apply to the Legal Aid Board for prior authority for expenditure against the estimates of fees and costs. The consequences of these nonsensical arrangements are serious in the extreme[103] and have already persuaded some of the handful of properly qualified independent forensic scientists to refuse further legal aid work in favour of more lucrative business elsewhere. They also help to ensure that scientists in the FSS are discouraged from entering the independent sector.

In regard to the cost implications, it should be pointed out that the early instruction of a competent forensic scientist for the defence can lead to substantial savings of public money. In cases where the strengths and soundness of the prosecution's scientific evidence can be authoritatively confirmed, the defendant's best interests may be served by an early plea of guilt. Alternatively, where the evidence is exposed as weak, flawed or misunderstood, the case may be withdrawn altogether. Accordingly, the Runciman Commission has called for legal aid to be more readily available, especially so that the private sector laboratories can operate effectively.[104]

Suggested Remedies

Rejected Suggestions

A number of suggestions have been made for improving the reliability of forensic science evidence and its interface with the criminal justice system. Ideas canvassed have included: a move towards a system of corroboration such as exists in Scotland; the creation of a single organisation to serve the needs of both the police/prosecution and the defence, but which is independent of both; the setting up of a separate, single organisation mirroring the FSS, but serving the defence alone; and, most radical of all, a fundamental change in the criminal justice system from an adversarial to an inquisitorial process including the appointment of experts by the court or by some sort of *juge d'instruction*.

All of these possible avenues of reform present drawbacks when examined in detail.[105] For example, the Scottish system of corroboration, which requires each case to be examined by two forensic scientists,[106] in practice appears to make no difference to the overall quality and balance of the work produced by the police laboratories there. This is probably because the scientists of each side in the case approach their examinations from the same point of view, having the same information at their disposal and responding to it in very much the same way and at the same time. Though one failure does not discredit a system, it is interesting to recall the case against John Preece.[107] Preece was convicted in 1973 of rape and murder on the basis of semen, hair and fibre analysis. His convictions were quashed in 1981. Dr Alan Clift's work was publicly discredited, even though it had been properly corroborated by another scientist.

---

[103] The same complaints are, of course, often made by solicitors dependent on legal aid payments. See: Law Society, *Response to the Legal Aid Efficiency Scrutiny* (London, 1986) p. 10.

[104] *Runciman Report*, ch. 9 paras. 49, 55.

[105] For further details, see: Walker, C., and Starmer, K., (eds.) *Justice in Error* (Blackstone Press, London, 1993) pp. 90–97; Mansfield, M., *Presumed Guilty* (Heinemann, London, 1993) ch. 14.

[106] See further Chapter 16.

[107] See: [1981] *Criminal Law Review* 783; Parliamentary Commissioner for Administration, *Fourth Report* (1983–84 HC 191); Jones, C.A.G., *Expert Witnesses* (Clarendon Press, Oxford, 1994) p. 230.

Suggestions which attempt to reform the quality of forensic services through institutional change are equally problematical. For example, the concept of a single, independent organisation which can offer forensic services both to the police/prosecution and the defence seems unconvincing. There is always going to be a substantial imbalance between police/prosecution and defence demands, which will create perceptions of acting for one side or another. In addition, the role of the forensic scientist is not, as described earlier, entirely reactive to customer requests; the scientist must also be ready to hatch lines of inquiry which the lay person may not be in a position to conceive. Accordingly, it is notable that the FSS continues to regard the police as its primary customer[108] and continues not to be regarded as an available resource by many defence solicitors. Indeed, it is difficult to see how one scientist from one FSS laboratory could effectively test and probe the findings, and in particular the professional opinions, of a colleague at another. There is also a danger that the police would take their business elsewhere if they felt that the FSS response to immediate police needs could be weakened by an increased volume of non-police work. Likewise, the Northern Ireland Forensic Science Laboratory (NIFSL), which has only one police force as its 'natural' customer, namely the Royal Ulster Constabulary (RUC), once remarked that it viewed agency status as risky to its relationship with the police.[109] Nevertheless, it has been relaunched as the Northern Ireland Forensic Science Agency (FSANI). As to the MPFSL, in evidence to the Home Affairs Committee,[110] the Metropolitan Police referred to the unique character of 'a single laboratory [the MPFSL] and a single customer'. It does not seem likely that these perceptions will be at all affected by the merger with the FSS, though the latter's commercial interests will no doubt in principle be assimilated by the MPFSL.

Comparisons have been drawn between the roles of forensic scientists and medical experts, such as forensic pathologists, who routinely advise the police one day and the defence the next. Such comparisons are fatally flawed. Unlike forensic scientists, medical experts rarely play any part at all in searching for, and providing evidence about, the identity of the perpetrators of crime. Rather, they are principally concerned with, for example, the nature of injuries and how and when these might have been caused. Against this background, it is difficult to see that, so far as disinterestedness is concerned, their roles have much in common.

If a single joint organisation is not possible, then what about a national forensic service for the defence to rival that of the FSS?[111] There would be formidable problems in locating the necessary teams of trained and experienced experts. In any event, be it in a university or otherwise, centralising forensic science expertise for the defence in a single organisation would lead to narrowing of horizons,

---

[108] *Ibid.*, p. 222. Close liaison exists, such as weekly meetings with police Scientific Support Managers and attendance at CID conferences and case briefings. See, for example: HMI, *Report on the West Yorkshire Police for 1993* (1994) para. 4.15.

[109] See: H.L. Committee, p. 50. The RUC Chief Constable revealed that police officers were formally part of the NIFSL's Serious Crime Unit: *Annual Report for 1991* (1992) p. 38. The NIFSL rarely acted for the defence, and there is a dearth of independent alternatives in Northern Ireland: Standing Advisory Commission on Human Rights, *17th Report* (1992–93 HC 54) ch. 6 para. 14, p. 275.

[110] *The Forensic Science Service* (1988-89 HC 26) Vol. II p. 129.

[111] A new defence-oriented forensic service was advanced by the Bar Council (Submission to Royal Commission, para. 16.2), having long attracted the support of JUSTICE as part of its campaign (*A Public Defender* (1987) para. 55) and see also Ormrod, Sir R., 'Evidence and proof' (1972) 12 *Medicine, Science and the Law* 12.

introspection and complacency as well as politicking, rivalry and polarisation so far as its relations with the FSS were concerned. Indeed, in evidence to the Home Affairs Committee, the Home Office expressed concern about 'any suggestion of centralising defence work . . . since this could inhibit the development of defence facilities'.[112] A public forensic defender system[113] based on salaried employees would also be vulnerable to underfunding.

For some of the reasons already discussed, it is difficult to see how a single scientist, whether appointed by the parties or the court, could function adequately and in equal measure for all parties concerned in a criminal investigation and subsequent trial, whether the legal framework was inquisitorial or adversarial. The multifaceted role to be fulfilled would not sit comfortably with the level of involvement and commitment needed at each stage of the work and seems to run the risk of requiring such impartiality as to render nugatory the scientist's contributions. In any event, a single expert is unlikely to be able to adduce convincingly all the possible legitimate but differing viewpoints which might be adopted but would reflect best their own traditions and agendas.[114] Over and above these difficulties, there are a number of concerns seemingly inherent in an inquisitorial system which involves the appointment of experts by the court.[115] For instance, as a court appointee, there might be a tendency for the expert's findings, and any opinions offered, automatically to be regarded as stamped with the court's seal of approval. In the possible absence of a ready means of challenging scientific evidence, the expert might well be encouraged to go beyond the proper limits of his or her expertise. The court itself, or the *juge d'instruction*, might be tempted to look more favourably on experts it knew were likely to endorse its own views. In any event, it is difficult to see that the court, as opposed to a rival expert, would be in a position effectively to question any expert in order properly to test the evidence.[116] For similar reasons, the suggestion by the House of Lords Select Committee,[117] since unthinkingly endorsed by the Royal Commission,[118] that experts be allowed to make statements after their examination should also be rejected. It once again reflects the mistaken belief that science, unlike other testimony, cannot be an interpretation rather than an undiluted reflection of reality.[119] The better view, put forward by the Royal Commission though not consistently applied by it, is that:[120]

---

[112] *The Forensic Science Service* (1988–89 HC 26) Vol. II p. 195.

[113] Sargant, T. and Hill, P., *Criminal Trials* (Fabian Research Series No. 348, London, 1986) p. 17.

[114] Roberts, P. and Willmore, C., *The role of forensic science evidence in criminal proceedings* (Royal Commission on Criminal Justice Research Study No. 11 HMSO, London, 1993) at p. 135; Jasanoff, S., *Science at the Bar* (Harvard University Press, 1995) p. 44.

[115] Compare: Sargant, T. and Hill, P., *Criminal Trials* (Fabian Research Series No. 348, London, 1986) p. 28; Howard, M.N., 'The Neutral Expert: a plausible threat to justice?' [1991] *Criminal Law Review* 98; Spencer, J.R., 'The neutral expert: an implausible bogey' [1991] *Criminal Law Review* 106, 'Court experts and expert witnesses' (1992) 46 *Current Legal Problems* 213.

[116] The Runciman Commission rejected the idea of a court appointed expert, though more for reasons of complexity than principle: ch. 9 paras. 67, 74. See further, Roberts, P., 'Forensic science evidence after Runciman' [1994] *Criminal Law Review* 780 at p. 789.

[117] HL Select Committee, para. 5.31.

[118] *Runciman Report*, ch. 9 para. 73. The Government also rejected the idea as giving 'a second chance to a witness who has performed badly under cross-examination': Lord Chancellor's Department, Home Office and Law Officers' Department, *The Royal Commission on Criminal Justice: Final Government Response* (Home Office, London, 1996) para. 167.

[119] Compare Frankel, M.S., 'Ethics and the forensic sciences' (1989) 34(3) *Journal of Forensic Sciences* 763; Saks, M.J., 'Prevalence and impact of ethical problems in forensic science' (1989) 34(3) *Journal of Forensic Sciences* 772.

. . . it would lead to a confusion of roles of precisely the kind that we believe that the criminal justice system should avoid. Moreover, since we are firmly of the view that where disagreement persists it must remain possible for the issues to be tested in examination and cross-examination at the trial, it follows that the experts who give evidence must do so on behalf of either the prosecution or the defence and not on behalf of the court.

These objections do not apply to the further suggestions of the House of Lords Select Committee and Royal Commission that the experts should meet at pre-trial conferences with lawyers from their own side and pre-trial reviews with experts from the other side in order to clarify the issues and differences between them.[121] Given that this is technical evidence which is at the limits of the understanding of jurors, it seems right to encourage preliminary evaluation by appropriate experts. However, this exercise should be limited to factual assertions rather than interpretations and inferences, the advance disclosure of which on the part of the defence seems to shift both the conduct of the case to scientists as well as the burden of proof, as does the further suggestion by the Runciman Commission that the defence should disclose evidence from experts who are not being called at trial.[122]

The Runciman Commission's Approach

All in all, the adversarial system appears to offer the best scope for properly testing and challenging scientific evidence, but only if police/prosecution forensic science services produce initially evidence of a high probative standard and only if the defence is effectively empowered to react effectively to the scientific resources of the prosecution. The latter consideration requires reforms in the areas of legal aid, pre-trial meetings and full prosecution disclosure, all of which have already been considered.

As for quality standards, there is at present almost no legal regulation[123] of the forensic science profession. Yet, in response to the diversity and complexity of forensic science and to the imperfect market in the services supplied, there is a pressing need for a statutorily constituted and empowered governing Council,[124]

---

[120] *Runciman Report*, ch. 9 para. 17. The power to appoint experts in the USA has fallen into disuse: Alldridge, P., 'Forensic science and expert evidence' (1994) 21 *Journal of Law & Society* 136 at p. 141.

[121] H.L. Select Committee, paras. 5.18, 5.30; *Runciman Report*, ch. 9 paras 43, 44, 63; JUSTICE, *Science and the Administration of Justice* (1991). There is a great deal of enforced exchange of expert information through the operation of the rules on prosecution disclosure and the Crown Court (Advance Notice of Expert Evidence) Rules 1987 SI 716 (as amended by 1997 SI No. 700) and the Magistrates' Courts (Advance Notice of Expert Evidence) Rules 1997 SI 705. Both sets of rules have not operated perfectly in practice: Brayne, H., 'Disclosing expert evidence and Crown Court trials' (1988) 52 *Journal of Criminal Law* 64. Prosecution disclosure was at fault in *R v Ward* (1992) 96 Cr App R 1. As for defence disclosure, problems arise for the prosecution as the Rules do not apply when the defence wishes to dispute the prosecution forensic evidence rather than to call further evidence of their own, though to place further duties of disclosure at this point seems again to transcend the normal burden of proof. See further Roberts, P., 'Forensic science evidence after Runciman' [1994] *Criminal Law Review* 780 at p. 786.

[122] *Runciman Report*, ch. 9 para. 65.

[123] By the Criminal Justice (Scotland) Act 1980, s.26, scientists approved by the Scottish Secretary can present evidence by certificate; about 30 forensic pathologists are listed by the Home Office: see Home Affairs Committee, *The Forensic Science Service* (1988–89 HC 26) Vol. II p. 181.

[124] The Forensic Science Society cannot readily perform this function as membership is based on interest rather than qualification.

perhaps like the General Medical Council or the Law Society.[125] This Council would be responsible for formulating, implementing and maintaining arrangements for the effective regulation of all the forensic science professions. In this way, the defence (and the prosecution) could be more sure of instructing a scientist whose work is of a high standard. It is essential that accreditation should cover all aspects, beginning with the individual scientists and extending to the ways in which they work and the analytical tests they carry out. Accreditation and regulation should be entirely independent of the FSS, or of any Government department or university. In this way, it could provide suitable benchmarks both for the FSS and especially for independent scientists.[126]

So far as the scientists are concerned, each should be certified in specific fields of expertise on the grounds of qualifications and experience.[127] This should be undertaken by peer review under the auspices of a properly constituted and empowered governing Council drawn partly from relevant professional bodies, including the Royal Society of Chemistry and the Institute of Biology, and partly from practitioners who have the respect of the profession as a whole. Thereafter, the Council should be required to monitor and to regulate the scientists' work against a Code of Conduct and competence standards, all centred upon individual professionalism.

As to the scientists' work, there are already quality management systems available, especially those recognised by the National Measurement Accreditation Service (NAMAS)[128] and British Standard ISO 9000, which cover different aspects of work from its organisation to performance of the analytical tests themselves. The FSS laboratories have now obtained accreditation on both systems.[129] The proposed governing Council should consider the stringency and coverage of these standards.[130] The consideration of the standards of methodologies and processes could fill an important gap concerning the recognition *in abstracto* of forensic science innovation.[131] It is not suggested that there should be the certification of a particular test *in abstracto*, but there would be the opportunity for the scrutiny of techniques and the level of acceptance in the scientific community of a given test or process, with the implication of assurances as to reliability before the professional conscience of an accredited scientist could allow for its utilisation in court. Regulations, which could cover issues such as testing which destroys samples, the recording of processes, defence presence during tests and access to equipment and

---

[125] See Medical Act 1983; Solicitors Act 1974.

[126] Likewise, accreditation by the American Society of Crime Laboratory Directors' Laboratory Accreditation Board was suggested by Office of the Inspector General of the Department of Justice, *The FBI Laboratory: An Investigation into laboratory practices and alleged misconduct in explosives-related and other cases* (Washington, 1997).

[127] Compare the case of Kevin Callan: Forensic Science Working Group, *Report* (Royal Society of Chemistry, London, 1997) para. 2.7.

[128] The Service is part of the National Physics Laboratory, an arm of the DTI. See: NAMAS M10/M11; HL Select Committee, para. 3.32. The work of accrediting laboratories against these standards is now governed by the UK Accreditation Service (which is licensed by the DTI).

[129] *Annual Report* (1993–94 HC 517) p. 5. But Scottish laboratories are not accredited: Forensic Science Working Group, *Report* (Royal Society of Chemistry, London, 1997) para. 1.26.

[130] The H.L. Select Committee recommends that laboratories should make public their quality assessment trials (para. 3.13) and that NAMAS standard setting should extend to sampling processes (para. 3.34).

[131] On the latter, see: Sargant, T. and Hill, P., *Criminal Trials* (Fabian Research Series No. 348, London, 1986) p. 27; Alldridge, P., 'Recognising novel scientific techniques' [1992] *Criminal Law Review* 687; *Daubert v Merrell Dow* (1993) 509 US 579.

records, the storage and retention of records and samples, might be set by a code of practice under the Police and Criminal Evidence Act, the compliance with which would then have a direct bearing on admissibility.[132]

In evidence to the Home Affairs Committee,[133] the Home Office was not persuaded by the case for formal regulation of the forensic science profession. While admitting to varying standards among defence scientists, it doubted that the problem justified any new measures to deal with it. Nevertheless, virtually all forensic services and their main customers now accept the need for external accreditation, and most also support the idea of a professional body to enforce standards.[134] This concept received a powerful endorsement from the House of Lords Select Committee, which suggested that forensic scientists should be individually registered with a Board fostered by the Home Office on proof of competence.[135] Non-registered persons could still be employed by the parties and be heard in court but would be more likely to be challenged and discredited as to their expertise.[136] Furthermore, the weight of opinion expressed to the Runciman Commission favoured a better regulated range of forensic facilities operated by more proficient personnel, both in the public and private sectors, with more generous legal aid for the latter.[137] There also exists a precedent for greater oversight in Scotland, where the Standing Committee on Forensic Science in Scotland considers (though does not register or accredit) standards and quality in forensic sciences, which are almost entirely based in four police laboratories.[138]

This regulatory model gained approval from the Runciman Commission itself. At the heart of its preferred scheme would be a Forensic Science Advisory Council,[139] whose functions would comprise the following: the accreditation of testing procedures[140] and the setting of qualifications for staff;[141] the development of codes of practice (covering, *inter alia*, professional ethics and duties of disclosure) and requirements as to training and accreditation;[142] the reporting on the state of forensic services and the encouragement of private sector facilities.[143] Though much of the scheme is to be welcomed, one concern is the limited range of personnel to be covered. Not only does it not apply to other forms of expert

---

[132] See further Lord Chancellor's Department, Home Office and Law Officers' Department, *The Royal Commission on Criminal Justice: Final Government Response* (Home Office, London, 1996) para. 161; Givelber, D., 'Meaningless acquittals, meaningful convictions: do we reliably acquit the innocent?' (1997) 49 *Rutgers Law Review* 1317 at p. 1383.

[133] *The Forensic Science Service* (1988–89 HC 26) Vol. II p. 194. The FSS also rejected the concept of an independent governing body: p. 15. The Committee itself (para. 84) was not convinced, though largely because of the then very limited number of independent forensic services.

[134] See: H.L. Select Committee.

[135] H.L. Select Committee, paras. 3.52–3.61.

[136] See: *R v Silverlock* [1894] 2 QB 766; *R v Robb* (1991) 93 Cr App R 161.

[137] See: Submissions of Amnesty International, para. 4.6; CPS, para. 12.3.24; Home Office, p. 8; Law Society, paras. 4.31, 4.35, 4.37, 4.38; Liberty, p. 63; Police Service, p. 149.

[138] Scottish Office, *Firm and Fair* (Edinburgh, HMSO, 1994) paras. 9.25–9.28. For opposing views as to the success of this system, see Bustill, A., 'The Scottish forensic science scene' (1991) 36 *Journal of the Law Society of Scotland* 397; Jensen, E., 'The Scottish forensic science scene' (1992) 37 *Journal of the Law Society of Scotland* 10.

[139] *Runciman Report*, ch. 9 para. 2.

[140] *Ibid.*, para. 30. There should of course also be regulations as to the records to be kept of the procedures: Alldridge, P., 'Recognising novel scientific techniques' [1992] *Criminal Law Review* 687 at p. 695.

[141] *Runciman Report*, para. 32.

[142] *Ibid.*, para. 36.

[143] *Ibid.*, paras. 34, 55.

witness,[144] but it is left to the FSS to set standards for the front-line troops of forensic science, namely SOCOs/SCEs.[145] Another concern is whether there is sufficient commitment to the private sector which will have to be paid from legal aid funds.[146]

Finally, just as standards should be raised for scientists, so one should expect lawyers to be properly trained to understand and handle forensic evidence. Thus, the House of Lords Select Committee called for appropriate training in forensic science matters,[147] as did the Runciman Commission.[148] Current proposals of the legal professions make no reference to this deficiency.[149]

Reforms since the Runciman Commission

There have been no official reforms in response to the Runciman Commission's oversight recommendations in regard to forensic science and expert evidence, though issues of disclosure and pre-trial hearings have been dealt with as part of larger reforms.

As for disclosure,[150] the rules are in the Criminal Procedure and Investigations Act 1996. One difficulty concerns the categorisation of forensic scientists. The duties under the Act apply to police officers and prosecutors, and so at first sight they do not appear to apply to third parties such as scientists. But it might be argued that forensic scientists fall directly within the prosecution team, and this was the interpretation of 'the forensic scientists who gave evidence for the prosecution at the trial' in *R v Ward*.[151] Yet, it is less certain that forensic scientists who are not called at trial necessarily fall into this category.[152] Fortunately, it has been recognised at common law, in *R v Maguire*,[153] that for the purposes of duties of disclosure, there could be 'no cause to distinguish between members of the prosecuting authority and those advising it in the capacity of a forensic scientist.'. These common law rules are preserved by the Act, and its Code of Practice also requires communications between the police and experts to be retained, but it is unfortunate that draft statements of opinion are not included in this duty.[154] Though they may legitimately alter in the light of later information, the process of the formulation of an expert's view, the pressures upon it and the strength of it should be as open as possible.[155]

---

[144] *Ibid.*, paras. 75, 76. See Phillips, E., 'Testing the truth' in McConville, M. and Bridges, L., *Criminal Justice in Crisis* (Edward Elgar, Aldershot, 1994). But a Home Office Policy Advisory Board for Forensic Pathology was established in 1991.

[145] *Runciman Report*, para. 41.

[146] Redmayne, M., 'The Royal Commission and the forensic science market' in McConville, M. and Bridges, L., *Criminal Justice in Crisis* (Edward Elgar, Aldershot, 1994) p. 228.

[147] H.L. Select Committee, para. 5.33.

[148] *Runciman Report*, ch. 8 para. 89, ch. 9 para. 79.

[149] Law Society, *Policies for Completing the Academic Stage of Legal Education for Solicitors* (1992); Lord Chancellor's Advisory Committee on Legal Education and Conduct, *Review of Legal Education: The Initial Stage* (1994).

[150] See further Chapter 7.

[151] (1993) 96 Cr. App. R 1 at p. 23.

[152] Compare: Niblett, J, *Disclosure in Criminal Proceedings* (Blackstone, London, 1997) at p. 88.

[153] (1992) 94 Cr. App. R 133 at p. 147.

[154] Code of Practice, paras. 5.4, 5.6. It may be doubted whether the Code applies by virtue of s. 26 directly to the forensic scientists rather than to the police who receive the reports. Forensic scientists have no legal duties to investigate aside perhaps from the duty arising from a contract with a customer.

The Criminal Procedure and Investigations Act 1996 also provides for preparatory hearings[156] under Part III in lengthy or complex cases where it might clarify a material issue (such as forensic reports). Part IV then allows binding pre-trial rulings to be issued. The effect is to allow a more judge-driven inquisitorial system,[157] including perhaps, the use of court-appointed experts, but whether judges will in fact seize powers to investigate evidence in this way rather than to manage cases in terms of time and efficiency remains to be seen.

Aside from disclosure, there has been an abject failure to bring about any structural reform. The Government rejected any statutory model and at best could see 'some value' in a non-statutory body.[158] This stance is disgraceful but perhaps not entirely unexpected. It is certainly not the case that the Home Office, the responsible department, is uninterested in forensic science. For example, the Home Secretary has called the national DNA database 'the biggest breakthrough since fingerprints',[159] and, as already decribed, the Home Office has done much to encourage, the greater use of forensic techniques. This support was especially signalled by the Criminal Justice and Public Order Act 1994[160] which extends the circumstances in which bodily samples could be taken and paved the way for a DNA National Register (with extra powers in 1997 to deal with known sex and violent offenders and burglars).[161] These changes go further than the Runciman Commission which mainly called for the reclassification of certain sampling from 'intimate' to 'non-intimate', thereby dispensing with consent, as well as some minor extensions of sampling powers.[162]

Yet, regulation along the lines suggested by the Runciman Commission would cost money, and so like other recommendations which not only improved the safeguards against abuse for the individual but also involved some immediate expenditure, such as the Criminal Cases Review Authority,[163] it was accorded a lower priority than those measures which can immediately expand police or sentencing powers.[164] In the absence of central direction, it has been left to the piecemeal efforts of individual private bodies, such as the British Academy of Experts, to attempt to define minimum standards[165] but without either the universal coverage or authority to do so effectively. The forensic profession became so alarmed by this official neglect that in 1996 the Royal Society of Chemistry established a committee under Lord Dainton to consider such matters. The Forensic Science Working Group duly accepted the need for regulation via registers and codes, as applied by a Forensic Science Registration Council which would be

---

[155] A good example is the reformulation of the time of death in the *Confait* case: Jones, C.A.G., *Expert Witnesses* (Clarendon Press, Oxford, 1994) p. 224.

[156] See Chapter 9.

[157] See Redmayne, M., 'Process gains and process values' (1997) 60 *Modern Law Review* 79 at p. 93.

[158] Lord Chancellor's Department, Home Office and Law Officers' Department, *The Royal Commission on Criminal Justice: Final Government Response* (Home Office, London, 1996) paras. 152, 168. It also rejected an independent oversight body for the projected DNA database: para. 14.

[159] *The Times*, 11 April 1995 p. 11.

[160] See also Prisons Act 1952, s.16A (as amended in 1994); Transport and Works Act 1992, s.31; Prisoners and Criminal Proceedings (Scotland) Act 1993, s. 28; Armed Forces Act 1996, ss. 11, 12.

[161] Criminal Evidence (Amendment) Act 1997.

[162] *Runciman Report*, ch. 2 paras. 14–38. See Creaton, J, 'DNA profiling and the law' in McConville, M. and Bridges, L., *Criminal Justice in Crisis* (Edward Elgar, Aldershot, 1994).

[163] *Runciman Report*, ch. 10; Home Office, *Criminal Appeals and the Establishment of a Criminal Cases Review Authority* (1994).

[164] See HC Debs. vol. 280 col.185wa 27 June 1996.

[165] The Academy introduced a code in 1993 for its members concerning qualifications, laboratory facilities, and record-keeping: Code of Practice (1993) *The Lawyer* 9 March p. 28.

distinct from any new professional body for forensic practitioners.[166] The Council is now being established with Home Office endorsement.[167]

Another prominent member of the forensic science profession, Professor Caddy, also renewed the calls for wide-ranging reform in his 1996 report about possible contamination in IRA cases processed by Fort Halstead.[168] His preferred model was an official Inspectorate of Forensic Services which would have the legal right to enter any laboratory and to inquire into suspected miscarriages of justice. It would also regulate individual scientists who would have to prove adequate qualifications before they are allowed to register and then to appear in court. At very least, he suggested a private Institute for Forensic Sciences covering all relevant groups and interests. The Government announced immediately that it accepted in principle the recommendation of external and independent monitoring but noted that it went further than Runciman's advisory model.[169] There was also no commitment as to a timescale for implementation or as to which model would be preferred.

What if such reforms were to be implemented? It is suggested that an oversight and standard-setting structure could have assisted with several of the forensic controversies of recent years. For example, there could have been earlier understanding of the nature and limitations of DNA profiling, the results of which seemed to be accepted without question at first but later came under scrutiny.[170] For example, in *R v Hammond*,[171] DNA evidence produced by the MPFSL was rejected at an Old Bailey trial because the source of the evidence was not fully disclosed, the population base against which the defendant's sample was compared was insufficiently representative and there were doubts about the interpretation of a 'match'. This case came at the end of 1992, but one wonders how many cases had produced guilty verdicts (or more likely still guilty pleas) without proper consideration of these issues which did not in any event reach Court of Appeal level until 1994.[172] A form of expert pre-analysis could be helpful, since English law has no threshold test for the initial recognition of forensic techniques, and so courts become very reliant on the experts chosen to appear for the parties, experts who might be neither very representative nor very qualified. This is not to say that the American test in *Frye v US*,[173] that the scientific technique must be shown to

---

[166] Forensic Science Working Group, *Report* (Royal Society of Chemistry, London, 1997) para. 1.19, ch. 6. There would be specific registration panels for Crime Scene Examiners, Fingerprint Examiners, Forensic Medical Examiners, Forensic Pathologists and Forensic Scientists.

[167] See HC Debs. vol. 312 col. 449wa 21 May 1998, Mr Jack Straw.

[168] See Caddy, B., *Assessment and Implications of Centrifuge Contamination in the Trace Explosive Section of the Forensic Explosives Laboratory at Fort Halstead* (Cm 3491, HMSO, London, 1996) App. 4.

[169] HC Debs. vol. 287 col. 769, 17 December 1996, Mr Michael Howard.

[170] See: Hall, A., 'DNA fingerprinting' (1990) 140 *New Law Journal* 203; Thompson, W.C. and Ford, S., 'Is DNA fingerprinting ready for the courts?' (1990) *New Scientist* 31 March p. 38; Macdonald, P.M., 'DNA profiling' 1990 *Scottish Law Times* 285; Fennell, C., 'Beyond reasonable doubt' (1990) 8 *Irish Law Times* 227; Young, S.J., 'DNA evidence' [1991] *Criminal Law Review* 264; Sufian, J., 'DNA in the Courtroom' (1991) *Legal Action Group Bulletin* Feb 7; Easteal, S., McLeod, N. and Reed, C., *DNA Profiling* (Harwood, Reading, 1991); Evett, I.W., 'DNA statistics' (1992) 156 *Justice of the Peace* 583; *Jakobetz v US* (1992) 955 F 2d 786, cert den 121 L.Ed. 2d 63 (1992).

[171] Ames, J., 'DNA evidence comes under scrutiny' (1992) 89/46 *Law Society's Gazette* 16 December p. 7; Farrington, D., 'Unacceptable evidence' (1993) 143 *New Law Journal* 806, 857.

[172] *R v Deen, The Times*, 10 January 1994; *R v Gordon, The Times*, 27 May 1994. The meaning of a 'match' was raised in the latter.

[173] 293 F 1013 (1923). See Black, B., 'A Unified Theory of Scientific Evidence' (1988) 56 *Ford L Rev* 595; Imwinkelried, E., 'The "Bases" of Expert Testimony: The Syllogistic Structure of Scientific Testimony' (1988) 67 *North Carolina Law Review* 1; 'Note: Proposals for a Model Rule on the

have general acceptance by the scientific community, is desirable or that one should alternatively place one's faith in the abstract certification by an expert committee.[174] Even the US Federal courts, in *Daubert* v *Merrell Dow Pharmaceuticals Inc.*,[175] have now recognised that the test has been superseded by the Federal Rules of Evidence.[176] Peer review and acceptance remain relevant, but the inquiry is more flexible than the *Frye* test, being based on principles, methodologies and error rates in specific cases rather than 'cosmic' outcomes.[177] The trouble with abstract certification is that it does not tell the court enough about what has been done in the circumstances of a particular case.[178] So, what is being suggested here is that a form of oversight authority could ensure that experts who did appear were indeed properly qualified and provide benchmark standards against which the tests carried out could be judged. The latter is the approach of the US DNA Identification Act 1994,[179] which allows funding only for laboratories which meet certain standards and also seeks to establish quality assurance methods.

Another example where some independent expert body could provide some reassurance concerns the proposals to alter the fingerprint standards. A 16-point standard was adopted after 1924 by agreement of both Home Office and the Director of Public Prosecutions.[180] Though never legally established, the standard required that before an identification can be claimed in court, there must be 16 points of similarity between a fingerprint at the scene of a crime and the inked samples taken from suspects or convicts. It was accepted by the Metropolitan Police after 1924 (before which 12 points sufficed) and in other police forces by 1953. The decision in principle to scrap this (or any other) standard was adopted in 1996,[181] following the ACPO Crime Committee's *Report of the Quality of Fingerprint Evidence Review*.[182] It is true that the old rule is in many ways

---

Admissibility of Scientific Evidence' (1986) 26 *Jurimetrics Journal* 235; Imwinkelried, E., 'The evolution of the American test for the admissibility of scientific evidence' (1990) 30 *Medicine, Science and the Law* 60.

[174] Compare Alldridge, P., 'Recognising novel scientific techniques' [1992] *Criminal Law Review* 687 at p. 694.

[175] (1993) 509 US 579. See Green, M.D., 'Expert Witnesses and Sufficiency of Evidence in Toxic Substances Litigation: The Legacy of Agent Orange and Bendectin Litigation' (1992) 86 *Northwestern University Law Review* 643; Becker, E.R. & Orenstein, A., 'The Federal Rules of Evidence After Sixteen Years – The Effect of 'Plain Meaning' Jurisprudence, the Need for an Advisory Committee on the Rules of Evidence, and Suggestions for Selective Revision of the Rules' (1992) 60 *George Washington Law Review* 857 at pp. 876–85.

[176] See Rule 702: 'If scientific, technical, or other specialised knowledge will assist the trier of fact to understand the evidence or to determine a fact in issue, a witness qualified as an expert by knowledge, skill, experience, training, or education, may testify thereto in the form of an opinion or otherwise.'

[177] Some state courts have retained the *Frye* test: Meaney, J.R., 'From Frye to Daubert' (1994) 35 *Jurimetrics* 191.

[178] Consider National Research Council, DNA Technology in Forensic Science (National Academy Press, Washington, 1992); Robertson, B. and Vignaux, G., 'Why the NRC Report on DNA is wrong' (1992) 142 *New Law Journal* 1619.

[179] 47 USC s.3796kk–2. See Shapiro, E.D. and Reifler, S., 'Forensic DNA analysis and the US Government' (1996) 36 *Medicine, Science and the Law* 43.

[180] See Evett, I.W. and Williams, R.L., *A Review of the Sixteen Point Fingerprint Standard in England and Wales* (Home Office, 1995). In 1978, it was agreed by the National Conference of Fingerprint Experts that a match of 8 points or more could constitute proof beyond reasonable doubt, and it was accepted in 1984 that evidence of at least this standard could be put before a court in an exceptionally serious case if supported by an expert of high standing.

[181] 'ACPO plan to scrap 16-point fingerprint match standard' (1996) 104 *Police Review* 19 April p. 5.

[182] Thames Valley Police, 1996.

unsupportable[183] and is based on historical fallacy.[184] There is no magic in the figure of 16 (or 12) either in fact or law.[185] It is also pertinent that these standards are not universal – in certain serious cases, there can be evidence of fewer points of similarity given by established experts.[186] The constructed nature of the standard is also demonstrated by the fact that standards in other countries are often different, even in such comparable jurisdictions as Australia, New Zealand and the USA.[187] It must also be accepted that in contemporary times, it is becoming outmoded as the methods of generating fingerprints from crime scenes become ever more sophisticated.[188] Fingerprinting – dactyloscopy – is not an exact science but involves judgment as to what is a 'match' between images which may be incomplete, indistinct, contaminated or distorted through the pressure or angle of the finger.[189] In addition, recent rules of disclosure mean that lawyers on both sides become aware of partial identifications more so than in the past. However, the 16-point standard did serve to set a very high probability threshold which chimed well with the notion of proof beyond reasonable doubt – the evidence was always viewed as incontrovertible and so worthy of collection[190] and presentation. Thus, it must be understood that the rule served legal, and not just scientific, purposes. Most of all, one should be 'astonished'[191] at how these changes are being managed. Much of the impetus for the rule changes came from pressure from the Audit Commission in 1988, which called for greater utilisation of fingerprinting.[192] Since then, the rule changes have been effectively pushed through by police, without consultation of Parliament, public or lawyers or judges and without the establishment of any nationally agreed or assured standards of training or experience for fingerprint experts (the vast majority of whom are employed by the police rather than the FSS). Though these quality standards are seen as an essential concomitant to the removal of a numerical standard,[193] there is no mechanism to ensure independent setting or oversight of standards and no date set by which they should

---

[183] See Evett, I.W., 'Expert evidence and forensic misconceptions of the nature of exact science' (1996) 36 *Medicine, Science and the Law* 118.

[184] ACPO Crime Committee, *Report of the Quality of Fingerprint Evidence Review* (Thames Valley Police, 1996) p. 5. There are also conceptual flaws: Stoney, D.A. and Thornton, J.I., 'A critical analysis of qualitative fingerprint individuality models' (1986) 37 *Journal of Forensic Sciences* 1187.

[185] On the position in law, see *R v Buisson* [1990] 2 NZLR 542.

[186] This was accepted in 1984 and 'partial' identifications now amount to 5–10 per cent of the total (33 cases in 1994): ACPO Crime Committee, *Report of the Quality of Fingerprint Evidence Review* (Thames Valley Police, 1996) p. 3.

[187] See *ibid.*, p. 8. In the USA, the figure is usually (though not fixed) around 10 to 12 points: Moenssens, A.A., *et al.*, *Scientific Evidence in Criminal and Civil Cases* (4th ed., Foundation Press, New York, 1995) p. 514.

[188] See Lee, H.C. and Gaensslen, RE. (eds.), *Advances in Fingerprint Technology* (Elsevier, New York, 1991).

[189] Evett, I.W. and Williams, R.L., *A Review of the Sixteen Point Fingerprint Standard in England and Wales* (Home Office, 1995) p. 11.

[190] See Robertson, B.W.N., 'Fingerprints, relevance and admissibility' [1990] *NZ Recent Law Review* 252 at p. 257 (in New Zealand, a 12–point standard operated).

[191] Jessel, D., 'The Lund Lecture: television, science and the law' (1997) 37 *Medicine, Science and the Law* 4 at p. 9.

[192] Police Papers No. 2: *Improving the Performance of the Fingerprint Service* (London, 1988) paras. 16, 20. This was followed by a review of the standard in 1988/89 by Evett and Williams: Evett, I.W. and Williams, R.L., *A Review of the Sixteen Point Fingerprint Standard in England and Wales* (Home Office, 1995).

[193] See ACPO Crime Committee, *Report of the Quality of Fingerprint Evidence Review* (Thames Valley Police, 1996) p. 18.

be achieved (though the projected start date for the end of the 16-point standard was 1 April 1998).

A final example where there could be a role for an expert oversight body concerns the current fashion for Bayesian theorem, which, it has been claimed, can form a common language between science and law.[194] The theorem uses information about known events to make calculations as to the probabilities of unproven events. For each piece of evidence, a 'likelihood ratio' is calculated. This is found by dividing the statistical probability of an event being true by the probability of it not being true. The likelihood ratios are then combined with prior odds to compute an overall probability, thereby converting 'prior odds' to 'posterior odds'. Bayes' Rule itself, an eighteenth century mathematical model, is well known and well accepted within science, but the controversy here is whether it is meaningful in the context of the highly complex and uncertain world of a criminal investigation in which the calculation of prior odds is extremely difficult and even more so when that evidence is put, often out of the expected sequence, to a jury. The difficulties (and predominant paradigms)[195] of the latter in understanding and applying the theorem convinced the Court of Appeal in *R* v *Adams*[196] to order a retrial on the basis that 'common sense' rather than mathematical modelling should be the basis for jury verdicts. But an expert body may be able more effectively to discern and explain the appropriate uses of the theorem. Certainly the emphasis on prior odds may usefully dilute the likelihood ratios, which in the case of DNA have seemed to overwhelm a full consideration of the evidence in context.

Conclusion
Given that forensic evidence is available to be investigated in only 1:200 cases[197] and that resources do not stretch to its analysis and submission in all possible cases, the hope that science may provide an antidote to the police construction of criminality, especially through interrogation, seems forlorn. Even when it is available, this chapter highlights the dangers of placing faith in the infallibility of scientists, just as it has proven mistaken to believe in the total honesty of all police detectives. The fond belief that the Police and Criminal Evidence Act 1984 or the Runciman Commission have remedied all ills is even less well-founded in regard to forensic, as compared to police, practices.[198] The Act has extended police discretion to obtain physical evidence in several important respects[199] but does little to impose regulation upon the police. It is wholly silent on the competence of forensic scientists and expert witnesses. Thus, there remain problems, especially about the standards employed in analysis and the soundness of the interpretation

---

[194] Robertson, B. and Vignaux, G.A., *Interpreting Evidence: Evaluating Forensic Science in the Courtroom* (Wiley, Chichester, 1994); Redmayne, M., 'Science, evidence and logic' (1996) 59 *Modern Law Review* 797.

[195] Smith, R., 'Forensic pathology, scientific expertise and the criminal law' in Smith, R. and Wynne, B. (eds.), *Expert Evidence* (Routledge, London, 1989).

[196] [1996] 2 Cr App R 467. See also *R* v *Doheny and Adams* [1997] 1 Cr App R 369; *R* v *Adams (No. 2), The Times* 3 November 1997.

[197] Police Service, Submission to the Royal Commission (1991) para. 1.1.19.

[198] Standards demanded elsewhere are little better: *California* v *Trombetta* 467 US 479 (1984); *Arizona* v *Youngblood* 488 US 51 (1988).

[199] See: ss.8, 9, 18, 32, 54, 61–63. The powers to search for property are in general rather better regulated than the powers to take bodily samples, which may reflect the general failure in English common law to recognise a right to privacy: *Malone* v *MPC (No. 2)* [1979] Ch 344.

of results, with the grave danger that the jury will be seduced by the purity of the science without fully considering the impurity of its application. As well as the notorious cases cited earlier which gave rise to the foundation of the Runciman Commission, examples of an over-eagerness to draw inferences from forensic evidence include in recent times the unresolved case of Patrick McLaughlin in 1985[200] and that of Danny McNamee, acquitted in 1998 of involvement in IRA bomb-making some eleven years after his conviction.[201]

It follows that the avoidance of confessions and reliance instead upon other sources of evidence may solve some problems but will highlight several more. Nevertheless, a progressive programme of reform could be derived from the foregoing discussion of forensic science. Relevant measures would need to promote healthy growth in independent forensic science and to ensure that scientific evidence was properly tested and balanced at trial and was therefore more likely to be sustainable thereafter. Despite the overwhelming support for a stronger and more regulated range of forensic services, three difficulties may persist.

First, there is the ever-present problem of funding. The Police and Criminal Evidence Act was implemented during a decade of unprecedented growth in police budgets, which allowed for new facilities and training without unduly prejudicing other priorities. By contrast, forensic services would need to be expanded, not simply redeployed, and at a time of public spending retrenchment. It has earlier been argued that financial considerations are at the core of the non-implementation of several Runciman Commission recommendations.

Secondly, the proper extent of the reforms in the forensic area, as opposed to their direction, remains largely unconsidered. For example, it might be asked why fingerprints are currently collected and analysed by the police without reference in the vast majority of cases to scientists or independent laboratories. The answer seems in the main to be historical; fingerprinting was developed two or three decades before the establishment of independent laboratories.[202] Even the Runciman Commission brushes away any inquiry with the comment that the 'expertise lies in the main with police forces themselves and not with the forensic science laboratories.'.[203] However, the location may be changing to some extent as sophisticated forms of fingerprint detection nowadays involve complex processing and may be subject to mistakes of implementation or interpretation at the stage of obtaining the print, typology and matching and then inferences drawn from its presence.[204] In addition, the implication that police 'expertise' means objectivity

---

[200] [1988] 3 All ER 431; *The Times*, 26 November 1986 pp. 1, 20. His fingerprints were detected on a bin-liner in which bombs had been wrapped. The owners of other prints were not charged. See Woffinden, B., 'The influence of justice' (1990) *Counsel* May p. 14.

[201] See *The Times*, 28 October 1987 pp. 1, 3; 18 December 1998 p. 15; Channel 4, *Trial and Error* (http://www.channel4.com/, 1996); Jessel, D., 'The Lund Lecture: television, science and the law' (1997) 37 *Medicine, Science and the Law* 4 at p. 8. McNamee's prints were taken from electrical equipment found in bombs. He admitted working as an electrician in Dundalk but alleges a mistaken match as well unfounded inferences from the presence of his fingerprints. His conviction was quashed on the grounds of non-disclosure of evidence linking the equipment to Desmond Ellis (see *R v Ellis, The Times*, 31 October 1991, pp. 1,3). He later attempted an escape from prison: *The Guardian*, 12 September 1994 p. 1.

[202] See: *R v Castleton* (1910) 3 Cr App R 74.

[203] *Loc. cit.* ch. 2 para. 46. Equally, fingerprinting is uncritically viewed as 'routine and unproblematic' by Redmayne, M., 'The DNA database' [1998] *Criminal Law Review* 437 at p. 443.

[204] See Campbell, D., 'Fingerprints' [1985] *Criminal Law Review* 175; Kind, S.S., *The Scientific Investigation of Crime* (Forensic Science Services, Harrogate, 1987).

cannot be assumed, as the change of standards perhaps demonstrates. Thus, forensic science should be defined in wide terms if the quality of justice is to be improved.

The third and final problem concerns how forensic evidence is handled and the particular danger that tests adverse to the contentions of the prosecution will be disregarded and suppressed. This leads to the observation that acceptable forensic detection ultimately depends not only on the imposition by society of training, rules, sanctions and supervision but also on the internalisation by scientists of the ethics behind that training and so on. As has been found to be indispensable in relation to interrogation practices, it is necessary to impact upon the whole culture with which the police approach investigations.[205] Thus, attempts have been made to develop an ethical approach to the business of interrogation, a trend which has now received official support from the Home Office in its *Guide to Interviewing*.[206] A corresponding approach to forensic evidence should spark debate as to what bodily tests should be permissible under compulsion, how the tests should be conducted, what inferences may be safely drawn, how evidence is presented to the police, defence and court, and the storage of samples and data about them. The debate has barely begun in the UK but may be more advanced elsewhere.[207]

In conclusion, those who advise 'more detection, less interrogation'[208] may be looking for a chimera – forms of evidence which can be presented in court unsullied by fallible human process.[209] In reality, all forms of evidence may be subject to misconceptions and misrepresentations, so there is little to be gained from wholly excluding or wholly relying on given forms of evidence. At the end of the day, 'the criminal justice system cannot be made "miscarriage proof"'.[210] It is important to consider the likely errors which can arise with each type and to devise strategies to minimise the mistakes and to make them detectable. However, it is important above all to instil a conscience about justice, freedom and truth in those with responsibility to act on behalf of the State in the criminal justice system.

---

[205] See Chapter 3.

[206] 1992. The booklet followed Home Office Circular 22/1992.

[207] See Law Reform Commission of Canada, *Working Paper 34: Investigative Tests* (Ottawa, 1984). Compare the unprincipled views of the Home Affairs Committee, *Annual Report of the Data Protection Registrar* (1990–91 HC 115) para. 26.

[208] McConville, M., 'Wanted: more detection, less interrogation' *The Times*, 2 March 1993 p. 31.

[209] See Kuhn, T., 'Scientific paradigms' in Barnes, B., (ed.), *Sociology of Science* (Penguin, London, 1972); *The Essential Tension: selected studies in scientific tradition and change* (University of Chicago Press, 1977), *The Structure of Scientific Revolutions* (3rd ed., University of Chicago Press, 1996); Neufeld, P.J., 'Have you no sense of decency?' (1993) 84 *Journal of Criminal Law and Criminology* 189; Jones, C.A.G., *Expert Witnesses* (Clarendon Press, Oxford, 1994) pp. 5, 273.

[210] Greer, S., 'Miscarriages of justice reconsidered' (1994) 57 *Modern Law Review* 58 at p. 73.

7

Disclosure: Principles, Processes and Politics

Ben Fitzpatrick

Introduction

When a prosecution is brought by the State, the resources available to the investigating and prosecuting authorities will inevitably dwarf those of all but the most affluent defendant. Such a disparity manifests itself in a number of ways. A defendant is relatively disadvantaged in finding out, in simple terms, *what is going on*: with what wrongdoing is he or she charged; when is he or she required to attend court; whom he or she should contact for advice or assistance; what would be an appropriate line of defence; what are the implications of bail? The language and practices of the criminal process are markedly exclusive – there would, of course, otherwise be little need for intercessionary lawyers. This discursive élitism conspires with the massive differentials in information access that pertain between State and individual, in a forum in which the nexus of knowledge and power is at its most pronounced. Were it not for remedial legal rules such as the burden of proof and legal aid to offset the imbalance, the implied assertion at the heart of the adversarial process, namely that a trial proceeds on the basis of so-called 'equality of arms'[1] would have an utterly hollow ring.

The rules governing the disclosure of evidence between prosecution and defence operate to some extent to mitigate the potential harsh effects of the disparity in investigative, legal and forensic resources between them, and thus as some kind of counter to the awesome machinery of state. They should also be reflective of where the initiative and burden of proof lies in criminal process. As Andrew Ashworth remarks:[2]

> The principle is that defendants should have the same access to documents, to records, and to other evidence as the prosecution . . . It derives strength from

---

[1] Equality of arms has long been recognised as 'an inherent element of a fair trial' under Article 6 of the European Convention: *X* v *Germany*, Appl. no. 1169/61, (1963) 6 YBEC 520 at 574. See Harris, D., O'Boyle, M. and Warbrick, C., *Law of the European Convention on Human Rights* (Butterworths, London, 1995) pp. 207–210.

[2] Ashworth, A., *The Criminal Process: An Evaluative Study* (1st ed., Clarendon Press, Oxford, 1994) pp. 66, 67.

the presumption of innocence, and its conception of fairness is that it would be wrong for a system to have one side with either procedural or practical advantages over the other. This would be especially wrong when that party is the State, with its immense power and resources, and the other party is the individual citizen, invariably much the poorer in terms of resources and support.

It is the purpose of this chapter to address the changes in the law governing disclosure, up to and including the most recent regulatory scheme contained in the Criminal Procedure and Investigations Act 1996 (CPIA 1996).[3] I also hope to locate the current law in an appropriate political context, with a view to determining its adequacy for securing a meaningfully level playing field for prosecution and defence.

Changes in the Law relating to Disclosure

The law governing disclosure has been through a number of more or less identifiable stages. For current purposes, discussion is to be limited to disclosure of evidence by the prosecution to the defence.[4] In the beginning, in the absence of a statutory scheme or forceful and coherent precedent, there were no rules to speak of. Authorities, such as they were, suggested, and no more than suggested, that there *might* be a duty either to serve an unused witness statement on the defence, or at least to furnish the defence with particulars of that witness, in order to facilitate the contacting of the witness by the defence, should they so desire.[5]

The disclosure debate was catalysed by the occurrence of a number of cases, the outcomes of which may have been affected by the lack of uniformity and, apparently, rigour in disclosure practices among regional investigating and prosecuting authorities.[6] In an attempt to impose order and coherence on a fragmented and arguably capricious system, the Attorney-General, in December 1981, published a set of *Guidelines*[7] for the disclosure of evidence between prosecution and defence. The Guidelines, although lacking the formal force of law, did take on some kind of quasi-legislative authority, in so far as they have been held either to

---

[3] The substantive law relating to public interest immunity is unchanged by the CPIA 1996 and so is considered in Chapter 8.

[4] There were few requirements in the other direction, the main exception being disclosure of an alibi defence under the Criminal Justice Act 1967, s.11.

[5] In *R v Bryant and Dickson* (1946) 31 Cr App R 146, it was suggested that there was no duty to serve an unused witness statement on the defence; it was sufficient to make the name and address of the witness known to the defence. Whether this is a particularly authoritative decision is questionable, as the defence had, in the particular circumstances, ample opportunity to take a statement from the witness themselves. In *Dallison v Caffery* [1965] 1 QB 348, a strong Court of Appeal, comprising Lord Denning MR, Diplock LJ, and Dankwerts LJ, hinted at the existence of a duty to furnish the defence with unused witness statements (the view taken by Lord Denning MR) or of the lesser duty, to make a witness available for the defence (the view of Diplock LJ). Both of these expressions of the scope of the duty of disclosure were *obiter*, and Dankwerts LJ did not concern himself at all with the question. In *R v Mills* [1998] 1 Cr App R 43, the House of Lords considered that *Bryant and Dickson* should no longer be regarded as good law, as the duty of disclosure, whatever its current scope at common law, had become unquestionably broader since that case.

[6] See for example *Baksh v R* [1958] AC 157; *R v Hassan and Kotaish* (1968) 52 Cr App R 291; *R v Cooper and McMahon* (1975) 65 Cr App R 215; (1978) 68 Cr App R 18; *R v Leyland Justices, ex parte* Hawthorn (1979) 68 Cr App R 269. The nadir of the pre-regulated disclosure era was arguably the time of the trials in the 1970s of the *Birmingham Six*, the *Guildford Four*, the *Maguire Seven*, Judith Ward, and the *Bridgewater Four*; see Chapter 2. The era firmly ended with the decisions in *R v Maguire and others* [1992] 2 All ER 433 and *R v Ward* [1993] 1 WLR 619.

[7] See (1982) 74 Cr App R 302.

confer a 'legitimate expectation' on a party that they will be complied with, such that a failure to do so could constitute a possible ground for judicial review; or to give rise to a material irregularity in a trial if compliance with them had not taken place.[8] As O'Connor rightly observes, although preferable to a total absence of possibility of redress, such guidelines are a convoluted and inappropriate reflection of the fundamental right to fair disclosure:[9]

> This has been a desirable, though makeshift, resource . . . However welcome, these are rather abstruse ways of conferring authority upon one of the basic foundations for a fair trial.

Implicit in O'Connor's argument is the suggestion that the rule of law demands utter transparency and relative accessibility in at least formulating legal argument on an issue of such magnitude.

As for the contents of the Guidelines, they created a presumption in favour of disclosure of evidence to the defence. Guideline 2 stated:

> In all cases which are due to be committed for trial, all unused material should normally . . . be made available to the defence solicitor if it has some bearing on the offence(s) charged and the surrounding circumstances of the case.

The presumption was subject to a number of caveats, in which a discretion not to make disclosure is vested in the prosecutorial authorities. According to Guideline 6:

> There is a discretion not to make disclosure – at least until counsel has considered and advised on the matter – in the following circumstances:
>
> (i)   There are grounds for fearing that disclosing a statement might lead to an attempt being made to persuade a witness to make a statement retracting his original one, to change his story, not to appear at court or otherwise to intimidate him.
>
> (ii)   The statement (e.g. from a relative or close friend of the accused) is believed to be wholly or partially untrue and might be of use in cross-examination if the witness should be called by the defence.
>
> (iii)   The statement is favourable to the prosecution and believed to be substantially true but there are grounds for fearing that the witness, due to feelings of loyalty or fear, might give the defence solicitor a quite different, and false, story favourable to the defendant. If called as a defence witness upon the basis of this second account, the statement to the police can be of use in cross-examination.
>
> (iv)   The statement is quite neutral or negative and there is no reason to doubt its truthfulness – e.g. 'I saw nothing of the fight' or 'He was not at home that afternoon.' There are however grounds to believe that the witness might change his story and give evidence for the defence – e.g. purporting to give an account of the fight, or an alibi. Here again, the statement can properly be withheld for use in cross-examination.

---

[8] See O'Connor, P., 'Prosecution Disclosure: Principle, Practice and Justice', in Walker C., and Starmer, K., (eds.) *Justice in Error* (Blackstone Press, London, 1993) at pp. 107, 108.

[9] See *ibid.* at p. 108.

There was a further discretion not to make disclosure in the case of 'sensitive' evidence, the disclosure of which would compromise the public interest (such as through an adverse effect on national security, or on the safety of an informant).[10]

The most notable characteristic of the quasi-law constituted or reflected by the Attorney-General's Guidelines was the degree of discretion vested in the prosecution in respect of the decision to disclose. Albeit that there was a presumption in favour of disclosure, the judge of whether any of the exempting grounds in Guideline 6 were satisfied was to be the prosecutor. Given the subjective nature of the prosecutor's judgment, both contemplated and endorsed by the Guidelines, one can imagine that any legal challenge in respect of non-compliance would only be successful in very limited circumstances.[11]

The Guidelines nevertheless contemplated the disclosure of a broad range of materials, not merely unused witness statements. That this placed potentially onerous burdens on the prosecution, in terms of the assimilation and copying of documentation to the defence, was recognised by Henry J, during the litigation arising from allegations of insider-dealing in the Guinness group of companies, which effectively ushered in the next, most liberal, epoch of disclosure regulation.[12] Albeit that the burdens on the prosecution might be extreme, the presumption in favour of disclosure outlined in the Attorney-General's Guidelines was not merely reiterated but was arguably strengthened by the Guinness case. It was made clear that disclosure would be required, of preparatory materials and memoranda, as well as the unused statements themselves.[13] Of equal significance was the assertion that the prosecution were not to be the judge of what material could be of relevance to the defence case.[14] Thus, the prosecution were only to have a discretion as to the making of disclosure where a public interest issue arose. To allow the prosecution a general discretion would be to allow them to be arbiter in their own cause. These changes were reflected in a further circular about disclosure, the 'Guinness Advice', issued by the Director of Public Prosecutions in 1992.[15]

Needless to say, considerable consternation was caused among prosecutors and investigators, who quite realistically feared extreme increases in administrative costs and a considerable erosion of some of their tactical advantages. It was felt that prosecutors were being compelled to facilitate the undertaking of so-called 'fishing expeditions' by defence teams, who might unmeritoriously either win the case through a war of attrition from which the prosecution were ground into withdrawal and discontinuance, or through the deployment of tenuous defences for which there was fragile support in the reams of material to which the defence would have access.

Nonetheless, the next development in the law governing disclosure did little to allay the fears of prosecutors, founded or otherwise. In fact, the Court of Appeal in the notorious case of *Judith Ward*,[16] did quite the opposite. Quashing Ward's

---

[10] See Chapter 8.

[11] Compare the test for the validity of so-called primary prosecution disclosure under the CPIA 1996, s. 3 discussed below.

[12] (Unreported but described in part in O'Connor, P., 'Prosecution Disclosure: Principle, Practice and Justice', in Walker C., and Starmer, K., (eds.) *Justice in Error* (Blackstone Press, London, 1993), Central Criminal Court, 1990). The decision of the Court of Appeal is reported as *R v Saunders and others* [1996] 1 Cr App Rep 463. See also Chapter 5.

[13] See trial transcript, p. 6D.

[14] *Ibid.*, at p. 7C.

[15] Walker C. and Starmer, K., (eds.) *Justice in Error* (Blackstone Press, London, 1993) pp. 123–7.

[16] [1993] 1 WLR 619.

convictions for explosives offences in respect of the M62 coach bombings, the Court of Appeal, addressing a litany of instances of inappropriate non-disclosure, emphatically asserted the fundamentality of disclosure to the fairness of the trial process. Recognising the cultural and professional affiliations arising among members of the prosecution team, broadly construed to include prosecutors, police and, in this particular case, forensic scientists employed by the Crown, the Court firmly stated that there was no place in the criminal process for the jealous guarding of material.[17] If material could either weaken the prosecution case or strengthen the defence case, then it should be disclosed. Furthermore, in the case of material in respect of which a public interest issue may have arisen, the Court swept away the discretion to make disclosure vested in the prosecution, which had been left untouched by the Guinness Guidelines. After *Ward*, the arbiter of whether such material ought to be disclosed was to be the court.[18]

If *Ward* represented something of a high point from the perspective of defence teams, the next test laid down by the courts, in *Keane*,[19] was simultaneously favourable and unfavourable to them. Although the test governing the need for disclosure remained broad, the case appeared to return to the prosecution a degree of power in actually making the assessment of whether the criteria of the test were satisfied. The test for whether the prosecution should make disclosure was to be one of materiality. Lord Chief Justice Taylor observed:[20]

I would judge to be material in the realm of disclosure that which can be seen on a sensible appraisal by the prosecution:

(1)   to be relevant or possibly relevant to an issue in the case;
(2)   to raise or possibly to raise a new issue whose existence is not apparent from the evidence the prosecution proposes to use;
(3)   to hold out a real (as opposed to fanciful) prospect of providing a lead on evidence which goes to (1) or (2).

There seemed to be something of a shift taking place, which could quite easily be understood in pragmatic terms, towards expediting the prosecution process and

---

[17] *Ibid.*, at pp. 674–5.

[18] *Ibid.*, at pp. 680–1. The Court of Appeal accepted the submission that the prosecution must give notice of their withholding of material on the grounds of an asserted public interest immunity, in order that, should the defence wish, the issue of whether such immunity existed could be adjudicated upon by a court. In the exceptional case in which the prosecution was not willing to have the matter adjudicated upon, the prosecution would inevitably have to be abandoned. This approach caused a number of difficulties for prosecutors who were concerned that the necessity of having a full hearing *inter partes* to bring about a decision on the issue of whether immunity existed might, for example, compromise the security of informants, by making them known to the defence. As a consequence, the procedures suggested in *Ward* have been subject to a degree of refinement in subsequent cases. It is now open to the prosecution, in circumstances in which an *inter partes* hearing would effectively disclose that which was sought to be withheld in the public interest, to make an *ex parte* application to the court for a ruling on the issue. Normally, the defence would be given notice that such an application was being made, although they would not normally be told the nature of the evidence being tested. In exceptional circumstances, where even the knowledge of the defence that an *ex parte* application was being made would irretrievably undermine the efficacy of the prosecution, it is possible to make the application without giving notice of the application to the defence. See *R* v *Davis, Rowe and Johnson* [1993] 1 WLR 613; Chapter 8.

[19] [1994] 1 WLR 746.

[20] *Ibid.*, at p. 752, adopting the test suggested by Jowitt J in *R* v *Melvin and Dingle* (unreported, Central Criminal Court, 1993).

presumably enhancing public confidence in it, by returning key decisions to the prosecution, while attempting to retain a sense of principle by maintaining broad criteria to govern whether material should be disclosed. Whether this balance of pragmatism and principle was, or could be, satisfactorily achieved is questionable. It became a particularly live question with the arrival of the next epoch of disclosure regulation, the CPIA 1996. It is to that legislation and its background that this chapter now turns.

The Statutory Regime of the CPIA 1996 – the Background

As some of the points made in the foregoing chapters have amply suggested, the past 20 years have witnessed a period of considerable public anxiety concerning the nature and role of the criminal justice process and agencies. From the time of the series of public disturbances in the inner cities of Britain in the early 1980s,[21] through the period of intense division engendered by the miners' dispute and the manner in which it was policed and politicised,[22] up to the uncovering of the series of high-profile miscarriages of justice in the late 1980s and early 1990s,[23] the 'neutrality' and 'objectivity' of the criminal justice system was called into question in a most profound manner. It began to become clear to the public, the consumers of the criminal justice product, that agency decisions which could have a profound effect on them were as likely to be based on occupational practices and informal policies as on hard and fast legislative rules. If there was a climate of opinion, it appeared to be in favour of rendering processual decisions more predictable, and accountable, and, in some sense, just. The preferred model for the criminal justice system was one that exhibited characteristics of so-called due process. The high points of preoccupation with due process were arguably the enactment of the Police and Criminal Evidence Act 1984[24] and the establishment of the Royal Commission on Criminal Justice in 1991 in response to the successful appeal of the *Birmingham Six*.[25]

However, it appears that at some point, the concerns which gave rise to the Runciman Commission, expressed in its primary terms of reference, namely to secure the acquittal of the innocent and the conviction of the guilty,[26] were hijacked by the apparently innocuous need to have regard to 'the efficient use of re-sources'.[27] It seemed that the *due* in due process was something of a fragile concept. As the political discourse of law and order resumed its traditional position of prominence, so it became possible to translate the systemic iniquity of miscarriages of justice into the inevitable, almost *natural* consequence of a rights-oriented process which was capable of engendering frustration in the results-geared agents who administered it. If the rules did not facilitate successful investigation and prosecution, one could hardly blame police and prosecutors for

---

[21] See Scarman, L., *The Brixton Disorders: 10–12 April 1981* (Cmnd 8427, HMSO, London, 1981).
[22] See for example Lustgarten, L., *The Governance of Police* (Sweet & Maxwell, London, 1986) ch. 8; Reiner, R., *The Politics of the Police* (2nd ed., Harvester Wheatsheaf, 1992) pp. 239–49; Fine, B. and Millar, R, *Policing the Miners' Strike* (Lawrence & Wishart, London, 1985); Green, P., *The Enemy Without* (Open UP, Milton Keynes, 1990).
[23] See Chapter 2.
[24] See Chapters 3, 4.
[25] See Chapter 2 for the *Runciman Report*.
[26] *Runciman Report*, at pp. i, ii.
[27] *Ibid*.

bending those rules, or the courts for taking a lenient view towards the rules being bent. A system which professed to hold dear the rights of those going through it was seen as being susceptible to exploitation by those suspects or defendants with the wherewithal, or the experience, to do so. It was possible to reinterpret successful appeals against miscarriages as merely technical triumphs for those involved. The taint of blameworthiness on successful appellants could not necessarily be expunged merely by an indictment, however searing, of the system which failed them.

Thus, the *Runciman Report*, born from a desire, and indeed a need, to make clear statements about the limits of official power in the investigation and prosecution of crime, grew into a blueprint for a bureaucratic model of the criminal process with an ill-disguised crime control/law and order subtext. Recommendations of the *Runciman Report* which accorded with the managerial preoccupations of Government, a preoccupation-which will be discussed in more detail below, such as the retention of a higher proportion of criminal cases at summary level, were adopted.[28] Where vestiges of due process were recognised by the Commissioners, such as in their marked scepticism towards the removal of the right to silence, they were brushed aside by Government and rationalised in terms of the need to restore faith in a system more concerned with the rights of 'criminals' than with the protection of the public.[29] The future of criminal justice was to be based around a reconceptualisation of the role of agencies, designed to present a more acceptable face to law-abiding citizens coming into contact with it or paying for it. The closure of 'technical' escape routes to unmeritorious suspects and defendants, and the correlative, implicit rearrangement of the criminal process more in the form of a truth-finding, inquisitorial endeavour would make the system more palatable. The benefit would be to those who felt alienated not so much by its capacity for error, as by the difficulties it encountered in attempting to deliver the goods in terms of both *obtaining* and *sustaining* convictions while simultaneously making such error.

As has been observed above, a key process-error in a number of the high-profile miscarriages cases related to the disclosure of evidence by the prosecution to the defence. It has been shown how the law governing disclosure has changed to accommodate the diverse needs of both sides in a criminal matter. We have, as Niblett suggests, come almost full circle in this field of law.[30] We began with the absence of any firm rules and therefore almost absolute discretion vested in local investigators and prosecutors. Then the Attorney-General's Guidelines stated the presumption in favour of disclosure but tempered it with wide discretionary powers in the prosecutor not to make disclosure in certain circumstances. The Guinness Guidelines and the judgment of the Court of Appeal in *Ward* imposed, in no uncertain terms, particularly onerous duties on prosecutors, but then in *Keane*, began to reverse the process by suggesting that the appropriate judge of materiality is the prosecutor. That this tendency should have continued, given the reconfiguration and rerationalisation of the criminal justice process which appears to be

---

[28] *Runciman Report*, ch. 6 para. 13.

[29] See Chapter 5. The provisions relating to the right to silence which eventually formed the Criminal Justice and Public Order Act 1994, ss. 34 to 37, were claimed as the triumph of Conservative Home Secretary, Michael Howard, who viewed them as an integral part of his '27-point plan to crack down on crime', which he announced in his speech to the annual Conservative Party conference in October 1993. See further Chapter 5; Wasik, M. and Taylor, R., *Blackstone's Guide to the Criminal Justice and Public Order Act 1994* (Blackstone Press, London, 1995) pp. 1–2, ch. 3.

[30] Niblett, J., *Disclosure in Criminal Proceedings* (Blackstone Press, London, 1997) at p. 83.

current, should come as no surprise. It has thus far culminated in the mandatory involvement of the defendant in the disclosure process, which is in keeping both with the 'truth-finding' justifications offered in defence of the body of significant changes which the criminal justice process is undergoing, and which is also utterly consonant with the bureaucratic 'rationalisation' of the system in terms of better, more efficient case-management and processing.

The CPIA 1996 was the specific product of a consultation process, the roots of which are to be found in the *Runciman Report*.[31] The *Report* countenanced the implementation of a scheme of reciprocal disclosure between prosecution and defence, in which the initial duty to disclose placed on the prosecution would have remained substantially as was the case at common law. The defence would respond to the prosecution disclosure with a general statement of their case, perhaps in a standard form document. Further, so-called secondary prosecution disclosure would be based upon defence requests for more information.

The Government followed up these recommendations by issuing a Consultation Paper, in which they unsurprisingly agreed in principle with the concept of reciprocal disclosure.[32] There was less concordance in the Consultation Paper with the scope of the original duty of disclosure on the prosecution as conceived by the *Runciman Report*. The drive towards efficiency demanded that less onerous duties be placed on the police and prosecution in the first instance.[33] Accordingly, the Consultation Paper expressly aimed to . . . move away from the current catch-all approach to an approach which places proper weight on the professionalism and integrity of the prosecutor, investigator and adviser.'.[34] That the then current approach was given the negative epithet 'catch-all' illustrates the regard in which it was held. Not only was such an approach inconsistent with the efficient administration of criminal justice, but it also, as has been observed above, could be portrayed to the public as being productive of inappropriate results. In a remark to the House of Commons, during the passage through Parliament of the CPIA 1996, which helps to situate the legislation in a broader politico-legal context, the then Home Secretary, Michael Howard, suggested that 'it is professional criminals, hardened criminals and terrorists who disproportionately take advantage of and abuse the present system.'.[35] Presumably these are the same hardened criminals who would 'play the system' by cynically demanding the fullest possible disclosure from the prosecution in the hope of pursuing the kind of 'fishing expedition' in search of evidence which the new legislation so clearly frowns upon.

The Bill passed through Parliament, not so much on an explicit law and order ticket, as on the back of efficiency – the quest for quicker and more appropriate resolution of cases. The reciprocal disclosure of evidence between prosecution and defence would, it was argued: facilitate earlier identification of the issues; produce clarity for a jury at the start of a trial and thus enhance the possibility of a 'correct' verdict being reached; enable weak cases to be weeded out in as expeditious a manner as possible, and discontinued; facilitate the identification of cases in which it might be suitable and possible, rather than go to a contested trial, to amend the indictment and procure a guilty plea; and prevent the employment of unmeritorious

---

[31] *Runciman Report*, ch. 6 paras. 33–73. See Glynn, J., 'The Royal Commission on Criminal Justice: Part 4: Disclosure' [1993] *Criminal Law Review* 841.

[32] *Disclosure: A Consultation Document* (Cm 2864, HMSO, London, 1995).

[33] See for example, *ibid.*, paras. 13, 14, 17.

[34] *Ibid.*, para. 40.

[35] HC Debs., vol. 235 col. 26, 11 January 1994.

'ambush' defences.[36] The actual *existence* of a system of reciprocal disclosure was by this stage taken for granted. While this is not a textbook on the technical processes envisaged by the Act,[37] it is to the mechanics of the new system of disclosure that this chapter now turns.

The Statutory Regime of the CPIA 1996 – the Contents

Primary Prosecution Disclosure

In all cases to which Part I of the CPIA 1996 applies,[38] the prosecution must make what is referred to as primary disclosure. While the defence will have presumably already had disclosed to them, under a variety of other statutory provisions, material which forms the basis of the prosecution case,[39] the CPIA 1996 itself is

---

[36] It is suggested by Niblett (*Disclosure in Criminal Proceedings*, Blackstone Press, London, 1997, at p. 222) that the making of opportunistic requests for information, and the deployment of such 'ambush defences' are of themselves wrong and do not depend for their wrongness on how often they occur. Research has suggested however, that the prevalence of ambush defences is not as wide as those who criticise their use might suggest. See for example, Report of a Working Party of the Bar Council, *The efficient disposal of business in the Crown Court* (London, 1992) para. 630; Leng, R., *The Right to Silence in Police Interrogation* (Royal Commission on Criminal Justice Research Study No. 10, HMSO, London, 1993) ch. 5; Zander, M. and Henderson, P., *Crown Court Study* (Royal Commission on Criminal Justice Research Study No. 19, HMSO, London, 1993) pp. 14, 15. In such a context, it would be disturbing if the largely empty fear of such defence tactics were used as a legitimating device for the promulgation of Draconian disclosure provisions.

[37] For texts dedicated to the CPIA 1996, see Card, R., and Ward, R., *The Criminal Procedure and Investigations Act 1996* (Jordan, London, 1996); Leng, R., and Taylor, R., *Blackstone's Guide to the Criminal Procedure and Investigations Act 1996* (Blackstone Press, London, 1996); Niblett, J., *Disclosure in Criminal Proceedings* (Blackstone Press, London, 1997); Corker, D., *Disclosure in Criminal Proceedings* (Sweet & Maxwell, London, 1997). For tactics under the legislation, see Corker, D., 'Maximising disclosure' (1997) 147 *New Law Journal* 961. The new statutory regime also prompted the explicitly defence-oriented practitioner text, Ede, R. and Shepherd, E., *Active Defence: A Solicitor's Guide to Police and Defence Investigation and Prosecution and Defence Disclosure in Criminal Cases* (Law Society, London, 1997).

[38] Part I applies to contested summary cases (s. 1(1)) in which the defendant has an option to make disclosure under s. 6. The remaining types of cases to which Part I applies involve the mandatory scheme of defence disclosure under s. 5, and it is on this scheme that the remainder of this chapter will focus. They are essentially those cases that are heard, for whatever reason, at Crown Court level. The types of case are listed in s. 1(2): indictable offences which are committed for trial; indictable cases of serious or complex fraud which are transferred to the Crown Court for trial under the Criminal Justice Act 1987; indictable child abuse cases which are transferred to the Crown Court under the Criminal Justice Act 1991, s. 53; summary offences which are included in indictments by virtue of being based on the same facts as indictable offences, under the Criminal Justice Act 1988, s. 40; cases for which a voluntary bill of indictment is preferred.

[39] For purely summary cases, there is no right to advance disclosure of the prosecution case, although requests for such disclosure are routinely granted as if an either-way case were involved, especially in courts where pre-trial review systems operate: Mulcahy, A., Brownlee, I. D. and Walker, C. P., 'PTRs, court efficiency and justice' (1994) 33 *Howard Journal of Criminal Justice* 109–124; Leng, R., and Taylor, R., *Blackstone's Guide to the Criminal Procedure and Investigations Act 1996* (Blackstone Press, London, 1996) p. 12. In relation to cases triable either way but which are, in the event, tried summarily, advance disclosure may be obtained by the defence, of either (at the discretion of the Crown Prosecution Service) copies of the prosecution evidence or a summary of the prosecution case: Magistrates' Courts (Advance Information) Rules 1985 (SI No. 601). As regards evidence in cases which will be heard in the Crown Court, this may be broken down into the following types: evidence required to be tendered at committal proceedings (under the CPIA 1996 Sched. 1); evidence supplied in relation to transferred child abuse cases, under the Criminal Justice Act 1991, Sched. 6 para. 4; evidence supplied in relation to transferred serious fraud cases under the Criminal Justice Act 1987, s.5(9); evidence supplied under the Indictments (Procedure) Rules 1971 (SI No. 2084) r. 9(1)(a).

concerned with the disclosure of *unused* material. Under section 3(1)(a), the prosecutor must disclose to the defence:

> . . . any prosecution material which has not previously been disclosed to the accused and which in the prosecutor's opinion might undermine the case for the prosecution against the accused . . .

The 'might undermine' test is clearly intended to narrow the duty of disclosure from that at common law, where 'materiality' was the guiding criterion.[40] Naturally, the duty to disclose is not just limited to material which would have a critically deleterious effect on the prosecution case. Indeed, in such circumstances, one would expect that a prosecution would not proceed in the first place.[41] Nonetheless, the implication is that material which is of merely 'small peripheral effect'[42] will not be subject to disclosure. As well as being relevant in terms of effect, the material must also be relevant in terms of the issues in the case. Unused material which goes to establishing whether the facts in issue in a particular case have been made out, or which goes to a collateral issue, such as the credibility of a witness, appears to be encompassed by the duty to make primary disclosure. Some guidance as to what types of material should be disclosed under section 3 can be found in the Consultation Paper:[43]

> If part of the prosecution case is a statement by a witness that he saw the accused near the scene of the crime shortly after it was committed, it will be necessary to disclose a statement by another witness that he saw a person of a different description from the accused at the same time and place.[44]
> If the defendant has told the police in an interview that he was acting in self-defence, it will be necessary to disclose the statement of any witness who supports this but whom the prosecution does not regard as truthful.[45]
> If the victim died of a hammer blow and part of the prosecution case is a forensic test showing that the bloodstains on a hammer found buried in the accused's back garden matched those of the victim, it will be necessary to disclose a negative test showing that the fingerprints on the hammer did not match those of the accused.
> If the prosecution is aware that its main witness has a previous conviction, it must disclose it to the defence, since it may affect the weight to be placed on his testimony.[46]
> If the prosecution is in possession of a psychiatric report showing that its main witness has a history of psychiatric disorder with a tendency to fantasise, it should disclose the report since it clearly undermines the credibility of that witness.

---

[40] See HL Debs. vol. 567 col. 1437, 18 December 1995, Baroness Blatch.

[41] According to the Code for Crown Prosecutors (at para. 5.1), a prosecution should only proceed if the Crown Prosecutor is satisfied that there exists 'a realistic prospect of conviction'.

[42] HC Debs vol. 272 col. 776, 27 February 1996, David Maclean.

[43] *Disclosure: A Consultation Document* (Cm 2864, HMSO, London, 1995) para. 42. See also Card, R. and Ward, R., *The Criminal Procedure and Investigations Act 1996* (Jordan, London, 1996) para. 2.36, at pp. 26, 27; HL Debs. vol. 569 col. 867, 19 February 1996, Baroness Blatch.

[44] See *R v Taylor and Taylor* (1994) 98 Cr App R 361.

[45] See *R v Mills* [1998] 1 Cr App R 43.

[46] See *R v Collister and Warhurst* (1955) 39 Cr App R 100.

If the prosecution is aware that a prosecution witness has applied for a reward for information leading to the conviction of a person for a criminal offence, it must disclose this to the defence.[47]

If previous versions of witness statements *are* inconsistent with the final version served on the defence, they must be disclosed . . .[48]

What is unclear is whether the notion of 'undermining the prosecution case' is taken to cover material which does just that but in ways not detailed already, or whether it should also cover material which may provide evidence of the existence of an available defence. It appears to be the case that during Parliamentary debates on the CPIA 1996, the former was contemplated but not the latter.[49] However, this is not borne out even by the examples from the Consultation Paper cited above, which refer to the possibility of disclosure of material which may support the existence of the defence of self-defence, albeit that the prosecution do not regard the witness concerned as a witness of truth. Moreover, such a restricted approach would be conceptually specious to say the least. It would overlook the fact that concepts familiar to the criminal lawyer, such as *actus reus*, *mens rea*, and indeed the notion of a *defence* have no discrete existence, but are merely analytic devices which can be deployed to determine whether or not a criminal offence has been made out. Thus, according to Roger Leng and Richard Taylor:[50]

If something is undermined it is likely to fall or fail. A prosecution case is likely to fail if found to have some internal inconsistency or flaw. Equally the prosecution case is likely to fail if the accused is successful in establishing an alternative hypothesis to explain the events in question, or the accused establishes a discrete defence. . . .

It is to be hoped that this interpretation of the 'might undermine' criterion will be employed, albeit that there may be some conflict between such an interpretation and the intention of Parliament.

It is worthy of note at this stage that whoever it is who makes the decision about what to disclose – as we shall see, there is some contention as to whether in practice this will be a Crown Prosecution Service or a police decision – the test of whether the decision has been exercised validly is to be undertaken on a *subjective* basis. It is the 'opinion of the prosecutor' that is to count in determining whether the material in question might indeed undermine the case for the prosecution. The key issue that this raises for current purposes is that the decision on what to make the subject of primary disclosure is unlikely to be susceptible to judicial review, provided it is taken rationally and by a party with the power to take it.

---

[47] See *R* v *Taylor and Taylor* (1994) 98 Cr App R 361.

[48] See *Baksh* v *R* [1958] AC 157.

[49] An amendment which would have obliged the prosecution to make primary disclosure of material which would have assisted the defence, as opposed to that which would simply undermine the prosecution case, was rejected in the interests of efficiency. It was felt that such a duty would have called for disclosure of material which might not have ultimately been used. See HL Debs. vol. 567 cols. 1436–47, 18 December 1995. It is not clear why the situatuion which has prevailed in the CPIA 1996 will necessarily involve the disclosure *only* of material of which the defence ultimately make use. See generally Leng, R., and Taylor, R., *Blackstone's Guide to the Criminal Procedure and Investigations Act 1996* (Blackstone Press, London, 1996) at pp. 13–15.

[50] *Ibid.*, at p. 14.

Defence Disclosure

The principal novelty of the CPIA 1996 resides in its launch of a scheme of mandatory[51] defence disclosure. The duty on the defence to make appropriate disclosure arises where the prosecution make or purport to make primary disclosure. However, the concept of reciprocity which apparently underpins the CPIA 1996 is rather specious. As already noted, the phraseology used in connection with prosecution primary disclosure renders almost absolute the security of the prosecution in respect of review of primary disclosure decisions and allows the pre-trial process to proceed unhindered, as it is sufficient that the prosecutor 'purports to comply' with the duty which requires only that he or she 'genuinely believe' that he or she has disclosed.[52] On the other hand, the prosecution will *always* become entitled to defence disclosure, however poor their efforts at the primary disclosure stage, whereas the entitlement of the defence to secondary disclosure is dependent on meeting threshold criteria in respect of the quality of the defence statement.

As to the scope of the duty on the defence to make disclosure, the Runciman Commission had suggested that it would be appropriate and sufficient in most cases to go no further than the ticking of boxes on a standard form, indicating just the name of the generic defence which it was proposed to run. There would be more complex cases in which the services of counsel could be employed in the formulation of the defence, but these would undoubtedly be a minority.[53] This proposed duty had expanded by the time of the Consultation Paper:[54]

> The defence would be required to provide sufficient particulars of its case to identify the issues in dispute between the defence and the prosecution before the commencement of the trial . . . The exact details of what would need to be disclosed by the defendant in each case would depend on the particular defence to be advanced. The Government envisages that the details will include . . . the name and address of any witnesses the defendant proposes to call in support of that defence, or a written statement of fact or opinion which the defendant proposes to adduce as expert evidence, or any evidence which might support a defence of, for example, consent or self-defence or duress.

The CPIA 1996 itself, building upon the broader conception in the Consultation Paper, requires that a 'defence statement' be given by the defence to the prosecutor and the court. The defence statement is defined in section 5(6) as a written statement:

(a)   setting out in general terms the nature of the accused's defence,
(b)   indicating the matters on which he takes issue with the prosecution, and

---

[51] The CPIA 1996, s. 6 also devises a scheme of *voluntary* disclosure in relation to cases going to summary trial, in respect of which, once the duty of primary prosecution disclosure (under s. 1(1), and defined under s. 3(1)) has been met, the defence *may* furnish the prosecution with a defence statement, which will both trigger the prosecution duty of secondary disclosure (under s. 7) and give rise to the possibility of sanctions in respect of a defence disclosure which, albeit that it is made, is in some way defective (under s. 11(2)). These sanctions are discussed in more detail below.

[52] HL Debs. vol.567 col. 1456, 18 December 1995, Baroness Blatch.

[53] *Runciman Report*, ch. 6, para. 68. The position in Scotland is in many ways comparable; see chapter 16.

[54] *Disclosure: A Consultation Document* (Cm 2864, HMSO, London, 1995) para. 51.

(c)   setting out, in the case of each such matter, the reason why he takes issue with the prosecution.

It can be seen quite clearly that this duty is far broader than that envisaged by the *Runciman Report*.[55] Not only must the defence furnish the prosecution with the general line, or indeed simply the legal name, of their defence, but they must also render specific details of their dispute with the prosecution version of events.

A benign interpretation of this provision would suggest that such defence disclosure maximises the potential for the defendant to acquire further knowledge of the prosecution case, through the process of secondary prosecution disclosure outlined below. Indeed, it was suggested by the Solicitor-General that worthwhile secondary prosecution disclosure depended on the provision of a suitable defence statement. The prosecutor could only make such disclosure if:[56]

> . . . the defence has, to use a colloquialism, set its stall out for the prosecution to be able to say: 'That is the issue, that is the issue, and that is the issue. Now what material do I have which I ought to disclose because it might reasonably assist the defence?'

This presents a rather rosy picture of the prosecution as a disinterested and collectively coherent endeavour, in which agencies co-operate in a thoroughly transparent manner, such that the flow of information among these agencies, and indeed the defendant, is full, free, frank and fair. For reasons which will be examined below, it is submitted that this is a naïve conception.

The defence statement is of considerable significance, not just to the manner in which the prosecution will subsequently conduct the case, but to the defence themselves and how the defence will proceed. At present it is considered good practice by legislators, investigators and one might suggest also by prosecutorial authorities, not merely to get an explanation from a suspect/defendant at the earliest possible opportunity, but also to get them to stick to that story line. This can be rationalised in terms of the rhetoric of both a conventional law and order perspective – a suspect/defendant with nothing to hide will simply repeat the same explanation without falling foul of discrepancies between versions, as they have no reason not to render their fullest co-operation to the authorities. It also fits with, more cynically, an efficiency point of view – the less opportunity that suspects/ defendants have to change their story, the more quickly the case can be processed. In keeping with both of these rationales, the defence statement is something of a straitjacket for the defendant, and it comes as no surprise to find that there are potential sanctions for the defendant who does not play the game. Section 11(1) of the CPIA 1996 posits a defendant who:

(a)   fails to give the prosecutor a defence statement under s. 5;

(b)   gives the prosecutor a defence statement under that section but does so after the end of the prescribed period;

(c)   sets out inconsistent defences in a defence statement given under s. 5;

---

[55] Though, it should be noted, in some respects narrower than that posited in the Consultation Document. No specific provision is made for the disclosure of witness contact details in s. 5(6).

[56] HC Standing Committee B col. 69 16 May 1996 Sir Derek Spencer.

(d)   at his trial, puts forward a defence which is different from any defence set
out in a defence statement given under that section . . .

Such a defendant would be subject to the possibility under section 11(3) of the
court, or any other party with leave of the court, making such comment as appears
appropriate, and to the further possibility of the drawing, by the court or jury, of
such inferences as appear proper in deciding whether the accused is guilty of the
offence in question.[57] The clear message is that those comments or inferences will,
of course, be adverse to the defence, especially as the side-note to section 11 refers
to 'faults' in disclosure by the accused.

Secondary Prosecution Disclosure

Once the defence has complied with the duty of disclosure imposed upon it by
section 5, a further duty on the prosecution crystallises, namely that to make
secondary disclosure. Under section 7(2) of the Act, the prosecutor must:

(a)   disclose to the accused any prosecution material which has not been
previously disclosed to the accused and which might be reasonably expected to
assist the accused's defence as disclosed by the defence statement given to the
prosecutor . . . ; or
(b)   give to the accused a written statement that there is no material of a
description mentioned in paragraph (a).

The key issue that distinguishes the processes of primary and secondary prosecution
disclosure is that, whereas the test for the validity of primary disclosure is *subjective*,
being concerned with the opinion of the prosecutor, the adequacy of secondary
disclosure is governed by an *objective* test, namely what *might be reasonably expected*
to assist the accused's case in the prescribed manner. As such, the latter would appear
to be more susceptible to judicial review and indeed challenge on appeal.

Issues Arising from the CPIA 1996

The institution of a reciprocal system of disclosure might be taken to signal a
reappraisal of the purposes and values underpinning the criminal process. Equally,

---

[57] Commentators have drawn attention to the link between these provisions and the Criminal Justice
and Public Order Act 1994, ss. 34 to 38, which allow for the drawing of inferences from the suspect
or defendant's silence or any inconsistencies in his or her account of events. See Card, R. and Ward,
R., *The Criminal Procedure and Investigations Act 1996* (Jordan, London, 1996) at pp. 44, 45, para.
2.67; Leng, R. and Taylor, R., *Blackstone's Guide to the Criminal Procedure and Investigations Act
1996* (Blackstone Press, London, 1996) at pp. 26–8; Sprack, J., 'The Criminal Procedure and
Investigations Act 1996: (1) The Duty of Disclosure' [1997] *Criminal Law Review* 308 at pp. 312,
313; Niblett, J., *Disclosure in Criminal Proceedings* (Blackstone Press, London, 1997) at p. 224. It
appears that the case law generated under the relevant provisions of the Criminal Justice and Public
Order Act 1994 may offer some guidance as to the scope, nature and effect of inferences that can
be drawn in the case where defence disclosure is defective. It is worthy of note in this context that,
since *R v Cowan* [1995] 4 All ER 939 suggested that an adverse inference cannot, in the context of
the Criminal Justice and Public Order Act 1994, form part of the prosecution's *prima facie* case,
with the result that a defendant cannot be convicted solely on the basis of an adverse inference, it
is probably the case, by analogy, that an adverse inference permitted as a result of defective
disclosure cannot form a part of the prosecution's *prima facie* case. It certainly cannot form the
whole case: s. 11(5).

the process of reappraisal might well be viewed as being rather superficial, and perhaps, aptly for the political discourse of the day, as an exercise in rebranding, where the image of the system portrayed to citizen-consumers is altered while the underlying substance remains fundamentally unchanged. It might be suggested that in this postmodern age, this type of ideological-based critique and the positing of a fixed 'reality' concealed beneath a veneer of rhetoric is misplaced. It is arguable however, that with the current Labour administration being both so firmly entrenched for the foreseeable future and already having secured a considerable reputation for politics of style over substance, of public relations over policies, there has never been a time when it has been so appropriate to attempt to identify any realities lurking beneath the surface of day to day politico-legal discourse.

In terms of the CPIA 1996 itself, the ideal-type situation involves a co-operative enterprise through which prosecution and defence generate a co-authored narrative specifying the areas of dispute between them. However, the mere existence of areas of dispute between them highlights that the criminal process, as currently operating, is not about co-operation, but about conflict. It does not require the calling into question of the personal integrity of investigatory or prosecutorial agents,[58] or indeed suspects or their lawyers, to highlight the professional culture and systemic factors which could militate against the making of full disclosure. The development of the prosecution case has been described as an exercise in construction.[59] Far from being a legal-rule based operation, it is guided as much by less formal institutional practices and regimes. The collective self-perceptions of investigatory agents lead to an institutional understanding of the prosecution process as being one of, for want of a less crude phrase, having found the culprit, then attempting to secure a conviction by the most expeditious route. It is deeply questionable whether the establishment of the 'independent' Crown Prosecution Service has done much to obviate the problems of such an attitude. While the Service depends for its information on the investigations conducted by the police, then its independence is very much of a formal rather than substantive nature. However much Crown Prosecutors may genuinely profess their detachment from the aligned nature of the investigation process, they are shackled by their dependency on that very process for the material which enables them to do their job. This is as much a problem to do with disclosure (to the prosecutor) as it is with any aspect of the prosecution case. Although the decision of whether and what to disclose rests with the prosecutor, this decision is fettered by the provision of material by the police. The prosecutor makes that decision based on the material generated by the attitudes and methodologies of others. Conversely, the prosecutor cannot disclose what he or she does not know of. It can be seen that a police perception of the case as something to be 'won' could understandably compromise the making of effective disclosure and has done on several occasions.[60] Police practice, however well-intentioned, can quite easily reverse any presumption in favour of disclosure, with the result that a prosecutor is unable to make a fully-informed decision on whether to make disclosure.[61] On receipt of a subsequent defence statement, itself presumably

---

[58] By which the Government apparently set so much store. See *Disclosure: A Consultation Document* (Cm 2864, HMSO, London, 1995) para. 40.

[59] See for example McBarnet, D, *Conviction: Law, the State and the Construction of Justice* (MacMillan, London, 1981); McConville, M., Sanders, A., and Leng, R., *The Case for the Prosecution* (Routledge, London, 1991).

[60] See for example, the cases mentioned in Chapter 2.

[61] The Code of Practice promulgated under the CPIA 1996, ss. 23, 25, designed to articulate

shaped by the (in)adequacy of primary disclosure, it might not be too far-fetched to suggest that, contrary to the Solicitor-General's explanation, rather than being an exercise in benevolent truth-finding, assistance to the defence and the expeditious functioning of the criminal process, the consideration of possible secondary prosecution disclosure might become focused on determining ways in which the defence case itself can be undermined and the prosecution case bolstered.

The New Statutory Regime in Context

The CPIA 1996 is very much a child of its time. In an era in which political ownership of the twin discourses of both law and order and limited public expenditure, has been claimed by both major political parties, the delivery of 'ordered society' to the electorate is to be done in as efficient a manner as possible.[62] The beginnings of this managerialist drive were felt first early in the 1980s, when there occurred the importation of management techniques from the private sector into the public service arena.[63] The watchwords of efficiency, economy and effectiveness were used as marketing devices to persuade the citizen-consumer that the (minimal) responsibilities of State were being discharged appropriately.[64] As this actuarial discourse began, and continues, to permeate criminal justice agencies,[65] as it undoubtedly has,[66] one senses that the 'three Es' have become firmly entrenched, not as a means to achieving a further end of 'justice', but as the rhetorical and real embodiment of justice itself. As Redmayne shrewdly observes, the language of managerialism facilitates the presentation of

mechanisms for the securing of the objectives of the Act, envisages a key role for the (police) disclosure officer, who is to be responsible for revealing material to the prosecutor during the course of an investigation and any subsequent proceedings, and disclosing it to the accused, and perhaps crucially, for examining records created during the investigation and compiling the schedules of unused material for the perusal of the prosecutor, who will then make the decision on whether to make disclosure. The disclosure officer is the vital link between investigation and prosecution agencies. It is disappointing that no requirement of seniority or specific attributes (such as forensic or even administrative training) attaches to the post of disclosure officer; compare the position of custody officers under the Police and Criminal Evidence Act 1984, s. 36. Conversely, one might well wish to avoid placing experienced, prosecution-socialised, case-hardened, senior officers in such a position, for fear of the greater difficulties they might possess in displaying the objectivity that the post of disclosure officer professes to require. Either way, the disclosure officer is possessed of a singular lack of independence.

[62] For a detailed overview, which suggests ultimately that there are acute tensions between the two aims of delivering, on the one hand, law and order, and on the other hand, bureaucratic efficiency, see Brownlee, I., 'New Labour – New Penology?: Punitive rhetoric and the limits of managerialism in criminal justice policy' (1998) 25 *Journal of Law & Society* 313.

[63] This began with the Financial Management Initiative (see: Treasury and Civil Service Select Committee, *Efficiency and Effectiveness in the Civil Service*, Cmnd 8616, 1982).

[64] See generally, *Citizen's Charter* (Cm 1599, HMSO, London, 1991); Rhodes, R., 'The Hollowing Out of the State: the changing nature of the public service in Britain' (1994) 65 *Political Quarterly* 138; 'The New Governance: governing without government' (1996) XLIV *Political Studies* 652.

[65] The use of agency status is itself a symptom of managerialism. See P.M.'s Efficiency Unit, *Improving Management in Government* (see HC Debs. Vol. 127, col. 1149, 18 February 1988); Baldwin, R., 'The Next Steps' (1988) 51 *Modern Law Review*; Drewry, G., 'Forward from F.M.I.' [1988] *Public Law* 503; Lewis, N., 'Reviewing change in Government' [1994] *PL* 105; *Next Steps Review* (Cm 3579, HMSO, London, 1996).

[66] Amongst the immense literature, see Jones, C., 'Auditing Criminal Justice' (1993) 33 *British Journal of Criminology* 187; Ryan, M. and Ward, T., *Privatization and the Penal System* (Open University Press, Milton Keynes, 1989); Leishman, F., Cope, S. and Starie, P., 'Reinventing and restructuring: towards a "new policing order"' in Leishman, F., Loveday, B. and Savage, S., eds., *Core Issues in Policing* (Longman, London, 1996).

highly contentious processual reforms in politically neutral, consumer-friendly terms.[67] Who, after all, would argue *against* efficiency? Certainly, there are no signs that post-Thatcher administrations of any complexion are ready to do so.

In terms of more traditional measures of the criminal justice process, one might view the CPIA 1996 as a healthy move away from the *competitive* trial and the theatrical *faux*-truth of adversarialism. It might also be suggested that an inquisitorial approach, geared more explicitly towards truth-finding might more easily command support from a public less alienated from the relevant processes. This is a public which is very much 'on message' in their acceptance of a technocratised discourse of law and order – a public for whom the detection and punishment of crime are of course legitimate and overriding concerns. However, viable inquisitorialism demands independence in investigation, a degree of independence that is simply not delivered by the formal separation of investigative and prosecutorial powers. As long as the Crown Prosecution Service rely on the police for information, as they continue to do in the construction of files, and in terms of the question of whether and what to disclose, then they remain players on the same side, laden with the cultural baggage of prosecution and labouring under the same pressures imposed by the twin demands of law and order and audit. Within such parameters, this is half-baked inquisitorialism of an ideologically reprehensible kind. Just as Kafka's Josef K. (a no doubt morally complex character) is 'encouraged' to co-operate with the faceless, and apparently innocuous prosecutorial machinery which is ultimately his downfall, so today's defendant, bereft of a *right not to co-operate*, cajoled into breaking his or her silence, manoeuvred into doing what is effectively prosecutorial leg-work, becomes a key-player in their own downfall.[68] That this is justified by recourse to a false labelling of the relevant processes as truth-finding is a disturbing double bind.

European Considerations

The domestic implications of the Criminal Procedure and Investigations Act 1996 are complex and have understandably formed the focus of analyses that have been undertaken thus far. However, as we have now incorporated by the Human Rights Act 1998 selected provisions of the European Convention on Human Rights, future analysis must be sensitive to the relationship between the current disclosure legislation and the 'superstatute' that the Human Rights Act 1998 represents.[69] The question that needs to be addressed is the possibility that the legislation breaches Article 6 of the Convention, the relevant parts of which state:

(1) In the determination of . . . any criminal charge against him, everyone is entitled to a fair and public hearing . . .

---

[67] Redmayne, M., 'Process Gains and Process Values: The Criminal Procedure and Investigations Act 1996' (1997) 60 *Modern Law Review* 79 at p. 93.

[68] Kafka, F., *The Trial* (Secker & Warburg, London, 1950). A particularly disturbing theme in Kafka's text, and, at the risk of appearing melodramatic, a similarly unsettling feature of the current disclosure regime, is the manner in which State and prosecutorial power are naturalised through powerful crime control and administrative rhetoric.

[69] By this I mean that the Human Rights Act will be both *substantive*, in that it will incorporate certain rights into domestic law, and *mechanistic*, in that it will provide a framework of procedures for determining the legitimacy of domestic legal provisions. The procedural mechanisms are beyond the scope of this chapter.

(2)   Everyone charged with a criminal offence shall be presumed innocent until proved guilty according to law.

The existing jurisprudence of the Convention suggests that considerable leeway is given to the individual States in the conducting of their domestic criminal processes, whether they be of an adversarial or inquisitorial nature.[70] One can expect a similar leeway to be given to individual pieces of domestic legislation under the judicial processes prescribed in the Human Rights Act, of whether domestic legislation requires some form of review. However, there are already suggestions that the disclosure provisions might have such an effect on the burden of proof in a criminal case as to be in conflict with the presumption of innocence in article 6(2) of the European Convention and the corresponding provisions of the Human Rights Act.[71] Furthermore, there are a number of pending cases which have more directly challenged the fairness of non-disclosures, as detailed in Chapter 8.

Conclusions

The disclosure provisions in the CPIA 1996 did not, given their politico-legal context, come as a surprise. Nonetheless, it is suggested that they are the product of a period of reappraisal, at State level, of the purposes and values underlying a criminal process. They form a part of a broader and deeper reconceptualisation of that process which seeks to satisfy the public demand for an *effective* criminal justice system, mindful of the fears of those who see it as a protective device, and the political need for an *efficient* system, capable of delivering the goods without upsetting the books. It can be seen that terms such as effectiveness and efficiency are meaningless outside the context in which they are deployed. They are terms which carry an acutely situational package of values; terms which while imbued with a doubtless positive rhetorical flavour, are effectively purchased with the compromise of other values. It seems that the provisions reflect an exchange of due process values for bureaucratic values and political (in its most pejorative sense) gain. That this exchange should have taken place at all ought to be an occurrence subjected to the closest public scrutiny. What makes the taste of the changes all the more unpleasant is the manner in which the suspect-citizen-defendant-consumer is brought on board as a naturalised key player in an *adversarial* process, which the disclosure provisions seek to dress, unconvincingly, in a thin layer of inquisitorialism. Until prosecutorial and investigatory authorities can themselves consistently demonstrate the kind of stewardship of material so eloquently categorised by O'Connor as 'trusteeship',[72] then it is submitted that one should view with extreme cynicism the coercion of suspects and defendants into facilitating the performance of what has, not surprisingly, been conventionally viewed as part of the prosecution task: namely, proving the prosecution case.

---

[70] See *Edwards* v *United Kingdom*, Appl. No. 13071/87, (1993) 15 EHRR 417; Field, S. and Young, J., 'Disclosure, Appeals and Procedural Traditions: *Edwards* v *United Kingdom*' [1994] *Criminal Law Review* 264.

[71] See Leng, R., 'Losing Sight of the Defendant: The Government's Proposals on Pre-Trial Disclosure' [1995] *Criminal Law Review* 704 at p. 710.

[72] O'Connor, P., 'Prosecution Disclosure: Principle, Practice and Justice', in Walker C. and Starmer, K., (eds.) *Justice in Error* (Blackstone Press, London, 1993) at p. 118.

The Act was the brainchild of a Conservative criminal justice ministry. The philosophy behind the legislation has been firmly adopted by the succeeding Labour administration. We live in an age in which the rhetoric of 'togetherness' and 'people's' politics (and passivity) is prominent in the lexicon of the nation. If the current law, in its method of 'involvement' of the defendant in his or her own prosecution, represents some kind of attempt to sell the criminal justice system as a 'people's process', then this is inclusionary politics of a very worrying kind.

8

Public Interest Immunity and Criminal Justice

Clive Walker with Geoffrey Robertson

The Relationship to Miscarriages of Justice

Public interest immunity (PII) may be defined as the branch of the law of evidence dealing with claims arising from public interest grounds to exemption from the normal processes of disclosure.[1]

> The doctrine of public interest immunity prevents material from being disclosed and adduced in the usual way, whenever it is held that the public interest in non-disclosure outweighs the public interest that, in the administration of justice, the courts should have the fullest possible access to all relevant material.

The claims are not confined to state agencies, but most of the case-law development has arisen from that source and has related to concerns about injury to national defence, foreign relations, and the effective functioning of public services including policing services. A full history and description of PII will not be given here, especially as much of it resides within civil rather than criminal cases.[2] Suffice to say that the doctrine has given rise to much uncertainty and controversy because of its obvious potential for undermining the fairness of a trial. Non-disclosure of any kind can have this impact, as already related in Chapter 7. However, when a defendant or a trial court is confronted with a demand for overriding secrecy based on higher State interests than the fair resolution of an action, one is reminded of doctrines of State necessity such as would be favoured by Stuart kings.

---

[1] Richardson, P.J., (ed.), *Archbold: Criminal Pleading, Evidence and Practice* (Sweet & Maxwell, London, 1998) para. 12.27. See generally Niblett, J., *Disclosure in Criminal Proceedings* (Blackstone Press, London, 1997) chs. 9, 10; Ede, R. and Shepherd, E., *Active Defence* (Law Society, London, 1997) ch. 13. 'Relevant material' might include oral testimony; see *McCann and Others* v *United Kingdom*, Appl. no. 18984/91, Ser.A no. 324, (1996) 21 EHRR 97; *Re Ministry of Defence's Application* [1994] NI 279.

[2] See especially *Duncan* v *Cammell Laird & Co. Ltd* [1942] AC 624; *Conway* v *Rimmer* [1968] AC 910; *D* v *NSPCC* [1978] AC 171; *Burmah Oil* v *Bank of England* [1980] AC 1090; *Air Canada* v *Secretary of State for Trade (No. 2)* [1983] 2 AC 394; *R* v *Chief Constable of the West Midlands Police ex parte Wiley* [1995] 1 AC 274.

This concern may be exaggerated, for one of the uncertainties relating to PII is its application to criminal cases. There has been a school of thought that it is essentially a civil law development where only money or reputation and not liberty are at stake. So, it should have no application to criminal justice, on the grounds that the public interest in doing justice to the individual and the ethic of prosecutorial fairness will always outweigh any other competing public interest. Certainly, some ministerial pronouncements tended in this direction,[3] but it has long been accepted by the courts that claims to PII could be made in certain circumstances, the most important being to protect the identities of police informants.[4] Other recognised categories relevant to criminal proceedings have proliferated in recent years, including the location of premises used for police surveillance and the identity of the owner,[5] information upon which a search warrant is based,[6] and police reports, manuals and methods.[7] But this list leaves unanswered whether other categories of claims could be made, especially whether a claim could be made by a Government minister for classes of documents (such as national security matters, foreign relations or internal memoranda between ministers and civil servants, the disclosure of which could damage future operations or relationships) rather than a content claim based on specific sensitive content.[8] Equally uncertain is the precise weight to be given to the interests of justice and the concerns behind the PII claim – is there an effective trade-off or does PII only apply, respecting the paramount objective of avoiding a miscarriage of justice, where the material is wholly irrelevant to the defence[9] or perhaps even to any issue between the parties?[10]

The role of PII has widened in recent years, as already noted, and there are further expansionary pressures because of changes in policing in the United Kingdom. One reason is the increasing part played by the Security Services in policing activities. This role began with the conferment of a lead role for the

---

[3] Viscount Kilmuir, L.C., stated that PII should not attach to materials 'which are relevant to the defence in criminal proceedings': HL Debs, vol. 197 col. 743, 6 June 1956.

[4] On informers, see *Marks* v *Beyfus* [1890] 25 QBD 494; *R* v *Hennessey* (1978) 68 Cr App R 419; *R* v *Hallett and others* [1986] *Criminal Law Review* 462; *R* v *Agar* (1990) 90 Cr App R 318; *R* v *Slowcombe* [1991] *Criminal Law Review* 198; *Blake* and *Austin* v *DPP* (1993) 97 Cr App R 169; *R* v *Vaillencourt* [1993] *Criminal Law Review* 311; *R* v *Reilly* [1994] *Criminal Law Review* 279; *R* v *Turner* [1995] 2 Cr App R 94; *R* v *Haghighat-Khou* [1995] *Criminal Law Review* 337; *R* v *Baker* [1996] *Criminal Law Review* 55; *R* v *Adams* [1997] *Criminal Law Review* 292; *Savage* v *Chief Constable of Hampshire* [1997] 2 All ER 631. On a wider range of informants, see *D* v *NSPCC* [1978] AC 171; *Kaufmann* v *Credit Lyonnais Bank* (1995) 7 Admin LR 669.

[5] *R* v *Rankine* [1986] QB 861; *R* v *Brown and Daley* (1987) 87 Cr App R 52; *R* v *Johnson (Kenneth)* (1988) 88 Cr App R 131; *R* v *Hewitt*; *R* v *Davis* (1992) 95 Cr App R 81; *Blake and Austin* v *DPP* (1993) 97 Cr App R 169; *R* v *Grimes* [1994] *Criminal Law Review* 213.

[6] *Taylor* v *Anderton, The Times*, 21 October 1986.

[7] *Evans* v *Chief Constable of Surrey* [1988] QB 588; *Gill and Goodwin* v *Chief Constable of Lancashire, The Times*, 3 November 1992; *O'Sullivan* v *Commissioner of the Metropolitan Police, The Times*, 3 July 1995; *Taylor* v *Anderton* [1995] 1 WLR 447.

[8] See Niblett, J., *Disclosure in Criminal Proceedings* (Blackstone Press, London, 1997) pp. 150–2. Governmental PII certificates began to be issued on such grounds even where the material was disclosable under the Attorney-General's Guidelines issued in 1982 (for which see Walker, C. and Starmer, K., *Justice in Error* (Blackstone Press, London, 1993) ch. 6). The practice was exposed in the Matrix Churchill case (see below).

[9] See *R* v *Langford* [1990] *Criminal Law Review* 653; *DPP* v *Morrow* [1994] *Criminal Law Review* 58.

[10] See *R* v *Yirtici* (LEXIS, 1996). Here the Court of Appeal quashed a conviction where the suppressed material (the identity and statement of an undercover police officer) was wholly hostile to the defence; but its relevance was undoubted and the possibility of successful cross-examination had to be allowed.

Security Service (MI5) in intelligence gathering against Republican terrorism.[11] The Security Service Act 1996[12] then allowed a much broader range of intervention in respect of serious crimes, and there has even been talk of the Secret Intelligence Service (MI6) being given a similar role.[13] The intervention of these agencies will inevitably give rise to claims that even to identify their presence, let alone their activities, could be sensitive. The other reason why PII can be expected to gain in prominence concerns the impetus of policing techniques in the past decade. Very much under the influence of the Audit Commission,[14] the police have been encouraged to engage in proactive, targeted approaches to crime, which translate in practical terms into a greater use of techniques such as informers and surreptitious surveillance, all of which is again the fare of PII. With these trends in mind, it is important to gauge whether the potential for injustice to the individual has been properly recognised and combated.

Recent Inquiries into PII

Runciman Report

As illustrated by the case of Judith Ward,[15] the problems presented to the Runciman Commission often arose out of the non-disclosure even of the existence of materials rather than a claim for suppression on grounds of their sensitivity. Nevertheless, the Commission did examine the grounds and the procedures for non-disclosure on grounds of 'sensitivity' which may attract PII.

The procedures were viewed as being put on a firmer footing following the *Ward* case, in which it was emphasised that it was not for the prosecution to be a judge in its own cause but that a claim had to be left to the court, with notice to the defence.[16] In view of concerns about alerting criminals to the possible existence of agents and informers, the requirement of notice was modified in *Davis, Rowe and Johnson*.[17] Notice must be given to the defence whenever possible, but there may be cases when it is in the public interest not to reveal the category of materials giving rise to potential PII and there may be highly exceptional cases when even the fact of application to the court need not be notified. These procedures were viewed by the Runciman Commission as largely satisfactory, subject to ensuring that designated High Court or circuit judges always consider any *ex parte* application.[18]

As for the grounds of PII, the Runciman Commission actually argued for the widening of the category of suppression. Information given in confidence to the police (by someone not falling in the category of informer) or information about commercial security arrangements would form a category of 'sensitive' information over and above existing categories of PII.[19]

---

[11] See HC Debs Vol. 207 col. 297, 8 May 1992.

[12] See: Intelligence and Security Committee, *Annual Reports 1995* (Cm 3198, HMSO, London, 1996), *1996* (Cm 3574, HMSO, 1997).

[13] See speech by Foreign Secretary, Robin Cook, Kuala Lumpur, 28 August 1997, as reported in Wall, D., *The Chief Constables of England and Wales* (Dartmouth, Aldershot, 1998) p. 76.

[14] Audit Commission, *Helping with Enquiries* (London, 1993), *Streetwise* (London 1996). See also Chapter 1.

[15] (1992) 96 Cr. App. R 1. See Chapter 2.

[16] *Runciman Report*, ch. 6 para. 44.

[17] [1993] 1 WLR 613.

[18] *Runciman Report*, ch. 6 para. 48.

[19] *Runciman Report*, ch. 6 para. 47.

This survey by the Runciman Commission is grimly disappointing. Rather than considering how public interest immunity can work against the primary interests of justice – the conviction of the guilty and acquittal of the innocent – the constant refrain is on the costs and difficulties presented to the police alone, and even commercial interests seem to be prioritised over individual justice. Fortunately, the *Runciman Report* had little impact on the development of PII. To its credit, the Government was not convinced by the recommendations for expansion, believing it would be neither possible to define 'sensitive' with any precision nor would it be justifiable.[20] In addition, there were to be no special procedures for PII decisions arising from work of the Criminal Cases Review Commission; the proposal that issues could be taken before a single Lord Justice has been rejected.[21]

Scott Report

The impact of PII was rather more dramatised in the prosecutions arising from the export of materials to Iraq, which formed the subject of the *Scott Report*.[22] To some, the story is 'boring',[23] but the liberty and reputations of several individuals crucially rested upon the interpretation and application of PII in their cases and it would not be the first time in recent years that miscarriages of justice could only be understood and averted by painstaking attention to detail.

The principal case[24] concerned three directors of an engineering company, Matrix Churchill, who were prosecuted by H.M. Customs and Excise for the

---

[20] Lord Chancellor's Department, Home Office and Law Officers' Department, *The Royal Commission on Criminal Justice: Final Government Response* (Home Office, London, 1996) para. 76. But the word does appear under later legislation.

[21] *Runciman Report*, ch. 10 para. 31; Lord Chancellor's Department, Home Office and Law Officers' Department, *The Royal Commission on Criminal Justice: Final Government Response* (Home Office, London, 1996) para. 195.

[22] *Report of the Inquiry into the Export of Defence Equipment and Dual-Use Goods to Iraq and Related Prosecutions* (1995–96 HC 115) ('*Scott Report*').

[23] Tomkins, A., *The Constitution after Scott* (Clarendon Press, Oxford, 1998) p. 167. Compare Leigh, I., 'Matrix Churchill, supergun and the Scott inquiry' [1993] *Public Law* 630; Zuckerman, A.A.S., 'Public interest immunity – a matter of prime judicial responsibility' (1994) 57 *Modern Law Review* 703; Leigh, I., 'Reforming public interest immunity' [1995] 2 *Web Journal of Current Legal Issues* 89; Leigh, I. and Lustgarten, L., 'Five volumes in search of accountability: the Scott Report' (1996) 59 *Modern Law Review* 695; Oliver, D., 'The Scott Report' [1996] *Public Law* 357; Thompson, B. and Ridley, F.F., (eds.), *Under the Scott-light: British Government seen through the Scott Report* (Oxford University Press, 1997).

[24] There were other relevant cases (see *Scott Report*, Vol.III, Sections H, J). One concerned Ordnance Technologies Ltd (Ordtec), which exported components to Iraq without any licence at all. A PII certificate was signed but not deliberated upon, as the defendants pleaded guilty in February 1992. An appeal against conviction was allowed on the basis of non-disclosure of policy and guideline documents governing the grant of export licences and knowledge of the use of Jordan as a conduit for arms to Iraq: *R v Blackledge* [1996] 1 Cr App R 326. The use of the PII certificates in the trial but not in the appeal was criticised by the *Scott Report*, Vol. III, Section J para. 6.66, 6.93. An earlier appeal, attacking the validity of the export control regulations, had failed: *R v Phillips*; *R v Grecian*; *R v Blackledge*; *R v Mason*, The Times, 29 May 1995. The second case involved BSA Tools Ltd. The trial was abandoned after the Matrix Churchill case. In the third case, *R v Schlesinger*; *R v Dunk*; *R v Atlantic Commercial Ltd* [1995] *Criminal Law Review* 137, guilty pleas had been entered to illegal arms shipments to Iraq in 1982 and 1983. The convictions were quashed when it was later revealed that, in order to save all Governments from embarrassment, the Foreign and Commonwealth Office had secretly dissuaded the Iraqi and the Jordanian Embassies from allowing their personnel to appear as witnesses who would otherwise have testified that the end users were to be Jordan and Sudan. A final case was *R v Redfern and another* (1992) 13 Cr App R(S) 709 (export of aircraft tyres).

exportation of machine-tool equipment contrary to controls on trade with Iraq in relation to defence equipment and dual-use goods.[25] The company directors had obtained a Department of Trade and Industry licence but were alleged to have misled civil servants as to the true purpose of the goods. In response, their defence was that the Secret Intelligence Service was fully informed throughout as to the transactions (one of the directors, Paul Henderson, had expressly volunteered the information). Furthermore, they claimed that the relevant minister, Alan Clark, had also been generally aware of the potential breach of the embargo but, for the sake of securing trade in the face of international competition, was apparently equally prepared to ride roughshod over United Nations sanctions and actually encouraged the directors to submit a misleading application for a licence. To prove these points, the defence sought discovery of various documents, realising that there must be 'a paper mountain'[26] within Whitehall to support their claims and forcing the prosecution team to institute searches for the documentation which would not otherwise have been volunteered even to the prosecution. In response, four Government ministers signed claims to PII;[27] these were largely class claims which were said to be necessary to protect intelligence information and informers, as well as internal documents between ministers and officials relating to the formation of policy. The Secretary of State for Trade and Industry, Michael Heseltine, objected to giving his authorisation in this blanket fashion, but the ministers were advised by the Attorney-General that they were obliged to sign the certificates if satisfied the information fell within the specified class.[28] Heseltine wrote to the Attorney-General, voicing his concerns about potential injustice, but this letter was not passed to prosecuting counsel.[29] In the event, discovery was ordered by the trial judge in regard to two of the three categories of sensitive documents (internal notes and security/intelligence information, but not informants). Fortified by this information, the resultant cross-examination of Alan Clark effectively secured a concession on the second defence, at which point (on 9 November 1992), the 'demolished'[30] prosecution invited the court to acquit.

Reviewing these events, the *Scott Report* reached several important conclusions – whether these were findings or recommendations depends on whether Sir Richard Scott adopted the correct or a wishful interpretation of the law as it stood around 1995. The fundamental issue is whether PII has any role whatever in criminal prosecutions. The only recent authority suggesting a general relevance for PII in criminal cases was *R* v *Governor of Brixton Prison, ex parte Osman*.[31] However, the case arose from a habeas corpus application, and, though this jurisdiction was said to be on all fours with criminal proceedings for PII purposes, the *Scott Report* viewed it as *obiter* and even mistaken.[32] In reply, it must be conceded that the

---

[25] See *Scott Report*, Vol.III, Section G; Robertson, G., *The Justice Game* (Chatto & Windus, London, 1998) ch. 15.

[26] Robertson, G., *The Justice Game* (Chatto & Windus, London, 1998) p. 317.

[27] They were drafted by an Assistant Treasury Solicitor who sought to take a view which was generous to Government interests: *Scott Report*, Vol.III, Section G para. 13.95.

[28] Compare *Savage* v *Chief Constable of Hampshire* [1997] 1 WLR 1061: PII may be waived at the instigation of the informant, at least in a civil case brought by that person.

[29] *Scott Report*, Vol. III, Section G paras. 13.71, 13.125.

[30] Robertson, G., *The Justice Game* (Chatto & Windus, London, 1998) p. 337.

[31] [1992] 1 All ER 108. See also *R* v *Latimer and others* [1992] 1 NIJB 89 at p. 100.

[32] *Scott Report*, Vol. III, Section G para. 18.84, 18.86; Scott, Sir R., 'The acceptable and unacceptable uses of public interest immunity' [1996] *Public Law* 427; Scott, Sir R., 'The use of public interest immunity claims in criminal cases' [1996] 2 *Web Journal of Current Legal Issues*.

narrow but well-established application of PII to informers and other defined categories listed above suggests that there is no blanket exemption for criminal proceedings[33] and that the withholding of 'sensitive' materials has been accepted in principle in several other recent cases.[34] Consequently, the more realistic approach would be to explore what extra restrictions over and above those in civil cases on PII might be desirable in view of the more important rights at stake for the criminal defendant.[35]

Along these lines, it seems to be already accepted by the courts that any claims to PII should automatically be scrutinised by the courts, rather than expecting the defendant to make out a case for inspection.[36] Another procedural issue to be considered was whether ministers are under an obligation to sign a PII certificate – on the Government's view, it is for the courts to discern the impact of the PII claim but it is the duty of the minister to put the matter before the court.[37] This view principally relied upon some *dicta* by Lord Justice Bingham in *Makanjoula v Commissioner for the Metropolitan Police*,[38] to the effect that PII is imposed on the parties rather than being a tactic at their disposal. However, the meaning of this statement is unclear, and the *Scott Report* took the view that there was no obligation to assert PII if the minister believed either that disclosure would not be damaging to Government interests or that non-disclosure would be damaging to the defence.[39] If a view is formed along these lines, then it should be for counsel for the department (and not the prosecution) to advocate it to the trial court so as to avoid any conflicts of interest between Governmental wishes and the administration of justice.[40] In *R v Horseferry Road Magistrates' Court, ex parte Bennett (No. 2)*,[41] there was even voluntary disclosure by the Crown Prosecution Service without prior court order, though Simon Brown LJ felt that this procedure should be subject to Treasury Solicitor approval.[42]

As for substantive limits, at the very least, Scott concluded, class claims should have no future role, especially class claims based on the protection of candour between ministers and officials:[43]

---

[33] The point seems to be accepted in the *Scott Report*, Vol. III, Section K para. 6.16. See further *R v Clowes* [1992] 3 All ER 440; *R v Ward* (1992) 96 Cr App R 1; *R v Davis, Rowe and Johnson* [1993] 1 WLR 613; *R v Keane* [1994] 1 WLR 746; *R v Brown (Winston)* [1995] 1 Cr App R 191.

[34] See Walker, C. and Starmer, K., (eds.) *Justice in Error* (Blackstone Press, London, 1993) ch. 6; ch. 7.

[35] This approach is taken in the later paper; Scott, Sir R., 'The use of public interest immunity claims in criminal cases' [1996] 2 *Web Journal of Current Legal Issues*. See also Gull, A., 'Public interest immunity and the right to a fair trial' (1997) 2 *Journal of Civil Liberties* 5 at p. 25.

[36] *R v K* (1993) 97 Cr App R 342.

[37] *Scott Report*, Vol. III, Section G para. 13.100. See also Mitchell, A., 'Disclosure – whose responsibility?' (1993) 137 *Solicitors' Journal* 854.

[38] [1992] 3 All ER 617 at p. 623. See Davenport, B.J., 'Waiver and public interest immunity' (1989) 105 *Law Quarterly Review* 547.

[39] *Scott Report*, Vol. III, Section G paras. 18.52, 18.54, Section K paras. 6.4, 6.18. See Allan, T.R.S., 'Public interest immunity and ministers' responsibilities' [1993] *Criminal Law Review* 660; Ganz, G., 'Matrix Churchill and public interest immunity' (1993) 56 *Modern Law Review* 564.

[40] *Scott Report*, Vol.III, Section K para. 6.19.

[41] [1994] 1 All ER 289. See Lord Justice Simon Brown, 'Public interest immunity' [1994] *Public Law* 579.

[42] Some argue that the referral to the Treasury Solicitor is now redundant because of the decisions in *ex parte Wiley* (Niblett, J., *Disclosure in Criminal Proceedings* (Blackstone Press, London, 1997) p. 123), but the same case suggests that in the case of a police inclination to disclose, there should be consultations with other chief constables, the police authority, the Attorney-General and possibly the Home Secretary: *R v Chief Constable of the West Midlands Police ex parte Wiley* [1995] 1 AC 274 at p. 297 per Lord Woolf. For an example, see *R v Adams* [1997] *Criminal Law Review* 292.

. . . I find it particularly bizarre and unacceptable that in respect of documents that are *prima facie* disclosable and whose contents do not justify any PII contents claim, the Government can properly put forward a PII class objection to their disclosure to a defendant seeking to establish his innocence in a criminal trial.

Class claims can be avoided by the effective use of content claims, a point seemingly accepted by the security services,[44] As for contents claims, these might validly be made on the basis of 'substantial harm',[45] but the *Scott Report* was next concerned to distinguish criminal cases from any balancing approach between competing interests which might occur in civil cases.[46] There was no real trade-off in criminal cases, since the public interest is always:[47]

. . . in favour of disclosure if there is any real possibility that the withholding of the document may cause or contribute to a miscarriage of justice . . . there is no real balance to be struck. The only issue for decision is whether the document might be of assistance to the defence.

In any event, the *Scott Report* demanded that PII certificates be more informative and should schedule the documents to be protected, a safeguard both for the courts and for the minister being asked to sign.[48]

The Reform of PII

The Criminal Procedure and Investigations Act 1996 (CPIA 1996)

It remains possible under the CPIA 1996[49] to withhold material where disclosure would be contrary to the public interest, but section 21(2) expresses that the Act is to have no impact on common law rules relating to the substantive definition of PII.[50] However, the relationship between common law and statute is not quite so straightforward. A PII-based objection to disclosure need only arise if the material is, under the rules of discovery, disclosable in the first place. It is clear from Chapter 7 that that the ambit of the primary duty of disclosure by the prosecution has been significantly reduced by the CPIA 1996.[51] Equally, the rules which deal with disclosure by the defence will result in the further delimitation of the duty of

---

[43] *Scott Report*, Vol. III, Section K paras. 6.6, 6.16, 6.25.

[44] See Scott, Sir R., 'The use of public interest immunity claims in criminal cases' [1996] 2 *Web Journal of Current Legal Issues*.

[45] *Scott Report*, Vol. III, Section K para. 6.18.

[46] See *Conway v Rimmer* [1968] AC 910.

[47] *Scott Report*, Vol. III, Section K para. 6.12. But compare the dicta cited at para. 6.13.

[48] *Scott Report*, Vol. III, Section K paras. 5.1, 6.18, 6.23.

[49] Sections 3(6), 7(5), 8(5), 9(8).

[50] Matters of procedure have been to some extent codified from *R v Davis, Johnson and Rowe* [1993] 1 WLR 613. See CPIA, 1996 ss. 14, 15, 23, 24; the Crown Court (Criminal Procedure and Investigations Act 1996) (Disclosure) Rules 1997 (SI No. 698) and the Magistrates' Court (Criminal Procedure and Investigations Act 1996) (Disclosure) Rules 1997 (SI No. 703) for the procedure to be followed where the prosecution make an application for an order for non-disclosure. See also Niblett, J., *Disclosure in Criminal Proceedings* (Blackstone Press, London, 1997) ch. 10.

[51] The rule of 'materiality' has been replaced by one of 'undermining'. For the former rule, see *Scott Report*, Vol. III, Section K paras. 6.7.

disclosure as the nature of what is or is not the defence argument emerges.[52] It therefore follows that fewer claims to PII are likely to arise in the future.[53] This result was intended by the Home Office in its paper on *Disclosure*, which expressed concern about the increasing disclosure of material which is 'marginal at best' having the effect of placing informants' lives in danger or causing the abandonment of prosecutions.[54] The examples given in the paper do indeed illustrate the hard choices to be made between fairness to the accused and police imperatives, but whether a case is made out for curtailment of the interests of the accused and whether the assessment of marginality is accurate is rather less convincing.

In this way, whilst the rules as to PII have been reformed generally in favour of the defence, as shall next be described, this generosity is largely diluted by the reduction of the antecedent duty to disclose. One step forward, two steps back.

Ministerial and Judicial Clarifications

Many of the Scott Report's assertions about the existing or future disposition of the law on PII were initially dismissed vehemently by the Government.[55] However, further reflection, in part motivated by the belief that there had been a major change in the law because of *ex parte Wiley*[56] and perhaps also by political deals to retain the support of dissident Conservative backbenchers, produced a remarkable change of heart. In December 1996, it was announced that a new approach would be taken to Governmental claims to PII, and the details were set out in a paper, *Public Interest Immunity*, issued by the Treasury Solicitor.[57] In detail, the paper accepts and seeks to implement many of the conclusions of the *Scott Report*. Accordingly, it is accepted that ministers must exercise a personal discretion and therefore consider the competing interests involved.[58] The demand that ministers take responsibility for signing PII certificates chimes with a number of post-*Scott Report* cases which equally suggest that the minister has at least a public law duty to balance public interests before signing a certificate.[59] The result has been that ministers are being given more information about the reasons for the claim and time to consider them and are divulging more information in their certificates,[60]

[52] CPIA, s. 8(2). This limitation was supported by the *Scott Report*, Vol.III, Section K para. 6.18.

[53] See Treasury Solicitor, *Public Interest Immunity* (London, 1996) para. 2.10. Between 1992 and late 1995, there were 28 PII certificates signed by Home Office ministers: HC Debs. vol. 267 col. 668wa, 28 November 1995.

[54] Home Office, *Disclosure* (Cm 2864, HMSO, London, 1994) para. 14.

[55] Tomkins, A., *The Constitution after Scott* (Clarendon Press, Oxford, 1998) pp. 187–94; Birkinshaw, P., 'Government at the end of its tether' (1996) 23 *Journal of Law and Society* 406 at p. 423.

[56] The belief may be largely mistaken; compare: Treasury Solicitor, *Public Interest Immunity* (London, 1996) para. 2.2 and Ganz, G., 'Matrix Churchill and public interest immunity: a postscript' (1995) 58 *Modern Law Review* 417, 'Volte-face on public interest immunity' (1997) 60 *Modern Law Review* 552 at p. 553. See also Webb, R.C., 'Public interest immunity: the demise of the duty to assert' [1995] *Criminal Law Review* 556.

[57] See HC Debs. vol. 287 col. 949, 18 December 1996; HL Debs vol. 596 col. 1507, 18 December 1996; Ganz, G., 'Volte-face on public interest immunity' (1997) 60 *Modern Law Review* 552; Supperstone, M. and Coppel, J., 'A new approach to public interest immunity' [1997] *Public Law* 211; Walker, P. and Costigan, T., 'Public interest immunity: a new approach' (1997) 2(1) *Judicial Review* 35; Leigh, I., 'Public interest immunity' (1997) 50 *Parliamentary Affairs* 55; Forsyth, C., 'Public interest immunity: recent and future developments' (1997) 56 *Cambridge Law Journal* 51.

[58] Treasury Solicitor, *Public Interest Immunity* (London, 1996) para. 2.3.

[59] See *R v Chief Constable of West Midlands ex parte Wiley* [1995] 1 AC 274; *Bennett v Commissioner of Police for the Metropolis* [1995] 2 All ER 1.

[60] Treasury Solicitor, *Public Interest Immunity* (London, 1996) paras. 4.5, 6.5.

points reflected in the *Ordtec* appeal.[61] The assertion of any class claim to PII is to end, and so there is to be no blanket protection for pre-determined classes of material.[62] Instead, a minister must be satisfied that real harm (meaning serious or substantial harm)[63] to the public interest would arise from the disclosure of the content of a specific document. The relevant harms are those recognised as overriding duties of disclosure in the Code of Practice on Access to Government Information[64] such as to individual privacy, regulatory processes, international relations, or economic interests.[65] At the same time, the courts have grown readier to examine claims on their merits.[66]

In summary, the 1996 paper represents 'a remarkable improvement',[67] but it is far from perfect. Some of its deficiencies concern the scope of its application. The most glaring defect is that it applies only to claims to PII by Government departments and only within England and Wales. As for Scotland, the position has long been distinct in that PII claims are confined to Government departments, though the courts have hither to not been allowed to inspect materials which are the subject of a claim to privilege.[68] However, Northern Ireland developments have more closely followed English models,[69] save that the Standing Advisory Commission on Human Rights has pointed out the special problem in 'Diplock' criminal cases that the judge who reads the documents is also the trier of fact, though its suggestion that the Director of Public Prosecutions could act as the preliminary scrutiniser instead of the trial judge may overestimate the detachment of that official from prosecution interests.[70] One might add that a similar problem exists in English summary cases.[71] Justices who heard a PII application will also have conduct of the trial, so they can keep under review any unfairness from the suppression.[72] But if they have suppressed the evidence and continue to do so, then they face a dilemma. Can they continue to sit on the substantive hearing without creating an appearance of unfairness through their possession of such secret evidence?[73] Alternatively, can they disqualify themselves from trial when that

---

[61] *R v Blackledge* [1996] 1 Cr App R 326. *The Independent* published some of the suppressed materials (parts of which had been disclosed by the court) but was cleared of contempt: *Attorney-General v Newspaper Publishing Plc* [1997] 1 WLR 926.

[62] Treasury Solicitor, *Public Interest Immunity* (London, 1996) paras. 2.3, 3.3, 4.1, 5.6.

[63] HC Debs. vol. 287 col. 951, 18 December 1996. This seems to correspond with the test in *R v Chief Constable of West Midlands, ex parte Wiley* [1995] 1 AC 274 at p. 281, but see further Supperstone, M. and Coppel, J., 'A new approach to public interest immunity' [1997] *Public Law* 211 at p. 212.

[64] (http://www.open.gov uk/m-of-g/code.htm, 1994). See Open Government (Cm 2290, HMSO, London, 1993).

[65] Treasury Solicitor, *Public Interest Immunity* (London, 1996) paras. 4.2, 4.3, 5.1.

[66] *R v Brown (Winston)* [1995] 1 Cr App R 191 at p. 200.

[67] Tomkins, A., *The Constitution after Scott* (Clarendon Press, Oxford, 1998) p. 199.

[68] See *Admiralty v Aberdeen Steam Trawling Co.* 1909 SC 335; *Rogers v Orr* 1939 SC 492; *Glasgow Corporation v Central Land Board* 1956 SLT 41; *Parks v Tayside RC* 1989 SLT 345; McShane, F.M., 'Crown privilege in Scotland: the demerits of disharmony' 1992 *Juridical Review* 256, 1993 *Juridical Review* 41. However, the legal position may now be more fluid owing to later judicial reinterpretations of the general rules of disclosure (see further Chapter 16).

[69] Northern Ireland Office, *Disclosure in Criminal Cases* (Belfast, 1995).

[70] *19th Report* (1993–94 HC 495) ch. 3 para. 14, 15. According to *R v Harper and another* [1994] NI 199, if the view is taken by the Crown that the trial judge should not see the document because it is prejudicial to the defendant, then it will be necessary for another judge to rule on the issue of materiality or of public interest immunity.

[71] *R v Bromley Magistrates' Court, ex parte Smith and Wilkins* [1995] 2 Cr App R 285.

[72] There is now no duty to keep the matter under review though there may be an application to reconsider: CPIA, s. 14. Compare CPIA, s. 15.

[73] Davies, F.G., 'Procedural unfairness arising from public interest immunity applications' (1997) 161 *Justice of the Peace* 957, 971.

means that another bench, unaware of the nature of the PII material and its possibly emergent relevance, will sit? Later guidance suggests they should continue to sit.[74] As for the limit in the 1996 paper to Government departments, the implication is that there is no application to policing organisations (or to other agencies[75]) despite the concerns expressed earlier that their reliance on PII may well increase in coming years and despite their continued use of class claims[76] or at least joint contents/class claims[77] post-*ex parte Wiley*.

Even in regard to the Government departments to which it applies, the impact of the statement is neither wholly clear or satisfactory. A policy paper from HM Treasury Solicitors' Office cannot actually alter the law, so, it is hard to avoid the conclusion that the sovereign instrument of legislation should be used for the sake of completeness and clarity.[78] There is also still the issue of whether there can be any 'balancing' in criminal cases, which even the *Scott Report* views as suffering from 'some degree of ambiguity'.[79] Certainly, the Home Office in its 1994 paper felt that 'the balance of interests test' should continue to apply.[80] Even the 1996 paper asserts that the same principles apply to civil and criminal cases, though it recognises that the balance is likely to favour the defendant in criminal cases.[81] Next, the 1996 statement does not wholly represent the demise of class claims; it certainly cannot abolish them, and ministers retain the right to engage in 'class reasoning' in connection with indirect or long-term harm arising from the disclosure specified documents.[82]

The *Scott Report* was opposed to legislation,[83] but one wonders whether the Government or the judges have since done enough to ward off parliamentary intervention. Furthermore, the impetus of European Convention cases implemented through the Human Rights Act, may also eventually demand reform.[84] Though PII claims were accepted (at least under Article 2 of the European Convention) as a fair limitation in the context of a coroner's hearing in *McCann v United Kingdom*

---

[74] See *R v Crown Prosecution Service, ex parte Warby* (1993) 157 *Justice of the Peace* 190; *R v Bromley Magistrates' Court, ex parte Smith and Wilkins* [1995] 2 Cr App R 285; *R v South Worcestershire Justices, ex parte Lilley* [1995] 4 All ER 186; *R v Stipendiary Magistrate for Norfolk ex parte Taylor* [1998] *Criminal Law Review* 276. See Carroll, A.J., 'Disclosure and public interest immunity in magistrates' courts' (1996) 160 *Justice of the Peace* 94.

[75] These might include, for example, the Serious Fraud Office and other financial regulators. See *Lonrho Plc v Fayed (No. 4)* [1994] 1 All ER 870; *Kaufmann v Credit Lyonnais Bank* (1995) 7 Admin LR 669.

[76] For example, in *Taylor v Anderton* [1995] 1 WLR 447, reports and working papers prepared by investigating officers in response to complaints against the police were recognised as forming a new class-based PII. See also *Kelly v Commissioner of the Police of the Metropolis, The Times*, 20 August 1997.

[77] Niblett, J., *Disclosure in Criminal Proceedings* (Blackstone Press, London, 1997) p. 138.

[78] This was the view of Lord Irvine in 1996: HL Debs vol. 596 col. 1510, 18 December 1996.

[79] *Scott Report*, Vol. III, Section K para. 6.19.

[80] Home Office, *Disclosure* (Cm 2864, HMSO, London, 1994) para. 69.

[81] Treasury Solicitor, *Public Interest Immunity* (London, 1996) paras. 1.9, 2.6. A balancing exercise is retained in Richardson, P.J., (ed.), *Archbold: Criminal Pleading, Evidence and Practice* (Sweet & Maxwell, London, 1998) para. 12–44c, but '[i]f admission of the evidence is necessary to prevent a miscarriage of justice, balance does not arise'. There must also be disclosure if the material is relevant to the issue between the prosecution and the defence, even though on its face it is directly contrary to the defence case: *R v Yirtici* (LEXIS, 1996).

[82] See HC Debs. vol. 287 col. 951, 18 December 1996. See also Treasury Solicitor, *Public Interest Immunity* (London, 1996) paras. 5.2, 5.11.

[83] *Scott Report*, Vol. III, Section K para. 6.18. The 1996 paper is equally opposed to legislation: Treasury Solicitor, *Public Interest Immunity* (London, 1996) para. 1.8.

[84] See Wadham, J., 'Prosecution disclosure, crime and human rights' (1997) 147 *New Law Journal* 697.

(concerning the 'Gibraltar Three', shot dead by the SAS),[85] the Court in *Edwards v United Kingdom*[86] has already stated that 'it is a requirement of fairness under Article 6(1), indeed one which is recognised under English law, that the prosecution authorities disclose to the defence all material evidence for or against the accused'. In the event, the applicant had not sought to challenge in the Court of Appeal the non-disclosure of the report of the police investigation on behalf of the Police Complaints Authority. But pending cases will examine the operation of PII in criminal proceedings and may prove more demanding. The pending cases include principally[87] *Jasper* v *UK*,[88] *Rowe and Davis* v *UK*,[89] and *Fitt* v *UK*,[90] which concern complaints that information withheld from the defence on PII grounds resulted in violation of defendants' right to a fair trial under Article 6. All were argued along similar lines, and all were declared admissible by the Commission in September 1997.

In *Rowe and Davis* v *UK*, the non-disclosure related to arrangements between the police and informants, reward payments to the latter, as well as a report following an investigation by the Police Complaints Authority. The Government contended that fairness to the accused remained 'paramount', but there was in its view no breach of Article 6 from either the procedures laid down by the Court of Appeal (which included the possibility of *ex parte* hearings, either with or without notice) or from the non-disclosure of material relevant to the case but which appeared to assist the prosecution rather than the defence or of material 'passing the low threshold of relevance . . . [but] of relatively minor importance to the accused.'.[91]

The application of Barry Fitt arose out of a conviction for the attempted armed robbery of a Royal Mail van. The police had been informed of the plans and had kept the van under observation. The sources of the police information (which the applicant believed to include an agent provocateur) were suppressed following an *ex parte* application (with notice), as were parts of the statement of a co-conspirator (who pleaded guilty). The Government's submission (in February 1997) was in very similar terms to that in *Rowe and Davis*.[92]

In the case of *Jasper* v *UK*, Eric Jasper was convicted in 1994 of the importation of three tonnes of cannabis from Belgium concealed in frozen meat in his lorry. He claimed ignorance of the presence of the drugs, but the prosecution case pointed to his possession of a false passport and a large sum of cash, as well as documents which indicated that he had received telephone instructions as to delivery. Following an *ex parte* application by the prosecution (notified to the defence), the judge ordered that materials be withheld on PII grounds. The defence then

---

[85] *McCann and Others* v *United Kingdom*, Appl. no. 18984/91, Ser. A no. 324, (1996) 21 EHRR 97. Protection was also afforded to vulnerable witnesses in *Stanford* v *UK.*, Appl. no. 16757/90, Ser. A. vol. 282-A (1994); *Doorson* v *Netherlands*, Appl. no. 20524/92, 1996–II, [1996] 22 EHRR 330.

[86] Appl. no 13071/87, Ser. A no. 247-B, (1993) EHRR 417 para. 36. See Field, S. and Young, J., 'Disclosure, appeals and procedural traditions' [1994] *Criminal Law Review* 264. Compare *Preston and Preston* v *UK*, Appl. no. 24193/94, [1997] EHRLR 695.

[87] See also *Cannon* v *United Kingdom*, Appl. no. 29335/95, (1997) 3 EHRLR 280.

[88] Appl. no. 27052/95.

[89] Appl. no. 28901/95. This case arises from the decision in *R* v *Davis, Rowe and Johnson* [1993] 1 WLR 613. See Chapter 7.

[90] Appl. no. 29777/96.

[91] Appl. no. 28901/95 at pp. 13, 14.

[92] Appl. no. 29777/96 at pp. 13, 14.

requested the prosecution to indicate whether, apart from the materials subject to the PII application, there was other relevant evidence, especially relating to informants, telephone intercepts or surreptitious observations. The prosecution confirmed that no materials related to informants or surreptitious observations but declined to answer further. The judge accepted that no answer need be given, nor PII claimed, in relation to telephone intercepts because of the impact of the Interception of Communications Act 1985 which seeks to avoid any revelation that an intercept has or has not been made. The Court of Appeal accepted that not all unused materials had been disclosed and that telephone intercepts could be of importance to the defence in confirming the source and content of the instructions received as to delivery. However, having reviewed the transcript of the *ex parte* hearing, the Court of Appeal accepted the verdict of non-disclosure of the trial judge, so the appeal was dismissed. In the interpretation of the Government (which was submitted in November 1996), it was sufficient either that the material was not relevant or, although relevant, the balance favoured the public interest in non-disclosure.[93] The latter is an especially disturbing claim which, if it remains a fair representation of the law despite all the efforts of the *Scott Report* and the froth of the 1996 statement, must surely undermine the principle of equality of arms in the preparation of one's own case and the testing of that of one's adversary.

A powerful case can be made that PII claims are both unnecessary and undesirable in the criminal justice system. How can Government ministers make judgments about what material is of relevance to the defence, and why should their opinions relating to damage to the public interest have the formal authority of a certificate? Where the prosecution seek to withhold material evidence because of some special damage its revelation may do, they should be put to proof in the ordinary way, by calling witnesses and leaving them open to cross-examination. Although the defence will necessarily be handicapped by not having read the document at issue, the biased assumptions and opinions so often expressed by ministers in PII certificates, which come more from the precedents on the Treasury Solicitors' word processor than from any careful and informed ministerial judgment, can at least be challenged directly and openly.

---

[93] Appl. no. 27052/95 at p. 16.

9

Trial Procedures

John Jackson

Adversarial Justice

The adversarial trial is often pinpointed as the focal point of the Anglo-American criminal process. Unlike inquisitorial systems which represent a continuous process of proof, with perhaps a number of phases of investigation supervised and conducted by judicial figures in serious cases,[1] the adversarial system focuses on one particular event – the contested trial. The problem with such a system is that it means that there is very little direct supervision of police or pre-trial conduct. But the advantage is often claimed to be that whatever happens before the trial, the defendant is at liberty to put the prosecution to proof at the trial and the prosecution must then adduce all its evidence in one single concentrated trial and have it tested by trained advocates acting for the defence. Adversarial trial procedures are thus commonly held out as the best protection to the defendant against unsafe convictions. As George Carman, one of the most formidable advocates in the UK, has put it,[2] 'the cut and thrust of advocacy, the testing of evidence by skilled and competent advocates with a judge acting as umpire, that is the best system we have devised for getting at the truth'.

It is increasingly being questioned, however, whether adversarial procedures do offer the best protection to defendants or indeed to other persons, such as victims of crime, who have an interest in the outcome of criminal proceedings. The first point to make is that these procedures are very rarely invoked in practice. The common law theory of evidence whereby defendants are found guilty by means of a formal adversarial process in which evidence against the defendant is presented by the prosecution and tested by the defence before an impartial adjudicator is a mere caricature of the truth because in practice the vast majority of defendants plead guilty.[3] In the adversarial system of justice the parties are relatively free to negotiate the outcome of cases between themselves with little scrutiny exercised

---

[1] For a description of the French system which is commonly characterised as an inquisitorial system, see Chapter 17.

[2] See the BBC 2 documentary, *The Verdict*, 13 November 1996.

[3] In England and Wales the plea rate is well over 90 per cent in magistrates' courts and around 65 per cent in Crown Courts: see Ashworth, A., *The Criminal Process: An Evaluative Study* (2nd ed., Oxford University Press, Oxford, 1998) pp. 268, 269.

by the courts. When a defendant pleads guilty to an offence, the judicial function is confined to determining whether the defendant's plea is voluntary or not. If satisfied that the plea is voluntary, the court accepts the defendant's guilt and the sole remaining question will be the sentence. If we could be satisfied that guilty pleas genuinely reflected the defendant's guilt, we might be satisfied with this process but we shall see that considerable effort has gone into creating incentives for defendants to plead guilty which can result in injustice being done.

Apart from incentives to plead guilty, there is little point in defendants contesting the case against them if there is no real opportunity of mounting a successful challenge to the prosecution evidence. If adversarial procedures are to protect the accused effectively, the prosecution must not only bear a heavy burden of proof but the defence must also be able to operate in an approximate position of 'equality of arms' so that they have an equal opportunity to present evidence and contradict evidence produced by the prosecution.[4] Yet, as the Court of Appeal recognised in the *Birmingham Six* and *Judith Ward* appeals, a disadvantage of the adversarial nature of criminal procedings is that the parties are not evenly matched in resources.[5] Nowhere is this clearer than in summary trials, where legal aid may be restricted in certain kinds of cases, with historically wide inconsistencies between courts,[6] and where there is still no right to disclosure when defendants face purely summary charges.[7] Even in the Crown Court where defendants receive legal aid and are in a better position to test the prosecution case, there are doubts about whether the defence can ever adequately match the resources of the State. The role of lawyers in the criminal process and the extent to which the defence obtain disclosure of evidence have already been considered.[8] Apart from trying to bolster up the resources of the defence, another attempt to protect the defence against the superior resources of the State has been to impose strict evidentiary controls on various kinds of prosecution evidence but as we shall see there has been a tendency to loosen rather than tighten these evidentiary constraints in recent years.

The spate of miscarriages of justice against innocent defendants in the late 1980s raised questions about whether adversarial trial procedures could protect defendants against unreliable prosecution evidence. Apart from this, however, there has also been concern about the way in which these procedures treat witnesses, and particularly victims who have an interest in the outcome of the proceedings. There is now increasing frustration on the part of victims that justice is denied to them at court because of the way their cases are dealt with.[9] Of course, there is an

---

[4] The European Commission and Court of Human Rights have recognised the principle of equality of arms as endemic in the notion of a fair trial under Art. 6 of the Convention: see Harris, D.J., O'Boyle, M. and Warbrick, C., *Law of the European Convention on Human Rights* (Butterworths, London, 1995) pp. 207-210.

[5] *R v McIlkenny and others* [1992] 2 All ER 417; *R v Ward* (1992) 96 Cr App R 1.

[6] See Young, J., Moloney, T. and Sanders, A., *In the Interests of Justice?* (Legal Aid Board, London, 1992); Young, R. and Wall, D., *Access to Criminal Justice* (Blackstone, London, 1996) ch. 6. In July 1993 the National Audit Office criticised the way criminal legal aid was granted and the Lord Chancellor issued new guidance in May 1994 in order to promote greater consistency.

[7] The accused has now a right to disclosure of material undermining the prosecution case in summary as well as indictable cases under s. 3(1) of the Criminal Procedure and Investigations Act 1996, but oddly enough no right to disclosure of the evidence on which the prosecution case is based, see Leng, R. and Taylor, R., *Guide to the Criminal Procedure and Investigations Act 1996* (Blackstone, London, 1996) pp. 12, 13.

[8] Chapters 4, 7.

[9] See Pollard, P., 'Public safety, accountability and the courts' [1996] *Criminal Law Review* 152.

inevitable clash between the interests of victims and defendants in any criminal procedure. The price we pay for ensuring that innocent people are not convicted is that guilty people may sometimes go free. But adversarial procedures put victims in a particularly difficult position because they are structured as a contest between two parties only, the prosecution representing the public interest (not just the interests of the victim) and the defence. It is not surprising then that this contest may overshadow the interests of the victim. The public interest may lie more in getting an offender convicted whatever the actual charge, while the victim's interest may lie as much in ensuring that the charge reflects the true gravity of the harm inflicted as in the actual conviction of the offender.[10] If, as invariably happens, the case never goes to trial, the victim's story may never be heard or presented properly. If the case goes to trial, witnesses and victims are put into the front line of the adversarial battle with little protection offered from the court.[11] It is common to hear rape victims, for example, complaining after the trial that they felt they were on trial as much as the defendant.[12]

It was against this background of concern about adversarial trial procedures that the Royal Commission on Criminal Justice was asked to make recommendations for reform and in particular to consider whether the courts should have a greater investigative role both before and during the trial.[13] Before we consider this possibility, it is proposed to examine in more detail the respects in which trial procedures may contribute to injustice to the defendant and the victim. We shall consider in turn the different modes of trial that are available, the phenomenon of plea bargaining, the rules of evidence which operate at trial and the role of the judge.

Mode of Trial

Whatever form trial procedures take, it is particularly important that there is confidence in the tribunal of fact which determines the case at the end of the day. There are only two modes of trial available to defendants in England and Wales. The vast majority of defendants are tried summarily which means trial by a bench of lay magistrates or by a 'stipendiary' professional magistrate. Alternatively, defendants who are committed to the Crown Court and who plead not guilty are tried by jury. Over the years, Parliament has gradually eroded the right of defendants to elect for trial by jury. In 1976 the James Committee recommended that a number of offences be transferred to the sole jurisdiction of magistrates,[14] and section 15 of the Criminal Law Act 1977 responded by making certain offences which were triable either way (that is, either in the magistrates' court or in the Crown Court), such as various public order offences and drink driving offences, purely summary. Only spirited opposition in the House of Lords at the time prevented the classification of thefts under £20 becoming summary offences

---

[10] See Sanders, A. and Young, R., *Criminal Justice* (Butterworths, London, 1994) p. 24.

[11] See Rock, P., *The Social World of an English Crown Court: Witnesses and Professionals in the Crown Court Centre at Wood Green* (Clarendon, Oxford, 1993) ch. 2.

[12] See Lees, S., *Carnal Knowledge: Rape on Trial* (Hamish Hamilton, London, 1996) p. 32.

[13] See Royal Commission on Criminal Justice, *Report*, (Cm 2263, HMSO, London, 1993) p. iii ('*Runciman Report*').

[14] *Interdepartmental Committee on the Distribution of Criminal Business between the Crown Court and the Magistrates' Court* (Cmnd 6323, HMSO, London, 1975).

only. Despite these changes, pressures for further restrictions continued largely on grounds of cost and delay, so the Criminal Justice Act 1988, sections 37 and 39 made the offences of taking a motor vehicle, driving while disqualified and common assault purely summary.[15] This downgrading of offences continued in 1995 when all criminal damage offences less than £5000 became summary only.[16]

Apart from making more offences purely summary, attempts have been made to ensure that magistrates hear most of the offences which are triable either way. Section 49 of the Criminal Procedure and Investigations Act 1996, for example, requires magistrates to hear the defendant's intention as to plea before deciding the venue, thus ensuring that defendants who plan to plead guilty are kept within the jurisdiction of the magistrates. More radically, suggestions have been made to abolish the defendant's right to elect for jury trial in triable either way offences. The Royal Commission on Criminal Justice was concerned that too many defendants who elected for trial by jury ended up pleading guilty. In order to 'secure a more rational division of either way cases', the Commission proposed that where prosecution and defence could not agree on the mode of trial it should be left to magistrates to decide.[17] The proposal provoked a storm of protest and was shelved by the Government, but it was floated again in the dying days of the last Conservative Government as a means of reducing delays and costs and the current Labour Government has made the proposal the subject of further consultation.[18]

As more serious offences are reclassified as summary and as more triable either way offences are tried summarily, it becomes imperative that defendants in the magistrates' courts receive a fair trial. The Royal Commission was content to remark that 'magistrates conduct over 93 per cent of all criminal cases and should be trusted to try cases fairly', a classic *non sequitur*.[19] Although there is an absence of recent research on the subject, there are increasing doubts about the fairness of magistrates' justice. As already mentioned, defendants can be refused legal aid and disclosure is not required in summary cases. There are also doubts about the fairness of the system which appoints magistrates.[20] The local advisory committees which advise the Lord Chancellor on the appointment of lay magistrates are neither open nor representative.[21] The benches selected display a clear over-representation of middle-class persons and an under-representation of women and members of ethnic minorities.[22] One study concluded that advisory committees operate racist criteria in selecting magistrates, such as 'being assimilated into the English way of

---

[15] For discusson see Emmins, C.J. and Scanlan, G., *Guide to the Criminal Justice Act 1988* (Blackstone, London, 1988) pp. 84–8.

[16] Criminal Justice and Public Order Act 1994, s. 46. The proposed next steps were set out in Home Office, *Mode of Trial* (Cm 2908, HMSO, London, 1995).

[17] *Runciman Report*, ch. 6, para. 13.

[18] See HC Deb vol. 291, cols. 429–442, 27 February 1997. The idea was mooted following the publication of the (Narey) Report on *Review of Delay in the Criminal Justice System* (Home Office, London, 1997). See now Home Office, *Determining Mode of Trial in Either-Way Cases: A Consultation Paper* (London, 1998).

[19] *Runciman Report*, ch. 6, para. 18. For criticism of the Royal Commission's approach towards magistrates' courts, see Bridges, L. and McConville, M., 'Keeping faith with their own convictions: the Royal Commission on Criminal Justice', and Jackson, J.D. 'Trial by jury and alternative modes of trial', in McConville, M. and Bridges, L. (eds.), *Criminal Justice in Crisis* (Elgar, London, 1994).

[20] For recent trenchant criticism, see Darbyshire, P., 'For the New Lord Chancellor and Home Secretary: an essay on the importance and neglect of the magistracy' [1997] *Criminal Law Review* 627.

[21] See Home Affairs Committee, *Judicial Appointments Procedures* (1995–96 HC 52).

[22] For discussion see Raine, J.W., *Local Justice* (T & T Clark, Edinburgh, 1989) pp. 43–66. For the

life' as a criterion of suitability for the selection of black magistrates.[23] Another barrier to representativeness apart from the selection procedures is the demands of the office, which require persons to 'have time to carry out the full range of magisterial duties'.[24] Concerns about the representativeness of magistrates raise questions about their independence and impartiality. These doubts are further fuelled by concerns about the close ties between the magistracy and the police, and about the ability of magistrates to avoid becoming case-hardened.[25] Research has shown that magistrates have a tendency to accept police evidence too readily, although the research concluded that most convictions were in accord with the weight of the evidence.[26]

One solution to the concerns about lay magistrates would be to increase the number of stipendiary magistrates. To an extent this strategy is already being implemented in England and Wales. Though their numbers have been constant in London, their presence in the provinces has recovered from the low point of 10 in 1974 and is now higher than ever.[27] Stipendiaries are perceived to be quicker and cheaper than lay justices and better able to cope with the more complex and serious cases being tried in the magistrates' courts. The Royal Commission favoured a more 'judicious employment' of stipendiary magistrates,[28] but there are doubts about whether their deployment improves the quality of justice. Stipendiary magistrates may be just as susceptible to 'case hardening' as lay magistrates and they may be no better at finding the facts than them.

It is not surprising that persons who want to plead not guilty see the Crown Court as offering a better chance of acquittal than the magistrates' court because of a number of clear advantages.[29] First of all, almost all accused are granted legal aid in the Crown Court. Secondly, defendants are granted disclosure of the prosecution case, as well as the chance to have the case dismissed at committal, although under the new modified form of committal proceedings proposed in the Criminal Procedure and Investigations Act 1996 live witnesses will no longer be able to be called and magistrates will assess the sufficiency of the prosecution case purely on the basis of written statements.[30]

The most important advantage claimed for process in the Crown Court is, of course, the jury. Although increasingly playing a less significant role in terms of the number of cases heard, the jury continues to play a vital role in characterising

---

most recent comment, see Darbyshire, P., 'For the New Lord Chancellor and Home Secretary: an essay on the importance and neglect of the magistracy' [1997] *Criminal Law Review* 627.

[23] King, M. and May, C., *Black Magistrates* (Cobden Trust, London, 1985).

[24] Lord Chancellor's Department, 'The qualities looked for in a Justice of the Peace' (1988) 44 *The Magistrate* p. 78.

[25] Enright, S. and Morton, J., *Taking Liberties* (Weidenfeld and Nicolson, London, 1990) pp. 96–9.

[26] Vennard, J., *Contested Trials in Magistrates' Courts* (Home Office Research Study no. 71, HMSO, London, 1981).

[27] See Seago, P., Walker, C. and Wall, D., *The Role and Appointment of Stipendiary Magistrates* (University of Leeds and Lord Chancellor's Department, 1995). See further Chapter 10.

[28] *Runciman Report*, ch. 8, para. 103.

[29] Riley, D. and Vennard, J., *Triable Either-Way Cases: Crown Court or Magistrates' Court* (Home Office Research Study no. 98, HMSO, London, 1988), Hedderman, C. and Moxon, D., *Magistrates' Court or Crown Court? Mode of Trial Decisions and Sentencing* (Home Office Research Study no. 125, HMSO, London, 1992). McConville, M., Hodgson, J., Bridges, L. and Pavlovic, A., *Standing Accused* (Clarendon, Oxford, 1994) at p. 212, report that the acquittal rate is 'significantly lower' in magistrates' courts (22.7 per cent) than in the Crown Court (50.2 per cent).

[30] For commentary see Leng, R. and Taylor, R., *Guide to the Criminal Procedure and Investigations Act 1996* (Blackstone, London, 1996) pp. 73–81.

the fairness of the English criminal process. The institution of the jury has been variously heralded as trial by one's peers, as an example of participatory democracy and as a safeguard against the abuse of State power and oppressive laws and prosecutions.[31] The historical justification for these claims is dubious, but there are clear advantages for defendants in trial by jury as compared with trial by magistrates. One benefit of jury trial is that jurors are not usually made privy to inadmissible evidence which may prejudice the tribunal of fact.[32] Another is that the principle of random selection appears to be a better foundation for impartiality and independence than the principle of selection by unaccountable advisory committees appointed by the Lord Chancellor. However, this principle is not fully observed. Governments have taken steps both to increase the opportunities for the prosecution to influence the composition of the jury while at the same time decreasing the opportunities for the defence to do so. In 1978 and 1980, the Attorney-General issued guidelines permitting the prosecution to make checks regarding the suitability of jurors in certain cases involving national security and terrorism.[33] The prosecution are also given a wide brief to carry out criminal record checks on jurors in any case. A further step taken in the Criminal Justice Act 1988, section 118, was to abolish the defence right of peremptory challenge on the ground that it enabled the accused to rig juries in their favour. Although this move was later followed up with a *Practice Direction* restricting the prosecution's corresponding right to stand by jurors,[34] the abolition of the peremptory challenge has made it particularly difficult for the defence to challenge jurors whom they think are unsuitable. There are other methods of challenge, such as a challenge to the array (an objection to the whole panel of jurors) and a challenge for cause, but these are difficult to mount successfully as they require reasons to be given.[35] As the court discourages the questioning of jurors, it is very difficult to show that a particular juror would be biased. The abolition of the peremptory challenge has also prevented accused persons from ethnic minorities ensuring that members of their communities are represented on the jury. There was a period during the 1970s and 1980s when some judges were prepared to stand by jurors to ensure a multi-racial jury in racially sensitive cases, but the Court of Appeal has since held that the power of the judge to stand by jurors is limited to removing jurors who are not competent to serve on a jury.[36] The Royal Commission recommended that the prosecution or defence should be permitted to apply to the judge in exceptional cases for the selection of a jury containing up to three people from ethnic minority communities.[37]

Research has suggested that ethnic minorities are under-represented on British juries.[38] It does not necessarily follow that accused persons from ethnic minorities

---

[31] For a critique of these claims, see Darbyshire, P., 'The lamp that shows that freedom lives: is it worth the candle?' [1991] *Criminal Law Review* 740.

[32] For discussion of the problems of shielding non-jury triers of fact from inadmissible evidence, see Jackson, J. and Doran, S., *Judge without Jury: Diplock Trials in the Adversary System* (Clarendon, Oxford, 1995) and Wasik, M., 'Magistrates: knowledge of defendants' previous convictions' [1996] *Criminal Law Review* 851.

[33] See *Note* [1980] 2 All ER 457 and *Note* [1980] 3 All ER 785.

[34] [1988] 3 All ER 1086.

[35] See Buxton, R., 'Challenging and discharging jurors' [1990] *Criminal Law Review* 225.

[36] *R v Ford* (1980) 89 Cr App R 278.

[37] *Runciman Report*, ch. 8, paras. 62–4.

[38] Baldwin, J. and McConville, M., *Jury Trials* (Clarendon, Oxford, 1979) pp. 97, 98.

are at greater risk of wrongful convictions. Research has also found that it is difficult to predict verdicts on the basis of general characteristics such as age, sex, class, race or social class.[39] But very little is known about the actual behaviour of juries, because researchers are forbidden by the Contempt of Court Act 1981, section 8, to investigate jury deliberations.[40] It has been argued that bias may intrude into the courtroom in a more subtle way than by overt racial or class prejudice.[41] Until more is known about jury behaviour, it would be wrong to underestimate the effect of excluding members of an accused's community from the jury, since there then may be no one on the jury who is able to understand and explain the accused's actions.

Although the institution of the jury is still capable of evoking considerable passion, as the outcry against the proposal to abolish the right to elect for trial in either-way offences has indicated, there is less confidence in its decision-making prowess than in the past. Much of the concern has been generated by those who consider that the jury too often acquits the guilty,[42] but there are also concerns that juries on occasions convict the innocent.[43] There has also been a specific concern that the length and complexity of serious fraud cases render them inappropriate for jury trial.[44] All this suggests that we need to know more about what kind of issues juries are good at deciding and what issues they may need greater help or guidance on. In their research into Diplock trials in Northern Ireland, the author and Sean Doran found that judges may be better placed to deal with issues involving identification evidence and scientific evidence, while juries may be better equipped to determine questions of credibility.[45] There is also the suggestion that in certain cases of an emotionally charged nature such as child abuse cases, judges may be better equipped to bringing a colder, unemotional outlook to bear than juries. Until more research is undertaken, it is impossible to reach firm conclusions but there is a case for giving defendants a right to waive jury trial in cases where they believe that they may not receive a fair trial.[46]

Plea Bargaining

There are obvious savings to be made when defendants are persuaded to plead guilty, and it is therefore natural that efforts have been made to encourage this form of case disposal. The principal mode of encouragement has been to offer some

---

[39] Sealy, A.P. and Cornish, W.R., 'Juries and their verdicts' (1973) 36 *Modern Law Review* 496; Baldwin, J. and McConville, M., *Jury Trials* (Clarendon, Oxford, 1979) pp. 99–105.

[40] Compare *Runciman Report*, ch. 1 para. 8.

[41] See, for example, Hans, V.P. and Vidmar, H., *Judging the Jury* (Plenum, New York, 1986) pp. 136–42.

[42] Under the Criminal Procedure and Investigations Act 1996, ss. 54–7 retrials may now be ordered in cases of tainted acquittals.

[43] These are discussed by Baldwin, J. and McConville, M., *Jury Trials* (Clarendon, Oxford, 1979) ch. 5. In the Crown Court study conducted for the Royal Commission on Criminal Justice, judges and prosecution barristers thought that jury convictions went against the evidence or the law in 2 per cent of cases: see Zander, M. and Henderson, P., *Crown Court Study* (Royal Commission on Criminal Justice Research Study No. 19, HMSO, London, 1993) pp. 170, 1.

[44] See Roskill Committee, *Fraud Trials Committee Report* (HMSO, London, 1986); Home Office, *Juries in Serious Fraud Trials* (London, 1998).

[45] Jackson, J. and Doran, S., *Judge without Jury: Diplock Trials in the Adversary System* (Clarendon, Oxford, 1995) ch. 8.

[46] See Doran, S. and Jackson, J., 'The case for jury waiver' [1997] *Criminal Law Review* 155.

inducement whereby it is made more palatable for defendants to consider pleading guilty. Without any form of inducement, defendants might in many cases be disposed to plead guilty. In a study conducted some years ago by Bottoms and McClean in Sheffield, about two-thirds of the defendants interviewed said that they pleaded guilty because they were guilty.[47] But the study also found considerable evidence of changes of plea where some pressure was brought to bear on defendants at the last minute. In a later study in Belfast magistrates' court and Crown Court surveying cases where defendants had originally pleaded not guilty, 48 per cent of the 229 cases sampled began with an initial plea of not guilty and ended with a change of plea.[48] The most common reasons given by defendants were 'to get a lower sentence' or because 'my lawyer told me to' or because they were guilty. In their observations of the encounters that take place between lawyers and clients, McConville and others encountered a daily process of haggling between prosecution and defence lawyers in both the magistrates' courts and the Crown Court, with prosecutors often offering 'sweeteners' to defence lawyers to induce a guilty plea.[49]

It has been claimed that there are three kinds of negotiations that can take place over the decision to plead guilty: the charge bargain, the fact bargain and the plea bargain.[50] The charge bargain occurs when the defence offers to plead guilty to a lesser charge or the prosecution offers to accept a plea of guilty to a lesser charge. The fact bargain occurs when the defendant agrees to change his plea on the faith of a promise by the prosecution to present the facts in a particular way. Finally, the plea bargain proper occurs as the result of an understanding on the part of the defendant that he or she will receive a lower sentence as a result of a plea of guilty. This kind of bargain differs from the others because it brings the judge into the process. An understanding of what a sentence will be can only be gained from the judge in the case.

Whilst there has been considerable reluctance on the part of English judges to admit that any kind of plea bargaining occurs,[51] it is now legislative policy that pleas of guilty should attract a lighter sentence than a plea of not guilty. This sentencing discount has been formalised in section 48 of the Criminal Justice and Public Order Act 1994. But there remains much less acceptance of the idea that judges should become involved in discussions on sentence prior to trial. In *R v Turner* the Court of Appeal accepted that barristers might want to discuss cases with judges before trial but the judge should not indicate what sentence was in mind unless it would take a particular form regardless of the plea.[52] The governing rationale is that the defendant's full freedom of choice must not be compromised when deciding how to plead. Despite this restriction, however, a number of decisions since *Turner* have revealed that certain trial judges are prepared to indicate what reduction they might give to a sentence if the defendant pleads

---

[47] Bottoms, A.E. and McClean, J.D., *Defendants in the Criminal Process* (Routledge & Kegan Paul, London, 1976).

[48] Jackson, J., Kilpatrick, R. and Harvey, C., *Called to Court: A Public View of Criminal Justice* (SLS Publications, Belfast, 1991).

[49] McConville, M., Hodgson, J., Bridges, L. and Pavlovic, A., *Standing Accused* (Clarendon, Oxford, 1994) chaps. 8 and 10.

[50] Ashworth, A., *The Criminal Process: An Evaluative Study* (2nd ed., Oxford University Press, Oxford, 1998) ch. 9.

[51] See Baldwin, J. and McConville, M., *Negotiated Justice* (Martin Robertson, London, 1977).

[52] [1970] 2 QB 321.

guilty,[53] and a study conducted for the Royal Commission on Criminal Justice found that the vast majority of prosecution and defence barristers and a majority of judges favoured a relaxation of the *Turner* rule so as to permit judges approached by defence counsel to give an indication of the highest sentence they would give on a guilty plea.[54] The Royal Commission favoured this approach and recommended a new scheme to this effect known as the 'sentence canvass'.[55]

Defenders of plea bargaining argue that it is an efficient method of disposing of cases which ensures a conviction that might not otherwise be secured if the case were to go to trial and that it works to the advantage of both defendants and victims. Defendants obviously derive the advantage of reduced charges and a reduced sentence, while victims are spared the ordeal of giving evidence in court. But there are arguments of principle against plea bargaining, sentence canvassing and indeed any form of sentencing discount. Critics have argued that any rule which operates as an incentive to waive the right to be tried contradicts the spirit of the presumption of innocence.[56] More critically, there is a concern that defendants may be induced into pleading guilty when they are truly innocent.[57] The courts have insisted that the accused must have a complete freedom of choice whether to plead guilty or not guilty and have taken a stand against defendants being being told directly about the sentence a judge has in mind, but they have also said that counsel must be completely free to give the accused the best advice they can, and in their study McConville and others found that a great deal of effort went in to persuading defendants to plead guilty. The idea that the prosecution should be put to proof was not accepted as valid or realistic, and barristers deployed a range of techniques which commonly involved manipulating the defendant into accepting a plea.[58]

If plea bargaining has the effect of causing certain defendants to plead guilty to crimes they did not commit, it can also result in the converse situation, the dropping or reduction of charges which the accused did commit or playing down the seriousness of the accused's conduct. Once a defendant has pleaded guilty to a charge the prosecution will give an account of the facts of the case to the court. If the defendant wishes to contest the version of the facts given, this may be done in what is known as a 'Newton' hearing.[59] But clearly it is in the defendant's interest to get the prosecution to agree a version of events which reflects as favourably as possible on him or her, and this is where fact bargaining can come in. Recent research found that when domestic assault charges were downgraded, prosecutors played down the seriousness of the incident when they described it in court.[60] So, for example, if the charge were downgraded to common assault, the

---

[53] See the examples given in Ashworth, A., *The Criminal Process: An Evaluative Study* (2nd ed., Oxford University Press, Oxford, 1998) pp. 281–2.

[54] Zander, M. and Henderson, P., *Crown Court Study* (Royal Commission on Criminal Justice Research Study No. 19, HMSO, London, 1993).

[55] *Runciman Report*, ch. 7, para. 51.

[56] See, for example, Ashworth, A., 'Plea, Venue and Discontinuance' [1993] *Criminal Law Review* 830.

[57] Estimates vary as to the numbers of innocent defendants who plead guilty: see Ashworth, A., *The Criminal Process: An Evaluative Study* (Oxford University Press, Oxford, 1994) pp. 269–70.

[58] McConville, M., Hodgson, J., Bridges, L. and Pavlovic, A., *Standing Accused* (Clarendon, Oxford, 1994) ch. 10.

[59] For discussion see Ashworth, A., *The Criminal Process: An Evaluative Study* (2nd ed., Oxford University Press, Oxford, 1998) p. 276. But see Crown Prosecution Service, *Offences Against the Person Charging Standard* (London, 1996).

[60] See Cretney, A. and Davis, G., *Punishing Violence* (Routledge, London, 1995) pp. 141–2.

description could be modified from 'threatening someone with a knife' to 'showing a knife to someone'.

The most recent version of the Victim's Charter offers victims a chance to explain how the crime has affected them and consideration is being given to how so-called 'victim impact statements' should be used by prosecutors and the courts. This raises difficult questions as to how far victims' views should be taken into account on prosecution and sentencing decisions and as to how far victims' rights should be recognised in the criminal justice system.[61] But it is at least arguable that victims are entitled to expect that an accurate portrayal will be given of the offence in which they were involved, and it is far from certain that present methods of case disposal allow this to happen.

The Treatment of Evidence

A number of the traditional rules of evidence may be viewed against the background of a concern to protect the innocent.[62] Mention has been made of the high standard of proof in criminal cases. In addition a number of rules such as the rules relating to similar facts, character, corroboration, restrictions on cross-examination of the accused, hearsay, confessions and opinion evidence provide controls over the quality of the evidence that is adduced against the accused. There are at least three ways in which these rules offer protection to the accused. First, they provide careful regulation over the admission of certain kinds of evidence, such as evidence of an accused's convictions, which may be over-valued by the tribunal of fact. Secondly, they control the admission of certain kinds of evidence, such as confession evidence, which may not have been properly obtained against the accused. Thirdly, they guard against the admission of certain kinds of evidence, such as hearsay evidence, which may be difficult for the defence to challenge effectively.

In recent years, however, there has been a very evident relaxation of evidential constraints over the admissibility, use and evaluation of evidence in criminal trials. The rules of evidence have been increasingly seen as barriers to truth-finding, as more faith is placed on the common sense of trial fact-finders to reach accurate decisions on the basis of all the relevant evidence put before them. This principle of free proof influenced many of the proposals of the *Eleventh Report* of the Criminal Law Revision Committee which contained the most comprehensive package of evidence reforms in the post-war era.[63] Although shelved at the time because of the outcry against its proposals limiting the right of silence, many of its proposals have since borne fruit. These include the relaxation of the strict voluntariness requirements which governed the admissibility of confessions at common law, the admissibility of convictions of third parties, and the provisions extending the admissibility of hearsay in criminal cases.[64] Even the controversial silence proposals which enable triers of fact to draw common-sense inferences from the silence of the accused in certain circumstances have seen the light of day

---

[61] See Ashworth, A., 'Victim Impact Statements and Sentencing' [1993] *Criminal Law Review* 498, Victim Support, *The Rights of Victims of Crime* (London, 1995).

[62] Galligan D.J., 'More scepticism about scepticism' (1988) 8 *Oxford Journal of Legal Studies* 249; Zuckerman, A., *The Principles of Criminal Evidence* (1989, Clarendon, Oxford).

[63] Criminal Law Revision Committee, *Evidence (General)* (Cmnd 4991, HMSO, London, 1972).

[64] See Police and Criminal Evidence Act 1984 (PACE), ss. 74, 76, Criminal Justice Act 1988 ss. 23, 24.

in the Criminal Justice and Public Order Act 1994,[65] along with the abolition of corroboration requirements.[66]

These changes have taken place despite the growing concern in the 1980s about miscarriages of justice. The Royal Commission on Criminal Justice did not favour any changes in the right of silence, but it generally recommended a greater rather than a lesser relaxation of the rules of evidence, supporting the abolition of corroboration requirements, a simplification of the similar fact evidence rules and a relaxation of the hearsay rule.[67] It also rejected suggestions that there should be a tightening of the rules relating to confessions. Section 76 of the Police and Criminal Evidence Act 1984 (PACE) replaced the old voluntariness test (under which confessions had to be excluded if they were obtained as a result of threats or inducements exercised by a person in authority) with a new test requiring confessions to be excluded where they have been obtained by oppression or by anything said or done likely to render them unreliable. At first sight this test goes to the very issue of preventing the admission of unreliable confessions, but the test is not one of actual unreliability, and the provision has been interpreted as requiring that something is said or done in the course of questioning which is out of the ordinary, such as a failure to comply with the rule that an independent person be present during interviews with juveniles, mentally disordered and mentally handicapped persons.[68] The test falls short of requiring exclusion when the PACE rules are breached, and, despite the importance attached in PACE to tape-recording police interviews and to suspects having access to solicitors, the Royal Commission specifically rejected suggestions that confessions should be excluded where they had not been tape-recorded or made or confirmed in the presence of a solicitor.[69]

A question that remains to be answered is whether confessions in response to police interrogation can ever be truly reliable when the whole system of police detention and interrogation is designed to elicit confessions from suspects. Many of the recent miscarriage cases have demonstrated the dangers of relying on unsupported confessions, and this has prompted the question whether confessions should be corroborated before persons can be convicted on their basis. The Royal Commission by a majority rejected the proposal that confessions should not be allowed to go before a jury in the absence of any supporting evidence, but it did recommend that juries be warned about convicting on the basis of confession evidence.[70] The Commission's rejection of any corroboration or supporting evidence requirement was based on concern about the potential number of cases where guilty defendants would walk free, and it was sceptical about whether such a requirement would offer significantly greater safeguards against wrong convictions. Certainly the existence of other supporting evidence is no guarantee against wrongful conviction if such evidence is itself dubious. Corroboration by dubious scientific analysis of concocted or coerced confessions hardly assisted the *Birmingham Six*. A further point which was not made by the Commission is that

---

[65] See Chapter 5.

[66] See ss. 32–9.

[67] For comment on its approach, see Jackson, J., 'The Royal Commission on Criminal Justice: the evidence recommendations' [1993] *Criminal Law Review* 817.

[68] See *R v Goldenberg* (1988) 88 Cr App R 285; *R v Crampton* [1991] *Criminal Law Review* 277.

[69] *Runciman Report*, ch. 4, paras. 43–55.

[70] *Runciman Report*, ch. 4 paras. 56–87. See also Chapter 15.

corroboration requirements risk spawning a wealth of case law which could distract the courts' attention from the crucial issues of the quality of the confession evidence and how the confession came to be made.

The loosening of evidential constraints puts greater responsibility on to the courts to safeguard against wrongful convictions. Judges retain discretion over the ultimate admissibility of evidence, and they have wide powers to warn juries about the effect of certain kinds of evidence. Throughout the course of this century the courts have developed a judicial discretion to exclude evidence whose prejudicial value is outweighed by its prejudicial effect. Although the use of this discretion has been quite limited, it has served as a means of excluding a clearly unreliable piece of evidence such as a confession made by an accused suffering from some mental disability.[71] For example, the Court of Appeal has held that where a confession is made by a significantly handicapped defendant and comprises the entire case against him, the case should be withdrawn if the confession is unconvincing.[72] One problem is that judges need to be able to recognise unreliable confessons. Experts now claim that there are two types of false confession – the 'coerced compliant' confession and the 'coerced internalised' confession.[73] The former is usually the result of forceful or persistent questioning, while the latter is the result of a belief on the part of the suspect of actual commission of the crime. The restrictive rules on expert evidence for a time prevented experts testifying about the likelihood of a person making a false confession unless the person was suffering from a recognised mental illness or was educationally subnormal, but the courts are now more amenable towards admitting expert evidence of a defendant's likely mental state at the time of the police interview.[74]

Apart from excluding clearly unreliable confessions, the courts have also taken a tough stance against the admission of confessions which have been obtained in breach of the PACE rules. We have seen that Parliament does not require the exclusion of confessions because they have been obtained in breach of PACE, but section 78 gives the courts a statutory discretion to exclude evidence which would have such an adverse effect on the fairness of the proceedings that it would not be proper to admit it. The English courts have traditionally been reluctant to exercise any exclusionary jurisdiction in respect of a breach of pre-trial procedures on the ground that their role at the criminal trial is to ensure a fair trial for the accused and not to discipline or punish the police.[75] Nevertheless, the courts have rather surprisingly interpreted section 78 as permitting them to exercise a stricter control over the pre-trial process than might have been expected. In one decision the Lord Chief Justice indicated that proceedings may become unfair where there has been an abuse of process because evidence has been obtained in deliberate breach of procedure laid down in an official code of procedure.[76] This suggests that the courts are giving a wide meaning to 'proceedings', taking the view that proceedings up to the trial are part of the overall criminal process because there is an intimate

---

[71] See, for example, *R v Miller* [1986] 1 WLR 1191.

[72] *R v Mackenzie* (1993) 96 Cr App R 98.

[73] See Pattenden, R., 'Should confessions be corroborated?' (1991) 107 *Law Quarterly Review* 319; Gudjonsson, G.H., *The Psychology of Interrogations, Confessions and Testimony* (Wiley, Chichester, 1992).

[74] See for example *R v Raghip, Silcott and Braithwaite, The Times*, 9 December, 1991.

[75] *R v Sang* [1979] 2 All ER 1222.

[76] *R v Quinn* [1990] *Criminal Law Review* 581. See commentary of D.J. Birch.

connection between what happens in the investigatory process and what happens at trial. Adopting this approach, the Court of Appeal has held that significant and substantial breaches of the codes of practice under PACE inevitably have an adverse effect on the fairness of the proceedings because Parliament has laid down the standards of fairness in the codes.[77] The courts have been particularly concerned to use section 78 to exclude confessions obtained in breach of the duty to record interviews contemporaneously and to a lesser extent confessions obtained after wrongful denial of access to legal advice.[78] They have not, however, considered that every breach has such an adverse effect on the fairness of the proceedings that justice requires exclusion and they have persisted in disclaiming any disciplinary role.[79] Some decisions have instead stressed the need for a causal link between the breach and the obtaining of the evidence, requiring that the accused has been prejudiced by the breach.[80] But it may be argued that if the courts have a responsibility to ensure that accused persons are not wrongly convicted, then in so far as rules such as the recording provisions and rights such as access to legal advice assist in preventing false convictions, the exclusion of confessions obtained in breach of them can be justified, however reliable the actual confession in any particular case, because it illustrates the courts' commitment to protecting the innocent.[81]

The courts have also proved to be quite vigilant in protecting accused persons against the dangers of identification evidence. Section 78 of PACE has been used to exclude identification evidence which has been obtained in breach of the identification code issued under PACE.[82] The courts have been equally alive to the more general dangers of identification evidence. Following a series of miscarriages of justice caused by defective identification evidence in the 1970s, the Devlin Committee recommended that, in the absence of any supporting evidence, visual identification evidence should not be allowed to go to a jury unless there were 'exceptional circumstances' which reduced the risk of misidentification.[83] Parliament did not act on these recommendations, but shortly after the publication of the report the Court of Appeal laid down specific guidelines, known as the *Turnbull* guidelines, governing the way in which a judge should direct a jury when the evidence against a person rests substantially on identification evidence based on personal impression.[84] These guidelines require judges to withdraw cases altogether where the quality of the evidence is poor and there is no supporting evidence; the judge should otherwise give a detailed warning to the jury of the special need for caution before acting on such evidence. Although some earlier decisions appeared

[77] *R v Walsh* (1989) 91 Cr App R 161. See further Chapter 10.
[78] See for example *R v Doolan* [1988] *Criminal Law Review* 747; *R v Delaney* (1988) 88 Cr App R 338; *R v Keenan* [1989] 3 All ER 598; *R v Canale* [1990] 2 All ER 187 (breaches of recording provisions); *R v Samuel* [1988] QB 615. Cf. *R v Alladice* (1988) 87 Cr App R 380; *R v Dunford* (1990) 91 Cr App R 150 (breach of legal advice provisions).
[79] *R v Mason* [1987] 3 All ER 481 at p. 484; *R v Delaney* (1988) 88 Cr App R 338; *R v Keenan* [1989] 3 All ER 598 at p. 609.
[80] See Birch, D.J., 'The pace hots up: confessions and confusions under the 1984 Act' [1989] *Criminal Law Review* 95.
[81] See Jackson, J.D., 'In defence of a voluntariness doctrine for confessions: *The Queen v Johnston* revisited' (1986) 21 *Irish Jurist* 208.
[82] See, for example, *R v Samms* [1991] *Criminal Law Review* 199; *R v Nagah* (1990) 92 Cr App R 344.
[83] *Report of the Secretary of State for the Home Department of the Departmental Committee of Identification in Criminal Cases* (1975–76 HC 338, HMSO, London, 1976) paras. 4.61–4.65.
[84] *R v Turnbull* [1977] QB 224

to confine the impact of the guidelines to 'fleeting glimpse' sightings,[85] it is now clear that the cases in which the warning can be dispensed with are 'wholly exceptional'.[86] One such exceptional case would seem to be where there is a purported recognition of a familiar face over a considerable period of time in perfectly good conditions of lighting.[87] But as recognised in *Turnbull* itself, mistakes can be made even in recognition cases, and it is arguably better to make the jury aware of the possibility of mistake even in apparently clear cases.

Even when a warning is issued, it may be questioned whether enough has been done to safeguard against mistaken identification evidence. The Royal Commission was confident that if the guidelines laid down in *Turnbull* were strictly applied, identification evidence should be capable of being assessed properly.[88] But there is a dearth of empirical evidence on what effect such warnings have on juries.[89] Another problem is that the guidelines are not specific enough to provide sufficient guidance in particular cases. If, for example, good quality identifications can be mistaken as well as bad quality identifications, how is a jury to assess the reliability of an identification in a particular case?[90] There is an argument that no matter how good the quality of the identification, convictions should not be based solely on identification evidence based on personal impression. Such a requirement would go against the trend which has been to abolish any corroboration requirements. The courts have enthusiastically endorsed the abolition of the corroboration requirements by making it clear that in future it will be up to individual judges to decide in the individual circumstances of each case whether any warning is required in respect of a witness who may be unreliable and whether such a warning should ask jurors to look for supporting evidence.[91] But a distinction can arguably be made between assessing the credibility of witnesses, which is usually considered within the competence of a tribunal of fact, and assessing the reliability of certain kinds of evidence such as identification evidence which are notoriously difficult to assess because the usual tools of assessment – cross-examination and demeanour of the witness – are not so effective.

The courts have also tried to be vigilant in protecting defendants against the risk of juries taking a hostile attitude against them. We have already mentioned the discretion to exclude evidence whose probative value is outweighed by its prejudicial effect. More recently the courts have stopped cases where they have believed that defendants would not get a fair trial because of adverse media attention.[92] By contrast, the courts do appear in certain instances to be placing more faith in juries. One example is in the area of similar fact evidence where the courts have stressed that 'striking similarity' is not a prerequisite to the admissibility of

---

[85] See, for example, *R v Curry*; *R v Keeble* [1983] *Criminal Law Review* 737.

[86] *Shand v R* [1996] 1 All ER 511.

[87] *R v Bentley* (1991) 99 Cr App Rep 342.

[88] *Runciman Report*, ch. 1 para. 9.

[89] See Law Commission, *Evidence in Criminal Proceedings: Previous Misconduct of a Defendant* (HMSO, London, 1996) paras. 6.35–38, App. D.

[90] See Dennis, I.H., 'Corroboration requirements reconsidered' [1984] *Criminal Law Review* 316; Jackson, J.D., 'The insufficiency of identification evidence based on personal impression' [1986] *Criminal Law Review* 203.

[91] *R v Makanjuola*; *R v Easton* [1995] 3 All ER 730.

[92] See, for example, the trial of police officers charged with perjury in the *Birmingham Six* case, *The Times,* 8 October 1993. See Chapter 13.

bad character evidence,[93] and have decided that the question whether the evidence of multiple complainants in sexual offences may have become contaminated by collusion is a matter of weight to be determined by the jury rather than a matter of admissibility to be decided by the judge.[94] According to Lord Griffiths in *R* v *H*, 'with better educated and more literate juries the value of those old restrictive rules of evidence is being re-evaluated and many are being discarded or modified.'.[95]

This trust in juries has also been a hallmark of the courts' approach towards scientific evidence. Despite concern about the independence of forensic scientists evidenced in such cases as the *Maguire Seven* and the case of *Judith Ward* and growing understanding of the limitations of the forensic techniques adopted by the scientific community, the UK courts have tended to permit expert evidence to be admitted with little scrutiny as to its reliability. The assumption has been that the ordinary processes of examination and cross-examination are capable of exposing any deficiencies in scientific evidence and that juries are capable of assessing the weight of such evidence.[96] But it may be questioned whether juries are as well equipped as judges to understand the complexities of forensic evidence.[97] It needs to be stressed that scientific evidence can only be effectively challenged if the defence are given full disclosure of all the material that has some bearing on the case and sufficient scientific resources to mount their own investigations. This raises questions of pre-trial disclosure and forensic services outside the scope of this chapter, but there are limits on what the courts can do to ensure that the defence are given full 'equality of arms' to pursue their own investigations.[98]

One respect in which the courts may provide the defence with adequate means to challenge evidence is in ensuring that the defence are given the opportunity at trial to cross-examine those witnesses who have important evidence to give in relation to the case. The hearsay rule has traditionally given the parties this opportunity, but, as already mentioned, this rule is being gradually eroded. Under section 23 of the Criminal Justice Act 1988, first-hand documentary evidence is now admissible if the maker of the statement is dead, ill, outside the UK and cannot be brought back, cannot be found despite all reasonable steps taken, or if the statement is made to a police officer and the maker does not give oral evidence through fear or because of being kept out of the way. This opens the door to conviction upon written as opposed to oral evidence, although the courts are given the final say by means of a statutory discretion to exclude evidence where in an individual case it may not be in the interests of justice to admit the evidence. Section 25 gives the courts a statutory discretion to exclude such evidence and in the case of documents prepared for the purpose of pending or contemplated criminal proceedings or a criminal investigation, section 26 requires that the leave of the court be given. In a Privy Council case interpreting earlier legislation, it was held that there was nothing inherently unfair in an accused being convicted on the

---

[93] *R* v *P* [1991] 2 All ER 859.
[94] *R* v *H* [1995] 2 All ER 865.
[95] *Ibid.*, at p. 878.
[96] See Jackson, J., 'The role of experts in UK criminal procedure' in Nijboer, N., Callen, C.R. and Kwak, N. (eds.), *Forensic Expertise and the Law of Evidence* (Royal Netherlands Academy of Arts and Sciences, Amsterdam, 1992); Smith, R., 'Forensic pathology, scientific expertise and the criminal law' in Smith, R. and Wynne, B., (eds.), *Expert Evidence* (Routledge, London, 1989).
[97] See Bawdon, F., 'Who checks forensics?' *The Times*, 24 May 1996.
[98] See further Chapter 6.

sole evidence of a sworn deposition statement.[99] In this case a witness had identified the three co-accused as the murderers of the deceased at a preliminary inquiry and was himself murdered before trial. But statements made to the police are different from statements taken at an oral preliminary inquiry because they give the defence no opportunity to cross-examine the makers. In the leading case on the interpretation of section 26, the Court of Appeal considered that the court must consider the quality of the evidence adduced and how far any potential unfairness arising from the defendant's inability to cross-examine on the statement could be effectively counterbalanced by a warning from the judge to the jury about relying on evidence which had not been tested by cross-examination.[100] But it is very difficult to know how juries are likely to regard such a warning. It would appear that no single objection will automatically lead to hearsay evidence being excluded – neither the fact that the statement contains identification evidence, nor the fact that it is the only evidence against the accused, nor the inability to cross-examine.[101] The crucial question is the quality of the evidence. But this raises the question whether quality can be assessed without the benefit of cross-examination. There have been a number of decisions of the European Court of Human Rights which have indicated that it is a breach of Article 6 of the European Convention for convictions to be based upon evidence which the defence were never given the opportunity to question.[102]

One of the purposes of the hearsay provisions in the 1988 Act was to protect victims against the need to give evidence when they are too fearful to give evidence. This raises the difficult question of the balance which has to be struck between the rights of defendants and the interests of witnesses and victims. In a recent judgment concerned with the question whether in a drug trafficking case the defendant had the right to question witnesses who had given evidence anonymously against him, the European Court of Human Rights recognised that the principles of fair trial require that the interests of the defence are balanced against those of witnesses or victims called upon to testify.[103] The interests of the defence may well require that the defence are given some opportunity to cross-examine prosecution witnesses, but there are doubts about whether these should extend so far as to enable defendants personally to subject their victims to lengthy questioning in the witness box, as happened in a highly publicised case when a rape victim was subjected to six days of questioning.[104]

One question which this case raised was whether judges were doing enough to protect vulnerable witnesses in the witness box. There has been particular criticism of the way in which judges have applied section 2 of the Sexual Offences (Amendment) Act 1976 which requires judges in rape cases to exclude evidence of the complainant's sexual experience with third parties except where it would be unfair to the defendant to refuse to allow the evidence to be adduced. Judges have

---

[99] *Scott v R* [1989] 2 All ER 305.

[100] *R v Cole* [1990] 2 All ER 108.

[101] See, for example, *Scott, Cole, R v Setz-Dempsey* (1994) 98 Cr App R 23, *R v Batt and Batt* [1995] *Criminal Law Review* 240.

[102] See, for example, *Ludi v Switzerland*, Appl. no. 12433/86, Ser. A no. 238, (1993) 15 EHRR 173; *Saidi v France*, Appl. no 14647/89, Ser A vol.261-C, (1994) 17 EHRR 251. For discussion see Law Commission, *Evidence in Criminal Proceedings: Hearsay and Related Topics* (Cm 3670, HMSO, London, 1997), pp. 60–63.

[103] *Doorson v Netherlands*, Appl. no 20524/92, 1996–II, (1996) 22 EHRR 330.

[104] See Gibbs, F., 'In terror of the accused', *The Times*, 17 September 1996; Report of the Inter-departmental Working Group on the treatment of Vulnerable or Intimidated Witnesses in the Criminal Justice System, *Speaking Up for Justice* (Home Office, London, 1998).

been criticised for taking too generous a view of the circumstances in which cross-examination of such evidence is admitted.[105] More generally, the Royal Commission on Criminal Justice urged judges to intervene to prevent witnesses being subjected to bullying or intimidatory tactics by counsel.[106] This raises questions about the role of the judge in the adversarial trial.

The Role of the Judge

The traditional role of the judge in the adversarial trial is to adopt an umpireal stance, and there is a considerable literature on the dangers that arise when a judge is seen to descend into the dust of the conflict.[107] Judicial intervention is considered particularly dangerous in jury trials, because the judge may then unduly influence the jury.[108] On the classical umpireal view, the judge's primary duty to ensure a fair trial requires that the proceedings are conducted fairly according to the rules of evidence and procedure but does not require a searching examination of the truth. The *locus classicus* is *Jones* v *National Coal Board* where Denning LJ said that judges should ask questions of witnesses 'only when it is necessary to clear up any point that has been overlooked or left obscure'.[109]

The author has argued elsewhere, however, that there are at least three respects in whch this umpireal characterisation of the judicial role is a misleading one.[110] First, umpires apply rules, but judges do much more than apply rules. We have already referred to the fact that judges exercise considerable discretion to admit or exclude evidence with profound consequences one way or another for the prosecution or defence case. Secondly, judges in practice stray well beyond the confines of the umpireal ideal in their questioning of witnesses. The Court of Appeal has sanctioned the questioning of witnesses which goes far beyond the narrow boundaries of simply clarifying evidence, and has tended to focus on whether the interventions prevented the defence from presenting their case rather than on whether they were compatible with the adversarial ideal.[111] Thirdly, even as an ideal characterisation of the judicial role, the umpireal analogy is misleading. Aside from powers to question witnesses, judges have always had a number of well-recognised powers that are not typically umpireal but which border on the realm of the inquisitorial.[112] These include powers to amend the indictment, to call witnesses and to withdraw weak cases from juries.[113] Moreover, not only are judges empowered to undertake certain active fact-finding responsibilities, they may be

---

[105] See, for example, Temkin, J., 'Sexual History Evidence: The ravishment of s. 2' [1993] *Criminal Law Review* 3; McColgan, A., 'Common law and the relevance of sexual history evidence' (1996) 16 *Oxford Journal of Legal Studies* 275.

[106] *Runciman Report*, ch. 8.

[107] *Yuill* v *Yuill* [1945] 1 All ER 183, at p. 189. See Frankel, M.E., 'The search for truth: an umpireal view' (1975) 123 *University of Pennsylvania Law Review*, 1031; Saltzburg, S.A., 'The unnecessarily expanding role of the American trial judge' (1978) 63 *Virginia Law Review* 1.

[108] *Ibid.*, p. 56.

[109] [1947] 2 QB 55, at p. 64.

[110] See Jackson, J., 'Judicial Responsibility in Criminal Proceedings' (1996) 49 *Current Legal Problems* 59.

[111] *R* v *Hamilton* [1969] *Criminal Law Review* 486. Compare *R* v *Matthews and Matthews* (1983) 78 Cr App R 23; *R* v *Gunning*, unreported, 7 July 1980. For a review of the authorities see Doran, S., 'Descent into Avernus' (1989) 139 *New Law Journal* 147; Pattenden, R., *Judicial Discretion and Criminal Litigation* (Clarendon, Oxford, 1990) pp. 98–102; Jackson, J. and Doran, S., *Judge without Jury: Diplock Trials in the Adversary System* (Clarendon, Oxford, 1995) pp. 104–110.

[112] Jackson, J. and Doran, S., *Judge without Jury: Diplock Trials in the Adversary System* (Clarendon, Oxford, 1995) pp. 179–96.

under a duty to do so. At the end of the trial, for example, judges have to sum up the evidence before the jury, with a duty to put before the jury any defence or defence issue which has arisen on the evidence even if this has not been specifically raised by defence counsel.[114]

The problem has been that judges have not always exercised these greater fact-finding responsibilities as fairly as they might have done. In a number of notable miscarriage cases judges have made extremely damning and inaccurate observations before the jury on summation. In the *Carl Bridgewater* trial, for example, the judge told the jury that they might have no hesitation 'in concluding that the farm was raided that day by a number of men, possibly four, and that they went there in two vehicles: one a light blue Cortina Estate, and probably also a Transit or Bedford type of van, and that they arrived at the farmhouse itself shortly before a quarter to four and left by about 4.40 or 4.45'.[115] In fact the state of the evidence was much less conclusive than this. Eye-witnesses were far from agreed about the number of men seen at the farm; no one saw two vehicles at or near the farm, and no one saw four men there or in the vicinity, either together or separately.[116] In this case, as in so many others, the judge was not content merely to summarise the evidence; he also commented in a manner extremely prejudicial to the defence. The judge referred to the evidence of a convicted prisoner who gave evidence against the accused as perhaps 'unusually convincing for a man of his background'.[117] Another tendency on the part of judges has been to speculate on the testimony without offering any evidence for what is suggested.[118] In the course of the summing-up in the trial of the *Birmingham Six* case, which serves as a classic example of one-sidedness, the judge attempted to discredit the prison doctor by suggesting that he must have been covering up for his colleagues.[119] It is one thing to comment on the answers given by a witness; it is quite another to make sweeping comments on the motives for a certain testimony.

The Royal Commission considered that judges should no longer be able to comment on the credibility of the evidence when they sum up on the facts to the jury.[120] Of course, judges can still make errors of fact in their summing-up, and in addition to recommending that defence counsel should have a duty to intervene to correct the judge on legal matters, the Commission could also have recommended that counsel should correct the judge on matters of fact.[121] An even better procedure may be to encourage judges to engage more openly in discussion with counsel on the facts as well as the law *before* summing-up. [122]

---

[113] Pattenden, R., *Judicial Discretion and Criminal Litigation* (Clarendon, Oxford, 1990) pp. 41–3, 102–4, 170–1.

[114] Doran, S., 'Alternative defences: the "invisible burden" on the trial judge' [1991] *Criminal Law Review* 878.

[115] Foot, P., *Murder at the Farm: Who Killed Carl Bridgewater?* (Sidgwick & Jackson, London, 1986) p. 135.

[116] *Ibid.*, pp. 135, 136.

[117] *Ibid.*, p. 164.

[118] See, for example, *R v Robson* [1992] *Criminal Law Review* 655.

[119] Woffinden, B., *Miscarriages of Justice* (Hodder and Stroughton, London, 1989) p. 405. See also Chapter 10.

[120] *Runciman Report*, ch. 8, para. 23.

[121] As is the practice in certain jurisdictions such as Northern Ireland and the Republic of Ireland, see Ryan, E. and Magee, P., *The Irish Criminal Process* (Mercier Press, Cork, 1983) pp. 362,363.

[122] The courts have recommended this procedure in relation to the issue whether a warning should be given that a witness's evidence may be unreliable: see *R v Makanjuola; R v Easton* [1995] 3 All ER 730.

Although the Royal Commission urged greater restraint on the part of judges at the stage of summing-up, it considered that judges ought to take a more interventionist approach both before, as well as during, the trial. Accordingly, it made a number of recommendations to widen the scope for judicial involvement. Instead of making a theoretical assessment of the relative merits of adversarial and inquisitorial procedures, the Commission preferred to be guided by, as it put it, 'practical considerations' in order to make the existing system serve the interests of justice and efficiency.[123] It recognised the force of many of the criticisms of the adversarial system which is said to turn a search for truth into a contest played between opposing lawyers, but its recommendations seemed more motivated by a concern for efficiency than a concern for truth-finding. Its recommendations for greater use of preparatory hearings before trial, more structured pre-trial disclosure and sentence canvassing were all designed to increase the degree of judicial management over criminal cases before trial. Its recommendations for judges to stop weak cases and to cut out time-wasting tactics at trial were designed to increase trial efficiency.

The essence of many of the pre-trial recommendations appears to have been accepted in spirit if not in detail.[124] As reported in the previous edition, policies of case management were being pursued long before the Royal Commission had reported.[125] Pre-trial reviews can be traced back to the middle of the 1970s in the case of some Crown Court centres and they became well established in magistrates' courts in the early 1980s. Since the Commission's report the Government has implemented a scheme for pleas and directions hearings whereby all cases are to be initially listed for hearing after they have been transferred to the Crown Court,[126] and the Criminal Procedure and Investigations Act 1996 extends the current provisions for pre-trial hearings in serious fraud cases to all Crown Court trials. Judges may now order a pre-trial hearing in any case where an examination of the indictment suggests that the trial is likely to be so long and complex that substantial benefits are likely to accrue from such a hearing.[127] Section 31 of the Act gives the judge extensive powers during the hearing to make binding rulings on issues of disclosure and admissibility in advance of the trial.

The Future of Trial Procedures

Many of the changes towards greater managerial judging made in the wake of the Royal Commission's report have profound implications for the future of adversarial trial procedures. It remains to be seen how judges respond to the more managerial role that they are being urged to adopt, but recent changes have the potential to shift the focus of the criminal process from the adversarial trial towards pre-trial procedures and to shift the judicial role still further away from the umpireal ideal.[128] This is taking place in the absence of any significant debate as to whether this change is desirable. For the reasons already given, it was always

---

[123] *Runciman Report*, ch. 1, para. 12.
[124] See further Home Office, *Improving the Effectiveness of Pre-trial Hearings in the Crown Court* (Cm 2924, HMSO, London, 1995).
[125] See pp. 154–6 of Walker, C. and Starmer, K., (eds.), *Justice in Error* (Blackstone Press, London, 1993).
[126] See *Practice Direction* [1995] 1 WLR 1318.
[127] Criminal Procedure and Investigations Act 1996, s. 29.
[128] See Redmayne, M., 'Process Gains and Process Values: the Criminal Procedure and Investigations Act 1996' (1997) 60 *Modern Law Review* 79.

misleading to describe the judicial function in criminal proceedings as purely umpireal. However, the new changes extend judicial power to influence proceedings beyond the trial stage into pre-trial proceedings. Some have argued that the greater involvement of judges in pre-trial hearings will mean that they will effectively determine guilt or innocence in many cases.[129]

Rather than seek to limit this judicial influence, it may be better to recognise that judges have a legitimate interest in influencing the outcome of proceedings and to work out a theory of judicial responsibility which recognises this interest as well as the need to give both sides a chance to present their case. This means shedding the traditional umpireal and inquisitorial caricatures that have so long haunted the judicial function and replacing them with a new vision of the judicial role. It has been argued elsewhere that truth-finding is best served by a dialectic process of fact-finding which encourages as active an interplay between all interested participants as is possible within the constraints of time and resources.[130] In this process interested parties must be free to assert and challenge evidence, but the ultimate triers of fact must be as free as possible to determine what evidence should be heard and to probe the evidence that is presented.

This may well mean greater judicial involvement in pre-trial proceedings. It has been argued that rather than permit the majority of cases to be settled out of court, an open court hearing should be required in all cases and that the true choice facing the accused should not be whether to plead guilty or not guilty, but to choose to have the case heard by a judge or by jury.[131] Thus even where the accused has not contested the charges, the evidence would at least be subjected to scrutiny by a judge – a 'slow' plea as such hearings are known in the United States[132] – even if in many cases the assessment of the evidence would be a formality. In this way defendants would have the protection of some formal scrutiny of their case. Prosecutors might be under less pressure to drop charges in order to obtain pleas and victims would in consequence see their cases determined in open court rather than bargained out of court.

A truly dialectic theory would also suggest that present trial structures should be changed to accommodate more active involvement on the part of the tribunal of fact. We may have to resign ourselves to the diminution of exclusionary rules of evidence and to think more in terms of inclusionary rules regulating participation between all parties within the spirit of inclusive dialogue.[133] This may require clearer rules on the extent to which, and the stage at which, triers of fact should intervene in the course of the trial and in jury trials clearer lines of responsibility between judges and juries on questions of fact, with more thought given to how best to maximise the contribution of both judges and juries in accordance with the respective strengths of lay and professional decision makers.[134]

---

[129] See, for example, Field, S. and Thomas, P., 'Justice and Efficiency? The Royal Commission on Criminal Justice' (1994) 21 *Journal of Law and Society*, 14.

[130] Jackson, J.D., 'Two methods of proof in criminal procedure' (1988) 51 *Modern Law Review* 549.

[131] Jackson, J. and Doran, S., *Judge without Jury: Diplock Trials in the Adversary System* (Clarendon, Oxford, 1995) p. 301.

[132] See Mather, L., *Plea Bargaining or Trial?* (Lexington, Mass., 1979) pp. 149, 50; Doran, S., Jackson, J.D. and Seigel, M.L., 'Rethinking Adversariness in Nonjury Criminal Trials' (1995) 23 *American Journal of Criminal Law* 1 at p. 6.

[133] For further argument, see Jackson, J.D., 'Analysing the new evidence scholarship; towards a new conception of the law of evidence' (1996) 16 *Oxford Journal of Legal Studies* 309.

[134] See Jackson, J. and Doran, S., 'Judge and jury: towards a new division of labour in criminal trials' (1997) 60 *Modern Law Review* 759.

Trial procedures must also take account of the interests of economy and efficiency which have been the driving force behind recent changes. But the need for greater efficency in our trial procedures must not be at the expense of justice. With the forthcoming incorporation of the European Convention on Human Rights into domestic law, trial procedures will come increasingly under the spotlight of international human rights standards and the demand for procedures which guarantee a fair trial to all interested parties will become ever more pressing. No procedure can ever protect against the risk of error. That is why at the end of the day we will still require rules of evidence to allocate risks of error in such a way as to protect the innocent so far as possible. But we may also need to think more radically about whether our adversarial trial procedures are achieving the best justice that is possible within existing resources.

10

The Judiciary

Clive Walker (with Appendix by James Wood)

'The function of the judiciary within the constitution of the United Kingdom is to ensure that justice is done so far as possible . . . to both the defendant and society in criminal trials . . .'[1] Does the judiciary live up to this mission statement? If miscarriages of justice occur, then not only is the defendant treated very unjustly, but also society (including the victims of crime) has not been accorded the gains in terms of safety, retribution and possible rehabilitation which should flow from an accurate conviction. This chapter will examine possible failings which arise from the personnel by which justice is administered. Taking the argument that case outcomes are constructions of fact as mediated by social and professional perspectives,[2] it must be worthwhile to examine some aspects of the performance of the judiciary, who are undoubtedly major players within the criminal justice system.

The Performance of Summary Justice

Attention should first be turned towards the magistrates' courts where well over 90 per cent of the business of criminal justice is in fact transacted.[3] This focus was not apparent to the Runciman Commission which naïvely took for granted the ability of magistrates to handle virtually any case to an acceptable standard of justice.[4] Yet, the system produces a large number of dissatisfied defendants as well as a significant proportion of successful appeals.[5] Consequently, many commentators have asserted that Crown Courts, despite all their imperfections, offer clear advantages to defendants in due process terms over trial by magistrates which may suffer from case-hardening, lower levels of legal representation and more generally an impetus towards a crime control ethos (as shown by high rates of guilty pleas

---

[1] Home Affairs Committee, *Judicial Appointments Procedures* (1995–96 HC 52) para. 3.
[2] McConville, M., Sanders, A. and Leng, R., *The Case for the Prosecution* (Routledge, London, 1991).
[3] See Derbyshire, P., 'An essay on the importance and neglect of the magistracy' [1997] *Criminal Law Review* 627.
[4] *Runciman Report*, ch. 6 para. 18.
[5] There were 10,441 appeals against conviction (3494 successful) in 1996: Home Office, *Criminal Appeals, England and Wales 1995 and 1996* (Research and Statistics Directorate, London, 1998).

and low rates of acquittals).[6] One radical response to these inherent imperfections is to abolish magisterial justice and to substitute the universal use of juries.[7] But this idea will not be pursued. It is not that the prospect is wholly undesirable or impossible, especially if notions of communitarian and restorative justice advance further.[8] However, it is certain that the ancient role of the justices of the peace[9] will in fact persist for the foreseeable future. So how might apprehensions about the standard of justice in magistrates' courts be answered within that system?

The Professionalisation of Local Justice

One response might be the professionalisation of justice on the assumption that standards of decision-making will thereby be improved. To a significant extent this strategy is already being implemented by the growing role of stipendiary magistrates in England and Wales.[10] Though their numbers have long been static in London, their presence in the provinces has recovered from the low ebb of ten in 1974 and is now higher than ever.[11] The reasons for this trend are several. One is simply mechanical – that the process of appointment has become simpler and no longer depends on local petition.[12] However, the main motivation seems to reflect concerns about efficiency in the light of the growth in workload of magistrates' courts and the tendency to reclassify as summary more complex and serious cases. Such court business demands frequent and prolonged attendance at court as well as legal expertise, factors which make life difficult for part-time amateurs. There have also been concerns about court delays and inefficiencies,[13] and stipendiaries are widely perceived to be quicker and cheaper than lay justices.[14]

The use of salaried professionals in summary courts is of course widespread in many other common law jurisdictions (including Scotland, Northern Ireland and the Republic of Ireland).[15] However, the wholesale replacement of the lay magistracy is not, and never has been, Government policy for England and Wales. The employment of stipendiaries as sole judicial actors would historically be viewed as a threat to judicial independence. Furthermore, there are fundamental principles of democracy and the protection of individual rights which call for

---

[6] See Carlen, P., *Magistrates' Justice* (Martin Robertson, London, 1976); Sanders, A. and Young, R., *Criminal Justice* (Butterworths, London, 1994) ch. 6. The effective acquittal rate of those pleading not guilty (about 170,000 defendants) is around 23 per cent, which is less than half the Crown Court rate.

[7] Mansfield, M., *Presumed Guilty* (Heinemann, London, 1993) ch. 17.

[8] The Crime and Disorder Act 1998 in particular will attempt to deflect juvenile misbehaviour from the formal criminal justice system towards youth offending teams.

[9] See Skyrme, Sir T., *History of Justices of the Peace* (Barry Rose, 1991).

[10] See Seago, P., Walker, C. and Wall, D., *The Role and Appointment of Stipendiary Magistrates* (University of Leeds and Lord Chancellor's Department, London, 1995). See further Chapter 9.

[11] In February 1998, there were 42 provincial stipendiaries and 49 Metropolitan stipendiaries; the number of lay magistrates in January 1996 stood at 30,326 active lay magistrates, an increase of 26 per cent on the 1979 figure of 24,021 and also a record high.

[12] See now Justices of the Peace Act 1997, s. 11.

[13] See: *Magistrates' Courts: Report of a Scrutiny* (Home Office, London, 1989).

[14] See: *Working Group on Pre-Trial Issues* (Home Office, London, 1991) para. 174. Stipendiaries were used on a temporary basis to dispense swift justice during the Miners' Strike in 1984–5: Rutherford, A. and Gibson, B., 'Special hearings' [1987] *Criminal Law Review* 440.

[15] See: Legal Studies Department, *Guilty Your Worship: A Study of Victoria's Magistrates' Courts* (La Trobe University, 1980); Skyrme, Sir T., *History of the Justices of the Peace* (Barry Rose, 1991) Vol. 3; Doob, A.N., Baranek, P.M. and Addario, S.M., *Understanding Justices* (University of Toronto, 1991).

representative[16] (and therefore predominantly lay) and local[17] involvement at all levels of justice. Equally, the extinction of stipendiaries seems far from practicable. In the first place, despite the yearly upward trend in the overall number of lay justices, a significant number of benches are finding it increasingly difficult to appoint suitable persons. Secondly, it would probably require at least another 3,000 lay justices completely to replace the existing stipendiaries, and this would mean benches of over 700 to run the larger city courts. So, the consensus seems to be around the idea of a basically lay system but with a stipendiary element which is essentially supplementary and supportive to the lay magistracy:[18]

> The Lord Chancellor has no plans to work toward the appointment of stipendiary magistrates in every town with a population exceeding 70,000. Stipendiary magistrates appointments are to commission areas and the Lord Chancellor will consider such appointments normally when he receives requests from those areas and he considers that the workload warrants that course. The Lord Chancellor has full confidence in the ability of the lay magistracy to cope with the bulk of work. The purpose of stipendiary appointments is to support the lay magistracy.

To be true to the principles of 'democratic consideration',[19] even this conservative model may have implications for trials conducted by stipendiary alone.[20] Certainly, it has long been suggested that the 'sound element' of lay experience should be retained in trials which means that stipendiaries should always sit with lay justices,[21] even though it has always been common for stipendiaries to sit alone in criminal matters so as to save time through not having to consult.[22]

In summary, with over 30,000 lay justices still operative within the system, it cannot be claimed that professionalism predominates. Nevertheless, stipendiaries are key figures in a growing number of magistrates' courts, and so their importance transcends their modest numbers. Yet, does their advance improve the quality of summary justice?

There are undoubted advantages in terms of speed, convenience and appropriate legal expertise, all matters which have a bearing on the delivery of justice. Nevertheless, it is rather less certain that professional justice is unfailingly superior to lay justice and should supplant it. After all, verdicts depend on facts as well as law, and there are many who rightly believe that the fresh lay minds of the jury are perhaps more accurate fact-diviners than lawyers. Even if that superiority in performance is dismissed as fanciful, community involvement and standard setting in summary justice is nevertheless highly desirable as a political and social policy and can be secured to some extent by the involvement of lay justices. It follows that a greater presence of stipendiaries should not affect boundary lines in the allocation of judicial work as between magistrates' courts and Crown Court. It has been suggested that a way of relieving pressure on the latter would be to reallocate

---

[16] Property qualifications for justices of the peace were abolished in 1906.
[17] A requirement as to residence was established by the Qualifications of the Justices of the Peace Act 1414.
[18] HC Deb vol. 220 col. 376 wa, 8 March 1993, John M. Taylor.
[19] *Report of the Royal Commission on the Selection of Justices of the Peace* (Cd 5250, 1919) p. 12.
[20] In the absence of a lay element, a safeguard adopted is that the stipendiary must give reasons for the verdict: Samuels, A., 'Vision for the future' (1991) 47(4) *The Magistrate*; Crowther, E., 'By god, is he right?' (1993) 157 *Justice of the Peace* 286.
[21] *Royal Commission on Justices of the Peace* (Cmd 7463, HMSO, London, 1948) para. 246; Lord Williams, 'Judges' in Bean, D., *Law Reform for All* (Blackstones, London, 1996) p. 74.
[22] *Royal Commission on Justices of the Peace* (Cmd 7463, HMSO, London, 1948) para. 244.

a class of cases for trial by the stipendiaries (or perhaps stipendiaries sitting with two lay justices).[23] Consideration could be given to an enhanced jurisdiction (up to two or three years' imprisonment) for a trial tribunal consisting of a stipendiary and two lay magistrates. However, this proposal has important implications for the function of the jury which is seen more effectively to embody the desired attributes of local lay involvement than even lay justices.

Balancing these factors, the Lord Chancellor's Department's Working Party report on *The Role of the Stipendiary Magistrate* concluded in 1996 that the appropriate role for stipendiaries is to supplement rather than to supplant lay magistrates, so the report advocates what are apparently only modest, largely managerial changes. First, it suggests greater clarity as to the special skills of stipendiaries and therefore their appropriate work allocation so as to make efficient and effective use of their talents. Their special skills are mainly legal and procedural expertise, court craft and speed, so an appropriate work diet includes technically complex issues, interlinked cases, matters involving national interests.[24] But there is encouragement for stipendiaries to undertake routine business, as has been made clear by the Lord Chancellor.[25] They differ in their rate and perhaps manner of dispatch of the load, but the nature of the load should not be exceptional. At the same time, there is wide recognition that hearings which either involve legal expertise or have to be timetabled over more than one day are likely to be especially appropriate for stipendiaries who have the expertise and time available. Such work is not common in most magistrates' courts. Of course, it would be equally possible to have allocation rules at either extreme of this suggestion. Stipendiaries could be fed exactly the same case diet as lay justices without exception, so that their main advantage would be efficiency rather than any form of craft or expertise. Conversely, stipendiaries could be supplied with special court lists, consisting entirely of items such as lengthy trials, complex legal cases and sensitive hearings. It is doubtful whether any court (perhaps outside one or two in London) could supply such a fare on a regular basis. One special area of workload to consider is the use of stipendiaries in Youth Courts. It is arguable that the use of stipendiaries sitting alone in these courts is inappropriate as there is meant to be more informality at such a hearing. A lay element is therefore desirable, and complaints have been raised when stipendiaries have sat alone.[26] However, the Crime and Disorder Act 1998, section 36, now allows Metropolitan Stipendiary magistrates to sit alone without proof of special circumstances.[27]

Next, the Report concluded that there should be an increase in the absolute number of stipendiaries. Furthermore, there should be a greater spread by appointments of 'semi-attached' stipendiaries (especially from London, where there is spare capacity) to multiple commission areas for up to 10 days per year per area.[28] Thus, consideration should be given to appointing stipendiaries to serve

---

[23] Bartle, R., 'Why stipendiaries?' (1986) 54(4) *Medico-Legal Journal* 236 at p. 245.

[24] Para. 5.3.

[25] Lord Chancellor's Department, *Judicial Statistics* (Cm 2623, HMSO, London, 1994) p. 93. But it is expected that stipendiaries will take cases lasting several days or ones involving difficult points of law.

[26] Gledhill, K., 'Youth on trial' (1994) 138 *Solicitors' Journal* 470.

[27] Compare Youth Courts (Constitution) Rules 1954 (SI No. 1711) r. 2, 12(3).

[28] Lord Chancellor's Department Working Party, *The Role of the Stipendiary Magistrate* (London, 1996) ch. 8.

within England and Wales, or within a more restricted jurisdiction but considerably wider than the present commission areas (possibly the Bar circuits). More imaginative use could be made of the existing Metropolitan stipendiaries, where the lay bench feels particularly squeezed.[29] A similar idea was put forward by the General Council of the Bar to the Royal Commission on Justices of the Peace but was viewed as having the practical difficulty of being able to predict when and where the stipendiary would be required and also courting the danger of discouraging lay justices.[30] More recently, the Lord Chancellor's Department has floated the idea of a unified stipendiary bench, each member with national jurisdiction to achieve the greatest flexibility.[31]

It is remarkable how modest these changes would be. Their implementation has been likewise hesitant, with the only tangible result being an increase in the maximum number of provincial stipendiary appointments from 40 to 50,[32] not enough to ensure national coverage, even 'semi-attached' cover. They do have more radical implications for London, where the roles are reversed and stipendiaries predominate. However, that issue is left for the future.

Finally, stipendiaries are not the only professionals who might be thought to threaten the local independence of lay magistrates in their judicial work. It is arguable that a more potent threat comes from the justices' clerks, who have been empowered under section 117 of the Courts and Legal Services Act 1990 (as amended) to undertake a range of judicial work on their own authority.[33]

The Centralisation of Local Justice

A further trend to be scrutinised for its impact on the standard of justice is the centralisation of local justice. One way in which centralisation can be achieved is again through the growing use of stipendiaries. On this ground, there is the fear that the concept of local justice will erode as the links with local communities, as reflected through the backgrounds, experience and outlooks of judicial appointments, are diluted. But are stipendiaries any less reflective of local interests than the lay magistracy, and is localism in any event consistent with justice?

In answer to the first two questions, lay magistrates do seem to view themselves as representing the locality and its values, so that 'a threat to the community is a threat to the magistracy (the custodians of the community) and vice versa.'[34] The supposition is that stipendiaries are more mobile and aloof appointees than lay magistrates, who must as part of their job description have links with the locality to which they are appointed.[35] Magistrates must live within 15 miles of the boundary of the Commission area.[36] In this way, the infusion of stipendiaries could

---

[29] See: Badge, P.G.N., 'The role of stipendiary magistrate' (1989) 45 (11) *The Magistrate* 196.

[30] Cmd 7463 para. 215.

[31] Lord Chancellor's Department, *Creation of a Unified Stipendiary Bench* (London, 1998).

[32] Maximum Number of Stipendiary Magistrates Order 1996, SI No. 1924.

[33] The Crime and Disorder Act 1998 s. 49 also gives greater powers to single magistrates. For the background, see Narey Report (Home Office, *Review of Delays in Criminal Justice System*, 1997); Lord Chancellor's Department, *The Future Role of the Justices' Clerk* (London, 1998).

[34] Brown, S., *Magistrates at Work* (Open UP, Buckingham, 1991) p. 111, 112.

[35] Resident magistrates are, of course, the model in Northern Ireland but even here identification with the locality is felt to be important: Report of a Committee on County Courts and Magistrates' Courts in Northern Ireland (Cmnd 5824, HMSO, London, 1974) para. 34.

[36] Justices of the Peace Act 1997, s. 6(1).

render justice a national rather than local concept – the nationalisation of justice. It must be admitted that the concept of geographically situated justice is itself troublingly vague, but such a 'bench ethos'[37] seems to be embedded in the alleged existence of such factors as a 'mass of situationally evolved knowledge'.[38] For example, one study found that 'differences in perceptions of local crime are important in explaining sentencing variation.'.[39] Interestingly, the same study seemed to show that the stipendiary is less influenced by local factors,[40] which might follow from the fact that they are far less likely to have spent their professional life (as private lawyers or court clerks) in that area and that they are far more mobile as judges, as they are regularly called to sit on benches outside their commission area.

As well as possible threats to localism from stipendiaries, probably a more serious trend is the managerialism and administrative consolidation which dilutes any claim to localism. Thus, the imposition of managerialism to local justice which has resulted in the closure of many courts and therefore the danger of distancing the local courts from the community,[41] a trend which continues despite the predictions of some.[42] This trend was given a boost by the Home Office's *Consultation Paper on the Size of Benches*[43] which pressed for the abolition of benches with fewer than 12 magistrates and for the reduction in petty sessional divisions. So the number of benches has been reduced from nearly 650 to under 400 as a result. Clerkships have also been whittled away from 307 in 1980 down to 209 in 1995. The number of magistrates' courts committees (105 in 1992) is also to be reduced substantially.[44] The administrative squeeze has also been backed by cash limits from 1992 onwards, all of which prompted the closure of smaller courthouses in favour of larger inner-city court buildings. This combination of changes could be said to have reduced localism in two ways. One is to remove the physical and symbolic link between localities and magisterial justice,[45] though one might argue that the geographical bounds of a 'community' are now considerably wider than they used to be because of the spread of the private motor vehicle, so that the shrinking of the court boundaries is in correspondence with the expansion in manageable drives to work, shops or entertainment. The other is to provide for more effective methods of central direction by the Lord Chancellor's Department, especially through the Magistrates' Courts Committees. The logical next step would be to rationalise further in terms of the provision of judicial administration. In this way, as justice becomes less localised, why should magistrates' courts

---

[37] Brown, S., *Magistrates at Work* (Open UP, Milton Keynes, 1991) p. 101.

[38] Carlen, P., *Magistrates' Justice* (Martin Robertson, 1976) at p. 75.

[39] Parker, H., Sumner, M. and Jarvis, G., *Unmasking the Magistrate* (Open UP, Milton Keynes, 1989) p. 82.

[40] *Ibid.*, p. 80.

[41] See *Magistrates' Courts: Report of a Scrutiny* (Home Office, 1989) (the 'Le Vay Report') Raine, J., *Local Justice* (T & T, Edinburgh, 1989); Raine, J. and Willson, M., *Managing Criminal Justice* (Harvester Wheatsheaf, Hemel Hempstead, 1993); Police and Magistrates' Courts Act 1994 Pt. IV; see Friedland, M.L., *A Place Apart* (Canadian Judicial Council, Ottawa, 1995) ch. 9; Alugo, C., Richards, J., Wise, G., Raine, J., 'The magistrates' court and the community' (1996) 160 *Justice of the Peace* 329.

[42] Raine, J. and Willson, M.J., 'Beyond managerialism in criminal justice' (1997) 36 *Howard Journal* 80.

[43] 1986. See: Raine, J.W. and Wilson, M.J., *Managing Criminal Justice* (Harvester Wheatsheaf, Hemel Hempstead, 1993) p. 106.

[44] Magistrates' Courts Service Inspectorate, *4th Annual Report* (1997–98 HC 248) para. 10.

[45] Concern on this ground is expressed by the Home Affairs Committee, *Report on Judicial Appointments* (1995–96 HC 52–I) para. 198.

buildings be distinct from Crown Court buildings? Why should there be separation of the staff working in them? And most controversial of all, in the absence of any practical need for, as opposed to abstract ideology of, localism, why is there a need for lay justices to reflect local connections? In this way, the very rationale of the lay bench comes into question:[46]

> Local knowledge, as every magistrate understood, was often a valuable aid to the work in the courtroom; indeed it was arguably the fundamental currency of the local justice process. Without it, was there sufficient justification for sustaining a volunteer-based magistracy?

Even if more characteristic of lay magistrates than of professional magistrates, is local justice either desirable or good quality justice?[47] A basic reason why stipendiaries are seen as exceptional must be that they do not comply with established features of English criminal justice which involve lay and local involvement. It follows that stipendiaries have historically been viewed as exceptional and, in a sense, irregular features of the system. Their introduction and deployment has often been founded upon pragmatic rather than principled grounds which are often negative rather than positive in nature – in other words because the 'normal' solutions are in a state of partial failure or crisis. The paradigmatic method of assigning guilt or innocence in the common law world is meant to be a jury. The jury has important symbolism for criminal justice – justice becomes communal rather than dictatorial, and the process involves the demystification of legal substance and process.[48] In its absence, justices of the peace may be an acceptable compromise so long as the following features pertain: they comprise local people and lay people (these reflect cherished attributes of the jury) and they confine their activities to less serious cases – ideally cases where liberty is not at stake. Thus, there are fundamental principles of democracy and the protection of individual rights which call for representative (and therefore predominantly lay) and local[49] involvement at all levels of justice. In this way, local justice can involve trial by one's peers, as well as benefiting from local knowledge and sensitivity to local needs.[50] So, all recent major studies have supported continuance of a fundamentally lay and local system. For example, the Royal Commission on Justices of the Peace in 1948[51] concluded that 'both on principle and on grounds of practical convenience, the present system ought to be retained . . .'. The *Le Vay Report* was also concerned that its reforms should not affect a model of 'an independent lay magistracy, delivering local justice in local courts. . . .'[52] This sense of 'local justice' was endorsed in the subsequent White Paper, *A New Framework for Local Justice*.[53] And it has been noted that the Lord Chancellor's Department's report on *The Role of the Stipendiary Magistrate* equally accepted the predominance of local lay justice.

---

[46] Raine, J.W. and Wilson, M.J., *Managing Criminal Justice* (Harvester Wheatsheaf, Hemel Hempstead, 1993) p. 116.
[47] See: Bankowski, Z.K., Hutton, N.R., McManus, J.J., *Lay Justice?* (T & T Clark, Edinburgh, 1987).
[48] See: Cornish, W.R., *The Jury* (Pelican, London, 1971).
[49] A requirement as to residence was established by 2 Henry V c. 1.
[50] Raine, J.W., *Local Justice* (T & T Clark, Edinburgh, 1989) pp. 30–32.
[51] Cmd 7463 para. 213.
[52] *Magistrates' Courts* (Home Office, London, 1989) vol.1 para. 12.2.
[53] Lord Chancellor's Department, (Cm1829, HMSO, London, 1992), para. 1.

On the other hand, despite the case for local lay justice, criticism arises whenever local difference actually emerges on the grounds that localism in this way infringes concepts of justice in the sense of equal treatment.[54] For example, Liberty complained in a report *Unequal Before the Law* in 1992[55] that like cases were not being treated alike in terms of magisterial custodial sentencing differentials, and the explanations are often that such disparities must be based on 'the proclivities of sentencers or . . . the sentencing traditions generated within local jurisdictions . . .'.[56] Disproportionate legal aid grants/refusals are also treated as problematic.[57] Conversely, professional, non-local background may actually assist independence by ensuring greater standardisation which will engender public confidence in judicial standards. Stipendiaries may then have an advantage of remoteness, but in reality, stipendiaries do not move from one commission area to another and so are just as likely as lay magistrates to pick up on local quirks and local needs.

While local involvement may be problematic in terms of its compliance with the universal nature of 'justice', it may serve other political ideals by helping to democratise and demystify the process of justice. The administration of local justice should be transparent and acceptable to the local populace, who should be educated in its operations. One way[58] to ensure this is to recruit them to its operations, as is supported by the Home Affairs Committee:[59]

> . . . we conclude that there is a role for lay magistrates in the justice system today. We consider that the administration of justice at a local level by members of the community may act as a bridge between the public and a court system which might otherwise seem remote.

Ultimately then, the case for local justice seems to rest in terms of public confidence and involvement in the criminal justice system – collective gains – rather than the achievement of justice to the individual. Assuming this primary aim does not actually produce a worse standard of justice for the individual, then it can legitimately be pursued. However, the recognition that this is a danger should lead to some curbs on the powers of the magistrates' courts so as to minimise the damage which this desirable social exercise in judicial democratisation might inflict on any individual defendant. Thus, it may be wise to remove, or at least severely curtail, the magistrates' powers to imprison[60] so as to minimise the impact of disparities in sentencing[61] which have consequences which are by no means

---

[54] Alugo, C., Richards, J., Wise, G. and Raine, J., 'The magistrates' court and the community' (1996) 160 *Justice of the Peace* 329.

[55] Custodial sentences made up 4.96 per cent of the total in 1990, but individual petty sessional divisions varied from 17.44 per cent to 0 per cent. See also: Hood, R., *Sentencing in Magistrates' Courts* (Stevens, London, 1962); Acres, D., 'Consistency and sentencing' (1987) 151 *Justice of the Peace* 343.

[56] Parker, H., Sumner, M. and Jarvis, G., *Unmasking the Magistrate* (Open UP, Milton Keynes, 1989) p. 16. See also: Tarling, R., *Sentencing Practice in Magistrates' Courts* (Home Office Research Study 56, Home Office, London, 1979).

[57] See: Young, R. and Wall, D., *Access to Criminal Justice* (Blackstone Press, London, 1996) ch. 7.

[58] Other ways have included open days, school visits and even community meetings (the magistrates' courts committees must meet in public at least once per year): Alugo, C., Richards, J., Wise, G. and Raine, J., 'The magistrates' court and the community' (1996) 160 *Justice of the Peace* 329 at p. 330.

[59] Home Affairs Committee, *Judicial Appointments Procedures* (1995–96 HC 52) para. 198.

[60] Liberty, *Unequal Before the Law* (London, 1992).

trivial.[62] In any event, the achievement of local justice cannot be secured if the lay justices actually appointed are not perceived as representative of the community. This problem will be considered next.

The Ownership of Summary Justice

A study by the House of Commons Home Affairs Committee, *Judicial Appointments Procedures*, expressed concerns that lay magistrates were not sufficiently representative of the community[63] and that the appointments process was partly to blame for this failing. Nor, might one add, is there any attempt to ensure accountability after appointment in any obvious sense of that term. So could the representativeness of lay justices be achieved more effectively?

Reform of the existing model of appointment of lay justices does not seem likely. The expectation of the Home Affairs Committee that a greater role for grace and favour establishment figures, in the shape of Lord Lieutenants, in the appointments process of magistrates as chairs of advisory committees will somehow enhance representativeness or public confidence seems very wide of the mark.[64] There are many praiseworthy initiatives being taken at a local level to recruit more widely, including the placing of advertisements. However, the reliance on volunteers along this path will always favour the retired (or at least non-employed), the politically active, and the comfortably-off.

An alternative (or perhaps additional) approach would be to co-opt magistrates from the community in the same way as jurors (save that service would have to extend over a longer period). This would cause difficulties and expense for the training programmes now thought necessary, and panels of three are less likely to be seen as representative than jury panels of 12.[65] Nevertheless, it would be a far more effective way both of ensuring representativeness and also of achieving the civic education of a wider section of the public.[66]

Another method of community involvement is by elections. Though the elected judges may not themselves be representative individuals, they can at least claim a mandate to represent community wishes and are subject to the periodic accountability of elections. Judicial posts in most states in the USA are elective, though elections bring with them the criticism of emphasising democratic credentials at the expense of constitutionalism. Thus, the vital role of the judiciary is to guard against majoritarianism and its crude impact on individual rights and unpopular minorities. By contrast, US judicial elections can be unsavoury 'high salience events' which reflect all too readily the will of 'the impassioned majority'.[67]

---

[61] See Parker, H., Sumner, M. and Jarvis, G., *Unmasking the Magistrate* (Open UP, Buckingham, 1989).

[62] McBarnet, D., 'Magistrates' courts and the ideology of justice' (1981) 8 *British Journal of Law & Society* 181.

[63] This is especially the case in London: Darbyshire, P., 'For the new Lord Chancellor – some causes for concern about magistrates' [1997] *Criminal Law Review* 861.

[64] Home Affairs Committee, *Judicial Appointments Procedures* (1995–96 HC 52) paras. 222, 225. The proposal was accepted by the Government: *Response to the Home Affairs Committee, Judicial Appointments* (Cm 3387, HMSO, London, 1996) para. 66.

[65] See *Williams v Florida* (1970) 399 US 78; *Clogrove v Battin* (1973) 413 US 149.

[66] In line with theories of assocative democracy (see: Hirst, P., *Associative Democracy* (Polity Press, Cambridge, 1994)), there are now proposals to open up local Government functions to citizen involvement (Department of the Environment, *Modernising Local Government*, 1998), so one might view magisterial work in the same light.

[67] Croley, S.P., 'The majoritarian difficulty: elective judiciaries and the rule of law' (1995) 62 *University*

Consequently, more 'open' versions of judicial elections seem to be gradually withering away in favour of a process of closed nomination of the professionally qualified followed by electoral confirmation.[68] One might summarise that elections, whether open or closed, could be useful devices for reinforcing the desired quality of localism, but these advantages may be at considerable cost to the fundamental characteristics of the judicial role such as actual and perceived independence and impartiality.

Conclusions

A balance of cultures, professional versus varied lay experience, national view versus parochialism, could help to maintain a healthy system which is neither too remote nor too beholden to a given local or professional clique. The result is not, however, a mixture. The predominant form of judicial actor should remain the lay justice, with stipendiaries in a supportive, complementary role – relieving un-manageable workloads or taking cases which lay justices find too hot or too heavy to handle. The quality of justice delivered by lay justices may be improved by some of the radical selection procedures set out earlier, though only at some cost in terms of training and support.

Another issue for the future is accountability, which should arise at two levels in a system which vaunts its localism. One is accountability for judicial work, a difficult objective to square with judicial independence. It may be said that there is legal accountability, such as through appeal to the Crown Court or by legal review in the Divisional Court. But legal cultures which are categorised as local are not discussed or approved by the general local public. One might argue that judicial independence would be compromised if they were, but these arguments have been faced down in regard to constabulary independence, in respect of which periodic local liaison committee meetings allow for consultation, report and complaint, though not direction or censure, by the public.[69] Secondly, there is still little accountability in administrative terms – all that is required is that each magistrates' courts committee must hold one meeting a year in public. As a result, there is only weak accountability between individual clerks and the magistrates' courts committees and between those committees and the paying (local) authority, yet accountability is not addressed in any of the recent policy papers. Perhaps the explanation is that new managerialism, which drives through changes such as the

---

of Chicago Law Review 689 at pp. 726, 734. Elections are not even a good method for producing a representative bench: p. 789. See also: Shapiro, M.H., 'USC Symposium on judicial election, selection and accountability' (1988) 61 Southern California Law Review 1555; Scheuerman, K.E., 'Rethinking judicial elections' (1993) 72 Oregon Law Review 459.

[68] For example, under the California Constitution, justices of the Supreme Court and the courts of appeal are subject to confirmation by the voters after being reviewed by the Judicial Nominees Evaluation Commission and the Commission on Judicial Appointments: http://ca94.election.digital. com/e/cand/judicial.html. Three California Supreme Court Justices were defeated in 1986 over attitudes to the death penalty: Thompson, R.S., 'Judicial independence, judicial accountability, judicial elections and the California Supreme Court' (1986) 59 Southern California Law Review 809. See also: Stephens, R.F., 'Judicial election and appointment at the State level' (1989) 77 Kentucky Law Journal 741; Canon, B.C., 'Judicial election and appointment at the State level' (1989) 77 Kentucky Law Journal 747; Handberg, R., 'Selection and retention of judges' (1994) 49 University of Miami Law Review 127; Achenbach, J., 'Selection and retention of judges' (1994) 49 University of Miami Law Review 155.

[69] See: Police and Criminal Evidence Act 1984, s. 106.

greater usage of stipendiaries, depicts consumers (including the local community) as consumers of services rather than active citizens. The opposition, from lay magistrates, has been pitched at an ideological level, but it is equally an ideology in which the relationship with the community is one way rather than reflexive. In other words, there is selection from the community but not necessarily responsiveness to it. However, the insertion of a professional magistracy does bring into question the justifiability and working of local justice and may, along with other changes, expose at the same time the strength of the ideology as well as the weaknesses of its application. If mechanisms of accountability were to be instituted, then the position of the stipendiary as local justice might actually become less anomalous, for there would be a link for professionals with community wishes not currently provided. Thus, not only lay justices would be able to claim that they represent community justice, and harmony of judge and judged could achieved by a more democratic method than a feeling in the bones of the magistrate.

The Performance of the Higher Criminal Courts

Despite for the most part being the processors of guilty pleas,[70] the judiciary in the Crown Court, Court of Appeal and House of Lords are seen as the chief practitioners of due process values. Undoubtedly, the accoutrements of due process are more in evidence – much fuller and freer legal advice, formal discovery and slow, deliberate and open procedures with a detached umpire. Yet these features will count for little if the judges exercise their wide discretions in favour of crime control models of justice in which guilt is largely assumed.

The fear that a judge can so influence trials as to contribute to miscarriages has unfortunately been realised all too readily in recent miscarriage cases.[71] The point is exemplified by the conduct of Bridge J (later Lord Bridge) in the *Birmingham Six* trial in Lancaster Castle in June 1975, as documented by James Wood in the Appendix to this chapter,[72] and by the grudging attitude of the Court of Appeal in the *Maguire* case which was criticised by the May Report.[73] Reduction of future error is most likely to be achieved by reforms to the systems of judicial appointments and training and by a variety of other reforms.[74]

Appointments

Deficiencies in the process of the appointment of the judiciary have long been debated. Though greater light has now been cast upon the mechanics of the

---

[70] Sanders, A. and Young, R., *Criminal Justice* (Butterworths, London, 1994) ch. 7.

[71] Compare the conduct of Judge Thayer in the trial of Sacco and Vanzetti in Massachusetts in 1921: Ehrmann, H.B., *The Case That Will Not Die* (W.H. Allen, London, 1970).

[72] Compare the vindication of judicial conduct by Lord Chief Justice Taylor, 'In defence of the judiciary' (1992) 142 *New Law Journal* 1673.

[73] May, Sir John, *Report of the Inquiry into the circumstances surrounding the convictions arising out of the bomb attacks in Guildford and Woolwich in 1974, Second Report* (1992–93 HC 296) paras. 1.4–8. The same attitude was displayed in the quashing of the conviction of Danny McNamee, the Court of Appeal claiming that he would still have been convicted 'as a matter of probability' even if full disclosure had been made: *The Times*, 18 December 1998 p. 15.

[74] See generally: Pannick, D., *Judges* (Oxford University Press, 1987); Harlow, C. (ed.), *Public Law and Politics* (Sweet & Maxwell, London, 1986) ch. 10; Brazier, R., *Constitutional Reform* (2nd ed., Oxford University Press, 1994) ch. 12.

system,[75] its actual nature still appears unsatisfactory since it owes rather too much to personal connections within the Bar and an emphasis upon the skill of advocacy.[76] The result is a judiciary drawn from a very narrow range of experience, social class, gender[77] and race which is often felt to be out of touch with common reality but which is self-perpetuating.[78] This defect is arguably more serious for magistrates than for higher judiciary, where the predominant characteristic is meant to be legal technical expertise rather than common-sense appraisal and on behalf of whom the jury can represent a cross-section of society. Nevertheless, as stated by the Home Affairs Committee in its report on *Judicial Appointments Procedures*, the judiciary cannot be representative but its composition does have an impact on public perceptions of it.[79] And any form of bias or narrowing of the field of possible candidates can result in appointments of the second-rate.

Therefore, it is suggested that the circle from which judges are drawn should be widened and might include, for example, solicitors, legal academics and especially the chairs of tribunals.[80] If it is not acceptable to select, for example, academics as judges, then at least more use could be made of their expertise in the drawing up of judgments especially in the Court of Appeal and House of Lords where, too often, curt and unreferenced statements are both unpersuasive and unclear. There is a system of judicial assistants in the Court of Appeal, but it involves part-time junior lawyers and confirms rather than alleviates the mediocre standards at which the judges currently aim in the articulation of their reasoning.[81] The use of law clerks in the US Supreme Court (since 1882) has become controversial, both in terms of their selection and role.[82] But there is no inevitability that only white male Harvard graduates should be employed or that judges should abdicate their responsibilities for selection of cases or the drafting of judgments; the point is to assist and enrich argumentation.

In addition, the process as well as the field must be altered. The present system is considered to involve too many 'cloak-and-dagger' tactics to secure confidence,[83] and it is also too amateurish to secure the best results.[84] Some changes

---

[75] See: Lord Chancellor's Department, *Judicial Appointments* (1986, 1990); Home Affairs Committee, *Judicial Appointments Procedures* (1995–96 HC 52).

[76] See: Law Society, *Judicial Appointments* (London, 1991); Bindman, G., 'Changing the judiciary' (1992) 142 *New Law Journal* 1035; Stevens, R., 'Unpacking the judges' (1993) 46 *Current Legal Problems* 1.

[77] As at 1 February 1998, 7 out of 97 High Court judges, 30 out of 547 circuit judges and 69 out of 862 recorders were female.

[78] A word-of-mouth appointments system is also arguably discriminatory: Bindman, G., 'Appointing judges without discrimination' (1991) 141 *New Law Journal* 1692; Hayes, J., 'Appointment by invitation' (1997) 147 *New Law Journal* 520.

[79] Home Affairs Committee, *Judicial Appointments Procedures* (1995–96 HC 52) para. 11.

[80] Sargant, T. and Hill, P., *Criminal Trials* (Fabian Research Series, London, 1986) p. 13; Partington, M., 'Training the judiciary in England and Wales: the work of the Judicial Studies Board' (1994) 13 *Civil Justice Quarterly* 319 at p. 322. But compare Home Affairs Committee, *Judicial Appointments Procedures* (1995–96 HC 52) para. 164. Some have suggested a professional judicial cadre: Mullin, C., 'Miscarriages of justice in the UK' (1996) 2(2) *Journal of Legislative Studies* 8 at p. 19.

[81] Graffy, C., 'The risks of justice on the cheap' (1997) Jan/Feb *Counsel* 16. There is no such system in the House of Lords: Lord Williams, 'Judges' in Bean, D., *Law Reform for All* (Blackstone Press, London, 1996) p. 75.

[82] Posner, R.A., 'Will the Federal courts of appeals survive until 1984?' (1983) 56 *Southern California Law Review* 761; Mahoney, J.D., 'The Second Circuit review – 1986–1987 term: foreword: law clerks: for better or for worse?' (1988) 54 *Brooklyn Law Review* 321; Oberdorfer, L.F. and Levy, M.N., 'On clerkship selection: a reply to the bad apple' (1992) 101 *Yale Law Journal* 1097; Mauro, T., 'Justices give key role to novice lawyers' (1998) *USA Today* 13 March.

[83] Mansfield, M., *Presumed Guilty* (Heinemann, London, 1993) ch. 20.

[84] Lord Williams, 'Judges' in Bean, D., *Law Reform for All* (Blackstone Press, London, 1996) p. 70.

have occurred in response to these criticisms – most evidently the advertising of vacant posts and the setting of criteria for appointment.[85] However, a more systematic approach would be to place the process within the hands of a body which is more clearly independent from professional ties than the present incumbents (who consist of the Lord Chancellor, as principally advised by the Lord Chief Justice, the Master of the Rolls, the Vice Chancellor of the Chancery and the President of the Family Division).[86] The idea of a Judicial Appointments Committee has been mooted over many years,[87] and its impact would not *per se* improve the representativeness of the judiciary so long as the principal criterion remains technical expertise[88] but it would enhance confidence.[89] The proposal was rebuffed by Lord Chancellor Mackay[90] and then by the Home Affairs Committee looking into judicial appointments.[91] Though adopted as a Labour Party policy guide in 1995, Lord Chancellor Irvine has also dropped the idea in favour of a continuation of secret soundings but with an annual report to Parliament,[92] a disappointing compromise which is not likely to achieve the objectives of net-widening, fairness, and confidence.

Another method of community confidence-building already canvassed in relation to magistrates is the use of elections, but a more likely route for some degree of popular approbation of the higher judiciary is by way of legislative confirmation. This occurs for appointments to the US Supreme Court, which are subject to confirmation by the Senate. Despite some highly politicised debates (such as in the rejection of Robert Bork in 1987),[93] there does now seem to be some interest in this process within England and Wales, especially in anticipation of the greater political role to be played by the courts in response to the Human Rights Act 1998.[94]

Training

Substantial improvements have been secured in the training of judges (including supervision of the training of the lay magistracy[95]) since the reconstitution of the Judicial Studies Board in 1985.[96] However, two serious criticisms may be levied against the current model. The first concerns the scale of its activities. Only just

---

[85] This began in 1993 and extended to High Court posts in 1998. See Wheatley, D., 'And a good judge too?' (1994) 144 *New Law Journal* 784; Lord Chancellor's Department, *Developments in Judicial Appointments Procedures* (London, 1994).

[86] See Rozenberg, J, *The Search for Justice* (Hodder & Stoughton, London, 1994) p. 72.

[87] See Abel-Smith, B. and Stevens, R., *In Search of Justice* (Penguin Press, London, 1968) p. 192; Law Society, *Judicial Appointments* (1991) para. 5.01; JUSTICE, *The Judiciary in England and Wales* (London, 1992) p. 2.

[88] Stevens, R., *The Independence of the Judiciary* (Clarendon Press, 1993) p. 163.

[89] Thomas, C. and Malleson, K., *Judicial Appointments Commissions* (Discussion Paper 6/97, Lord Chancellor's Department, London 1997).

[90] *The Times*, 22 April 1993 p. 9.

[91] Home Affairs Committee, *Judicial Appointments Procedures* (1995–96 HC 52) para. 142.

[92] (1997) *The Times*, 27 May 1997 p. 1; (1997) 94/39 *Law Society's Gazette* p. 4.

[93] Rader, R.A., 'The independence of the judiciary: a critical aspect of the confirmation process' (1989) 77 *Kentucky Law Journal* 767.

[94] Hague, W., 'Change and tradition: thinking creatively about the constitution' (http://www. conservative-party.org.uk/, February 1998).

[95] See Justices of the Peace Act 1997, s. 64; Reeves, P., 'Sitting in judgment' (1994) 91(20) *Law Society's Gazette* 20, 23.

[96] See: Judicial Studies Board, *Reports*, 1979–82 (1983), 1983–87 (1988), 1987–91 (1992), 1991–95 (1995), 1995–97 (1997). See Heaton-Armstrong, A., 'Judges should go back to school' (1993) 143 *New Law Journal*; Partington, M., 'Training the judiciary in England and Wales: the work of the Judicial Studies Board' (1994) 13 *Civil Justice Quarterly* 319.

over 2 per cent of judicial time (measured in days rather than weeks or even years as in Continental systems) is expended on initial or refresher training,[97] and there is little scope for either expansion or elaboration of the information provided within existing financial resources or the available time of the judiciary to tutor or be tutored.[98] The result is especially deficient in regard to training after appointment,[99] a feature criticised by the *Runciman Report* but which prompted only a marginal increase in the programme in 1996 which did not meet the target of refresher training every three years, though this is now in sight.[100] There are also special difficulties with training the very significant proportion of those acting in the Crown Court who are part-timers, namely recorders and assistants.[101] Only so much can be achieved by the current model of 'stealthy evolution'.[102]

The second defect, insularity, arises from the insistence of the Board that instruction should for the main part be provided by established representatives of the profession to be entered.[103] In other words, tutor-judges are seen as the predominant and only truly credible teachers of judges,[104] and there is hostility to the idea that other professionals within the legal system, law teachers or legal interest groups have an equally important perspective and would combat inefficient and unskilled teaching methods and the perpetuation of insular judicial misconceptions and myths.[105] The insularity may now be on the wane, with more mixed personnel involved in training in regard to the Children Act 1989, the Criminal Justice Act 1991 and the Human Rights Act 1998 and a much broader array of speakers being used in refresher seminars. There is also a welcome move towards professionalisation with directors of studies (still judges, of course) being appointed after 1995.[106]

A final criticism raised by the Runciman Commission was the need for greater judicial awareness of gender issues; however, the Judicial Studies Board has exceeded the requirement by adding human awareness training on top of the existing work carried out through its Ethnic Minorities Advisory Committee (which was created in 1991).[107]

Other reforms

Though training may reduce the frequency of poor judicial performance, there is still a need for monitoring both as to output and quality. The *Runciman Report* expressed some disquiet in this regard:[108]

---

[97] Judical Studies Board, Report 1987–91, para. 31.

[98] *Ibid.* 1991–95, paras. 2.1, 2.12, 2.13. See also Lord Williams, 'Judges' in Bean, D., *Law Reform for All* (Blackstone Press, London, 1996) p. 73.

[99] See Judicial Studies Board, *Report* 1991–95 (1995) para. 2.19.

[100] *Runciman Report*, ch. 8 para. 97; Judicial Studies Board, *Report* 1991–95 (1995) para. 4.14, 1995–1997 (1997) para. 2.3.

[101] As at 1 February 1998, there were 547 circuit judges, 862 recorders, 354 assistant recorders (plus 61 in training). See Rozenberg, J., *The Search for Justice* (Hodder & Stoughton, London, 1994) pp. 109–111.

[102] Partington, M., 'Training the judiciary in England and Wales: the work of the Judicial Studies Board' (1994) 13 *Civil Justice Quarterly* 319 at p. 335.

[103] Judicial Studies Board, *Report* 1987–91 (1991) paras. 4, 11, 11.3.

[104] Judicial Studies Board, *Report* 1991–95 (1995) paras. 2.9, 4.4.

[105] See *Runciman Report*, ch. 8 para. 100.

[106] Judicial Studies Board, *Report* 1991–95 (1995) para. 2.18.

[107] *Runciman Report*, ch. 8 para. 95; Judicial Studies Board, *Report* 1991–95 (1995) para. 2.23; Reeves, P., 'Racial awareness – training for the legal profession' (1994) 158 *Justice of the Peace* 55.

[108] *Runciman Report*, ch. 8 para. 98.

> We are . . . less than satisfied that adequate monitoring arrangements are in place and find it surprising that full-time judges seldom if ever observe trials conducted by their colleagues . . . we recommend that the judiciary as a profession should have in place an effective formal system of performance appraisal.

The view of the *Runciman Report* that there should be more monitoring of performance during training and performance appraisal thereafter added weight to the more fully argued call by JUSTICE for a Judicial Standards Commission to measure performance and to respond to complaints.[109] Reforms along these lines had already been vetoed by Lord Lane.[110] However, in response to the later pressure, Lord Chief Justice Taylor instituted a more informal system of inter-judicial appraisal,[111] save that the performance of Assistant Recorders is now more formally monitored.[112] It follows that there is arguably more oversight of judicial performance in summary process, where the Magistrates' Courts Service Inspectorate could at least note mechanical problems such as delay, though this still leave problems such as inattentiveness or rudeness. The case of Harman J, who resigned in February 1998 over the deplorable delays he had created in his handling of a civil case,[113] illustrates clearly that all levels of the judiciary, full-timers included, would benefit from systematic and independent oversight, a far better approach than awaiting appeals, complaints under Article 6 of the European Convention on Human Rights (via the Human Rights Act) or 'the more informal scrutiny of the media'.[114] The experience of North America suggests that formats can be devised which are not threatening to judicial independence.[115]

Indicators of Judicial Performance

Have the judges in the higher criminal courts in fact responded appropriately to the criticisms of performance acknowledged by the Court of Appeal in cases from the late 1980s onwards and further highlighted by the *Runciman Report*? The shortcomings already detailed indicate that there has been no systemic approach to

---

[109] JUSTICE, *The Judiciary in England and Wales* (London, 1992) p. 14. See Salter, D., 'Some observations on a report by Justice – the judiciary in England and Wales' (1993) 12 *Civil Justice Quarterly* 329.

[110] Zander, M., *A Matter of Justice* (Oxford University Press, 1989) p. 129.

[111] Reeves, P., 'Sitting in judgment' (1994) 91/20 *Law Society's Gazette* p. 20. These ideas were rejected by Lord Taylor: Rozenberg, J., *The Search for Justice* (Hodder & Stoughton, London, 1994) pp. 117–121.

[112] Government Response to the Home Affairs Committee, *Judicial Appointments* (Cm 3387, 1996) para. 14. Before a trainee assistant recorder, for example, is authorised to sit alone, he or she must undertake an induction programme, which includes the training course run by the Judicial Studies Board, but also involves a period of sitting-in with an experienced circuit judge in the Crown Court (the pupil-master judge) who is required to report to the Lord Chancellor. In addition, the pupil-master judge in respect of assistant recorders (and the equivalent supervising judges in respect of certain other categories of judicial office-holders) is expected now to undertake an element of in-court observation so as to provide further advice and appraisal to newly appointed part-time judges and to enable better assessment of their suitability for appointment to full-time judicial office (see *Runciman Report*, ch. 8 para. 97).

[113] *The Times*, 14 February 1998 pp. 1, 2.

[114] HL Debs. vol.574 col.220wa, 16 October 1996, Lord Mackay.

[115] For further discussion, see Friedland, M.L., *A Place Apart* (Canadian Judicial Council, Ottawa, 1995) ch. 7; Malleson, K., 'Judicial training and performance appraisal: the problem of judicial independence' (1997) 60 *Modern Law Review* 655

reform. In particular, because of the failures in the appointments process, one cannot be sure that a new mind-set has been instilled within the judiciary, though the contemporary judges have learnt to be less openly irritated by claims of miscarriage.[116] Certainly, they are 'no longer the right-wing ideologues some people still imagine them to be.'.[117] Lord Taylor was depicted as more liberal and more open than Lord Lane,[118] and, in turn, Lord Bingham has actually praised TV programmes like *Trial and Error* and *Rough Justice*, a far cry from the 'mere entertainment' disparagement of Lord Lane.[119] Rather than further personalise this survey, one might consider instead more objective performance indicators. Those chosen relate to the following issues: the admissibility of evidence obtained by police questioning or other police tactics; the interpretation of the 'right to silence'; the attitude of the Court of Appeal to its own powers; and its attitude to miscarriages of justice in general.

Admissibility of evidence obtained by police questioning or other police tactics The reforming sweep of PACE, which produced a coherent and comprehensive overhaul of pre-trial policing, encouraged new, more interventionist judicial attitudes in regard to the actions of the police in securing evidence to be put before the courts, whether on arrest or during subsequent detention as part of the process of interrogation.[120] By 1990, it was possible to argue that the courts viewed the regulation of police practices as an important aspect of procedural fairness, and amongst the reasons given was disillusionment with the police.[121] These changes have been mainly founded upon section 78 of PACE.[122] Its impact has to be considered necessary to achieve fairness in the proceedings. Nevertheless, within their own terms, the English judges have been active,[123] basing themselves largely on the principles of protection of the fundamental rights of the accused as they impact either upon the reliability of the evidence or, more generally, the integrity of the system.[124] The rate and impact of judicial intervention has been described as 'striking', with not only many cases turning on such issues but also many defendants actually succeeding in their arguments.[125]

Though the thresholds of admissibility in sections 76 and 78 of PACE can prevent the admission of unreliable or unconscionable confessions, these gate-keeping devices have their limits. For instance, reliability is not to be understood as ruling out confessions simply on the grounds that they were made whilst the suspect was experiencing the abnormal stress and pressure which is part and parcel of the purpose of police interrogation.[126] The judges will not therefore readily

---

[116] See the remarks of Lords Denning and Lane in the Appendix to this chapter.

[117] Rozenberg, J., *The Search for Justice* (Hodder & Stoughton, London, 1994) p. 6.

[118] *Ibid.*, p. 34.

[119] Willis, J., 'Justice by television', *The Guardian*, 30 July 1997 p. 7.

[120] See further Chapters 4, 9. It is intended to give only an overview in this passage.

[121] Feldman, D., 'Regulating treatment of suspects in police stations: judicial interpretations of detention provisions in PACE' [1990] *Criminal Law Review* 452 at p. 468.

[122] See Grevling, K., 'Fairness and the exclusion of evidence under section 78 of the Police and Criminal Evidence Act 1984' (1997) 113 *Law Quarterly Review* 667. See further Chapter 9.

[123] See Birch, D., 'The Pace hots up' [1989] *Criminal Law Review* 95; Berger, M., 'The exclusionary rule and confession evidence' (1991) 20 *Anglo-American Law Review* 63.

[124] Ashworth, A., 'Excluding evidence as protecting rights' [1977] *Criminal Law Review* 723.

[125] See Zander, M., *The Police and Criminal Evidence Act 1984* (2nd ed., Sweet & Maxwell, 1990) p. 201. See also 3rd ed., 1995, Pt. VIII.

[126] See *R v Goldenberg* (1988) 88 Cr App R 285; *R v Crampton* [1991] Crim LR 277.

admit that 'normal' people have the potential to make false confessions.[127] Nor will they convert the rules about admissibility into disciplinary sanctions against the police, so as to enforce compliance with decent standards of behaviour.[128] The American exclusionary rule is consequently considered to be of dubious value: uncertain and unproductive in terms of outcomes,[129] as well as of questionable relevance to England and Wales with its less fragmented and more regimented police forces.[130] The courts have also insisted that account be taken of fairness to public as well as to defendant, which allows for ends to justify means unless a long-term view is taken of the value of the integrity of the criminal justice system.[131]

Further misgivings arise from the fact that it is in any event the expressed intention of Parliament that the normal protections for police detainees are to be reduced in the case of terrorist suspects by reference to special legislation in the Prevention of Terrorism (Temporary Provisions) Act 1989 and the Northern Ireland (Emergency Provisions) Acts 1996–8. As the *Final Report* of the May Inquiry comments:[132]

If all the safeguards of PACE are necessary to avoid miscarriages of justice then it must be recognised that in terrorist cases greater risks of injustice are accepted than in the ordinary course of criminal cases.

There has been no evident response from the judiciary to respond to these fears by construing narrowly the relevant powers.

Interpretation of the curtailment of 'right to silence' The championing of due process values is also a trait absent from the judicial reactions to the curtailment of the 'right to silence' under the Criminal Justice and Public Order Act 1994, sections 34 to 37.[133] On the whole, the judges have been accommodating towards

---

[127] See Pattenden, R., 'Should Confessions be Corroborated?' (1991) 107 *Law Quarterly Review* 319; Gudjonsson, G.H., *The Psychology of Interrogations, Confessions and Testimony* (Chichester, 1992).

[128] See *R v Alladice* (1988) 87 Cr App R 380; *R v Delaney* (1988) 88 Cr App R 338; *R v Keenan* [1989] 3 WLR 1193; *R v Canale* (1990) 91 Cr App R 1; *R v Dunford* (1990) 91 Cr App Rep 150. Compare: Oaks, D.H., 'Studying the exclusionary rule in search and seizure' (1970) 37 *University of Chicago Law Review* 665; Kaplan, J., 'The limits of the exclusionary rule' (1974) 26 Stanford Law Review 1027; Loewy, A.H., 'The Fourth Amendment as a device for protecting the innocent' (1983) 81 Michigan Law Review 1229; Orfield, M.W. Jr., 'The exclusionary rule and deterrence' (1987) 54 *University of Chicago Law Review* 1016.

[129] See Loewy, A.H., 'The Fourth Amendment as a device for protecting the innocent' (1988) 81 *Michigan Law Review* 1229.

[130] Philips Commission, paras. 4.126, 4.127.

[131] See *R v Smurthwaite* [1994] 1 All ER 898 at p. 903; Choo, A.L.-T., *Abuse of Process and Judicial Stays of Criminal Proceedings* (Clarendon Press, Oxford, 1993) p. 13. Compare *R v Powell* [1992] RTR 270 at 276.

[132] May, Sir John, *Report of the Inquiry into the circumstances surrounding the convictions arising out of the bomb attacks in Guildford and Woolwich in 1974, Final Report* (1993–94 HC 449) para. 21.8.

[133] See Dennis, I., 'The Criminal Justice & Public Order Act' [1995] *Criminal Law Review* 4; Pattenden, R., 'Inferences from silence' [1995] *Criminal Law Review* 602; Broome, K., 'An inference of guilt' (1997) 141 *Solicitors' Journal* 202; Tregilgas-Davey, M., 'Inferences from silence' (1997) 161 *Justice of the Peace* 525, 'Adverse inferences and no comment interviews' (1997) 141 *Solicitors' Journal* 500; Williams, J., 'Inferences from silence' (1997) 141 *Solicitors' Journal* 566; Black, J.S.W., 'Inferences from silence' (1997) 141 *Solicitors' Journal* 741, 772. The same point can be applied to the judicial treatment of other evidential safeguards: Zuckerman, A., 'Miscarriages of justice and judicial responsibility' [1991] *Criminal Law Review* 492.

the changes and see themselves as part of the project rather than a break on its progress.[134] There has been little reflection of the disquiet about its utility and acceptability, including to a majority of the Runciman Committee.[135] Accordingly, it has been accepted that it has general application to a wide range of cases,[136] and that neither legal advice to remain silent[137] nor mental backwardness or instability[138] block the drawing of inferences. The progress has been swifter and more pronounced than the judicial handling of equivalent measures in Northern Ireland.[139]

Next, there has been no determined effort to read in the constraints imposed by the European Convention. In a prescient remark, Lord Taylor had suggested that if Ernest Saunders were to be successful in the European Court of Human Rights after failing in the Court of Appeal, then the English legislature would have to consider giving effect to the European ruling, though the courts could do little since 'Parliament has made its intentions quite clear' though it might still be possible for the judges to exclude evidence under section 78 of PACE given 'the background setting' of compulsion.[140] In the event, despite the reversals for the United Kingdom Government in *Saunders* v *United Kingdom*[141] and in *(John) Murray* v *UK*[142] and despite the fact that these cases have emerged post-enactment and so would not require defiance of the sovereign will of Parliament, neither legislature nor courts have reacted to Lord Taylor's lead.[143] For example, in *R* v *Staines, R* v *Morrissey*,[144] the Court of Appeal under Lord Bingham viewed the position as 'very unsatisfactory' but not sufficiently so as to manufacture an interpretation which disapplied the irreconcilable provisions under section 177 of the Financial Services Act 1986.

Attitude of the Court of Appeal to its own reformed powers Perhaps the most telling indicator of whether there has been any change in attitudes of the judiciary towards miscarriages of justice concerns the willingness of the Court of Appeal to police the performance of the courts themselves. Much depends on changes in attitude, since the new wording in the Criminal Appeal Act 1995 makes little objective difference.[145] Instead, the *Runciman Report* relies upon blandishments directed towards the Court of Appeal to be readier to overturn jury verdicts without providing any clear legislative signal that they must do so.[146]

---

[134] As predicted by Zander, M., 'You have no right to remain silent' (1996) 40 *Saint Louis University Law Review* 659 at p. 671.

[135] See Chapter 5.

[136] *R* v *Cowan* [1995] 4 All ER 935; *R* v *Argent* [1997] 2 Cr App R 27.

[137] *R* v *Condron* [1997] 1 Cr App R 185.

[138] *R* v *Friend* [1997] 1 WLR 1433; *R* v *Law-Thompson* [1997] *Criminal Law Review* 674; *R* v *A* [1997] *Criminal Law Review* 883.

[139] See Jackson, J.D., 'Curtailing the right to silence' [1991] *Criminal Law Review* 404, 'Inferences from silence' (1993) 44 *Northern Ireland Legal Quarterly* 103, 'Interpreting the silence provisions' [1995] *Criminal Law Review* 587.

[140] *R* v *Saunders* [1996] 1 Cr App R 463 at p. 478.

[141] Appl. no. 19187/91, 1996–VI, (1997) 23 EHRR 313.

[142] Appl. no. 18731/91, 1996–I, (1996) 22 EHRR 29.

[143] See Nash, S. and Furse, M., 'Self incrimination, corporate misconduct and the ECHR' [1995] *Criminal Law Review* 854; Munday, R., 'Inferences from silence and the European Human Rights law' [1996] *Criminal Law Review* 370.

[144] [1997] 2 Cr App R 426. See also *R* v *Law-Thompson* [1997] *Criminal Law Review* 674; *R* v *Kelly and Sandford, The Times*, 29 December 1998.

[145] But see Smith, J.C., 'Criminal appeals and the CCRC' (1995) 145 *New Law Journal* 533, 572, 'Appeals against conviction' [1995] *Criminal Law Review* 920.

[146] *Runciman Report*, ch. 10 paras. 46, 59.

Since the 1995 Act has come into force,[147] the cases suggest no sudden taste for harder scrutiny or deeper scepticism. This attitude was expressed in general in *R v Graham*,[148] while in *R v Hickmet*,[149] the Court felt it necessary to emphasise that the new grounds of appeal were no narrower than the previous version – hardly encouraging the thought that they could actually be wider. The loss of the proviso to section 2 of the revised Criminal Appeal Act 1968[150] has made little difference; the Court said in *R v Foley*[151] that if the strength of the case remained overwhelming, then the convictions would be upheld as 'safe'. Throughout, the Court emphasises that the safeness of a conviction is the criterion and so points to the interests of the system rather than integrity of rights. It follows that appeals have failed even where basic unfairness has occurred through non-disclosure (as in *R v Mills*)[152] or where a trial judge's mistake (a ruling on admissibility) influenced a plea of guilt and therefore avoided the proper testing of evidence (*R v Chalkley and Jeffries*).[153] There is a certain arrogance in these rulings; how can the Court be sure the same outcome would have occurred if the processes had been observed properly? Such rulings ignore the integrity of the system and the primacy of jury decision making.[154] Similarly, in the case of Eddie Guilfoyle, the Court admitted fresh evidence under section 23 but then cast doubt in advance on whether it was likely to have the slightest impact, hardly evidence of an open mind.[155]

Statistical evidence[156] as to appeals reveals some rise in both applications and especially of quashings around the time of the major Irish miscarriage of justice cases. One might surmise that the attendant publicity encouraged more appeals, though other factors could include rapid changes in criminal justice laws leading to errors and uncertainties and greater contact with lawyers through *pro bono* work.

In the light of the foregoing statistics, it may be commented that no dramatic change has occurred in appeal practices, and some commentators have attributed the fundamental difficulty as residing in excessive deference to the finality of jury system.[157] Certainly, these considerations, along with the necessary rationing of judicial resources, mean that it will never be sufficient simply to claim innocence by way of an appeal.[158] But changes in attitude towards the proper transaction of

---

[147] For the earlier period, see Thornton, P., 'Miscarriages of justice: a lost opportunity' [1993] *Criminal Law Review* 926.

[148] [1997] 1 Cr App R 302.

[149] [1996] *Criminal Law Review* 588.

[150] 'Provided that the Court may, notwithstanding that they are of opinion that the point raised in the appeal might be decided in favour of the appellant, dismiss the appeal if they consider that no miscarriage of justice has actually occurred.'

[151] *The Times*, 17 March 1997. See also *R v Farrow* (1998) *The Times*, 20 October.

[152] [1997] 3 WLR 458.

[153] [1998] QB 848.

[154] An exceptional case where misdirections and mistakes in conduct of the trial resulted in overturning of a conviction occurred in the case of Elizabeth Forsyth, the legal adviser of fugitive businessman Asil Nadir: *The Times*, 18 March 1997 p. 29.

[155] *R v Guilfoyle* [1996] 3 All ER 883.

[156] Source: Home Office, Criminal Appeals in England and Wales 1995 and 1996 (Home Office, London, 1998). These figures in Table 10.1 slightly underestimate judicial intervention, since around 150 appeals per year are abandoned.

[157] Nobles, R. and Schiff, D., 'The never ending story' (1997) 60 *Modern Law Review* 293 at p. 303.

[158] Friendly, H.J., 'Is innocence irrelevant? Collateral attack on criminal judgments' (1970) 38 *University of Chicago Law Review* 142.

Table 10.1: Appeals against conviction to the Court of Appeal.

Year	Total appellants	Convictions quashed (%)
1985	1397	169 (12)
1986	1892	162 (9)
1987	1192	134 (12)
1988	1267	131 (10)
1989	1578	174 (11)
1990	1634	198 (12)
1991	1711	223 (13)
1992	1871	299 (16)
1993	1967	314 (16)
1994	2462	320 (13)
1995	2551	277 (11)
1996	2403	263 (11)

fundamental judicial business is possible – for example, it has been achieved in sentencing during the past decade when severity has markedly increased without legislative change (at least until the Crime (Sentences) Act 1997). Lord Chief Justice Bingham has attributed this trend to the impact of 'the vocal expression of opinion by influential figures that custody is an effective penalty'.[159] Presumably if judges can be influenced in their perceptions as to sentencing, then they can be influenced as to the viability of appeals. Unfortunately, the *Runciman Report* provided no clear signal that there were to be major changes, while, in the intention of the Government, the subsequent Criminal Appeal Act 1995 simply 'reflects the current practice of the Court of Appeal'.[160] It is not that no change could be secured or that finality and respect for the jury had to predominate to this extent over respect for individual rights; rather, a decision was taken that it was politically inopportune to alter the balance.

Attitude of the judiciary to miscarriages of justice in general In the view of some commentators, there was a retrenchment of attitudes once the Runciman Commission had reported, which reflected 'a determination . . . to draw a firm line under the era of miscarriages of justice.'.[161] Even before that time, the handling of the appeals of the *Maguire Seven* was grudging and criticised by the May Inquiry.[162] More recently, Lord Justice Rose in the *Bridgewater Four* case graciously said that 'this is another case of a miscarriage of justice which is a matter of regret to this Court'. But he then assumed the arrogant position of speaking for an imaginary jury following an imaginary trial, and managed to conclude that 'There remains evidence on which a reasonable jury properly directed could convict.'.[163] Clearly, the assertion that the Court of Appeal, when it quashes a conviction, 'does not

---

[159] NACRO, *Criminal Justice Digest*, vol. 95, January 1998 p. 20.

[160] Lord Chancellor's Department, Home Office and Law Officers' Department, *The Royal Commission on Criminal Justice: Final Government Response* (Home Office, London, 1996) paras. 178, 180.

[161] Jessel, D., 'The Lund Lecture: television, science and the law' (1997) 37 *Medicine, Science and the Law* 4 at p. 14.

[162] See Chapters 2, 6.

[163] *The Times*, 31 July 1997 p. 4. See further Chapter 2 and the case of Danny McNamee (*The Times*, 18 December 1998, p. 15).

pronounce on the innocence or guilt of those whose convictions no longer stand'[164] was not true in the past and is not true now.

There are three more specific indicators of retrenchment. One is the refusal to respond to criticisms of how their summing-up on the facts can introduce bias, as illustrated by the *Birmingham Six* case in the Appendix.[165] The Court of Appeal rejected any change in practice in *R v Brower*.[166] Likewise, the layout of the courts still involves the use of a dock.[167] The third indicator is the obstacles placed in the path of investigative journalists seeking to find evidence about miscarriages of justice.[168] Until a judgment in the High Court in 1996, the Prison Service had increasingly refused permission for access by journalists invited to talk to prisoners who protested their innocence unless they signed an undertaking that any material obtained during the visit would not be used for professional purposes, and in particular for publication by the journalist or anyone else. Such visits had been undertaken as friends rather than in an explicit journalistic capacity, for the rules about access would normally disbar such visits:[169]

> Visits to inmates by journalists or authors in their professional capacity should in general not be allowed and the governor has authority to refuse them without reference to headquarters . . . Where, exceptionally, a journalist or author is permitted to visit an inmate in his or her professional capacity, or is allowed general access to the establishment, he or she will be required to give a written undertaking that no inmate will be interviewed except with the express permission in each case of the governor and the inmate concerned, that interviews will be conducted in accordance with such other conditions as the governor considers necessary, and that any material obtained at the interview will not be used for professional purposes except as permitted by the governor. No inmate should be permitted to accept any payment or gratuity in exchange for an interview or for a radio or television appearance.

Two journalists (Bob Woffinden and Karen Voisey) had refused to sign the undertaking. In *R v Secretary of State for the Home Department, ex parte Simms and O'Brien*,[170] Latham J, referring to freedom of expression under Article 10 of the European Convention, found for the prisoners and, implicitly, for the journalists. It was recognised that the involvement of journalists at this post-appeal stage is often vital. Neither prisoner had legal advice, and a responsible journalist would in any event want to act responsibly by checking facts. However, the Court of Appeal concluded that a convicted prisoner had no right to communicate orally

---

[164] Nobles, R. and Schiff, D., 'Miscarriages of justice: a systems approach' (1996) 59 *Modern Law Review* 299 at p. 299.

[165] Wolchover, D., 'Should judges sum up on the facts?' [1989] *Criminal Law Review* 781; Mansfield, M., *Presumed Guilty* (Heinemann, London, 1993) p. 252.

[166] [1995] *Criminal Law Review* 746. Summing-up is limited in Scotland: *King v HM Advocate* 1985 SCCR 322.

[167] Sargant, T. and Hill, P., *Criminal Trials* (Fabian Research Series, London, 1986) p. 12; Law Society, *Submission* (1991) para. 3.79; Liberty, *Submission* (1991) p. 46; Zander, M., 'The Royal Commission's Crown Court survey' (1992) 142 *New Law Journal* 1730.

[168] See Chapter 13.

[169] Prison Service Standing Order number 5, s A, paras. 37, 37A.

[170] *The Times*, 17 January 1997. See Foster, S., 'Free speech and the regulation of solicitors' correspondence' (1997) 147 *New Law Journal* 252; Hill, P., 'The voice inside' (1997) 94/3 *Law Society's Gazette* 25.

with the media through a journalist. Lord Justice Kennedy concluded that the restriction was:[171]

> . . . part and parcel a sentence of imprisonment . . . He can no longer go where he wishes. He is confined. He can no longer speak to those outside prison or receive visits from anyone other than his lawyer and his relatives and friends . . . Lest it be thought that the efforts of Simms and O'Brien to establish their innocence are being some way unfairly curtailed it is worth remembering that they can still have access to lawyers and correspond with journalists – just like any other prisoner.

So, Lord Justice Kennedy emphasised that the prisoners remained free to correspond with the journalists by post.[172] But this right is also significantly fettered in the case of those wishing to dispute their convictions, since they are then subject to the constraints of Standing Ord 5, s. B, which deals with correspondence. Paragraph 34 of that section provides:

> General correspondence . . . may not contain the following: (9) material which is intended for publication or for use by radio or television (or which, if sent, would be likely to be published or broadcast) if it . . . is about the inmates' own crime or past offences or those of others, except where it consists of serious representation about conviction or sentence or forms part of serious comment about crime, the processes of justice or the penal system.

This is not to say there should be complete freedom of access, for that might cause a serious risk of distress to victims and their families. But in many cases, safeguards could be imposed through the defence lawyers who hold the case papers – that access should be granted in appropriate circumstances and subject to undertakings as to the material published about the case. After all the Home Office and the police do not seem averse to discussions or even reconstructions of solved crimes, so it is control of the message which seems to be important.

By way of balance, the Court of Appeal has given a warm welcome to the Criminal Cases Review Commission. Thus, Rose LJ, in *R v Mattan*,[173] observed that:

> the Criminal Cases Review Commission is a necessary and welcome body, without whose work the injustice in this case might never have been identified . . . no one associated with the criminal justice system can afford to be complacent . . . injustices of this kind can only be avoided if all concerned in the investigation of crime, and the preparation and presentation of criminal prosecutions, observe the very highest standards of integrity, conscientiousness and professional skill.

---

[171] *R v Secretary of State for the Home Department, ex parte Simms and O'Brien, ex parte Main* [1998] 2 All ER 491 at p. 501.

[172] But they may be prohibited from making telephone calls to the media: *R v Secretary of State for the Home Department, ex parte Bamber* (1996); *Bamber v UK*, Appl.no. 33742/96, [1998] EHRLR 110.

[173] *The Times*, 5 March 1998.

However, whether the same attitude will be taken if faced with errors of more recent origin or if the referrals become a flood rather than a trickle remains to be seen.

The final proviso is that there has been a considerable improvement in the treatment of witnesses and victims in the courts process. However, it is noticeable that the main movers in these changes have either been pressure groups (Victim Support) or the official agencies (such as the Court Service).[174] The judges have been less adaptable, for example in regard to rules designed to protect rape survivors.[175] So the improvement in the plight of these court users has tended to be motivated by administrative concerns for the 'consumers' of court services rather than by a judicial conversion to the centrality of the protection of rights.

Conclusions

The higher judiciary are now more aware of the possibility of pre-trial abuses and error than previous generations. They are also (with some exceptions) becoming much more aware of how to present themselves to the press and public as being informed and fair. However, until systemic changes take place within the areas of appointments, training and support facilities, it is unlikely that there will be a sustained change in their approach to allegations of miscarriages of justice.

---

[174] See especially Courts Service, *Courts Charter* (HMSO, London, 1995).
[175] See Chapter 2.

Appendix – Extracts from the Transcript of the Trial of the *Birmingham Six*, Lancaster, June 1975[176]

James Wood

Though legally correct in every respect, Bridge J brought his authority to bear upon the jury so as to ensure the outcome he clearly desired.[177] He commenced his summing-up by reassuring the jury of the quality of the advocacy they had heard:

> All counsel have presented their cases with the utmost skill . . . no valid point has been missed on either side . . .

However, he then revealed that he had formed a clear view as to which side had been the more persuasive:

> The Judge is not an advocate for any party, or he certainly should not be. He tries in summarising the evidence to hold the scales fairly and to present a balanced picture of the evidence on both sides . . . Some Judges tell juries that in doing that they will express no views of their own . . . I never say that to any jury, because I think that is attributing to oneself a superhuman capacity. I do not think any of us can be so detached . . . I have naturally formed an impression of the conclusion to which the evidence leads . . . and I think, however hard a judge tries to be impartial, inevitably his presentation of the evidence is bound to be coloured by his own view.

Lest the jury should be left in any doubt as to what his view was or which side he favoured, he proceeded to tell them the reason for one of their long absences from court:

> I had to hear all the evidence about the confessions, both from the police witnesses and from the defendants . . . I decided, as you know, that the evidence was admissible.

Thereafter, the judge divided up his summing into chapters and, at the conclusion of each, chose to make comments damning of the defence contentions. A few examples will suffice to give the flavour of this approach.

---

[176] See: *The Times*, 16 August 1975 p. 1, *The Times*, 31 March 1976 p. 9, [1980] 2 All ER 227, [1981] 3 WLR 906, [1988] 1 WLR 1, *The Times*, 29 January 1988 p. 5, *The Times*, 22 March 1988 p. 1, (1988) 88 Cr. App. R 40, *The Times*, 1 April 1991, [1992] 2 All ER 417.

[177] See also Mansfield, M., *Presumed Guilty* (Heinemann, London, 1993) ch. 20.

First, when dealing with the conflict of scientific evidence between Dr Skuse (for the prosecution) and Dr Black (for the defence), Bridge J commented:

I have read the transcript of Dr Black's evidence and I discover that there is a point when I ask him a question. I said to him 'Dr Black, is this conclusion of yours based on anything other than your theorising?' and he said 'Oh, my Lord, to talk of theorising is rather unfair, is it not?' Is it? If Dr Black was not theorising, what was he doing? I am afraid that I have made my views on this issue . . . pretty plain.

Similarly, when dealing with the alleged beatings and confessions, Bridge J rehearsed the evidence which was capable of supporting the defence version of events and dismissed it. In response to Dr Harwood, the prison doctor who gave evidence of the defendants' injuries and their probable infliction by the police, Bridge J commented:

. . . can you believe one single word of what Dr Harwood says? There are inescapably many perjurers who have given evidence. If Dr Harwood is one of them, is he not the worst? The profession of medicine is an honourable and noble one, and doctors, I had always supposed were dedicated not only to the interests of their patients but also were men of integrity and truth. If this man has come to this court deliberately to give you false evidence, he is certainly not fit to be a member of the honourable profession upon which, by perjuring himself, he has brought terrible shame.

Of the wounds seen by the defence solicitors prior to their clients' beatings in prison, he said:

Is it entirely coincidence that [they] all showed discoloration of the chest, scratch marks, scrawls and scrapes. Are those the sort of injuries that the police are likely to inflict – obviously visible but not one would have thought causing any intense pain? If a man wants to inflict injuries upon himself, what more obvious place in which to do it than by scratching his chest?

Finally, he tried to make the police conspiracy to deceive and fabricate alleged by the defence sound so outrageous as to be far-fetched:

If the defendants are giving you honest and substantially accurate evidence, there is no escape from the fact that the police are involved in a conspiracy to commit a variety of crimes which must be unprecedented in the annals of British criminal history.

The jury were by this time no doubt well satisfied that the views of the judge were reasonable and that their duty was to absolve the police by convicting the defendants. What is surprising is that it took the jury until the following day to reach the required verdict.

The woeful performance of the judiciary continued in the later proceedings connected with the *Birmingham Six*. Thus, during the appeal in March 1976, Lord Chief Justice Widgery highlighted his lack of concern for the men's plight and his lack of attention to the evidence by stating that he could not recall the origin of Walker's black eye – but he doubted whether it mattered very much. The men's injuries at the hands of the police were nothing 'beyond the ordinary'.

Next, after the *Six* had begun civil proceedings for assault against the police, Lord Denning struck out their action and showed again the true colours of the judiciary:[178]

> If the six men win, it will mean that the police were guilty of perjury, that they were guilty of violence and threats, and the confessions were involuntary and were improperly admitted in evidence and that the convictions were erroneous. That would mean the Home Secretary would either have to recommend that they be pardoned or he would have to remit the case to the Court of Appeal. This is such an appalling vista that every sensible person in the land would say: It cannot be right these actions should go further.

When the case was referred back to the Court of Appeal in 1987, the judges again indicated their hostility to the defendants. Lord Chief Justice Lane concluded the 168 page judgment with these words:

> As has happened before in References by the Home Secretary to this Court . . . the longer this hearing has gone on the more convinced this court has become that the verdict of the jury was correct.

Even at the second, and final, reference in 1991, it was the concession of the prosecution rather than insight from the court that made the outcome certain. Thus, the court indicated at a preliminary hearing that it would not be spoiling its Christmas by looking at the papers and so securing an early release.

---

[178] *McIlkenny v Chief Constable of West Midlands Police Force.* [1980] 2 All ER 227 at pp. 239, 240.

11

Post-conviction Procedures

Nick Taylor with Mike Mansfield

Introduction

In the last decade the Court of Appeal has quashed the long-standing convictions of the *Guildford Four*, the *Maguire Seven*, the *Birmingham Six* and the defendants in a host of other now notorious miscarriages of justice.[1] The pressure created by the intensity and scale of such mistakes led the Government to establish the Royal Commission on Criminal Justice (the 'Runciman Commission')[2] which reported in 1993. As Sanders and Young commented,[3] 'never before had the due process protections for suspects against wrongful conviction appeared to require such urgent repair work.'. However, such urgent repair work would not be forthcoming:[4]

> The Report of the Royal Commission on Criminal Justice (Runciman Commission) is a sham. It is a document that is slip-shod in its use of empirical evidence, slippery in its argumentation, and shameful in its underlying political purposes.

Though the then Home Secretary, Kenneth Baker, had said that its 'aim . . . will be to minimise so far as possible the likelihood of such events happening again',[5] it was surprising then that no detailed analysis of any wrongful convictions took place, especially of those cases which motivated the very establishment of the Commission itself.

Whilst it is accepted that some mistakes in a criminal justice process are an inevitable consequence of human fallibility, the health of that process may be evaluated not only on the number of errors it may make but also (amongst other factors) on its ability to recognise and rectify those mistakes. The failure of the British criminal justice system in regard to both the recognition and the rectification of its mistakes in recent years has been abject. Therefore, as part of its remit,

---

[1] For a brief summary of these major cases, see Chapter 2.

[2] Royal Commission on Criminal Justice, *Report* (Cmnd 2263, HMSO, London, 1993).

[3] Sanders, A. and Young, R., *Criminal Justice* (Butterworths, London, 1994) p. 2.

[4] Bridges, L., 'Normalising injustice: The Royal Commission on Criminal Justice', (1994) 21 *Journal of Law and Society* 20. See also, McConville, M. and Bridges, L., *Criminal Justice in Crisis* (Edward Elgar, Aldershot, 1994).

[5] Bridges, L., 'Normalising injustice: The Royal Commission on Criminal Justice' (1994) 21 *Journal of Law and Society* 20.

the Runciman Commission deliberated upon 'the arrangements for considering and investigating allegations of miscarriages of justice when appeal rights have been exhausted'.[6] There was almost unanimous agreement for reform in this area though little agreement on the form it should take.[7] It was of little surprise therefore that the Runciman Commission recommended that an independent body would take over the role exercised by the Home Office in the post-appeal structure. The Government largely accepted the proposals and implemented them in the Criminal Appeal Act 1995. This Act set up the independent Criminal Cases Review Commission which commenced its work in April 1997.[8] There are, of course, a wide range of other reforms that are necessary to reduce the number of wrongful convictions, some of which are considered elsewhere in this book. However, the aim of this chapter is to consider the reforms brought about by the Criminal Appeal Act 1995 in relation to the establishment of the Criminal Cases Review Commission and to evaluate its potential to provide a greater level of accessibility to the Court of Appeal. The reforms made in relation to the Court of Appeal itself will also be considered to determine if an efficient and effective and fair safety net to root out miscarriages of justice has finally been established.

Up to this point, for an appellant who maintained he or she had been wrongfully convicted but whose appeal under section 1 of the Criminal Appeal Act 1968 had been unsuccessful, the only option available to secure a further review of the case prior to the Criminal Appeal Act 1995, would be to lodge a petition with the Home Office.[9] Under section 17 of the Criminal Appeal Act 1968 the Home Secretary was empowered to refer a case back to the Court of Appeal where a person had been convicted on indictment, for a new determination as to conviction or sentence or both, as 'he thought fit'. The Court of Appeal then treated the referral as if it were a 'normal' appeal.[10] This power could be exercised at any time, even after the usual time limit for appeals had been exhausted or the Court of Appeal had refused leave to appeal. Alternatively, in rare cases the Home Secretary could choose to grant a pardon, though they were largely granted only in cases involving minor offences where there was no right of appeal, or in summary cases where a reference to the Court of Appeal was not available.[11] As a result, the final

---

[6] *Runciman Report*, ch. 11 para. 1.

[7] For example, see Buxton, R., 'Miscarriages of justice and the Court of Appeal' (1993) 109 *Law Quarterly Review* 66; O'Connor, P., 'The Court of Appeal: re-Trials and tribulations' [1990] *Criminal Law Review* 615; Wadham, J., 'Unravelling miscarriages of justice' (1993) 143 *New Law Journal* 1650; Thornton, P., 'Miscarriages of justice: a lost opportunity' (1993) *Criminal Law Review* 926; JUSTICE, *Remedying Miscarriages of Justice* (London, 1993); Mansfield, M., *Presumed Guilty* (Heinemann, London 1993).

[8] See generally Home Office, *Criminal Appeals and the Establishment of a Criminal Cases Review Authority* (HMSO, London, 1994); Thornton, P., 'Righting the wrongs' in Birks, P.B.H. (ed.), *Pressing Problems in the Law Volume 1: Criminal Justice and Human Rights* (Oxford University Press, 1995); Owers, A., 'Not completely appealing' (1995) 145 *New Law Journal* 353; Smith, J.C., 'Criminal appeals and the CCRC' (1995) 145 *New Law Journal* 533, 572, 'Appeals against conviction' [1995] *Criminal Law Review* 920; Malleson, K., 'A broad framework' (1997) 147 *Justice of the Peace* 1023; Bindman, D., 'Righting wrongs' (1997) *Law Soc Gazette* 94/2 12; Malet, D., 'The new regime for the correction of miscarriages of justice' (1995) 159 *Justice of the Peace* 716, 735.

[9] *R v Pinfold* [1988] 1 QB 462. The Court of Appeal held that it had no jurisdiction to entertain a second application for leave to appeal in the same case even where fresh evidence had been discovered since the earlier appeal.

[10] Criminal Appeal Act 1968, s. 17(1)(a).

[11] Further, see, Smith, A.T.H., 'The prerogative of mercy, the power of pardon and criminal justice', [1983] *Public Law* 398; Wolfgarten, A., 'Free pardon', (1986) 130 *Solicitor's Journal* 157.

safeguards of the criminal process against such miscarriages of justice operated at the sole discretion of the Home Secretary. The role of the Criminal Cases Review Commission in respect of alleged wrongful convictions is in many ways similar to that previously operated by the Home Office. It has no power to determine the status of cases for itself but, if certain criteria are established, can refer a case back to the Court of Appeal. In order to determine its potential effect, therefore, one must consider the critical differences between the two procedures.

Preparing the Application

Traditionally, the process whereby the Home Secretary might refer a case back to the Court of Appeal took a considerable amount of time, thereby rendering it of little practical value to those serving shorter sentences. Even in the most serious of cases the Home Secretary rarely moved on his own initiative.[12] In practice, a convicted person had to persuade the Home Secretary to act by forwarding a petition to the Home Office. As the Home Office, acting through its C3 department, received around 700–800 such petitions every year,[13] it was vital that an individual petition was clearly written and well drafted if it was to catch the eye of the relevant officials. On receiving a petition civil servants within the Home Office would look for any new and relevant considerations contained within it which had not previously been dealt with by the Court of Appeal. If a prisoner was unable to present coherently and precisely these often technical issues, the case would not be considered further. In some circumstances a prisoner may have been able to persuade a legal adviser to work on their behalf for little or no remuneration if the case appeared to represent a gross injustice, but such occasions were rare. Failing this the support of friends and family could be invaluable in ensuring that the case retained media exposure and possibly the support of influential public figures.[14] Voluntary organisations such as JUSTICE and Liberty may have been able to provide assistance in some cases, though the sheer demand for their help meant that they had reluctantly to ignore a number of cases through a lack of funds.[15] Thus, at the initial filtering stage in the post-appeal process a wrongfully convicted person may already have lost their final opportunity to secure justice through their inability to construct for themselves a convincing petition, or may simply lack the necessary funds to enlist the assistance of a legal adviser.

The establishment of the Commission is designed in part to remove some of these initial practical obstacles from the petitioner. Though in the vast majority of cases an applicant will bring his or her own case to the attention of the Commission, this does not necessarily have to be the case. Section 14 of the 1995 Act allows the convicted person to apply to the Commission, or indeed anyone

---

[12] HC Debs. Standing Committee B, col. 39, 23 March 1995.

[13] Home Office, *Memoranda* (1991) p. 20, para. 4.44.

[14] In 1982, the Home Affairs Select Committee commented that, 'in practice the [Home Office] decision to act may depend upon the amount of pressure that is brought to bear on the Home Secretary by people of influence': *Report on Miscarriages of Justice* (1981–2 HC 421), para. 10. See also *Government Reply* (Cmnd 8856, 1983); Tregilgas-Davey, M., 'Miscarriages of justice within the English legal system' (1991) 141 *New Law Journal* 668; Brandon, R. and Davies, C., *Wrongful Imprisonment* (Allen and Unwin, London, 1973) ch. 6.

[15] Following the establishment of the Commission, JUSTICE announced that it would gradually give up its casework on individual miscarriages and return to its original, more policy-oriented oversight of the criminal and civil legal systems: *The Times*, 17 June 1997 p. 41.

acting on their behalf. Furthermore, the Commission is also given the power to consider a case without any application having been made. The possibilities of this arising would appear to be in cases where, for example, the application of one party may throw doubt upon the conviction of a co-defendant or where evidence unearthed in one case renders a series of convictions open to doubt, as occurred, for example, with a number of cases dealt with by the now disbanded West Midlands Serious Crime Squad.[16] In theory this represents a change in emphasis from a body very reluctant to encourage applications to one more dedicated to rooting out miscarriages of justice.[17] However, given that the Commission will undoubtedly have a heavy caseload, certainly in its initial stages, the extent of its proactive role may be considerably limited in practical terms by financial constraints at the very least.

For the majority who will have to bring their own case to the attention of the Commission a user-friendly application form is available, though its use is not essential. Such a form is intended not only to help the applicant structure the case but will also ensure as far as possible that the Commission elicits the essential information it requires as soon as possible. The guidance offered by the form could also have the effect that an applicant may be able to present a reasonably strong case without legal assistance, or is able to obtain effective assistance within the very narrow legal aid boundaries which operate at this stage in the process. The ability to carry out this task without legal assistance will, however, be dependent upon how effectively an applicant is able to draft the application to satisfy the criteria the Commission chooses to use to filter the cases it receives.

The 1995 Act does not provide any statutory guidance as to the criteria to be used by the Commission when filtering or prioritising its workload, but 'informal' criteria will inevitably develop over time. The process of making an application to the Commission will therefore not be a simple form-filling exercise but will require an understanding of how the Commission will view certain cases and types of evidence. The benefit of legal advice to ensure that the case is presented as effectively as possible will consequently be increasingly invaluable if a case is to receive the attention it merits. The value of legal assistance at this stage in the criminal process is emphasised considerably when it is recognised that those people in the most difficult position when formulating a petition, namely those of limited ability and resources are also, as the major miscarriages of justice have illustrated, those most likely to suffer injustice.

The Runciman Commission suggested that 'adequate arrangements for granting legal aid'[18] should be made to persons making representations to the Commission. The Government's response was to ensure that legal assistance could still be obtained under the 'Green Form' scheme as was the case when formulating a petition to the Home Office, and it was claimed that this would be 'adequate' as a solicitor would not be required once the Commission began its non-adversarial investigations. Thus, the provision of legal aid was not addressed in the 1995 Act. Nonetheless, even taking into consideration the more user-friendly application procedure, the basic two hours of advice initially available under the 'Green Form'

---

[16] See Chapter 2.

[17] The term 'miscarriage of justice' in this sense is restricted to wrongful convictions and unjust sentences. For a detailed consideration of the meaning of the term see Chapter 2.

[18] Quoted by the *Runciman Report*, ch. 11 para. 32.

scheme cannot be sufficient in any but the most straightforward of cases. Though the Commission will be engaged in non-adversarial investigations when considering a case before it, the applicant's solicitor could still be a vital contact in clarifying a particular case. If the applicant is unable to retain legal services, it could prove to be considerably detrimental. This may result in a number of cases continuing to be fought primarily by dedicated journalists and pressure groups. Given that the poor quality of the petitions produced for the Home Office was counterproductive for all parties in terms of wasted time and resources, extensions to the 'Green Form' scheme must be more readily granted to improve the quality of justice both expected and received. The Legal Aid Board anticipates an increase in demand for legal aid under the Green Form scheme when the Commission becomes fully operational. One can only hope that this extra drain on resources will not militate against the possibility of extensions being granted.[19]

Consideration of the Application

Under the previous referral process the initial hurdle of preparing and presenting the petition was considerable. A petition before the Home Office was initially evaluated by civil servants who, operating within strict self-imposed guidelines, would not consider referring cases to the Home Secretary without new evidence or other considerations of substance not available at the original trial. If such evidence was not forthcoming, this would invariably result in a simple rejection of the application. If the petition, however, appeared to provide *prima facie* grounds for re-examining the case, then further investigations could be carried out. Given that C3 was vastly under-staffed[20] and under-resourced for the task it was expected to perform, the quality of such examinations was open to doubt. In some situations the relevant police force was asked to re-investigate the case, though it was somewhat naive to expect them to unearth their own or their colleagues' potential misconduct.

   Following any re-investigation, if C3 was of the opinion that a miscarriage of justice might have occurred, the matter would then be passed on to the Home Secretary who held the final decision in regard to a referral to the Court of Appeal. However, as far as the Home Secretary was concerned, the overriding principle governing the use of his discretionary power was the need to avoid the appearance of any executive interference with the role of the judiciary. The position was summed up by the Home Office:[21]

   Successive Governments have taken the view that it is fundamental to our system of justice that questions of guilt or innocence are matters for the court to decide, free from interference from ministers. Juries are arbiters of fact and it is not for the Home Secretary to seek to set aside a verdict simply because he or others who have interested themselves in a case have drawn a different conclusion about a convicted person's guilt based on their own assessment of the evidence which was before the court. Similarly, questions of law are matters for the judge, not the Secretary of State; it is not for him to substitute his view on such questions.

---

[19] Legal Aid Board, *Annual Report 1995–6* (1995–6 HC 505) p. 38, para. 6.12.

[20] In 1995 C3 comprised 21 staff at the Home Office; there were 3 officials in Northern Ireland.

[21] Home Office, *Memoranda* (1991), para. 4.5.

Therefore, the Home Secretary considerably limited his statutory discretion and would normally only refer a case if there was 'new' evidence available.[22] The effect of this criterion was considered by Sir John May:[23]

> . . . there is no doubt that the criterion so defined was and is a limiting one and has resulted in the responsible officials within the Home Office taking a substantially restricted view of cases to which their attention has been drawn . . . The very nature and terms of the self imposed limits . . . have led the Home Office only to respond to the representations which have been made to it in relation to particular convictions rather than to carry out its own investigations into the circumstances of a particular case . . .

The Runciman Commission in turn commented that 'the role assigned to the Home Secretary . . . under the current legislation is incompatible with the constitutional separation of powers as between the court and the executive.'[24] This intractable problem could only be overcome by a body truly independent of the executive and therefore unfettered by the constitutional constraints experienced by successive Home Secretaries.

The constitutional independence of the Commission is provided for in section 8(2), whereby it 'shall not be regarded as the servant or agent of the Crown or as enjoying any status, immunity or privilege of the Crown . . . '. Though the Home Secretary must prepare an annual report for Parliament on the work and progress of the Commission,[25] he is not involved with the selection procedure, does not determine the number of staff, does not set the working structure of the Commission, and crucially, is not involved in its decision-making role. Appointments, however, are made by the Crown on the recommendation of the Prime Minister contrary to the view of the Runciman Commission that members be appointed by the more apolitical Lord Chancellor.[26] Though this potentially allows the possibility of political influence compromising the independence of the body, the fact that the selection procedure has complied with the requirements of the Nolan Committee[27] on *Standards in Public Life* suggests some degree of political independence. However, as the Nolan Committee found that supporters of the country's governing party were disproportionately appointed to quangos,[28] it remains a disappointment that the 1995 Act did not preclude entirely political motivations for appointments by excluding politicians from the process.

Applications for membership were publicly advertised,[29] and the actual selection procedure was run by the Home Office. Candidates were interviewed, independent-

---

[22] The Home Secretary's decision not to refer a case to the Court of Appeal under s. 17 was susceptible to challenge by way of judicial review, see *R v Secretary of State for the Home Department, ex parte Garner* [1989] COD 461; *R v Secretary of State for the Home Department, ex parte Hickey (No. 2)* [1995] 1 WLR 735. The self-imposed limitations have, however, been held to be lawful see *R v Secretary of State for the Home Department, ex parte Pegg* [1991] COD 46; *R v Secretary of State for the Home Department, ex parte McCallion* [1993] COD 148.
[23] *Runciman Report*, ch. 11 para. 7.
[24] *Ibid*, ch. 11 para. 9.
[25] Criminal Appeal Act 1995, sch. 1, para. 8.
[26] *Runciman Report*, ch. 11 para. 14; Criminal Appeal Act 1995, sch. 1, para. 1.
[27] *Committee on Standards in Public Life* (Cmnd 2850, 1995).
[28] *Ibid*. vol.1, p. 70, para. 22.
[29] HC Debs, vol 256, col 25, 6 March 1995.

ly assessed and 'rigorously tested for their analytical skills'.[30] At least one third of the Commission's membership must be legally qualified, and at least two thirds 'shall be persons who appear to the Prime Minister to have knowledge or experience of any aspect of the criminal justice system . . .'.[31] Though the Runciman Commission suggested that the independence of the Commission would be emphasised further if its Chair was not a serving member of the judiciary, this too was rejected by the Government. As established in April 1997 the Commission has 14 members, ten of whom are part-time. They will have fixed terms of five years renewable to a maximum of ten years.[32]

The apparent desire to appoint members with wide-ranging legal experience in addition to a perspicacious lay element must also be welcomed when compared with the cohort of civil servants responsible for evaluating petitions in C3 who lacked any formal legal training. The Government considered that 'the most important qualifications for the work which the [Commission] will undertake are likely to be an ability to assess and interpret facts and behaviour; patience and sensitivity; and an open-minded determination to get to the root of what are often complex and enigmatic problems'.'[33] Whilst these are valuable qualifications there must also be a strong commitment to uncovering miscarriages of justice.[34] Chris Mullin MP asserted that 'it is important that the Commission is not seen as any old quango, but as a body that includes members with a track record of scepticism towards the official version of events.'.[35] The appointment of a Chairman, Sir Frederick Crawford, who is a prominent member of the Freemasons, does not outwardly inspire confidence that this will be achieved regardless of his personal characteristics.[36] Mullin further suggested that the Commission should be served by people of the calibre of Ludovic Kennedy and Paul Foot who have worked tenaciously to uncover injustice in the past, perhaps in place of some of the prosecutors, accountants and businessmen who make up a half of the Commission.[37] However, the chief executive of the Commission has recently insisted that 'we have a team of people who are very committed to rooting out miscarriages.'.[38] Whilst this must be a minimum prerequisite for appointment to the Commission, it is, as Schiff and Nobles recognise, unlikely that the Prime Minister would recommend the appointment of, for example, members of an organisation such as Liberty who have dedicated their careers to such objectives and may be more willing to refer cases to the Court of Appeal.[39] Instead, the current Commission

---

[30] Stacey, G., 'Taking a case to the Criminal Case Review Commission' (Proceedings of a Seminar held in Belfast, 12 April 1997, British Irish Rights Watch, 1997) p. 15.

[31] Criminal Appeal Act 1995, s. 8(6).

[32] Schedule 1, para. 2(3)–(5).

[33] Home Office, *Criminal Appeals and the Establishment of a Criminal Cases Review Authority* (HMSO, London, 1994) para. 81.

[34] See Wadham, J., 'Unravelling miscarriages of justice' (1993) 143 *New Law Journal* 1650.

[35] HC Debs, Standing Committee B, col 39, 23 March 1995.

[36] See *The Times*, 16 August 1996, p. 2; *The Guardian* 15 August 1996, p. 1.

[37] The first Commissioners were Sir Frederick Crawford (Chair, ex-University Vice-Chancellor), Laurence Elks (corporate lawyer), Jill Gort (barrister and tribunal chair), Tony Foster (chemicals business executive), Karamjit Singh (ex-Police Complaints Authority), Fiona King (ex-CPS), Professor Leonard Leigh (London School of Economics), James McKeith (forensic psychiatrist), David Kyle (ex-CPS), John Leckey (coroner), Barry Capon (local government), Edward Weiss (accountant), John Knox (ex-SFO), Baden Skitt (ex-police).

[38] Stacey, G., 'Taking a case to the Criminal Case Review Commission' (Proceedings of a Seminar held in Belfast, 12 April 1997, British Irish Rights Watch, 1997) p. 16.

[39] Schiff, D. and Nobles, R., 'Criminal Appeal Act 1995: the semantics of jurisdiction' (1996) 59

'membership is heavily weighted towards the prosecuting authorities',[40] and it is perhaps unfortunate that it also largely reflects the white, male, middle class background that is so often a feature of judicial institutions.

In order to refer a case to the Court of Appeal the Commission is given statutory guidance rather than retaining the discretion available to the Home Secretary. The Commission, under section 13(1), must 'consider that there is a real possibility that the conviction . . . would not be upheld were a reference to be made . . . ' . This 'real possibility' can be realised through 'an argument, or evidence, not raised in the proceedings . . . '. This is effectively wider than the Home Office review and may ensure the criteria for referrals are more easily satisfied. No longer will there be a need to provide 'new evidence' as interpreted by the Home Office, which was a cause of many failed petitions; evidence which was available at the original trial but not used may also be advanced. This change is welcome. Whilst respect should be paid to the principle of finality in judicial proceedings, this must bow, under the requisite conditions, to the interests of justice in an individual case. The Home Office minister also explained that the section would permit a referral if, for example, 'incompetent advocacy prevented an important aspect of the applicant's case from being put to the jury.'.[41] If such criteria cannot be fulfilled, a reference can still be made if there are 'exceptional circumstances which justify . . . it.'.[42] Such exceptional circumstances may include, for example, where the court has developed the law by accepting arguments which it previously had rejected.[43]

Clearly, the referral criteria outlined in the 1995 Act would initially appear to be more favourable to applicants. However, this largely depends upon how the Commission choose to interpret such words and how receptive the Court of Appeal is to receiving such cases. In addition, the criteria would appear to be little different from the test ultimately used by C3, and clarified by Simon Brown LJ in *R v Secretary of State for the Home Department, ex parte Hickey (No. 2).*[44] He stated, 'the Secretary of State should to my mind ask himself this question: could the new material reasonably cause the Court of Appeal to regard the verdict as unsafe?'.[45] The new test under the 1995 Act, 'is there a real possibility that the conviction . . . would not be upheld . . . ', will still mean that the Court of Appeal will have to be second-guessed but that would appear to be unavoidable given the present machinery whereby the Commission has no power to determine a case for itself and the Court of Appeal must give its own independent decision in every case. The interpretation of 'real possibility' in section 13 would appear to be vital. During the Committee Stage of the Criminal Appeals Bill the minister responsible simply stated that the word 'real' makes 'possibility' slightly firmer.[46] Were this to be interpreted restrictively, however, it could represent a considerable hurdle to an

Modern Law Review 573 at p. 578.

[40] Mansfield, M., 'Pressure points' (1997) 35 *Red Pepper* 15.

[41] HC Debs. Standing Committee B, col. 126, 30 March 1995.

[42] Criminal Appeal Act 1995, s. 13(2).

[43] It is interesting to note that when the words 'exceptional circumstances' appeared on the Commission's application form and were submitted to the Plain English Campaign, they were substituted with the words 'very rare': Stacey, G., 'Taking a case to the Criminal Case Review Commission' (Proceedings of a Seminar held in Belfast, 12 April 1997, British Irish Rights Watch, 1997) p. 22.

[44] [1995] 1 All ER 490.

[45] *Ibid.*, at p. 496.

[46] HC Debs. Standing Committee B, cols.133, 134, 30 March 1995.

applicant. The ultimate interpretation of this phrase by the Commission will be largely dependent upon the attitude adopted by the Court of Appeal. Undoubtedly the Home Office were influenced by judicial pronouncements of disapproval of their referrals,[47] and this in turn was reflected in the fact that they invariably only referred cases virtually guaranteed to succeed.[48] Certainly, under the 1995 Act the executive will no longer be seen as interfering with the role of the judiciary and the Court of Appeal may as a result prove to be more receptive to referrals than in the past. If this is so, it in turn is likely to lead to a liberal interpretation of the criteria by the Commission. Nonetheless, whether liberal or restrictive, the Commission's criteria for referral will be too dependent upon the attitude of the Court of Appeal. Early indications are quite promising, for the Court of Appeal has given a warm welcome to the Criminal Cases Review Commission. As noted in Chapter 10, Rose LJ, in *R v Mattan*,[49] called the Criminal Cases Review Commission 'a necessary and welcome body'. However, whether the same attitude will be taken in regard to errors more recent than 1952 or if the referrals become a flood rather than a trickle remains to be seen. Therefore, a better solution would have been to adopt the test forwarded by JUSTICE that there be a referral where there is 'an arguable case that there has been a wrongful conviction.'.[50] A more radical solution would have been to give the Commission the power to make recommendations to the Court of Appeal. Either solution would have prevented the Commission from having to second-guess the Court of Appeal and would have enabled them to determine their own fresh and independent position in regard to individual cases.

Re-investigations

Those applications which are made to the Commission which are well-drafted and provide evidence which has not been before the courts previously will present few difficulties. They can be swiftly considered and, if necessary, referred to the Court of Appeal. However, in the past a particular problem faced by a number of applicants is that their case would not be forwarded without fresh evidence. Yet it would often be difficult to find such evidence without further investigations being carried out. JUSTICE have found that a large number of the people who write to them alleging a miscarriage of justice do not have new arguments which could be placed before a court but do have points which require further investigation.[51] Though the referral criteria of the Commission are wider than those of the Home

---

[47] During the unsuccessful first appeal by the *Birmingham Six*, Lord Lane commented, 'as with many cases referred by the Home Secretary to the Court of Appeal, the longer this case has gone on, the more this court has been convinced that the jury was correct': *R v Callaghan and Others* (1989) 88 Cr App R 40. The then Home Secretary, Douglas Hurd, said that he had learned from a rebuke such as this that doubts a Home Secretary might have about an individual case were not welcomed by the Court of Appeal: *The Independent*, 3 October 1991 p. 1. See also O'Connor, P, 'The Court of Appeal: re-trials and tribulations' [1990] *Criminal Law Review* 615 at p. 617: 'Judicial distaste for the whole reference procedure has verged at times upon open hostility.'.

[48] This was illustrated in the *Runciman Report*, ch. 11 para. 5. From 1989 to 1992 49 appellants had their cases referred to the Court of Appeal. Of those 45 had their convictions quashed, with two others being granted a re-trial. For further statistics, see HC Debs. vol. 269 col. 373, 15 January 1996.

[49] *The Times*, 5 March 1998.

[50] JUSTICE, *Remedying Miscarriages of Justice* (London, 1993).

[51] Stacey, G., 'Taking a case to the Criminal Case Review Commission' (Proceedings of a Seminar held in Belfast, 12 April 1997, British Irish Rights Watch, 1997) p. 3.

Office in that the evidence need not necessarily be 'fresh', many applicants will still be faced with the problem of trying to persuade the Commission to use its resources in carrying out further investigations. As the quality of re-investigations under the old reference procedure was heavily criticised[52] it is vital to the success of the Commission that it is seen to have thorough and, as far as is possible, transparent investigative processes.

Michael Mansfield has commented that, 'the theme which runs through most miscarriages of justice is clear and constant. It is the failure of the police to conduct a proper investigation.'.[53] This applies not only at the prosecution stage but also at the stage when re-investigations have been carried out at the request of C3.[54] As a result there was considerable demand for the responsibility for re-investigating cases to be transferred from the police to, for example, an investigative arm of the Commission.[55] The Runciman Commission concluded to the contrary, stating that 'given the size and scope of inquiries that sometimes have to be made in these cases and the resources required, there is in our view no practicable alternative to the police carrying out the investigation.'.[56] Nevertheless, they further recommended that in major cases the Commission should have powers analogous to those of the Police Complaints Authority to oversee investigations and, when necessary, appoint investigating officers from a force other than the one which carried out the original investigation.

The Government largely accepted these recommendations and stood fast against giving the Commission an ability to investigate cases with its own staff:[57]

> The Government has no intention of funding a team in the Commission whose job would be to operate as a mini police force, duplicating work which could, and should, be done by the police . . . We envisage its doing investigative work from time to time but, generally the right people to investigate will be the police
> . . .

So, the Commission is given no powers to appoint any in-house investigative staff and thus any re-investigations that do take place will be carried out by the police.[58] Under the 1995 Act the Commission can require the appointment of an investigating officer to carry out inquiries,[59] and can insist that the investigating officer be from a different force than the one which carried out the original investigation.[60]

---

[52] JUSTICE, in 1983 asked if it was 'reasonable to expect the police diligently to investigate a complaint which might reveal that they or their colleagues were incompetent or negligent or simply wrong'. See Editorial [1983] *Criminal Law Review* 577.

[53] Mansfield, M., *Presumed Guilty* (Heinemann, London, 1993) p. 184. See also Mullin, C., 'Miscarriages of justice in the UK' (1996) 2(2) *Journal of Legislative Studies* 8 at p. 17.

[54] For example, in the case of the *Birmingham Six* a total of four re-investigations were carried out before the convictions were quashed by the Court of Appeal. Even then one could argue it was not scrupulous police work that led to their release but the painstaking work of family, friends and others dedicated to their case.

[55] For example, see: Thornton, P., Mallalieu, A. and Scrivenor, A., *Justice on Trial* (Civil Liberties Trust, London, 1992.

[56] *Runciman Report*, ch. 11 para. 28.

[57] HC Debs. vol 263, cols 1371–72, 17 July 1995.

[58] Or other relevant institutions who carried out the original investigation into a particular case such as Customs and Excise, the Serious Fraud Office, and the Inland Revenue.

[59] Criminal Appeal Act 1995, s. 19(1).

[60] *Ibid.*, s.19(4)(b).

The Commission can also direct that a particular person shall not be appointed[61] or, should they be dissatisfied with his or her performance, they can require that the officer be removed.[62] It is interesting to note, however, that the Commission's powers do not extend to the actual appointment of the investigating officer; that is the task of the Chief Constable of the force responsible for the original investigation.[63] As Malet suggests, 'In short, the 1995 Act takes a trusting attitude to the police.'.[64]

In many respects this is the same investigative personnel as worked under the agency of C3. Ultimately the police are investigating themselves, and the conflict of interests which arises is readily apparent. In his report on the Brixton disorders Lord Scarman commented, 'Critics of the system have argued that complainants will always be dissatisfied so long as the police perform this task, because it is contrary to natural justice that anybody should be judge in their own cause.'.[65] Even if a different force is employed from the one which carried out the original investigation the governing influence of police occupational culture may work to blunt the impact of fresh minds. The Commission differs from C3 in that section 20 of the 1995 Act permits it to direct investigations and supervise them in much the same way as currently performed by the Police Complaints Authority. Whilst this represents a more proactive role for the Commission than that taken by C3, it is far from adequate.

Though the police may carry out thorough and comprehensive investigations in a large majority of the cases which are referred to them by the Police Complaints Authority, the way in which this role is perceived by the public is equally important in determining its efficacy so that justice should be seen to be done. A number of studies have been carried out to measure the degree of 'user' satisfaction with the Police Complaints Authority. In 1987 Brown's study[66] found that 60 per cent of those sampled considered themselves to be 'very dissatisfied' with the complaints process. Interestingly, this dissatisfaction was seemingly not so much connected to the outcome of the complaint but with a range of other factors such as the actual nature of the investigation. Complainants felt that the overall standards of investigation were superficial and two-thirds of those 'dissatisfied' felt there was a pro-police bias. This was even recorded on occasion amongst complainants whose allegations were substantiated. A 1991 survey by Maguire and Corbett[67] found the 'dissatisfaction' rate to be higher still at 74 per cent, with many complainants viewing the procedure as lacking independence. This apparent lack of public confidence in the police investigating themselves is not confined to this country but is a problem reflected in similar jurisdictions.[68] Though this general

---

[61] *Ibid.*, s.19(6).

[62] *Ibid.*, s.20(5).

[63] *Ibid.*, s.19(2) and s. 22(4)(a).

[64] Malet, D., 'The new regime for the correction of miscarriages of justice' (1995) 159 *Justice of the Peace* 716, at p. 736.

[65] Report of an Inquiry by the Rt. Hon. The Lord Scarman, *The Brixton Disorders 10–12 April 1981* (Cmnd 8427, London, HMSO, 1981) para. 7.18.

[66] Brown, D., *The Police Complaints Procedure: A Survey of Complainants' Views*, (HORS 93, HMSO, London, 1987).

[67] Maguire, M. and Corbett, C., *A Study Of The Police Complaints System*, (HMSO, London, 1991).

[68] For examples, see: London Strategy Policy Unit, *Police Accountability and a new Strategic Authority for London* (Police Monitoring and Research Group Briefing Paper No. 2, London, 1987); Victoria Government, *Report of the Board of Inquiry into Allegations Against Members of the Victoria Police Force* (Government Printer, Melbourne, 1987); Queensland Government, *Report of a Commission of*

perception may serve to mask a largely effective system in most cases, it cannot, if replicated in the post-appeal process, effectively restore public confidence in the system.

Much will depend on the level of supervision and direction to be taken by the Commission. A proactive role could ensure that whilst the police continue to carry out re-investigations using their comprehensive understanding and experience of police practices and culture, real scrutiny of their role could be established. Members of the Commission could actively participate in the re-investigation process by, for example, accompanying the investigating officer in interviews and briefings. Commenting on the Police Complaints Authority, Maguire stated:[69]

> One of the main lessons . . . seems to be that any outside body which hopes to play an effective part in the control of a complex and powerful organisation like the police cannot hope to do so at arm's length. The prerequisites include gaining some understanding of the organisational culture, learning how to extract key pieces of information, and establishing good relationships with, and gaining the respect of, internal investigators.

Nevertheless, the evidence Maguire has collated from considering the 'supervisory' role of the Police Complaints Authority has suggested that the supervision is rarely so proactive. In the vast majority of cases a passive role is taken whereupon supervision merely amounts to reading through the files prepared by the police. JUSTICE have argued that, at the very least, the Commission should be under a duty to supervise the investigation process rather than merely doing so where it thought the public interest demanded it.[70] Arguably this does not go far enough, since a duty of supervision similar to that of the Police Complaints Authority is clearly not enough. Recognition of the need for an independent element in the investigation of complaints against the police as 'desirable in principle' has been made by the House of Commons Home Affairs Committee in December 1997, and the Home Office in response has positively suggested that independent investigators such as former military officers, Customs officials, lawyers, accountants or Government departmental specialist investigators could be appointed to the Police Complaints Authority.[71] Thus, less than a year after the Commission began its work, the foundations upon which its investigative work are based are impliedly being called into question.

Perhaps a more effective solution would be to provide the Commission with its own branch of experienced police officers to carry out investigations on its behalf. This would ensure that the Commission had access to a concentrated pool of expertise which could be swiftly mobilised and, importantly, could be more easily

---

Inquiry Pursuant to Orders in Council (Queensland Government Printer, Brisbane, 1989); Landau, T., *Public Complaints Against the Police: A View from Complainants* (University of Toronto, 1994); MacMahon, M., 'The situation of complaints in Toronto' (1988) 12 *Contemporary Crises* 301.

[69] Maguire, M. and Corbett, C., *A Study Of The Police Complaints System* (HMSO, London, 1991) p. 194.

[70] *The Electronic Telegraph*, 24 February 1995 (http://www.telegraph.co.uk). An Opposition amendment to the Criminal Appeal Bill attempted to strengthen the supervisory role of the Commission by suggesting it should take place in all but exceptional cases. It was rejected by the Government as expensive and unnecessary: HC Debs. Standing Committee B, col. 158, 30 March 1995.

[71] Home Affairs Committee, *Police Disciplinary and Complaints Procedures* (1997–98 HC 258–I) para. 81, *The Times*, 24 March 1998 p. 2.

supervised as they worked in tandem with other Commission members. Such a suggestion was criticised in the Home Office's *Discussion Paper* as being uneconomical and wasteful as in a vast number of cases the issues are straightforward and more easily dealt with by members of the original force who are familiar with the issues.[72] However, the very element often required in such cases is a fresh approach to the investigation. In the immediate aftermath of cases such as the *Birmingham Six*, the general consensus was that they were straightforward[73] and the original forces familiar with the issues would certainly have dismissed them very easily. If the Commission were able to finance its own investigations in this way, it could also ensure that investigations were more thorough. Under the 1995 Act the police are expected to fund re-investigations out of their own budgets. It would be ingenuous to expect them to divert scarce funds towards unearthing their own mistakes. Even the Chairman of the Commission has expressed the worry that without separate budgetary requirements for police re-investigations, 'this may limit their inclination and capacity to undertake investigations for the Commission willingly and expeditiously'.[74]

There have been suggestions that if confidence is to be fully restored to the post-appeal process, then the investigative element should be completely independent of the police. Mansfield refers to the successful commission in Hong Kong established to investigate corruption within the police and legal institutions.[75] However, there is considerable evidence to suggest that without the necessary knowledge and experience of police culture and operations it is very difficult to overcome the resistance to external 'interference'. The effect of police culture in creating the 'them and us' climate is so strong that Goldsmith suggests that the possibility of 'complete independence of investigation . . . is a myth'.[76] In Loveday's observation of police investigations of their own misconduct in the United States,[77] it appears that those systems which appeared to be the most effective involved the use of the police and civilians working together rather than an wholly independent service. Yet, more could be done to marry the undoubted experience and skill of current officers with independence. In particular, such officers should be seconded to the Commission, and there may still be a role for investigators from other professions (such as lawyers) to act as directors and supervisors.

Disclosure

In *ex parte Hickey* in 1994, Simon Brown LJ ensured through his judgment that when the Home Secretary was minded to reject an applicant's petition on the basis of evidence gathered in any further inquiries, the applicant should be given an opportunity to make representations upon such material before a final decision is

---

[72] Home Office, *Criminal Appeals and the Establishment of a Criminal Cases Review Authority* (HMSO, London, 1994) para. 58.
[73] For example, this is reflected in the incredulity with which Lord Denning addressed the evidence in a civil action against the police alleging that the *Birmingham Six* had been assaulted: *McIlkenny* v *Chief Constable of the West Midlands* [1980] 2 WLR 689 at p. 706.
[74] *The Daily Telegraph*, 9 April 1997, p. 11.
[75] Mansfield, M., *Presumed Guilty* (Heinemann, London, 1993) p. 263.
[76] Goldsmith, A., *External Review and Self Regulation, in Complaints Against the Police: The Trend To External Review* (Oxford University Press, 1988) p. 32.
[77] Loveday, B., 'Police complaints in the USA' (1988) 4 *Policing* 172.

made. The practice up to that date had been simply to provide a formal rejection of a petition without an explanation given as to the reasons, thereby ensuring that an applicant was in a very difficult position when seeking to submit further applications. Simon Brown LJ stated, 'elementary fairness surely requires that [the prisoner] should have an opportunity to address these fresh obstacles and that principle dictates that advance disclosure is required.'.[78] In response, the Home Office planned that '[t]he Commission will, and we intend that it should, be governed by the same duty of fairness and the same resulting duty of disclosure as the Divisional Court set out [in *ex parte Hickey*].'.[79] It is worth noting, however, that there is no general duty under the 1995 Act to disclose all the information gathered during any re-investigation, the Government preferring to rely upon the flexible approach in *ex parte Hickey* whereunder the demands of fairness may change in each individual case. This is regrettable. The Commission may operate in the spirit of fairness and openness, but in light of the inadequacies of C3, such principles ought to be guaranteed by a more onerous statutory duty (under section 14) than to state reasons.

The Commission has a wide power to obtain documents from public bodies under section 17 of the 1995 Act 'where it is reasonable to do so.'. It also has the power to direct that material should not be damaged, destroyed or altered. The provisions of section 17 do not extend to any information in regard to a minister's previous consideration of the case. Without this provision it was officially suggested that the Commission would have been 'vulnerable to the charge of having been unduly influenced by the views taken during the earlier consideration of the case by a different authority'.[80] Yet, if the Commission is expected to take a line independent of police reports and opinions, why could its members not rise above the dismissive attitudes of officials? A greater level of co-operation between C3 and the Commission could have ensured a smoother and quicker transition period. As it stands, the Commission is taking on a huge workload at the same time as recruiting and training staff. This inevitably means there is an increasing backlog of cases, some of which will have no merit, but in others innocent people will remain imprisoned for longer simply as a result of the transition. One wonders if part of the reason for the curtain drawn around C3 was to prevent future political damage (or even legal action or greater payments of compensation) when its abject failures became apparent to applicants.

Resources

Undoubtedly the Commission will be better resourced than C3. In addition to the 14 Commission members, it will also employ around 65 staff though the exact number will depend on the volume of work received. Its annual budget of between £4 million and £5 million also represents a substantial increase in resources when compared to the estimated £750,000 annual running cost of C3.[81] However, though the resources will increase, there will also be a substantial increase in the workload

---

[78] *Ex parte Hickey* [1995] 1 All ER 490 at 499.
[79] HC Debs. Standing Committee B, col. 144, 30 March 1995. This is now reflected in the Criminal Appeal Act 1995, s. 14(6).
[80] HC Debs. vol 263, col 1529, 17 July 1995. See now s. 18.
[81] Editorial, 'Cheap options for criminal cases review' (1994) 144 *New Law Journal* 449.

of the Commission. It was suggested in 1995 that the Commission would initially have twice the caseload of the previous body, around 1400,[82] whilst the Commission itself is making assumptions of around 1600. The estimate is a difficult one to make as there appears to be some evidence that, in the last months of the Home Office procedure, cases were being held back in anticipation of a more liberal outlook from the Commission.[83] Following its first week of operation the Chairman of the Commission questioned 'whether we can cope with the workload'. The size of the task was a 'formidable' prospect such that 'a single complicated fraud case, or even a modest number of forensic studies, could far exceed the Commission's current budget for investigations'.[84] Likewise, after one year, perhaps the principal message to government in its first Annual Report was that staff and facilities were inadequate to cope with the case-load.[85]

In addition to the power to refer Crown Court conviction issues, the Commission is also entrusted with the task of accepting and evaluating applications in regard to Crown Court sentencing issues and to conviction and sentencing issues in the magistrates' court. Whilst these provisions must be welcomed as miscarriages of justice can and do occur at summary level, they will add considerably to the workload and expense of the Commission. At such an early stage in the life of the Commission an evaluation of its resource needs is impossible. It is likely, however, that its funds will be vastly over-stretched and therefore an important question will be how it prioritises its available funds through filtering the cases it receives.

The Court of Appeal

The fact that the Commission cannot make determinations about a case on its own behalf means that it remains clearly subordinate to the Court of Appeal. Thus, whilst the Commission may ensure that the post-appeal process is more accessible, albeit not much, the crux of the reforms brought about by the 1995 Act depends upon how the Court of Appeal chooses to interpret its own role in the process. If it chooses to interpret its role restrictively this may largely nullify any benefits brought about by the establishment of the Commission.

The Court of Appeal has had considerable theoretical and practical problems with miscarriages of justice for the duration of its existence since 1907. Both before and after that date, judicial attitude towards criminal appeals was often hostile, with fears that there would be an avalanche of undeserving appeals which would incur great cost for the judicial system both in financial terms and in the damage they would do to general public confidence in the whole judicial process, the latter based on the primacy afforded to the notion of finality in legal proceedings and especially of a jury verdict. As a result the powers which have been available to the Court have been considerably under-used through a lack of will or through confusion about its role.[86] This reluctance is repeated throughout

---

[82] HC Debs. vol 256, col 25, 6 March 1995.

[83] Stacey, G., 'Taking a case to the Criminal Case Review Commission' (Proceedings of a Seminar held in Belfast, 12 April 1997, British Irish Rights Watch, 1997) p. 18.

[84] *The Daily Telegraph*, 9 April 1997, p. 11.

[85] *Annual Report 1997–98* (Birmingham, 1998) pp. 7, 9.

[86] Malleson, K., 'Appeals against conviction and the principle of finality' (1994) 21 *Journal of Law and Society* 51; Pattenden, R., *English Criminal Appeals 1844–1994* (Clarendon Press, Oxford, 1994) p. 210.

the litany of recent miscarriages. In 1988 Lord Denning said, in reference to the growing agitation for the release of the *Birmingham Six*, 'It is better that some innocent men remain in jail than the integrity of the English judicial system be impugned.'.[87] The task of ensuring that the Court of Appeal is more liberal in its attitude towards referred cases is central to the successful improvement of the post-appeal process.

The Runciman Commission recognised that 'the Court of Appeal should be readier to overturn jury verdicts than it has shown itself to be in the past.'.[88] The Commission suggested that this could be achieved by redrafting the grounds of appeal, then set out in section 2(1) of the Criminal Appeal Act 1968, but its members were divided as to what the new formula should be. This in a sense sums up the essential difficulty with reforming the Court of Appeal. The actual words of any new section are unlikely in themselves to bring about a change in its practice; more important is how the Court chooses to interpret its own role. Indeed, in many areas the Runciman Commission recognised that the Court of Appeal already had adequate powers but was simply too reluctant to use them. This is not a new phenomenon but has existed throughout the life of the Court of Appeal itself.[89]

Certainly, the three alternative grounds for appeal in the 1968 Act were imprecise and overlapped[90] and so were replaced by a simpler single ground of appeal in the 1995 Act, namely, an appeal against conviction would be allowed by the Court of Appeal if it thought the conviction was 'unsafe'.[91] There have been questions as to the extent to which this section might change the approach of the Court but, if history is to offer any guidance, the statutory language may be of little consequence as 'it will continue to be the judges who shape the review process.'.[92] It is perhaps somewhat ironic that prior to the 1995 Act the Court of Appeal was by then displaying a less rigid approach to its role and powers. In some respects therefore the changes brought about by the 1995 Act may not be necessary. However, as Chris Mullin recognised, though there has been 'an improvement of attitude following the change of personnel in that court . . . they could of course change back again'.[93] The fact that a more liberal attitude was adopted by the Court whilst still being 'guided' by the 1968 Act is a prime example that tinkering with the words of the grounds for appeal is unlikely of itself to provide any significant changes and is effectively nothing short of an exercise in semantics.

The success of the Commission is wholly dependent upon how the Court of Appeal chooses to exercise its own powers. In effect, this represents little change from that of C3. Though a convicted person might have an improved opportunity to present his case at the referral stage, this matters little if the Court of Appeal

---

[87] Mansfield, M., *Presumed Guilty* (Heinemann, London, 1993) p. 261.

[88] *Runciman Report*, ch. 11 para. 3.

[89] Malleson, K., 'Appeals against conviction and the principle of finality' (1994) 21 *Journal of Law and Society* 151 at pp. 153–4.

[90] See O'Connor, P., 'The Court of Appeal: re-trials and tribulations' [1990] *Criminal Law Review* 615; Buxton, R., 'Miscarriages of justice and the Court of Appeal' (1993) 109 *Law Quarterly Review* 66; Smith, J.C., 'The Criminal Appeal Act 1995: appeals against conviction' [1995] *Criminal Law Review* 920; Darbyshire, A., 'Criminal Appeal Act 1995' (1996) 140 *Solicitor's Journal* 486.

[91] Criminal Appeal Act 1995, s. 2.

[92] Malleson, K., 'Appeals against conviction and the principle of finality' (1994) 21 *Journal of Law and Society* 151 at p. 155. For a survey of the impact since 1995, see Chapter 10.

[93] HC Debs. vol 258, cols 951–952, 26 April 1995.

continue to turn their faces against the possibility that a jury can make substantial errors which justice demands be corrected. Though there are some commendable aspects to the 1995 Act one is left with the feeling that a real opportunity to make meaningful changes has been lost.

Conclusion

It is difficult to foresee any further legislative reform in the post-appeal process for some considerable time. In any event, one could argue that the Commission ought to be given a reasonable opportunity to prove itself. But, as presently constituted, the Commission is not equipped to make a substantial impact upon the continuing number of miscarriages of justice given the primacy of the Court of Appeal. As long as the Court of Appeal retains its current role in the post-conviction process, wrongfully convicted persons will have to wait a considerable time for justice to be done, if indeed it ever will be.

The single most important change must therefore be to ensure that the Court of Appeal is more receptive to cases of potential injustice. One way in which this might be achieved is to give the Commission the power to make recommendations to the Court of Appeal when a case is referred. If the Commission reasonably believes that a miscarriage has occurred, it should recommend a re-trial, with difficult questions concerning admissibility being dealt with by the Commission's own independent bank of lawyers. As has been noted the Court of Appeal are very reluctant to overturn the verdict of a jury, so the most effective solution in a case of potential miscarriage is to present the case before another jury. There has been considerable opposition to this in the past, with detractors citing the problem of delay affecting the ability of witnesses to recall the necessary facts effectively and that testimony would be shaped by the initial cross-examination. Whilst this would be a concern in some cases, the argument is perhaps over-stated. The concern of delay is somewhat muted when prosecutions are raised years after the original crime.[94] If a re-trial was not possible in an individual case, the Commission should have the ability to recommend that the verdict be quashed. Whilst the final determination in the case would lie with the Court of Appeal, if they were to uphold a conviction contrary to the wishes of the Commission, they would have to provide compelling reasons for so doing – the onus would be weighted in favour of acquittal.

Under such a system, it would be imperative that the Commission should have its independence strengthened by taking personnel selection out of the hands of the Prime Minister and entrusting it to a Parliamentary Select Committee. In this way the selection procedure would be wholly transparent and accountable and as a result should be less prosecution-orientated than the current membership. In addition to the powers currently available to the Commission an ability to carry out competent investigations would be strengthened by providing it with seconded police officers and perhaps lawyers, as suggested earlier. Ultimately, however, it alone must be responsible for the direction of investigations, and it must be an active participant in the process. This could ensure that there is not only a tenacity

---

[94] See *R* v *Quinn, The Times,* 31 March 1990; The Crown Prosecution Service, *Annual Report,* 1995–6, p. 38, para. 6.5(d); Choo, A., *Abuse of Process and Judicial Stays of Criminal Proceedings* (Clarendon Press, Oxford, 1993) ch. 3.

to uncover injustice but also the necessary expertise to carry out detailed investigations against the backdrop of the all-pervasive police culture.

It will also be critical that applicants at this stage of the appeal procedure be considered more favourably for legal aid. If the legal aid budget has to be increased considerably to cater for those appealing post-conviction, is this an argument to suggest legal aid should be denied or that the pre-trial and trial procedures are made somewhat more secure to ensure that the post-conviction procedure really is a 'safety net' to catch those rare mistakes rather than simply a further bite at the cherry?

The fear that a more accessible post-conviction process will damage the principle of finality is a strong argument. Certainly finality produces public confidence in the criminal process but not if it is at the expense of justice. As Lord Atkin commented in 1933, 'Finality is a good thing, justice is better'.[95] Appeal Court judges need to be reminded of this fact, and also that real finality in criminal proceedings is not something that should be manufactured, but should be brought about by judgments of quality. If the post-conviction procedure is in frequent use, this should not be a signal for the Court of Appeal to become unyielding, but rather it should provide a signal that all is not well with the initial investigation and trial procedures. It is totally inadequate to build a review commission on what are effectively rotten foundations which are unlikely to be shored by increasing political competitiveness to produce a hard-line crime control model.[96] What price the possibility of a similar discussion in twenty years following another multitude of major miscarriages?

---

[95] Malleson, K., 'Appeals against conviction and the principle of finality' (1994) 21 *Journal of Law and Society* 151.

[96] Editorial, 'Turning the clock back' (1997) 147 *New Law Journal* 481.

12

Victims of Miscarriages of Justice

Nick Taylor with James Wood

Introduction

In 1952, Richard Donnelly observed, 'Although unprosecuted crime is a serious social menace, few disasters are more tragic than the condemnation of an innocent person to imprisonment . . .'.[1] Since the presumption in favour of liberty and innocence is such a widely held and basic right,[2] it is not difficult to appreciate the gross injustice caused by any wrongful conviction. As stated in the previous chapter, the fairness and efficacy of the British criminal justice system can be measured not only by the number of mistakes it makes but also on its ability swiftly to recognise and rectify such mistakes. However, the State's responsibility in relation to wrongful convictions should not, and does not, end with the quashing of such a conviction. In addition, the State's victim should also be compensated for the gross injustice that has occurred and the consequent injury caused. Additionally, it ought to afford him or her the chance to reintegrate into the society from which they may have been displaced. The aim of this chapter is to analyse the adequacy of schemes of official compensation available to victims of miscarriages of justice currently in existence and how such compensation schemes are operated.

The Consequences of Wrongful Imprisonment

Within the United Kingdom imprisonment is the heaviest penalty that can be exacted upon an offender, and thus remains the most potent weapon available to a court.[3] The effect of such a loss of liberty even when arguably justifiable is

---

[1] Donnelly, RC., 'Unconvicting the innocent' (1952) 6 *Vanderbilt Law Review* 36.

[2] Ashworth, A., *The Criminal Process. An Evaluative Study* (2nd ed., Clarendon Press, Oxford, 1998) pp. 50–52.

[3] The death penalty was largely abolished by the Murder (Abolition of Death Penalty) Act 1965 and the Northern Ireland (Emergency Provisions) Act 1973, s. 1, and for offences of high treason (Treason Act 1814, s. 1) and piracy with violence (Piracy Act 1837, s. 2) by the Crime and Disorder Act 1998, s. 36 (consequent upon the bringing into force of Protocol 6 of the European Convention on Human Rights).

far-reaching,[4] though undoubtedly the effects can be exacerbated greatly for those wrongfully convicted.

The most obvious burden to be endured by the wrongfully convicted person is the time spent incarcerated. Ironically, for a person who maintains their innocence throughout their trial and imprisonment the ultimate sentence may in some cases be longer than is standard for a particular crime due to the fact that often they will not plead mitigating circumstances or show the necessary remorse for their alleged actions. Gerard Conlon explained, 'Mitigation to me means getting leniency for something you've admitted, something you've done. I'd maintained my innocence all through remand, committal and trial.'.[5] Following the guilty verdict at the trial of the *Guildford Four*, he said to the junior barrister, 'I don't care about the sentence. I've been found guilty of something I haven't done, and you're not going to get up and be begging for me and making it sound as though I have.'.[6] In October 1995 Michael Hickey, one of the men wrongly convicted for the murder of Carl Bridgewater,[7] turned down an offer of parole wishing instead to leave prison with his name cleared. He subsequently spent a further 16 months imprisoned before being released on bail in February 1997, prior to his conviction being finally quashed later that year.

The physical and mental burden of imprisonment can be intolerable for many but the accompanying feelings of frustration and bitterness felt by those who are innocent can often be overwhelming.[8] Vincent Hickey is alleged to have slashed his wrists whilst serving his seventeenth year in prison, and is also reported to have turned to drugs and to have had an eating disorder.[9] For those wrongly convicted of certain serious crimes, such as murder, crimes of a sexual nature, or those involving children, there also exists the threat of physical abuse from other prisoners, and possibly prison staff or the police.[10] Michael Hickey's refusal to be segregated from fellow prisoners under Rule 43 led to considerable ill-treatment from some prisoners, though he considered that as an innocent man there was no reason to isolate himself, believing that accepting segregation would suggest he was accepting his sentence. Gerard Conlon recalls how he had to remain in solitary confinement on the punishment block at Wandsworth Prison for his own safety, following an earlier attack on Gerry Hunter, one of the *Birmingham Six*.[11]

Research suggests that a particular fear held by long-term prisoners is that they will in some sense 'deteriorate' in prison. Whilst evidence as to the reality of this

---

[4] See, for example, Martin, J.P. and Webster D., *The Social Consequences of Conviction* (Heinemann, London, 1971); Cohen, S. and Taylor, L., *Psychological Survival: The Experience of Long Term Imprisonment* (Penguin, Harmondsworth, 1972); Sapsford, R., *Life Sentence Prisoners: Reaction Response and Change* (Open UP, Milton Keynes, 1983) chs. 2, 3; Bettsworth, M., *Marking Time* (Macmillan, London, 1989).

[5] Conlon, G., *Proved Innocent* (Penguin Books, London, 1990) p. 131.

[6] *Ibid*.

[7] Foot, P., *Murder at the Farm* (Penguin, London, 1988).

[8] See *The Guardian*, 23 April 1996 p. 1. A medical expert suggested that the *Birmingham Six* suffered irreversible trauma as a result of their wrongful convictions and ill-treatment, as severe as that suffered by brain damaged accident victims.

[9] *The Times*, 2 March 1996, p. 4.

[10] Vivid accounts of physical abuse towards the *Birmingham Six* are recounted in Mullin, C., *Error of Judgment* (2nd ed., Chatto and Windus, London, 1990). See also, HC Debs. Standing Committee B, col 85, 23 March 1995. Many allegations of police brutality were also made against the West Midlands Serious Crime Squad prior to the disbandment of the squad in 1989. See, Kaye, T., *Unsafe and Unsatisfactory* (Civil Liberties Trust, London, 1991).

[11] Conlon, G., *Proved Innocent* (Penguin Books, London, 1990) p. 139. See also, Hill, P. and Burnett, R., *Stolen Years: Before and After Guildford* (Doubleday, London, 1990) ch. 6.

remains ambiguous, it nevertheless appears that long term imprisonment leads to depression of self-image and a strong feeling of powerlessness, especially amongst those serving indeterminate sentences.[12] But the very people whose sentence may effectively be indeterminate include those who believe they are innocent and continue to contest the conviction. They may harbour hopes of imminent release for many years without ever knowing when, or even if, it will ever materialise.[13] Ann Whelan, mother of Michael Hickey, said of her son, 'He looked at life through mesh and bars for nearly two decades. When you're in prison for something you didn't do, every day is torture. We have to remember he went in as a teenager and he's got to learn to be an adult.'.[14] Whilst this does not necessarily suggest deterioration, it certainly suggests that the prison sentence hampered Hickey's development.

If a person is imprisoned, even for a short spell, the prisoner's family must learn to live with the stigma that comes with such a punishment.[15] Again, for those convicted of the most serious of crimes, such as the *Guildford Four*[16] and the defendants in the Carl Bridgewater case, this can result in physical abuse for not only the prisoner but also for the family. One of the *Bridgewater Four*, James Robinson, said that the experience had been 'a terrible thing, not just for us but for our families. It smashes you up over the years.'.[17] Nick Molloy, the son of Pat Molloy who died in 1981 whilst serving a sentence for the manslaughter of Carl Bridgewater, was a schoolboy when his father was convicted. He remembers being regularly being beaten at school, spat at in the street and abused in the town.[18] The pressure that this brings to bear on those on the outside can, and often does lead to physical illness and the breakdown of marriages. Frederick Whelan, stepfather of Michael Hickey, is said himself to have suffered three nervous breakdowns as a result of the Bridgewater convictions.[19] The wrongfully convicted person may also be denied the opportunity to see their children's formative years. Carole Richardson, one of the *Guildford Four*, had to endure the loss of her child-bearing years.

The economic effects of wrongful imprisonment can also have an enormous impact upon a family. The convicted person may very well have been the major financial contributor in the household. Without such income the family may face such dire consequences as the loss of the family home. Association with the convicted person may also mean that it becomes very difficult for the remaining family members to obtain work. In addition, as the family continue to contest the conviction beyond the appeal stage, their legal expenses will soar. At the post-conviction stage the provision of legal aid will invariably be restricted to two

---

[12] See Sapsford, R., *Life Sentence Prisoners: Reaction Response and Change* (Open UP, Milton Keynes, 1983).

[13] For example, determined to draw attention to his case, Michael Hickey staged the longest rooftop protest in history, when he scaled the roof of Gartree prison for 89 days during the winter of 1983–4, an act which almost cost him his life. This action obviously did not bring forward any release date but cost Hickey two further months in solitary confinement.

[14] *The Times*, 1 July 1997, p. 10.

[15] See *The Independent*, 12 July 1995, p. 4; Bettsworth, M., *Marking Time* (Macmillan, London, 1989).

[16] See Kee, R., *Trial and Error* (Hamish Hamilton, London, 1986); McKee, G. and Franey, R., *Time Bombs* (Bloomsbury, London, 1988).

[17] *The Guardian*, 21 February 1997, p. 1.

[18] *The Observer*, 23 February 1997, p. 6.

[19] *The Times*, 22 February 1997, p. 6.

hours worth of advice under the Green Form scheme. It will certainly not cover the considerable amount of time that the solicitor might spend with the family seeking the necessary evidence that could lead to the conviction being quashed.[20] With so many priorities upon the family income, even visiting the prisoner as he or she is moved from one prison to another becomes financially onerous. For example, during Gerard Conlon's 14 years' imprisonment, he was moved on 18 occasions through 12 different prisons spanning the length of the country. The consequences of this for the family are not merely financial, however, but affect any semblance of 'normal' family life.

Though many victims of wrongful convictions may not suffer all of these consequences or to such a devastating degree, their plight should not be under-estimated. Even for less serious crimes a family can be shunned by their community – a reaction that often continues even when the verdict itself may have been quashed.[21] In the light of all of these costs of wrongful conviction, there is no feasible direct remedy for their spoiled lives, or indeed, those of their family. Nonetheless, there are currently two ways by which the Home Office seeks to make compensation payments to victims of miscarriages of justice. These are by way of a monetary payment which is either *ex gratia* or falls under section 133 of the Criminal Justice Act 1988.

The *Ex Gratia* Compensation Scheme

Prior to the Criminal Justice Act 1988 a person who had been pardoned or whose conviction was quashed had no legal right to compensation despite the fact that a gross miscarriage of justice might have occurred. In certain instances, however, the Home Secretary would offer an *ex gratia* payment from public funds, though for many years there was little official guidance as to when or how claims would be assessed. In 1973 Brandon and Davies stated that, 'we have come across many cases of people wrongly imprisoned, and very few where they have been compensated for it . . . The compensation paid, when it is paid, is obviously nothing like enough. A bare repayment of wages lost is . . . scarcely sufficient compensation for the damage likely to be suffered.'.[22]

In July 1976, in response to a Parliamentary question, the Home Secretary outlined the procedure followed when assessing the amount by way of an *ex gratia* payment to be made to a person wrongly convicted:[23]

> A decision to make an *ex gratia* payment from public funds does not imply any admission of legal liability. The payment is offered in recognition of the hardship caused . . . notwithstanding that the circumstances may give no grounds for a claim for civil damages.

Any payment made was to be at the discretion of the Home Secretary, though he would seek the advice of an independent assessor. A memorandum would be drawn

---

[20] See, for example, Mansfield, M., *Presumed Guilty* (Heinemann, London, 1993) p. 262.
[21] See Mullin, C., 'Miscarriages of justice in the UK' (1996) 2(2) *Journal of Legislative Studies* 8 at p. 10.
[22] Brandon, R. and Davies, C., *Wrongful Imprisonment* (Allen and Unwin, London, 1973) p. 200.
[23] HC Debs. vol 916, cols 328–30, 29 July 1976.

up including the circumstances of the case and any special features of the case that might be considered relevant to the amount of compensation to be paid. The claimant and his or her solicitor could comment on the memorandum and submit any further facts they thought relevant before it would be considered by the independent assessor. In making the assessment, the assessor was to apply principles analogous to those governing the assessment of damages for civil wrongs, including both pecuniary and non-pecuniary loss. Since the payment to be made was *ex gratia*, and therefore wholly at the discretion of the Home Secretary, he was not bound to accept the assessor's recommendation 'but it is normal for him to do so.'.[24]

The following year the House of Commons was informed as to how cases were selected for *ex gratia* payments:[25]

> In exceptional cases . . . the Home Secretary may authorise an *ex gratia* payment from public funds, but this would not normally be done unless there had been some misconduct or negligence on the part of the police or some other public authority . . . as long as an accused person is not required to prove his innocence it is difficult to justify automatic compensation on acquittal . . . Any other procedure for allowing compensation in selected cases only would involve invidious discriminations that might reflect upon those not compensated.

This statement reflected the fact that the Home Office wished to avoid a situation whereby a refusal to compensate particular claimants suggested they were somehow less 'innocent' than a successful claimant.

The House of Commons Home Affairs Committee in 1982[26] unearthed details of the *ex gratia* payments made between 1972 and 1981. A total of 47 payments were made to a total of 44 people.[27] Whilst records were not kept of unsuccessful compensation claims, the Home Office staff responsible estimated that fewer than 10 per cent of claims received resulted in an *ex gratia* payment. The highest awards totalled £25,000 and £22,000 both made in 1981, though a large proportion of claims were less than £5000. Examples of awards include £2000 paid to Luke Dougherty in 1973 for eight months spent in prison following a wrongful theft conviction, £10,000 paid to Tom Naughton in 1977 for the three years he spent in prison on the basis of a wrongful conviction for armed robbery, while Albert Taylor, released in 1979 after serving five years of a life sentence for murder, received £21,000 following the quashing of his conviction.[28]

Though these arrangements were gradually becoming more transparent, they remained open to criticism. In a 1982 Report[29] JUSTICE criticised the reliance upon the Home Secretary's discretion in determining the right to compensation for wrongful conviction, arguing that it should be a legally enforceable right, with

---

[24] *Ibid*, col 330.

[25] HC Debs. vol 929, cols 835–36, 1 April 1977.

[26] Home Affairs Committee, *Report on Miscarriages of Justice* (1981–2, HC 421). See also *Government Reply* (Cmnd 8856, HMSO, London, 1983).

[27] 47 payments made to 44 people can be explained by the fact that the three defendants in the *Confait* case each received payments on two separate occasions.

[28] For further examples of *ex gratia* awards see, JUSTICE, *Report on Compensation for Wrongful Imprisonment* (London, 1982) paras. 14–27; Zander, M., *Cases and Materials on the English Legal System* (7th ed., Butterworths, London, 1996) p. 536.

[29] JUSTICE, *Report on Compensation for Wrongful Imprisonment* (London, 1982).

applications being made to an independent 'Imprisonment Compensation Board'. A further criticism of the involvement of the Home Secretary was that such a scheme could not meet the UK's international obligations under Article 14(6) of the UN International Covenant on Civil and Political Rights (ICCPR):[30]

> When a person has by a final decision been convicted of a criminal offence and when subsequently his conviction has been reversed, or he has been pardoned, on the ground that a new or newly discovered fact shows conclusively that there has been a miscarriage of justice, the person who has suffered punishment shall be compensated according to law, unless it is proved that the non-disclosure of the unknown fact in time is wholly or partly attributed to him.

An *ex gratia* compensation scheme dependent upon the discretion of the Home Secretary would not appear to be 'according to law' as demanded by the ICCPR The phrase 'according to law' has been interpreted under the European Convention on Human Rights in *Malone* v *United Kingdom*.[31] The European Court stated that 'it would be contrary to the rule of law for the legal discretion granted to the executive to be expressed in terms of an unfettered power: the law [has] to indicate the scope of any such discretion . . .'. One would expect a similar interpretation to be applied under the ICCPR. The UN Human Rights Committee doubted the UK's compliance with Article 14(6) whereupon the Government decided to review its position.[32]

In November 1985 the results of the review were conveyed to Parliament.[33] Despite Article 14(6) of the ICCPR, the Home Secretary announced that he had no intention of establishing a statutory scheme but would continue to pay compensation to those who applied for it, who had been wrongly imprisoned and:

(a) who had been pardoned by the Queen; or,

(b) whose conviction had been quashed by the Court of Appeal or the House of Lords either after a reference back to those courts under s. 17 of the Criminal Appeal Act 1968, or after the time normally allowed for an appeal by those courts had elapsed; or,

(c) where the Home Secretary was satisfied that the imprisonment resulted from a serious default on the part of a member of a police force or of some other public authority.

In future he would also pay compensation to any person where it was required by the UK's international obligations or where he considered that there were exceptional circumstances (such as facts emerging at the trial or at an appeal brought within time that completely exonerated the defendant). He would not, however, pay compensation simply because the prosecution was unable to sustain the burden of proof at the trial. He further stated that he would regard himself bound by the decision of the independent assessor in relation to the quantum of compensation.

---

[30] Cmnd 6702, HMSO, London, 1977.

[31] *Malone* v *United Kingdom*, Appl. no. 8691/79, Ser. A vol. 82, (1985) 7 EHRR 14. See also Harris, D.J., O'Boyle, M. and Warbrick, C., *Law On The European Convention On Human Rights* (Butterworths, London, 1995) pp. 285–90.

[32] Ashman, P., 'Compensation for wrongful imprisonment' (1986) 136 *New Law Journal* 497.

[33] HC Debs. vol 87, cols 691–692, 29 November 1985.

Though the Home Secretary considered that this scheme met both the 'spirit and purpose' of the UK's international obligations, the scheme still lacked legal force and was wholly dependent upon the discretion of the Home Secretary of the day. In this respect, despite the re-statement of the scheme, it continued to fail the requirements of the ICCPR.[34] The scheme lacks independence in that it is the Home Secretary who determines whether or not there has been serious default on the part of the police or the courts – the very person who, through his or her position, may not want to recognise such conduct or to deem it 'serious'. If justice is done in an individual case, it will certainly not be seen to be done. Little guidance is given to prospective applicants about how they can apply for an *ex gratia* payment.

The lack of certainty surrounding the scheme was highlighted in *R v Secretary of State for the Home Office, ex parte Chubb*.[35] The applicant spent 15 months in prison before his conviction was finally quashed by the Court of Appeal. He applied to the Home Secretary for an *ex gratia* compensation payment but was refused. The applicant claimed that the Home Secretary's statement in 1985 made the position in relation to the payment of *ex gratia* awards analogous to the position of the Criminal Injuries Compensation Board and it was therefore subject to judicial review. The Court held, however, that the Home Secretary retained complete discretion in regard to such payments, and in 1985 he had merely stated that in exceptional cases he would make a payment. The lack of any administrative rules upon which such payments were to be based therefore meant the payments were not judicially reviewable in this respect.

The capricious nature of the *ex gratia* scheme was further illustrated in *R v Secretary of State for the Home Department, ex parte Harrison*.[36] After the applicant had had his one year conviction quashed, he sought *ex gratia* compensation from the Home Secretary for the time he had spent in prison. The application was refused without any reasons being given, and the applicant therefore sought an order of certiorari quashing the decision contending that the criteria upon which the decision was based had been kept confidential and that the details ought to be disclosed to him so that he could make representations on his own behalf. The Home Secretary did indeed use criteria beyond those stated in his 1985 Parliamentary answer, including the criterion that, on a balance of probabilities, the claimant was more likely than not to have been innocent. The applicant was never aware that his guilt or innocence was in issue as part of the application; had he known this, he might have been able to address the issue. As confidential criteria had been used, it was argued that the Home Secretary had acted unfairly in reaching his decision. However, the Court held that as the payments were *ex gratia*, with no obligation upon the Home Secretary to make them, he could establish his own rules for dispensing them, provided he did not act fraudulently or with bias. Therefore, reasons did not need to be given when an application was refused.

It is possible that the trend towards more openness in more recent judicial review decisions of the courts will eventually impact upon this area.[37] Until then, the

---

[34] See Ashman, P., 'Compensation for wrongful imprisonment' (1986) 136 *New Law Journal* 497.

[35] [1986] *Criminal Law Review* 809.

[36] [1988] 3 All ER 86.

[37] For example, see *R v Secretary of State for the Home Department, ex parte Wilson* [1992] 2 All ER 576; *Doody v Secretary of State for the Home Department* [1993] 3 All ER 92; *R v Secretary of State for the Home Department, ex parte Duggan* [1994] 3 All ER 277; *R v Secretary of State for the Home Department, ex parte Hickey (No. 2)* [1995] 1 All ER 490.

position cannot reflect the 'spirit and purpose' of the ICCPR. Farquharson J stated in *ex parte Harrison*, '. . . at one end of the scale the rules of natural justice require that the procedures of a public tribunal are akin to those of a court of law. In contrast, when a decision is being made . . . by a minister in his closet . . . he is required only to act fairly in the sense that his decision is free from bias or fraud.'.[38] A compensation procedure 'according to law' should be clear, precise and accessible to the public.

The Statutory Compensation Scheme

The scale of the miscarriages of justice unfolding in the late 1980s arguably would have forced the Government's hand towards the implementation of a statutory compensation scheme. However, in a somewhat unexpected turn, the Government announced the introduction of such a project in November 1987. In the House of Lords an amendment was moved to the Criminal Justice Bill[39] to introduce a statutory compensation scheme for 'victims' of miscarriages of justice. This became section 133 of the Criminal Justice Act 1988, with effect from October of that year. For the first time the Home Secretary now had a duty and not merely a discretion to pay compensation, but only in the limited circumstances covered in section 133. The *ex gratia* scheme continues to operate in those cases which may fall outside the Act.[40]

The procedure by which a claim for statutory compensation is made is in many ways similar to that under the *ex gratia* scheme. Section 133(2) requires that a positive application for compensation must be made to the Secretary of State. The question of whether or not there is a right to compensation in a particular case is then determined by the Home Office following the criteria in section 133(1):

> . . . when a person has been convicted of a criminal offence and when subsequently his conviction has been reversed or he has been pardoned on the ground that a new or newly discovered fact shows beyond reasonable doubt that there has been a miscarriage of justice, the Secretary of State shall pay compensation . . . to the person who has suffered the punishment . . . or, if he is dead, to his personal representatives . . .

The section also contains a proviso that if the new evidence arises from non-disclosure by the convicted person either wholly or in part, compensation will not be payable.

There are undoubtedly a wider range of areas than those outlined in section 133 in which compensation could justifiably be demanded for miscarriages of justice. For example, JUSTICE[41] recommended in 1982 that persons whose conviction had been quashed following a normal appeal should at least be entitled to apply for compensation. Equally, there are compelling arguments to suggest that compensation ought to be available at even earlier stages in the prosecution process, such as

---

[38] *Ex parte Harrison* [1988] 3 All ER 86 at p. 91.
[39] HL Debs. vol. 490, cols 398–9, 19 November 1987.
[40] However, neither will avail a company which has suffered financial loss because of the treatment of its officers: *R v Home Secretary, ex parte Atlantic Commercial Limited, The Times*, 10 March 1997.
[41] JUSTICE, *Report on Compensation for Wrongful Imprisonment* (London, 1982) para. 7.

for a person who has spent time in custody awaiting trial whereupon the prosecution offers no evidence, or where a person is detained in police custody and then released without charge. There is the opportunity to sue for false imprisonment or malicious prosecution in such cases, but establishing these causes of action is notoriously difficult.[42] There remains a valid argument to suggest, therefore, that persons who have been wrongfully denied their liberty, or have wrongfully been the subject of some other criminal punishment, should be entitled to apply for compensation of some kind. Such a scheme, however, would undoubtedly be very difficult to apply and would be much more costly. Whilst such drawbacks are not insurmountable, they do lend some rationale for the narrow remit of the current scheme. It has also been confirmed that the presumption of innocence under Article 6(2) of the European Convention does not require a broader compensation scheme.[43]

The Criminal Justice Act 1988 makes no attempt to define what the term 'miscarriage of justice' means but provides that statutory compensation will only come into effect in very specific circumstances, namely, when a conviction has been pardoned or quashed on an appeal out of time, or on a reference back to the Court of Appeal.[44] Thus, for the purposes of the Act, a miscarriage of justice only occurs when a decision is reversed beyond the normal stages of trial and 'standard' appeal. These criteria invariably take a considerable amount of time to satisfy and possibly reflect a guiding factor behind state compensation: that it is not a payment in recognition of a miscarriage of justice *per se* but is designed to recognise 'the hardship caused by the conviction,' which, at this stage in the process, should be a significant hardship suffered by a minimal number of people.

The Home Office interpretation of section 133 was considered in *R* v *Secretary of State for the Home Department, ex parte Bateman*.[45] In 1987 Andrew Bateman was convicted and sentenced to a term of six years' imprisonment for conspiracy to handle stolen cheques and obtain goods by means of the cheques. In 1990 the Home Secretary referred the case to the Court of Appeal under the provisions of section 17 of the Criminal Appeal Act 1968. That appeal was allowed in October 1991, whereupon Bateman immediately applied for compensation, but was rejected. He was then given leave to apply for judicial review. In explaining itself to the Divisional Court, the Home Office had rejected his application on the basis that the Court of Appeal had quashed his conviction because certain statements had been wrongly admitted in evidence at the trial. In the Home Office's interpretation, this discovery of a judicial error did not amount to the emergence of a 'new or newly discovered fact' for the purposes of section 133(1). In opposition, the applicant argued that the construction of the statute was such that only in the case of pardons was the right to compensation dependent upon the 'ground that a new or newly discovered fact shows beyond reasonable doubt that there has been a miscarriage of justice'. This interpretation was rejected by the Court. Section 133

---

[42] See Fridman, G.H.L., 'Compensation of the innocent' (1963) 26 *Modern Law Review* 481; Shelbourn, C., 'Compensation for Detention' [1978] *Criminal Law Review* 22; Rogers, W.H.V., *Winfield and Jolowicz on Tort* (14th Ed., Sweet and Maxwell, London, 1994) ch. 4 and pp. 572–80.

[43] *Masson and Van Zon* v *Netherlands*, Appl.nos. 15379/89 and 15346/89, Ser. A, no. 327, (1996) 22 EHRR 491 para. 49.

[44] For a wider discussion of what may be included within the term 'miscarriage of justice', see Chapter 2.

[45] [1993] COD 494, DC, [1994] COD 504, CA.

is based largely upon Article 14(6) of the ICCPR which, as recognised by McCullough J, is virtually identical to the terms of Article 3 of the Seventh Protocol (1984) to the European Convention for the Protection of Human Rights and Fundamental Freedoms.[46] Paragraph 23 of the Explanatory Memorandum relating to the Seventh Protocol states in relation to Article 3:

> The Article applies only where the person's conviction has been reversed or he has been pardoned, *in either case* on the ground that a new or newly discovered fact shows conclusively that there has been a miscarriage of justice. [*emphasis supplied*]

Thus, the effect of the judgment is to deny a right to compensation in cases where a conviction has been quashed on the ground of wrongfully admitted evidence. The Home Secretary still retained the discretion to award Bateman an *ex gratia* payment, but this too was denied as the Parliamentary statement of 1985 established that compensation would only be paid following a wrongful conviction or charge that has resulted from 'serious default on the part of a member of a police force or of some other public authority'. In *R* v *Secretary of State for the Home Office, ex parte Harrison*,[47] it was determined that a wrong decision by a judge exercising a judicial discretion does not constitute a serious default on the part of a public authority.

In a further case, Katrina Howse[48] sought compensation for the fourteen days she spent wrongfully convicted. From 1985 she was convicted on a number of occasions for trespassing on the Greenham Common Military Airbase and sentenced under by-laws later declared *ultra vires* by the House of Lords.[49] However, the invalidity of the by-law did not amount to the discovery of a new fact which would provide her with a statutory right to compensation.[50] Furthermore, there were no 'exceptional circumstances' or default on the part of a public authority through which she could obtain an *ex gratia* payment.

Whilst the compensation scheme under the Criminal Justice Act 1988 might in theory meet the requirements of the ICCPR, it could be argued that the narrow interpretation now adopted still fails to reflect the 'spirit and purpose' of the international obligation and equally fails to respect the individual rights violated in these cases.

Procedure under the Criminal Justice Act 1988

Following a determination that there is a right to compensation, a form is sent to the applicant on which a claim for interim payments may be made.[51] Such

---

[46] Protocol 7 will be ratified as part of the process of incorporation of the Convention by the Human Rights Act 1998, but it is not expected to require legal changes to rights of appeals: *Rights Brought Home* (Cm 3782, HMSO, London 1997) para. 4.15; HL Debs vol. 58361. SP4 18 November 1997, Lord Williams.

[47] [1988] 3 All ER 86.

[48] *R* v *Secretary of State for the Home Department, ex parte Howse*, [1993] COD 494, DC, [1994] COD 504, CA.

[49] *DPP* v *Hutchinson* [1990] 2 AC 783. See also *Bugg* v *DPP* [1993] 2 WLR 628.

[50] Though her case had not been referred back to the Court of Appeal, it had satisfied the initial qualification under s.133 in that it was an appeal out of time. Under the misconception that the Home Secretary had power to quash her convictions, initially she wrote to him but, having been advised to apply for leave to appeal out of time, she did so and all her convictions under the by-laws were reversed by the Reading Crown Court in June 1991.

payments are speedily made by the Home Office, usually within days of release in order that the applicant is not faced with the further trauma of, for example, being homeless and unable to pay for rented accommodation. Though Gerard Conlon was provided with five-star hotel accommodation by an excited media upon his release,[52] the victims of the more mundane miscarriages must look after themselves, thus making swift interim payments an essential element of the compensation scheme.

Accompanying the form for interim payments are guidance notes for successful applicants. These indicate a number of areas in which compensation will be payable and enable the applicants to provide a detailed statement of their claim. Compensation payments under the statutory scheme, as under the *ex gratia* scheme, are calculated in a way analogous to the calculation of damages for civil wrongs. Personal pecuniary losses include a calculation of the loss of earnings and the reduction in future earning capacity. This may be as a result of the fact that the applicant is considerably older than when first imprisoned, thus effectively reducing employability, or, more simply, that he or she has lost touch with the modern world through serving a long sentence. In February 1997, one of the *Birmingham Six*, Paddy Hill, provided evidence of this: 'You try to get a job and people ask you whether you have been trained on IBM computers. I have to say I don't even know how to work a television set.'.[53] The complex calculations involving such things as loss of pension rights may also mean that securing the services of a forensic accountant could prove invaluable. Other losses that may be compensated include the cost of the applicant's legal assistance and the potentially considerable travel expenses incurred by the family when visiting the applicant over the years.

Non-pecuniary losses may also be claimed, though they are by their very nature extremely difficult to quantify. In the libel case, *John v MGM Ltd*,[54] Sir Thomas Bingham stated, 'It has often, and rightly, been said that there can be no precise correlation between a personal injury and a sum of money. The same is true, perhaps even more true, of injury to reputation'.[55] In many miscarriages of justice the victim may very well have been subjected to severe character assassination by prosecuting authorities seeking to justify their actions, and this may have been echoed by the mass media. A sum to compensate such injuries would obviously be very difficult to ascertain and would be unlikely to reflect the irreparable damage caused to a person's reputation by the criminal label.[56] Though the injury done to a person's character in treating them as a criminal is in many cases extreme, this is not reflected in compensation payments:[57]

It was with some irony that on the same day as details of John Preece's *ex gratia* award were leaked in the press [£77,000 for eight years in prison for a wrongful

---

[51] These payments can be substantial. In October 1989 the Home Office announced that three of the *Guildford Four* would receive immediate interim payments of £50,000, and the fourth, Paul Hill, would receive £10,000 (a reduction because at the time he still stood convicted on a separate charge of murder in Belfast). See *The Times*, 31 October 1989, p. 1.

[52] Conlon, G., *Proved Innocent* (Penguin Books, London, 1990).

[53] *The Guardian*, 22 February 1997, p. 6.

[54] [1996] 2 All ER 35.

[55] *Ibid.* at p. 54.

[56] For example, at the sentencing of Michael Hickey in November 1979, Drake J referred to him as 'a hardened, dangerous criminal': *The Guardian*, February 21 1997, p. 2.

[57] Ingman, T., *The English Legal Process* (6th ed., Blackstone Press, London, 1996) p. 173.

murder conviction] the newspapers reported that Billy Bremner, the former Leeds United and Scotland footballer, had been awarded libel damages of £100,000 by a jury over allegations . . . that he offered bribes to influence the results of football matches.

An additional problem associated with many of the recent high profile cases is that there is no precedent for the types of sums that ought to be awarded in such catastrophic situations. Nevertheless, levels of awards for identifiable damage such as chronic mental illnesses, including post-traumatic stress disorder and the various psychiatric problems which have been a recurrent theme in cases of wrongful conviction, can be based on the levels of damages awarded for such injuries in other areas of the civil law.

Statutory compensation payments do not, however, appear to entitle the family of an applicant to claim for their own losses beyond their travel expenses. In many respects the distress and harm caused to the parents, spouses and children of the applicant can be as grievous as that suffered by the applicant. The Home Office note for guidance confirms that the payment of statutory compensation, as with *ex gratia* payments, is not an admission of liability but is offered in recognition of the hardship caused by the miscarriage of justice. If this is really the rationale for payment, then recognition should be given to the fact that the ramifications of such a miscarriage extend well beyond the applicant, and in many cases result in ruined lives.

Once an application has been drawn up, it is submitted to an independent assessor under section 133(4). Schedule 12 of the Criminal Justice Act 1988 provides the terms on which an assessor is appointed, removed, retired and remunerated. Sir David Calcutt QC is the current independent assessor. To date few statutory compensation awards have been finalised in the major miscarriage cases, though some of the offers made have courted controversy. Whilst Gerard Conlon is reported to have settled for a final payment in the region of £400,000, members of the *Birmingham Six* were 'insulted' at similar offers and are set to challenge these 'full and final' offers in the High Court.[58] Guidance is provided as to the levels of awards only in respect of 'harm to reputation or similar damage' by section 133(4A).

Such offers do not appear to compare favourably with the available guidance as to the appropriate level of compensation taken from awards of damages made in cases of false imprisonment.[59] In *Lunt* v *Liverpool City Justices*,[60] an appeal was made by the plaintiff against an assessment of damages for a total of forty two days' wrongful imprisonment of £13,500. The Court of Appeal made it clear that the sum is not to be calculated by an hourly rate but is largely based on the humiliation and discomfort suffered. Reference was made to the case of *Walter* v *Alltools*[61] in which Lawrence LJ said, 'A false imprisonment does not merely affect

[58] *Daily Telegraph*, 22 April 1996, p. 1; *The Guardian*, 22 April 1996, p. 7.
[59] See Clayton, R. and Tomlinson, H., *Civil Actions Against the Police* (2nd ed., Sweet and Maxwell, London, 1992). An award of £6250 was made in an action for breach of contract and negligence against a solicitor whose lamentable performance had resulted in a wrongful conviction set aside over two years later (but not imprisonment): *McLeish* v *Amoo-Gottfried & Co., The Times*, 13 October 1993.
[60] (1991, LEXIS).
[61] (1944) 171 LTR 371.

a man's liberty; it also affects his reputation. The damage continues until it is caused to cease by an avowal that the imprisonment was false.'.[62] Mr Lunt was of impeccable character and reputation. Though the Court found that the damage to his reputation was of a relatively minor kind since his imprisonment was not the subject of any widespread publicity, nor did the imprisonment flow from any accusation of crime but from a non-payment of rates, nonetheless the appropriate award in the circumstances should be one of £25,000. Though the Court emphasised that the case was not setting any standard to be followed as each case must be dealt with on its own facts, the award was nevertheless brought more closely in line with other such judicial awards. These include, for example, *Wershof* v *Commissioner of Police for the Metropolis*,[63] in which a young solicitor went to the family jewellers' shop where his younger brother was in dispute with the police as to whether a ring on sale in the jewellers' shop was stolen or not. The plaintiff was subsequently arrested and firmly marched out of the shop in front of his brother and employees and customers in the shop. He was detained in a police cell for about one hour before being charged and released on bail. The sum awarded at first instance was £1,000. In *Reynolds* v *Commissioner of Police for the Metropolis*,[64] the plaintiff was arrested in the early hours of the morning and taken to a police station in a journey that took two and a half hours. She was detained until 8 p.m., and did not return home until 11 p.m. The jury assessed the damages at £12,000. In *Houghton* v *Chief Constable of Greater Manchester*,[65] the plaintiff had been to a fancy-dress party dressed as a policeman and carrying a truncheon. He was arrested shortly after midnight on suspicion of possessing an offensive weapon and detained for two and a half hours. The court awarded a sum of £600. Though these cases do not establish a mathematical scale of damages, they do provide broad guidance and emphasise the importance of the individual facts of a case in determining the correct sum rather than purely accounting for the length of wrongful imprisonment.

More recently, in *Thompson* v *Metropolitan Police Commissioner, Hsu* v *Metropolitan Police Commissioner*,[66] Lord Woolf sought to provide general guidance and clarification as to the directions to be given to a jury to assist them in assessing the damages to be awarded in cases involving unlawful conduct by the police towards the public. He stated that, 'In a straightforward case of wrongful arrest and imprisonment the starting point is likely to be about £500 for the first hour during which the plaintiff has been deprived of his or her liberty. After the first hour an additional sum is to be awarded, but that sum is to be on a reducing scale . . .'. He further suggested that a period of twenty-four hours would equate to about £3000, again followed by a reducing daily scale. Aggravating features could increase the award and 'can include humiliating circumstances at the time of arrest or any conduct of those responsible for the arrest or the prosecution which shows that they had behaved in a high-handed, insulting, malicious or oppressive manner either in relation to the arrest or the imprisonment.'. Exemplary damages

---

[62] *Ibid.* at p. 372.
[63] [1978] 3 All ER 540.
[64] [1982] *Criminal Law Review* 600.
[65] (1986) 84 Cr App Rep 319.
[66] [1997] 2 All ER 762. Further on the guidelines, see Cragg, S. and Harrison, J., 'New guidelines for police misconduct damages' (1997) *May Legal Action* 22; Spencer, J.N., 'Damages in civil cases: ordinary, aggravated and exemplary damages' (1997) 161 *Justice of the Peace* 456.

were unlikely to be less than £5000 or more than £50,000. Though the Home Office does not accept any legal liability when making compensation payments for miscarriages of justice, a parallel should still be drawn with these cases of false imprisonment in terms of the methods used to calculate an appropriate sum.[67]

In some miscarriages of justice involving lengthy sentences and considerable aggravating factors, such as in the cases of the *Birmingham Six* and the *Guildford Four*, compensation payments based on similar calculations ought to be very substantial, and certainly more than, for example, an award of £316,000 compensation offered to Paddy Hill for the 16 years he spent in prison. Following the complexity and seriousness of the aggravating factors in these cases, coupled with the apparent desire to keep the amount of compensation payments to a minimum, it is of little surprise that a number of legal challenges against the assessment criteria will be made before satisfactory final payments are formulated. It is timely that the Criminal Cases Review Commission has usurped the role of the Home Office in referring possible miscarriages of justice to the Court of Appeal, for if the Home Office were faced with a further series of cases in which compensation payments might be substantial, the conflict of interests is obvious.

Conclusion

Though it took a long time to establish a right to statutory compensation in national legislation,[68] its scope does broadly reflect the minimum requirements of the ICCPR and the Seventh Protocol of the European Convention on Human Rights. Whether the minimum is acceptable or desirable is another matter, and perhaps the onus is on the Home Office to interpret applications more generously in various ways. First, though an appellant may technically have a conviction quashed on the basis of a misdirection, this should not prevent an application on the basis of a lack of new evidence if this nevertheless existed in abundance but was not necessary for the court's decision. If the compensation scheme is to recognise satisfactorily the level of hardship caused by a wrongful conviction, then the Home Office must interpret the legislation to include rather than exclude people such as Katherine Howse and Andrew Bateman. Secondly, one could argue that the qualification in section 133 of the Criminal Justice Act 1988, that proof of a miscarriage of justice must be beyond reasonable doubt before compensation is paid, is too narrow. It certainly suggests that two classes of quashed convictions have been created which is the very situation the Home Secretary has sought to avoid under the *ex gratia* scheme and which is contrary to principle:[69]

It is questionable whether any country which purports to maintain a presumption of innocence can without betraying that principle demand positive proof of innocence before awarding compensation, especially where there has been an acquittal.

---

[67] But it must be admitted that the *Thompson* guidelines cannot be applied mathematically and can be 'departed from in order to reflect factors which, whilst not justifying aggravated or exemplary damages, worsen the plaintiff's loss or damage': Gatty, D., 'Police case note' (1998) January *Legal Action* 15, citing in authority *Hussain* v *Chief Constable of West Midlands Police* (unreported, 1997).

[68] In 1982, the UK was the only member country of the Council of Europe with no statutory compensation scheme: JUSTICE, *Report on Compensation for Wrongful Imprisonment* (London, 1982) para. 5.

[69] Shelbourn, C., 'Compensation for detention' [1978] *Criminal Law Review* 22 at p. 26.

The position adopted in section 133 virtually demands such proof of innocence, and so compensation is withheld from many deserving claimants. Thirdly, the task of the assessor when determining a payment must be to seek to compensate the applicant fairly and openly, an assessment which ought not to have a particular regard to keeping a firm grip on the purse strings. Compensation should not be a balancing exercise but an opportunity to make amends as far as is possible.

In reality, whilst no amount of monetary compensation can fully 'make amends' for a wrongful conviction, it can ease the burden for many applicants.[70] What is undoubtedly lacking for those who have wrongfully suffered a loss of liberty, especially for an extended period, is any form of rehabilitation programme. For prisoners who have rightly served long sentences, there are retraining schemes to help them find employment, somewhere to live and generally readjust into society. For the wrongfully convicted there is nothing. One problem is that the wrongfully convicted are often unaware of their release date until, in some cases less than a week before it occurs, and therefore it is difficult to provide rehabilitation programs inside the prison. For example, Gerard Conlon describes how he was given less than two days' notice of his release after spending 14 years in prison. Confirmation of the rumours of his release came from a radio news broadcast rather than the prison governor.[71] Yet, there is no reason why help cannot be provided as part of a compensation package. Without such help the original wrongful conviction can continue to wreck lives, no matter how much monetary compensation is provided. Paddy Hill said, following the release of the *Bridgewater Three*, 'There is not a week goes by when I don't wish I was back in prison.'.[72] Only five months after being released from prison following his conviction for the murder of Carl Bridgewater, Michael Hickey was fined £200 for the theft of a ring. His solicitor explained that, 'there is a deep sense of despair which pervades his life . . . [he trusts] precisely nobody.'.[73] Following his 18 years' imprisonment, he was given little assistance to readjust into society. Indeed, Hickey's mother claimed that the theft was essentially to demonstrate the very fact that he had left prison with nothing and still had not received compensation.

As a number of legal challenges against the level of statutory compensation awards appear in the offing, an evaluation of the statutory scheme in terms of the sums it has offered is not flattering. Certainly the sums suggested to date do not compare favourably with damages for wrongful imprisonment and do not reflect a transparent assessment procedure. The decisions in the recent cases of *Lunt* and *Thompson* and *Hsu* provide a sound basis from which to establish fair and proportionate payments, and these must be taken on board by the independent assessor. In addition, one could suggest that the scheme should be operated more swiftly. Though it is accepted that in a number of cases the serious nature of the long-term effect of the psychological harm suffered may not allow swift payments

---

[70] This does not apply to all. In 1976, at the age of 23, Stefan Kiszko was convicted of the murder of a schoolgirl. The conviction was quashed in 1992 following the discovery of evidence that he could not have been the murderer (see Chapter 2). Less than two years after his release, Mr Kiszko died at the age of 41. A family friend commented, 'After being released, Stefan could not rouse himself and never recovered from what happened . . . He could not face the world.': Sanders, A. and Young, R., *Criminal Justice* (Butterworths, London, 1994) p. 185.

[71] See Conlon, G., *Proved Innocent* (Penguin Books, London, 1990) ch. 28.

[72] *The Times*, 22 February 1997, p. 6.

[73] *The Times*, 1 July 1997, p. 10.

to be assessed, the delays currently experienced are inexcusable. Thus, even though the statutory scheme has the relatively narrow remit of providing monetary compensation to a small group, it delays too long in paying too few too little. Since the scheme remained largely untouched by the Criminal Appeal Act 1995[74] any reform is unlikely in the near future, and it is regrettable therefore that although miscarriages will undoubtedly still occur, the State response will still be to throw an initial downpayment at an applicant (albeit not enough!) rather than to ensure that he or she has some lasting quality of life.

---

[74] 'The Government has concluded . . . that there should be no change to the present arrangements for deciding whether compensation should be awarded and for determining the amount of such awards.': Home Office, *Criminal Appeals and the Establishment of a Criminal Cases Review Authority: A Discussion Paper* (HMSO, London, 1994) para. 94.

13

The Role and Impact of Journalism

Mark Stephens and Peter Hill

A   MEDIA INTERFERENCES IN TRIALS –
MARK STEPHENS

It is appropriate that as I write (in late November 1996) O. J. Simpson has just taken the stand in a civil trial across the Atlantic brought by the family and friends of his late wife, Nicole Brown-Simpson and her friend, Ronald Goldman. I am, however, undecided as to whether I should use this introduction to my chapter as it gives away the fact that I began to write well after the deadline for submissions; I'll risk it for the sake of a story. That is really what this chapter is all about – risking it for the sake of a story.

My prime concern in this section, and indeed in much of the work I do as a lawyer who often represents people who are themselves, or by reason of an action or situation in the public eye, is media interference in the course of justice. Having spoken with Peter Hill whose viewpoint is put forward in the second half of this chapter, I feel that it may be necessary to qualify my concern. My reason for doing so is neither that I am inspired to retract all that I have ever believed in to come into line with his opinions, nor is it because our views are irreconcilable. Rather, in speaking to Peter Hill, I came to comprehend for the first time exactly how great the discrepancy is between the visions of lawyer and journalist. Account must also be taken of the fact that some, but not all, of the dangers of interference with the course of justice are the sole responsibility of the media.

Media Interferences with Justice

My starting point has been for some time that I am for justice, somehow representing if not 'good' at least 'truth', while the journalist's prime objective is 'the story' – at whatever cost, he is able and willing to risk it ('it' being justice, dignity, and others' liberty or whatever). Peter's primary concern, as I perceive it, is the investigation and exposure for the public good of miscarriages of justice. Peter explains the subjects of investigation as being of a tripartite nature, the three elements involving: serious breaches of law, loopholes in the law or government which create weaknesses in the system, and 'consumer journalism' involving perhaps the abuse of the supposed spirit, if not the letter, of the law. My concern with regard to journalistic 'investigation' and press coverage and that which I would happily call 'consumer journalism' (although it does not correspond with Peter's use of the phrase) is the very specific area of media 'interference' prior to, and during, active trials.[1]

I believe in every individual's right to a fair trial; I also believe in freedom of expression. In demanding that the media should temper and regulate that which is published, I am not condoning censorship. Rather, I am making a plea for truth, honesty and above all else integrity on the part of the media. In the absence of those qualities my concern is that the legal profession should be aware of, and equipped to respond to, media interference and that we should have adequate and enforced legislation to prevent or combat the ill-effects of such interference.

Images of the O. J. Simpson trial will never leave us: the chase, the courtroom, the merchandise, the French and Saunders parody. We are forced to ask exactly what sort of challenge can a further civil trial present to a man who has already performed on a world stage? Is Simpson's civil trial only occurring at all because of the media which surrounded the original trial for the murders of Simpson's wife and her friend? I think that the answer has to be 'yes'.[2] At the end of any trial the likelihood is that one party will be disgruntled or distraught, feeling that they have been wronged or let down by the legal system. Usually though, that sense of failure or injustice is founded in a belief that they are 'right' and that the other party is 'wrong'. It is not usually because the outcome of the trial or the decision of judge or jury do not measure up to the opinion of a transglobal audience. But in the O. J. Simpson trial that is exactly what happened. We look back now, bandying about phrases such as 'media circus', recalling the hysteria, the opinion-mongering, and we explain it, at least in part, as relating to the American way. Everything, including the media and the legal system, is bigger, brighter, bolder, brasher and better for a story. But the nature of this beast is not peculiar to our transatlantic cousins.

Shortly after O. J. Simpson had been found innocent – or at least not guilty in the court of Judge Ito – another judge, Roger Sanders, this time sitting in an English court, saw fit to dismiss from that court the charges against Geoff Knights, perhaps best known for his girlfriend's (*Eastender's* actress, Gillian Taylforth) novel way of dealing with his pancreatitis. The judge declared that the media intervention in the case had been such that a fair trial was made impossible.[3] This was a courageous decision on his part, but the real issue is whether he had any other option in making it and why it became necessary to dispose of the case in this way. The prosecution actually sought to appeal against the decision on the basis that the judgment was wrong; intriguingly, the appeal was filed one day out of time and therefore did not go ahead. The powerful sway of media opinion had not long before shown itself as a guiding factor and a key element in the trial of Michelle and Lisa Taylor.[4]

---

[1] For the meaning of 'active', see Contempt of Court Act 1981, s. 2(3) and sch. 1.

[2] *People v Simpson* (Case Number BA097211, California, 1995). See http://www.islandnet.com/walraven/simpson.html; Schmalleger, F, *Trial of the Century: People of the State of California vs. Orenthal James Simpson* (Prentice Hall, New Jersey, 1996).

[3] *R v Knights, The Times*, 5 October 1995, p. 1. See Crowther, E., 'Publish and then be damned' (1996) 160 *Justice of the Peace* 20. A decision was later taken not to bring contempt proceedings against the *Daily Mail, Daily Mirror, The Sun, The Star*, and *Today: The Times*, 1 August 1996 p. 3

In that particular case the media in general and especially tabloids, including *The Sun* and *The Star* in particular, went beyond intimating a set of facts but actually constructed a set of facts using manipulated photographs from a video-recording in order to present a story other than, and in the eyes of the media better than, the truth. What was in reality a civil greeting between bridegroom and wedding guest became at the hands of the tabloids an impassioned embrace between a killer and her lover under headlines such as 'Judas Kiss' and 'Cheat's Kill'. *The Sun* ran Michelle's presence at the wedding under the title 'The "Killer" Mistress who was at lover's wedding'. A large arrow ran from the word 'Killer' to Michelle Taylor's face on the cover of the paper. Even the perspective of the broadsheets was one of assumed guilt.

Having been convicted of murder and accessory to murder respectively, Michelle and Lisa Taylor had their sentences quashed when their convictions were found to be unsound at appeal. Lord Justice McCowan, presiding over the Taylors' release, stated that he found it 'quite impossible to say that the jury were not influenced in their decision by what they read in the press'.[5] Lord Justice McCowan also specifically requested that the Attorney-General, Sir Nicholas Lyell, should address the issue. For reasons which he elected not to disclose even under pain of judicial review,[6] the Attorney-General decided that his intervention was either unnecessary or unwise. The most significant and damning consideration relating to Sir Nicholas Lyell's omission to act has to be the plight of Michelle and Lisa Taylor themselves. Had the media succeeded in their campaign of unsubstantiated accusation, they would have been wrongly imprisoned for approximately 20 years.

Perhaps the closest event that this country has seen to the O. J. Simpson saga is the treatment of the late Fred and Rosemary West. Arguments by the latter on appeal that her trial was prejudiced by media reporting were, however, rejected.[7] Even if she had been successful at appeal, Rosemary would still be guilty in the mind of the public. Likewise how many people, despite the total lack of evidence implicating him, the ultimate collapse of the case against him, and his acquittal, think of Colin Stagg as inextricably entwined with the murder of Rachel Nickell and will continue to do so until someone else is convicted, by which time the damage will anyway have been done?[8]

There is of course a difference between being innocent and being not guilty, and it is often the media which not only explains but also creates this distinction. A failure by the prosecution to discharge the burden of proof is of little consequence to those covering the story because, quite simply, the media works on 'probabilities' rather than 'beyond reasonable doubts'.

---

[4] *R v Taylor; R v Taylor* (1994) 98 Cr App Rep 361. See Naylor, B., 'Fair trial or free press' (1994) 53 *Cambridge Law Journal* 492.

[5] (1993) 98 Cr App Rep 361 at p. 369.

[6] *R v Solicitor-General ex parte Taylor and Another, The Times,* 14 August 1995.

[7] *R v West, The Times,* 3 April 1996. The *Gloucester Citizen* was fined soon afterwards for its reporting of the committal of Fred West: *The Times,* 26 April 1996 p. 8. Compare *R v Kray* (1969) 53 Cr App R 412; *R v Savundranayagan* [1968] 1 WLR 1769; *R v McCann* (1991) 92 Cr App R 239; *R v Reade, The Times,* 16 October 1993; *R v Wood, The Times,* 11 July 1995; *R v Knights, The Times,* 5 October 1995 p. 1.

[8] See Gibb, F., 'Police tactics on trial', *The Times,* 15 September 1994; Gibb, F., 'Stagg case increases pressure on Lyell to curb media coverage', *The Times,* 16 September 1994; Doherty, M., 'Watching the detectives' (1994) 144 *New Law Journal* 1525; Scrivener, A., 'Mistrial by media?', *The Times,* 25 February 1997.

Particular Failures Connected with Media Interferences with Justice

The Police

In both the trials of the Taylor sisters and of Colin Stagg evidence of something between ineptitude and foul play on the part of the police was a feature. It would be easy to allow evidence of police misbehaviour to overshadow and negate the seriousness of media misbehaviour. I am not saying that dishonesty on the part of the police is of no importance: what I am saying is that the regulation of the media and the enforcement of the Contempt of Court Act 1981 and common law *sub judice* rules relating to media coverage of trials are just as important. Nevertheless, the issue of inappropriate reporting on the part of the media is entwined with equally inappropriate behaviour on the part of the police. The Police Discipline Rules lie neglected whilst it is known that as part of the interdependent relationship between police and press, it is often the police who give reporters their leads.[9] Indeed it could be argued that to some degree it is the police who control crime reporting.[10] Of course such journalists are valuable to the police for the investigative work which they are able to do through funding from a particular publication or broadcasting body and perhaps by means which the police could not officially countenance. In cases of murder or abduction the police actively encourage police conferences to enable them to 'plant' questions with journalists and to disseminate information contained in exchanges with journalists which could not directly be volunteered by the police. It is not unusual for the police to employ behavioural psychologists to study footage of such conferences in an attempt to ascertain more about the character of any participant.

The Attorney-General

The dismissal from court of the case against Geoff Knights,[11] and the initial conviction of the Taylor sisters demonstrate more than adequately the danger and gravity of consequences of the failure to abide by the Contempt of Court Act 1981. It seems near ironic that section 1 of the Act provides for strict liability, that is: 'the rule of law whereby conduct may be treated as a contempt of court as tending to interfere with the course of justice in particular legal proceedings regardless of intent to do so'. The media have grown accustomed to exploiting the general presumption that the Contempt of Court Act is an unenforced and unenforceable piece of legislation. If the Attorney-General fails in his duty to enforce such legislation, it seems hypocritical to expect the media to abide by it. And so the issue shifts from the accountability of the press 'risking it for the sake of a story' to the accountability of the Government 'risking it for the sake of their political allies'. It is of course the Government's allies in the tabloid press who would be first in the firing-line were the Contempt of Court Act to be properly enforced.

So, the final courtroom battle in the case relating to the Taylor sisters concerned the accountability of the Attorney-General in the matters of contempt beyond the

---

[9] Schlesinger, P. and Tumber, H., *Reporting Crime* (Clarendon Press, Oxford, 1994); Lord Chancellor's Advisory Committee on Legal Education and Conduct, *Lawyers' Comments to the Media* (1997) para. 28 *et seq.*

[10] See Ferguson, G., 'Set the agenda' (1995) 103 *Police Review* 26; Morton, J., '*R v OJ Simpson*' (1995) 11 *Policing* 325.

[11] *R v Knights, The Times*, 5 October 1995 p. 1.

face of the court. This challenge to fair trials, if anything, is what should have been exhibited to the public attention at the time. But instead, the cuttings files were reopened, and 'those pictures' were exhumed again along with all the misplaced furore which accompanied them on their first exposure. Despite the fact that the constitutional dangers should have been fully aired in public in this set of proceedings, this concern was not in the least attractive to the media (with the exception of the rarefied category of legal journalism). The media hounds' reaction to the serious nature of the affair was to drag their own, by now taxidermal, body of effects out of the filing cabinet. Besides being less than helpful to the proceedings themselves, this revival of the media's Taylor sisters showcase provided an ironic echo of the original trial. A particularly pertinent editorial in *The Independent*[12] stated that the Taylor sisters' application for judicial review was to be welcomed, 'as open(ing) the debate about whether the Contempt of Court Act strikes the right balance between press freedom and impartial justice.'. The editorial referred to Sir Nicholas Lyell's decision, 'not to prosecute five tabloid newspapers which had published material that was found to have prejudiced their original trial.'. Even the Court of Appeal held their coverage to have been 'unremitting, extensive, sensational, inaccurate and misleading'[13] and commented that:[14]

> What, in fact, they did was not reporting at all; it was comment, and comment which assumed guilt on the part of the girls in the dock. But the Press is no more entitled to assume guilt in what it writes during the course of a trial, than a police officer is entitled to convince himself that a defendant is guilty and suppress evidence, the emergence of which he fears might lead to the defendant's acquittal . . .

One has to ask oneself following this feature in *The Independent* why the Attorney-General still failed to act.[15] The moment was obviously right for a reassessment of both legislation and self-regulation in the area: the writer of the feature in *The Independent* actually voiced a truth to which few journalists admit in saying that, 'Newspapers are tempted to break the rules because they fear that their rivals will steal their readers by publishing everything they can find.'. A representative of *The Sun* voiced the same sentiment on Greater London Radio, but this still failed to provoke the Attorney-General into action.

There exist of course, certain non-legislative and non-governmental remedies for the problems which we are encountering. However, the existence of regulatory and disciplinary bodies such as the Press Complaints Commission (PCC) should not permit the relevant legislation to lie redundant, the Attorney-General to ignore his duty or editors to take the law into their own hands. The limited powers of the PCC may only be activated once something has been published and thus once the damage has been done. In my opinion, prevention is better than cure, particularly when that cure cannot guarantee the reinstatement of rightful liberty or the restoration of innocence in the perception of others.

---

[12] 28 July 1995.
[13] (1993) 98 Cr App Rep 361 at p. 368.
[14] *Ibid.* at p. 369.
[15] The negative decision was actually taken under his authority by the Solicitor-General. See *The Times*, 29 July 1995 p. 2; *R v Solicitor General, ex parte Taylor, The Times*, 14 August 1995.

The Operative Legal Rules

Even if the law were to be properly enforced, there would still be problems. The Contempt of Court Act's strict liability rule applies only to publications whilst proceedings are 'active', but it is not only within that period that damage may be inflicted.[16] Furthermore, common law contempt is almost unworkable; the necessary 'intention' to impede or prejudice the administration of justice is near impossible to prove and again the media are not only aware of this fact but keen to take advantage of it.[17]

Media Involvements with Justice

The Televising of Court Proceedings

Over recent years there has been a move to, or perhaps a mode for, the concept of televising trials.[18] I am unwilling, however, to believe that this aspiration, at least on the part of the media, is founded in a desire to allow justice to be seen to be done or to genuinely demythologise the courts and their workings. I would welcome sensible proposals for the demystifying of the law providing that they did not put justice in jeopardy. The interests of much of the media with relation to trials has been evidenced by the furore surrounding plaintiffs such as George Michael[19] and Gillian Taylforth. Currently, all the publicity surrounding these media magnets' court appearances was focused outside the courtrooms. Obviously this focus was necessitated by the prohibition on filming court proceedings in England and Wales.[20] Yet, offered the option, would the media, with general public lasciviously in tow, suddenly lose all interest in the private whys, wherefores and wardrobes of such people and develop a profound interest in the legal proceedings in which they were involved? It remains far more exciting to deliberate over exactly how many millions George Michael spent on his battle with Sony and to tot up the acreage of Armani he sported during the hearing than to be forced to concentrate on the nature of contract law and European Community regulations on business competition.

The broadcast of 'The Trial', an experimental series of Scottish trials filmed with the approval of Lord Hope and the subject of much conjecture,[21] offered an

---

[16] The courts have equally concluded the reverse, that not all comment during the 'active' period is necessarily contemptuous: *A-G v News Group Newspapers* [1986] 3 WLR 365.

[17] See *Davis v Eli Lilley (No. 2), The Times*, 23 July 1987; *In re Channel 4 TV Co.* [1988] *Criminal Law Review* 237; *A-G v Newspaper Publishing* [1987] 3 All ER 276, *The Times*, 28 February 1990; *A-G v Times Newspapers* [1992] 1 AC 191; *Re an Application by Derbyshire CC* [1988] 1 All ER 385; *A-G v News Group Newspapers* [1988] 3 WLR 163; *A-G v Sport Newspaper* [1992] 1 WLR 1194.

[18] See Report of the Working Party of the Public Affairs Committee of the General Council of the Bar, *Televising the Courts* (1989); Walker, C. and Brogarth, D., 'Televising the Courts' (1989) 153 *Justice of the Peace* 637; Hytner, B., 'Televising the courts' (1992) 13 *Journal of Media Law & Practice* 174; Caplan, J., 'Televising the courts' (1992) 13 *Journal of Media Law & Practice* 176; Thaler, P., *The Watchful Eye* (Praeger, New York, 1994).

[19] See *Panayiotou and Others v Sony Music Entertainment (UK) Ltd, The Times*, 30 June 1994.

[20] See Criminal Justice Act 1925, s. 41.

[21] See Gibb, F., 'Courting the cameras', *The Times*, 18 January 1994 p. 35; Catliff, N., 'Court on camera', *The Times*, 8 November 1994 p. 37; Linklater, M., 'Court on camera' (1994) *The Times*, 15 November 1994 p. 18; Munday, R., 'Televising the courts' (1995) 159 *Justice of the Peace* 37, 57; Webster, S., 'Lights, camera, action . . . M'lud' (1994) 138 *Solicitors' Journal* 1176.

appearance of the media and legal systems apparently in harmony. Ultimately however, one was left with the sense that there was no truth in the semblance; that this was life imitating artifice. The problem, not assisted by the format of the programme interspersed as it was with views of Edinburgh and Scottish sunsets, was that the trial appeared to occur in a vacuum despite the inevitable 'before and after' footage. The series itself and the reaction of the invited audience from the legal profession to a special screening of 'The Trial' induced the then Lord Chief Justice to close his mind completely to the replication of the exercise in England and Wales.[22]

What tends to be overlooked in the televised trials debate is the fact that the only proceedings in which filming would be permitted are those at which the public may anyhow attend; and the fact that some fairly extensive editing would be required. Compliance with the current contempt of court legislation would determine that the broadcast of trials would occur only following judgment. But could this be guaranteed? Would such legislation be overturned along with the very authority to film proceedings? Contemporaneous broadcasting could well result in the ridiculous fervour generated in America during trials such as those of O.J. Simpson, William Smith Kennedy[23] and the Menendez brothers.[24]

Media Payments to Participants in Court Proceedings

Ironically the Americans do not seem to suffer from one of the most potentially corruptive practices of the English media: the payment of witnesses. The issue first came to mass attention in the prosecution of Brady and Hindley in which the chief prosecution witness admitted receiving ongoing payments from a newspaper in return for information. The Attorney-General, despite his belief that such arrangements could seriously jeopardise the administration of justice, said that he could find no evidence that any testimony had been affected.[25] In 1974 the Phillimore Report on Contempt of Court[26] concluded that the potential risks of financial incentives to witnesses were sufficiently grave to prompt an enquiry and to contemplate the creation of legislation rendering the practice in certain forms a criminal offence. Twenty-two years later it is estimated that 19 witnesses in the West cases received payment or at least contracted with the media,[27] including Janet Leach who acted as the appropriate adult during Fred's police interviews and who categorically denied any arrangement with the media both in her statement and on oath. It was only after Mirror Group Newspapers informed the prosecution that Ms Leach had an agreement with them that she admitted as much in cross-examination.

The issue of payments to witnesses has been the subject of comment by Government,[28] House of Commons Select Committee[29] and Press Complaints

[22] See 'Lord Chief Justice's "no" to court TV' (1996) 146 New Law Journal 274.

[23] State v Smith (No. 91–5482–CF.A02, 1991). See Hutt, S.H., 'Note: in praise of public access' (1991) Duke LJ 368; Denno, D.W., 'Perspectives on disclosing rape victims' names' (1993) 61 Fordham L Rev 1113

[24] People vs. Lyle and Erik Menendez (Case no. BA 068880, California, 1995). The Menendez brothers were convicted of murder on 20 March 1996, for the killings of their parents. They are serving life prison terms. See http://www.courttv com/casefiles/menendez/.

[25] See Lord Chancellor's Department, Payments to Witnesses (HMSO, London, 1996) para. 11.

[26] See Committee on Contempt of Court, Report (Cmnd 5794, HMSO, London, 1974).

[27] Lord Chancellor's Department, Payments to Witnesses (HMSO, London, 1996) para. 13.

[28] Lord Chancellor's Department, Payments to Witnesses (HMSO, London, 1996).

[29] National Heritage Committee, Press Activity Affecting Court Cases (1996–97 HC 86).

Commission,[30] but promised reform has not yet taken place and seems increasingly unlikely.[31]

The Relationships between Lawyers and the Media

In America lawyers are becoming court-step game show hosts, actually publicising their endeavours and discussing their strategies.[32] The steps of our domestic courts are relatively uncluttered by lawyers playing host to the media: it is more often the case that when a lawyer appears in the media making a statement about one of his cases, a large proportion of the legal profession throw up their hands in horror and accuse that lawyer of inviting media interference. It is vital to recognise that with or without the participation of the lawyer a debate will still rage if the situation is sufficiently provocative. Whilst a barrister can slip from court as he slips from his wig and gown, solicitors and their accompanying clients are prey for the waiting media. It is my belief that it is for a solicitor to inform the debate where it is strictly necessary, and it is interesting that unease about the 'celebrity lawyer' was recently found to be largely misplaced by the Lord Chancellor's Advisory Committee on Legal Education and Conduct.[33]

Accordingly, in England and Wales, one (albeit extra-curricular) part of a solicitor's duty to his client is to recognise the forum created by the media and to treat it in a dignified and judicious manner. The legal profession can potentially do as much if not more harm by failing or refusing to acknowledge the platform which they are lent, than by stepping onto it (after sufficient preparation naturally). For some clients the offer of the opportunity to tell their story and perhaps earn some money is too great to resist. A wronged client with the promise of national press coverage and no guidance is a dangerous thing – to himself, his case, and even his lawyer.

So, the media can be a useful tool for members of the profession and certain of their clients, provided it is treated in the correct manner. As I said when I was working for Princess Anne's former maid in *Joyce* v *Sengupta*,[34] there are two kinds of lawyers: the 'fixed paradigm' type and the creative sort. The former treats the law as a rigid set of 'cans' and 'cannots', while the latter treats it as an art form, skilfully manipulating its rich pattern to evolve a solution. But the old adage 'all publicity is good publicity' simply is not true. Any type of media contact

---

[30] *Moving Ahead* (1996). See Code of Practice, para. 9.

[31] See *The Times*, 30 October 1996 p. 5, 17 December 1998 p. 2. The desirability of further restrictions is disputed: Pannick, D., 'No need to act on witness payments', *The Times*, 19 November 1996 p. 41; Stott, R., 'Lawyers blame the press for prejudicing fair trials' *The Times*, 20 November 1996 p. 25.

[32] This applies both to prosecution and defence: Dershowitz, A.M., *The Best Defense* (Random House, New York, 1982), *Reversal of Fortune: Inside the von Bülow case* (Random House, New York, 1986) *Reasonable doubts: The O.J Simpson case and the criminal justice system* (Simon & Schuster, New York, 1996); Clark, M. with Carpenter, T., *Without a Doubt* (Viking, New York, 1997). Even jurors have published their experiences: Kennedy, T., Kennedy, J. and Abrahamson, A., *Mistrial of the Century* (Dove Books, Beverley Hills, 1995); Wrightsman, L.S., Posey, A.J. and Scheflin, A.W., *Hung Jury: the diary of a Menéndez juror* (Temple University Press, Philadelphia, 1995). There is also the televised outlet, Court TV, for their frequent appearances: see http://www.courttv com/.

[33] Lord Chancellor's Advisory Committee on Legal Education and Conduct, *Lawyers' Comments to the Media* (1997) para. 62. The Law Society Code of Practice for Advocates para. 6.3 states that personal views or opinions on clients' cases must not be offered; the Bar Code of Conduct, para. 604 relates to any comment.

[34] [1993] 1 WLR 337.

should be entered into with a great deal of caution, careful preparation and even a pinch of salt. The reasoning behind the need for caution and preparation are obvious: consider how much the media need to know for your purposes and not theirs; consider what the tone of any media exposure should be; guard against allowing inappropriate utterances to escape and saying things which could be taken out of context; and make an informed decision as to whether or not your client should be in the public eye at all. Will public recognition with a particular legal issue ruin their career and sully their reputation, or will it in fact provide protection? For example, in the case of a lesser-known client involved with potentially dangerous issues, it is true to say that people only notice that somebody has disappeared if they were aware of their existence in the first place. The pinch of salt is a vital ingredient because to some extent the media will always express what they want, whether this entails lending a story a political bias, a prejudgment intimation of innocence or guilt or publishing a full blown 'error'. During Fred and Rosemary West's saturation of the press one tabloid paper adorned its cover with a large photograph accompanied by an authoritative character assassination. Thus was Rosemary West introduced to the nation: except that the photograph was not of Rosemary West but of a wholly unconnected individual. Obviously this potentially fatal mistake was entirely the fault of the publication in question. However with this sort of lack of responsibility on the part of the media, it is vital that the solicitor should be constantly aware of such potential disasters before they hit the headlines.

Conclusion

It is again appropriate that, as I conclude this section (in March 1997), O. J. Simpson has been found liable for compensation for the battery and unlawful deaths of Nicole Brown-Simpson and Ronald Goldman in the civil trial brought against him in Los Angeles. Things have been rather different this time; this time the jury agreed with the media. The paper which I have before me screams in three inch high letters from its cover, 'OJ DID IT': they have been waiting for two and half years to use that headline. I am undecided as to whether I should use this conclusion to my chapter as it gives away the fact that I finished writing well after the renewed deadline for submissions; I'll risk it for the sake of a story.

B   THE ROLE OF THE JOURNALIST – PETER HILL

Mark Stephens's comment that his starting point as a lawyer was that he is 'for justice, somehow representing if not "good" at least "truth"', and the journalist's objective is 'the story' illustrates the gap between the two professions and the need for this chapter. In the past 20 years we have seen an increase in criticism of the system of justice by the media. This has been coupled with an onslaught by the judiciary against journalists who have pointed out the errors in the system. Co-operation between the media and those within the legal system and the media has traditionally been hierarchical: the lawyer expecting the reporter to record slavishly whatever is said without change or comment. That situation has enhanced the reputation of neither profession. During the 1980s the bitterness of the judiciary became so great that whilst improvements were introduced in other areas of the system, nothing was done to improve relations with the media.

As a journalist who has suffered from the wrath of the Lord Chief Justice[35] on the question of truth, I could respond to Mark's comment in similar fashion. I search for the truth; yet in the 17 years during which I have worked on alleged miscarriages of justice, I have yet to find a court primarily interested in what I would define as 'the truth'. The concept of truth depends on the rules one uses to define it.

Justice in our courts sometimes seems to have little to do with the truth. Lawyers and jurists are concerned with 'the case', or 'guilt', or 'innocence'. The truth may lie somewhere else, lost in inadmissible evidence and lack of investigation. The search for 'guilt' is a consequence of the desire for finality, the ultimate goal of the system of justice. Unfortunately, the rules laid down to produce finality diminish the value of the 'truth' produced by the courts. Truth at trial is not necessarily the whole truth. It is a limited scenario bounded by rules of evidence and even, lamentably, by the court's budget and timetable. The journalist's foundation for the truth can be equally unreliable. However, when the journalist gets it wrong, it is for different reasons, for the test of truth in journalism is different from that used in the courts.

The Legal Determination of the 'Truth'

I could offer many examples of this difference from my own experience but shall settle on the latest. In January 1997, there was a judgment in the Court of Appeal in one of the cases on which I have worked.[36] The appellant was Paul Malone, convicted in 1987 of four armed robberies. The appeal was dismissed, yet six months later the Police Complaints Authority accused five of the investigating officers of giving false and misleading evidence at the trial.[37] The demands by Malone's defence team that these same policemen should be called to give evidence at the appeal had been turned down. Two areas of the evidence in this case reflect the different aims that jurists and journalist have in their search for truth.

All four convictions depended on a woman's identification of Malone's car. She had been walking past a public house near to the scene of one of the robberies. The public house had a car park at the side with a high wall around it. As she walked along the pavement towards the entrance to the car park, a man ran past her, then turned into it – around the end of the wall. She then saw a car emerge from the car park and she remembered the registration number. The police later discovered that it was Malone's car. Malone admitted he had been in the car-park – but denied he was the man the woman had seen running into it. The key question at the trial was the time of this incident. The woman told the jury it happened at around 1:15p.m. The robbery was not reported until 1:25p.m., and there was no

---

[35] *R v Mycock* (Court of Appeal, 5 December 1985, No 6605/85). See Hill, P., 'TV Justice: rough and unready' *The Guardian*, 24 November 1992 p. 18.

[36] *R v Malone* (Court of Appeal, January 1997). See also *R v Secretary of State for the Home Dept, ex p Malone* [1995] 1 WLR 734; Mullin, J., 'Justice on trial: day at the races "led to 15-year jail term"', *The Guardian*, 5 January 1993 p. 5; Hill, P., 'Taking the politics out of justice' (1994) 144 *New Law Journal* 1270.

[37] *The Times*, 7 June 1997.

particular reason for a ten minute delay. But the jury obviously concluded that the running man was the robber – and it was therefore Malone.

At the appeal, Malone's counsel raised a second question. He argued that the witness could not be certain that the running man was the driver of the car. His point was a difficult one to express in words. The running man and the woman were moving at different speeds, and there was a high wall between them for some of the time. At the original trial the prosecution had produced police photographs which did not show the different lines of sight available to the woman during the incident. Moreover, all the police photographs had the cars in the car park clearly visible, yet it was accepted that the woman could only have seen the cars after she had passed the high wall and reached the car park entrance. Counsel argued that there could have been two men: the man who ran past the woman might not have been the man she saw getting into the car. He pointed out that the running man was out of her sight for a significant period. She was unsure of the clothing and had no other evidence to provide a link. To demonstrate how long the man must have been out of her sight, counsel attempted to introduce a video reconstruction of the incident. Scripted by an expert witness often employed to calculate possible lines of sight, the video showed the woman's different viewpoints as she walked along the pavement.

The expert's scientific approach to the problem of the varying lines of sight had prompted him to seek a baseline for the synchronisation of the actions under scrutiny. He fixed on a most remarkable fact in the woman's evidence – she remembered the car's number plate. Her evidence showed that there was only one position where she could have had a clear view of it. The expert therefore could calculate the various positions and times for the incident from this base position. He could therefore calculate where she must have been when her view was restricted by the high wall, when the running man passed her and when she could see the man getting into the car. The video demonstrated that what the woman had told the court at trial could not be wholly true.

The appeal judges refused even to see the video before declaring it inadmissible. They said that 'though tendered on the basis that it involved expertise, it was in reality no more than an attempt to prove by argument that (the witness) could not have seen the events she described.'. And they added, 'It did not need an expert's opinion to inform the jury that (she) could not have seen into the . . . car park until her line of sight cleared the wall.'. They considered that the still photographs submitted by the police had been sufficient for the jury to appreciate the truth of the woman's testimony. There was no reference to the baseline produced by the expert witness as a firmer foundation for the truth – because they refused to listen to him, wholly in line with Lord Justice Lawton's dictum that:[38]

An expert's opinion is admissible to furnish the court with scientific information which is likely to be outside the experience and knowledge of a judge or jury.

As a journalist, I claim no superiority in knowledge or experience in such matters to the average juror. However, I believe that 'truth' is best served by taking into account all the available data. Moreover, when that data is deemed insufficient, or

---

[38] *R v Turner* [1975] QB 834 at p. 841.

when better methods of evaluation are available, I think it right to seek more information and take advantage of any additional methods of evaluation. The average juror might well agree with me. The irony of this episode in the Court of Appeal is that the video might well have been admissible in the original trial. Because the police had introduced still photographs which failed to show the line of sight of the witness, the defence might have been able to introduce the video as a legitimate, indeed superior, means of contradicting the police evidence.

There was a second incident in the *Malone* appeal which provoked even less curiosity on the Appeal Court bench. A new witness was produced who had apparently seen a robbery at the same time and location as one of the robberies for which Malone had been convicted. This new witness, an ambulance driver, had immediately told the police about it – and was told they knew about it. He could only add to their knowledge of the incident by mentioning some letters on the registration plate of the getaway car and that it was a blue Cortina driving northwards from the scene. Malone agreed he had been driving in the locality – in his red Escort. But his route was in exactly the opposite direction to that of the blue Cortina seen by the ambulance man. During Malone's first interrogation the police put it to him that he knew about a Cortina. They even told him its registration number in full. The Court of Appeal was very concerned that the ambulance driver's evidence had not been disclosed to the defence. However the judges decided that disclosure had not been essential – because Malone's solicitor could have followed up the lead himself. After all the police had told Malone the registration number of the Blue Cortina. As for the ambulance driver, they concluded that what he had seen 'had nothing to do with the robbery'.

One wonders if a juror would have agreed with the Court of Appeal. It is not often that the average man in the street sees something seemingly suspicious. In this particular instance the ambulance driver saw a man dash across a pavement with something like a cash bag in his hand, jump into a car and speed off down the road with little regard for the safety of others. Coincidentally, according to the truth as determined by the Court of Appeal, another such man (Malone) committed a robbery at about the same time, in the same block. He too dashed off along the pavement with a bag in his hand, jumped into his car and sped off down the road with little regard for others. There were two key differences between these two incidents. The man seen by the ambulance driver drove north and was never investigated by the police; Malone drove south and was found guilty of robbery. Significantly, neither the police nor the Court of Appeal were interested in the name of the owner of the Cortina.

Given such decisions, are journalists really to believe – and publish – that those who work within the system of justice are wholly concerned with the 'truth'? They understand that English courts are limited in what they can do. Courts review and decide, but do not investigate. They may ask counsel for further clarification, but they never ask for further investigation to be made.[39]

A classic example occurred in 1985 in the case of Anthony Mycock in the Court of Appeal,[40] when Lord Chief Justice Lane chose to accept as the 'truth' one part

[39] The Criminal Cases Review Commission is capable of being called upon by the Court of Appeal to make further investigation, but this system is, as yet, untried. See Criminal Appeal Act 1968, s. 23A. (as amended).

[40] *R* v *Mycock*, (Court of Appeal, 5 December 1985, No 6605/85).

of the evidence of a hysterical, suggestive woman. She was the supposed victim in a case of burglary and robbery which had been referred back by the Home Secretary. Lord Lane chose to believe her even after he had accused her of lying to him.

At issue was whether the crime for which the appellant had been convicted had even taken place. Lord Lane decided that, although the appellant was not guilty, one part of the crime had certainly taken place.[41] He pointed to a part of the woman's evidence where she had described her assailant as having a 'helmet-shaped tattoo' on his hand. He decided that this assailant must have been the appellant's brother, named Gary ('Gaz').[42] Lord Lane concluded in his judgment:

> The other remarkable fact is . . . that Gaz or Gary Mycock had on the base of his left thumb a tattoo in the shape of a heart.

A ten-year-old child could have checked this. But Lord Lane did not. He relied on the evidence of one of the investigating officers, Detective Sergeant Fury, who said:

> He has a tattoo on the base of his left thumb . . . looks something like a heart, I am not quite sure.

In fact, DS Fury had already told the court that he had not seen Gary Mycock close enough to examine his hands for two years. Gary Mycock was sitting outside the courtroom when DS Fury said these words. Though no part of his brother's appeal case, he was available to provide evidence to the Court of Appeal and the Lord Chief Justice knew it. He was not called. Even more than a decade later we can still discover the 'truth' with our own eyes. Gary Mycock's tattoo is still on his hand. It is not the 'helmet' shape that Fitzpatrick described. It is not 'something like a heart' as described by DS Fury. It is not 'heart-shaped' as described by the Lord Chief Justice. It is the four letters 'A.C.A.B.'.[43] Yet legally, to this day, the 'truth' is that the four letters are 'heart-shaped'.

One wonders what the average juror might have made of this episode: yet the courts jealously protect such silliness. If the incident had occurred at trial, and a juror had met up with Gary Mycock outside the courtroom by chance – and seen the 'real truth' – the jury would certainly have been dismissed. In cases of miscarriage of justice there are numerous examples of courts not searching assiduously for the truth. Large amounts of evidence pertinent to the full picture of the crime are left out of trials because they are deemed to be not relevant to the guilt of the accused.

Routine courtroom tactics further add to the confusion around the truth. Counsel lead witnesses demanding 'yes' or 'no' to questions. They justify this on the grounds of obtaining clarity for the jury. But it can sometimes mean that the jury does not hear the full story. Witnesses often leave the box bemused at this because

---

[41] The assault, but not the burglary. The 'burgled goods' had already been proved to have been disposed of by the 'victim' herself and were all accounted for.

[42] Gary Mycock was never arrested or tried for this crime, nor did he fit any physical description given by the 'victim'.

[43] A common tattoo, an acronym for 'All Cops Are Bastards'.

they have not told the 'whole truth' that they swore to tell. Scientific evidence can produce even greater confusion, for experts are paid to put alternative arguments using selective evidence about facts where there is often a genuinely assessable truth.[44]

The Journalistic Determination of the 'Truth'

Most journalists look for the full story beyond the 'legal truths'. However, their work lacks the regulation and professional discipline that bind lawyers. Journalists have no effective regulatory body other than the organisations which employ them. Establishing standards of probity requires some kind of professional discipline. So too does fair representation and balance of that evidence. However, the means of establishing such discipline in journalism do not lie in the law. Good reporting is not founded in law, but in the journalistic ethic.

In the system of legal justice, 'truth' is decided by a court – the case then ends and the lawyer goes on to the next case. The journalist works in a different societal context. If something untrue is published the journalist responsible suffers retribution in a most direct way. The audience stops listening. This does not occur in the legal system. Perhaps people stopped listening to Lord Lane after the final *Guildford Four*[45] appeal, though I doubt it. I suspect that people did not stop listening to Lord Denning after his appalling comments on the *Birmingham Six* case:[46]

If the six men win it will mean the police are guilty of perjury . . . this is such an appalling vista that every sensible person in the land would say: It cannot be right.

Criminal lawyer associations support the opinions of the judiciary, no matter how ill-balanced and biased they may be. We ignore their decisions and strictures at our peril – regardless of whether we privately think.

Credibility and reliability of judgment are, however, supremely important to journalists. If you wish to ruin a journalist, do not accuse him or her of breaking the law – for the public will often condone that. Accuse them of lying – for the public does not easily forgive a journalist who is proved to be a liar. Although the prestige of some publishers, such as the BBC or *The Times* may lend authority to the journalists they employ, this offers no protection from the public when mistakes about truth are made. No publisher is immune from the loss of reputation that follows the publication of poorly researched articles. Those with the greatest prestige suffer most from the slightest blemish. It follows that the journalist treats 'truth' carefully. Mere publication, with the source, of the 'truth' as established in a court may not be sufficient, for the public may simply not believe it. The ultimate journalistic 'truth' does not therefore rely on rules of evidence, precedent, or courtroom privilege. The journalist turns to concepts such as 'common sense' in deciding truth. In effect, this is what the public will accept as being the truth on consideration of the available evidence.

---

[44] For a detailed analysis of the misuse of forensic evidence, see Chapter 6.
[45] See *The Times*, 20 October 1989.
[46] *McIlkenny* v *Chief Constable of the West Midlands Police Force* [1980] 2 All ER 227 at pp. 239, 240.

Editorial balance in journalism is judged by a similar yardstick. Just as the primary duty of the reporter is to present a truthful rendition of the immediate events, the primary duty of the editor is to ensure the various elements of the story are balanced so as to present a truthful picture in the wider context. To do this, the editor tries to define what the public at large will accept as a fair balance in reporting. This is normally defined as 'the public good'. The judiciary sometimes claim to act 'in the public interest',[47] but one might suggest that judges live in a world slightly less associated with the common man than does the journalist.

These different approaches to the 'truth' may cause the journalist and the lawyer to disagree on a fundamental point of principle. Unlike the lawyer, the journalist may sometimes consider that breaking the law is acceptable if it will lead to the presentation of a more truthful picture of a situation where 'the public good' may be in jeopardy. For example, in the investigation and publication of Government secrets, the moment when the wind began to blow in the journalists' favour may well have been when the new Official Secrets Act was enacted in 1989. Most journalists consider that the new offences in the Act, in so far as they replace section 2 of the 1911 Act,[48] will never be invoked, because the Act fails to recognise the validity of a public interest defence. The jury's decision in the *Clive Ponting* case[49] made it very clear that the public believes in a public interest defence even if told by a judge to put it out of their minds. So, when the journalist feels there will be strong public support for publication, he or she will almost always decide to 'publish and be damned' – whilst reaching for a copy of Article 10 of the European Convention on Human Rights.[50] Recent judgments offer mixed responses to such daring.

First, until a judgment in the High Court in 1996, the Home Office had regularly refused prisoners permission to invite journalists to visit them to discuss their cases. Journalists had been asked to make a declaration that they would not use any information gained for journalistic purposes. In *R v Secretary of State for the Home Department, ex parte Simms and O'Brien*,[51] Latham J, referring to Article 10 of the ECHR, found for the prisoners and, implicitly, for the journalists. However, the Court of Appeal concluded that a convicted prisoner had no right to communicate orally with the media through a journalist.[52]

Secondly, the Contempt of Court Act 1981 has generally been used to punish journalists who refuse to disclose a source, despite the terms of section 10, by which:[53]

---

[47] See especially the decisions to prevent the Channel 4 re-enactments of the *Ponting* and *Birmingham Six* cases: *R v Ponting, The Times*, 29 January 1985; *In re Channel 4 TV Co. Ltd* [1988] *Criminal Law Review* 237; *Channel 4 v UK*, Appl. no. 14132/88, 61 DR 285 (1989). See also *Director of Public Prosecutions v Channel 4* [1993] 2 All ER 517.

[48] See the Departmental Committee on s. 2 of the Official Secrets Act 1911 ('the Franks Committee') (Cmnd 5014, HMSO, London, 1972); Reform of s. 2 of the Official Secrets Act 1911 (Cmnd 7285, HMSO, London, 1978); Reform of s. 2 of the Official Secrets Act 1911 (Cm 408, HMSO, London, 1988).

[49] *R v Ponting* [1985] *Criminal Law Review* 318.

[50] Significant judgments in favour of press reporting include *Evans, Sunday Times and Times Newspapers v UK*, Appl. no. 6538/74, Ser.A vol. 30, (1979) 2 EHRR 245, 3 EHRR 317, 615; *The Observer and The Guardian v UK*, Appl. No 13585/88, Ser. A no. 216, (1992) 14 EHRR 153; *The Sunday Times v UK (No. 2)*, Appl No. 13166/87, Ser. A, No 217, (1992) 14 EHRR 229, (1991) *The Times*, 27 November 1991.

[51] *R v Secretary of State for the Home Department, ex parte Simms and O'Brien, ex parte Main* [1998] 2 All ER 491. See Foster, S., 'Free speech and the regulation of solicitors' correspondence' (1997) 147 *New Law Journal* 252; Hill, P., 'The voice inside' (1997) 94/3 *Law Society's Gazette* 25.

[52] *Ibid.* See further Chapter 10.

No court may require a person to disclose, nor is any person guilty of contempt of court for refusing to disclose, the source of information contained in a publication for which he is responsible, unless it be established to the satisfaction of the court that disclosure is necessary in the interests of justice or national security or for the prevention of disorder or crime.

But the European Court of Human Rights[54] later found in favour of a journalist, William Goodwin, after an English judge had required him 'in the interests of justice' to disclose the identity of a source of a story published in *The Engineer* about the financial solvency of Tetra Ltd.[55] The Strasbourg Court was concerned that such interference in the journalist's work could affect the accuracy of the press. The Court also feared that the 'public watchdog role of the press' might be disproportionately undermined. It would seem that the European Court of Human Rights places regard for the 'public good' above any contrary British interpretation of interests of justice.[56]

The most common and vehement criticism by lawyers of journalistic 'truth' is the accuracy of reporting trials or appeals. These criticisms are sometimes well-founded, yet the way forward to better reporting is not the enforcement of legislation[57] that seeks to limit the right to disseminate information. Journalists may choose to disregard such laws, but they are foolish if they disregard the basic requirements of successful journalism – credibility and fair balance. We therefore need training, support and discipline to help journalists achieve this.

The primary causes of poor published accounts are the two fundamental editorial problems – ignorance and commercial pressure. People outside the profession assume that editors know more than their reporters of the details of a story. That is rarely so. They have many responsibilities and cannot spend time checking all the facts they are given. Although they are usually aware of the various situations journalists find themselves in which can affect the accuracy of reporting, they can usually do little to help the journalist in the field. If a reporter takes something down wrongly, there is no way of even discovering the fault – until it is too late.

Commercial pressure affects the accuracy and balance of reports of criminal trials, because basic human instincts enter the reporting and editorial process. If a terrible crime has been committed, such as the murder of a young woman, many of the women in the area are afraid and many of the local men are suspected of the murder. There is a general feeling among the public that someone has to be found guilty – and quickly. Such communal emotions may be of little consequence to lawyers, but they are very important to the journalist. After the initial curiosity

---

[53] See *A-G* v *Lundin* (1982) 75 Cr App R 90; *Secretary of State for Defence* v *Guardian Newspapers* [1984] 3 WLR 986; *Maxwell* v *Pressdram* [1987] 1 WLR 298; *In re an Inquiry under the Company Securities (Insider Dealing) Act 1985* [1988] 2 WLR 33; *X* v *Y* [1988] 2 All ER 648.

[54] *Goodwin* v *UK*, Appl. no. 17488/90, 1996–II, (1996) 22 EHRR 123.

[55] *X* v *Morgan-Grampian* [1990] 2 WLR 1000. See Palmer, S., 'Protecting journalists' sources' [1992] *Public Law* 61; Cram, I., 'When the interests of justice outweigh freedom of expression' [1992] 55 *Modern Law Review* 400.

[56] More restrictive British views still persist: *Camelot Group* v *Centaur Communications* [1998] 2 WLR 379.

[57] Current statute law can actually encourage false or vague reporting, The Official Secrets Act 1989 may be used against a journalist who publishes something based on an authoritative source – yet if what is published is merely without documentary or authoritative provenance, prosecution may be avoided.

about the crime wanes, the free market in publishing exerts pressure on the media to calm those fears. People tend to watch and read what they wish to see. Editors are pressured to satisfy the demand. During murder investigations the police are similarly pressured. They sometimes respond, as some journalists, with slipshod methods. This is where many reporting mistakes begin – and become published, unchecked by the editor. Public pressure fosters close, unhealthy, relations between police and crime reporters. Each uses the other. The police feed reporters tantalising titbits that make sensational headlines. The headlines, in turn, help the police. Each side feels that the end justifies the means. The collusion continues when someone is charged and brought before the courts. Pictures are released, the names of witnesses 'surplus to requirements' are secretly handed over. Reporters are given tips on which bits of evidence are the most damning. Given this scenario, it is not surprising that some crime reporters have a built-in bias against the defence.

Editors realise that there is a good reason for crime reporters to foster contacts with the police. The prime reason may be simply a matter of knowing what cases are coming up or how long they will be. Being first with the news is a basic requirement in the publishing marketplace. However, more importantly, provenance can be strengthened by such friendships. First-hand sources, preferably with documentation, are important to accurate reporting. The police are more likely to supply this illicitly than anyone else in the criminal process. But whilst this relationship produces authoritative sources in the reporting stage, it can seriously disturb the balance of the editorial process. In similar fashion, court reporters often become close friends with court officials and counsel. They need to check spellings and take a second look at complicated evidence. But the pay-off for this illicit privilege may be the slanted report. The consequence of such contact with persons involved in the adversarial system of the courts need not be biased by design. It may be simply a mistaken impression which grows into a journalist's 'fact'. However, if such a 'fact' is subsequently revealed to be untrue, the editor involved may feel powerless to change the underlying personnel problem. Crime reporters can rarely be replaced – they have hard-won contacts, invaluable for information and documents. Similarly, court reporters need to have excellent shorthand – yet most journalists rely on tape recorders these days. This background categorises those most close to the system of justice as an élite band of trusted employees – usually without fear of competition, or indeed, contradiction.

The courts could do much to help reporters increase their journalistic credibility by offering a more simple means of achieving it. Allowing tape-recorders[58] or access to recordings of proceedings[59] would admit a much wider group of journalists to the court rota. With more reporters able to report court proceedings there would be more competition for the places – and consequently more trustworthy, accurate and fair reporting. Greater accessibility to trial transcripts would also help journalists to spend more time on their balance as well as their facts. This system would give journalists what all editors want – accurate information from a first-hand source leading to greater credibility. But it would

---

[58] See *Practice Direction (Tape Recorders in Court)* [1981] 1 WLR 1526.

[59] At present, access to such information is largely dependent upon administrative guidance (especially Home Office Circulars 78/1967, 80/1989 and Lord Chancellor's Department, Court Business no. 9/89, item B.1904).

also give the lawyers involved some degree of control through an avenue of complaint.

Co-operation with the press might go even further. If a proper press office were set up at all Crown Court centres, press briefings on big cases could be organised at the end of each session. Many journalists would welcome this. Sometimes rulings by judges are obscure and would benefit from an informal, less legalistic explanation.[60] A particularly important quote could be handed out as routine, so there would be no need of a 'friend' among counsel. The advantage of offering such special services to journalists is that if the court felt unfair reporting were taking place these privileges could be withdrawn either from the individual reporter or the offending publisher. Such a system would help counteract the commercial pressures that can produce lack of balance in court coverage and sharpen the editors' perception of the problems of balance and style.

Such a system is already in place in a similar institution. When television entered the House of Commons in 1989, a Select Committee of the House first took evidence from the major broadcasters, then selected specialist advisers – and produced a report for the House which was effectively a code of conduct for television coverage.[61] These rules were designed to produce accurate and balanced reporting by the journalists – most of whom had little experience of reporting the proceedings of the Commons. The handbook that the broadcasting organisations produced from this report was detailed enough to include instructions on cutaways, wide shots of the Commons, and the recording of casual conversations of Members during speeches. This handbook also tells journalists the areas of the House where they may go with permission – or even without permission – and areas which are strictly off-limits. The similarity of the courts to the House of Commons is obvious. Both have clear rules of procedure and conduct. Members of each enjoy privilege against prosecution. In both proceedings members of the public are admitted with certain restrictions.

Confidence in the system has produced improvements. When Commons coverage first began, journalists still had to take shorthand notes or transcribe speeches from the video recordings, even though Hansard and Committee proceedings were being transcribed onto computer disk. Now all proceedings are available electronically.[62] Immediate access to these transcriptions helps the journalists to produce a more fair balance in reporting the proceedings because there is less labour required for transcription – and more time available for editorial considerations.

Such a system could benefit reporting of trials. If the Lord Chancellor were to encourage the formation of a committee of representatives of the media and the

---

[60] Note that the Lord Chancellor's Department has latterly advised judges to provide journalists with a written note of their remarks about sentencing in cases likely to attract media attention: (1997) 94/13 *Law Society's Gazette* 5.

[61] House of Commons Select Committee on Televising Proceedings of the House (1988–89 HC 141). See also: House of Commons Select Committee on Broadcasting, *The Arrangements for the Permanent Televising of the Proceedings of the House* (1990–91 HC 11); Ryle, M., 'Televising the House of Commons' (1991) 44 *Parliamentary Affairs* 185; Walker, C. and Brogarth, D., 'Televising the Courts' (1989) 153 *Justice of the Peace* 637.

[62] The proceedings are now even available to the public via the world wide web: http://www.parliament.uk/. Compare the minimal publication of law reports (House of Lords cases since 14 November 1996 may be seen at http://www.parliament.the-stationery-office.co.uk/pa/ld/ldjudinf.htm, otherwise there are just a handful of other cases available through the Lord Chancellor's Department at http://www.open.gov uk/). Many more cases can be accessed through Smith Bernal's Casebase (http://www.Smithbernall.com/).

judiciary to regulate special privileges granted to the press in our courts, we might achieve a level of fairness of reporting of trial similar to the balance achieved by Westminster reporters.

Ultimately, editors know that the meaning of any communication lies within the mind of the receiver of the information. It follows that the style of a report of a court case will depend on which section of the public the publication is designed for. We may care to define this difference in style as the broadsheet versus the tabloid; however, the underlying principle is that the citizen of limited education and intelligence has an equal right with a professor of law to take an interest in what is going on in our courts. The means by which the two satisfy that interest will be different. The language and content of the reports they appreciate will therefore be different – but the editorial balance should remain the same.

The fault in the current system is that the free market in publishing encourages some editors to extend this concept of catering for the audience by pandering to their prejudices. Their reports demonstrate a lack of appreciation of, or care for, the distinction between style and balance. The prejudiced reader may prefer to read unbalanced reports, but such a biased editorial practice breaches the essential journalistic guideline – for it hardly serves the 'public good'. In this category of bad reporting and unbalanced editing I would place the tabloid newspapers' sensational photo stories showing Michelle Taylor kissing Michael Shaughnessy at his wedding. A system of granting privileges to journalists could counterbalance this further weakness in the system. Market forces are essentially finance-led. If a publication that has produced unbalanced reports in the past finds it must pay more to get information from the courts that its rivals get for nothing, it will soon reform its ways.

Miscarriages of Justice, the Truth and the Journalist

There is probably no other area of reporting on the system of justice that provokes such violent reaction against journalists than revelations of the ultimate weakness of our judicial system – that it can send innocent people to jail. The particular threat of such journalists is to the very heart of the system of justice – its ability to achieve finality in a case. The reputation of any legal system depends on its ability to produce finality. Yet the journalist apparently determines to prove the jurists have failed in this task.

I believe that the judiciary who complain about journalists should look first to themselves. The English Court of Appeal came into being because the Adolf Beck case in 1896[63] demonstrated that the system of justice was incapable of delivering what it was created to deliver – a final and conclusive verdict. Greater learning and wisdom was, supposedly, brought to the process by the new court. However, from the moment of its creation the Court of Appeal adopted practices and principles that frustrated attempts to produce finality – even though, ironically, they were adopted in its name. The Court soon came to rely on its authority to assert finality, rather than the wisdom of its judgments.[64] For example, the judges decided that

---

[63] See *Report of the Committee of Inquiry* (HMSO, London, 1904); Criminal Appeal Act 1907; Watson, E.R., *The Trial of Adolf Beck* (Hodge, London, 1924).

[64] See further Chapter 11; Malleson, K., 'Appeals against conviction and the principle of finality' in Field, S. and Thomas, D.A., (eds), *Justice and Efficiency?* (1994) 21(1) *Journal of Law & Society*.

evidence which had already been heard by the Court of Appeal could never be presented again. This exclusion was then extended to evidence that had not come before the jury because the defence (for whatever reason) had decided not to present it.[65] The Court also determined that it should have no jurisdiction to entertain a second application for leave to appeal in the same case – even where fresh evidence had emerged since the dismissal of the earlier appeal.[66]

When the Home Secretary was brought into the process to prompt referrals back to the Court,[67] the innovation merely hindered the courts further in finding finality. The Home Secretary's input sometimes had less to do with justice than the political climate of the day. Petitions were rarely granted during Party Conferences when law and order was the issue of the day. Certain other niceties were observed. In theory the Home Secretary could refer cases 'if he thinks fit',[68] but in practice he always required 'new evidence'.[69] Moreover, there was never any suggestion that a different decision should, or could have been reached by the courts on the same facts. Perverse juries were ignored, as were ill-advised and prejudicial comments by judges and ineffective lawyers.

As a result of these many restrictions on the admissibility of evidence, finality in our courts has become determined by rules very similar to those which determine 'truth'. Indeed, finality and truth are inextricably linked. A lack of finality is 'a lurking doubt'. It usually involves some questioning of the truth as established at trial. The journalist places such rules of admissibility of evidence into the same category as the supposed truths established in the courts. It is not surprising therefore that the journalist becomes the next port of call for the innocent convict. After all, here is somebody who does not believe the judges but who has the skills, experience, contacts and professional motivation to conduct a thorough and independent reinvestigation.

It is unfortunate that we have not yet invented a better system of continuing the search for finality – or truth. It seems that only journalists can investigate the suspected truths that were rejected by the court and perhaps firm them up enough to first persuade a mass readership, and then later the courts, to accept them. The newly-created Criminal Case Review Commission has yet to prove that it can close the gap in the system. Until it does, the alternative is to consider better regulation of the present *ad hoc* system of involving journalists.

Turning to this issue of regulation, as with inaccurate and unbalanced reporting, the central problem in this situation is that there is no real control over journalists who reinvestigate cases. Lawyers must take some of the blame for this. When the courts have finished with a case, it seems that most of the rules about confidentiality and contempt are forgotten. Journalists looking into a supposed miscarriage of justice will inevitably wish to see all the available documentation because it is 'first-hand and documentary source' material. However, many of the documents they need are, technically, confidential – even though prisoners will happily hand them over. Such documents include solicitors' letters, briefs to counsel – even expenses sheets. Most importantly the bundles usually contain disclosed documents

---

[65] *R v Stafford and Luvaglio* [1968] 3 All ER 752.
[66] *R v Pinfold* [1988] 1 QB 462.
[67] See Criminal Appeal Act 1968, s. 17 (now repealed by the Criminal Appeal Act 1995).
[68] Criminal Appeal Act 1968, s. 17.
[69] See Royal Commission on Criminal Justice, Report (Cm 2263, HMSO, London, 1993) ch. 11 para. 6; *R v Secretary of State for the Home Department, ex parte Hickey* (No. 2) [1995] 1 WLR 735.

not used in the trial. This disclosure is a dangerous practice which may eventually work against the best interests of the convicted person in the case. An even greater danger exists. Journalists can then write about a miscarriage of justice without the permission of either the prisoner or solicitor. Miscarriage of justice is too important a matter to be open to such dangers. As responsible professionals, solicitors may find themselves in deep trouble. Some form of regulation is needed to protect them, their clients and, indeed, the journalists.[70]

One form of regulation would be for solicitors involved in a suspected miscarriage of justice to require of journalists who wish to see case documents to enter a legal agreement to act as an agent of the solicitor. In return, the solicitor or convict would contract sole rights on the publication of the outcome to the journalist. This would not only satisfy requirements of confidentiality, but would give the solicitor some control over the journalist's activities. Perhaps most importantly, such a system should keep the endeavour within the contempt of court laws.[71] A further advantage would be that the journalist would need to make a greater commitment to the case both in finance and time. A better investigation should result.

Conclusion

All the above suggestions to produce better, more balanced reporting of trials and other legal processes have an underlying element – greater co-operation between the legal system and the media. Most lawyers have a poor attitude towards the media. That is often returned by a journalistic contempt for the narrow confines of the law.

Historically, the judiciary have the worst record in this disdain.[72] Lord Taylor's *ouverture* showed that if judges thought more carefully before jumping to conclusions about the motives of the press they would get better coverage. Moreover, if they gave more reasoned comments on some of their more obscure decisions, rather than falling back on the authority, the majesty and the mystique of the courts to support their judgments, they would find themselves more respected, when now they are merely feared. The contempt for journalists spreads down the legal ranks. Many at the lower levels in the system firmly believe that the less the media know, the more easily they can be blamed – and kept in their proper place. That, in turn, protects the mystique and the majesty of the law, but it serves neither the public's right to information nor justice itself.

Such attitudes belong to a bygone age. If people are to accept the decisions of the courts, there must be transparency. The people should be able to recognise that in each case, be it trial or appeal, there is genuine wisdom behind the core premises of the system of justice. Lawyers are trained to accept the court's rules without question, but the public is not. To accept the lawyers' 'truth' and the court's 'finality', the public must agree that there is validity in the rules concerning the

---

[70] Regrettably, the Criminal Procedure and Investigations Act 1996, ss. 17, 18, appear to increase the dangers for journalists and their solicitor or litigant informants.

[71] Restrictions by way of contempt of court can persist in documents not read out in open court: *Harman* v *Home Office* [1982] 2 WLR 338; Rules of the Supreme Court (Amendment) Order 1987 SI No. 1423; *A-G* v *Newspaper Publishing* [1997] 1 WLR 926.

[72] See for example the comments of Lord Ackner, 'Cet animal est méchant' (Holdsworth Club, University of Birmingham, 1992).

conduct of trials, the rules of admissibility, the rules applied to petitions for appeals. They must see and acknowledge that there is wisdom and common sense behind what their judges decide. Such public enlightenment is most likely to be achieved through the media. The level of transparency in the system of justice will depend on the quality of journalism applied to it. This quality can only be achieved by an improvement in relations between the two professions. Better systems and regulations can improve co-operation and enhance the reputation of both.

Part Three

MISCARRIAGES OF JUSTICE IN OTHER JURISDICTIONS

14

Miscarriages of Justice in Northern Ireland

Brice Dickson

Introduction

The application of the criminal law in Northern Ireland has been a matter of some controversy for at least the past 30 years. Yet even those who have been most vocal about the law's theoretical deficiencies do not always have much to say about actual miscarriages of justice. The lack of a hue and cry has itself been used as evidence of the relative reliability of the system in this regard.[1] A myth has thus been constructed that Northern Ireland has had very few, if any, such miscarriages.

Pressure groups working in the field of civil liberties in Northern Ireland,[2] and not just those which might be expected to have a bias in favour of one or other of the paramilitary organisations,[3] know only too well that allegations of miscarriages of justice do abound. The campaigns around these cases may not always have as high a profile as some of the recent campaigns involving Irish prisoners in England, and for some cases there is no campaign to speak of at all. Nonetheless the convicted prisoners themselves, and their close families, contend strenuously to those who will listen that the convictions in question are unjust.

The type of injustice displayed in such cases varies because, as noted elsewhere in this book, the label 'miscarriage of justice' can be applied to a number of

---

[1] See, e.g., Hellerstein, W.E., McKay, R.B. and Schlam, P.R., *Criminal Justice and Human Rights in Northern Ireland: A Report to the Bar of the City of New York* (New York, 1987) p. 56. This view was refuted in Human Rights Watch, *Human Rights in Northern Ireland* (New York, 1991) pp. 95–100. See also, Lawyers' Committee for Human Rights, *At the Crossroads: Human Rights and the Northern Ireland Peace Process* (New York, 1996) pp. 79–82.

[2] In September 1995, Jane Winter of British-Irish Rights Watch produced a catalogue of 39 individuals who were alleging a miscarriage of justice. The Committee on the Administration of Justice, a civil liberties group in Belfast, also has documentation on a great number of alleged miscarriages. Cases are regularly highlighted in its monthly newsletter, *Just News*, especially by Paul Mageean, the CAJ's Legal Officer. In the April 1997 issue, for example, 10 possible miscarriages of justice are summarised (including three in England). Anyone researching about miscarriages of justice in Northern Ireland must be greatly indebted to the work of both the CAJ and BIRW.

[3] During the last decade or so, Sinn Féin has produced several lists of alleged miscarriages of justice involving Republican prisoners in Northern Ireland (see http://www.vms.utexas.edu/~jdana/glorgafa.html and also http://larkspirit.com/ipow/). Ian Paisley Jnr, of the Democratic Unionist Party, has been prominent in the campaign to secure the release of the *UDR Four* (see also http://www.udp.org/prisoner.htm).

different situations. What most people would see as the paradigm of a miscarriage is where a person has been convicted completely without factual foundation: the prosecution has simply made a mistake of identity and charged someone who was not involved in the criminal incident at all (the 'wrong person' case).[4] Around this core there is a cluster of other situations which can cause equal concern. One of them arises where a person has been convicted of the wrong offence: he or she may indeed have been involved in a criminal incident, but not in the serious way the prosecution alleges (the 'wrong offence' case). Another is where a person who is rightly found guilty of an offence has been given a sentence which is wholly disproportionate to the behaviour in question (the 'wrong sentence' case).[5] Yet another is where a person has been convicted in circumstances where the proper legal procedures have not been adhered to: the person may well have committed an offence, but the rule of law has not been followed when that person was being processed through the criminal justice system (the 'wrong law' case). In this type of situation the injustice is exacerbated if the breach of the rule of law leads to the person's acquittal, for there may then be no other person who can be prosecuted for the offence, leaving the victim, and society at large, just as let down by the system.[6] There are, finally, many situations where, although a person has not been tried and convicted, he or she has still been processed by the criminal justice system in such a way as to have suffered a serious breach of his or her human rights (the 'wrong procedure' case). The dividing line between a breach of human rights and a miscarriage of justice is not always a clearly defined one, especially when the breach of rights takes the form of a deprivation of liberty.

Campaigners often fail to distinguish between these varieties of miscarriage, sometimes with the result that their campaigns do not attract the support, let alone the ultimate success, which they might otherwise enjoy. For this chapter, all of the situations mentioned above have been borne in mind. The scope of the inquiry is therefore much wider than that which forms the remit of the Criminal Cases Review Commission, a body which has jurisdiction in relation to Northern Ireland as much as it does in relation to England and Wales,[7] but which focuses on 'wrong person', 'wrong sentence' and 'wrong law' cases. A broader perspective is required if an overall assessment of the chances of a miscarriage of justice occurring in Northern Ireland is to be attempted. Inevitably the chapter will concentrate on cases involving the application of anti-terrorist laws, since they are the ones which

---

[4] An example of this in Northern Ireland is the case of Stephen Larkin, sentenced in 1995 to a 17 year prison term for attempted murder in 1993. After a retrial had been ordered by the Court of Appeal, he was acquitted in May 1996 because the judge could not be certain that the witnesses had identified the right man: see *Just News*, footnote 2 above, June 1996. (The IRA had claimed responsibility for the killing in question but had issued a statement denying that Larkin was a member of the IRA.)

[5] In *R v Murphy* [1993] NI 57 the Court of Appeal of Northern Ireland held that a 25 year sentence for attempted murder was not wrong in principle or manifestly excessive. In *Re Black's Application* [1993] NI 368 the Divisional Court held that it did not have jurisdiction on judicial review to set aside a sentence on the ground that it was so far outside the normal discretionary limits that its imposition amounted to an error of law.

[6] Particularly difficult are those cases where a person who has been acquitted of an offence later publicly admits that he or she was in fact guilty. Because of the common law defence of *autrefois acquit* he or she cannot be successfully prosecuted again for the same offence. An example of someone 'thumbing his nose' at the authorities is Eamon Collins, who has written about his IRA crimes in *Killing Rage* (Granta Books, London, 1997).

[7] Criminal Appeal Act 1995, esp. ss. 10, 12 and 27. See Northern Ireland Office, *Criminal Appeals and Arrangements for Dealing with Alleged Miscarriages of Justice in Northern Ireland* (Belfast, 1994).

have thrown up most of the difficulties, but reference must also made to 'ordinary' criminal law and procedure, some of which is applicable in terrorist cases too.

'Ordinary' Criminal Law and Procedure

When the Royal Commission on Criminal Justice was set up in 1991, its terms of reference made no mention of Northern Ireland. Interest groups wondered if this was an oversight. But when they inquired they were told that, although the Commission would not be looking at the situation in Northern Ireland, any useful findings it came up with would be extended to cover Northern Ireland. The assumption, in other words, was that Northern Ireland was not a special case: any arguments about the best way of reforming the criminal justice system in England and Wales would apply automatically in Northern Ireland also. What this rather arrogant assumption ignores, of course, is the fact that criminal law and procedure in Northern Ireland, even leaving to one side the 'emergency' criminal law and procedure, is in several respects significantly different from criminal law and procedure in England and Wales.[8] It follows that whatever changes are appropriate for England and Wales will not necessarily be appropriate for Northern Ireland. Regrettably this point was not taken on board when the Royal Commission finally reported.[9]

Policing Issues

The police's 'ordinary' powers in Northern Ireland[10] are, in theory at least, very similar to those in England and Wales, largely because the Police and Criminal Evidence (Northern Ireland) Order 1989 is modelled almost entirely upon the Police and Criminal Evidence Act 1984,[11] and the resulting Codes of Practice are almost identical too[12] (although the Code on Tape-Recording was not in place for Northern Ireland until July 1996). But the PACE legislation in both jurisdictions leaves many matters to the discretion of the police, such as whether there are 'reasonable grounds for suspecting' that a person has committed an offence,[13] whether there are 'reasonable grounds for believing' that access to a solicitor will lead to interference with evidence,[14] and whether there is 'sufficient evidence' to charge an arrested person.[15] In relation to each of these issues members of different

---

[8] For information on the criminal law, see Valentine, B., *Booklet of Criminal Offences in Northern Ireland* (4th ed., SLS Legal Publications (NI), Belfast, 1998), available from the author at the Bar Library, Royal Courts of Justice, Belfast. For a slightly dated, but still relevant, description of procedural matters, see Doran, S., 'Criminal Procedure in Northern Ireland' in Dickson, B. and McBride, D., (eds), *The Digest of Northern Ireland Law* (1st ed, SLS Legal Publications (NI), Belfast, 1988) and Valentine, B. and Hart, A., *Criminal Procedure in Northern Ireland* (SLS Legal Publications (NI), Belfast, 1989, and 1990 supplement).

[9] Cm 2263, HMSO, London, 1993. (*Runciman Report*).

[10] See Dickson, B., 'The Powers of the Police', and Jackson, J., 'Questioning Suspects' in Dickson, B., (ed.), *Civil Liberties in Northern Ireland: The CAJ Handbook* (3rd ed, CAJ, Belfast, 1997).

[11] SI No. 134. See the symposium papers published in (1989) 40(4) *Northern Ireland Legal Quarterly*. Michael Zander's *The Police and Criminal Evidence Act 1984* (3rd ed, Sweet & Maxwell, London, 1995) explains the law in Northern Ireland too.

[12] The changes made to the English and Welsh PACE Codes in 1991 and 1995 were not introduced in Northern Ireland at the same time, but they were incorporated into a new set of Codes effective in Northern Ireland from 29 July 1996.

[13] PACE (NI) Order 1989. Article 26(4)(b), concerning the power of arrest without warrant.

[14] PACE (NI) Order 1989. Article 59(8)(a), concerning the power to delay access to a solicitor for up to 36 hours.

[15] PACE (NI) Order 1989. Article 38(1), concerning the duties of custody officers before charge.

police forces can vary in their customs and practices. If the RUC's interpretation of what is reasonable or sufficient in the above circumstances differs from the interpretation adopted by forces in England and Wales, surely the Royal Commission should have taken these differences on board when making recommendations which were intended to impact on Northern Ireland? Of course no one knows for sure whether the interpretation adopted by police forces in different parts of the country does differ, but that is precisely one of the issues upon which the Royal Commission itself could have asked for research to be conducted.[16] There is little hard evidence that RUC officers have abused their powers or neglected their duties under the PACE (NI) Order[17] – the people appointed as lay visitors to designated police stations have been more than happy with what they have seen going on there since their visits started in 1991[18] – but it is quite conceivable that police malpractice continues, even though it is not always made the subject of a complaint, before the suspect arrives at the police station.[19]

Pre-trial and Trial Issues

Apart from the room for divergence of practice within the realm of police activities, there are significant differences between Northern Ireland and England in the areas of bail applications, prosecution policies, evidential provisions and trial procedures.

Northern Ireland's law on bail was left lagging behind that of England when no equivalent to the Bail Act 1976[20] was introduced, though it may well be – again there is a lack of research to demonstrate the point either way – that the practice in the two jurisdictions does not vary that much.

The Office of the Director of Public Prosecutions operates rather differently in England from the way its counterpart operates in Northern Ireland (even though the latter was set up some 13 years earlier[21]), at least on paper. Whereas the former issues a Code for Crown Prosecutors, indicating the factors to be taken into account when deciding whether to continue a prosecution,[22] and publishes an annual report on its activities, no such documents are produced in Northern Ireland. Challenging

[16] The study which comes closest to this is the work by Maguire, M. and Norris, C., *The Conduct and Supervision of Criminal Investigations* (Royal Commission on Criminal Justice Research Study No. 5, HMSO, London, 1992), but it does not look specifically at regional differences in the way that police discretions are exercised.

[17] In *R v C* [1997] NIJB 37 Sheil J, applying art. 76(1) of the PACE (NI) Order 1989, refused to admit the defendant's statements because he had not been cautioned prior to interview, in contravention of para. 10.1 of the Code on Questioning.

[18] Dickson, B. and O'Loan, N., 'Visiting Police Stations in Northern Ireland' (1994) 45 *Northern Ireland Legal Quarterly* 210.

[19] Research conducted in England and Wales for the Royal Commission on Criminal Justice revealed that 8.1 per cent of suspects were interviewed before arrival at the station and 74.3 per cent of these made a damaging admission or a full confession: Moston, S. and Stephenson, G.M., *The Questioning and Interviewing of Suspects outside the Police Station* (Royal Commission on Criminal Justice Research Study No. 22, HMSO, London, 1993) pp. 22 and 27. But the researchers concluded that interviews conducted outside the police station did not have an independent effect on the police's decision to charge or release; this does not mean, of course, that the prosecutors would make no use of the information gleaned from such interviews.

[20] Nor to the Bail (Amendment) Act 1993.

[21] By the Prosecution of Offences (Northern Ireland) Order 1972 (SI No. 538).

[22] Ashworth, A. and Fionda, J., 'The new Code for Crown Prosecutors: prosecution accountability and the public interest' [1994] *Criminal Law Review* 894.

prosecution decisions is difficult enough in England and Wales,[23] but in Northern Ireland, given the absence of written materials upon which to base a complaint, it is well-nigh impossible.[24]

As far as the law of evidence is concerned, there are many minor differences between the rules in Northern Ireland and those in England,[25] but the most important difference between the two jurisdictions, at any rate in 1991 when the Royal Commission started its deliberations, was that Northern Ireland has had curbs on a suspect's right to silence since the introduction of the Criminal Evidence (Northern Ireland) Order 1988.[26] One of the main outcomes of the Royal Commission, unintended though it may be,[27] was of course that similar curbs on the right to silence have since been introduced in England and Wales.[28] One might have thought that before taking such a step proper research into the operation of the 1988 Order in Northern Ireland would have been carried out, and that the Royal Commission would have been an ideal body to instigate that research. Some research was conducted, but only into the potential impact of a change to the law in England and Wales.[29]

Northern Ireland's criminal justice system also differs from the English and Welsh in institutional and procedural respects. At the lowest court level, for example, all magistrates in Northern Ireland are legally qualified individuals of at least seven years' standing as barristers or solicitors.[30] Appeals from their decisions go not to the Crown Court (on a full appeal) or to the Queen's Bench Division (on a point of law only, by way of case stated) but to the county courts[31] or the Court of Appeal respectively. When witnesses are waiting to give evidence at a trial they are allowed to sit in the body of the court until they are called, whereas in England they are kept outside the courtroom. The law concerning challenges to potential jurors is slightly different too. Important also is the fact that Northern Ireland's smallness means that the same police officers, prosecutors and judges are likely to be involved in criminal prosecutions time and time again. A certain sense of solidarity can thereby be established which, over time, may become inimical to a completely objective presentation and assessment of evidence. Too often a case

---

[23] *R* v *Chief Constable of Kent and Another, ex parte GL*; *R* v *Director of Public Prosecutions, ex parte RB* [1993] 1 All ER 756; *Elguzouli-daf* v *Commissioner of Police* [1995] QB 335; *R* v *DPP, ex parte C* [1995] 1 Cr App Rep 136. But see *R* v *DPP, ex parte Treadaway* (1997) LEXIS 31 July.

[24] But see Osborne, P., 'Judicial Review of Prosecutors' Discretion: The Ascent to Full Reviewability' AT (1992) 43 *Northern Ireland Legal Quarterly* 178 (noting *R* v *Chief Constable, ex parte McKenna* [1992] NI 116) and Spencer, J., 'Judicial Review of Criminal Proceedings' [1991] *Criminal Law Review* 259.

[25] See Jackson, J., *Northern Irish Supplement to Cross on Evidence* (SLS Legal Publications (NI), Belfast, 1983).

[26] SI No. 1987.

[27] See Chapter 5. A majority of the Royal Commission actually recommended that adverse inferences should not be drawn from silence at the police station.

[28] Criminal Justice and Public Order Act 1994, ss. 34–7.

[29] Leng, R., *The Right to Silence in Police Interrogation* (Royal Commission on Criminal Justice Research Study No. 10, HMSO, London, 1993); McConville, M. and Hodgson, J., *Custodial Legal Advice and the Right to Silence* (Royal Commission on Criminal Justice Research Study No. 16, HMSO, London, 1993). It has been left to pressure groups to fill the research gap; see, e.g., JUSTICE, *The Right of Silence: the Northern Ireland experience* (London, 1994).

[30] On 1 January 1996 there were only 92 stipendiary magistrates in England and Wales. Northern Ireland also knows nothing of the Magistrates' Courts Service Inspectorate, set up under the Police and Magistrates' Courts Act 1994.

[31] One judge sitting alone, not with two lay magistrates as in the Crown Court in England and Wales when it hears such appeals.

reduces itself to a police officer's word against that of an accused, and almost invariably it is the police officer who is believed. Criminal legal aid, however, is less problematical in Northern Ireland: an accused person, if granted such aid, makes no contribution towards its cost.

There are also difficulties which Northern Ireland shares with England, such as the absence of an independent forensic science service,[32] delays in bringing cases to trial (in Northern Ireland there are no time limits such as exist in England)[33] and an appellant's inability to argue on appeal that a mistake made by his or her lawyer(s) at the trial stage contributed to the miscarriage.[34] Moreover, Northern Ireland now operates under the same new rules on prosecution and defence disclosure in criminal proceedings as apply in England and Wales.[35] Coming into force as they did around the time of the uncovering of the miscarriage of justice suffered by the men convicted of Carl Bridgewater's murder in England (July 1997), they give little cause for hope that the risk of miscarriages occurring in the future is any less than that which has existed up to now. They may even land the United Kingdom in trouble in Strasbourg.[36] The arguments which have been presented against the new disclosure rules elsewhere in this book[37] are just as applicable in Northern Ireland, the more so since a higher proportion of prosecutions in Northern Ireland (many of which involve the 'emergency' criminal justice system) rely upon the evidence of informers: under section 3(6) of the Criminal Procedure and Investigations Act 1996, material must not be disclosed if the court, on application by the prosecutor, orders that it is not in the public interest to disclose it. In recent years the Northern Irish courts have not always been averse to ordering disclosure of sensitive material;[38] it is to be hoped that they will continue to lean in favour of the defence when the interests of justice so require.

Much of the controversy in this whole context relates to the burden and standard of proof in criminal cases. The orthodox principle, of course, is that the burden must always rest on the prosecution[39] and it must be satisfied 'beyond a reasonable doubt'. These are traditionally viewed as twin characteristics of a 'due process' model of criminal justice; once we begin to qualify them we move towards a 'crime control' model.[40] One of the risks of so doing is that a greater number of

---

[32] See Chapter 6.

[33] Prosecution of Offences (Custody Time Limits) Regulations 1987 (SI No. 299), as amended.

[34] From the point of view of a wrongly convicted accused, the legal prohibition on suing barristers (*Rondel* v *Worsley* [1969] 1 AC 141; *Kelley* v *Corston* [1997] 4 All ER 466) for negligent advocacy must seem like one contributing factor to the injustice being experienced.

[35] Criminal Procedure and Investigations Act 1996, sch. 4. In October 1996 the Northern Ireland Office produced a helpful Introductory Guide to the Act for Northern Ireland; this includes a copy of the Act as it applies in Northern Ireland. The provisions in Parts III (Preparatory Hearings) and VI (Magistrates' Courts), as well as some other sections, do not extend to Northern Ireland.

[36] Wadham, J., 'Prosecution disclosure, crime and human rights' (1997) 147 *New Law Journal* 697.

[37] See Chapter 7.

[38] *R* v *Latimer* [1992] NI 45 (*UDR Four* case, also sometimes known as the *Armagh Four* case), where the Court of Appeal ordered the Director of Public Prosecutions and RUC to produce documents to the court for inspection, including the report by a police investigator into allegations of irregularities by other police officers; *McSorley* v *Chief Constable of the RUC* [1993] NI 85, where Carswell J allowed the plaintiff to call for a copy of the statement made by a police witness which he had re-read prior to entering the witness-box to refresh his memory.

[39] This was described by Viscount Sankey LC in *Woolmington* v *DPP* [1935] AC 462 at 481 as a 'golden thread' always to be seen throughout the web of English criminal law.

[40] These terms were of course coined by Herbert Packer in *The Limits of the Criminal Sanction* (Stanford University Press, 1968).

innocent people will be wrongly convicted of crimes they did not commit. This can only be prevented if, alongside the qualifications to the long-standing principles, there are introduced new safeguards to ensure that the qualifications do not lead to abuses.

'Anti-terrorist' Criminal Law and Procedure

There have been specific anti-terrorist laws in place in Northern Ireland ever since its creation in 1921. In 1973, following the Report of the Diplock Commission,[41] they were modernised in the form of the Northern Ireland (Emergency Provisions) Act (EPA), which has since been amended many times and was most recently re-enacted in 1998.[42] Together with the Prevention of Terrorism (Temporary Provisions) Acts 1974–89 (PTA), these provisions have been subjected to numerous official reviews.[43] None of these, however, has specifically looked at the risk of miscarriages of justice occurring as a consequence of the emergency provisions. The discussion has been mainly concerned with the different question of whether the anti-terrorist measures intrude too greatly upon civil liberties.

Policing Issues

As regards the power of arrest, the main difference between the anti-terrorist law and the ordinary law is that the police can arrest someone if they have reasonable suspicion that he or she is involved in 'terrorism', even though terrorism as such is not an offence.[44] In other words, reasonable suspicion that a person is in some way connected with terrorist activities – perhaps by living close to where those activities have taken place, or by being related to someone who already has a criminal record for paramilitary activities – is enough to ground that person's arrest and subsequent detention. In the most recent large-scale review of anti-terrorist laws, conducted by Lord Lloyd of Berwick, a recommendation was made to correct this anomaly, not by limiting the power of arrest but by creating the new offences of 'active participation' in a terrorist organisation, whether or not proscribed, and 'being concerned in the preparation of an act of terrorism'.[45] Obviously there is great scope for arresting the wrong people even under the existing power, and the fact that, as Table 13.1 shows, three-quarters of all those arrested under it in Northern Ireland during the past 14 years have later been released without charge,

---

[41] *Commission to consider legal procedures to deal with terrorist activities in Northern Ireland* (Cmnd 5185, HMSO, London, 1972) (*Diplock Report*).

[42] In the wake of the Omagh bombing in August 1998, amendments to both the EPA and PTA were passed in the Criminal Justice (Terrorism and Conspiracy) Act 1998. In so far as this facilities the conviction of a person for membership of 'specified' prescribed organisations (by allowing under ss. 1 and 2 the use as evidence of the opinion of a senior police officer and the silence of the accused), it too could increase the risk of a miscarriage of justice.

[43] See: *Report of a Committee to consider, in the context of civil liberties and human rights, measures to deal with terrorism in Northern Ireland* (the *Gardiner Report*) (Cmnd 5847, HMSO, London, 1975), *Review of the Operation of the Northern Ireland (Emergency Provisions) Act 1978* (the *Baker Report*), (Cmnd 9222, HMSO, London, 1984), *Review of the Operation of the Prevention of Terrorism (Temporary Provisions) Act 1984* (the *Colville Report 1987*), (Cm 264, HMSO, London, 1987), *Review of the Northern Ireland (Emergency Provisions) Acts 1978 and 1987* (the *Colville Report 1990*), (Cm 1115, HMSO, London, 1990), *Inquiry into Legislation against Terrorism* (the *Lloyd Report*), (Cm 3420, HMSO, London, 1996); *Legislation against Terrorism* (Cm 4178, Stationery Office, London, 1998).

[44] Prevention of Terrorism (Temporary Provisions) Act 1989, s. 14 (this applies throughout the UK).

[45] *Lloyd Report*, paras. 6.13 and 8.17. The latter had been recommended as far back as 1975 by the *Gardiner Report*.

would suggest that that is exactly what has been happening. Most are kept in detention for two or three days, but some are kept for seven days. There is virtually nothing that can be done to challenge such detentions, even after release. Some would call this internment by another name.

Table 13.1: Numbers of persons arrested under the PTA in Northern Ireland and released without charge, 1984–97.[46]

Year	Numbers arrested under the PTA in Northern Ireland	Numbers released without charge or exclusion[47] (percentage)
1984	908	650 (72%)
1985	938	691 (74%)
1986	1,309	951 (73%)
1987	1,459	1,115 (76%)
1988	1,717	1,344 (78%)
1989	1,583	1,155 (73%)
1990	1,549	1,150 (74%)
1991	1,608	1,256 (75%)
1992	1,795	1,335 (74%)
1993	1,641	1,249 (76%)
1994	1,503	1,131 (75%)
1995	443	335 (76%)
1996	569	410 (72%)
1997	504	356 (71%)
Totals	17,526	13,128 (75%)

Arrest is of course a key stage in the criminal justice process because it lays the foundation for subsequent detention and interrogation. Having been given the opportunity to interrogate a suspect, it is natural for the police to want to make full use of the power. But it is worth stressing that the opportunity provided is a very large one. Arrest purely for the purposes of interrogation is not unlawful under the emergency laws.[48] Provided the police can show some grounds for suspecting the person's involvement in terrorism, it is easy for them to resist successfully any challenge to the reasonableness of the arrest. If an arrested person disputes the lawfulness of his or her arrest, the police must relate only in general terms the matters which constituted reasonable grounds for the arresting officer's suspicion.[49] It has been held by the House of Lords, moreover, that, although acting on a superior officer's orders cannot by itself provide reasonable grounds for suspicion, the arresting officer's suspicion does not have to be based on his or her own observations but can be based on information he or she has been given, perhaps

---

[46] Source: quarterly statistics issued by the Northern Ireland Office.
[47] Exclusion from Northern Ireland (see Prevention of Terrorism (Temporary Provisions) Act 1988 s. 6) has been relatively uncommon.
[48] *Ex parte Lynch* [1980] NI 126, where Lord Lowry LCJ (at p. 131) said that arrest under the Prevention of Terrorism Act is not the first step in a criminal proceeding against a suspected person on a charge but the first step in the investigation of a person's involvement in terrorism. See Walker, C., *The Prevention of Terrorism in British Law* (2nd ed., Manchester University Press, 1992) p. 161.
[49] *Clinton v Chief Constable of the RUC* [1991] 2 NIJB 53.

even by an anonymous informant.[50] In the words of Lord Hope: 'The question whether [the information] provided reasonable grounds for the suspicion depends on the source of his (*sic*) information and its context, seen in the light of the whole surrounding circumstances.'.[51] It is thus easy to see how police officers, who may themselves believe in the guilt of a suspect, but who otherwise have little objective evidence to substantiate this belief, can set a ball rolling towards a finding of guilt in a way which is hard to stop. In the absence of any requirement at the committal stage for anything other than a *prima facie* case to be made out against the accused,[52] and with the trial judge being permitted to supplement this *prima facie* case with inferences drawn from the accused's silence, a momentum can be built up which relentlessly leads to a conviction.

The EPA includes as many discretionary powers as the PACE legislation, and usually the consequences of their exercise are more severe for the detainee. Access to a solicitor can be delayed for up to 48 hours, not just 36, as can notification of the arrest to a relative or friend of the detainee.[53] In *John Murray* v *UK*[54] the European Court of Human Rights held that delaying access to a solicitor, when combined with the fact that inferences of guilt could be drawn from a detainee's silence in the face of police questioning with no solicitor present, was a breach of Article 6(3)(c) of the European Convention on Human Rights, the provision on the right to legal assistance. This was a case, therefore, of a 'wrong law' miscarriage. Of course the accused's conviction was in no way affected by the European Court's finding, and no compensation was ordered to be paid (just legal costs), but the ruling is a pointer to the need for reform. Unfortunately, despite being nearly three years old, the judgment has not yet led to any changes to the law, whether in Northern Ireland or in England and Wales. It must not be forgotten, moreover, that several solicitors in Northern Ireland have been intimidated by police officers; one prominent solicitor who was known for his defence of IRA suspects, Pat Finucane, was murdered and there have been strong suggestions that this resulted from collusion between police officers and Loyalist paramilitaries.[55] No one has yet been charged with the killing.

The changes to the law on the right to silence, introduced in Northern Ireland at the end of 1988, were directly responsible for the conviction of Dermot Quinn, now serving 25 years for the attempted murder of two police officers. He had been arrested in April 1988 but was released on remand some five months later when key witnesses refused to testify at the committal hearing. In July 1990, after the 1988 Order had been brought into force, Quinn was rearrested, and eventually he was convicted. The key witnesses again refused to testify, but this time the trial judge drew inferences from the defendant's silence in the face of police questioning, even though at the trial he produced an alibi which his employer corroborated.[56] Quinn

---

[50] *O'Hara* v *Chief Constable of the RUC* [1997] AC 286. See Hunt, A., 'Terrorism and reasonable suspicion by "proxy"' (1997) 113 *Law Quarterly Review* 540.

[51] [1997] AC 286 at p. 298.

[52] Of course these proceedings can themselves be the object of an application for judicial review: *Neill* v *North Antrim Magistrates' Court* [1992] 4 All ER 846; see Osborne, P., 'The floodgates of judicial review: once more unto the breach' (1993) 44 *Northern Ireland Legal Quarterly* 233.

[53] Northern Ireland (Emergency Provisions) Act 1996, ss. 46 and 47.

[54] Appl. no. 18731/91, 1996–I, (1996) 22 EHRR 29; noted at Dickson, B., 'The right to silence and legal advice under the European Convention' (1996) 21 *European Law Review* 424.

[55] See Lawyers Committee for Human Rights, *Human Rights and Legal Defense in Northern Ireland* (New York, 1993); Human Rights Watch, *To Serve Without Favor: Policing, Human Rights and Accountability in Northern Ireland* (New York, 1997) ch. 6.

maintains his innocence and has lodged a petition with the European Commission of Human Rights.[57] There are several other cases where application of the power to draw inferences from silence appears to have made the difference between innocence and guilt.[58] Advocates of the power will argue that this demonstrates its importance as a weapon in the fight against terrorist organisations, which train recruits in the art of saying nothing; civil libertarians will argue that to convict someone on the basis of their silence – or to allow that to be the factor which tips the otherwise evenly balanced scales in favour of guilt – is to undermine one of the basic principles of criminal justice, namely that a person must be assumed to be innocent until proven guilty.[59]

In Northern Ireland, unlike in England and Wales, a solicitor is not entitled to be present during the police interview with a terrorist suspect. A challenge to this practice was unsuccessful in the Northern Irish Divisional Court, despite *Murray v UK* being cited and fully considered.[60] Interviews with terrorist suspects are also not tape-recorded, unlike in cases governed by the PACE legislation or even under the PTA in England and Wales.[61] Instead, since the implementation of the Bennett Committee recommendations,[62] there have been closed-circuit television monitors and, under section 53 of the Northern Ireland (Emergency Provisions) Act 1996, the Secretary of State has made an order introducing the silent video-recording of interviews from the Spring 1998. The latter may be a more effective safeguard against police malpractices than the former, the use of which has certainly not led to any convictions being overturned, but the absence of audio-recording has meant that the potential for verbal abuse and threats remains very great.[63] The police were not issued with a guide on how to exercise their powers under the EPA and PTA until 1990, and this was not supplemented by statutory Codes of Practice until 1994.[64] There are substantial differences between the latter and the Codes issued under the PACE legislation.

---

[56] *R v Quinn* [1993] NI 351.

[57] Appl. no. 23496/94.

[58] E.g. the cases of Cahal Fox, Andrew Laverty, Ronan McCartan, Gary McKay and Kevin McCann, all documented in the British Irish Rights Watch dossier: see footnote 2 above. See also *R v McLernon* [1992] NI 168 (CA).

[59] It is wrong to assert that Continental legal systems adopt the opposite principle (as is commonly believed by prejudiced Anglo-Saxons), but there is no doubt that 'innocent until proven guilty' and 'the privilege against self-incrimination' are more germane to the Anglo-American criminal justice tradition than they are to those based on Roman law. French and German law, for example, do not have sophisticated rules forming a law of evidence for criminal cases; they even assume that a person's previous criminal record is very relevant to the determination of his or her guilt on a new charge. See generally Youngs, R., *English, French and German Comparative Law* (Cavendish, London, 1998) pp. 126–40.

[60] *R v Chief Constable of the RUC, ex parte Russell* (25 October 1996, Div Ct, unreported).

[61] See Walker, C. and Fitzpatrick, B., 'The Independent Commissioner for the Holding Centres: a review' [1998] *Public Law* 106 at p. 117. As a result of the EPA 1998, audio-recording is to be introduced in early 1999.

[62] *Report of a Committee of Inquiry into Police Interrogation Procedures in Northern Ireland*, (Cmnd 7947, HMSO, London, 1979) (*Bennett Report*).

[63] The Independent Commissioner for the Holding Centres, Sir Louis Blom-Cooper QC, has consistently argued in each of his annual reports since his appointment in 1993 that there should be both audio and video recordings, with restricted disclosure. The fact that he and his deputy can sit in on interviews is a safeguard, but in 1996 they sat in on only 24 out of the 6,000 or so which occurred: *Fourth Annual Report* (1996) p. 20. See Walker, C. and Fitzpatrick, B., 'The Independent Commissioner for the Holding Centres: a review' [1998] *Public Law* 106.

[64] Issued under the Northern Ireland (Emergency Provisions) Act 1991, s. 61 (now s. 52 of the 1996 Act). The non-statutory guide was also updated in 1994.

The RUC also seem to have operated for many years with no guidance as to how to take notes at interviews. It is at least very likely that, on occasions, notes were later altered to reflect the interpretation of events which the police themselves wished to portray.[65] Nor were police (or Court Service) practices regarding data storage very organised. Electrostatic Document Analysis (ESDA testing) has only recently come to light as a method for authenticating notes, but in many cases the RUC now claim to be unable to trace any records of notes taken at earlier interviews.[66] One would have thought that these would have been automatically retained in court files relating to the case. In one case an ESDA test showed that the police had tampered with eight to ten pages of interview notes, but the judge nevertheless accepted the police's word as to their veracity; to make matters worse, by the time the case came on for appeal the ESDA exhibits had mysteriously disappeared.[67]

At the heart of the emergency criminal justice system is the rule that an accused person's confession is inadmissible only if the police cannot prove that it was not obtained by torture, by inhuman or degrading treatment, or by violence or the threat of violence.[68] This is a significantly less exacting test than that applied in PACE cases, for it leaves open the possibility that confessions obtained by oppression, or in consequence of anything said or done which was likely to render them unreliable, could still be used as evidence.[69] Judges have, on occasions, thrown out a case because of the police's inability to satisfy the EPA test, but it is impossible to say how many cases satisfied the EPA test but would have failed the PACE test. Strangely, statistics do not seem to be maintained on the number of defendants who at their trial allege that they confessed to the police because of coercion. Several prisoners in Northern Ireland's jails continue to maintain their innocence on this ground.[70]

Some evidence of the extent of alleged police abuse is provided by the figures supplied in the annual reports of the Independent Commission for Police Complaints (the ICPC). Table 13.2 paints an alarming picture, especially in respect of the substantiation rate for complaints. The rather unhelpful comment repeated in several of the ICPC annual reports is that there was not enough evidence to prove the complaints beyond a reasonable doubt; it is only in the last few years that the ICPC has begun to press for that standard to be lowered,[71] and even today it

---

[65] This was the reason why three of the *UDR Four* were released by the Court of Appeal of Northern Ireland in July 1992: *R* v *Latimer* [1992] NI 45.

[66] E.g. Patrick Grimes, Joseph Harper, Peter Markey, Edward McClelland, Sean McKinley, Seamus Mullan and Eamonn Nolan, all documented in the British Irish Rights Watch dossier; see footnote 2 above.

[67] *R* v *Murray (Barry)*, *Just News* (the newsletter of the Committee on the Administration of Justice), Belfast, May 1993, p. 4.

[68] Northern Ireland (Emergency Provisions) Act 1996, s. 12(2). The phrase 'violence or threat of violence' was not added until 1987 (when judicial discretion to exclude otherwise admissible confessions was also officially recognised).

[69] The PACE test is in art.74(2) of the PACE (NI) Order 1989.

[70] E.g. Thomas Green, convicted of murder in 1987; immediately after signing a confession at Castlereagh Holding Centre, he collapsed and had to receive hospital treatment for low blood sugar. His case was highlighted in the *Belfast Telegraph* on 24 July 1997.

[71] A call echoed by Dr Maurice Hayes in his recent comprehensive review of the police complaints system: *A Police Ombudsman for Northern Ireland?* (Northern Ireland Office, 1997). The reform was not made by the Police (N.I.) Act 1998, which otherwise largely implemented the review, but it is due to be introduced in April 1999 (see Police Authority for Northern Ireland, *Policing: A New Beginning* (Belfast, 1998) para. 18.2).

suggests that the standard should still be as high as beyond a reasonable doubt in cases where the penalty the officer might pay for the alleged breach is very severe.[72]

Table 13.2: Complaints and allegations made by persons arrested under the anti-terrorist laws in Northern Ireland, 1988–97[73]

Year	Number of complaints by persons arrested under the EPA or PTA	Number of allegations of assault during interview	Number of allegations of assault prior to arrival at holding centre	Number of complaints upheld
1988[74]	170	132	5	0
1989	319	246	11	0
1990	492	328	20	0
1991	433	281	48	0
1992	395	271	27	0
1993	299	138	27	0[75]
1994	354	140	19	0
1995	191	80	12	0[76]
1996	85	26	7	0
1997	108	29	8	0
Totals	2,846	1,750	184	0

Pre-trial and Trial Issues

In terrorist cases, there is a lack of openness on the part of the Director of Public Prosecutions' Office, just as in the 'ordinary' criminal justice system. In some instances charges seem to be laid which are wholly inappropriate to the circumstances. Sometimes these serve as excuses for having the suspects remanded in custody for a prolonged period, sometimes they lead to even more drastic consequences. Two notorious examples of the former are the cases of the so-called *Beechmount Five* and *Ballymurphy Seven*.

The members of the first of these groups,[77] all aged 17 to 19, were arrested in May 1991 on suspicion of being involved in an elaborate lookout system prior to a rocket and gun attack on a police Landrover in which a police sergeant was killed. They were interrogated at Castlereagh Holding Centre (or 'Police Office' as the authorities insist upon calling it), denied access to a solicitor for more than two days, and charged with aiding and abetting murder as well as with the attempted murder of another police officer who was in the same Landrover. At the eventual

---

[72] *Triennial Review 1994–97* (1996–97 HC 195) p. 6.

[73] Source: the annual reports of the ICPC 1988–96. Note that one complaint can contain more than one allegation.

[74] From 29 February only, the date on which the ICPC came into being.

[75] But two officers were 'paraded' before their Divisional Commander and 'admonished'.

[76] But in one case a Detective Sergeant was 'admonished' for his interviewing technique and in two other cases 'constructive discussions' took place with four officers.

[77] Liam Coogan, Laurence Hillick, Jim McCabe, Kevin Mulholland and Mark Prior.

eight-week trial most of the time was taken up with testing the admissibility of a sample confession made by one of the accused, Mark Prior. There was a contest between his recollection of what had happened during his interrogation (some two years earlier) and the police officers' notes from that time. Not surprisingly, Prior could not remember exactly when he was told by the police (falsely) that his mother was near death, and the prosecution sought to use this lack of recall as an indication that the police had not used such intimidatory tactics. It became clear as the *voir dire* progressed that all of the defendants' alleged confessions were unsafe; the prosecution then began to suggest deals with the accused, whereby the serious charges would be dropped if guilty pleas were offered for less serious charges. The accused agreed to this, but mainly because they had already spent more than two years in custody and wanted desperately to be released. The outcome means that five young men spent two years locked up on remand and now have a criminal record even though there is no evidence against them besides their unsafe confessions. A preferable result would clearly have been the dropping of all charges. Another point illustrated by this case is that the rules on plea-bargaining in Northern Ireland are laxer than in England and Wales; the observation by the Court of Appeal in *R v Turner*[78] to the effect that a judge should never, subject to one exception, indicate to a barrister in a private meeting the sentence he or she is minded to impose for an offence, has no application in the province, but the barrister must not reveal to the accused what the judge said.[79]

In the *Ballymurphy Seven* case the young people were aged from 17 to 21; five of them were arrested in 1991[80] and two in 1992,[81] all on suspicion of involvement in IRA attacks on the RUC. Each of the seven was interrogated in the Castlereagh Holding Centre, deprived of access to a solicitor for up to 72 hours, allegedly coerced into signing written confessions prepared for them by their interrogators, charged with attempted murder, and remanded in custody to the adult prison on Belfast's Crumlin Road. The cases against all seven eventually collapsed, for four of them because the police could not show that they had secured their 'confessions' lawfully[82] and for three because the prosecution had not disclosed 10 boxes of relevant evidence to the defence, although, in his final judgment concerning these three,[83] Kerr J went out of his way to say that just because he was ordering their release this did not mean that he thought they were entirely innocent![84] With respect, it would have been more appropriate for the judge to comment on the failure of the criminal justice system to acquit the not-guilty at an earlier stage and to make suggestions as to how the system could be changed accordingly.[85] One

---

[78] [1970] 2 QB 321.
[79] *R v McNeill* [1993] NI 46 (CA).
[80] Michael Beck, Anthony Garland, Brendan McGrory, Hugh McLaughlin, and Stephen McMullan.
[81] Ciaran McAllister and Danny Pettigrew.
[82] Ciaran McAllister, Brendan McGrory, Stephen McMullan and Danny Pettigrew.
[83] *R v McLaughlin, Beck and Garland*, 3 March 1995 (unreported). Kerr J said the three men were 'the less than deserving beneficiaries of an inadvertent lapse on the part of the prosecution authorities' (to disclose material which was of potential assistance to the accused); he added: 'I do not consider this result as a resounding vindication of their innocence.'
[84] The same judge was just as equivocal when he acquitted Stephen Larkin at his retrial for attempted murder in May 1996 (see footnote 4 above).
[85] To be fair, Kerr J did call for audio recording of interviews at Castlereagh Holding Centre. His words were quoted and endorsed by Sir Louis Blom-Cooper QC, the Independent Commissioner for the Holding Centres, in his *Third Annual Report* (1995) p. 35. On the other hand, at an earlier date Kerr J had refused to throw out the charges when it was put to him that the European Court of Human

can sympathise with police and prosecutors who 'know' that an accused is guilty but who cannot prove it to the required standard, but the solution is not then to bend the rules but rather to establish new rules, with proper safeguards to ensure that they are not abused.

Inappropriate charges have also been at the heart of another prominent alleged miscarriage – that of the *Casement Three*. These men were convicted of counselling and procuring the murder of two army corporals who were killed after driving into a funeral parade on the Andersonstown Road in West Belfast in March 1988. The charge in question was added only at the committal stage, prior to which the men had enjoyed bail. Patrick Kane, Sean Kelly and Michael Timmons were each sentenced to life imprisonment, not for any direct involvement in the soldiers' deaths (no one has ever been prosecuted for pulling the trigger) but for supposed involvement in the beating of the soldiers at Casement Park prior to their being driven away to be murdered at Penny Lane, a few hundred yards away. All three cases certainly fall into the 'wrong offence' and 'wrong sentence' categories, and two (Kane and Kelly) possibly also into the 'wrong person' category, since they deny that they were even in Casement Park at the time of the beatings and the heli-tele evidence on this point is equivocal.[86] The main bone of contention is the judges' preparedness, both at the trial and on appeal, to apply the so-called doctrine of common purpose and thereby link the perpetrators of the beatings with the eventual killers. A recent judgment from the House of Lords in another case[87] demonstrates that the judges in Northern Ireland were wrong to apply that doctrine to the *Casement Three*. In June 1997 Patrick Kane secured his release, on the basis that the trial judge had not been shown evidence from a psychologist indicating that at the time of his interrogation Kane was not in a fit mental condition. The cases of Kelly and Timmons are currently being investigated by the Criminal Cases Review Commission, and the two were released (on licence) in October 1998.

One cannot help feeling that among the factors contributing to the injustice in the *Casement Three* scenario are the wish of the prosecutors to demonstrate to the public that some of the 'main' culprits on the day in question have received their just deserts, the desire of the judges not to appear to be too soft on violent crime, the traditional immunity from suit enjoyed by legal advocates, and the inflexibility of the review system once convictions have occurred and sentences have been meted out. The moral panic which the soldiers' terrible deaths engendered tended to blind the authorities to other important principles of justice, not the least of which is that like cases should be treated alike.[88] What the Northern Irish criminal justice system is often not good at displaying is a proportionate response to problems.[89]

Rights had ruled in *Murray v UK*, Appl. no. 18731/96, 1996–I, (1996) 22 EHRR 29, (see footnote 54 above) that denial of access to a solicitor, coupled with curbs on the right to silence, breached Article 6(3)(c) of the European Convention on Human Rights; he said domestic law must take precedence. This stance has been echoed by the English Court of Appeal: *R v Staines, R v Morrissey*, [1997] 2 Cr App R 426; *R v Law-Thompson* [1997] *Criminal Law Review* 674.

[86] For more details see Committee on the Administration of Justice, *The Casement Trials: A Case Study on the Right to a Fair Trial in Northern Ireland* (Belfast, 1992).

[87] *R v Powell, R v English* [1997] 4 All ER 545. The Northern Irish cases are nowhere mentioned.

[88] For instance, a man who drove the two soldiers to their place of execution received a seven-year sentence and was acquitted of murder.

[89] A comparable case is that of Christopher Sheals, who was sentenced to life imprisonment for conspiracy to murder even though there was very little evidence to link him to the killing in question

A reluctance to charge members of the security forces in cases where they have used lethal force only serves to point up the way in which the rule of law is partially applied in Northern Ireland.[90] Of course one cannot claim that a person who has been rightly convicted has suffered a miscarriage merely because someone else in similar circumstances has not been convicted (or even prosecuted), but the whole justice system is brought into disrepute if it is applied in such a discriminatory fashion. Eyebrows must also be raised when, even after a miscarriage has been uncovered and police malpractice revealed, the officers in question are not convicted of perverting the course of justice or of perjury. This is what happened in the case of four police officers charged after three of the *UDR Four* had been released from life sentences (after six years in prison) when the Court of Appeal found that the police had given untruthful evidence at the trial[91] and falsely authenticated some of the interview notes. One of the *UDR Four*, Neil Latimer, remains in prison because the appeal judges did not think that the degree of contamination of his various statements was enough to exonerate him; there is a vibrant campaign to secure his release on the basis that all of his confessions were false.

It should not be forgotten that it was in emergency law cases that the prosecution resorted to the use of supergrasses, a practice which was eventually condemned by the Court of Appeal of Northern Ireland amidst mass reversals of first instance decisions.[92] But the use of informers persisted and much evidence since presented by police officers in court has been based on information supplied by such anonymous sources. Lord Lloyd, moreover, has proposed that the law should be altered so as to permit telephone taps to be admissible as evidence in cases affecting national security.[93] In Northern Ireland this will make an already bad situation even worse: it is at present the only part of the United Kingdom where information is not provided, even by the official overseer of such practices,[94] on the number or type of telephone taps which are currently authorised. It is therefore extremely likely that the reliability of the evidence will be difficult to challenge in court as its provenance will be cloaked in public interest immunity.

(a young woman who had been visiting a Loyalist band hall). The Court of Appeal quashed the murder conviction because it was based on insufficient evidence, but it upheld the convictions on lesser charges (see *The Irish Times*, 6 December 1997).

[90] See Committee on the Administration of Justice, *Adding Insult to Injury?* (Belfast, 1993) and Amnesty International, *Political Killings in Northern Ireland* (London, 1994). The disparity between the treatment afforded members of the security forces who have been convicted of serious crimes and civilians in a similar situation is again stark. Private Ian Thain, the first soldier to be convicted of murder (*R* v *Thain* [1985] NI 457) was released after serving less than three years of a life sentence. Private Lee Clegg was comparably treated (convicted in June 1993, released in July 1995) even though the House of Lords had confirmed his conviction (*R* v *Clegg* [1995] 1 AC 482). Clegg is currently (December 1998) being retried. In both cases the rules were applied in a flexible way to allow reviews of the sentences to be conducted many years before they would otherwise have been due. Meanwhile many civilians languish in prison awaiting the normal application of the rules. For a more general critique of governmental interference in sentencing, see Dickson, B., 'Executive Involvement in Sentence Reduction', in Standing Advisory Commission on Human Rights, 21st Annual Report (1995–96 HC 467) p. 191.

[91] *R* v *Latimer* [1986] 9 NIJB 1; the first appeal is reported as *R* v *Latimer and others* [1988] 11 NIJB 1. See also on the second appeal [1992] NI 45.

[92] See Boyd, A., *The Informers* (Mercier, Dublin, 1984), Greer, S., *Supergrasses* (Clarendon Press, Oxford, 1995) and Morton, J., *Supergrasses and Informers* (Little, Brown and Co., London, 1995), Chapter 6.

[93] *Lloyd Report* (see footnote 43 above), para. 7.25.

[94] The Commissioner on Interception of Communications, appointed under s. 8 of the Interception of Communications Act 1985.

Such divergences from the norm might not be so serious if at the end of the day the credibility of evidence in terrorist cases was being judged by a jury. But juries, of course, were abolished for such cases in Northern Ireland by the Northern Ireland (Emergency Provisions) Act 1973. The trials are conducted by a judge sitting alone. That judge is meant to warn himself,[95] for example, of the dangers of acting on uncorroborated confession evidence and of inferring guilt merely from a suspect's silence. It would be easy simply to assert that trial by judge alone in such circumstances is bound to be more risk-laden from the miscarriage point of view than trial by judge and jury, but this is not borne out by the fact that the serious miscarriages which have come to light in England and Wales have all been judge and jury cases. The most detailed study of the issue has concluded that the quality of justice supplied in judge-only courts is not noticeably worse than that supplied in judge and jury cases, although there is an 'adversarial deficit' in non-jury trials.[96] There have certainly been instances of defendants being acquitted on appeal because the judges there thought that the trial judge had placed undue credence on the evidence of a police or army officer (in a way that a jury might not have done).[97] It is possible to argue that, while no single departure from the norm makes the emergency criminal justice system 'unfair', the holding of non-jury trials on top of all the earlier departures does constitute a breach of the internationally recognised fair trial standard.[98]

Conclusion

By no means everything in Northern Ireland's criminal justice system is wrong. There are some positive signs that the system is improving. Since 1995 the Independent Commissioner for the Holding Centres (and his deputy) have been permitted to sit in on police interviews with suspects. Since 1997 there has been video-recording (albeit silent) of what transpires at those interviews. The judges have occasionally been prepared to order a person's discharge if they are not satisfied that the police have not mistreated that person.[99] Many of the officials at the Northern Ireland Office are comparatively enlightened (and have produced much more by way of information and research in the past few years[100]). A local person[101] has been appointed to the Criminal Cases Review Commission. And there is now an inter-agency Criminal Justice Issues Group, chaired by a senior judge, which meets regularly to discuss problems in the criminal justice system.[102]

---

[95] These judges are, and always have been, male; there has never been a female member of the Supreme Court of Judicature in Northern Ireland.

[96] Jackson, J. and Doran, S., *Judge Without Jury* (Clarendon Press, Oxford, 1995) esp. pp. 292–7.

[97] *R v Miller, McFadden and McMonagle* (1995, unreported).

[98] See, e.g., Liberty, *Broken Covenants: Violations of International Law in Northern Ireland* (London, 1993) pp. 70–84; Hunt, P. and Dickson, B., 'Northern Ireland's Emergency Laws and International Human Rights' (1993) 11 *Netherlands Quarterly of Human Rights* 173.

[99] E.g. in the cases of *R v Collins* (1987) (unreported), *R v Nash* (December 1992) (unreported, but see *Just News*, January 1993), and four of the *Ballymurphy Seven* (see text and footnotes 79–84 above). In *R v Chief Constable of the RUC, ex parte Gillen*, the applicant was released on a writ of habeas corpus because there was a strong *prima facie* case that he had been assaulted by the police while in custody: *Just News*, February 1988, [1990] 2 NIJB 47. He was later awarded £7,500 in an out of court settlement: *Just News*, December 1990.

[100] E.g. the Digest of Information on the Northern Ireland Criminal Justice System (3rd ed., Northern Ireland Office, Belfast, 1998) and the annually distributed Research Strategy and Programme.

[101] John Leckey, who is also HM Coroner for the Greater Belfast area.

[102] In December 1996 it even distributed the first issue of a Newsletter.

Nevertheless, the allegations of miscarriage of justice are too numerous and vociferous to dismiss lightly. There is probably no single feature which is more responsible than others for such allegations in 'wrong person' or 'wrong law' cases, but the police can be blamed for following incorrect pre-trial procedures, the prosecution service for charging people with inappropriate offences, and judicial attitudes for disproportionate sentencing. It should be stressed, though, that as likely an explanation for miscarriages is the cumulative effect of dubious practices, coupled with the absence of safeguards in the application of those practices. In this sense it is often the 'ethos' of the system which is to blame rather than any particular actor or process.

15

Miscarriages of Justice in the Republic of Ireland

Dermot Walsh

Introduction

In the latter years of the 1980s the Irish legal and political establishment began to address the treatment of Irish persons in the British criminal justice system.[1] Through the machinery of the Anglo-Irish Conference the Irish Government repeatedly expressed its concern about the reliability of the convictions in cases such as the *Birmingham Six* and, generally, about an apparent bias in the British criminal justice process when dealing with Irish suspect terrorists. At one point the Irish Attorney-General even went so far as to refuse a British application for the extradition of a Fr Patrick Ryan to answer terrorist charges.[2] The refusal was explained on the ground that the Attorney-General could not be satisfied that Fr Ryan would get a fair trial in Britain. While the Irish Government's stance could be supported by the experiences of Irish suspects, it would appear that the Irish Government itself had not entered the fray with clean hands. The fact of the matter was that the Irish criminal justice process had also produced a few disturbing examples of likely miscarriages of justice; some of which were contemporaneous with the *Birmingham Six* saga. Embarrassingly for the Irish Government, these examples revealed that, in some respects, Irish criminal procedure was even more conducive than its British counterpart to the emergence of such cases and was less capable of rectifying injustice once it had occurred.

The Leading Cases

Two cases, in particular, illustrate very clearly how miscarriages could arise in the Irish criminal justice system, how that system was incapable of responding effectively and the steps that have been taken to remedy the inadequacies.

The first case, *People (Director of Public Prosecutions)* v *Meleady & Grogan*[3] (hereinafter referred to as *Meleady*) concerned mistaken identification. Although

---

[1] A summary of the Irish Government's representations to the British Government is given at Dáil Debates, vol. 402, cols 1089–1092 (1 November, 1990).
[2] Dáil Debates, vol. 385, cols 1199–1207 (13 December, 1988).
[3] [1995] 2 IR 517 (CCA); Supreme Court, unreported, 22 March 1995.

dating from 1984, the case is still ongoing today. The facts were that some youths took a car at night from the driveway of the owner's home. As the car was being driven away the owner jumped onto the bonnet. He managed to hold on for a few minutes, even though the front seat passenger was trying to knock him off with articles taken from inside the car. Subsequently, at the request of the police, the owner attended a sitting of the District Court where he identified Joseph Meleady and Bernard Grogan as the persons responsible. Both were convicted of taking and driving away a car without the owner's consent and were sentenced to five years' imprisonment. A retrial was ordered on appeal,[4] but they were convicted again and this verdict was upheld on appeal. The conviction, however, was based solely on an identification,[5] which in turn was based on what the owner could see at night looking through the windscreen of a moving car while lying on its bonnet and being subjected to attempts to force him off.

Meleady and Grogan always protested their innocence. Initially they were supported only by local opinion in their own neighbourhood, and by a few senior politicians and churchmen who took an active interest in their case. The public appeal of their case was boosted considerably by an RTE investigative documentary programme, broadcast in 1990, which revealed that fingerprint evidence found in the car was more consistent with the presence of three other individuals who actually claimed that they were the culprits. At the original trial one of these persons had given evidence that he was in the front seat of the car and that neither Meleady nor Grogan had been in the car. Although the prosecution did not lead any forensic evidence from the car, they put to the witness in cross-examination that his fingerprint had been found on a back seat window of the car. In fact, the forensic examination had revealed that the witness' fingerprint was on a front seat window. This critical information was kept hidden from the defence as was the fact that the car had been subjected to forensic examination. It followed that the defence were not made aware of the fact that no fingerprints from either Meleady or Grogan were found in the car. A subsequent internal investigation in the Chief State Solicitor's office revealed a memo written by a solicitor in the office in preparation for the committal proceedings against Meleady and Grogan on 18 May 1984. The memo stated that the car owner, and chief prosecution witness, had been shown a book of 50 photographs, in which he picked out one of the accused, before the official identification. This information had not been disclosed to the defence, nor was it revealed during the trial.

The dilemma facing the Irish Government was how to respond to these developments. There was no formal mechanism by which the case could be referred back to the courts for further consideration. The only option was a straight choice between direct executive interference in the administration of justice[6] or doing nothing. Eventually, after much prevarication,[7] the minister compromised by

---

[4] A retrial was ordered because at the appeal a third youth, Paul McDonnell, gave evidence that he, and not Meleady and Grogan, was in the car on the relevant night. Subsequently, McDonnell was charged and convicted of perjury.

[5] It is permissible to convict solely on the basis of identification evidence. However, the judge is obliged to deliver a strongly worded warning to the jury on the dangers of convicting on the basis of identification alone; *People* v *Casey (No. 2)* [1963] IR 33 at p. 39.

[6] The minister has the power, delegated by the Government, to remit or commute sentences imposed by the courts; Criminal Justice Act 1951 s. 23 as amended by the Road Traffic Act 1961, s. 124. The Government can advise the President to exercise the right to pardon and to remit or commute punishment imposed by the courts; Arts. 13.6 and 13.9 of the 1937 Constitution.

remitting the remaining seven months of Meleady's five year sentence of imprisonment. Grogan had already served his sentence by this time.

The second seminal example of a miscarriage of justice was one of a number of cases in which it was alleged that the original convictions were based on confessions which had been obtained by the use of ill-treatment in police custody. Most of these cases happened in the 1970s and concerned persons who had been arrested on suspicion of involvement in subversive activity. The objective of the arrests and corresponding interrogations seemed to be a mixture of procuring confessions, gathering intelligence about subversive organisations and intimidating members and supporters of such organisations. Amnesty International was sufficiently concerned about the volume and content of these allegations to carry out an investigation into them in June 1977.[8] After investigating 28 cases, 26 of which occurred between April 1976 and May 1977, it concluded that a number of persons concerned had been ill-treated while in police custody.[9] The nature of the abuses ranged from food and sleep deprivation over several days to severe physical beatings. Particularly significant was Amnesty's finding that the source of the ill-treatment was a group of plain-clothes detectives from the central detective unit in Dublin, who featured in nearly all of the cases irrespective of their location throughout the country. This confirmed a widespread public belief that there was a 'heavy gang' operating within the Garda Siochana with a brief to get results without any questions being asked about their methods.[10] It is hardly surprising, therefore, that the most disturbing example of an apparent miscarriage of justice in the Irish legal system is a confession case from this period, namely *People (Director of Public Prosecutions)* v *Kelly.*[11]

The facts of the *Kelly* case and its progress through the legal system reveal an embarrassing parallel with the facts and progress of the *Birmingham Six* case. Nicky Kelly was one of 21 persons arrested in April 1976 on suspicion of involvement in robbing a mail train and being a member of an unlawful organisation. The arrests were effected under section 30 of the Offences against the State Act 1939, which allows the police to detain a suspect for up to 48 hours without charge. In the event, charges were preferred only against Kelly and five others: Brian McNally, Osgur Breathnach, John Fitzpatrick, Michael Plunkett and Michael Barrett. By the time the case came on for trial in October 1978,[12] the charges against Barrett[13] had been dropped, Fitzpatrick was no longer available to be tried,[14] and Plunkett was discharged in the course of the trial. The sole evidence against Kelly and his remaining two alleged accomplices, McNally and Breath-

---

[7] As late as February 1990 the minister asserted that he could see no grounds for intervening in the case of Meleady who was still serving his sentence. In 1988 he had rejected a petition for Grogan's release.

[8] *Report of an Amnesty International Mission to the Republic of Ireland in June 1977* (London, 1977).

[9] *Ibid.* at p. 4.

[10] The Amnesty Mission was satisfied that the primary purpose of the ill-treatment was to secure confessions; *ibid*, at p. 4.

[11] [1982] IR 90, [1983] IR 1. For a detailed account of this case, see Joyce, J. and Murtagh, P., *Blind Justice* (Poolbeg Press, Dublin, 1984).

[12] The first trial, which commenced on 19 January 1978, had to be aborted owing to the death of one of the presiding judges.

[13] The only evidence implicating Barrett was that he was named as an alibi for Fitzpatrick.

[14] Owing to the State's failure to present the book of evidence within a reasonable time, the accused were discharged by the District Court in December 1976. Fitzpatrick took this opportunity to go 'underground' and so was unavailable when the State reinstated the case.

nach, was the confessions they had given during their interrogation in police custody. The Special Criminal Court, which sits without a jury, declared itself satisfied that the confessions were voluntary, and proceeded to convict and impose sentences of 12 years, 9 years and 12 years respectively. The circumstances in which the confessions were obtained, therefore, were of paramount importance.

Kelly's ordeal[15] commenced at 9.55a.m. on 5 April 1976 with his arrest under section 30. By the time he was charged before a District Court at 10.30p.m. on 8 April, he had dictated a detailed written statement admitting his participation in the robbery and taken police on a fruitless journey to places where he alleged the guns and money had been hidden. He later claimed, however, that his confession was false and had been forced out of him by a combination of physical beating, exhausting interrogation sessions, threats, and food and sleep deprivation. He was also denied access to a solicitor. It is important to point out at this stage that the interrogation experiences of McNally, Breathnach, Plunkett and Fitzpatrick mirrored that of Kelly. Their allegations of ill-treatment were firmly supported by compelling medical testimony from both their own doctors and from the prison doctor.[16] Indeed, Breathnach even had to be transferred from the police station to the hospital on account of his condition after 48 hours in police custody.

When the case finally went to trial, the sole issue was the admissibility of the confessions of Kelly, McNally and Breathnach. The police did not attempt to contest the strong medical evidence in support of the assertion that the confessions had been extracted by ill-treatment and oppression. Instead, they suggested that the accused had colluded to inflict the injuries on each other while remanded in police custody two to a cell. The credibility of this suggestion was undermined by several factors. First, the nature and extent of the injuries were such that they could only have been inflicted over a lengthy period of time accompanied by a considerable degree of noise. There was no evidence, however, that the police on duty in the station where the accused were remanded heard anything unusual from the cells. Secondly, Breathnach was in hospital at the relevant time, so his injuries could not have been inflicted by his co-accused. Thirdly, and most disturbing of all, is the fact that the police would not have been able to raise the suggestion of collusion had they not adopted the most unusual course[17] of requesting that the accused should be remanded into their custody for the night of 7 April, whereupon they irregularly housed them two to a cell. A very credible explanation for these unusual arrangements is that they were engineered by the police intentionally so that they could explain the injuries on the accused by suggesting that they were self-inflicted.

Despite the strength of the evidence in support of the accused's allegations, coupled with the weak and speculative nature of the police explanation, the trial court ruled the confessions admissible and proceeded to convict all three. The fourth, Plunkett, was discharged as the only evidence against him was an identification which collapsed during the trial. In the case of the three convicted,

---

[15] The facts are set out in *Kelly* v *Ireland*, Appl. no. 10416/83, (1984) D.R. 38 p. 158.

[16] In Kelly's case the medical evidence revealed bruising on the arms from the shoulder to the elbow, and over the mastoid bone. There was also bruising over the left shoulder blade, over the ribs, over the pubic bone and on his left hip and thigh. All the bruising was very tender and consistent with recent physical ill-treatment.

[17] At the trial evidence was given by station house officer Padden that in his lengthy experience he could not remember an adult ever being remanded to a police station and not to a prison.

however, the court accepted the police assertion that they were not ill-treated, that the questioning, although protracted and continuous, was not oppressive, and that even if there was a breach of the Judges' Rules[18] it was not sufficient to warrant exclusion.

Kelly absconded after the confessions were ruled admissible. McNally and Breathnach, however, appealed to the Court of Criminal Appeal which overturned their convictions.[19] In McNally's case this was done on the basis that the Judges' Rules had been breached, while in Breathnach's case the operative factor was oppressive questioning. Heartened by these developments Kelly returned to the jurisdiction, where he was arrested and placed in prison to serve the sentence that had been imposed on him in his absence. Ultimately, he appealed his conviction to the Court of Criminal Appeal.[20] Remarkably, in view of the outcome of McNally's and Breathnach's appeals, his conviction was upheld, as the Court could find no grounds for upsetting the trial court's findings.[21] Furthermore, the Court of Criminal Appeal did not accept that admitted breaches of the Judges' Rules were sufficient to overturn the conviction. A final appeal to the Supreme Court was similarly unsuccessful.[22] Given the very strong similarity between Kelly's case and those of his two co-accused, particularly McNally's, it is hardly surprising that a strong public perception of a miscarriage of justice emerged.[23] This perception has been enhanced by the fact that Kelly had to serve four years of his sentence before release and had to wait 16 years before being pardoned.

The question that must be addressed now is how cases such as *Meleady* and *Kelly* could have happened under the Irish criminal justice system. The answer lies primarily in a combination of broad police powers of arrest and detention, inadequate controls on the interrogation of suspects in police custody, judicial inconsistency in the application of the rules on the admissibility of confessions, a relatively weak appellate procedure, and the absence of a post-appellate procedure. Each will be considered briefly in turn.

Arrest

Police powers in Ireland mostly have followed the pattern of their counterparts in Britain, though without any fundamental review or codification equivalent to the Police and Criminal Evidence Act 1984. The courts have eschewed the notion of a general power of summary arrest available on suspicion of criminal activity.[24] Instead, at common law and by statute, the police have been conferred with a large number of powers which are defined by reference to specific types of criminal

---

[18] The 1918 version is still applicable in Ireland. See *People* v *Cummins* [1972] IR 312, at pp. 317, 318. In *People* v *McNally and Breathnach*, 2 Frewen 43 (16 February 1981) the trial court accepted that there was evidence of non-compliance with Rule IX (recording the statement in writing).

[19] *People* v *McNally and Breathnach*, 2 Frewen 43.

[20] Because he was appealing out of time he had to apply to the Court of Criminal Appeal for an extension of time. Initially, this was refused, but was granted on appeal to the Supreme Court; *People* v *Kelly (No. 1)* [1982] IR 90.

[21] *People* v *Kelly (No. 2)* [1983] IR 1.

[22] *Ibid.*

[23] The strong similarity in the cases was specifically cited by the Supreme Court as a factor which persuaded it to grant an extension of time to apply for leave to appeal; *People* v *Kelly (No. 1)* [1982] IR 90 at pp. 109, 115.

[24] *Dunne* v *Clinton* [1930] IR 366.

activity. Nevertheless, the result is that police officers enjoy a power of arrest in almost every situation in which they reasonably suspect an individual of committing a serious criminal offence.

The power of arrest which the police favour most in combating serious crime is found in section 30 of the Offences against the State Act 1939. The section 30 power was the one used to arrest the suspects in the *Kelly* case. Significantly, of all the arrest powers, it is the one which imposes the fewest restrictions on the police. It empowers a member of the force to arrest without warrant any person whom he or she suspects of an offence under the Act, or of a scheduled offence, or of having information about any such offence. The flavour of the power is conveyed by the fact that it is not even necessary for the police officer to suspect the individual affected of involvement in any criminal activity; it will be sufficient if the officer merely suspects him or her of having information about a relevant offence. In this respect the section 30 power is even broader than those available to a constable in Northern Ireland or Great Britain under the emergency legislation.

The immense scope of the power is also reflected in the range of offences to which it applies. The Act itself creates offences designed to protect the State against subversion. More significant, however, is the power it confers on the Government to extend section 30 to other existing offences simply by listing them in a statutory order. Such offences are designated 'scheduled offences'.[25] Although the 1939 Act was designed to protect the State against subversion, it is permissible to arrest under section 30 for a scheduled offence even if there are no subversive overtones.[26] The effect is that ordinary criminal suspects can now be drawn into the much harsher criminal process that has been designed primarily to deal with the challenge and threat posed by subversive suspects.[27] The implications of this for miscarriages of justice are revealed by the extent to which section 30, and the regime of which it forms an integral part, undermine the traditional safeguards for the suspect in the criminal process.

Not only can section 30 be used to deal with a wide range of situations, but it can also be used even where there are no reasonable grounds to connect the individual in question with a relevant criminal offence. Section 30 stipulates that a mere suspicion is sufficient. The courts have interpreted this to mean that a police officer need only have an honestly held suspicion coupled with the existence of at least some evidence upon which this subjective suspicion could reasonably be based.[28] The mere fact that a reasonable person would not have suspected in the same circumstances does not invalidate the arrest. Furthermore, the suspicion need not be personal to the arresting officer. It will be sufficient that he acted on the instructions of a superior officer who had the requisite suspicion.[29] The full significance of this low threshold for suspicion is revealed when arrests are made for membership of an unlawful organisation. The nature of this offence means that

---

[25] Currently, these consist of offences under the Malicious Damage Act 1861; the Conspiracy and Protection of Property Act 1875, s. 7; the Explosive Substances Act 1883; the Firearms Acts 1925–71; and the Offences against the State Act 1939.

[26] *People* v *Quilligan* [1987] ILRM 606 at pp. 617–38.

[27] The police have also managed to extend s. 30 to other non-scheduled offences; see Walsh D.P.J., 'The impact of antisubversive laws on police powers and practices in the Republic of Ireland: the silent erosion of individual freedom' (1989) 62 *Temple Law Review* 1105.

[28] Hogan, G. and Walker, C., *Political Violence and the Law in Ireland* (Manchester University Press, Manchester, 1989) at pp. 202–5.

[29] *People* v *McCaffrey* [1986] ILRM 687.

the police need not suspect an individual of engaging in any positive criminal act. Membership, by its very nature, is an ongoing state of being. Since all that is needed is a mere honest suspicion based on some evidence, it follows that a large number of people known to the police are constantly vulnerable to arrest under section 30. Matters such as associating with suspect subversives or selling IRA propaganda will be sufficient to ground a valid arrest.[30] It is not surprising, therefore, that a large number of arrests under section 30 are for membership. However, they do not usually result in charges. It would appear in practice that many of the arrests are effected primarily for the purpose of gathering intelligence information on subversive organisations.[31]

Detention and Interrogation

In Ireland police powers to detain an arrested person for questioning about an offence are based exclusively on statute. At the time of the *Kelly* arrests the only such power was provided by section 30 of the Offences against the State Act 1939. It has since been supplemented by section 4 of the Criminal Justice Act 1984 which permits detention for up to 20 hours in a wide range of offences, and section 2 of the Criminal Justice (Drug Trafficking) Act 1996 which permits detention for up to seven days in a narrower range of offences. Under section 30 a suspect can be held without charge for 48 hours. He or she is also obliged to assist the police by accounting for his or her movements and actions during any specified period and for all information in his or her possession concerning the commission of a relevant offence by any other person. Failure to co-operate is a criminal offence.[32] In the *Kelly* case the police made use of this provision to coerce the co-operation of the suspects. In the absence of countervailing safeguards for the suspect, the risk of a false confession being extracted in such circumstances is obvious. It follows that the law and procedure governing the treatment of persons in police custody are of critical importance in protecting against possible miscarriages of justice.

Up until 1987 the treatment of persons in police custody was governed by the 1918 version of the Judges' Rules, the Constitution and general laws such as those on the admissibility of confession evidence. There were no published regulations governing detention in police custody. This was painfully obvious to the suspects in the *Kelly* case. As well as allegations of physical abuse, their litany of complaints included: being moved around from one police station to another; their whereabouts being concealed from next of kin; no access to medical examination; no access to a solicitor; being deprived of adequate food and rest; being questioned for excessively long periods by an inordinately large number of detectives working in relays; being questioned without caution; notes of interrogations being written after interview; being confronted with co-accused; being left alone with co-accused; being subjected to threats; and being re-arrested immediately following on release. Assuming that all of these allegations were true, the most they amounted to was a breach of the Judges' Rules and a possible infringement of the

---

[30] See, for example, *O'Leary* v *Attorney-General* [1991] ILRM 454 and [1995] 2 ILRM 259.

[31] Between 1981 and 1986 (inclusive) the rate of charge of persons arrested under s. 30 was as low as 11 and did not exceed 20 per cent; Dáil Debates, vol. 369, cols 2559–60; vol. 371, col. 714 (18 November, 1986).

[32] Offences against the State Act 1939, s. 52. The constitutionality of this provision has been upheld by the High Court in *Heaney* v *Ireland* [1994] 2 ILRM 420.

constitutional right of access to a solicitor.[33] There were no regulations prohibiting any of these practices nor, of course, any specifying positively how a suspect should be treated in police custody.

Amnesty International identified the inadequacy of legal safeguards for the rights of the suspect in police custody as a particular cause for concern.[34] This was taken up by the O'Briain Committee, which was set up in 1977 by the Government to recommend safeguards for people in custody and to safeguard the police from untrue allegations. It reported in 1978 with a long list of substantive and procedural recommendations aimed at filling the void.[35] It was 1987, however, before an actual code for the protection of persons in police custody was actually promulgated.[36] The Code lays down standards on matters such as access to legal advice and medical examination, the structure and conduct of interrogations and on the suspect's rights while in police custody. Breach constitutes a disciplinary, as opposed to a criminal offence and does not result in the automatic exclusion of a confession. Moreover, it is unlikely that the Code will have as much impact as those under PACE. Nevertheless it does represent a substantial improvement on the earlier situation. As such it should make some contribution to nipping possible miscarriages of justice in the bud.

Unfortunately, the Code has been accompanied and succeeded by a substantial extension in the investigative powers at the disposal of the police. The powers to detain arrested suspects for further investigation under the 1984 and 1996 Acts have already been mentioned. The section 30 approach which had been perceived as the exception has now become the norm.[37] New and extensive powers to search, photograph, fingerprint and take forensic samples from suspects in police custody have been introduced.[38] Further restrictions on the right to silence are also a feature.[39] The combination of these provisions will result in a regime where more suspects are held in police custody for longer periods and in circumstances where they can be put under more pressure to co-operate with the police investigation. It is unlikely that the accompanying safeguards in the form of the Code will be sufficient to ensure that these measures do not produce false confessions in individual cases.

Admissibility of Confessions

In Irish law it is quite permissible to convict solely on the basis of a confession given by the accused while being questioned in police custody. Before such a confession can be admitted in evidence, however, the prosecution will have to establish beyond a reasonable doubt that it is voluntary and that it has not been obtained in circumstances which amount to a conscious and deliberate violation of

---

[33] It was not until 1989 that the Supreme Court recognised a constitutional right of access to a solicitor for a suspect in police custody; *People* v *Healy* [1990] ILRM 313.

[34] *Report of an Amnesty International Mission to the Republic of Ireland in June 1977*, at pp. 4–7.

[35] Prl. 158 (Dublin, 1978).

[36] Criminal Justice Act 1984 (Treatment of Persons in Custody in Garda Siochana Stations) Regulations, 1987 (SI No. 119).

[37] Walsh D.P.J., 'The impact of antisubversive laws on police powers and practices in the Republic of Ireland: the silent erosion of individual freedom' (1989) 62 *Temple Law Review* 1105 at pp. 1112–14.

[38] See the Criminal Justice Act 1984, s. 6(1)(c), (d) and (e) and the Criminal Justice (Forensic Evidence) Act 1990.

[39] Criminal Justice Act 1984, ss. 6, 15, 16, 18, 19.

the suspect's constitutional rights.[40] The standard test for voluntariness is that the confession must not have been obtained from the accused by fear of prejudice or hope of advantage held out by a person in authority,[41] or by oppression.[42] It is not even necessary that any blameworthiness should attach to the police. It will be sufficient if an investigating officer innocently said or did something that excited fear or hope in the mind of the suspect as a result of which he confessed. Furthermore, the constitutional protection afforded the suspect in police custody ensures that if the custody is or becomes unlawful owing to circumstances within the knowledge of the police, any confession given during the period of unlawful detention is automatically inadmissible.[43] Lastly, the trial judge can mop up any cases that fall through the net by exercising his discretion to exclude a confession where, owing to circumstances in which it was obtained, it would be unfair to the accused to admit it.[44] Where a confession is admitted, the trial judge is now under a duty to advise the jury, where appropriate, to have regard to the absence of corroboration.[45] In practice, of course, this requirement has little substantive effect as most of the contested confession cases (which are infrequent in Ireland) occur in the no-jury Special Criminal Court.

In theory these admissibility tests should provide an impregnable barrier against unjust conviction on the basis of confession evidence. In practice, however, the law has not always proved an effective filter, particularly where, as in the *Kelly* case, the trial is in the Special Criminal Court.[46] The distinctive feature of this court is that it sits with an uneven number of judges (not being less than three) and without a jury. Although it is not part of the normal court structure and does not have a permanent existence, it enjoys the same powers as the Central Criminal Court in matters of trial and sentence. Its jurisdiction covers all scheduled offences and can even extend to non-scheduled offences where the Director of Public Prosecutions has certified in any individual case that the ordinary courts are inadequate to secure the effective administration of justice and the preservation of public peace and order in relation to the trial of that case. In practice, most persons who are tried in the Special Criminal Court will have been arrested and detained under section 30 of the Offences against the State Act 1939. It follows that if they confessed under the section 30 interrogation regime, the admissibility and credibility of the confession will be determined by three judges without reference to a jury.

From the case law it is difficult to avoid the impression that the Special Criminal Court applies a less rigorous admissibility test. The *Kelly* case itself is a disturbing example. Although the Court accepted (it could hardly do otherwise given the

---

[40] Ryan, E. and Magee, P., *The Irish Criminal Process* (Mercier Press, Cork, 1983) pp. 113–15 and 156–76.

[41] *People* v *McCabe* [1927] IR 129.

[42] *People* v *Lynch* [1982] IR 64.

[43] *People* v *Madden* [1977] IR 336; *People* v *McLoughlin* [1979] IR 85.

[44] *People* v *O'Brien* [1965] IR 142; *People* v *Cummins*, [1972] IR 312; *People* v *Lynch* [1982] IR 64; *People* v *Shaw* [1982] IR 1; *People* v *Healy* [1990] ILRM 313.

[45] Criminal Procedure Act 1993, s. 10. The Government toyed briefly with the idea of introducing a strict corroboration requirement for confession evidence. The idea, however, excited virtually no debate.

[46] For a detailed analysis of the Special Criminal Court, see Hogan, G. and Walker, C., *Political Violence and the Law in Ireland* (Manchester University Press, Manchester, 1989) at pp. 227–44; Irish Council for Civil Liberties, *The Special Criminal Court* (Dublin, 1995).

medical evidence) that the accused had suffered serious injuries while in police custody, it concluded that these injuries must have been self-inflicted. In reaching this conclusion, however, the Court did not attempt any explanation as to how the accused persons could have managed to inflict such injuries upon themselves in police custody without the knowledge and intervention of the police. Nor did it see anything sinister about the improper police move to have the accused remanded into their custody and then to house them two to a cell contrary to regulations. It was as if the Court did not want to contemplate the possibility that the police version might not be the truth. The Amnesty International investigation in the late 1970s identified a similar judicial reluctance in the Special Criminal Court to exclude confessions on the ground of involuntariness. It concluded that:

> . . . the onus of proof has in effect been on the defence to establish beyond all reasonable doubt that the maltreatment did occur, rather than on the prosecution to prove that it did not.[47]

Once the Special Criminal Court has ruled a confession admissible, conviction is virtually a foregone conclusion. The same three judges who ruled on its admissibility decide what weight to attach to it. So far there has been no case of an admissible confession being followed by a refusal to convict.

Appeals

The very real possibility of a miscarriage of justice resulting from some of the confession cases emphasises the importance that must be attached to the appellate procedure. In Ireland, an accused who has been convicted in the Central Criminal Court or the Special Criminal Court has no right of appeal to the Court of Criminal Appeal; he or she must apply for leave. In practice this is nothing more than a technicality, as the merits of the appeal are often considered on the application.[48] The appeal, however, is conducted solely on the basis of the transcript of the trial.[49] Fresh evidence may be admitted but only with the leave of the court. Where the fresh evidence was available at the original trial but not used, leave will be granted only in exceptional cases.[50] Further appeal to the Supreme Court is possible, but only if the Court of Criminal Appeal or the Director of Public Prosecutions certifies that the decision involves a point of law of exceptional public importance and that it is desirable in the public interest that an appeal should be taken to the Supreme Court.[51]

In confession cases the capacity of the appellate procedure to repair miscarriages of justice is heavily dependent on the willingness of an appellate court to upset the trial court findings of fact and his application of the admissibility test to those facts. Unfortunately, the current state of the law on this aspect in Ireland does not hold out much hope for appellants. The role of an appeal court in criminal matters was explained as follows by the Court of Criminal Appeal in *People* v *Madden*:

---

[47] *Report of an Amnesty International Mission to the Republic of Ireland in June 1977*, at p. 8.
[48] See *Report of Committee to Inquire into Certain Aspects of Criminal Procedure* (Dublin, 1990) (*Martin Report*) at p. 6.
[49] Ryan, E. and Magee, P., *The Irish Criminal Process* (Mercier Press, Cork, 1983) at p. 427.
[50] *Ibid.*, at pp. 428–9.
[51] Courts of Justice Act 1924, s. 29.

... to review as far as may be required any rulings on matters of law, to review as far as may be necessary the application of the rules of evidence as applied in the trial, and to consider whether any inferences of fact drawn by the court of trial can properly be supported by the evidence; but otherwise to adopt all findings of fact.[52]

With respect to the trial court findings of fact, the Court made it clear that they should not be upset unless they were 'so clearly against the weight of testimony as to amount to a defeat of justice'.[53] This can pose a major problem for the accused in a confession case where the trial court has displayed a tendency to rely on the police version of events and where that version conflicts with the account given by the accused. Unless the accused can expose blatant internal contradictions in the police account, or a straight conflict between the police account and independent evidence, there will inevitably be some grounds upon which the trial court could have believed the police account. Typically that account will in turn offer some evidence upon which the trial court could reasonably have concluded that the confession was voluntary and that there was no room for the exercise of discretion.

An appellate court, therefore, will be left with very little room for manoeuvre in upsetting the trial court decision on the admissibility of a confession. Indeed, the *Kelly* case illustrates how an appellate court's attempt to deal at third hand with what happened behind the closed doors of the police interrogation room can actually enhance the appearance of injustice rather than produce the opposite effect. Although all the ingredients which had vitiated the convictions in both McNally's and Breathnach's cases were present in full measure in Kelly's case, the Court of Criminal Appeal still managed to uphold Kelly's conviction. It did this by adopting a subtly different approach to the relevant factors in Kelly's case compared with that in the cases of the other two. To make matters worse, the Court did not offer any convincing explanation for the difference in treatment. In supporting the trial court finding in Kelly's case that the confession was voluntary, the Court relied solely on the evidence of Kelly's conduct after he had confessed. By contrast, in Breathnach's case it had focused on the length and intensity of the interrogation sessions prior to confession. When dealing with the breach of the Judges' Rules in Kelly's case, the Court concentrated solely on whether the breach could have affected the accuracy of the record of the confession. By comparison, in McNally's case the Court focused on the adequacy of the justification proffered for the failure to comply with the Rules. The net result was that Kelly's conviction was upheld, and he was left to serve out a sentence of 12 years' imprisonment while his two co-accused were freed. Not only did the Court of Criminal Appeal not explain why it adopted a different approach to the two appeals, but it did not even feel it necessary to address its collective mind to the apparent injustice of the conflicting results. It is concerned primarily with the procedural fairness of the trial at first instance and with whether the trial court's findings can be supported by the evidence. It does not regard itself as having a general jurisdiction to act in a positive role to ensure that justice is done.[54]

---

[52] [1977] IR 336, at p. 340.

[53] *Ibid.*, at p. 339.

[54] *People v Mulligan* 2 Frewen 16. The broader approach adopted by the Court of Appeal in England

Remedying a Miscarriage of Justice

When a conviction was upheld on appeal in Ireland, that was effectively the end of the road for the individual concerned prior to December 1993. Serious doubts may linger, as in the *Meleady* and *Kelly* cases, about the fairness or reliability of the convictions, but there was no formal procedure whereby the matter could have been reopened. There was no procedure for referring a case back to the Court of Criminal Appeal for further consideration even on the basis of new evidence. The most that could have happened was the granting of a Presidential pardon on the advice of the Government.[55] Alternatively, the Government had the power to commute or remit, in whole or in part, a sentence imposed on a convicted person so long as the offence in question was not capital.[56] This power was exercised in both the *Meleady* and *Kelly* cases. The Presidential pardon, however, has been exercised on only two previous occasions since the establishment of the State in 1922.[57] The Government's decision to advise a Presidential pardon for Nicky Kelly in April 1992 can therefore be described as momentous, even if it was a long time in coming.

The official Government statement announcing Kelly's pardon explains that the decision was taken on the advice of the Attorney-General who, in turn, had consulted the Director of Public Prosecutions. The reasoning in the statement is both interesting and confusing. Almost the first half is devoted to the evidence of two linguistic analysts, who claimed that Kelly was not the author of his alleged inculpatory statement.[58] The opinion of the Director of Public Prosecutions was that this evidence would probably not have had any effect on the original decision to prosecute. However, the advice of the Attorney-General on this matter was that a court would regard such evidence as admissible and that it could not be said that such evidence would be disregarded. The statement then went on to consider the possible effect on the verdict or appeal and concluded that it could not be definitely asserted that it would not have led the courts to recognise the existence of a reasonable doubt over the voluntariness of Kelly's confession. It is not clear, however, whether this represented the advice of the Director of Public Prosecutions or the Attorney-General, or simply an awkward attempt by the Government to avoid stating its position on the textual analysis of Kelly's statement.

The second half of the statement would appear to contain the decisive part. It stated that the Attorney-General had advised the Government that it would be unsafe to accept Kelly's guilt as established beyond reasonable doubt. This opinion is based on three considerations, each of which, it is stated, would have been sufficient to have militated against a decision to prosecute. The strange aspect of this assertion is that two of the considerations were operative at the time of the trial[59] and the third was operative at the time of Kelly's appeal.[60] Stranger still is

in *R* v *Cooper* (1969) 53 Cr App R 82 was not approved by the Irish Supreme Court in *People* v *Egan* [1990] ILRM 780.

[55] Articles 13.6 and 13.9 of the 1937 Constitution.

[56] Criminal Justice Act 1951, s. 23.

[57] Thomas Quinn in 1940 and Walter Brady in 1943 (see *The Irish Times*, 30 April 1992).

[58] This evidence became public through an RTE documentary in November 1991, which gave a significant impetus to the review which resulted in the pardon.

[59] The first was the collapse of the identification evidence against Plunkett. The second was the implausibility of the police attempt to square Fitzpatrick's participation in the robbery with his alibi.

[60] The third point was the judgment in *People* v *Shaw* [1982] IR 1, as applied in *People* v *McNally and*

the fact that the textual analysis was not offered as one of the operative considerations. The effect is to give the impression that the miscarriage of justice was entirely excusable, even unavoidable. Perhaps such an over-sensitive approach is to be expected when the executive feels that it has to encroach upon the judicial domain. In the *Kelly* case, however, it is just as likely that the executive was hoping to avoid having to face up to skeletons in its own cupboard. Thus, if the Government and the Attorney-General had described the linguistic evidence as instrumental to the decision to pardon, it would have focused the spotlight once more on the veracity of Kelly's claim that he was forced to sign a false confession through police ill-treatment. That the executive had no stomach for such an eventuality is suggested by the fact that the Government was happy to accept the advice of the Attorney-General and the Director of Public Prosecutions to the effect that 'any further inquiry in to the circumstances of the case would be unlikely to produce any clearer resolution of the issues that arose in it.'.

As will be seen later, the Criminal Procedure Act 1993 now makes provision for alleged miscarriage of justice cases to be referred back to the Court of Criminal Appeal for further consideration. Nevertheless, the Presidential pardon still remains. Indeed, the 1993 Act provides a statutory procedure to be followed where a convicted person petitions the Minister for Justice with a view to the Government advising the President to grant a pardon. Unless the minister is satisfied that the case for a miscarriage of justice has not been made out or that it is one which should be dealt with by an application to the Court of Criminal Appeal, he or she should recommend to the Government that it should advise the President to grant a pardon. Alternatively, the minister could advise the Government to appoint a committee to inquire into the case. Such a committee will be a tribunal within the meaning of the Tribunals of Inquiry (Evidence) Acts 1921 and 1979 and may consist of one or more persons. The role of a committee is to receive such evidence and other information as it sees fit with a view to advising the Government on whether it should advise the President to grant a pardon. Where a Presidential pardon is granted pursuant to this statutory procedure, or where the minister for Justice is of the opinion that a newly-discovered fact shows that there has been a miscarriage of justice, the minister must pay compensation to the convicted person. In practice it is likely that the Presidential pardon procedure will be overshadowed in importance by the new procedure for taking a case back to the Court of Criminal Appeal. This is discussed later.

Another possibility, besides Presidential pardon, for a collateral attack on the soundness of a conviction based on confession evidence alone, is to sue the State for damages for ill-treatment suffered while under interrogation in police custody. In 1983 Kelly was persuaded by the Government to come off his hunger strike to pursue this course. The implication was that if he was successful, it would be tantamount to establishing that his conviction was unsafe and unsatisfactory. Despite encouraging Kelly to pursue this course, the authorities then sought to have his action struck out on the technical ground that the issues he sought to litigate had already been determined against him at the trial in the Special Criminal Court.

Breathnach, 2 Frewen 43. *The Shaw* case was interpreted as having laid down a more liberal approach to the admissibility of confessions (to the effect that a confession is admissible only if voluntary and the circumstances in which it was obtained did not fall below the required standards of fairness) than in *People* v *O'Brien* [1965] IR 142 (which demanded a deliberate and conscious violation of rights and the absence of any extraordinary excusing circumstances).

Basing himself substantially on the decisions of the English Court of Appeal and the House of Lords in the civil action brought by the *Birmingham Six*,[61] O'Hanlon J, in the Irish High Court, said that to allow Kelly to reopen the findings of the Special Criminal Court on the voluntariness of his confession in the course of his civil action would give rise to an issue estoppel and an abuse of the process of the court.[62] This could be avoided only if fresh evidence was adduced. Again, however, O'Hanlon was guided by the Court of Appeal and the House of Lords in defining the appropriate test to be applied to any fresh evidence adduced. It must be evidence of such a character as to change the whole aspect of the case; it must be evidence which could not, by the exercise of reasonable diligence, have been made available at the previous hearing; and it must be evidence which is well capable of belief in the context of the circumstances as a whole. Clearly, the prospects of using the civil action as a means of remedying a possible miscarriage of justice in a criminal case are no more attractive in Ireland now than they were in Britain for the *Birmingham Six*.

Reform

The *Meleady* and *Kelly* cases were very much alive as alleged miscarriages of justice throughout the period that the Irish Government was voicing its concerns about the treatment of Irish suspects in Britain. Those campaigning on behalf of Meleady and Kelly took full advantage of the opportunity to contrast the Irish Government's concern at the shortcomings in the British criminal justice system with its refusal to face up to even graver shortcomings at home. The Irish Government's position became even more untenable when justice was finally done in cases such as the *Guildford Four* and the *Birmingham Six*. The question being asked in Ireland was no longer whether the same could happen there, but whether something could be done about it when it did happen. Since the answer, for all intents and purposes, was 'No', it was hardly surprising that the Government moved to address the situation by the establishment of a committee of inquiry under the chairmanship of Judge Frank Martin.[63] The committee's terms of reference reflected two major aspects of the problem. First, it had to examine whether additional safeguards were needed to ensure that confessions made by suspects to the police were properly obtained and recorded. Secondly, it had to examine whether there was a need for a procedure where cases could be reviewed even though they had exhausted the normal appeals procedure. Although the Committee reported in March 1990, its recommendations were not implemented until December 1993 in the case of a review procedure and March 1997 in the case of the recording of confessions.

Post-conviction Review

The Criminal Procedure Act 1993 makes provision for the Court of Criminal Appeal to review alleged miscarriages of justice in cases where the normal appeal

---

[61] *Hunter* v *Chief Constable of the West Midlands* [1981] 3 WLR 906. See Chapter 2.

[62] *Kelly* v *Ireland* [1986] ILRM 318.

[63] The Committee set up by the minister for Justice in 1989 to inquire into certain aspects of criminal procedure accepted that mistaken identification had given rise to wrongful convictions in the past. See *Report of Committee to Inquire into Certain Aspects of Criminal Procedure* (Dublin, 1990), pp. 9, 10.

process has been exhausted. The jurisdiction of the Court can be invoked where a person alleges that a new or newly discovered fact shows that there has been a miscarriage of justice in relation to his or her conviction on indictment after the normal appeals process has been exhausted.[64] An application under this procedure is treated for all purposes as an appeal to the Court of Criminal Appeal.[65] The Court may affirm the conviction if it considers that no miscarriage of justice has occurred, or it may quash the conviction with or without an order for a re-trial.[66] It may also quash the conviction and substitute a verdict of guilty of another offence. These options are open to the Court in both miscarriage of justice applications and in ordinary appeals.

At the heart of this procedure is the allegation that new evidence has emerged suggesting that there may have been a miscarriage of justice.[67] The new evidence may be a fact which has only come to the notice of the convicted person after the conclusion of the relevant appeal proceedings. Equally it may have been something that was known but the significance of which was not appreciated by the convicted person during the earlier proceedings. It may even consist of a fact the existence and significance of which was appreciated by the convicted person, so long as there is a reasonable explanation for his or her failure to adduce evidence of it during the earlier proceedings. Significantly, it is not necessary that the new evidence actually shows that there has been a miscarriage of justice. Nor is there an executive filter which an applicant must survive before his or her case is referred to the Court. The application is made directly by the applicant to the Court. However, if the Court considers the application is frivolous or vexatious and can be determined without a full hearing, it may dismiss the application summarily without calling anyone to attend the hearing or to appear on behalf of the prosecution.[68] Where the Court does proceed to a full hearing of the application by way of appeal, it may direct the Commissioner of the Garda Siochana to carry out inquiries for the purpose of determining whether further evidence ought to be adduced.[69] In practice this will usually amount to an inquiry into the new evidence proffered by the applicant. The Court may also order the production of any document or exhibit, order the appearance of any compellable witness for examination and cross-examination, receive the evidence tendered by any witness and generally make such order as may be necessary for the purpose of doing justice in the case.

One of the vital ingredients of the new procedure is the provision for compensation. The question of compensation will arise where a person's conviction has been quashed pursuant to the miscarriage of justice procedure or on appeal, or where a person has been acquitted in any re-trial.[70] The Minister for Justice must pay compensation in any such case where the Court of Criminal Appeal (or the court of trial in the event of a re-trial) has certified that a newly-discovered fact[71]

---

[64] Criminal Procedure Act 1993, s. 2(1). The jurisdiction also extends to an allegation that a sentence imposed is excessive.

[65] *Ibid.*, s. 2(2).

[66] *Ibid.*, s. 3(1). It also has powers to quash a sentence and to impose a different sentence; s. 3(2).

[67] See Criminal Procedure Act 1993 s. 2(3) for the definition of a 'new fact' and s. 2(4) for the definition of a 'newly-discovered' fact.

[68] *Ibid.*, s. 5. This power also extends to applications for leave to appeal in ordinary appeal cases.

[69] *Ibid.*, s. 3(3). The Court also enjoys these powers in ordinary appeal cases.

[70] *Ibid.*, s. 9(1).

[71] Surprisingly, perhaps, the definition of a 'newly-discovered' fact for the purpose of compensation

shows that there has been a miscarriage of justice. The amount of compensation, which is only payable on application, is at the minister's discretion.[72] However, any person dissatisfied with the amount awarded may apply to the High Court to determine the amount which must be paid.[73]

The first case to be brought under the provisions of the 1993 Act was *Meleady*[74] which was taken to the Court of Criminal Appeal in February 1994 after the five year sentences had been served.[75] The Court concluded that the non-disclosure of the fingerprint evidence and the existence of the Walker memo to the defence rendered the convictions unsafe and unsatisfactory. Accordingly it quashed the convictions and sentences without ordering a retrial. Surprisingly, perhaps, the Court refused the defence application for a certificate that there had been a miscarriage of justice. Without this certificate Meleady and Grogan could not receive compensation for the five years which each had served in prison. The Court reasoned that the quashing of a conviction on appeal was not always synonymous with a miscarriage of justice. Even where a conviction was quashed without an order for a retrial it did not inevitably follow that there had been a miscarriage of justice within the scope of the 1993 Act. In the *Meleady* case the Court concluded that a certificate could not issue because the evidence of the chief prosecution witness had not been considered by a jury in a trial untainted by the irregularities revealed by the newly-discovered facts.

The defence appealed the refusal of the certificate to the Supreme Court which ruled that the Court of Criminal Appeal had erred in finding that a certificate could not issue simply because the newly-discovered material had not been considered by a jury.[76] Once an applicant has had his or her conviction quashed on appeal or has been acquitted on a retrial, he or she is entitled to have the Court of Criminal Appeal enter on an inquiry as to whether a newly-discovered fact shows that there has been a miscarriage of justice. No distinction can be drawn between those whose convictions have been quashed on appeal, and those who have been acquitted on a retrial. Accordingly, the Supreme Court remitted the case back to the Court of Criminal Appeal to consider whether there had been a miscarriage of justice.[77] Clearly, the Supreme Court was accepting that just because a newly-discovered fact has resulted in the quashing of a conviction without an order for a retrial, it does not automatically follow that a miscarriage of justice certificate must issue.

On the same day that the Supreme Court handed down its judgment in the *Meleady* case, it also handed down judgment in the second case to have been

---

differs from that which was sufficient to invoke the jurisdiction of the Court in miscarriage of justice cases. The former excludes the situation where the convicted person alleges that there is a reasonable explanation for his failure to adduce evidence of a fact the existence and significance of which was known to him or her at the earlier proceedings. See s. 9(6).

[72] Criminal Procedure Act, 1993, s. 9(4).

[73] *Ibid.*, s. 9(5).

[74] The *Kelly* case had been settled by a full Presidential pardon before the 1993 Act came into effect.

[75] *In re s. 2, Criminal Procedure Act 1993, People (DPP) v Meleady and Grogan* (unreported judgment of the Court of Criminal Appeal, 22 March 1995).

[76] *In the Matter of section 29 of the Courts of Justice Act 1924, in the matter of section 2 and section 9 of the Criminal Procedure Act 1993, the People (DPP) v Meleady and Grogan* (unreported, 4 March 1997).

[77] It is worth noting that in December 1996 the owner of the car involved was awarded £452,000 criminal injuries compensation for mental injuries and stress resulting from the case. See also Chapter 12.

brought under the 1993 Act, namely *The People (Director of Public Prosecutions) v Pringle*.[78] In this case the applicant had been convicted of capital murder and robbery and sentenced to death (later commuted to 40 years' imprisonment) in November 1980. In 1995 he appealed his conviction and sentence to the Court of Criminal Appeal under the terms of the 1993 Act. The basis of the appeal was new evidence which cast doubt on the credibility of one of two Garda officers who had taken a confession from the applicant while he was in police custody. The Court quashed the conviction without an order for a retrial but refused to issue a miscarriage of justice certificate. On the appeal against this refusal the Supreme Court confirmed that the onus was on the applicant to prove positively and on a balance of probabilities that a newly-discovered fact showed that there had been a miscarriage of justice. The mere fact of the conviction being quashed without an order for a retrial was not sufficient in itself. Because this requirement may not have been fully appreciated on account of the newness of the procedure, the Supreme Court remitted the case back to the Court of Criminal Appeal so that the applicant could argue his case on this basis.

The Supreme Court in *Pringle* explained that the primary meaning of a miscarriage of justice within the 1993 Act is that the applicant is innocent of the offence of which he was convicted. This would have to be established on a balance of probabilities by relevant and admissible evidence. Clearly, this formulation will significantly impair the scope for an award of compensation under the legislation. Many applicants who should never have been convicted will not be able to prove that they are innocent. Not only will this deprive them of the right to compensation for time unnecessarily spent in prison, but it will also disqualify them from being granted a miscarriage of justice certificate. Inevitably, there is a serious risk that the quashing of convictions in such cases will not be sufficient to clear the individuals concerned of the appearance of criminal wrongdoing. Their presumption of innocence will be technically intact, but their public reputation will remain under a cloud of suspicion. Admittedly, there is room in the Supreme Court's judgment to minimise further injustice flowing from this restrictive interpretation of a miscarriage of justice. The Court acknowledged that other cases might qualify such as, for example, where a prosecution should never have been brought as there was no credible evidence implicating the accused, or where the case involved such a departure from the basic rules of judicial procedure as to disqualify it from being described as judicial or constitutional procedure. Even these examples, however, reflect a very conservative approach to the potential of the 1993 procedure. It is unlikely, therefore, that the final decisions in the *Meleady* and *Pringle* cases will signify a new era of apology and compensation for cases of wrongful conviction.

Prevention of False Confessions

Procedures for correcting miscarriages of justice are very necessary, but they are no substitute for measures which will reduce the incidence of such cases. It is significant, therefore, that part of the remit of the Martin Committee was to examine whether additional safeguards were needed to ensure that confessions made by suspects to the police were properly obtained and recorded. This reflected

---

[78] [1995] 2 IR 547 (CCA), Supreme Court, unreported, 4 March 1997.

a reasonable assumption that greater transparency in the circumstances and manner in which suspects are questioned in police custody will lead to a reduction in the incidence of alleged miscarriages of justice. The Committee found that the present methods used to obtain and record confessions from suspects in police custody were less than reliable.[79] The mere fact of being in police custody was, in itself, sufficient to pose a risk to the voluntariness of a suspect's confession, while the procedure for recording the confession ensured that the end result was only a police officer's summary of what actually transpired. Subsequently, if an accused challenged his alleged confession in court, considerable delay, expense and inconvenience for all concerned would have to be expended in establishing what exactly happened behind the closed doors of the interrogation room. At the end of the day the court will be left with the difficult task of weighing up the oath of one person against another. There is no independent factor which can be used to determine the issue with the certainty that justice demands.[80]

While the Committee accepted that the current law and regulations governing the treatment of suspects in police custody were sufficient for the most part to ensure that justice was done,[81] it also felt that further, more radical measures were needed, not just to ensure that justice was done in all cases but also to simplify and shorten the lengthy trial procedure associated with the current approach.[82] Accordingly, the Committee recommended the introduction of audio-visual record- ing of the interrogation of suspects in police custody, and the acceptance of the tapes as admissible evidence at trial.[83] Basing itself on Canadian and Australian experience, the Committee concluded that the audio-visual recording would present a very accurate and reliable account of interrogation sessions and would obviate the need for separate admissibility hearings at the trial in the event of a challenge to the admissibility of a confession.

Regulations giving effect to the Martin Committee's recommendations on the recording of interrogations in police custody were not introduced until March 1997. The Criminal Justice Act 1984 (Electronic Recording of Interviews) Regulations 1997 make provision for the electronic recording of certain interviews in certain police stations. The interviews in question are those conducted with persons detained under section 4 of the Criminal Justice Act 1984, section 30 of the Offences against the State Act, 1939 or section 2 of the Criminal Justice (Drug Trafficking) Act 1996.[84] While these will cover a large number of interrogations, they fall significantly short of all interrogations in police custody. Interviews with persons who have gone to a police station voluntarily or who have been arrested but not detained under one of the three statutory provisions are not covered. Even

---

[79] *Report of Committee to Inquire into Certain Aspects of Criminal Procedure* (Dublin, 1990), pp. 22, 23.

[80] *Ibid.*, p. 26.

[81] It did make several recommendations for change in the regulations, including: the imposition of an obligation on the police to supply a suspect with a list of solicitors willing to attend at police stations (p. 41); wherever possible the number of officers in the interrogation room at any one time should be confined to two (p. 42); and that apart from specified circumstances a suspect should not be interrogated until a reasonable time for the attendance of his solicitor has elapsed (p. 43). It also suggested that consideration should be given to the introduction of a requirement for trial judges to give a warning to the jury on the dangers of convicting on the basis of confession evidence alone (p. 39).

[82] *Ibid.*, pp. 26, 27.

[83] *Ibid.*, pp. 32–9.

[84] Criminal Justice Act 1984 (Electronic Recording of Interviews) Regulations 1997, reg. 3(2).

interviews which are technically covered need not be recorded in certain circumstances such as where the equipment is not available or where the recording is not
practicable. The tape can also be switched off in order to take a break in the
interview.[85] The significance of the recording requirement is also undermined by
the fact that it only applies to police stations in which the recording equipment has
been installed.[86] As yet, very few police stations are equipped. Finally, it must also
be noted that the requirement to record interviews electronically can be satisfied
either by a sound recording of oral communication on tape or a video recording
with or without a soundtrack.[87] It follows that there is no obligation to make a
complete audio-visual recording of interviews.

When all of these limitations are taken into account it is apparent that the
electronic recording of interviews might not realise its full potential as a safeguard
against miscarriages of justice. Nevertheless, its introduction must be welcomed as
a step in the right direction. If it had been available in the interrogation of Nicky
Kelly and his co-accused, it is likely that that sorry episode in Irish criminal justice
history would never have happened.

Conclusion

It is too early to make any concrete assessment of the contributions that the recent
reforms will make to the correction and prevention of miscarriages of justice. The
full potential of the review procedure has not been helped by the restrictive
approach to the interpretation of a miscarriage of justice adopted by the Supreme
Court. Moreover, the regulations on the electronic recording of interviews in police
custody are not sufficiently comprehensive to ensure that all interviews of persons
subsequently charged with serious offences will have been recorded. Nevertheless,
the reforms represent a significant advance on the circumstances which prevailed
at the time of the *Meleady* and *Kelly* cases.

---

[85] *Ibid.*, reg. 7.
[86] *Ibid.*, reg. 3(1).
[87] *Ibid.*, reg. 2(1).

16

Miscarriages of Justice in Scotland

Clive Walker

Scotland can offer some contrasting models for criminal investigation and adjudication from which to draw experience in relation to miscarriages of justice in England and Wales.[1] The Scottish criminal process is not wholly distinct in nature:[2]

> Although centuries ago the Scottish criminal justice system had an inquisitorial aspect (which explains some of its present features) the system is now firmly adversarial, with the initiative being taken by the prosecution.

Nevertheless, this quotation points not only to an adversarial ethos shared with the English model but equally to at least one difference in practice, namely an ideological emphasis on a prosecution rather than a police controlled process. So, there are 'genuine and deep differences in tradition and in the design of institutions',[3] as a result of which two points of interest arise. One is to examine whether the Scottish process gives rise to miscarriages to a greater or lesser extent than the English process. The other is to consider any causes or responses which differ from recent English patterns. In this analysis, it is intended to concentrate on serious ('solemn procedure') cases tried before a jury either in the High Court of Justiciary or the Sheriff Court.[4]

The Catalogue of Miscarriage Cases

As with Chapter 2, the catalogue should be confined to examples from contemporary police, forensic and curial circumstances, and it may therefore be safe to leave out of the account infamous cases such as that of Oscar Slater, convicted in 1909

---

[1] See Royal Commission on Criminal Justice, *Report* (Cm 2263, HMSO, London, 1993) ('*the Runciman Report*') para. 1.13; Hill, P., 'Justice in Scotland?' (1994) 144 *New Law Journal* 1705.

[2] Brown, A.N., *Criminal Evidence and Procedure: An Introduction* (T. & T. Clark, Edinburgh, 1996) p. 16. See also Second Report of the Thomson Committee, *Criminal Procedure in Scotland* (Cmnd 6218, HMSO, Edinburgh, 1975) para. 8.03.

[3] Young, P., *Crime and Criminal Justice in Scotland* (Stationery Office, Edinburgh, 1997) p. 5.

[4] By the Criminal Procedure (Scotland) Act 1995, s. 3(6), the Sheriff Court may try all crimes except murder, treason, rape and breach of duty by magistrates. Between 1992 and 1997, there were 8414 (40%) persons called to the High Court in solemn procedure and 21149 (60%) to the Sheriff Court (statistics supplied by Fred Thorne, Scottish Office, 1999).

of murder but acquitted on appeal in 1928 (on the grounds of misdirection and amidst allegations of misidentification).[5] The concern about identification procedures arose more recently in the prosecution of Patrick Meehan, concerning the murder of Mrs Rachel Ross at her home in Ayr during a robbery in 1969.[6] Meehan was a criminal from Glasgow who admitted that, on the same night as the murder, he had been engaged in a burglary (with Jim Griffiths) in Stranraer. However, this alibi witness of dubious repute had gone berserk when the police arrived to arrest him, and two persons died (including Griffiths) in the subsequent exchanges of gun-fire. Meehan denied the murder[7] and complained of unfair treatment at an identification parade (where he was picked out by the husband of the victim) and the police planting of evidence on his dead accomplice. After further investigation by the defence, it was suggested strongly that two other criminals had been involved, Ian Waddell and, later, William McGuinness, who was publicly identified after his murder in 1976, when a member of his family related his confession to the murder (by coincidence, Joseph Beltrami, solicitor, acted for both McGuinness and Meehan). Waddell (who was also later murdered) was convicted of perjury following Meehan's trial and thereafter confessed several times to involvement in the crime. A royal pardon was granted to Meehan in 1976, but Waddell was acquitted of murder.[8] The subsequent inquiry by Lord Hunter, which took five years to unravel these affairs, did little to criticise the police for operating lax rules in relation to identification parades or for failing to follow up a sighting of McGuinness in Ayr on the day of the murder and even fancifully posited that all four men could have been involved.[9]

A further instance of misidentification resulting in miscarriage affected Maurice Swanson, convicted of a bank robbery in Glasgow in 1974.[10] He had been identified, originally from criminal records photographs and then at a formal parade, by two bank tellers. However, another man, convicted of three bank robberies a few months later, admitted to Swanson's alleged crime (Joseph Beltrami had again represented both men and so was fortuitously placed to make the link). His confession was initially disregarded, but after a palm print match was obtained at the bank, a royal pardon (the first in Scotland in the twentieth century) was granted to Swanson.

Misidentification continues to be alleged in the case of Stephen Windsor, found guilty in 1985 of armed robbery and attempted murder arising from the robbery of a Post Office van in Edinburgh's Wester Hailes area and a subsequent police chase.

[5] *Slater v HM Advocate* 1928 JC 94. See Millar, J.G., *Case of Oscar Slater* (Cmnd 7482, HMSO, London, 1914); Roughead, W. (ed.), *Trial of Oscar Slater* (4th ed., W. Hodge, Edinburgh, 1930); Kuppner, F., *A Very Quiet Street* (Polygon, Edinburgh, 1989); Toughill, T., *Oscar Slater: The Mystery Solved* (Canongate, Edinburgh, 1993); *The Glasgow Herald*, 6 September 1994, p. 14.

[6] See Kennedy, L., *A Presumption of Innocence* (Gollancz, London, 1976); Forbes, G. and Meehan, P., *Such Bad Company* (Harris, Edinburgh, 1982); Beltrami, J., *A Deadly Innocence: The Meehan File* (Mainstream Publishing, Edinburgh, 1989) (the author thanks the last-named for his additional comments).

[7] His request to give evidence under the influence of a 'truth drug' was rejected (*Meehan v HM Advocate* 1970 JC 11) as was his attempt to bring a private prosecution against police witnesses (*Meehan v Inglis* 1974 SLT (Notes) 61).

[8] Waddell had attempted to block the prosecution on the basis, *inter alia*, that Meehan's conviction had not been quashed: *HM Advocate v Waddell* 1976 SLT (Notes) 61; Gane, C., 'The effect of a pardon in Scots law' 1980 *Juridical Review* 18. Meehan was awarded £50,500 in compensation in 1984.

[9] *Report of an Inquiry by Lord Hunter into the whole circumstances of the murder of Mrs Rachel Ross at Ayr in June 1969* (1981–82 HC 444). See the comment at (1983) 76 SCOLAG Bulletin 7.

[10] See Beltrami, J., *The Defender* (revised ed., M. & A. Thompson, Edinburgh, 1988) ch. 4. The author thanks Joseph Beltrami for his comments on this case.

The name and address of one of two boys, who failed to identify him after his arrest and detention the same day (during which he claimed he was denied legal advice), was concealed from his defence, but this point was not clear to the High Court on his appeal (made in person without legal aid).[11] After tracing the boy in 1989, Windsor's attempt to have the case reviewed by the *nobile officium* jurisdiction (the Secretary of State having refused to make a referral in 1992 because he doubted the importance of the boy's evidence) was rejected in 1993.[12]

Other disputed convictions can be related to the quality or non-disclosure of forensic evidence. John Preece[13] was convicted in 1973 of rape and murder on the basis of semen, hair and fibre analysis. His convictions were quashed in 1981, when it was accepted that the evidence could have been interpreted in a less prejudicial way. The work of the Home Office scientist, Dr Alan Clift, was publicly discredited, even though it had been corroborated by another scientist. Another case of disputed forensic evidence is that of Andrew Smith, convicted in 1977 for killing Richard Cunningham in a bar fight in Larkhall. Smith, an amateur boxer, admits punching the victim once in self-defence but not kicking him on the ground. Defence pathologists support his claim that the fatal blow was from the fall following the punch and not the kick, alleged by prior forensic evidence.[14]

Forensic evidence (and its non-disclosure) is also a major theme of the continuing case of George Beattie.[15] Beattie, aged 18 at the time, had been convicted of the murder of a young woman in Carluke in 1973, and his first appeal was dismissed in the same year. The case was referred back to the Appeal Court in 1994 by the Secretary of State for Scotland, after re-examination in 1982 and 1984 by the television programme *Rough Justice*. The programme had argued that there had been insufficient disclosure of the time of death which, if more accurately assessed, could have tallied with his alibi. In addition, perhaps the most damning evidence against Beattie was that a tissue discovered a week later in a suit he was not wearing on the night of the crime contained a small spot of blood of a type which was said to match that of the victim, though it was of a common type and the later, undisclosed evidence suggested it was not a match at all since the blood sub-groups differed.[16] Beattie admitted to witnessing a murder, which meant he also had corroborative special knowledge for the purposes of Scottish evidential law (described below), though, at an undisclosed interview, he had been shown by the police a sketch of the crime scene (including, it is now alleged, the location of the body, where the girl's suitcase had been thrown and the mistakenly supposed murder weapon, a knife) and so could have learnt of important details in that way. His referred appeal was rejected in December 1994,[17] when Lord Hope said: 'In

---

[11] See *Windsor* v *UK*, Appl. no. 13081/87, inadmissible 14 December 1988. Complaints were also made about the denial of access to a car and guns allegedly used in the robbery and the denial of access to a solicitor. See also Appl. no. 16244/90, inadmissible 12 December 1991, Appl. no. 18942/91, inadmissible 6 April 1993 (concerning prison treatment).

[12] *Windsor, Petitioner* 1994 SLT 604. The purpose of the *nobile officium* is to prevent injustice or oppression where there are extraordinary and unforeseen circumstances and where no other remedy or procedure is provided by law.

[13] See: [1981] *Criminal Law Review* 783; Parliamentary Commissioner for Administration, *Fourth Report* (1983–84 HC 191); Jones, C.A.G., *Expert Witnesses* (Clarendon Press, Oxford, 1994) p. 230.

[14] *Scotland on Sunday*, 30 August 1998, p. 11

[15] See Hill, P., 'Justice in Scotland?' (1994) 144 *New Law Journal* 1705, 'Another weapon in the armoury' (1995) 145 *New Law Journal* 1620 (see also p. 1880).

[16] *The Scotsman*, 4 November 1994, p. 3.

[17] *The Glasgow Herald*, 3 December 1994, p. 1. However, the terms of the review were narrow since the appeal was dealt with on pre-1980 legislation, which meant that Beattie's defence team was not

our opinion, it cannot be said that the evidence of grouping of the deceased's blood on the MN system would on its own have had a material part to play in the jury's determination of a critical issue at the trial.'. A further campaign for a referral or a pardon is now pending, based additionally on the undisclosed evidence in the notebook of a police officer which relates the details revealed by the police to Beattie and Beattie's alleged statements.[18]

Police interviewing tactics and their 'selective' deployment of evidence lies at the heart of two further cases. One involves Alexander Hall, convicted for the murder of Lorna Porter in 1988. Following a previous unsuccessful appeal in 1989, his conviction was quashed in December 1998 when it was accepted that the failure to hear two witnesses not called at the trial was a miscarriage of justice.[19] The 'new' witnesses, James McAvoy and the woman with whom he had an affair, Jean Carroll, testified that the principal prosecution witness, James's brother, George McAvoy, had lied in 1987 about identifying Hall (and thereby corroborating Hall's confession) in an argument in the garden of his house with the victim. The defendant also disputed his alleged confession to the police, which had been made after being stopped for a motoring offence months after the murder in 1984, though there remains circumstantial evidence to link him to the murder and so a retrial is planned.

Another alleged 'construction' involves the 'Glasgow Two' – Thomas Campbell and Joseph Steele. Arising from incidents during the Glasgow 'ice-cream wars' (rivalry between competing van owners which the press speculated was based on the desire to monopolise trade in stolen goods and drugs), the two were convicted in August 1984 of setting fire to a house in which six members of the Doyle family, including Andrew 'Fat Boy' Doyle who was the driver of an opposition gang's ice-cream van, died.[20] After a trial at which allegations of intimidation and perjury abounded,[21] the two lost their appeals in 1985 but continued their protestations of innocence, which have included in the case of Steele three prison abscondences and in the case of Campbell hunger strikes and civil litigation.[22] Their convictions largely rested on evidence of an alleged confession by Campbell that the murders were 'a frightener which went too far' and a statement by Steele that 'I'm no' the one that lit the match', both corroborated by a key witness, William Love who testified that he overheard their plans to attack Doyle in a conversation in a pub. However, Love later claimed on a number of occasions from 1988 onwards, including on a BBC programme in 1993, *Rotten to the Core*, and on *Trial and Error* (Channel 4) in 1998, that he had lied about the pub conversation because he was

able to raise the issue of how the police 'fed' information to Beattie because Beattie did not give evidence at his trial and it was never suggested to the police witnesses under cross-examination: *Beattie v HM Advocate* 1995 SLT 275. Beattie was released on parole in 1995, after two previous periods of release.

[18] The author thanks Peter Hill for this information (http://www.justice.homepad.com). See also *The Glasgow Herald*, 16 November 1994, p. 15, 22 June 1995, p. 5.

[19] *The Scotsman*, 19 December 1998, p. 5.

[20] Four other defendants, Thomas Gray, Thomas Lafferty, George Reid and John Campbell received shorter sentences for assault and (in the case of Thomas Gray only) attempted murder regarding associated ice-cream vendettas, and Thomas Campbell was sentenced further for attacking one van with a shotgun. See Skelton, D. and Brownlie, L., *Frightener: the Glasgow ice-cream wars* (Mainstream, Edinburgh, 1992). The author thanks Thomas Campbell for his comments on this case.

[21] See *HM Advocate* v *Granger and Reynolds* 1984 SCCR 4; *Lord Advocate's Reference (No. 1 of 1985)* 1987 SLT 187; *Granger* v *UK*, Appl. no. 11932/86, Ser. A No. 174, (1990) 22 EHRR 469.

[22] See *Campbell* v *UK* Appl. no. 12323/86, (1988) 58 DR 148 (concerning the trial and appeal processes) and Appl. no. 13590/88, (1995) 15 EHRR 137 (concerning prison treatment).

promised bail on an unrelated armed robbery charge and that charges would not be pursued for his own part in an armed attack on Doyle's van. This explanation was backed by his sister, Agnes Carlton, who also gave evidence of Love's own involvement in a violent attack on Doyle's van. In addition, the terms of his alibi for the armed robbery excluded him from being at the bar where he heard the defendants' conversation. Nevertheless, Campbell and Steele's appeal was refused in 1985 and, after referral back in 1996 largely on the basis of Love's apparent perjury,[23] failed again in February 1998.[24] A second petition to the Secretary of State in March 1998, based, *inter alia*, on the confusion of the majority in the Appeal Court as to the extent of Love's involvement in shooting at Doyle (and therefore his degree of motivation to help the police on other matters), was rejected in December 1998.[25] A third petition was immediately lodged by Campbell, concerning the documentation before the court as to Love's admission of the shooting.[26]

Undue reliance upon unreliable and poorly evidenced confessions is alleged in the case of Raymond Gilmour, jailed in 1982 for the rape and murder of schoolgirl Pamela Hastie in Johnstone, Renfrewshire. He was convicted solely on the basis of two unsigned but self-corroborating confessions made to the police (the first arose a week after the murder, following a police interview on charges of indecent exposure, the second some months later allegedly after threats of violence in the back of a police car).[27] The confessions were inconsistent with several important features of the case, such as the sexual assault on the victim, the implement used to strangle her and the presence of a knife used in the attack.[28] An appeal was rejected soon after conviction,[29] and the Scottish Secretary refused to refer the case back to the Appeal Court (on the basis of the identification of another suspect and police abuses of Gilmour) in 1994[30] and again (based on, *inter alia*, psychological and forensic evidence) in 1997.[31]

The inflexibility of the appeals process, as experienced by Campbell and Steele, may further be illustrated by John McLay, jailed for killing a taxi driver in Glasgow in 1992. His co-accused, Stephen Harkins was acquitted despite his alleged confessions to six witnesses which were held on appeal in 1994 to be inadmissible hearsay on grounds of public policy (the danger of confederates attesting to spurious confessions by acquitted accomplices).[32] The case was referred back to the Appeal Court in December 1997 and awaits a hearing.

These well-documented cases should suffice to suggest that persistent and unresolved miscarriages of justice do occur in Scotland and that the causes broadly correspond to those in England and Wales. In response, there has been no Scottish

---

[23] He was not charged with this offence: *The Scotsman*, 4 February 1995, p. 3.

[24] *Campbell and Steele* v *HM Advocate* 1998 SLT 923.

[25] *The Scotsman* 2 December 1998, p. 1.

[26] The author thanks Thomas Campbell for this information.

[27] *The Guardian*, 27 March 1993, p. 8.

[28] *The Guardian*, 20 September 1994, p. 8.

[29] 1982 SCCR 590.

[30] *The Glasgow Herald*, 19 April 1994, p. 3. He was later convicted of an indecency offence whilst on release from prison: *The Glasgow Herald*, 4 April 1996, p. 5.

[31] *Scotland on Sunday*, 15 June 1997, p. 4.

[32] 1994 SLT 873. See now Scottish Law Commission, *Hearsay Evidence in Criminal Proceedings* (Report no. 149, HMSO, Edinburgh, 1995); Criminal Procedure (Scotland) Act 1995, s. 259(1) (but this is retrospective only in regard to a retrial and not to the appeal which can lead to a retrial: *Conway* v *HM Advocate* 1996 SLT 1293; *O'Neill* v *HM Advocate* 1996 SLT 1357).

Runciman Report, though several Scottish Office reviews have been held,[33] and reforms reminiscent of England and Wales, with a similar emphasis upon crime control, have been pursued through adaptation where possible. Closer attention must now be turned to the causal factors involved in Scottish miscarriages, the safeguards which have long existed and the reforms which have recently been undertaken.

Police and Prosecution

A strikingly fundamental difference from the English position is that Scottish policing powers have been left largely unconsidered and uncodified,[34] and, for 25 years, calls for fundamental review have been unheeded.[35] The powers of arrest without warrant are in part set out in the Criminal Procedure (Scotland) Act 1995, section 21, but are mainly creatures of common law whereunder they were 'never clearly defined',[36] a degree of vagueness which itself may breach Article 5(1) of the European Convention on Human Rights. Historically, the absence of regulation reflects a fundamental legal stance against 'cross-examination' or any form of interrogation on (or after) arrest: 'No extrajudicial confession, unless it be adhered to by the pannel [accused] in presence of the inquest [trial jury], can be admitted as evidence.'[37] Arrest itself is traditionally only justifiable on the evidence sufficient thereupon to found a criminal charge against the suspect,[38] but this stance against police[39] pre-charge interrogation has considerably weakened. The judges themselves have resiled from an absolutist approach. They have interpreted 'cross-examination' more literally and less as a synonym for any form of police interviewing. Consequently, they have preferred to emphasise the overall 'fairness' of the process not only in terms of the accused but also to the victim, the public or even the police. Questioning *per se* before charge[40] is not forbidden, but questioning which is unduly pressurised in the circumstances of the offence and the suspect offender is impugned.[41] The resultant legal position is remarkably vague and therefore unduly indulgent of police practices and their impacts.[42]

---

[33] Scottish Office, *Juries and Verdicts* (HMSO, Edinburgh, 1993); *Review of Criminal Evidence and Criminal Procedure* (HMSO, Edinburgh, 1993); *Sentencing and Appeals* (HMSO, Edinburgh, 1994); *Firm and Fair* (HMSO, Edinburgh, 1994).

[34] See generally Ewing, K.D. and Finnie, W., *Civil Liberties in Scotland* (2nd ed., W. Green & Son, Edinburgh, 1988) ch. 3. For reforms which have taken place, see Scottish Office, *Firm and Fair* (Cm 2600, HMSO, Edinburgh, 1994) ch. 9.

[35] See Second Report of the Thomson Committee, *Criminal Procedure in Scotland* (Cmnd 6218, HMSO, Edinburgh, 1975) para. 3.29; Home Affairs Committee, *Practical Police Cooperation in the European Community* (1989–90 HC 363) paras. 90, 127.

[36] Brown, A.N., *Criminal Evidence and Procedure: An Introduction* (T. & T. Clark, Edinburgh, 1996) p. 27. See *Peggie v Clark* (1868) 7 M 89; Gordon, G.H., *Renton and Brown's Criminal Procedure* (6th ed., W. Green, Edinburgh, 1996) ch. 7.

[37] Erskine, J., *An Institute of the Law of Scotland* (Bell & Bradfute, Edinburgh, 1821) vol. II p. 1229.

[38] The leading case is *Chalmers v Lord Advocate* 1954 SLT 177. See Griffiths, D.B., *Confessions* (Butterworths, Edinburgh, 1994) pp. 33–9; Gordon, G.H., *Renton and Brown's Criminal Procedure* (6th ed., W. Green, Edinburgh, 1996) ch. 24.

[39] Compare on non-police interrogators of fraudsters: *Styr v HM Advocate* 1993 SCCR 278.

[40] For the position after charge, see *Stark and Smith v HM Advocate* 1938 JC 170; *Fraser and Freir v HM Advocate* 1989 SCCR 82. It is legitimate to delay charge in order to continue with questioning: *Miller v HM Advocate* 1998 SLT 571.

[41] *Milne v Cullen* 1967 JC 21; *Jones v Milne* 1975 SLT 2; *Hartley v HM Advocate* 1979 SLT 26; *HM Advocate v Gilgannon* 1983 SCCR 10; *Lord Advocate's Reference (No. 1 of 1983)* 1984 SCCR 62; *Johnston v HM Advocate* 1993 SCCR 693; *Codona v HM Advocate* 1996 SLT 1100; *Black v Anderson* 1996 SLT 284; *Stewart v Hingston* 1997 SLT 442; Griffiths, D.B., *Confessions* (Butterworths, Edinburgh, 1994) pp. 44–71.

[42] See Maher, G., 'Balancing rights and interests in the criminal process' in Duff, A. and Simmonds,

Equally, there have been statutory dilutions, especially by the grant of police detention powers following the Criminal Justice (Scotland) Act 1980.[43] As consolidated within the Criminal Procedure (Scotland) Act 1995, section 13 permits the 'detention' of both suspects and witnesses in order to assist with police inquiries. In the case of suspects, they may be detained on reasonable suspicion of any offence and be questioned about their identity and any explanation in relation to the crime. This process must be completed 'quickly', but further detention and investigation may then be carried out under section 14 in relation to imprisonable offences. Pursuant to this power, the suspect may be detained for up to six hours in a police station where there is reasonable suspicion for the detention[44] but insufficient evidence to arrest on charge. As regards witnesses, section 13 also allows for a short period of detention outside the police station in order to establish details of the person's identity; but a refusal to co-operate may result in an arrest.[45] The powers are poorly defined in comparison with those under the Police and Criminal Evidence Act 1984, with no statutory codes of practice governing issues such as the meaning of reasonable suspicion or treatment whilst in custody nor clear sanctions for breach.[46] Furthermore, they do not forbid the pre-1980 practice of inquiries by 'consent' and 'voluntary' attendance at the police station which so concerned the Thomson Committee.[47] Alongside detention, there are also expanding powers under the Criminal Procedure (Scotland) Act 1995, sections 18 to 20[48] to take from detainees or arrestees fingerprints or other bodily samples, thus augmenting very indistinct common law powers.[49]

As already indicated, the accompanying safeguards are woefully inadequate. There is no regulation by statutory code equivalent to PACE nor has there ever been a set of expectations such as the Judges' Rules.[50] There is a statutory caution under section 14(9) of the 1995 Act, but it seems to be of little moment.[51] Though

---

N., (eds.), *Philosophy and the Criminal Law* (Steiner, Wiesbaden, 1984); *Blagojevic* v *HM Advocate* 1995 SLT 1189. The procedures for handling disputes about admissibility may also be distinct in Scotland in that there is a concern that trials within trials impinge on the role of juries to decide fairness; see Gordon, G.H., *Renton and Brown's Criminal Procedure* (6th ed., W. Green, Edinburgh, 1996) paras. 24.59 *et seq.*

[43] See Second Report of the Thomson Committee, *Criminal Procedure in Scotland* (Cmnd 6218, HMSO, Edinburgh, 1975) paras. 3.13–15; Gordon, G.H., *The Criminal Justice (Scotland) Act 1980* (W. Green, Edinburgh, 1981); Gordon, G.H., *Renton and Brown's Criminal Procedure* (6th ed., W. Green, Edinburgh, 1996) ch. 6.

[44] See *Wilson and Nolan* v *Robertson* 1986 SCCR 700.

[45] See Second Report of the Thomson Committee, *Criminal Procedure in Scotland* (Cmnd 6218, HMSO, Edinburgh, 1975) para. 6.02.

[46] See *Cummings* v *HM Advocate* 1982 SLT 487; *Grant* v HM Advocate 1989 SCCR 618.

[47] Curran, J.H., and Carnie, J.K., *Detention or Voluntary Attendance: Police Use of Detention under Section 2, Criminal Justice (Scotland) Act 1980* (Central Research Unit, Scottish Office, Edinburgh, 1986); MVA Consultancy, *Detention and voluntary attendance of suspects at police stations* (Central Research Unit, Scottish Office, Edinburgh, 1994).

[48] As amended by the Crime and Punishment (Scotland) Act 1997, s. 47. See Scottish Office, *Firm and Fair* (Edinburgh, HMSO, 1994) paras. 8.27–30; Scottish Law Commission, *Report on Evidence: Blood Group Tests and Related Matters* (Paper no. 120, HMSO, Edinburgh, 1989).

[49] See: Brown, A.N., *Criminal Evidence and Procedure: An Introduction* (T. & T. Clark, Edinburgh, 1996) pp. 41–4. At least these are mainly authorised by a sheriff's warrant (but see *Adair* v *McGarry* 1933 SLT 482; *Bell* v *Hogg* 1967 JC 49; *McHugh* v *HM Advocate* 1978 JC 12), whereas only searches under s.18(6) require higher authority and in that case from a police inspector and not a judge.

[50] See Royal Commission on Criminal Procedure, *Report* (Cmnd 8091, HMSO, London, 1981).

[51] *Scott* v *Howie* 1993 SCCR 81. However, common law cautions and reason-giving are strictly required: *Tonge, Jack and Gray* v *HM Advocate* 1982 SLT 506; *Walkinshaw* v *McIntyre* 1985 SCCR

only six hours' detention is permitted under the statutory provisions (albeit subject to additional time through the use of 'consent' or common law arrest), this period would be sufficient to cover around three-quarters of detentions in England and Wales,[52] and it is a crucial period in any interrogation.[53] Another disturbing omission is that the form of records to be made of interviews is not specified. For example, audio-taping is not required by law,[54] though it is widely utilised (but only for more serious offences and with the consent of the suspect) following guidance from the Scottish Office that it should be in place from 1988 onwards.[55] Judicial criticisms of 'verballing' by the police are apparently rare in Scotland,[56] but this form of abuse does figure in some of the illustrations of alleged miscarriages of justice listed earlier.

As for suspects' rights, section 17 of the 1995 Act grants an immediate and absolute right of access to a solicitor upon arrest and then to have a 'private interview' before examination or appearance in court.[57] However, this right relates to legal advice in connection with future court processes and impacts too late to affect the police phase of the investigation. There is also a right under section 15 for persons detained under section 14 to be informed on arrival at the police station of their right to send intimation of the detention to a solicitor (subject to possible delay). There is no right, however, to have any interview stopped in order to consult, and the failure to issue the notice of rights (or to act upon requests) may not affect admissibility of any statement.[58] Even if a duty solicitor is available,[59] neither detained nor arrested persons are entitled to the presence of a lawyer at interviews, though this in practice may be allowed to allay fears of inadmissibility of evidence,[60] and there are also some exceptional rights for solicitor attendance at identification parades or for clients charged (not simply detained or arrested) with murder, attempted or culpable homicide.[61] The lame reasons given for police opposition to greater access to legal advice are that it might compromise security,

---

389; *Forbes* v *HM Advocate* 1990 SCCR 69; Griffiths, D.B., *Confessions* (Butterworths, Edinburgh, 1994) pp. 56–8.

[52] See Brown, D., *PACE: Ten Years On* (Home Office Research Study no. 155, London, 1997).

[53] *John Murray* v *UK*, Appl. no. 18731/91, 1996–I, (1996) 22 EHRR 29 at para. 66. See also *Imbrioscia* v *Switzerland*, Appl. no. 13972/88, Ser A vol. 275, (1994) 17 EHRR 441 at para. 36.

[54] It was demanded as a condition of the admissibility of admissions in response to police interrogation: Second Report of the Thomson Committee, *Criminal Procedure in Scotland* (Cmnd 6218, HMSO, Edinburgh, 1975) para. 7.13. Video-recording was proposed at HL Debs. vol. 560 col. 370, 12 January 1995, Lord Macaulay.

[55] See Second Report of the Thomson Committee, *Criminal Procedure in Scotland* (Cmnd 6218, HMSO, Edinburgh, 1975) paras. 7.13, 7.15; *Lord Advocate's reference (No. 1 of 1983)* 1984 SCCR 62; Scottish Home and Health Department, *The Tape Recording of Police Interviews with Suspected Persons in Scotland* (1985); HC Debs. vol. 114 col. 55wa, 6 April 1987; Criminal Procedure (Scotland) Act 1995 s. 277; Griffiths, D.B., *Confessions* (Butterworths, Edinburgh, 1994) pp. 157–69.

[56] Griffiths, D.B., *Confessions* (Butterworths, Edinburgh, 1994) p. 3.

[57] See also Law Reform (Miscellaneous Provisions) (Scotland) Act 1985, s. 35, which deals with pre-charge arrests in connection with terrorism and allows access but not presence for advice purposes.

[58] *Cheyne* v *McGregor* 1941 JC 17; *Grant* v *HM Advocate* 1989 SCCR 618; Gordon, G.H., *Renton and Brown's Criminal Procedure* (6th ed., W. Green, Edinburgh, 1996) para. 24.51.

[59] The scheme is based on sheriff and district courts (Criminal Legal Aid (Scotland) Regulations 1996, SI No. 2555, r. 5), but the lists are notified to police as well as court clerks. The scheme arose following the (Hughes) Royal Commission on Legal Services in Scotland (Cmnd 7846, HMSO, Edinburgh, 1980) paras. 8.10, 8.11, 8.62.

[60] See *HM Advocate* v *Fox* 1947 JC 30; *Law* v *McNicol* 1965 JC 32; *Forbes* v *HM Advocate* 1990 SCCR 69.

[61] Criminal Legal Aid (Scotland) Regulations 1996, SI No. 2555, r. 5(1).

especially because of a shortage of manpower,[62] a shortage which has not hampered a significant increase in their interviewing activities. Yet, the blame for the lack of legal advice cannot be placed solely on the police, for 'it is the right of the solicitor concerned to choose whether or not to attend the police station to interview his client . . .'.[63] However, the practices of lawyers do seem to be changing. In 1990, one commentator observed that : 'In most cases, whether under solemn or summary procedure, a solicitor is unlikely to become involved until after the case is in court.'.[64] The same author concluded in 1997 that 'if a solicitor is told that a detained person has asked that he be informed of his detention and whereabouts, he may very well decide to attend at the police station . . .'.[65] The Scottish Legal Aid Board now has powers under the Crime and Punishment (Scotland) Act 1997, section 49 to regulate the conduct of solicitors offering assistance under a scheme. A Code of Practice was issued in 1998,[66] but it relates predominantly to court work and does not add any new duties in relation to attendance at police stations, perhaps a lost opportunity in the light of English experience.[67] Finally, the concept of 'appropriate adult' is unknown to Scottish law. After a prior ineffectual attempt in 1990, the Scottish Office issued a police circular in 1998[68] which demands that arrangements be put in place for the mentally disordered by the middle of 1999. Nevertheless, there is still no legal enforcement, and this requirement does not extend to juveniles.

These developments towards police station-focused investigation seem to cast some doubt on the reputed '[v]ery considerable reliance . . . placed on the integrity and judgment of the public prosecutor, especially in the early stages of a prosecution.'.[69] Admittedly, the prosecutors formally retain an upper hand in their relationships with the police and can issue directions to the latter under section 17(3) of the Police (Scotland) Act 1967: '. . . in relation to the investigation of offences the chief constable shall comply with such lawful instructions as he may receive from the appropriate prosecutor.'[70] However, most commentators report that it is rare for this power to be invoked explicitly,[71] and so prosecutors are

---

[62] Second Report of the Thomson Committee, *Criminal Procedure in Scotland* (Cmnd 6218, HMSO, Edinbourgh, 1975) para. 5.07.

[63] Sheehan, A.V., Hingston, D.R. and Crowe, F.R., *Criminal Procedure* (Butterworths, Edinburgh, 1990) p. 66.

[64] Stewart, A.L., *The Scottish Criminal Courts in Action* (Butterworths, Edinburgh, 1990) p. 86.

[65] *Ibid.* (2nd ed., Butterworths, Edinburgh, 1997), p. 93.

[66] *Code of Practice in relation to criminal legal assistance* (Edinburgh, 1998). The author thanks Colin Lancaster, SLAB, for information about the Code. Compare the even thinner booklet, Law Society of Scotland, *Code of Conduct for Criminal Work* (Edinburgh, 1998).

[67] See Chapter 4.

[68] *Interviewing people who are mentally disordered: 'Appropriate Adult' schemes* (Scottish Office, Circular 7/1998). The author thanks Alison Ross, Scottish Office, for this information.

[69] Brown, A.N., *Criminal Evidence and Procedure: An Introduction* (T. & T. Clark, Edinburgh, 1996) p. 16.

[70] Note also the possible issuance of instructions by the Lord Advocate under the 1995 Act, s. 12 for the police to report the occurrence of specified offences. Powers of this kind were rejected by the *Runciman Report*, ch. 5 para. 26.

[71] Brown, A.N., *Criminal Evidence and Procedure: An Introduction* (T. & T. Clark, Edinburgh, 1996) p. 17. However, Assistant Chief Constable A. Brown asserts that liaison is very close in the investigation of very serious crimes: 'DNA as an investigative tool' (1998) 38 *Science and Justice* 263. Furthermore, the Crown Office and Procuration Fiscal Service, *Annual Report 1997–98* (Edinburgh, 1998) p. 13, claims that Procurators Fiscal 'frequently instruct the police to carry out further inquiries.'.

largely dependent on the running made by the police[72] and do not even remotely approach the status of European investigating magistrates.[73] This relationship is largely admitted by the Crown Office itself, which has stated that:[74]

> Although the Procurator Fiscal may take the initiative in instructing investigation of an alleged crime, in practice in almost all cases the trigger for his involvement is a report, either from the police or from one of fifty other investigating agencies.

It is true that in serious cases, the procurator fiscal will later take precognitions (statements) from the key witnesses listed by the police, but this is done in order to confirm and perhaps clarify evidence rather than to explore new lines of inquiry,[75] and by the stage of precognition the defendant has long been charged and put before the courts.

In summary, the investigation of crime has become (if it were ever otherwise) as much a police affair in Scotland as it is in England and Wales, and the Scottish police seem to be far more beholden to the Scottish Office in regard to their investigative techniques, through controls such as circulars[76] and Her Majesty's Inspectorate of Constabulary, than to prosecutors. However, these controls seem to have little regard for the susceptibilities of suspects in police custody to provide misleading evidence.

Judicial Examination

From an English lawyer's perspective, some of the remarkable features of the Scottish process include the potential use of judicial examination and the rules on the corroboration of incriminating evidence, both of which are often depicted as protections against miscarriage of justice arising from police-based interrogation.

Judicial examination was revived in 1980 and is now set out in sections 35 to 39 of the Criminal Procedure (Scotland) Act 1995.[77] The objectives in 1980 were: to afford the accused an opportunity to state the defence's position at the earliest opportunity; to enable the prosecution to ask questions to block the later fabrication of defences at trial; and to ensure that admissions made to the police are confirmed

---

[72] Moody, S.R. and Tombs, J., *Prosecution in the Public Interest* (Scottish Academic Press, Edinburgh, 1982) pp. 45–7, 140.

[73] But compare Sheehan, A.V., *Criminal Procedure in Scotland and France* (HMSO, Edinburgh, 1975); Maher, G., 'Reforming the criminal process: a Scottish perspective' in McConville, M. and Bridges, L., (eds.) *Criminal Justice in Crisis* (Edward Elgar, Aldershot, 1994) pp. 65–7. See also Chapter 17.

[74] Crown Office and Procurator Fiscal Service, *Annual Report 1992–93* (Edinburgh, 1993) p. 4.

[75] Precognition is conducted in private at the office of the procurator fiscal, but if the witness is reluctant or unreliable, a warrant may be obtained and evidence can be taken on oath before a sheriff: Criminal Procedure (Scotland) Act 1995, s. 140(3). In either eventuality, the defence is not entitled to attend.

[76] See for example, Circular 6/1992, *The Use of Automatic Detection Devices for Road Traffic Law Enforcement*.

[77] Its origins lie in the Criminal Procedure (Scotland) Act 1887. See Second Report of the Thomson Committee, *Criminal Procedure in Scotland* (Cmnd 6218, HMSO, Edinburgh, 1975) ch. 8; Gordon, G.H., *The Criminal Justice (Scotland) Act 1980* (W. Green, Edinburgh, 1981); Macphail, I.D., 'Judicial examination' (1982) 27 *Journal of the Law Society of Scotland 296*; Gow, N., 'The revival of examinations' (1991) 141 *New Law Journal* 600; Macphail, I.D., 'Safeguards in the Scottish criminal justice system' [1992] *Criminal Law Review* 144; Gordon, G.H., *Renton and Brown's Criminal Procedure* (6th ed., W. Green, Edinburgh, 1996) para. 12.10 et seq.; Farmer, L., *Criminal Law, Tradition and Legal Order* (Cambridge UP, 1997) chs. 3, 4.

as undistorted (or otherwise).[78] By all accounts the procedure has made relatively little impact, with only patchy invocation,[79] and it has certainly not replaced or curtailed police questioning.

There has been an attempt to strengthen the process by limitations to the right to silence, which followed promises in the Scottish Office paper, *Firm and Fair* in 1994 to try to make more use of the device as a way of avoiding the later fabrication of defences and of providing early notice of lines of defence so that the prosecutor can investigate them.[80] Consequently, the amended version expressly allows questioning about the charge by the prosecutor designed to elicit an admission by the accused about any defence or declaration made at the examination.[81] If the accused declines to make in response 'any admission, denial, explanation, justification or comment', then this omission may be the subject of adverse comment at trial either by the prosecutor or the judge (or a co-accused)[82] but only where the defendant subsequently avers at trial something which could have been stated appropriately[83] at an earlier time.[84] The prosecutor may also engage in questioning about an extrajudicial confession to the police, though must disclose in advance a copy of the alleged confession.[85] Some saw the 1995 reforms as changing the judicial examination into 'an inquisitorial procedure which is inappropriate to the adversarial system we have',[86] but it might be closer to the truth that this is a form of adversary process with the prosecutor taking the place of the theoretically hobbled police interrogator. At the same time, there are limits to adversarial fervour, as there is still no Crown obligation to make use of the procedure at all.

Corroboration and other Evidential Safeguards

The general rule of evidence in Scotland is that there must be two witnesses (independent sources of evidence) to prove every 'crucial' fact (a fact establishing guilt) on which the Crown seeks to rely.[87] This evidential rule is vaunted as 'an

---

[78] Second Report of the Thomson Committee, *Criminal Procedure in Scotland* (Cmnd 6218, HMSO, Edinburgh, 1975) paras. 7.13, 8.14.

[79] It is used in only 15% of cases on petition: Scottish Office, *Firm and Fair* (Edinburgh, HMSO, 1994) para. 8.20.

[80] Scottish Office, *Firm and Fair* (Edinburgh, HMSO, 1994) para. 8.21; Criminal Procedure (Scotland) Act 1995, s. 36.

[81] See s. 36(1), (2), (4).

[82] See s. 36(8).

[83] The advice of a solicitor to remain silent may not protect the accused: *Gilmour v HM Advocate* 1982 SCCR 590; *Alexander v HM Advocate* 1990 SCCR 590; *McEwan v HM Advocate* 1992 SLT 317; *McGhee v HM Advocate* 1992 SLT 2; *Dempsey v HM Advocate* 1996 SLT 289.

[84] See s. 36(1), (8). If no evidence is led by the accused, there can be no comment: *Walker v HM Advocate* 1985 SCCR 150; *Dempsey v HM Advocate* 1995 SCCR 431. If there is comment, it must be restrained: *McEwan v HM Advocate* 1990 SCCR 401. There may also be adverse comment under the wider provisions in the Criminal Justice (Scotland) Act 1995, s. 32.

[85] See s. 36(3).

[86] HL Debs. vol. 560 col. 363, 12 January 1995, Lord Macaulay.

[87] See Scottish Law Commission, *Corroboration, Hearsay and Related Matters* (Report no. 100, Edinburgh, 1986); Macphail, I.D., 'Safeguards in the Scottish criminal justice system' [1992] *Criminal Law Review* 144; O'Gorman, C., 'The corroboration of confessions' (1993) 33 *Criminal Lawyer* 1; Gordon, G.H., 'At the mouth of the two witnesses' in Hunter, R.F., *Justice and Crime* (T. & T. Clark, Edinburgh, 1993); Griffiths, D.B., *Confessions* (Butterworths, Edinburgh, 1994) ch. 5; Gordon, G.H., *Renton and Brown's Criminal Procedure* (6th ed., W. Green, Edinburgh, 1996) para. 24.69 et seq.; Field, D. and Raitt, F.E., *The Law of Evidence in Scotland* (2nd ed., W. Green, Edinburgh, 1996) ch. 7; *Smith v Lees* 1997 SLT 690.

invaluable safeguard in the practice of our criminal courts against unjust conviction
. . .'[88] which accords 'superiority to the English'.[89] Its protection especially arises
from the demand that there must be 'some independent fact incriminating the
accused, altogether apart from the statements or confessions which he may have
made'.[90] The accused cannot even corroborate the confession by repetition or
voicing it in the presence of more than one person.[91] In regard to confessions, the
corroboration is designed 'to ensure that there is nothing phoney or quixotic about
the confession',[92] a healthy attitude of scepticism towards confession evidence
which chimes with Scottish legal history but, unfortunately, neither the view of the
Runciman Report[93] nor recent Scottish trends.

It has long been accepted that the second source of evidence need not be very
strong. It is simply evidence which 'supports or confirms' the direct evidence of a
witness and so can be circumstantial.[94] However, the corroboration rule has been
progressively weakened even from this tentative starting-point both by judicial
interpretation and statute.[95] The corroboration rule was already watered by the
Moorov doctrine: offences which are closely linked in time, character and
circumstances can be proven by the evidence of one witness for each, the
corroboration being the linked offence(s).[96] However, the courts have during the
past two decades established that in practice any corroboration needs to be even
less strong when the confession can be viewed as of high quality (for example
because of its clarity or because of the character of the defendant).[97] In addition,
the judges have tended to diminish the degree of independent verification supplied
by corroborative evidence by the widening of the 'special knowledge' or 'self-
corroborating' confession exception whereby an accused (such as George Beattie)
reveals facts which only the perpetrator of the crime could know (such as location
or witnesses or other details).[98] This apparent knowledge plus a confession is
sufficient for a conviction, but the combination is vulnerable to invention or
suggestion by the police, who are able not only to elicit a confession but to supply
the intimate details which offer the corroboration. The courts have not confined the
special knowledge to facts not known to the police and so have not done sufficient

---

[88] *Morton* v *HM Advocate* 1938 JC 50 at p. 55 per L J-C Aitchison.
[89] Gordon, G.H., 'At the mouth of the two witnesses' in Hunter, R.F., *Justice and Crime* (T. & T. Clark, Edinburgh, 1993) at p. 33.
[90] *Manuel* v *HM Advocate* 1958 JC 41.
[91] See: *Bainbridge* v *Scott* 1988 SLT 871; *McGougan* v *HM Advocate* 1991 SLT 908.
[92] *Sinclair* v *Clark* 1962 JC 57 at p. 62 per L J-C Thomson.
[93] Corroboration of confessions was recommended by a minority in the *Runciman Report* at para. 4.86, the majority believing that it would hamper perfectly sound convictions; see para. 4.68. See further Chapter 9.
[94] *Fox* v *HM Advocate* 1998 SLT 335 at p. 340 per Lord Rodger.
[95] See also Criminal Procedure (Scotland) Act 1995, s. 280.
[96] *Moorov* v *HM Advocate* 1930 JC 68. See McCannell, M.D., 'Parallel offences' (1995) 40 *Journal of the Law Society of Scotland* 439; Gordon, G.H., *Renton and Brown's Criminal Procedure* (6th ed., W. Green, Edinburgh, 1996) para. 24–87 et seq.; Field, D. and Raitt, F.E., *The Law of Evidence in Scotland* (2nd ed., W. Green, Edinburgh, 1996) p. 158. Compare Ferguson, P.W., 'Corroboration and similar fact evidence' 1996 *Scottish Law Times (News)* 339.
[97] *Hartley* v *HM Advocate* 1979 SLT 26 at p. 31 but see also *Meredith* v *Lees* 1992 SLT 802.
[98] *Manuel* v *HM Advocate* 1958 JC 41; *Wilson* v *HM Advocate* 1987 SCCR 217; *Hutchison* v *Valentine* 1990 SCCR 569; *Low and another* v *HM Advocate* 1994 SLT 277; *Mackie* v *HM Advocate* 1995 SLT 110; *Re Gilmour* 1994 SCCR 872; *Beattie* v *HM Advocate* 1995 SLT 275; *Hemming* v *HM Advocate* 1998 SLT 213; Brookens, D., 'Guildford: a warning' [1989] *Journal of the Law Society of Scotland* 448; McCannell, M.D., 'Special knowledge confessions' 1993 SLG 142; Griffiths, D.B., *Confessions* (Butterworths, Edinburgh, 1994) pp. 138–51.

to protect against false confessions.[99] The result is that, as in England, confessions are considered to be the best and most reliable form of evidence, whilst the corroboration rule is viewed as increasingly inappropriate.[100] The lesson seems to be that any attempt to impose a corroboration requirement in England would have to be clear and precise, otherwise its impact is likely to be minimised by prosecution pressures and judicial sympathies for the police and victims. By and large, there can be no great enthusiasm that this would be a worthwhile reform, and it is unrealistic nowadays to see it as 'a crucial safeguard' in Scotland.[101] Its impact, if any, is in any event confined to one problem amongst several which arise in connection with police interrogation. It may help to assure the court that the confession does disclose facts which are verifiable, but it does not establish that the defendant actually was the original source of those facts or that they were disclosed in circumstances free of oppression or violence.

Similar problems arise with identification evidence. As well as a warning to the jury,[102] identification does require corroboration (where, at least, it is a 'crucial' disputed fact).[103] However, this safeguard was significantly overrated by the *Bryden Report* in 1978:[104]

> . . . the public prosecution system with its sifting of evidence, the requirement for corroboration evidence, and the availability of the not proven verdict constitute safeguards inherent in the Scottish system of criminal justice which, in our opinion, significantly reduce the risk of wrongful conviction on the basis of identification evidence.

In response, it has been observed that 'the requirements of corroboration are at their weakest when what is to be corroborated is evidence of a kind regarded by most people as highly suspect.'.[105] Where there is one positive identification, then, akin to the treatment of confessions, very little corroboration is required, ignoring the inherent unreliability of such evidence. In *Nolan* v *McLeod*,[106] an identification which was 80 per cent sure was added to another identification by another witness which was 75 per cent sure, thereby producing proof beyond reasonable doubt. In *Murphy* v *HM Advocate*,[107] a positive identification could be backed by a 'resemblance identification' (based on just height and hair colour). In any event, the identification procedures (such as parades) are regulated only by Scottish Office guidance to the police,[108] the impact of which is uncertain in law.

---

[99] See *McAvoy* v *HM Advocate* 1982 SCCR 263; *Wilson* v *McCaughey* 1982 SCCR 398; Pattenden, R., 'Should confessions be corroborated?' (1991) 107 *Law Quarterly Review* 317 at p. 366.

[100] See: *Sinclair* v *Clark* 1962 JC 57; *Hartley* v *HM Advocate* 1979 SLT 26.

[101] Committee on Criminal Appeals and Alleged Miscarriages of Justice, *Report* (Cm 3245, HMSO, Edinburgh, 1996) ('*Sutherland Report*'), para. 3.4. Despite this depiction, the *Report* contains no discussion or suggestions for change, and the later Scottish Office paper, *Crime and Punishment* (Cm 3302, HMSO, Edinburgh, 1996) para. 15.14, equally makes no specific proposal.

[102] See *McAvoy* v *HM Advocate* 1991 SCCR 123. Compare *Bennett* v *HM Advocate* 1975 SLT (Notes) 90 and the Note by Lord Justice General, Criminal Trials (18 February 1977).

[103] See Field, D. and Raitt, F.E., *The Law of Evidence in Scotland* (2nd ed., W. Green, Edinburgh, 1996) pp. 147 et seq.

[104] *Identification under Scottish Criminal Law* (Cmnd 7096, HMSO, Edinburgh, 1978) para. 10.3. It also considered that a warning to a jury is unnecessary: para. 5.03.

[105] Gordon, G.H., 'At the mouth of the two witnesses' in Hunter, R.F., *Justice and Crime* (T. & T. Clark, Edinburgh, 1993) p. 61.

[106] 1987 SCCR 558.

[107] 1995 SLT 725.

[108] These are reproduced in Gane, C.H.W. and Stoddart, C.N., *Criminal Procedure in Scotland: Cases*

As applied to forensic evidence, as mentioned in Chapter 6, the rules of corroboration require each case to be examined by two forensic scientists, but this demand in practice appears to make no difference to the overall quality of the work produced by the police laboratories. This is probably because the scientists of each side in the case approach their examinations from the same point of view, having the same information at their disposal and responding to it in very much the same way and at the same time, as in the case of John Preece, outlined earlier. Similarly, in Beattie's case, the post-mortem examination was effectively conducted by one professional, with the other writing up the notes; there were not two independently produced examinations, which meant that the time of death was not accurately established and Beattie's evidence of alibi was thereby nullified. Finally, evidence of the victim's distress has been allowed to count as corroboration in sex offence cases, even though it cannot intrinsically link the crime to the defendant and means that there is in fact only one witness in a case.[109] As a result, it has been accepted in *Smith v Lees*[110] that it cannot corroborate physical acts but only the state of mind of the complainant.

The application of these rules of corroboration may not be met when there is a plea of guilt. John Boyle, absent without leave from the Army, wrongly confessed and pleaded guilty to an armed robbery, apparently because he preferred civilian to military prison. The conviction was set aside on appeal, and there were indications that not only was the conviction a factual error but also that there was no corroborative evidence.[111]

Other rules of evidence which may protect against miscarriages of justice have been likewise diluted. For example, it is no longer mandatory to give warnings about evidence from accomplices. In *Docherty v HM Advocate*,[112] Lord Emslie for one perceived no greater danger in an accomplice giving evidence against, rather than for, an accused.

Disclosure

The police are bound fully to 'report' an offence to the prosecutor, or at least, according to *Smith v HM Advocate*, everything that 'may be relevant and material to the issue of whether the suspected party is innocent or guilty . . .'.[113] This duty reflects the nominal subservience of police to prosecution. As between prosecution and defence, however, there has been, at least until very recently, considerable imbalance.

It would amount to a breach of the prosecution's duty to the court to pursue a case knowing there is undisclosed evidence proving innocence.[114] However, the

---

and Materials (2nd ed., W. Green, Edinburgh, 1994) pp. 160–2. The accused can apply for a sheriff's order that an identification parade be held: Criminal Procedure (Scotland) Act 1995, s. 290. The police can also apply: *McMurtrie v Annan* 1995 SLT 642.

[109] See Field, D. and Raitt, F.E., *The Law of Evidence in Scotland* (2nd ed., W. Green, Edinburgh, 1996) p. 162.

[110] 1997 SLT 690. See also *Fox v HM Advocate* 1998 SLT 335; Brown, A., 'Two cases on corroboration' 1998 SLT 71. The earlier judgment in *Stobo v HM Advocate* 1994 JC 28 was overturned, and Stobo's conviction was quashed after referral: *The Scotsman*, 5 December 1997 p. 13.

[111] *Boyle v HM Advocate* 1976 SLT 126. Boyle entered his plea contrary to the advice of his solicitor, Joseph Beltrami, whom the author thanks for his additional comments on this case.

[112] 1987 SLT 784 at p. 789. See also *Campbell v HM Advocate* 1998 SLT 923 at p. 931.

[113] 1952 JC 66.

[114] *Slater v HM Advocate* 1928 JC 94.

defence has not hitherto been entitled to access any evidence held by the prosecution even if potentially relevant to the case and tending to exculpate the accused. In *Higgins* v *HM Advocate*, Lord Cowie imperiously dismissed any such claim to fair process:[115]

> . . . we regard this ground of appeal as wholly without foundation, not to say impertinent. There is no obligation on the Crown to provide any list of witnesses other than those which are attached to an indictment, and there is no obligation on the Crown to disclose any information in their possession which would tend to exculpate the accused.

The practice latterly did not always follow this stricture – the Crown subsequently dissociated itself from *Higgins* and generally accepted a duty to disclose material which might assist the defence.[116] Nevertheless, as shown by cases such as Windsor and Beattie, it is an act of faith both extraordinary and misplaced that the police and prosecution in an adversarial system will always act fairly of their own volition or that the defence can effectively investigate all the evidence for themselves.[117] The Scottish Office consultation paper, *Review of Criminal Evidence and Criminal Procedure*, called in 1993 for greater disclosure but more to encourage early pleas of guilt than to ensure overall fairness. So, the position remained that the defence was not as a matter of course entitled to see Crown witness statements (including precognitions), and 'it is up to the defence to conduct its own interviews with witnesses – including prosecution witnesses – and prepare its case in light of those interviews and other investigations.'.[118] In this way, the defence is allowed to conduct its own investigations, including by the taking of precognitions from prosecution witnesses who can be required to attend before the sheriff in chambers for this purpose.[119] In the absence of fair rules as to disclosure, defence precognitions have increased in popularity,[120] but this gathering of statements arises after the protagonists have firmly established their positions[121] and it cannot reach into official records, such as the convictions records of witnesses.[122] By contrast to these rules as to prosecution disclosure, according to section 78 of the Criminal Procedure (Scotland) Act 1995, the defence must disclose 'special defences', i.e. an alibi, incrimination of a co-accused, insanity, self-defence, automatism and coercion. In this way, duties of disclosure are far more clearly placed on the defence than on the prosecution, and failure to observe the duty may result in the disbarment of a line of defence.

---

[115] 1990 SCCR 268. An attempt to obtain Crown materials by warrant was also rejected in *Campbell and Steele, Petitioners, The Scotsman*, 26 October 1995, p. 5.

[116] *HM Advocate* v *Ward* 1993 SCCR 595; *Beattie* v *HM Advocate* 1995 SLT 275; Brown, A.N., *Criminal Evidence and Procedure: An Introduction* (T. & T. Clark, Edinburgh, 1996) p. 67. There are pre-trial meetings between prosecution and defence: (1980) SLT (News) 42.

[117] HL Debs. vol. 560 col. 379, 12 January 1995, Lord Rodger.

[118] Scottish Office, *Towards a Just Conclusion* (Edinburgh, 1998) para. 2.3.

[119] Criminal Procedure (Scotland) Act 1995, s. 291. The practice is to employ private inquiry agents (often former police officers): Stewart, A.L., *The Scottish Criminal Courts in Action* (2nd ed., Butterworths, Edinburgh, 1997) p. 125.

[120] Compare *Low* v *MacNeill* 1981 SCCR 243; *Brady* v *Lockhart* 1985 SCCR 349; *HM Advocate* v *Campbell* 1997 SLT 577.

[121] The power arises only after committal and before trial: *Cirignaco, Petitioner* 1985 SCCR 157, *Gilmour, Petitioner* 1994 SCCR 872.

[122] *HM Advocate* v *Ashrif* 1988 SLT 567.

The erstwhile absence of any legal duty of prosecution disclosure undoubtedly provided the potential for challenge under Article 6 of the European Convention on Human Rights[123] and for miscarriages of justice. One example might be the case of *Steele and Campbell*.[124] If there had been fuller pre-trial disclosure by the Crown of the dealings between Love and the police, then more could have been put before the jury, without having to explain why on appeal the evidence was not raised sooner and whether the explanation could be verified by others (as discussed later). Recognising this obvious deficiency in the fairness of Scottish trial process, the High Court accepted in 1997 that the position in *Higgins* was no longer tenable. First, in *Hemming* v *HM Advocate*,[125] the public interest in a fair trial was said to outweigh potentially the Crown's interest in the privacy of witness statements: 'justice must be done and miscarriages of justice avoided'. This breakthrough was followed by a more comprehensive examination in *McLeod, Petitioner*, based on the principle that:[126]

> . . . the idea that the Crown could proceed with a trial without disclosing to the defence matter which would tend to exculpate the accused is wholly inconsistent with the basic premise of our law that the accused is entitled to a fair trial . . . The Crown have no interest in securing the conviction of any but the guilty and must be astute to avoid asking for the conviction of the innocent. When the Crown provide the defence with information which supports the defence case, they are therefore not acting out of a sense of charity but out of an awareness of their duty in a system which is tenacious of the presumption of innocence and jealous of the right to a fair trial.

In detail, the Court accepted that it should balance the public interest in disclosure and fairness to the defendant as against any Crown claim to public interest immunity; if there was no claim to immunity, then it could simply adjudicate on the ground that the disclosure would have to be shown to be of material assistance to the defence. Yet, on these latter grounds, the Court doubted that police interview notes with more than 40 uncited witnesses were disclosable (30 had been cited), despite the difficulties of the defence in tracing some of them and/or taking informative new statements so long after the event. In addition, the Court rejected the wider proposition that all statements and similar information generated in the course of an investigation which led to criminal charges should be made available to the accused unless there was a special reason for withholding a particular document. The Crown does have a duty to disclose at all times, including during trial, but only materials likely to be of material assistance to the defence.

These judgments represent an indubitable improvement in the achievement of fairness in Scottish criminal process. Yet, they have their limitations. The focus is on statements of witnesses to the police, which leaves unexplored the accessibility of other records, such as prior convictions or police disciplinary files; and Crown precognitions (unless before the sheriff) remain unobtainable. Other limits in the judicial formulations fall short of European Convention expectations: for example,

---

[123] See Chapter 7.

[124] 1998 SLT 923. The issue was raised on the basis of facts then known to the defence in *Campbell* v *UK*, Appl. no. 12323/86, (1998) 58 DR 148 but was declared inadmissible (6 March 1987).

[125] 1998 SLT 213 at p. 218 per Lord Osborne. See Ferguson, P.W., 'Disclosure in criminal proceedings' 1997 *Scottish Law Times* 181.

[126] 1998 SLT 233 at p. 244 per Lord Rodger. See Ferguson, P.W., 'Disclosure: the prosecutor's duty' 1998 *Scottish Law Times* 233.

that there will be disclosure of material which may undermine the credibility of a defence witness or material which may be relevant to sentence; and that there is a broad duty of third party disclosure extending to all agencies involved in the investigation;[127] and that disclosure is a duty of the prosecution rather than a response to the specification of a defence to the court in order to prove that disclosure is necessary. In any event, these court-based rules of disclosure remain cumbersome, for ultimately there must be a petition to the High Court under section 103(7) of the 1995 Act if sufficient disclosure is not forthcoming.

Trial Features

Trial procedures have been less dramatically altered. Many of the changes, as foreshadowed by the Scottish Office papers, *Review of Criminal Evidence and Criminal Procedure*[128] and *Firm and Fair*,[129] have reflected concerns about delay and efficiency rather than injustice, a trait likewise prevalent south of the Border.[130] Therefore, recent reforms have included: a reduced number of jury trials, even though they are already uncommon compared with England and Wales;[131] the mandatory use of intermediate diets in summary procedure and first diets in sheriff and jury cases;[132] the greater emphasis on judicial case management;[133] the abolition of the right to peremptory challenge to three jurors without cause;[134] and the encouragement to give sentence discounts for early and clear guilty pleas.[135]

There has been one other notable change, again in line with English developments and perhaps spurred by a decision to the contrary in *Dempsey* v *HM Advocate*.[136] It was established by the Criminal Justice (Scotland) Act 1995, section 32, that the previous prohibition on the prosecutor commenting on the failure of the accused to give evidence in solemn and summary procedures was to cease to have effect. Adverse comment may arise when the accused fails to lead evidence and is not confined to the situation where the defendant later puts forward a submission in defence which could have been stated earlier (unlike the position in regard to judicial examinations under the Criminal Procedure (Scotland) Act 1995,

---

[127] *Jespers* v *Belgium*, Appl. no. 8403/78, 27 D & R 61 at para. 56.

[128] Scottish Office, Edinburgh, 1993.

[129] Cm 2600, HMSO, Edinburgh, 1994, para. 2.4.

[130] Conversely, the *Runciman Report* considered Scottish models at several points, including the fuller facts adduced in indictments and curtailed prosecution opening speeches and summing up by the judge (ch. 8 paras. 7, 21).

[131] See Criminal Justice (Scotland) Act 1987, s. 58; Crime and Punishment (Scotland) Act 1997, s. 13; Maher, G., 'Reforming the criminal process: a Scottish perspective' in McConville, M. and Bridges, L., (eds.) *Criminal Justice in Crisis* (Edward Elgar, Aldershot, 1994) pp. 62–5. The share of solemn cases in the High Court increased from 14% in 1980 to 27% in 1992: Scottish Office, *Sentencing and Appeals* (HMSO, Edinburgh, 1994) para. 3.15.

[132] Scottish Office, *Firm and Fair* (Cm 2600, HMSO, Edinburgh, 1994) paras. 2.15–2.20. See Criminal Procedure (Scotland) Act 1995, ss. 71, 148. A 'diet' is a meeting at court for considering or hearing some aspect of the case.

[133] Scottish Office, *Firm and Fair* (Cm 2600, HMSO, Edinburgh, 1994) para. 2.37.

[134] Criminal Procedure (Scotland) Act 1995, s. 86. See *Juries and Verdicts* (HMSO, Edinburgh 1993); *Firm and Fair* (Cm 2600, HMSO, Edinburgh, 1994) para. 3.9; Ferguson, P.W., 'Jury vetting' 1997 *Scottish Law Times* 287.

[135] Scottish Office, *Firm and Fair* (Cm 2600, HMSO, Edinburgh, 1994) para. 4.14; Criminal Procedure (Scotland) Act 1995, s. 196. See 'Backdating sentences and imprisonment' (1995) *Journal of the Law Society of Scotland* 383. Compare the previous practices: Kelly, D., *Criminal Sentences* (T. & T. Clark, Edinburgh, 1993) p. 6.

[136] 1996 SLT 289.

section 36(8), and unlike the position under the Criminal Justice and Public Order Act 1994).[137] Such an attack on the right to silence should be confined to 'special circumstances' according to the Scottish Office,[138] but these are not specified in the legislation. It is possible that the practice will reflect that in relation to judicial comment on silence, which has long been allowed:[139] there must first be proven facts which raise a presumption that the accused has committed the crime and that in any event silence can only be one part of the story. Some commentators may doubt the importance of the reform:[140] 'In the long run things balance out: defence lawyers will require in providing effective assistance to their clients, to think more deeply about the tactical decision on giving evidence.'. Nevertheless, in the absence of legislative reforms in regard to disclosure and legal assistance at the police station and having regard to the fundamental right to be presumed innocent, one wonders whether these changes can be said to be fair or indeed 'balanced'. At least, compared with elsewhere in the United Kingdom, no reliance has been placed on silence in the police station. As indicated earlier, there is traditional distrust of any form of evidence gathering in the police station as 'the venue is a sinister one' and 'the dice are loaded against [the suspect]'.[141] It follows that there is a fundamental recognition of the privilege against self-incrimination,[142] though it is now subject to the obligations under sections 13 and 14 of the 1995 Act.

Other distinctly Scottish trial features have largely escaped attention. This category includes the three verdict system (including the verdict of 'not proven')[143] and the jury panel of 15 operating on a simple majority verdict.[144] It is claimed that the 'not proven' verdict offers an extra safeguard against marginal convictions, though it must be balanced against the fact that convictions can be sustained on the verdict of eight jurors (as opposed to at least 10 in England and Wales). The statistics overleaf (Table 16.1) suggest that the verdict is utilised in a significant number of cases and does contribute to a lower rate of proven charges compared to England and Wales. However, further investigations would have to be conducted into prosecution and judicial, as well as jury, practices in response to 'not guilty' pleas before one could be sure of its role.

Appeals to the High Court of Justiciary (the 'Appeal Court')

Continuing the previous theme, several of the reforms at appeal level have been again primarily reflective of cost-saving and efficiency objectives. These include

---

[137] See Chapter 5.
[138] HL Debs. vol. 560 col. 416, 12 January 1995.
[139] *Brown* v *Macpherson* 1918 JC 3, as interpreted in *Scott* v *HM Advocate* 1946 JC 90; *McIlhargey* v *Heron* 1972 JC 38; *Knowles* v *HM Advocate* 1975 JC 6; *Stewart* v *HM Advocate* 1980 SLT 245; *Dorrens* v *HM Advocate* 1983 SCCR 407; *HM Advocate* v *Hardy* 1983 JC 144; *McIntosh* v *HM Advocate (No. 2)* 1997 SLT 1320.
[140] Shiels, R.S., *Current Law Statutes 1995* (Sweet & Maxwell, London, 1995) pp. 20–37.
[141] *Chalmers* v *HM Advocate* 1954 SLT 177 at p. 184 per Lord Justice-General Cooper.
[142] *Livingstone* v *Murray* (1830) 9 S 161; *Wightman* v *HM Advocate* 1959 JC 44; *McHugh* v *HM Advocate* 1978 JC 12; *Upton* v *HM Advocate* 1986 SCCR 188; *White* v *HM Advocate* 1991 SCCR 555; PWF, 'The right to silence' 1987 *Scottish Law Times* 17.
[143] Scottish Office, *Firm and Fair* (Cm 2600, HMSO, Edinburgh, 1994) para. 3.19. The argument in favour is that it can allow a lingering or lurking doubt to found an acquittal: Beltrami, J., *The Defender* (revised ed., M. & A. Thompson, Edinburgh, 1988) pp. 137–8. The idea was rejected by the *Runciman Report*, ch. 8 para. 75.
[144] Scottish Office, *Firm and Fair* (Cm 2600, HMSO, Edinburgh, 1994) para. 3.21.

Table 16.1: The impact of the 'not proven' verdict[145]

	1995		1996		1997	
	Scottish High Ct/Sheriff Ct: Solemn cases (%)	English Crown Ct (%)	Scottish High Ct/Sheriff Ct: Solemn cases (%)	English Crown Ct (%)	Scottish High Ct/Sheriff Ct: Solemn cases (%)	English Crown Ct (%)
Discharged or directed acquittal	463 (10)	10426 (13)	567 (12)	8697 (10)	418 (8)	9298 (10)
Jury verdict: not guilty	399 (9)	5764 (6)	421 (8)	5466 (6)	392 (8)	5812 (6)
Jury verdict: not proven	191 (4)	N/A	175 (3)	N/A	185 (4)	N/A
Charge(s) proven	3432 (77)	78515 (83)	3846 (77)	74907 (84)	4117 (81)	80586 (84)
Total defendants	4485	94705	5009	89070	5112	95696

145 Source: Fred Thorne, Scottish Office, 1999; Lord Chancellor's Department, Judicial Statistics (Cm 3290, 3716, 3980, HMSO, London, 1996–98).

the abolition of direct access to the High Court (which is the only criminal appeal court for Scotland). There is now a sifting process of requiring leave to appeal from a single judge on note of appeal, with appeal against refusal to a full bench of three;[146] full appeals against sentence in solemn proceedings are now heard by two judges only.[147] Both were essentially conceived as resource-conserving measures and are not considered to infringe the rights of appeal required under the European Convention.

Aside from these matters, the constitution and performance of the Appeal Court has for many years engendered the deepest concerns about unremedied miscarriages of justice. There exists a single ground of appeal, which is set out (for solemn procedure) in section 106(3) of the Criminal Procedure (Scotland) Act 1995:[148]

> By an appeal . . . a person may bring under review of the High Court any alleged miscarriage of justice in the proceedings in which he was convicted, including any alleged miscarriages of justice on the basis of the existence and significance of additional evidence which was not heard at the trial and which was not available and could not reasonably have been made available at the trial.

As thus drafted (originally in 1980), there was no statutory definition as to the meanings of 'miscarriage of justice',[149] save for the one example of additional evidence.[150] The additional evidence must have been not reasonably available at the time of the trial, so defence incompetence or tactics not to use it could not as such be the basis for an appeal.[151] The Appeal Court did not treat as 'evidence' at all a change of story on the part of a witness or the defendant;[152] one has the feeling here that finality ruled over righteousness. In other respects, the Appeal Court declined to provide any clear definition of 'miscarriage',[153] though it did interpret the criterion as requiring a level of seriousness and materiality before a miscarriage 'properly so called' can be recognised.[154] In some ways the effect is similar in effect to the 'proviso' which used to exist expressly under section 2 of the Criminal Appeal (Scotland) Act 1926 until amendment in 1975,[155] the effect being that the court may decide not to overturn a conviction where some fault has occurred but, overall, no injustice has been sustained worthy of the legal label, 'miscarriage'.

---

[146] Criminal Procedure (Scotland) Act 1995, ss. 107, 180. See Scottish Office, *Sentencing and Appeals* (HMSO, Edinburgh, 1994) para. 5.20; Scottish Office, *Firm and Fair* (Cm 2600, HMSO, Edinburgh, 1994) paras. 1.7, 5.7, 5.8; *Sutherland Report*, para. 1.18). For the likely grounds, see Lord McCluskey, *Criminal Appeals* (Butterworths, Edinburgh, 1992) pp. 176–89.

[147] Criminal Procedure (Scotland) Act 1995, ss. 103, 173. See Scottish Office, *Firm and Fair* (Cm 2600, HMSO, Edinburgh, 1994) paras. 1.7, 5.11.

[148] For summary procedure, see s. 175(3). Appeal commenced under the Criminal Appeal (Scotland) Act 1926, which was made retrospective by Criminal Appeal (Scotland) Act 1927 (to deal with *Slater* v *HM Advocate* 1928 JC 94). For the possible disposals following an appeal, see ss. 118, 119.

[149] It was not recommended by the Thomson Committee and was not debated in Parliament: Gordon, G.H., *Renton and Brown's Criminal Procedure* (6th ed., W. Green, Edinburgh, 1996) para. 29–02.

[150] See Lord McCluskey, *Criminal Appeals* (Butterworths, Edinburgh, 1992) pp. 160–8.

[151] *McDonald* v *HM Advocate* 1987 SCCR 153; *Grimes* v *HM Advocate* 1988 SCCR 580.

[152] *Mitchell* v *HM Advocate* 1989 SCCR 502; *Jones* v *HM Advocate* 1989 SCCR 726; *Maitland* v *HM Advocate* 1992 SCCR 759; *Brodie* v *HM Advocate* 1993 SCCR 371; *McCormack* v *HM Advocate* 1993 SCCR 581. But compare *Marshall* v *MacDougall* 1986 SCCR 376.

[153] But see the examples in Lord McCluskey, *Criminal Appeals* (Butterworths, Edinburgh, 1992) pp. 176–90. Compare the Canadian Criminal Code, R.S., c. C-34, ss. 686(1), 690.

[154] Lord McCluskey, *Criminal Appeals* (Butterworths, Edinburgh, 1992) p. 172. See further Gordon, G.H., *Renton and Brown's Criminal Procedure* (6th ed., W. Green, Edinburgh, 1996) para. 29–12.

[155] See First Report of the Thomson Committee, *Criminal Appeals in Scotland* (Cmnd 5038, HMSO, Edinburgh, 1972) para. 39.

In the light of these restrictive approaches and following the failure of the Scottish Office to find a consensus for reform after the issuance of its own consultation paper,[156] the Sutherland Committee was appointed in 1994 to consider further appeal-related laws and practices.[157] The Committee noted that there were criticisms of the scope and application of the grounds for appeal, but it concluded that the basic ground of appeal should be retained.[158] This emphasis on the word 'miscarriage' is supportable, as it points to the overall treatment of the defendant in terms of justice, but whether it really improves on a formula such as 'unsafe' (as in the Criminal Appeal Act 1995, section 2) must be doubted.[159] The First Report of the Thomson Committee in 1972[160] rejected both the (then) English formula of 'unsafe and unsatisfactory' and the (then) proposed test of 'miscarriage of justice' on the basis that both allowed for the possibility of appeal on wider grounds than hitherto and that this indulgence was not necessary because of other putative safeguards against wrongful conviction (such as corroboration) and the assertion that no miscarriages had arisen because of error in fact. In reality, both 'miscarriages' and 'unsafeness' point to both the plight of the defendant as well as the interests of the system. Both words are inherently flexible,[161] so they are heavily affected by judicial perceptions and experiences of the reliability of different sources or types of evidence and the standing of the administration of justice in general.

It follows that much depends on the practices of the appellate judges, and one could argue that much clearer legislative guidance will be necessary, given a history of judicial reluctance to set aside convictions:[162]

Table 16.2: Appeals from High Court solemn trials

	1993	1994	1995	1996	1997
Total defendants at trial	1601	1228	1390	1420	1356
Total appeals	290	287	277	292	261
Appeal against sentence only	169	148	170	184	185
Appeal against conviction/or both	121	139	107	108	76
Conviction quashed	2	4	0	4	2
Sentence altered	30	27	24	31	49
Other appeal sustained	3	4	2	4	4
Dismissed	139	125	131	110	89
Abandoned	116	127	120	143	117

[156] Scottish Office, *Sentencing and Appeals* (HMSO, Edinburgh, 1993); Scottish Office, *Firm and Fair* (Edinburgh, HMSO, 1994) paras. 1.8, 6.2, 6.6, 6.17.

[157] Committee on Criminal Appeals and Alleged Miscarriages of Justice, *Report* (Cm 3245, HMSO, Edinburgh, 1996) ('*Sutherland Report*'). See also Millar, A.R., *Appeals in Scottish Criminal Courts: A Study of the Appeal Process* (Central Research Unit, Scottish Office, Edinburgh, 1993; Duff, P. and McCallum, F., *Grounds of Appeal in Criminal Cases* (Central Research Unit, Scottish Office, Edinburgh, 1996).

[158] *Sutherland Report*, paras. 2.12, 2.16, 2.29.

[159] Several Scottish practitioners believed the English formula to be more permissive: Duff, P. and McCallum, F., *Grounds of Appeal in Criminal Cases* (Central Research Unit, Scottish Office, Edinburgh, 1996) para. 5.9.

[160] First Report of the Thomson Committee, *Criminal Appeals in Scotland* (Cmnd 5038, HMSO, Edinburgh, 1972) paras. 16–19.

[161] See *Runciman Report*, ch. 10 para. 32.

[162] Source: Scottish Office, *Statistical Bulletin: Justice Services* (Edinburgh, 1999).

Compared with the figures for England and Wales,[163] the Scottish rate of appealing is higher (20%),[164] but the proportion of 'successful' outcomes is lower (14%). One apparent difficulty, shared with Northern Ireland, is that the self-same set of judges deal with trials conducted by their brethren.[165]

As already indicated, a restrictive pattern has likewise emerged in legal interpretations of the appeal jurisdiction. The Scottish formula, though direct and uncontradicted, has allowed for 'a conservative approach'[166] on the part of the Appeal Court, reflecting especially a reluctance to set aside convictions on the basis of significant trial procedure error or to allow fresh evidence or to question directly a jury verdict on grounds of lurking doubt. So the *Sutherland Report* recommended the fleshing out of the concept, 'miscarriage of justice', by examples which would afford more explicit guidance.[167] Four were considered in relation to solemn procedure, though these were to be without prejudice to others.[168]

The first concerned the case of fresh evidence which was expressly mentioned in section 106 of the 1995 Act. As already described, the Appeal Court demanded that the additional evidence must have been not reasonably available at the time of the trial. Consequently, additional evidence was not readily admitted, since it was not enough that a reasonable explanation could have been given for its prior omission if it did in fact exist at the time of the trial.[169] This approach was briefly challenged in 1995 in the case of *Church* and but was quickly reaffirmed in *Elliott*.[170] Therefore, the Sutherland Committee was minded to recommend the test of 'reasonable explanation' (as in section 4 of the Criminal Appeal Act 1995) and to apply it to any 'fresh' rather than 'additional' evidence.[171]

The second mooted example of a 'miscarriage' was the related situation where a witness wishes to change his or her testimony. For reasons of judicial policy (relating to finality and the dangers of perjury and intimidation),[172] the Scottish courts have set their face against accepting such changes of heart.[173] In response the Sutherland Committee considered that such evidence should be a relevant ground for appeal but must be supported by some additional and credible evidence.[174]

---

[163] See Chapter 1.

[164] See Scottish Office, *Sentencing and Appeals* (HMSO, Edinburgh, 1994) para. 5.2. The Appeal Court cannot increase a sentence on appeal by a defendant against conviction, though it may do so on an appeal against sentence: Criminal Procedure (Scotland) Act 1995, s. 118 (see for example *Donnelly* v *HM Advocate* 1988 SCCR 386; *Beattie, Petitioner* 1993 SLT 676).

[165] In practice, around 8 out of 26 High Court judges deal with appeals: Scottish Office, *Sentencing and Appeals* (HMSO, Edinburgh, 1994) para. 5.2.

[166] Gordon, G.H., *Renton and Brown's Criminal Procedure* (6th ed., W. Green, Edinburgh, 1996) para. 29–08.

[167] *Sutherland Report*, paras. 2.33, 2.58, 2.70.

[168] *Sutherland Report*, para. 4.1. For summary procedure and retrials after the quashing of a conviction, see *Sutherland Report*, paras. 2.79-84; *Boyle* v *HM Advocate* 1993 SLT 577, 1079, 1085.

[169] See *Salusbury-Hughes* v *HM Advocate* 1987 SCCR 38; *Williamson* v *HM Advocate* 1988 SCCR 56; *Craven* v *Macphail* 1990 SCCR 558; *Mackenzie* v *HM Advocate* 1995 SLT 743.

[170] *Church* v *HM Advocate* 1995 SLT 604 (see also 1996 SLT 383); *Elliott* v *HM Advocate* 1995 SLT 612; Scott, M., 'The cases of *Church* and *Elliott*' 1995 SLT 189; Ferguson, P.W., 'Fresh evidence appeals' (1995) 40 *Journal of the Law Society of Scotland* 264.

[171] *Sutherland Report*, para. 2.44, 2.53.

[172] Scottish Office, *Sentencing and Appeals* (HMSO, Edinburgh, 1994) paras. 6.15, 6.16.

[173] Defendants: *Mitchell* v *HM Advocate* 1989 SCCR 502; *Brodie* v *HM Advocate* 1993 SCCR 371; *McCormack* v *HM Advocate* 1993 SCCR 581. Third party witnesses: *Stillie* v *HM Advocate* 1990 SCCR 719; *Perrie* v *HM Advocate* 1991 SCCR 255; *Maitland* v *HM Advocate* 1992 SCCR 759.

[174] *Sutherland Report*, para. 2.58.

The third was the highly contentious ground that a jury's verdict is simply unreasonable even if it does not lack a sufficiency of technically admissible evidence to support it. As in England, the Appeal Court has hesitated to usurp the jury's function of assessment of credibility and reliability.[175] So, appeal on the basis of 'lurking doubt' can rarely be successful, though it is impliedly a lawful basis for appeal. The Sutherland Committee insisted that the rare possibility should be explicitly recognised, but then proceeded to set the standard at an almost impossible level – that a verdict was such that 'no reasonable jury, properly directed, could have reached'.[176]

Fearing the encouragement of 'a multitude of frivolous and unfounded appeals', the Sutherland Committee did not include in the list of conceivable examples a fourth possible category, the occurrence of defective legal representation.[177] Instead, the Committee was minded to follow the emergent viewpoint of the High Court in *Anderson* v *HM Advocate*.[178] The conduct of the defence can form the basis of an appeal, but only in the circumstance of where the defence has not been presented to the court, especially if contrary to express instructions or because of 'other conduct' which might include for example, inadequate preparation, but only if to the extent that it could be said that the defendant has been deprived of a fair trial. This forbearance on the part of the Sutherland Committee (which is also reflected by the absence of subsequent statutory intervention) may have been too trusting of the attitude of the judiciary. After all, James McAulay Anderson lost his appeal against assault, and the Appeal Court viewed as an understandable tactic rather than a dire failure that his solicitor-advocate failed to carry out instructions to explore the criminal record of the principal witness since it comprised offences of violence rather than dishonesty.

The Government's response in 1996, *Crime and Punishment*,[179] accepted the single appeal criterion of 'miscarriage of justice' and the specific recommendations as to the admission of fresh evidence if there was a reasonable explanation for its earlier omission, the overturning of a verdict which no reasonably directed jury could have reached, and also possible appeals on behalf of deceased convicts.[180] Other detailed Sutherland recommendations were rejected, including appeal on the basis of the acceptance of a witness's change of mind.[181] The setting out of examples was left for later consideration.[182] However, further concessions in the direction of the wishes of the *Sutherland Report* were made during the passage of the Crime and Punishment (Scotland) Act 1997, under the influence of backbench pressure set against the exigencies of the parliamentary timetable prior to the forthcoming General Election.

[175] *Reilly and others* v *HM Advocate* 1981 SCCR 201; *Rubin* v *HM Advocate* 1984 SLT 369; *Cameron* v *HM Advocate* 1987 SCCR 608; Lord McCluskey, *Criminal Appeals* (Butterworths, Edinburgh, 1992) p. 188.

[176] *Sutherland Report*, para. 2.70.

[177] *Sutherland Report*, paras. 2.75–78.

[178] 1996 SLT 155, reversing *McCaroll* v *HM Advocate* 1949 SLT 74. See 'Miscarriages of justice and legal practice' (1996) 41 *Journal of the Law Society of Scotland* 5; Gow, N., "Flagrant incompetency" of counsel' (1996) 146 *New Law Journal* 453; Shiels, R.S., 'Blaming the lawyer' [1997] *Criminal Law Review* 740; *McIntosh* v *HM Advocate (No. 2)* 1997 SCCR 389.

[179] Cm 3302, HMSO, Edinburgh, 1996 ch. 15.

[180] *Crime and Punishment* (Cm 3302, HMSO, Edinburgh, 1996) paras. 15.6, 15.7.

[181] *Ibid.* para. 15.9.

[182] *Ibid.* para. 15.9.

The law under the reformulated section 106(3) (as substituted by section 17 of the 1997 Act) is that the basic ground of appeal remains unchanged, though appeals may now be taken up on behalf of deceased persons[183] and may rely upon changes in the law of evidence in favour of the appellant which have occurred since trial.[184] In addition, several circumstances grounding appeal (leaving aside relatively uncontroversial grounds, such as error of law, misdirection by the judge or procedural irregularity)[185] have now been indicated and propound several extensions to the prior understandings.

First, there are new formulations relating to additional evidence cases:

(3) By an appeal under subsection (1) above a person may bring under review of the High Court any alleged miscarriage of justice, which may include such a miscarriage based on—

(a) subject to subsections (3A) to (3D) below, the existence and significance of evidence which was not heard at the original proceedings . . .

(3A) Evidence such as is mentioned in subsection (3)(a) above may found an appeal only where there is a reasonable explanation of why it was not so heard.

(3B) Where the explanation referred to in subsection (3A) above or, as the case may be, (3C) below is that the evidence was not admissible at the time of the original proceedings, but is admissible at the time of the appeal, the court may admit that evidence if it appears to the court that it would be in the interests of justice to do so.

(3C) Without prejudice to subsection (3A) above, where evidence such as is mentioned in paragraph (a) of subsection (3) above is evidence—

(a) which is—

(i) from a person; or

(ii) of a statement (within the meaning of section 259(1) of this Act) by a person, who gave evidence at the original proceedings; and

(b) which is different from, or additional to, the evidence so given,

it may not found an appeal unless there is a reasonable explanation as to why the evidence now sought to be adduced was not given by that person at those proceedings, which explanation is itself supported by independent evidence.

(3D) For the purposes of subsection (3C) above, 'independent evidence' means evidence which—

(a) was not heard at the original proceedings;

(b) is from a source independent of the person referred to in subsection (3C) above; and

(c) is accepted by the court as being credible and reliable.

The changes here are apparently substantial. First, the Appeal Court can now review on the basis of evidence not heard at 'the original proceedings' whereas the 1975 Act referred to 'the proceedings in which he was convicted'. This difference avoids the uncertainty that the appeal must be confined to matters relating to earlier

---

[183] 1997 Act, s. 20, inserting s. 303A of the 1995 Act.

[184] Compare *McLay* v *HM Advocate* 1994 SLT 873; *Conway* v *HM Advocate* 1996 SCCR 570.

[185] See Gordon, G.H., *Renton and Brown's Criminal Procedure* (6th ed., W. Green, Edinburgh, 1996) paras. 29–28 to 29–33.

court process[186] and also clarifies admissibility when a defendant has pleaded guilty and so there is no 'trial'.[187] However, it is regrettable that the wording excludes reliance upon evidence which was heard in the original proceedings, for such evidence could take on a new significance in the light of other wholly new evidence.[188]

Secondly, the Appeal Court can review on basis of 'evidence which was not heard', whereas the 1975 Act referred to 'additional evidence' not heard at the trial. In this way, it is sufficient that the evidence is fresh to the appeal proceedings, even if it has been in existence for some time. There must be satisfied a 'reasonable explanation' test as to why the evidence was not adduced earlier – effectively adopting the aberrant decision in *Church* v *HM Advocate*[189] – and certainly intended to be more flexible than the previous exacting test.[190] The result will be to allow lines of evidence which might have been raised at trial but were not perceived as significant until after the trial had unfolded.

Thirdly, the foregoing change should be sufficient to admit, *inter alia*, evidence from a prior witness or a new witness arising through a 'change of heart' or the recovery of memory, so that the later testimony differs from an earlier version which has been given in court. This form of additional evidence has to be supported (as stated in section 106(3C)) by a reasonable explanation which is further supported by independent evidence. As defined in section 106(3D), the independent evidence must involve a credible and reliable explanation and emanate from a third party (such as a relative or a doctor).[191]

The referred appeal of the *Glasgow Two – Campbell and Steele –* was the first occasion on which a witness's retraction of evidence was used as grounds for appeal since the change in the law in 1997. In this case, the retraction emanated from the key prosecution witness, William Love, who claimed he had been under police pressure to give evidence against the appellants.[192] The Appeal Court concluded, however, that there was no independent 'reasonable explanation' demanded by section 106(3D) as to why Love had not told the truth in the first place. This result is a characteristically mean interpretation. One can appreciate that further investigation might result in doubts as to the importance or credibility of the evidence now being adduced, but the story that Love lied in return for police bail and immunity from prosecution was accepted as credible for the purposes of section 106(3C) (the inability to show at trial that the witness was a liar being sufficient for (3A)). So, the case turned on whether there was independent evidence of the change of heart under (3D). The defence claimed that the independent element derived from Love's sister, Agnes Carlton,[193] but Lord Cullen, supported by Lord Sutherland, rejected this basis:[194]

---

[186] *Sutherland Report*, para. 2.30.
[187] *Carrington* v *HM Advocate* 1994 SCCR 567.
[188] See *Sutherland Report*, para. 2.58
[189] 1995 SLT 604.
[190] Gordon, G.H., *Renton and Brown's Criminal Procedure* (6th ed., W. Green, Edinburgh, 1996) paras. 29–36.
[191] HL Debs. vol. 579 cols. 34–39, 10 March 1997.
[192] 1998 SLT 923.
[193] The Court held she could not provide new evidence independent of Love's since there was no reasonable explanation under s. 106(3A) for her failure to give it at the trial when she was listed as a defence witness but not called, thereby rejecting allegations of police pressure on witnesses: *ibid.*, pp. 935, 936.

She is able to give evidence which, if it is true, indicates that Love would have wished to minimise his own involvement in the shooting. That could support the proposition that he gave false evidence as to his own involvement, but that does not tend to show that he was induced or pressured by others to give false evidence on other matters.

In this way, the Appeal Court demanded an extraordinarily close connection between the fresh evidence and the independent evidence.[195] It is true that Love's sister could not directly testify to the police's pressure, but it seems an unduly strict level of proof to demand it – presumably it would require evidence from a police officer that he had acted to pervert the course of justice. Does the law really require corroboration as to the reasons given by Love as to why he committed perjury rather than any relevant reasons or even simply the fact that he admitted he did? In other words, must the independent evidence be confined to, and even provide precise and proximate 'justification' for,[196] the reasonable explanation of the 'change of heart' of the witness rather than any other reasonable explanation? The purpose of the 1997 Act's new rule as to independent evidence was to avoid the possibility of intimidation by the defendants; this motivation was in no way alleged by his sister whose evidence should have been able to have been treated as an independent support that there had been a true change of heart. His sister showed, through her evidence as an eye-witness to the ice-cream van shooting, that Love had a reason for wishing to minimise his involvement.[197] Consequently, there should be (and there was) provided independent evidence for supporting the story of a genuine change of heart, which is not based on an explanation arising from the intimidation by the defendants, though it does not necessarily verify the positive reasons for the new stance in all respects; once this has been done, it is up to the court to accept the evidence but then to test it. This interpretation was taken in dissent by Lord McCluskey who suggested Mr Love and Mrs Carlton should be put into the witness box and subjected to cross-examination. In his view, even accepting there was a need for the independent evidence to be of the standard of corroboration, the sister had direct evidence of Love admitting involvement in the shooting at Doyle's van, which surely could be taken to be a strong motivation to blame others, no matter what the police said.[198] So, the interpretation of Lord McCluskey, based on an analysis of both the *Sutherland Report* and Parliamentary debates, does not demand that the explanation under section 106(3C) to be evidenced under section 106(3D) must be precisely that given by the 'change of heart' witness – it may instead come from the appellants or the deposition of a dead or missing witness.

---

[194] *Ibid.* at p. 941.

[195] Compare Poole, A., 'Remedies in miscarriage of justice cases' 1998 *Scottish Law Times* 65.

[196] Lord Sutherland rejected the idea that the general hope of personal advantage could ever be a sufficient justification under (3C) (at pp. 952–3). This demanded level of consistency and explanation seems to go beyond the legal test of 'reasonable explanation' (as well as raising the possibility of justifiable perjury) and was raised in the second petition of Campbell which was rejected by the Secretary of State on 1 December 1998.

[197] Lord Cullen mistakenly held that Love had not admitted the shooting at Doyle's van (*ibid.* at p. 941), but this mistake becomes irrelevant in his reasoning, for it is precisely the police pressure (and not the background shooting which made the police pressure all the more telling) which must be corroborated by the independent witness. This point seems to have been the main basis for the Secretary of State's rejection of the second petition on 1 December 1998 (letter supplied to the author by Thomas Campbell).

[198] *Ibid.* at p. 951.

After this very disappointing start in early 1998, the Appeal Court heard fresh evidence later the same year under these rules in the case of Alexander Hall. It accepted that the new witness, George McAvoy, had not come forward before because he wanted to deceive his wife about an affair with another woman.[199]

As well as the changes to the appeal ground of fresh evidence, s. 106(3) of the 1995 Act, as substituted by s. 17 of the 1997 Act, recites a further ground of appeal based on the unreasonableness of the verdict:

> (3)   By an appeal under subsection (1) above a person may bring under review of the High Court any alleged miscarriage of justice, which may include such a miscarriage based on . . .
>   (b)   the jury's having returned a verdict which no reasonable jury, properly directed, could have returned.

The meaning of section 106(3)(b) is not at all clear. In some ways, it is reminiscent of section 2(1) of the original Criminal Appeal (Scotland) Act 1926, but there the verdict had to be 'palpably wrong'[200] because it had to be shown that it 'cannot be supported having regard to the evidence'. Conversely, this new ground is not meant to be as wide as the concept of 'lurking doubt'.[201] Probably, it will be interpreted by the Appeal Court as amounting to no more than a legislative expression of the former practice; such a ground did arguably exist before 1995, but was not explicit and was always given short shrift.[202] The *Sutherland Report* envisaged its use as being exceptional, though perhaps broader than the 1926 test.[203] It is presumably meant to apply to a verdict in the absence of evidence to support an element of the charge, but it goes further than this as it omits the words in the 1926 Act. Intervention is not likely if the challenge is to the credibility and reliability of a witness who appeared before the trial court[204] or perhaps relates to issues which have been explicitly canvassed on both sides of the argument.[205] It cannot be based on new evidence but arises from a re-examination of the evidence before the jury. The ground was raised unsuccessfully in the *Campbell and Steele* case,[206] but only in relation to the conviction of Campbell for attempted murder (arising from the prior shooting at an ice-cream van).

Finally, the 1997 Act is silent on the grant of legal aid in connection with appeals. This aspect of practice has produced a troubling flow of litigation under the European Convention on Human Rights. In *Granger* v *UK*,[207] the applicant gave evidence to the police in the *Campbell and Steele* case, but then denied the essential facts at trial. He was convicted of perjury but was refused legal aid in connection with his appeal. The European Court found a breach of Articles 6(1) and 6(3), given the substantial period of imprisonment at stake, the fact that the Solicitor-General appeared for the Crown, the complex legal issues, and the

---

[199] *The Scotsman*, 8 July 1998, p. 5.
[200] *Webb* v *HM Advocate* 1927 JC 92; *McMillan* v *HM Advocate* 1927 JC 62.
[201] *Sutherland Report*, para. 2.69.
[202] *Rubin* v *HM Advocate* 1984 SLT 369; *Ginnity* v *HM Advocate* 1995 SLT 1080.
[203] *Sutherland Report*, para. 2.71.
[204] Gordon, G.H., *Renton and Brown's Criminal Procedure* (6th ed., W. Green, Edinburgh, 1996) para. 29–19, 29–20.
[205] See *R* v *Mailloux* [1988] 2 Can SCR 1029; *R* v *Burns* [1994] 1 Can SCR 656.
[206] 1998 SLT 923.
[207] Appl. no. 11932/86, Ser. A No. 174, (1990) 22 EHRR 469.

applicant's modest intelligence. By a *Practice Note* on 4 December 1990, the Appeal Court is advised to consider the merits of legal aid and to adjourn and make a recommendation to the Scottish Legal Aid Board in appropriate cases.[208] However, this concession has not ensured the grant of legal aid on a fair scale, and so the matter returned to the European Court in *Maxwell* v *UK*[209] and *Boner* v *UK*,[210] where further breaches were found, principally because of the heavy penalties being faced. Fairness to the accused demands proper representation in court, even in lines of argument adopted contrary to the advice of counsel.[211]

Post-appeal: Referrals and the Scottish Criminal Cases Review Commission

The Sutherland Committee also examined the system for dealing with post-appeal complaints of miscarriages of justice by which persons petitioned the Secretary of State who could refer the matter to the Appeal Court under section 124 of the Criminal Procedure (Scotland) Act 1995.[212] Under this provision, which was additional to the prerogative of mercy,[213] the Scottish Secretary could refer either the whole case to the High Court or particular points[214] at any time after conviction.[215] The decision, which would follow a departmental review of the court file and, exceptionally, responses to inquiries and further investigations by the Crown Office and police,[216] was legally reviewable but most unlikely to be impugned.[217] Like English counterparts wary of stepping into judicial territory, the Scottish Secretary demanded fresh evidence or considerations of substance,[218] and, as a result, the power was frugally used. Between 1984 and 1994, an average of 48 petitions per year were submitted to the Secretary of State, but only 19 referrals had been made between 1928 and the end of 1998 (with eight convictions quashed as a result).[219]

---

[208] See Scottish Office, *Criminal Legal Aid Review* (HMSO, Edinburgh, 1994) para. 4.55. Several pending complaints were settled as a result in 1992 and 1993: *Higgins* v *UK*, Appl. no. 14778/89; *PM* v *UK*, Appl. no. 15861/89; *Ritchie* v *UK*, Appl. no. 16212/90; *WW* v *UK*, Appl. no. 18123/91.

[209] Appl. no. 18949/91, Ser. A, No. 300-C, (1995) 19 EHRR 97, 1995 SCCR 1.

[210] Appl. no. 18711/91, Ser. A No. 300-B, (1995) 19 EHRR 246.

[211] Compare Finnie, W., 'The European Court of Human Rights and criminal legal aid in Scotland' 1995 *Scottish Law Times* 271.

[212] The power to ask the High Court of Justiciary to decide preliminary points of law under the 1926 Act, s. 16(3) was repealed following the First Report of the Thomson Committee, *Criminal Appeals in Scotland* (Cmnd 5038, HMSO, Edinburgh, 1972) paras. 49–51.

[213] *HM Advocate* v *Waddell* 1976 SLT (Notes) 61; Gane, C., 'The effect of a pardon in Scots law' 1980 *Juridicial Review* 18.

[214] *Slater* v *HM Advocate* 1928 JC 94; *Gallagher* v *HM Advocate* 1951 JC 38; *Higgins* v *HM Advocate* 1956 JC 69.

[215] In practice, a reference would not be made if appeal processes were still possible: Scottish Office, *Firm and Fair* (Cm 2600, HMSO, Edinburgh, 1994) para. 6.13.

[216] See *Sutherland Report*, paras. 5.12–19. The High Court of Justiciary has powers to initiate further investigations: Criminal Procedure (Scotland) Act 1995, s. 104(1). See *Crossan* v *HM Advocate* 1996 SCCR 279. But an investigative arm for the Appeal Court was rejected by the *Sutherland Report*, para. 5.45.

[217] *McDonald* v *Secretary of State for Scotland* 1996 SLT 16, distinguishing *Leitch* v *Secretary of State for Scotland* 1983 SLT 394. But the possibility of repeated applications under s. 124 rules out the *nobile officium* jurisdiction: *Windsor, Petitioner* 1994 SLT 604.

[218] *Sutherland Report*, para. 5.7.

[219] The author thanks Fred Thorne, Scottish Office for these statistics (letter dated 8 February 1999). See also Sutherland Report, paras. 5, 20–21. The list in full is at http://www.leeds.ac.uk/law/hamlyn/scot.htm. Up to 1972, there had only been three referrals: First Report of the Thomson Committee, *Criminal Appeals in Scotland* (Cmnd 5038, HMSO, Edinburgh, 1972) para. 46.

In the light of the arguments and experiences which had surrounded the English Criminal Appeal Act 1995, the Sutherland Committee recommended that there should be an independent referral body, along much the same lines and for much the same reasons (especially the principled argument of the separation of powers) as the Criminal Cases Review Commission.[220] Applications would normally be lodged by the convicted person, but it should be possible to pursue an appeal on behalf of a deceased person.[221] Its procedures and powers would also be very much on the English model, save that there was a firmer expectation that any investigations would be directed by the Crown Office rather than carried out 'in house'.[222] After consideration, the grounds for a referral would be where the Commission believes that a miscarriage of justice may have occurred and that it is in the interests of justice to make the reference.[223] One difference from England and Wales, justified by past and expected caseloads, would be the confinement of the Scottish body to solemn cases.[224]

The Government's initial reaction was negative. In its paper, *Crime and Punishment* in June 1996, it rejected the idea of a Scottish review body,[225] and this stance was also complacently reflected by Lord Chancellor Mackay when presenting the Crime and Punishment (Scotland) Bill:[226]

> Unlike in England, we have happily not had the widely publicised cases involving miscarriages of justice which have led to the setting up in England of the new Criminal Cases Review Commission.

However, the Scottish Criminal Cases Review Commission ('Scottish CCRC') was unexpectedly established by Part II of the Act,[227] following persistent parliamentary opposition in the days running up to prorogation prior to the General Election of 1997.[228] Under what becomes (by virtue of s. 25 of the 1997 Act) section 194C of the Criminal Procedure (Scotland) Act 1995, the Scottish CCRC can refer cases 'if they think fit' on grounds:

> that they believe—
> (a) that a miscarriage of justice may have occurred; and
> (b) that it is in the interests of justice that a reference should be made.

The referral does not have to await the exhaustion of appeal procedures,[229] but one assumes that it usually will. The body is empowered to take precognitions on oath under section 194H of the 1995 Act under warrant from a sheriff. In this way, it can compel oral statements from private sources, and this is backed by the powers

---

[220] *Sutherland Report*, para. 5.50.

[221] *Sutherland Report*, para. 5.61.

[222] *Sutherland Report*, paras. 5.65–72.

[223] *Sutherland Report*, para. 5.63. It follows that there would also be a power to recommend instead the exercise of the prerogative of mercy rather than to refer to a court: para. 5.69.

[224] *Sutherland Report*, para. 5.59. See also the fuller arguments in Scottish Office, *Sentencing and Appeals* (HMSO, Edinburgh, 1994) para. 7.55.

[225] *Crime and Punishment* (Cm 3302, HMSO, Edinburgh, 1996) para. 15.10.

[226] HL Debs. vol. 579 col. 190, 11 February 1997.

[227] Inserting ss. 194A-L of the 1995 Act.

[228] See HL Debs. vol. 579 col. 946, 19 March 1997; *Sunday Mail* 23 February 1997, p. 10.

[229] Compare *Sutherland Report*, para. 5.63.

to obtain documents under section 194I under order from the High Court. These are useful powers not possessed by the English equivalent.

The impact of the Scottish CCRC, which will start work in April 1999, is ultimately bounded by the performance of the Appeal Court to where cases will still be referred. Therefore, much will depend on whether the appellate bench is persuaded to change its narrow legalistic ways. Early evidence from the *Glasgow Two* case suggests it is too early to be confident that the scene has changed. In addition, it is arguable that valuable resources and time will be lost through the very process of establishment of the Scottish CCRC, whereas a unified United Kingdom Commission could have operated earlier and more effectively. Though Scotland has a distinct criminal process, it is not the case that its differences must be reflected in expensive offices and equipment or the reinvention of working systems, especially as there will be just seven part-time members to support.[230] So, the separation is most likely explained by reasons of historical symbolism rather than a determination to combat miscarriages of justice.

Conclusion

Many Scottish lawyers display a great deal of what might at best be described as complacency and at worst blind arrogance about the righteousness of their system.[231] Even in 1996, it was seriously contended by some that there were no significant problems within the appeals and post-appeals systems, with the assertion throughout that the existence of a public prosecutor as well as the rule about corroboration were all sufficient to avoid the creation of injustice.[232] A few judges have shown signs of being less sanguine, but even so, have continued to allow venerable due process restraints to be loosened through the pressures of crime control. The result is that the Scottish criminal process displays signs of drift and inconsistency. Three major pieces of legislation and several consultation papers have been produced, but the process has involved 'shallowness'[233] compared to the *Thomson* or even *Runciman Reports*. Whilst the occurrence of documented cases of miscarriage may have been, in comparison with the rest of the United Kingdom, a trickle rather than a torrent, this rate of production can be attributed to the happy absence of Irish terrorist cases and the less felicitous habit of denial of any blemish by the legal community especially at appeal and post-appeal level. It is by no means certain that the 1997 Act will effect a perception shift, for its trust in the

---

[230] Alistair Bonnington (BBC legal adviser); Professor Peter Duff (University of Aberdeen); the Very Rev Graham Forbes (Provost of St Mary's Cathedral, Edinburgh and a former lay inspector of constabulary); Andrew Gallen (solicitor and a member of the legal advisory group of the Scottish Consumer Council); Gerald Gordon (legal author and former Glasgow sheriff); and William Taylor (advocate and a member of the Criminal Injuries Compensation Board) plus, as chair, Professor Sheila McLean (University of Glasgow): *The Scotsman*, 4 December 1998, p. 10.

[231] Further evidence of this trait includes the near silence on the issue of miscarriages in legal journals (with some honourable exceptions, such as Professor Gerry Maher) and also by the very stunted training programme for the judiciary: Scottish Office, *Firm and Fair* (Cm 2600, HMSO, Edinburgh, 1994) para. 9.35; *Crime and Punishment* (Cm 3302, HMSO, Edinburgh, 1996) para. 7.18. A notable judicial exception is Lord McCluskey who played an extraordinarily active role in the debate on the 1997 Act. The author thanks Lord McCluskey for his observations on this chapter.

[232] *Sutherland Report*, para. 1.24, repeating the view of the Scottish Office, *Firm and Fair* (Cm 2600, HMSO, Edinburgh, 1994) para. 6.15 and of Lord Fraser, Scottish Office Minister, in HL Debs. vol. 559 col. 551, 29 November 1994.

[233] HL Debs. vol. 559 col. 565, 29 November 1994, Lord McCluskey.

Appeal Court is 'in defiance of past history'[234] and recent form. Aside from the appeals system, some other reforms have been undertaken, including the belated recognition by the courts that the rules on prosecution disclosure are indefensible. Nevertheless, the result is a piecemeal approach which creates major uncertainties and gaps. The root of many of the cases of miscarriages of justice which have been documented lies in the prosecuting authorities' growing reliance on confession evidence to secure convictions; the police's powers to obtain and record confessions continue to be disgracefully indulged by the courts and legislature.

For the future, there is some hope that a process of reform could be sparked by the passage of the Scotland Act 1998 and the advent of a Scottish Parliament. This possibility follows from the fact that Scottish criminal law and procedure are important symbols of nationhood. Its distinctiveness is enshrined in the Act of Union of 1707, which, by Article XIX, ensures 'That the Court of Session . . . And that the Court of Justiciary do . . . remain in all time coming . . .'. As a result, the High Court has political, if not legal, entrenchment, and it has been allowed to retain the final word on Scottish criminal law, so that the shaping and performance of criminal law and procedure remains 'linked to the history of the Scottish nation and national character.'[235] It follows that the Union Parliament has been very slow to intervene in radical ways which disrupt traditional features; if English reforms can be grafted on, then so be it, but major changes (such as PACE) have not been attempted. The hope now arises that a new Scottish forum, bolstered by a renewed national self-confidence, will be more able to accomplish change.[236] Like other small jurisdictions, it should be encouraged to study models from abroad (including England) and to have the confidence to say that Scottish ways are not always best. However, whether the Scottish Parliament and Executive will be ready to act is another matter, for it is equally possible that attachment to the 'nostalgic and romantic version'[237] of Scots law, as well as the powerful lobby of the largely self-satisfied legal community, will deter them from early action. Furthermore, the Westminster Parliament will remain a powerful player, since it can continue to legislate for Scotland and can be expected to continue to favour a crime control agenda.[238] In the event of hesitation under the Scotland Act, the Human Rights Act 1998 will surely blow away some of the dust which has settled on the system, especially around issues such as policing powers, access to solicitors and prosecution disclosure. The record of the Scottish judges on rights issues is again not inspiring, though it is true that in *T, Petitioner*,[239] they have now adopted the same approach to the Convention as in England and Wales. One way or another, there must be renewal so as to face up to the actual and potential occurrence of miscarriages of justice in Scotland.

---

[234] Scott, M., 'New criminal appeal provisions' 1997 *Scottish Law Times* 249 at p. 250.

[235] Farmer, L., *Criminal Law, Tradition and Legal Order* (Cambridge UP, 1997) at p. 22.

[236] See Lord Hope, 'Devolution and human rights' [1998] *European Human Rights Law Review* 367.

[237] Farmer, L., *Criminal Law, Tradition and Legal Order* (Cambridge UP, 1997) at p. 186.

[238] See s. 28(7) of the 1998 Act. Acts of the Scottish Parliament can affect Scottish criminal law and procedure (but for reserved matters, see ss. 29, 30, Sched. 4 para. 2(3), including matters already subject to Westminster legislation or mentioned in the Acts of Union (s. 37), save that the position of the High Court must be preserved (Sched. 5 para. 1(d)) and there are also some aspects of criminal law (such as drugs, firearms, national security and terrorism) which are to remain part of UK legislation (Sched. 5 Part II Head B).

[239] 1997 SLT 724. See Murdoch, J., 'Scotland and the European Convention' in Dickson, B. (ed.), *Human Rights and the European Convention* (Sweet & Maxwell, London, 1997).

17

The French Pre-Trial System

John Bell

In recent years, no European legal system has been content with its criminal procedure. The French review of its system of pre-trial investigation demonstrated a particular interest in the English adversarial system, while the English were contemplating the advantages of the investigating magistrate system.[1] In the end, the reforms of both systems have remained firmly in their traditional moulds, but the mutual understanding which recent debates have engendered will be important in an era of greater co-operation between judges, prosecutors and police within Europe.[2] No legal system will be able to avoid miscarriages of justice altogether, but it is important for lawyers of other systems to appreciate the points at which miscarriages are likely to occur so that they do not inadvertently contribute to them. Since the European Convention on Human Rights sets standards across Europe, it is important also to appreciate the ways in which different procedures can be equally successful in protecting the rights of the accused while permitting efficiency in the pursuit of offenders. The argument of this chapter will be that the central role played by a written file in the French pre-trial system is an important safeguard against miscarriages of justice since it renders the process more transparent and open to verification and account.

The interest of France to the common lawyer on the topic of preventing miscarriage lies principally in two aspects of its criminal justice system. First, professional judges, either as prosecutor (*procureur*) or as investigating magistrate (*juge d'instruction*) exert external control over police investigations and are themselves responsible for gathering evidence. Secondly, French criminal procedure is essentially written, thus enabling checking and challenge to materials used to establish guilt which are collected in the file (*dossier*) used by pre-trial, trial and appellate judges alike. Indeed, as Anton put it:[3]

---

[1] See Commission Justice Pénale et Droits de l'Homme, *Rapport sur la mise en état des affaires pénales* (Paris 1991) (hereafter Delmas-Marty Report); Leigh, L.H. and Zedner, L., *A Report on the Administration of Criminal Justice in the Pre-Trial Phase in France and Germany* (Royal Commission on Criminal Justice, Research Study No. 1; London, HMSO, 1992). For a valuable comparative debate, see Spencer, J. and Delmas-Marty, M. in Markesinis, B., *The Gradual Convergence* (Clarendon Press, Oxford 1994) ch. 2.

[2] As encouraged by the Treaty on European Union (Cm 1934, 1992) Title VI and the Amsterdam Treaty 1997 Art. 1.

The comparison between the French and Anglo-American trials is misleading for it is only a slight exaggeration to say that, while in England or in the US a *man* is on trial, in France it is a *dossier*.

The existence and use of the file is both a safeguard for the accused and a permanent record of what is said. It will be about the content of this file that most debate turns in the pre-trial stage. Although the French system is held out to be 'inquisitorial' in form, this is not a label the French would accept. They would rather see their system as having a mix of inquisitorial features (illustrated by the role of the investigating magistrate) with accusatorial features (such as the role of defence lawyers in formulating representations on the file and engaging in adversarial debate at the trial with the prosecution).[4]

The role of judges in the preliminary phases of the investigation of the offence, and the importance of the file throughout the proceedings give rise to a radical continuity between the various phases of the criminal process. One can identify three main phases: investigation (*enquête*), decision to prosecute and committal (*instruction*), and hearing and judgment. The continuity between phases lies in that the information from each stage forms part of the *file* which will form the ultimate basis of decision.

Miscarriages of justice can arise for a number of different reasons. In the first place, the evidence presented to a court can be defective. A modern example in France was of the 'Irishmen of Vincennes' in 1982 where policemen almost certainly planted weapons on a number of Irishmen, suspected of involvement with the IRA, staying in a hotel in Vincennes, and then charged them with gun-running. The policemen involved were eventually punished by the French courts.[5] A second problem with evidence occurs in respect of expert evidence. The adversarial approach of the English system makes the expert very much a person appointed by the police who is difficult to contradict.[6] As will be seen, the French situation is that the expert is appointed by the court, and is to that extent independent. On the other hand, the French judges do tend to rely on what the expert has found, and there is less of a culture critical to an expert's findings. A third problem lies in the context of interrogation of a suspect before trial, and the confessions which

---

[3] Anton, A., 'L'instruction criminelle' (1960) 9 *Am Jo Comp Law* 441 at p. 456. For an account of the importance of the file in a trial, see Johnson, C., 'Trial by dossier' (1992) 142 *New Law Journal* 249 and Sheehan, A., *Criminal Procedure in Scotland and France* (HMSO, Edinburgh, 1975) ch. 5. For instance, in the appeal of the police officers accused in the 'Irishmen of Vincennes' incident (see below footnote 5), witnesses were not heard despite defence protests on the ground that the Court of Appeal of Paris considered that it was 'neither useful nor necessary' to go beyond the file. Provided that the parties are heard at some stage, it does not matter that they do not submit all their representations at the formal trial: *Delta v France*, Appl. no. 11444/85, (1990) Ser. A, No. 191, (1993) 16 EHRR 574.

[4] Delmas-Marty Report, pp. 19 and 29. For an account of the French criminal justice system generally, see Vogler, R., *A Guide to the French Criminal Justice System* (Prisoners Abroad, London 1989) and West, A. *et al.*, *The French Legal System* (Fourmat, London 1992), ch. 5; also Trouille, H., 'A Look at French Criminal Procedure' [1994] *Criminal Law Review* 735.

[5] See *Le Monde*, 25 June 1991 and 26 September 1991. The successful charges against Michael Plunkett, Stephen King and Mary Reid, were reduced to suborning witnesses in that the police officers were instructed by the defendant superiors to hide the fact that the searches had been conducted in the absence of the accused in breach of procedural requirements. For background, see Holland, J. and McDonald, H., *INLA: Deadly Divisions* (Torc, Dublin, 1994) ch. 11.

[6] See Spencer, J.R., 'Court experts and expert witnesses: have we a lesson to learn from the French?' (1992) 45 *Current Legal Problems* 213.

may be made. The French system leaves interrogation predominantly to a judge, but, until recent reforms, has left the suspect with limited legal assistance in preparing for interrogations which may be, in practice, almost conclusive of guilt. For although a trial may involve rehearing of evidence (and there is no formal guilty plea), reliance will obviously be placed on what is said to the investigating magistrate. The role of the various judges in the criminal process may also pose problems for an accused, and the French jury is far less independent than the English one. It sits only in the very serious cases (some 2000 out of over 8 million criminal cases per year), and it sits with three judges. In one high profile case, Omar Raddad in February 1994, the defence complained that the judge's interventions swayed the jury members to convict the accused, even though the evidence against him was questionable.[7] Perverse verdicts are really out of the question. The only perverse decisions will come from judges themselves.[8] Finally, the conduct of cases by counsel may be less of a problem in France in that the day in court is far less important than in England. The preparation of the file is a significant part of the process, and will typically resolve many of the problems of criminal cases.

The French system underwent a number of reforms in 1993. The reforms of January 1993 under the Socialist Government were reversed in part under the subsequent right-wing Government in August 1993. The speed of change reflects the conflict which often arises between law and order and civil liberties, as well as the constraints imposed by public expenditure restrictions.[9]

Preliminary Points on the French system

Personnel

The significant actors in the French criminal process discussed here are the judicial police, prosecutors, judges, and lawyers. The judicial police are only one of a number of police forces. This category covers a separate criminal investigation force set up on a national level (National Police) or in small towns (*Gendarmerie*). Officers of this force have the powers relevant to criminal investigations. In addition, there are administrative, traffic, and frontier police forces, while telephone tapping is conducted by a separate police force (*Renseignements Généraux*). The judicial police conduct the investigation of minor offences on their own. In more serious cases, this will be done under the control of the *procureur* or the investigating magistrate. In practice, their control can be rather formal until the police produce a suspect, with a delegation of authority (*commission rogatoire*) being given by those superiors to the police in many cases. This is especially true

---

[7] On this case, see also Trouille, H., 'A look at French criminal procedure' [1994] *Criminal Law Review* 735, at note 29. For further discussion of the French jury see Munday, R., 'Jury trial, Continental style' (1993) 13 *Legal Studies* 204, 'What do the French think of their Jury?' (1995) 15 *Legal Studies* 65.

[8] For example, after members of Parliament granted an amnesty to those guilty of electoral funding irregularities, some judges delivered what can only be described as perverse verdicts. For instance, on 26 April 1990, the *tribunal correctionnel* of Vannes appealed to 'a recent development in the notion of public policy' to justify the imposition of a 30F fine on a woman convicted of fiscal fraud of over 700,000F. Other judges followed suit by releasing from detention a number of persons accused of crimes against property (see *Le Monde*, 4 and 8 May 1990).

[9] See Field, S. and West, A., 'A tale of two reforms: French defence rights and police powers in transition' (1995) 6 *Criminal Law Forum* 473.

of most ordinary criminal offences in which only the *procureur* will be involved in the pre-trial process. As Leigh and Zedner remark, 'the reality of many of these cases probably differs little from the reality in England and Wales save that the defence may be less favoured'.[10]

The *procureur* is a member of the judiciary who specialises in criminal prosecution. Because the role is judicial, he is under the Minister of Justice, whilst the police are under the Minister of the Interior. He or she decides to prosecute and conducts the case in court. In the pre-trial process, the *procureur* has powers to direct and supervise police investigations, and to interview witnesses or the accused. But, in some cases it will be necessary to call in the investigating magistrate, another member of the judiciary, assigned to this post. His or her main functions are in relation to serious offences and include powers to direct and supervise police investigations, but he or she may also issue search and arrest warrants in both serious and non-serious cases. He or she also directs the *procureur* in serious cases about the decision to prosecute. (The final decision remains formally that of the *procureur.*) The investigating magistrate will take charge either immediately or within a short period (at most 21 days) in the investigation of serious offences. The *Chambre d'accusation*, composed of three judges from the regional court of appeal, takes committal decisions in the most serious cases (*crimes*[11]), but also hears challenges to validity of pre-trial proceedings.

Trial judges will be a single judge in the lowest criminal court, the *tribunal de police*, three judges in the normal serious crimes court, the *tribunal correctionnel*, and in very serious criminal cases, the *cour d'assises* is composed of three judges and nine jurors in a single panel. In terrorist and military cases, the *cour d'assises* is composed of a panel of seven judges.[12]

Appeals are heard from the *tribunal de police* and the *tribunal correctionnel* by the regional court of appeal. The appeal takes the form of a rehearing based on the file, though witnesses are not normally heard at this stage. In the case of decisions of the *cour d'assises*, there is no appeal, except on a point of law to the *Cour de cassation*, the highest court in France, which also hears appeals on a point of law from the regional courts of appeal.

Among the many legal professions in France, the principal person involved in criminal cases is an *avocat*, who can advise and make representations on behalf of his or her client in pre-trial proceedings, as well as at trial or on appeal.

Content of the File (Dossier)

The French criminal file is made up of four elements which show that the courts judge the person, not the action. The first section contains evidence, i.e. records of

---

[10] Leigh, L.H. and Zedner, L., *A Report on the Administration of Criminal Justice in the Pre-Trial Phase in France and Germany* (Royal Commission on Criminal Justice, Research Study No. 1; London, HMSO, 1992) p. 14.

[11] The Penal code distinguishes between three classes of offences. The most serious (such as murder) are *crimes*, tried by the *cour d'assises*. The next most serious are *délits* (such as theft), tried by the *tribunal correctionnel*. The distinction between these two has much in common with the old common law distinction between felonies and misdemeanours. The third class is that of *contraventions*, which are typically regulatory offences (failure to carry identity documents, failure to observe many traffic regulations, and so on), and are tried by the *tribunal de police*.

[12] A typical case for this procedure would be the prosecution of Basque terrorists: see the Bidart case, *Le Monde*, 31 May 1991.

police investigation, questioning of witnesses and accused by police, *procureur* and investigating magistrate, expert reports, and so on. The second section contains detention records, showing when the accused was held, for how long, as well as medical reports which may have been made during this period. The third section is more general. It contains any personal and character details, such as criminal record, family and psychological history, including material that would be in social inquiry reports. Such information is used in pre-trial and trial procedures, even when it is not formally adduced as evidence.[13] There is no sense in France that it should be withheld until sentencing. The fourth section contains formal documents, such as copies of warrants.

The inclusion of reports or matters on a file may be challenged, for example on grounds that it has been obtained irregularly. This avoids the need to challenge admissibility at trial. Irregularity during the *instruction* is more likely to be excluded than at an earlier stage.

Pre-trial Procedures

The French system grants different powers to the police and judges depending on the nature of the offence at stake. In the ordinary procedure (*enquête préliminaire*), the police have limited powers. They can neither arrest nor search without instituting a judicial inquiry (*enquête judiciaire*), thus involving the investigating magistrate who has wider powers, but the police are then constrained to act on his authority. All the same, the power to detain a person in order to verify their identity is often invoked. Under art. 78–2 of the Code of Criminal Procedure, it is limited to where the person detained was about to commit a crime or to threaten the safety of persons or property, or where he or she has information concerning the investigation of a *crime* or *délit*. (Since 1993, the *procureur* may designate an area for a short time in which the police can require any person to prove their identity.[14]) But this does give some scope, along with powers to check the papers of foreigners, to detain suspected criminals where the flagrant procedure cannot be invoked. By contrast, in the flagrant procedure (*enquête flagrante*), there are wide police powers in the early days of the inquiry, albeit under control of *procureur*, but the investigating magistrate must be brought in to take over the case as soon as feasible. A flagrant offence is defined under art. 53 of the Code of Criminal Procedure as either a *crime* or *délit* which is being or has just been committed;[15] or where a person is found in possession of objects or there is other evidence that he has been involved in such an offence; or where the head of a household requires the police or *procureur* to investigate such an offence.

There are special terrorist and drugs procedures, under which the police have wider powers of search and detention, even where the offence is not flagrant. Under the Law of 3 September 1986, 'terrorism' is defined as individual or collective acts

---

[13] See the excerpts from a trial in Sheehan, A., *Criminal Procedure in Scotland and France* (HMSO, Edinburgh, 1975) pp. 211–14.

[14] Articles 78–2 and 78–3 of the Penal Code as amended by the *loi* of 10 August 1993.

[15] The central requirement is that the case is fresh, hence a rape is still flagrant if reported 28 hours after the event: Cass.crim. 26 Feb. 1991, Bartoli, D. 1991. IR 115. The procedure for flagrant offences is invoked by the officers of the *police judiciaire* (the equivalent of the CID) in 85 per cent of instances in which they are involved: Pradel, J., *Procédure pénale* (8th edn., Cujas, Paris 1995) para. 369 (hereafter Pradel).

involving certain offences against persons or property, or with arms or explosives with the object of causing serious public disorder by intimidation or terror.

L'Instruction

The investigating magistrate is a figure from the Jacobin State because he is close, in reality and in the imagination, to a functionary bearing the authority of the central State, able himself to investigate and to judge as did the criminal lieutenant and the intendant [of the Ancien Régime] in the past . . . The ideal of the investigating magistrate is of the man alone, empowered to manage a judicial situation, a search for the truth and a procedure, as a unity. By contrast, the accusatorial procedure emphasises the search by way of a process, the two-sided debate, the equality, at least in theory, of arms between the prosecution and defence.[16]

This description, given by leading criminal judges, brings out the peculiar position of the investigating magistrate within the French system. The secret procedure of the seventeenth century is now judicialised, turning this judge increasingly into the supervisor of the process, rather than the principal investigator. The role of the investigating magistrate is diminishing in France. In 1960, such a judge dealt with over 20 per cent of criminal cases; in 1990 a mere 8 per cent. All the same, his or her role remains significant for serious crimes.[17]

The judicialisation of the process has only gradually been accompanied by appropriate safeguards for the rights of the accused. It took until 1897 for some rights of the accused to be built into the system, permitting the suspect's lawyer to sit in on the later hearings by the investigating magistrate. The reforms of 1993 have given the defence lawyer a status almost equivalent to that of the prosecutor. He or she can now have access to the file at least four working days before any questioning of his client by the investigating magistrate and at any other time, providing this does not compromise the proper performance of the duties of the investigating magistrate. The accused is also able to challenge the content of the file during the investigation. The system thus depends both on the investigatory powers of the investigating magistrate and the protections afforded to the suspect.

Function of the Investigating Magistrate

The basic task of the *instruction* process is to decide whether there is a sufficient case to answer to warrant committal of the suspect to the courts for trial. The tasks of the investigating magistrate are specified in art. 81 of the Code of Criminal

---

[16] Bellet, P., Calvet, H. and Soulez-Larivière, D., *Libération*, 10 Dec. 1990.

[17] M. Delmas-Marty notes that this situation gives predominant power to the prosecutor and the police in all but the most serious cases: 'In the end, it is the prosecutor who is the wheel without which the machinery of the *instruction préliminaire* is unable to go round' (in Markesinis, B., *The Gradual Convergence* (Clarendon Press, Oxford 1994) p. 53). This position is confirmed by statistics. In 1996, 5,185,495 cases were referred to the *procureurs* in France. Of these, 4,114,672 did not lead to a prosecution and were *classés sans suite* ('filed for no further action'), although, among these, 90,128 cases were dealt with by alternatives to prosecution. Only 520,235 cases were directed to the courts and of these 43,671 were sent to the *juge d'instruction*. In addition to these criminal prosecutions, 9,440,058 fixed penalty fines were imposed, mainly for traffic offences. Figures from the Web-site of the Ministry of Justice: (http://www.justice.gouv.fr).

Procedure (CPP) of 1959: 'the investigating magistrate undertakes all investigating acts which he judges necessary to the revelation of the truth'. These acts will include gathering evidence, for example by ordering expert tests or reports, such as about ballistics, by reconstruction of the crime, or by directing further police investigation. In order to preserve evidence, even the *police judiciaire* may order expert reports. Experts are chosen from a list of court experts. Their reports can then be commented on if the case proceeds to the *instruction* phase.[18] Warrants may be issued for arrest or for searches, and this may include telephone tapping.[19] They will also involve formal questioning of witnesses, either by taking formal statements from them one by one or even staging a confrontation of witnesses to elicit truth. Most importantly, the investigating magistrate will question the suspect. There will be a first formal hearing (*l'interrogatoire de première comparution*) both to check details and to inform the suspect of the case against him and of his rights. Until 1993, no lawyer used to be present, but now under art. 116 of the Code of Criminal Procedure, the suspect is entitled to have a lawyer present. If he is only made aware that he is under suspicion at the first formal hearing, he is entitled immediately to telephone a lawyer and have him attend. At subsequent hearings, a lawyer will be present and the purpose is to get to the truth, and may involve challenging the suspect on statements by witnesses. The investigating magistrate then produces a report which sets out his or her own view on what should be done and instructs the *procureur* about the next steps to be taken in the case.

The investigating magistrate is seised of a case by the requisition from the *procureur*. This defines the ambit of the investigation *in rem*, and the magistrate will need further instructions from the *procureur* to deal with new offences turned up in the course of the investigation. Unlike the English magistrates in committals prior to the Criminal Procedure and Investigations Act 1996, the French investigating magistrate is not limited *in personam*, as she or he may investigate both persons named in the requisition or others whom they suspect of the offence. Indeed, there may be no person named by the procureur in the initial reference. A feature common to most civil law systems is the right of the victim of the crime to initiate the criminal process both to secure a criminal conviction and to obtain civil redress from the criminal court. A requisition to the investigating magistrate may thus come not only from the *procureur* but also from the civil party.

The investigating magistrate is a single individual appointed by the president of the *tribunal de grande instance*. Numbers are not large – about 10 per cent of the private and criminal law judiciary. Since they are divided over the country, they

---

[18] For a critical comment on the operation of experts in France, see Spencer, J.R., in Markesinis, B., *The Gradual Convergence* (Clarendon Press, Oxford 1994) pp. 40–43.

[19] The French law on telephone tapping has been strongly influenced by the European Court of Human Rights. Such tapping has been gradually permitted by the judges in the 1980s: Ass. plén., 24 Nov 1989, D. 1990, 34. Powers were revised in the light of the decisions of the ECHR of 24 April 1990 in *Kruslin* v *France*, Appl. no. 11801, Ser. A. vol. 176–B, (1990) 12 EHRR 547 and *Huvig* v *France*, Appl. no. 11105, Ser. A vol. 176-B, (1990) 12 EHRR 528. It was laid down that telephone tapping must not be conducted by artifice and its results are open to inspection and comment by the suspect and any other party: see e.g. Cass. crim. 17 Nov 1990, D. 1990 IR 221, and Cass. crim. 6 and 26 Nov 1990, D. 1991 IR 11 and 26. The Law of 10 July 1991 provides further safeguards and sets more detailed limits on the exercise of such a power: see Pettiti, L.E., 'Les Ecoutes téléphoniques et le droit français', AJDA 1992, 35. Current attitudes are well illustrated by Cass. crim 27 Feb. 1996, D. 1996, 346 in which telephone tapping undertaken by way of provocation of an offence and without the prior authorisation of an investigating magistrate was struck down as unlawful and the evidence excluded.

are as few as five in some towns.[20] The nominee may be removed on grounds of the good administration of justice where the *procureur* or one of the parties requests, but reasons must be given for such a decision (art. 84 CPP). The same power also exists in the *Cour de Cassation*. This was used in 1996 when the investigation of terrorist offences in Corsica was removed from the local courts to the Paris *Cour d'Appel*, provoking much criticism in judicial circles.

The three principal characteristics of the *instruction* process are that it is written and secret, but it is now subject to an *inter partes* debate (*le principe du contradictoire*). All the statements of the accused or witnesses are recorded in a *procès verbal*, and so the file is built up. In this way, every act of procedure is open to inspection. At any stage, the parties, through their lawyers, are permitted to submit written observations which are then put on file (art. 199, para. 2 CPP). The secrecy of the proceedings is an obligation essentially on the magistrate and the *procureur*, as well as the press.[21] They are not allowed to reveal details of the investigation to third parties. Although conceived as a safeguard of public order, it obviously also serves the function of privacy. In practice, however, the suspect and his lawyer frequently make statements to the press about their version of events. As long as they do not reveal information gleaned from the file, they will not be in breach of the duty of secrecy. In the section on the accused's rights, we will deal with the issue of how far the procedure is open to debate. The additional feature that strikes the English lawyer is the relative informality of the procedure. Questioning takes place in the magistrate's chambers and follows no set form. There are no time limits, and the process can take as long as is considered necessary. It is for the magistrate to be satisfied that everything has been covered for a decision on prosecution to be taken.

The most disturbing feature of the French procedure is the use made of the *commission rogatoire*. Under the current art. 81, para. 3, 'if the investigating magistrate is unable to carry out all the investigatory measures, he may give a *commission rogatoire* to officers of the judicial police so that they may carry out such investigatory acts as are necessary in the circumstances subject to the rules laid down for them'. Certain measures cannot be delegated in this way to the police but only to another judge, especially the issuing of an arrest warrant or questioning the accused (art. 152, para. 2, CPP). Such powers have been upheld by the *Conseil Constitutionnel* in relation to telephone tapping powers, even where the persons in question were telecommunications officials with the same status as officers of the judicial police.[22] Since there are so few investigating magistrates in France, it is impossible that they could cope even with the small proportion of cases which fall to them. It is necessary in most cases for the work to be undertaken by the police. In that searches, formal questioning of witnesses, requesting expert reports and so on may well be done by police officers, and yet will appear on the file which forms

---

[20] For discussion of numbers, see Boyer Chammard, G., *Les Magistrats* (Paris 1985) p. 75; Perrot, R., *Institutions judiciaires* (3rd edn., Cujas, Paris 1989) para. 168. These estimate that there are under 80 investigating magistrates for Paris and the caseload in a place like Marseilles might be 100 cases a year.

[21] The press is liable to punishment for breach of art. 38 of the Law of 29 July 1881 which prohibits the publication of documents in the criminal process before the public hearing: see TGI Paris, 5 Feb. 1996, *Libération*, D. 1996, 230 and see generally Chesterman, M., 'Contempt: In the Common Law, but not in the Civil Law' (1997) 46 *International and Comparative Legal Quarterly* 521.

[22] See CC decision no 90–281 DC of 27 December 1990, *Telecommunications Law*, RFDC 1991, 118; Bell, J., *French Constitutional Law* (Clarendon Press, Oxford, 1992) p. 148.

the basis for a judicial decision, a basic weakness in the control exercised by the investigating magistrate emerges, and this was noted by the Delmas-Marty report in 1990.[23] Whereas that report wanted the investigating magistrate to exercise control over all interference with liberty, this has been achieved, as will be seen, only to a limited extent. In reality, the police have more power than in England, for they are exercising the powers of a judge, but are subject to less control in that they do not require prior authorisation for searches. It is in this area that the conflict is most apparent between the theory of the system as one directed by the judge and the reality of personnel and resources.

Rights of the Accused

The rights of the accused are really the product of the last hundred years since the *loi Constans* of 8 December 1897 gave the suspect's lawyer access to the investigating magistrate's chambers and to the file. Following the 1993 reforms, the defence is more or less on an equal footing with the prosecution. But all hinges on the proactive approach of the lawyer in the process and his or her ability to read the file and anticipate issues which are emerging.

The principal safeguard of the suspect is therefore to have a lawyer. Once a person has been formally put under investigation, then he or she is informed of rights of access to a lawyer.

La mise en examen (formerly called *l'inculpation*) is a crucial stage in the pre-trial process. From that moment, a person becomes a suspect in the eyes of the law and not merely in the eyes of the police or the civil party. The person is formally under investigation with a view to prosecution, and the investigating magistrate prepares the case for a committal. To be made a suspect, there must be 'serious and concordant indications' of a person's criminal liability. At that stage, the rights of the accused become stronger, notably the right to silence and the right to a lawyer. *Mise en examen* does not automatically lead to prosecution. In 1996, there were 64,317 persons *mise en examen* of which 21 per cent were not prosecuted.[24]

The routes to this stage can be various. It may be that the *procureur* refers the case to the investigating magistrate with a person specifically named as suspect. On the other hand, the investigating magistrate may have become involved in questioning witnesses and then forms a view that a particular individual is a suspect. On either route, there has to be a moment when an individual is notified that he or she is under investigation (*mise en examen*). The normal view is that a person is under investigation no later than the formal first appearance before the investigating magistrate and is then informed of his or her rights to silence and to a lawyer.

This formal interview may not be the first time the person has been questioned by the investigating magistrate. Well-established case law requires that the

---

[23] See report p. 38 where it describes some of such investigation as 'secret, written, not open to both sides and more or less coercive'. Foreign commentators have noted this in identifying weaknesses within the French system: see Goldstein, A.S. and Marcus, M., 'The myth of judicial supervision in three "Inquisitorial" systems: France, Italy and Germany' (1977) 87 *Yale Law Journal* 240. Compare Langbein, J.H. and Weinreb, L.L., 'Continental criminal procedure' (1978) 87 *Yale Law Journal* 1549.

[24] Ministry of Justice (http://www.justice.gouv fr/chiffres/penale.htm).

magistrate should not inculpate a person 'until he has clarified whether the person did take part in the incriminating act in circumstances such as to give rise to his criminal liability'.[25] Nowadays the requisition presented by either the *procureur* or the civil party to the investigating magistrate may well name a suspect directly or indirectly. This is not necessarily sufficient to justify the inculpation of the person named. It may well be necessary for the investigating magistrate to check whether the allegations are substantiated. This will be the case particularly when the requisition is filed by the civil party. But to protect a potential suspect, art. 104 CPP requires the investigating magistrate to explain to the person named in the requisition that they are so named and that he has the right to be heard as a witness (without a lawyer) or as an 'assisted witness' (with a lawyer), or to be put under investigation immediately, with all the rights that confers.[26]

In order to avoid the device of interviewing a person as a witness rather than questioning the person as a suspect, with the formal constraints which that entails, art. 105 CPP provides that neither the investigating magistrate nor a policeman acting under a *commission rogatoire* may hear a person as a witness where there are serious and concordant indications of guilt with the design of impeding that person's rights of defence.[27] The sanction is not an automatic nullity of the questioning record, but the deliberate intention which the article requires would almost always lead to such a nullity. Such a protection does not apply to police questioning before a person has been referred to the investigating magistrate or *procureur*. Here it is permitted for the police to continue questioning, even after the person has made a confession.[28]

Rights of the suspect in detention. A suspect may be in pre-trial custody in two ways. First, during the preliminary investigation, he or she may be in police custody (*garde à vue*). Secondly, after *mise en examen*, the suspect may be remanded in custody (*détention provisoire*), usually in prison. The rights of the suspect are significantly different at these two stages, and it would be fair to say that, until *mise en examen*, the suspect lacks many of the rights which would be expected in the common law world.

Garde à vue Police custody is a major moment in the French criminal process. In 1990, some 347,107 persons were held in police custody, a figure which represents a 26 per cent increase on 1981. By the end of the process, substantial evidence will have been gathered which then is forwarded to the *procureur* and the investigating magistrate. Put by way of understatement in the explanatory memorandum introducing the criminal procedure Bill of 1992, the Ministry of Justice has stated that 'as far as the person kept in custody is concerned, his rights are very rudimentary. Furthermore, the role of the *procureur* in the control over custody is not asserted with adequate force.'. Leigh and Zedner note that 'while nothing in French law requires the overuse of detention, a tendency to do so seems

---

[25] Cass. crim, 8 Dec. 1899, D. 1903.1.457, note Le Pottevin.

[26] The intermediate category of 'assisted witness' was introduced by the Law of 30 Dec. 1987, but is not seen as conferring many advantages on the potential suspect: Pradel, J., 'De la réforme de l'instruction préparatoire', D. 1989 Chap. 1.

[27] See, e.g. Cass. crim 26 Sept. 1986, D. 1987 Somm.82.

[28] See Pradel, para. 433, and Cass. crim 17 July 1964, JCP 1965 II 14038, note PC. On the exclusion of evidence and the abuse of police powers, see Pakter, W., 'Exclusionary rules in France, Germany, and Italy' (1985) 9 *Hastings International and Comparative Law Review* 1, pp. 8–14, 28.

deeply ingrained in the legal culture and doubtless derives from a desire not to release a suspect until the truth has been ascertained'.[29] Recent reforms have sought to control the police more and to give the detainee access to legal advice. But the outcome is still a limited protection.

There is no power of arrest in the ordinary procedure (*enquête préliminaire*). But, under art. 78–2 CPP, the police may detain a person if it is necessary to verify his or her identity where he or she was about to commit a crime or where there is a threat to the safety of persons or property or to public order. All the same, the police do have a power under art. 77, para. 1, CPP to detain 'any person' where necessary for the investigation of an offence. In flagrant offences, in addition to a power of arrest, there is a power under arts. 62 and 63 CPP for the police to detain anyone whom they consider able to provide information, or against whom there are serious signs of guilt. Such detention in custody may continue for up to 24 hours, though it may be continued for a further 24 hours by the *procureur*.

The Delmas-Marty Commission was concerned that, although custody was formally approved by the *procureur*, in practice he intervened after the event and often by telephone. Since 1993, the *procureur* must be notified immediately of a detention, but there is no requirement of a formal appearance. But it is provided that an extension should only be authorised in a non-flagrant case where there are exceptional circumstances. There has thus been only a limited improvement, since the investigating magistrate still does not control this aspect of the process.

The police must keep a record under art. 64 CPP of the reasons for the detention, when it began and ended, duration of questioning and rest periods between questioning. Such records then go into the file used by the investigating and trial judges. But it is clear that there is no prohibition on the police questioning a suspect, unless he or she objects.

A persistent criticism by the French legal profession and academics is the absence of any right of the person detained to a lawyer. By contrast, there has long been a right to request a medical examination after 24 hours. Article 63–4 CPP now provides that, after 24 hours, the detainee is entitled to request an interview with a lawyer and to be facilitated in obtaining a lawyer through the head of the local Bar. The entitlement is to a private interview of up to 30 minutes. The lawyer is still not permitted to be present at the interview with the police. If the lawyer makes allegations of any irregularities in the questioning, these are sent to the *procureur* as soon as possible. Under the general implementing circular, the detainee is entitled to request an interpreter to facilitate conversation with the lawyer. This is a valuable, but limited reform. By the time the lawyer is brought in, a significant amount of questioning will have taken place and pressure will have been exerted. Even if this has not already achieved results, it is not clear that the interview with the lawyer will prevent the suspect giving in under the further questioning which will follow. The suspect has also been given the right to inform someone that he or she is being detained by the police.

The *procureur* will normally interview a person before making a requisition to the investigating magistrate. This interview is without a lawyer. The *Conseil Constitutionnel* upheld this in its *Security and Liberty* decision of 1981 on the

[29] Leigh, L.H. and Zedner, L., *A Report on the Administration of Criminal Justice in the Pre-Trial Phase in France and Germany* (Royal Commission on Criminal Justice, Research Study No. 1; London, HMSO, 1992) p. 53.

ground that, since the *procureur* was a member of the judiciary, this provided adequate safeguards for the suspect.[30]

Détention provisoire   The 1808 Code of Criminal Investigation had a presumption in favour of the detention of a suspect during the inquiries of the investigating magistrate. In its current form (since the Law of 9 July 1984), art. 137 CPP provides that 'the accused shall remain free unless, for reasons of the necessities of the investigation or as a security measure, he is submitted to *contrôle judiciaire*[31] or, exceptionally, he is remanded in provisional custody.'. Provisional custody is very significant in France. In 1970, there were 10,840 such remand prisoners (as we would call them) in French jails (37.5 per cent of the prison population). By 1994, the number had risen to 21,143 (44 per cent). The average period of detention also rose from 2.3 months in 1969 to 3.2 months since 1984.[32] In part, the numbers of remand prisoners and the period of their detention is accounted for by appeals and procedural delays outside the control of the investigating magistrate. Nevertheless, delay is also caused by the slowness of the investigatory procedure. The average period for investigation by the investigating magistrate is 16.1 months (16.7 months for *crimes*).[33] It is thus crucial to examine the safeguards for the rights of the prisoner.

The investigating magistrate is required to hear the affected parties before taking a decision to remand a person into provisional custody (art. 145 CPP).[34] The decision can only be justified by the need to preserve evidence, to protect public order or the accused or witnesses and the investigating magistrate must give reasons for a detention. On the other hand, he or she does not have to give reasons for refusing a prosecution request to remand the suspect in custody. Furthermore, there are time-limits on the use of custody. In the case of *crimes* the period is a year, though this can be renewed. In the case of *délits* the period is four months, which can be extended once by a further four months. Since 1987, a maximum length for custody in the case of first-time offenders accused of *délits* and not liable to more than five years' imprisonment has been set at six months in total, and for other offenders at two years. These periods are still long, and France has been found in breach of Article 5 of the European Convention on Human Rights in a number of recent cases for excessive periods of detention. As the European Court of Human Rights pointed out in *Tomasi v France*, the existence of reasonable suspicion that a person has committed an offence is a necessary condition to justify his or her detention, but after a period of time, it cannot be a sufficient justification without other reasons in support.[35]

---

[30] Paragraph 30 of CC decision no. 80–127 DC of 19 and 20 January 1981, in Bell, J., *French Constitutional Law* (Clarendon Press, Oxford 1992), p. 312.

[31] *Contrôle judiciaire* imposes conditions on freedom, such as might be imposed as bail conditions in this country.

[32] Figures drawn from Pradel, p. 526.

[33] Ministry of Justice (http://www.justice.gouv fr/chiffres/penale.htm).

[34] Indeed, the presence of the *procureur* with the investigating magistrate after the suspect has gone out may be treated as vitiating the decision to remand the suspect in custody: Cass. crim, 19 Sept. 1990, D. 1991, 91, note Mayer.

[35] *Tomasi v France*, Appl. no. 12850/87, (1992) Ser. A, No 241–A, (1993) 15 EHRR 1: here a detention of nearly five years and seven months before acquittal was held to be unjustified. For further examples of findings of excessive detention see, for example, *Letellier v France*, Appl. no. 12369/86, Ser. A, No. 207, (1992) 14 EHRR 83 (2 years and 10 months); *Birou v France*, Appl. no. 13319/87, Ser. A, No. 232–B, (1992) 14 EHRR 738 (5 years and 3 months); *Kemmache v France*, Appl. no.

Questioning The lawyers of the parties (prosecution, defence, and civil party) have the right to attend, or at least to see the results of, any questioning. They are entitled to be present for the questioning of the suspect and the civil party, and may even suggest questions to be asked. Under art. 102 CPP, witnesses are heard by the investigating magistrate and his clerk alone.[36] The material produced from each question session before the investigating magistrate is reduced to writing and is signed by the person(s) questioned. Comments may then be submitted by any party on what has been said or on questions which have not been asked. These formal records and comments are kept on file and will be used at committal and trial. The parties may also ask for further expert reports to be made (art. 156, para. 1 CPP).

From the first interview, the suspect has a right to a lawyer. The lawyer has to be informed at least five days before any proposed interview of the suspect by the investigating magistrate and has a right to see all the file at least four days before each hearing. Thus, there are no surprises, and the lawyer can prepare the case with the accused.

Nullity of L'instruction

The French law on the consequences of illegalities in the pre-trial process is complex and difficult to operate. In part this is due to the substantive rules which apply, but it is also due to the intricate procedure by which illegalities are challenged. The normal process involves an application to strike out offending items in the file, and this will take place before trial. Challenges may also be made at trial to the inclusion of material on file. But the trial court cannot raise a procedural irregularity of its own motion unless the ground is one of lack of jurisdiction.[37] This might arise where an investigating magistrate was not territorially competent to authorise a search.

Under art. 173 CPP, all parties will be able to challenge the inclusion of material on the file during the course of the investigation by the investigating magistrate. Nullity is imposed either for breach of a substantial formality or for breach of any provision which infringes the rights of the party concerned (either defence or civil party). But after 20 days from the closure of the investigation process, all procedural irregularities will be purged and will be unchallengeable (art. 175 CPP). Unless a suspect is competently advised by a lawyer, both the present and future positions could result in a procedural irregularity in the pre-trial period going unchallenged.

When dealing with illegally obtained evidence, it is important to identify the way in which it is illegally obtained. Where an irregularity occurs in the preliminary police investigation, this cannot be annulled since it has no formal status.[38] In general, only those acts which are undertaken after the *instruction* has commenced are liable to be annulled. (Though, of course, there are some matters for which the law does prescribe nullity, such as interviewing a person as a witness in order to defeat the supect's rights of defence (art. 105 CPP, discussed above).)

14992/85, Ser. A, No. 218, (1992) 14 EHRR 520 (8 years and 6 months).

[36] The presence of the *procureur* does not invalidate such proceedings, provided that he does not intervene in the questioning and there is no prejudice to the rights of the accused or the civil party: Cass. crim 19 June 1990, D. 1991, 15, note Coste.

[37] Cass. crim 25 Feb. 1991, *Dometz*, D. 1991 IR 158.

[38] Cass. crim 12 March 1898, D. 1898.1.208.

Evidence gathered as a result of illegal searches, as well as any consequent confessions, may well be annulled.[39] In principle, the evidence gathered at the investigation stage has no binding probative force. The trial judge(s) (and jury) can make of them what they like. An attempt to nullify evidence arising from irregular detention was introduced into the Code of Criminal Procedure in 1981, but removed in 1983. Thus, in the ordinary procedure, the irregularity of acts of investigation arising from abuse of *garde à vue* or illegal searches does not lead to their nullity and to the exclusion of evidence 'unless it is shown that the inquiry into and the determination of the truth have thereby been fundamentally compromised'.[40]

During the *instruction* by the investigating magistrate, irregular decisions may be taken, and the resulting evidence may be included on file. Some specific legal provisions do prescribe nullity as a sanction for breach, such as those dealing with searches and seizures, as well as bodily searches and the notification of lawyers of interviews with their suspect client (arts. 56, 57, 59, 76, 95 and 96 CPP). But there is also art. 172 CPP which provides that there shall also be nullity in the case of substantial breaches of other provisions concerning the *instruction*, especially where there are breaches of the rights of the defence. This creates the potential for a wide category of nullities, which has been restricted by the Law of 6 August 1975. By virtue of that law, art. 802 CPP now provides:

> In cases of procedures prescribed by the law on pain of nullity or of failure to observe substantial formalities, except those for which article 105 makes provision, any court, including the *Cour de cassation*, which receives an application for nullity or which raises such an illegality of its own motion, shall not order a nullity unless the breach has the effect of infringing the interests of the party in question.

As Pradel points out, this significantly reduces the scope of nullity.[41] Only where there is a public interest (for example in judges keeping within their own jurisdictional area), or a private interest (such as prejudice to the accused), will a nullity be ordered.

The overall position is, thus, that illegally obtained evidence may well not be excluded from the file, and the real sanctions, if they operate, are frequently only disciplinary.

Appeals

The pre-trial procedure is of the greatest sophistication in serious offences (*crimes*) because they are tried by the *cour d'assises* from which there is no appeal, unlike in other criminal cases. Only the civil party may contest an acquittal by the *cour*

---

[39] Pakter, W., 'Exclusionary rules in France, Germany, and Italy' (1985) 9 *Hastings International and Comparative Law Review* 1 at pp 34–7, e.g. Cass. crim 21 July 1982, JCP 1982 IV 346. A much criticised example is the decision of the *Cour de cassation* to quash an alcohol test conducted by the police when they were 'invited' to enter a man's house after the legal hour for searches (i.e. after 9 p.m.): *Le Monde*, 21–22 July 1991.

[40] Cass. crim, 17.3.1960, *Kissari*, JCP 1960 II 11641; Pakter, W., 'Exclusionary rules in France, Germany, and Italy' (1985) 9 *Hastings International and Comparative Law Review* 1 at p. 13; Pradel, paras. 502, 503. The evidence of parties is not excluded unless it has been obtained by unlawful means: see Cass. crim 15 June 1993, Bull. crim no. 210.

[41] Para. 503.

d'assises, and this is because of the consequences for the person's civil action for damages. In the case of other courts, there is a right of appeal given to all parties (art. 497 CPP). The hearing is based on the file and is, in principle, a rehearing. If the court finds a defect, it can not only quash the decision, but also decide itself on the merits by *évocation* of the case to itself (art. 520 CPP). In all cases a decision may be sent to the *Cour de cassation* for a point of law.

Since 1808, *révision* of a decision may be invoked in the case of *crimes* or *délits* for the rare cases where, for instance, the victim of a murder is found alive, there has been perjury of witnesses, or a subsequent trial produces a contradictory finding (art. 622 CPP). Such cases may arise where a witness has subsequently been convicted of perjury.[42]

This scope for appeal is very limited, and so a Law of 8 June 1895 (amended in 1989) provides that where after conviction, 'a fact occurs or a new fact is discovered or a new element unknown to the court at the date of trial arises such as to give rise to a doubt on the guilt of the accused' (art. 622 CPP), then the case can be submitted to the *Cour de cassation*. Until 1989, it was necessary to show that this new feature was such as to show that the innocence of the convicted person was probable. Again, until 1989, the case could only be submitted by the Minister of Justice (*Garde des sceaux*), but now it may be submitted also by the convicted person or his family or heirs (art. 623 CPP). A number of famous cases, such as Dreyfus and Danval, have led to acquittals under this provision.[43] In the latter case, a person was convicted of arsenical poisoning only for it later to be discovered that a peculiar kidney complaint had caused the death. The availability of the criminal file makes it all the easier to reopen a case. A more recent example concerned a conviction for child abuse which was quashed where it was proved that the victim had imagined the events on the basis of what really had happened to her sister.[44] More commonly, the cases for revision involve findings of mental illness which affected the convicted person, but were not investigated at trial.[45]

On such a reference, the *Cour de cassation* sits as a court of five judges which will investigate the case. This *instruction* process allows the court to give a *commission rogatoire* to the police to conduct investigations much as in the procedure under the control of the investigating magistrate. As in that process, the convicted person is able to make representations, and the *ministère public* at the *Cour de cassation* gives his or her observations. The usual outcome of a successful investigation is that the decision of the trial court is quashed and a retrial ordered by a court of co-ordinate jurisdiction. If this is no longer possible or useful, such as if the innocence of the convicted person is now certain, then the conviction is simply quashed (art. 625, para. 5 CPP).

Conclusion

The best in the inquisitorial system is the recognition of the importance of the phase preparatory to trial and the affirmation of strict rules governing the search

---

[42] See Cass. crim 13 Nov 1968, D. 1969, 219; but this will not apply where the witness is acquitted of perjury, even though the evidence at trial may call into question the safety of the conviction: Cass. crim 26 Jan. 1994, Bull. crim no. 37.

[43] Cass. ch. réun. 12 July 1906, *Dreyfus*, D. 1908.1.553; Cass.crim. 28 Dec. 1923, *Danval*, D.P. 1924.1.66.

[44] Cass. crim 9 May 1994, Bull.crim no. 176.

[45] See Cass. crim 3 May 1994, D. 1995 Somm. 144.

for and preservation of evidence during this period . . . The best in the accusatorial system is to promote the judges as a genuinely neutral umpire by separating the judicial and investigative functions, which permits a new balance of power between the prosecution and defence . . . [46]

The benefits of the inquisitorial system have to be viewed in the context in which it operates. They relate to the way miscarriages are prevented, are monitored, and are cured.

The French system has three strategies for preventing miscarriages of justice. It offers judicial supervision of the investigation process by either the investigating magistrate or by the *procureur*. In practice, this is limited in the phase of police investigation and judicial supervision is more often a review of what has been found and checking that it is correct. The reason for the more limited role is simply one of resources, rather than the idea of the investigating magistrate itself. The second aspect is the role of the independent court expert who provides the relevant forensic evidence on which the court will rely. More recently, the interview with the lawyer at the police station has been added to identify when suspects may have been subjected to unfair pressure or where other irregularities have occurred and the *procureur* needs to be involved.

At the monitoring phase, the role of the written file is critical. The most important feature is the checkability which arises from the written file and the access which the suspect's lawyers have to it. There is a way of checking that no improperly-obtained evidence is on file before the case comes to trial, and this streamlines the system significantly. The open access to the file also minimises the dangers of non-disclosure of exculpatory evidence such as occurred in the *Judith Ward* case.[47] The file also makes an appeal easier. A second feature here is the way the law structures the *instruction* phase so that there is less emphasis on the day in court and a more careful preparation of the case by lawyers who will have long familiarity with it and who will ensure that the various phases before trial will ensure that the innocent person does not appear at trial.

The French processes of nullity of the *instruction* appeal and *révision* provide more avenues for curing miscarriages through the normal court process than exist in English law. The willingness of the French to allow appeals on new evidence is one of the good features of their system. The *révision* process is long-standing and frequently used, so there has not been the pressure for a body to investigate miscarriages of justice outside the judicial system.

The 1993 reforms have gone some way towards improving the rights of the defence. But the principle that the investigating magistrate should be guardian of liberty met with the difficulty that resources were not adequate to ensure enough such judges were in post. It was also noted that the speed of investigation could be slowed by less use of detention.[48] There are obvious compromises between protecting rights and securing speedy and effective justice. The French are still struggling to get the balance right.

Leigh and Zedner conclude their study into inquisitorial systems on behalf of the Runciman Commission with the following remark:[49]

---

[46] Mme M. Delmas-Marty, *Le Monde*, 21 November 1991.

[47] *R v Ward* [1993] 1 WLR 619.

[48] See Field, S. and West, A., 'A Tale of Two Reforms: French Defence Rights and Police Powers in Transition' (1995) 6 *Criminal Law Forum* 473 at pp. 489–90.

We do not believe that the examining magistrate is a real protection against overbearing police practices save in rare cases where physical brutality is involved. Furthermore, despite the fact that only ten per cent of cases go before the *juge d'instruction*, the system is overburdened and works slowly.

There is much truth in this comment. Even if it were working better, the investigating magistrate system forms only one part of a complex structure which is not directly comparable with anything which exists in England and Wales. What we can learn is that supervision over the police by independent persons and the continuity and availability of evidence in a file can be safeguards against miscarriages of justice. But my own view would be that the system of the single pre-trial case-file, cumbersome though this can be, has merits which are worth exploring more than the system of the investigating magistrate.

---

[49] Leigh, L.H. and Zedner, L., *A Report on the Administration of Criminal Justice in the Pre-Trial Phase in France and Germany* (Royal Commission on Criminal Justice, Research Study No. 1; London, HMSO, 1992) at p. 68. A good example of police brutality being detected is the *Tomasi* case (Appl. no. 12850/87, (1992) Ser. A, No 241–A, (1993) 15 EHRR 1). But in this case, the police brutality was not prevented by the later supervisory control by the investigating magistrate.

Part Four

MISCARRIAGES OF JUSTICE IN SUMMARY

18

Concluding Remarks

Helena Kennedy and Keir Starmer

It is hard to believe that it was less than ten years ago[1] that Lord Chief Justice Lane and his co-judges made plain their outrage at the allegations submitted by the lawyers for the *Birmingham Six* against the police and dismissed the appeal. No one who sat for any length of time in that court doubted that the appeal would fail. Lord Lane's abhorrence of the slightest slur on the police sat heavily with those who were conducting the appeal of the *Guildford Four* which followed some months later. They agonised about the plan of campaign for the legal argument, debating all sorts of formulae for softening criticism of the police.[2] Then, out of the blue, the independent police enquiry into the case led to the discovery of evidence which supported conclusively the appellants' claims that they had been subjected to police misconduct.

The convictions of the *Guildford Four*, *Birmingham Six* and many others fell like a pack of cards. Yet it is interesting to speculate what would have happened if the *Guildford Four* appeal had proceeded and the Crown had not withdrawn its opposition. For years the criminal justice system had been propped up by complacency and arrogance. And, as it was, no apology attended the release of the *Birmingham Six*, and no expressions of shame came from the bench that our system had so profoundly failed these people. Whatever the failings of the system, the judiciary and legal profession clearly did not feel that they had any accounting to do. Far from being humbled by these experiences, there are still members of the judiciary who are resentful and angry that they have come under scrutiny at all.[3]

In the intervening years, there has been debate, analysis, official and unofficial reports and even some tinkering with the criminal justice system (not all for the good), but precious little focus on the personnel charged with administering criminal justice. Few people now doubt the fact that some police officers engage in very serious malpractice. Yet the system for accountability has not been altered.[4]

---

[1] These events were in 1989. The appeal was eventually allowed in 1991. See Chapter 2.

[2] See Kennedy, H., *Eve Was Framed* (Vintage, London, 1993) pp. 8, 9.

[3] These include Lord Denning who had to retract adverse comments made in *The Spectator*: *The Times*, 3 January 1991. Former Conservative MP, David Evans, paid libel damages for similar allegations: *The Times*, 10 July 1998.

[4] See further House of Commons Home Affairs Committee, *Police Disciplinary and Complaints Procedure* (1997–98 HC 258–I).

Every year, hundreds of litigants obtain substantial damages as compensation for serious police misconduct. Yet, it continues to astonish victims of police mal-practice and the public alike that, in nearly every case, no disciplinary action is taken after such damages awards.

The case of Kenneth Hsu is a typical example.[5] Called to Mr Hsu's premises by a lodger who claimed that she had been prevented from collecting her belongings, three police officers forced their way into Mr Hsu's house. When he tried to prevent them, the officers twisted his arms behind his back, placed him in a neck lock, punched him in the face, struck him across the face with a set of keys and kicked him in the back. Mr Hsu was also racially abused. He was taken to the police station and, nearly two hours later, left to walk home in bare feet. When Mr Hsu brought civil proceedings for damages, the police's justification for the arrest was rejected by the jury, who accepted that the police officers concerned had fabricated their note-book entries and lied on oath. The jury were so appalled by these events that they awarded Mr Hsu £20,000 compensatory damages and £200,000 exemplary damages (later reduced to £35,000 on appeal). Yet none of the officers has been disciplined.

For its part, the Crown Prosecution Service[6] has also failed to live up to expectations. The *Glidewell Report*[7] into the workings of the CPS, published in June 1998, concluded that in various respects there has not been the improvement in the effectiveness and efficiency of the prosecution process which was expected to result from setting up the CPS in 1986. The *Butler Report* is likely to be more direct. This was commissioned following the debacle in 1997 concerning a number of decisions by the CPS not to prosecute any police officer following two deaths in police custody and a High Court finding that police officers had tortured a suspect during interrogation. In one of the cases, that of Derek Treadaway,[8] the 87-page reasoned judgment of the High Court judge who awarded £50,000 in damages against the West Midlands Serious Crime Squad failed to impress the local Assistant Chief Crown Prosecutor. In his view, despite the judge's finding that four long-standing police officers had lied to him when they denied placing plastic bags over Mr Treadaway's head to persuade him to sign a pre-prepared 'confession', there was no realistic prospect of securing a conviction for assault. That decision was eventually quashed, but the current Stephen Lawrence Inquiry under Sir William Macpherson hardly inspires greater confidence in the speedy conviction of the guilty and the acquittal of the innocent.

Putting deliberate wrongdoing on one side, snapshots of everyday practice are not very flattering. In theory, meticulous care is required by the police, the CPS and defence lawyers if the risk of miscarriages of justice is to be reduced. But, in practice, such care is a rarity. Ordinary members of the public constantly allude to bungled investigations, the disorganisation of the CPS and the appalling standard of advocacy in court. Yet no one dares to champion the rights of victims of miscarriages to sue for negligence. The insistence of the judiciary that the police and the CPS owe no duty of care to those who suffer because of their shortcom-

---

[5] See *Thompson* v *Commissioner of Police for the Metropolis, Hsu* v *Commissioner of Police for the Metropolis* [1997] 2 All ER 762.
[6] Set up under the Prosecution of Offences Act 1985, the CPS began to operate in 1986.
[7] *Review of the Crown Prosecution Service* (Cmnd 3960, Stationery Office, London, 1998).
[8] See *R* v *DPP, ex parte Treadaway, The Times*, 18 November 1997.

ings[9] has now been refuted by the European Court of Human Rights in *Osman and Osman v UK*.[10] Meanwhile, the judicial reasoning that to impose a duty of care on the police, the CPS and lawyers in court would have an inhibiting effect on the discharge of their functions continues to bemuse and infuriate doctors, dentists and architects who enjoy no such immunity.

In reality, the criminal justice system is riddled with assumptions which have either not been tested or, when tested, have been found to be unwarranted. Cases of domestic violence provide an example of this.[11] After years of turning a blind eye, failing to prosecute and taking little action against perpetrators, some of the key issues of domestic violence have gradually been addressed. Marital behaviour behind closed doors was for a long time deemed a 'no go' area for law enforcement. This reluctance of the law to become involved accounts for much of the past difficulty in pursuing legal remedies for child abuse, both physical and sexual, and for rape, unless it involved being jumped on in an alley.

Many police forces have now developed domestic violence units with specially trained officers conducting the investigations. The spotlight must now move to the CPS and the courtroom. Lawyers and judges often regard prosecution as inappropriate because it might harm family relationships, and see their role as preserving the marriage. In a *World in Action* television programme, 'The right to rape', shown in 1989, about rape as part of the pattern of domestic violence within marriage,[12] Sir Frederick Lawton, a retired Appeal Court judge, explained that if it were open to wives to bring prosecutions for rape, albeit against a background of domestic violence, it would prohibit any chance of rehabilitation of the marriage and would have a deleterious effect on children – as though rape itself, rather than prosecution, might not already have had that effect.[13] The dogged refusal of the CPS to give reasons for its decisions where it decides not to prosecute or discontinues proceedings in domestic violence cases often adds insult to injury.

Even where prosecutions are brought, recent research suggests that most rape victims are dissatisfied with the way in which the CPS handled their case.[14] More generally, a woman at magistrates' courts can meet a hostile environment. If her husband is on bail, he often sits in the hallway feet away from her, harassing her and coercing her into dropping the charges. If he is in the cells, the same pressure may be exercised by his family or mates. The initial questioning of the woman is sometimes antagonistic, justified by those who are supposed to be on her side as testing the strength of any case they could bring and letting her see what is going to come from those who will represent her husband.

The increased scrutiny of all aspects of the criminal justice system over the last ten years has led to a better understanding of what that system is and how it

---

[9] See *Elguzouli-Daf v Commissioner of Police* [1995] QB 335.
[10] Appl. no. 23452/94, (1998) *The Times*, 5 November.
[11] See Hoyle, C., *Negotiating Domestic Violence* (Clarendon Press, Oxford, 1998).
[12] See *Daily Telegraph*, 25 September 1989 p. 4.
[13] These views are stated by him (as chair) in the Criminal Law Revision Committee, *15th Report: Sexual Offences* (Cmnd 9213, HMSO, London, 1984) para. 2.66. The legal possibility of prosecution has now been accepted: *SW and CR v UK*, Appl. nos. 20166, 20190/92, Ser. A, vol. 335–B, C, (1996) 21 EHRR 363.
[14] Victim Support, *Women, Rape and the Criminal Justice System* (London, 1996). For a review of treatment at all stages, see Report of the Interdepartmental Working Group on the Treatment of Vulnerable or Intimidated Witnesses in the Criminal Justice System, *Speaking Up for Justice* (Home Office, London, 1998).

operates. However, as the issues discussed in this book demonstrate, there is no quick fix, and the parameters of debate should not be too tightly drawn. Deliberate malpractice and negligence may never be fully eradicated, but equally they should not be allowed to flourish under rules made by lawyers for the benefit of other lawyers. There is no reason why a brain-surgeon should be required to exercise reasonable care, but the police, CPS and lawyers in court should not. The claim that it is the criminal justice system that anonymously fails and not the personnel is unsustainable.

General Bibliography

The objective behind this collection is to highlight works which touch on multiple issues relating to miscarriages of justice or are leading works on more specific topics. Further sources about a given topic may be found in the footnotes to the relevant chapter.

UK Official Reports

Caddy, B., *Assessment and Implications of Centrifuge Contamination in the Trace Explosive Section of the Forensic Explosives Laboratory at Fort Halstead* (Cm 3491, HMSO, London, 1996)

Committee on Criminal Appeals and Alleged Miscarriages of Justice, *Report* (Cm 3245, HMSO, Edinburgh, 1996)

Duff, P. and McCallum, F., *Grounds of Appeal in Criminal Cases* (Central Research Unit, Scottish Office, Edinburgh, 1996)

Home Affairs Committee, *Miscarriages of Justice* (1981–82 HC 421) and *Government Reply* (Cmnd 8856, HMSO, London, 1982)

Home Office, *Criminal Appeals and the Establishment of a Criminal Cases Review Authority: A Discussion Paper* (HMSO, London, 1994)

Home Office, *Disclosure* (Cm 2864, HMSO, London, 1994)

Home Office, *Improving the Effectiveness of Pre Trial Hearings in the Crown Court* (Cm 2924, HMSO, London, 1995)

Home Office, *Juries in Serious Fraud Trials* (London, 1998)

Home Office, *Mode of Trial* (Cm 2908, HMSO, London, 1995)

Home Office, *Protecting the Public* (Cm 3190, HMSO, London, 1996)

Home Office and Northern Ireland Office, *Legislation against Terrorism* (Cm 4178, Stationery Office, London, 1998)

Home Office Working Group, *The Right to Silence* (London, 1989)

Lord Chancellor's Department, Home Office and Law Officers' Department, *The Royal Commission on Criminal Justice: Final Government Response* (Home Office, London, 1996)

May, Sir John, *Report of the Inquiry into the circumstances surrounding the convictions arising out of the bomb attacks in Guildford and Woolwich in 1974, Interim Report* (1989–90 HC 556), *Second Report* (1992–93 HC 296), *Final Report* (1993–94 HC 449)

Narey, M., *Review of Delay in the Criminal Justice Process* (Home Office, London, 1997)

Northern Ireland Office, *Committal Proceedings in Northern Ireland* (Belfast, 1995)

Northern Ireland Office, *Criminal Appeals and Arrangements for Dealing with Alleged Miscarriages of Justice in Northern Ireland* (Belfast, 1994)

Northern Ireland Office, *Disclosure in Criminal Cases* (Belfast, 1995)

Report of the Departmental Committee, *Evidence of identification in criminal cases* (1975–76 HC 338)

Report of the Inquiry into the Export of Defence Equipment and Dual-Use Goods to Iraq and Related Prosecutions (1995–96 HC 115)

Report of the Inter-departmental Committee, *The Court of Criminal Appeal* (Cmnd 2755, HMSO, London, 1965)

Report of the Inter-departmental Working Group on the Treatment of Vulnerable or Intimidated Witnesses in the Criminal Justice System, *Speaking Up for Justice* (Home Office, London, 1998)

Royal Commission on Criminal Justice, *Report* (Cm 2263, HMSO, London, 1993)

Royal Commission on Criminal Justice, *Research Studies:*

Leigh, L.H. and Zedner, L., *Report on the Administration of Criminal Justice in the Pre-Trial Phase in France and Germany* (Royal Commission on Criminal Justice Research Study No. 1, HMSO, London, 1992)

Baldwin, J., *Preparing the Record of Taped Interviews* (Royal Commission on Criminal Justice Research Study No. 2, HMSO, London, 1992)

Baldwin, J., *The Role of Legal Representatives at the Police Station* (Royal Commission on Criminal Justice Research Study No. 3, HMSO, London, 1993)

Baldwin, J. and Moloney, T., *Supervision of Police Investigation in Serious Criminal Cases* (Royal Commission on Criminal Justice Research Study No. 4, HMSO, London, 1992)

Maguire, M. and Norris, C., *The Conduct and Supervision of Criminal Investigations* (Royal Commission on Criminal Justice Research Study No. 5, HMSO, London, 1992)

Robertson, G., *The Role of Police Surgeons* (Royal Commission on Criminal Justice Research Study No. 6, HMSO, London, 1993)

Clare, I. and Gudjonsson, G., *Devising and Piloting an Experimental Version of the Notice to Detained Persons* (Royal Commission on Criminal Justice Research Study No. 7, HMSO, London, 1993)

Evans, R., *The Conduct of Police Interviews with Juveniles* (Royal Commission on Criminal Justice Research Study No. 8, HMSO, London, 1992)

Steventon, B., *The Ability to Challenge DNA Evidence* (Royal Commission on Criminal Justice Research Study No. 9, HMSO, London, 1993)

Leng, R., *The Right to Silence in Police Interrogation* (Royal Commission on Criminal Justice Research Study No. 10, HMSO, London, 1993)

Roberts, P. and Willmore, C., *The Role of Forensic Science Evidence in Criminal Proceedings* (Royal Commission on Criminal Justice Research Study No. 11 HMSO, London, 1993)

Gudjonsson, G. *et al.*, *Persons at Risk During Interviews in Police Custody* (Royal Commission on Criminal Justice Research Study No. 12, HMSO, London, 1992)

McConville, M., *Corroboration and Confessions* (Royal Commission on Criminal Justice Research Study No. 13, HMSO, London, 1993)

Levi, M., *The Investigation, Prosecution and Trial of Serious Fraud* (Royal Commission on Criminal Justice Research Study No. 14, HMSO, London, 1993)

Bock, B.P., *Ordered and Directed Acquittals in the Crown Court* (Royal Commission on Criminal Justice Research Study No. 15, HMSO, London, 1993)

McConville, M. and Hodgson, J., *Custodial Legal Advice and the Right to Silence* (Royal Commission on Criminal Justice Research Study No. 16, HMSO, London, 1993)

Malleson, K., *Appeals against Conviction and the Principle of Finality* (Royal Commission on Criminal Justice Research Study No. 17, HMSO, London, 1993)

Plotnikoff, J. and Woolfson, R., *Information and Advice for Prisoners about Grounds for Appeal and the Appeals Process* (Royal Commission on Criminal Justice Research Study No. 18, HMSO, London, 1993)

Zander, M. and Henderson, P., *Crown Court Study* (Royal Commission on Criminal Justice Research Study No. 19, HMSO, London, 1993)

Fitzgerald, M., *Ethnic Minorities and the Criminal Justice System* (Royal Commission on Criminal Justice Research Study No. 20, HMSO, London, 1993)

Irving, B. and Dunningham, C., *Human Factors in the Quality Control of CID Investigations and a Brief Review of Relevant Police Training* (Royal Commission on Criminal Justice Research Study No. 21, HMSO, London, 1993)

Moston, S. and Stephenson, G.M., *The Questioning and Interviewing of Suspects outside the Police Station* (Royal Commission on Criminal Justice Research Study No. 22, HMSO, London, 1993)

Royal Commission on Criminal Procedure, *Report* (Cmnd 8092, HMSO, London, 1981)

Scottish Office, *Appeals in the Scottish Criminal Courts* (Edinburgh, 1993)

Scottish Office, *Crime and Punishment* (Cm 3302, HMSO, Edinburgh, 1996)

Scottish Office, *Criminal Legal Aid Review* (Edinburgh, 1994)

Scottish Office, *Firm and Fair: Improving the Delivery of Justice in Scotland* (Cm 2600, HMSO, Edinburgh, 1994)

Scottish Office, *Juries and Verdicts* (Edinburgh, 1993)

Scottish Office, *Review of Criminal Evidence and Criminal Procedure* (Edinburgh, 1993)

Scottish Office, *Sentencing and Appeals* (Edinburgh, 1994)

Standing Advisory Commission on Human Rights, *19th Report* (1993–94 HC 495)

Standing Advisory Commission on Human Rights, *20th Report* (1994–95 HC 506)

Standing Advisory Commission on Human Rights, *21st Report* (1995–96 HC 467)

Treasury Solicitor, *Public Interest Immunity* (London, 1996)

Commentaries

Allen, R.J., 'Reform: the system: the Simpson affair, reform of the criminal justice process, and magic bullets' (1996) 67 *Colorado Law Review* 989

Ashworth, A., 'The Royal Commission on Criminal Justice: Part 3: plea, venue and discontinuance' [1993] *Criminal Law Review* 830

Ashworth, A., *The Criminal Process: An Evaluative Study* (2nd ed., Clarendon Press, Oxford, 1998)

Ashworth, A., 'Crime, community and creeping consequentialism' [1996] *Criminal Law Review* 220

Blom-Cooper, Sir L., *The Birmingham Six and other Cases: Victims of Circumstances* (Duckworth, London, 1997)

Brandon, R. and Davies, C., *Wrongful Imprisonment: Mistaken Convictions and their Consequences* (Allen, London, 1973)

Bridges, J., 'Normalising injustice: the Royal Commission on Criminal Justice' (1994) 21(1) *Journal of Law and Society* 20

Bridges, L., and McConville, M., 'Keeping faith with their own convictions' (1994) 57 *Modern Law Review* 75–90

British Irish Rights Watch, 'Taking a Case to the Criminal Case Review Commission' (Proceedings of a Seminar held in Belfast, 12 April 1997)

Buxton, R., 'Miscarriages of Justice and the Court of Appeal' (1993) 109 *Law Quarterly Review* 66

Carrington, K., *et al.*, *Travesty!* (Pluto Press, Leichhardt, 1991)

Choo, A.L-T., *Abuse of Process and Judicial Stays of Criminal Proceedings* (Clarendon Press, Oxford, 1993)

Committee on the Administration of Justice, *The Casement Trials: A Case Study on the Right to a Fair Trial in Northern Ireland* (Belfast, 1992)

Committee on the Administration of Justice, *Adding Insult to Injury?* (Belfast, 1993)

Damaska, M.J., *The Faces of Justice and State Authority* (Yale University Press, 1986)

Davies, M., Croall, H. and Tyrer, J., *Criminal Justice* (2nd ed., Longman, London, 1998)

Dennis, I., 'Miscarriages of justice and the law of confessions: evidentiary issues and solutions' [1993] *Public Law* 291

Dixon, D., *Law in Policing: Legal Regulation and Police Practices* (Clarendon Press, Oxford, 1997)

Douzinas, C. and Warrington, R., 'A well-founded fear of justice: law and ethics in postmodernity' in Leonard, J. (ed.), *Legal Studies as Cultural Studies* (State University of New York, Albany, 1995)

Douzinas, C. and Warrington, R., *Justice Miscarried* (Harvester Wheatsheaf, London, 1995)

Du Cann, C., *Miscarriages of Justice* (Muller, London, 1960)

Ede, R. and Shepherd, E., *Active Defence* (Law Society, London, 1997)

Fennell, P., Harding, C., Jorg, N. and Swart, B., (eds.), *Criminal Justice in Europe: A Comparative Study* (Clarendon Press, Oxford, 1994)

Field, S. and Thomas, P.A., (eds.), *Justice and Efficiency* (1994) 21(1) *Journal of Law & Society* 21(1) (special issue, Blackwell, London)

Forensic Science Working Group, *Report* (Royal Society of Chemistry, London, 1997)

Ganz, G., 'Volte-face on public interest immunity' (1997) 60 *Modern Law Review* 552

Givelber, D., 'Meaningless acquittals, meaningful convictions: do we reliably acquit the innocent?' (1997) 49 *Rutgers Law Review* 1317

Glynn, J., 'The Royal Commission on Criminal Justice: Part 4: Disclosure' [1993] *Criminal Law Review* 841

Greer, S., 'Miscarriages of justice reconsidered' (1994) 57 *Modern Law Review* 58

Hill, P., 'Justice in Scotland?' (1994) 144 *New Law Journal* 1705

Hill, P. and Young, M., *Rough Justice* (BBC, London, 1983), *More Rough Justice* (Penguin, London, 1986)

Hodgson, J., 'Justice undermined' (1997) 29 *Criminal Justice Matters* 4

Hodgson, J. and McConville, M., 'Silence and the Suspect' (1993) 143 *New Law Journal* 659

Hogan, G. and Walker, C., *Political Violence and the Law in Ireland* (Manchester University Press, 1989)

Huff, C.R., Rattner, A. and Sagarin, E., *Convicted But Innocent: Wrongful Conviction and Public Policy* (Sage, Thousand Oaks, 1996)

Ingraham, B.L., 'The right of silence, the presumption of innocence, the burden of proof, and a modest proposal: a reply to O'Reilly' (1996) 86 *Journal of Criminal Law & Criminology* 559

Jackson, J., 'Royal Commission on Criminal Justice: Part 2: the evidence recommendations' [1993] *Criminal Law Review* 817

Jackson, J. and Doran, S., *Judge without Jury: Diplock Trials in the Adversary System* (Clarendon Press, Oxford, 1995)

Jackson, J. and Doran, S., 'Judge and jury: towards a new division of labour in criminal trials' (1997) 60 *Modern Law Review* 759

Jessel, D., 'The Lund Lecture: television, science and the law' (1997) 37 *Medicine, Science and the Law* 4

Jessel, D., *Trial and Error* (Headline, London, 1994)

Jones, C.A.G., *Expert Witnesses* (Clarendon Press, Oxford, 1994)

JUSTICE, *Home Office Review of Criminal Convictions* (London, 1968)

JUSTICE, *Miscarriages of Justice* (London, 1989)

JUSTICE, *Remedying Miscarriages of Justice* (London, 1993)

JUSTICE, *Unreliable Evidence? Confessions and the Safety of Convictions* (London, 1994)

JUSTICE, *Disclosure: A Consultation Paper, the JUSTICE Response* (London, 1995)

Kennedy, H., *Eve Was Framed* (Vintage, London, 1993)

King, M., *The Framework of Criminal Justice* (Croom Helm, London, 1981)

Leng, R., 'Losing sight of the defendant' [1995] *Criminal Law Review* 704

Leo, R., 'Police interrogation and social control' (1994) 3 *Social & Legal Studies* 93

Lewis, D. and Hughman, P., *Just How Just?* (Secker & Warburg, London, 1975)

Liberty, *Broken Covenants: Violations of International Law in Northern Ireland* (London, 1993)

McConville, M. and Bridges, L., (eds.) *Criminal Justice in Crisis* (Edward Elgar, Aldershot, 1994)

McConville, M. and Mirsky, C., 'The disordering of criminal justice' (1993) 143 *New Law Journal* 1446

McConville, M. and Mirsky, C., 'Balancing acts and constitutionalism' (1993) 143 *New Law Journal* 1579

McConville, M., Sanders, A. and Leng, R., *The Case for the Prosecution* (Routledge, London, 1991)

Maguire, M. and Norris, C., 'Police investigations: practice and malpractice' (1994) 21 *Journal of Law & Society* 72

Malet, D., 'The new regime for the correction of miscarriages of justice' (1995) 159 *Justice of the Peace* 716, 735.

Malleson, K., 'Appeals against conviction and the principle of finality' (1994) 21 *Journal of Law and Society* 151

Malleson, K., 'A broad framework' (1997) 147 *Justice of the Peace* 1023

Mansfield, M., *Presumed Guilty* (Heinemann, London, 1993)

Morgan, D. and Stephenson, G., (eds.), *Suspicion and Silence: the right to silence in criminal investigations* (Blackstone Press, London, 1994)

Mulcahy, A., Brownlee, I.D. and Walker, C.P., 'PTRs, court efficiency and justice' (1994) 33 *Howard Journal of Criminal Justice* 109

Mullin, C., *Error of Judgment* (3rd ed., Poolbeg, Dublin, 1990)

Mullin, C., 'Miscarriages of justice in the UK' (1996) 2(2) *Journal of Legislative Studies* 8

Newburn, T., *Crime and Criminal Justice Policy* (Longman, London, 1995)

Niblett, J., *Disclosure in Criminal Proceedings* (Blackstone Press, London, 1997)

Noaks, L. *et al.*, (eds.) *Contemporary Issues in Criminology* (Wales University Press, Cardiff, 1995)

Nobles, R. and Schiff, D., 'Miscarriages of justice: a systems approach' (1996) 59 *Modern Law Review* 299

Nobles, R. and Schiff, D., 'The never ending story' (1997) 60 *Modern Law Review* 293

O'Connor, P., 'The Court of Appeal: re-trials and tribulations' [1990] *Criminal Law Review* 615

O'Reilly, G.W., 'England limits the right to silence and moves towards an inquisitorial system of justice' (1994) 85 *Journal of Criminal Law & Criminology* 402

O'Reilly, G.W., 'Criminal law: comment on Ingraham's "moral duty" to talk and the right to silence' (1997) 87 *Journal of Criminal Law & Criminology* 521

Owers, A., 'Not completely appealing' (1995) 145 *New Law Journal* 353

Packer, H.L., *The Limits of the Criminal Sanction* (Stanford University Press, 1969)

Pattenden, R, *English Criminal Appeals 1844–1994* (Clarendon Press, Oxford, 1996)

Pollard, C., 'Public safety, accountability and the courts' [1996] *Criminal Law Review* 152

Poole, A., 'Remedies in miscarriage of justice cases' (1998) *Scottish Law Times* 65

Redmayne, M., 'Process gains and process values' (1997) 60 *Modern Law Review* 79

Reiner, R., 'Royal Commission on Criminal Justice: Part 1: Investigative powers and safeguards for suspects' [1993] *Criminal Law Review* 808

Roberts, P., 'Forensic science evidence after Runciman' [1994] *Criminal Law Review* 780

Roberts, P., 'Science in the criminal process' (1994) 14 Oxford Journal of Legal Science 469

Roberts, P., 'What price a free market in forensic science' (1996) 36 *British Journal of Criminology* 37

Rose, D., *In the Name of the Law* (Jonathan Cape, London, 1996)

Rozenberg, J., *The Search for Justice* (Hodder & Stoughton, London, 1994)

Runciman, W.G., 'An outsider's view of the criminal justice system' (1994) 57 *Modern Law Review* 1

Sanders, A. and Young, R., *Criminal Justice* (Butterworths, London, 1994)

Sargant, T. and Hill, P., *Criminal Trials* (Fabian Research Series No. 348, London, 1986)

Schiff, D. and Nobles, R., 'Review: *Justice in Error*' (1994) 34 *British Journal of Criminology* 383

Schiff, D. and Nobles, R., 'Criminal Appeal Act 1995' (1996) 59 *Modern Law Review* 573

Scott, M. 'New criminal appeal provisions' (1997) *Scottish Law Times* 249

Scott, Sir R., 'The use of public interest immunity claims in criminal cases' [1996] 2 *Web Journal of Current Legal Issues*

Scott, Sir R., 'The acceptable and unacceptable uses of public interest immunity' [1996] *Public Law* 427

Scraton, P., 'Denial, neutralisation and disqualification: the Royal Commission in context' [1982] *Statute Law Review* 98

Smith, A.T.H., 'The right to silence in cases of serious fraud' in Birks, P.B.H. (ed.), *Pressing Problems in the Law Volume 1: Criminal Justice and Human Rights* (Oxford University Press, 1995)

Smith, J.C., 'Criminal appeals and the CCRC' (1995) 145 *New Law Journal* 533, 572

Smith, J.C., 'The Criminal Appeal Act 1995: appeals Against conviction' [1995] *Criminal Law Review* 920

Stockdale, E. and Casale, S., *Criminal Justice under Stress* (Blackstone Press, London, 1992)

Supperstone, M. and Coppel, J., 'A new approach to public interest immunity' [1997] *Public Law* 211

Thornton, P., 'Miscarriages of justice: a lost opportunity' [1993] *Criminal Law Review* 926

Thornton, P., 'Righting the wrongs' in Birks, P.B.H. (ed.), *Pressing Problems in the Law Volume 1: Criminal Justice and Human Rights* (Oxford University Press, 1995)

Uglow, S., *Criminal Justice* (Sweet & Maxwell, London, 1995)

Walker, C.P., *The Prevention of Terrorism in British Law* (2nd ed., Manchester University Press, 1992)

Walker, C.P., 'Review in error' (1995) 35 *British Journal of Criminology* 661

Walker, C.P. and Starmer, K., *Justice in Error* (Blackstone Press, London, 1993)

Walker, C.P. and Stockdale, R., 'Forensic science and miscarriages of justice' (1995) 54 *Cambridge Law Journal* 69

Wall, D., 'Legal aid, social policy and the architecture of criminal justice' (1996) 23 *Journal of Law & Society* 549

Warbrick, C., 'Self incrimination and the European Convention on Human Rights' in Birks, P.B.H. (ed.), *Pressing Problems in the Law Volume 1: Criminal Justice and Human Rights* (Oxford University Press, 1995)

Wisotsky, S., 'Criminal law symposium: miscarriages of justice: their causes and cures' (1997) 9 *St Thomas Law Review* 547

Woffinden, B., *Miscarriages of Justice* (2nd ed., Avon, 1989)

Young, R. and Sanders, A., The Royal Commission on Criminal Justice' (1994) 14 *Oxford Journal of Legal Studies* 435

Zander, M., 'The Royal Commission strikes back' (1993) 143 *New Law Journal* 1507

Zander, M., 'Where the critics got it wrong' (1993) 143 *New Law Journal* 1338, 1364

Zander, M., 'You have no right to remain silent' (1996) 40 *Saint Louis University Law Review* 659

Zuckerman, A., 'Miscarriages of justice and judicial responsibility' [1991] *Criminal Law Review* 492

Zuckerman, A., 'Miscarriages of justice – a root treatment' [1992] *Criminal Law Review* 323

Zuckerman, A., 'A strategy for reducing the incidence of miscarriages of justice' (1993) 44 *Northern Ireland Legal Quarterly* 3

World Wide Websites

A comprehensive and constantly updated list of relevant sites, including the addresses of the Criminal Cases Review Commission, the Forensic Science Service and the organisation, Scandals in Justice, can be found at: UK Criminal Justice Web Links < http://www.leeds.ac.uk/law/ccjs/ukweb.htm >. In addition, there is a resource site specifically connected with the contents of this book at the address of UK Law Online: < http://www.leeds.ac.uk/law/hamlyn/miscarri.htm >.

Index